FEB 2 7 2024

Circassia

Circassia

BORN TO BE FREE

Adel Bashqawi

Copyright © 2017 by Adel Bashqawi.

Library of Congress Control Number: 2017913354
ISBN: Hardcover 978-1-5434-4763-7
Softcover 978-1-5434-4764-4
eBook 978-1-5434-4765-1

All rights reserved. No part of this book may be reproduced or transmitted in any form or by any means, electronic or mechanical, including photocopying, recording, or by any information storage and retrieval system, without permission in writing from the copyright owner.

Any people depicted in stock imagery provided by Thinkstock are models, and such images are being used for illustrative purposes only.
Certain stock imagery © Thinkstock.

Print information available on the last page.

Rev. date: 09/15/2017

To order additional copies of this book, contact:
Xlibris
1-888-795-4274
www.Xlibris.com
Orders@Xlibris.com
760560

Contents

Foreword: by Merabi Chukhua ... ix
Introduction ... xi

1 Circassia ... 1
2 The Circassian Independence ... 23
3 The Russian-Circassian War (1763–1864) ... 83
4 A View on the Circassian Genocide ... 145
5 The Circassian Flag, the Homeland, the Circassian Identity ... 270
6 The So-Called 450-Year Association with Russia ... 286
7 Language, Culture, and IT ... 293
8 Commemoration of the Twenty-First of May ... 332
9 The Circassian Legal Status and the Right to Self-Determination ... 359
10 Circassian Political Activism ... 390
11 Recognizing the Circassian Genocide ... 440
12 Institutionalization of Ideological Invasion ... 472
13 Developments that Imposed Themselves on the International Scene ... 510
14 Humanitarian Issues ... 521
15 The 2014 Sochi Winter Olympic Games ... 555
16 Appendices ... 588

Index ... 641

Dedication

This work is dedicated to our courageous ancestors, the Circassian heroes who exerted all they could to protect their historic homeland. They have passed on the message of goodness and love to future generations.

I also want to thank my dear wife and our beloved children for the great support, understanding, and devotion bestowed on all my endeavors.

FOREWORD

by Merabi Chukhua

Humanity remembers many of the brutalities committed against the peoples. Of them, the genocide of Circassians perpetrated by the Russian Empire in the nineteenth century is one of the most terrible and hardest crimes. As a result of these bloody events, 90 percent of the Circassian population was killed or forced to leave their homeland. Even though Circassians left their native land, they remain undefeated. More than 150 years have passed since then, but the hard consequences of Circassian genocide have not been yet eradicated. Throughout this period, both the Russian Federation and the world's political forces had a deathly silence on this issue. This silence was broken by the historic resolution of the Parliament of Georgia on May 20, 2011. In the world, Georgia became the first state that recognized genocide, gave the exact legal-political assessment of Circassian tragedy, and restored historical justice.

Genocide's perception has left a great trace on the ethnopsyche of Circassians: many Circassians still do not eat fish caught in the Black Sea because they consider it to be fed with the body of their ancestors. In the Circassian language, the word "Tlapqghakwad" (literally "loss of the nation") appeared, denoting the genocide. For the obvious reasons, this word has been reflected in none of the Circassian dictionaries issued in Russian Federation.

World history knows various genocide cases: Bosnia, Chechnya, Ruanda, but Circassians' genocide is unique, as Circassians lost three-fourth of their population, sovereignty, and the main, their homeland. So Circassians are scattered in more than fifty countries in the world. They deserve refugee status, but unfortunately cannot benefit from it.

It is of utmost importance that modern Circassian ethnicity does not forget the horrors that took place in the nineteenth century. Having perceived these tragic events, actually catastrophe by Circassian consciousness adequately, it involuntarily and subconsciously qualifies it as the genocide. How surprising it would be, all these are more appropriately and rightly noted by Russian historian I. Kutsensko:

> – It is impossible to hide the truth about genocide. In the Adyghe republics the memories of this event still alive, are being enriched with new details, cause great interest. Especially the memories of the painfully tragic, bloody past are revealed on May 21 – in every anniversary year of the Caucasus War. This day has become a mourning day for many people. Thus genocide has long been recognized by the main instance – by mass consciousness of indigenous population and even by a significant part of the Russians. It remains unrecognized only by the formal political leadership of Russia and its obedient local administrations.

The present book is written just under this spirit: the Circassian public figure and patriot Adel Bashqawi living in Jordan, who, as a result of the Russian genocide, naturally cannot forget the homeland and spends nights in the memory of a lost native land because he is a direct descendant of Circassians fighting for freedom and a victim who was exiled from his homeland.

The Circassians' struggle for freedom is still going on. I believe that the book is a part of this fight. It will easily find a way to the hearts of fighters fighting for revival. Those who take the Circassian tragedy to the heart naturally become a member of the Circassian community. Today, we are all Circassians because it is impossible to know about this genocide and not to sympathize with it, to do nothing to eradicate its consequences. I believe that everything in this world will change, justice will be restored, and one day, mankind will see the victorious Circassian people, who today are united due to thinking about homeland and future.

Merabi Chukhua
Professor TSU, Director of the Circassian (Adyghian) Cultural Center
Georgia, Tbilisi

Introduction

Two Circassians from Jordan took an unusual journey in the mid-1960s (during the Soviet era) that took them back to where their families had originated. It began in Amman, Jordan, by road. They drove their car to Turkey via Syria. Back then, it was not possible to travel by personal car across the land borders between Turkey and the Georgian Soviet Socialist Republic. They had to board a ferry across the Black Sea along with their car, heading to Batumi.

At the time, tourist visas were obtained from the Soviet embassy. This limited the destination only to select permitted areas (which was mainly Georgia in this case). Upon arrival, they picked up the car and then proceeded to Tbilisi. The next day, they met an Armenian who lived in Tbilisi, to deliver a personal letter and some presents from his son who was living in Amman.

The two friends enquired about a possible way to travel to the Circassian part of the North Caucasus. They left Tbilisi in the early morning, as instructed, and for the first time, they drove across their original homeland. They continued until they reached a hotel in the city of Krasnodar. They walked into the lobby looking for accommodations while speaking English. They tried to speak Adygha (the Circassian language), and the receptionist started to communicate with them in Adygha, even speaking their own Shabsough dialect.

They explained that they were Circassians who came to visit their motherland to meet with the people. Even though they had no previous reservation, the man offered them rooms. He then made a phone call to his acquaintances. Suddenly, Circassians from his village were flocking to the hotel to meet with the two friends. They invited them for a Circassian feast and were warmly greeted by all; Circassian food was provided, and they enjoyed native music and dancing until almost midnight. They thanked the Almighty God for linking them with Circassians.

They later returned to the hotel, even though they were offered to stay the night. And when other Circassians from other villages in the area heard of the sudden visitors, they came and invited them for the next day. They promised to pick them up from the hotel in the morning. They were planning to tour the area, especially the Black Sea port of Tuapse, where their ancestors were deported from in 1864.

On the next day, the hosts came to accompany them to the next hosting place. However, there was a surprise waiting for everybody; KGB agents came to the hotel. They requested to see documents and passports. Upon seeing the presented passports, the two friends were told that their visas were not valid to travel beyond the permitted tourist zone. They had to say goodbye to their countrymen. A KGB officer accompanied them on their drive back to Tbilisi.

Those two friends were my late father, Mohiddin, and his late friend, Yacoub Tamokh.

The idea for writing a book about Circassia has been on my mind since I was a youth. I have always thought about an abandoned homeland, a people in exile, wasted rights, and a forgotten issue. That is because I am a descendant of victims who were forcibly expelled from their homeland across the Black Sea to live in exile due to colonial ambitions.

I feel the time is right to publish this book because even though data was available at hand, it needs to be presented in a realistic and nonbiased way.

It is based on the facts of eyewitness statements, documents, and unbiased books and novels that included memoirs and biographies. A proper method is utilized to collect data from various reliable sources. They are availed to those who are eager to know legitimate evidence on the Circassian issue. Most importantly, it clarifies information that was ambiguous or published in a unilateral way that relied on propaganda and hypotheses.

The Russian-Circassian War (1763–1864) took a remarkable dimension in the Circassians' history for the past centuries. The biggest genocide committed in the nineteenth century resulted in a catastrophic Circassian exodus. I elaborate on the Circassians' background, a look at Russia's background, and the formation of the Russian Empire's strategic goal of annexing Circassia, the involvement of the tsars in the long war, and the Cossacks' role and acquisition of others' properties while serving the goals of the Russian Empire.

The Circassian genocide has occupied a special attention and capacity for the way it affected the fate of a nation. Barbaric methods steered the Circassians to a situation of total destruction while the Russian Empire reached a brilliant victory. This provided the opportunity to decide the fate of a nation that half of it was systematically murdered while 90 percent of the survivors were deported away from their residence of origin. The Russians imposed tragic and unfavorable conditions and resettled Circassia with strangers.

In this book, I also cover various activities and proceedings that take place in the "Circassian World," both in the Circassian homeland and in diaspora. Circassians are proving that they are more concerned with their national status than ever before. Activities and positive efforts are taking place in many locations through utilizing national and social activities and motions. Lectures, conferences, seminars, and gatherings are arranged in culture, language, history, and social fields as well as present and future prospects. The spread of internet use all over the world allowed Circassians to utilize modern information and technology for their national benefit. "The Circassians and IT" is a blessing for a nation that suddenly found itself oppressed and distributed all over the world.

It is noticed how Circassian identity would be the most important element in preserving Circassians. It is an important tool as it achieves the need for coherence and cohesion among the world's Circassians. If the situation doesn't improve, Circassians will have their national and indigenous identity at risk. Attaining unity will lead the process of sharing the feeling of belonging to a common nation and origin. There are concerned people who call to help the Circassians across the world to protect their identity and unity. This coordination energizes the psychological and emotional elements needed to enhance the process. They have similar beliefs and common aspirations expressed among the people involved. They need to protect their indigenous national identity against narrow nationalism.

For a change, Circassians discovered themselves virtually united again. The strength and the impact of this miraculous achievement led to a growing global mobility of Circassians in all fields. This has led to the exchange of information on the Circassian Question, which has been disseminated to the public. This has assisted the different issues of the Circassian Question to gain supporters.

I also talk about the yearly painful commemoration of May 21 (Circassian Memorial Day), which reminds the younger generation of the fate of their ancestors and lets the world know what happened when the Russian-Circassian War ended.

The Circassian flag was made and became a national symbol (marine green color, with three crossed arrows and twelve stars in gold) when it was declared by Circassian tribes in a special ceremony in the midst of the tsarist-waged Russian-Circassian War. The national flag consecration was attended by members of the main Circassian tribes.

Even though more than 150 years have passed since the great Circassian catastrophe, time has not yet come to convey the case to the international courts and arenas, except on a very limited scale. The international community must be informed of the various issues that have impacted the existence of Circassians as a people and as a nation. They are entitled to have the right to maintain their respected character. It is unavoidable to gain this accomplishment and to recover the legitimate rights of this small European nation.

Conditions should be created and devoted to discuss the real issues, where a peaceful solution that cites justice for the cause must be reached using legal and peaceful means. Freedom and human dignity are not a favor from anyone, but natural rights to be practiced by every human being. Circassians need to redress their legitimate rights, and equity must be granted.

The Russian government, being the successor of the Russian Empire and other successive regimes, must give restitution. Crimes and their consequences should be recognized and apologized for, in accordance with international law. A fair compensation must be disbursed, and the right of return, followed by the legitimate right of self-determination, must be given. All other outstanding problems should be resolved.

People should not be driven to despair as it leads to loss of hope and confidence. The winds of displacement, dispersion, diaspora, alienation, and exile should be avoided and resisted. Optimism and solidarity should prevail to overcome weakness and discord. This will be a cornerstone to preserve the culture, heritage, language, and the nation.

1

Circassia

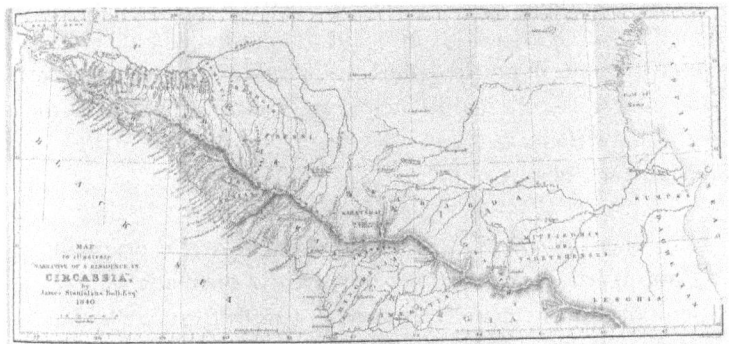

Map Of Circassia 1840

Circassia has a confirmed history of more than six thousand years, consistently and positively contributing to humanity. Circassian civilization and culture originated in northwestern Caucasus and has existed for a long time. Circassia is situated within the Caucasus Plateau and is considered a natural obstacle. It contains Mount Elbrus, the highest peak in Europe, with an elevation of 18,510 feet above sea level.

The Circassian homeland is in southeastern Europe. It is in a strategic area situated in the northwestern part of the Caucasus mountain range. It lies on the northeastern shores of the Black Sea, extending between the Sea of Azov and Abkhazia.

The Circassians are the original inhabitants of the northwestern Caucasus: "An agricultural and cattle-breeding culture arose in the Northwest Caucasus in the early Bronze Age. By 3,000 B.C., the Dolmen culture, whose name comes from the distinctive megaliths used as grave markers, had arisen here and reached its peak; it lasted until the last quarter of the second millennium B.C. The area where the Caucasian dolmens are found is the ancestral home of the Adyghe-Abkhaz tribes. Today, there are five dolmen fields in the republic with about 200 whole and partly ruined dolmens."[1]

Circassia was not born out of circumstances, whims, or fantasies, nor was it built by conquering the innocent and oppressed. On the contrary, it is known in history as the homeland of the indigenous Circassian people who participated in the process of the advancement of human civilization. During this process, they had to endure a high cost of self-preservation and existence as one of the nations of the Caucasus while being identified by their distinctive homeland.

This region has witnessed, over thousands of years, many attempts by invaders and colonizers to control Circassia in the form of wars and campaigns of aggression, characterized by hit-and-run tactics. The Circassians were always vigilant, exercising their right to protect their freedom and national dignity. Every time they were subjected to attempts of their homeland being occupied and their nation being dominated, they took refuge in the Caucasus mountains, continuing their resistance against their aggressors until, eventually, they could expel or eliminate them.

Walter Richmond says,

> How the Circassians, who call themselves Adyghe, originally came to occupy the North-Eastern shore of the Black Sea is yet another story of exile. They are most likely the descendants of the Haitians, who developed an advanced society in central Anatolia as early as the third millennium BCE. When the Hittites invaded ca. 2,000 BCE, many migrated to the northeast and occupied the land between the modern cities of Sukhumi and Anapa along the coast of the Black Sea. They eventually separated into the Abkhaz, Abaza, Circassian, and Ubykh peoples (although most Circassians consider the Ubykhs a Circassian tribe). Known as Zigei (a corruption of Adyghe?) to the Greeks and Romans, the Circassians had commercial and political ties with both peoples and had built a set of fortified cities by the early Middle Ages. The Mongols, who destroyed their civilization in the thirteenth century, referred to them as the Jerkes, literally "one who blocks a path." Originally a term used to describe all the peoples of the North Caucasus, the Russian variant of the term, Cherkes, became attached exclusively to the Adyghe people by the nineteenth century and was translated into "Circassian" in Western Europe.[2]

According to the Unrepresented Nations and Peoples Organization (UNPO), "The formation of the Circassian people over the millennia had taken place in close contact with the tribes of Western Asia, Greeks, Cimmerians, Scythians, and Sumerian's. The main Circassian settlements were located in the northwestern foothills and plains of the lower reaches of the Kuban and on the east coast of the Black Sea from the mouth of the Don to Abkhazia. Circassian society of that time can be described as early feudal, and farming was the leading economic sector. Cattle and horse-breeding, fishing, and crafts were well developed. The celebrated Silk Route passed through the territory of historical Cherkessia (Circassia), as shown by various archaeological finds. The Circassians first emerged as a coherent entity somewhere around the tenth century A.D., although references to them exist much earlier."[3]

Circassians consist of twelve main tribes that are represented on their green flag by twelve golden stars above three crossed arrows that symbolize union and peace. They were commonly called by others Circassians or "Cherkess" (a Western term derived from the Greek Kerketos and the Turkic Cherkess).[4] However, their self-designated name and language is called Adyghe. The Adyghe consist of twelve main tribes: Abzakh (not to be confused with Abkhaz), Besleney, Bjedugh, Hatuqwai, Kabarday, Temirgoy, Mokhosh, Natkhwaj, Shapsugh, Ubykh, Yedjerikway, and Jana. Many of these tribes don't exist anymore because of the devastating war that was imposed on them.

> Circassia was a small independent nation on the northeastern shore of the Black Sea. For no reason other than ethnic hatred, over the course of hundreds of raids, the Russians drove the Circassians from their homeland and deported them to the Ottoman Empire. At least 600,000 people lost their lives to massacre, starvation, and the elements while hundreds of thousands more were forced to leave their homeland. By 1864, three-fourths of the population was annihilated, and the Circassians had become one of the first stateless peoples in modern history.[5]

Throughout their existence, Circassians have developed qualities that characterized them. They are known for their courage, devotion, altruism, liberality, politeness, sincerity, and modesty. These qualities formed what came to be known as the "Khabze," a word in the Adyghe language that means "law and order." The "Khabze" is the conduct, behavior, and etiquette, explained as "a whole philosophical and religious system," "a system that determines the identity of the Circassian people."

Khabze is not a prohibitionist system. Khabze is not built on bans and restrictions. Khabze shows way in which a person is developed in harmony with oneself, with others, with nature, and the outside world.[6]

It is worth mentioning a statement of truth regarding some false information circulated against the Circassians: "The Circassians participated in the slave trade themselves, a fact that has been regularly used by the Russians to justify their actions, although the accusation rings somewhat hollow when one considers that the Russians practiced institutionalized slavery on a far more massive scale all the way until 1861. Also, despite Russian claims that slaves were the only goods the Circassians traded in, the truth is that the Circassians also sold furs, leather, wax, honey, copper, hard woods, jewelry, and other goods to the Turks."[7]

Until the commencement of the Russian-Circassian War in 1763, the Circassians shared a friendly coexistence with the different people who passed through the region. Some of these people stayed tentatively, such as the ancient Greeks, Venetians, Genoese, and Romans: "In the thirteenth to fifteenth centuries, the Genoese constructed trading posts on the coastal regions of Circassia and Abkhazia."[8] Other people who passed through the region remained permanently in the North Caucasus. They include those of Persian and Turkish origins, who eventually settled in and inhabited the Caucasus region. Some of them had resided next to some Circassian tribes and got along with them. Still, Circassians were able to stay in their homeland, which they inherited from their ancestors.

Ibrahim Köremezli said, "Until the Russian conquest, Circassians maintained a very archaic social structure altering from tribe to tribe." Describing the Circassians' way of life, he continued, "Such a way of life prevented Circassians to develop a centralized authority but to live in a tribal confederation; however their devotion to independent way of life protected their freedom against any foreign domination. This and other cultural characteristics of Circassians played a role in the Circassian resistance against Russia."[9]

The Russian expansion in Circassia began before the Muscovites' era, but then extended to become inherited as a legacy characterized by the desire to control the destinies of others. This started from the reign of the first tsar, Ivan IV (Ivan the Terrible), and continued into the reigns of the following tsars, emperors, communist leaders, and current Russian leaders.

A series of wars took place between the Russians and the Circassians. This occurred from the infancy of the establishment of a Russian state, such as the Kievan Rus era, which was led by Prince Sviatoslav, who "had captured part of Taman Peninsula, laid the foundation of Tmutarakan town, at the present location of the Taman village, and had established the Princedom of Tamatarkha."[10]

The Muscovites, and those who succeeded them, initially started with intermittent skirmishes and wars in many directions. The Circassians, other nations of the Caucasus, and others had been opposing the Russian tendency to capture and subjugate all peoples and nations around them until the Russian Empire declared an uncompromising aggressive war against the Circassians. This war, which lasted for 101 years, was to control Circassia, eliminate the presence of the Circassian nation on its soil, and control the Circassian coast on the Black Sea. It is considered the longest war that the Russian state had ever fought throughout its history. It is called the Russo-Circassian War, or the Russian-Caucasian War. This is unlike what the Russian government calls it, the Caucasian War, in an attempt to eliminate its major participant regarding its occurrence and repercussions.[11]

With friend and foe both letting them down, the Circassians faced famine, disease, deprivation, murder, genocide, and the destruction of all elements of their homeland by a scorched-earth policy that was declared and delivered by the invading forces and their mercenaries. The result was the complete occupation of Circassia. Half the total of the Circassian population was lost during this war. However, the real tragedy experienced by the Circassians, which they are still suffering from to this day (more than 150 years after the occupation), is the alienation of 90 percent of the total population from their beloved homeland into exile, as they are still living in a large dispersion that consists of dozens of countries. It was the result of a forced mass expulsion in favor of the imperial plans of the invaders.

The other 10 percent, who are still residing in their homeland, were administratively divided and diluted. They are now a population of several minorities who must live in six nonhomogeneous, nor geographically contiguous, enclaves that were dictated and implemented by the successive Russian regimes imposing a fait accompli on the Circassians. After vacating the Circassian land from most of its population, they replaced them by settlers from different origins and nationalities to keep the indigenous Circassians as strangers and minorities in the places where they resided, that is, their homeland.

Various conditions affected the Circassians in their new environment, whether in dispersion or in the homeland in the north Caucasus. These conditions changed the Circassians as they adjusted to the new circumstances around them.

> The Circassians in the Soviet Union underwent forced resettlement onto kolkhozy and into new villages in the

lowlands. Traditional housing styles were replaced with standard Soviet rural brick homes with small plots around them. Some Circassians have moved to the new local cities and have established themselves in modern urban life. The Circassians in Turkey are still largely peasants, with a few that have taken up military careers. The Ubykhs still persist as a distinct type of Adyghe, but their language is now spoken only by one man and one woman. In Jordan, the Circassians are concentrated in and around Amman, where they own a great deal of property and have been entrusted with the state electrical and power monopoly. They enjoy Circassian radio and television but are not allowed to publish in their language. In Syria, the Circassians were concentrated in five villages in the Golan Heights. After the 1967 Arab-Israeli War, these Circassians withdrew into Syria, specifically to slum districts of Damascus. Finding their settlements unacceptable, they petitioned the United States in the mid-seventies to be granted asylum. The United States initiated a program with the aid of the Tolstoy Foundation of New York City to enable many of these Circassians to immigrate into America, where they settled in New Jersey and New York City. In Israel, the two villages of Circassians appear to enjoy relative freedom and have a tradition of serving Israel as an elite border patrol. In the United States, the Circassian communities are largely urban. Here there is considerable tension and debate between those few who came directly from the Caucasus and the vast majority who have come from the Middle East as to the purity of their traditions and the best way to salvage their heritage, for there is considerable anxiety that they are destined for extinction as a people. Some harbor dreams of a repatriation of all Circassians to the Caucasus, and there is a movement, based in Holland, dedicated to achieving that end by peaceful means. It might be mentioned that the only Ubykhs outside of Turkey reside in southern California.[12]

For Circassians, the importance of their homeland and its fate were never forms of political essay or subjects of bargaining. On the contrary, their homeland has always been, and will persist as, the most precious asset that Circassians own. It is redeemed by the hearts and souls of the Circassians and is considered as an identity and affiliation.

Deportation and Displacement

The Circassian deportation was proven to be planned by the Russian army.[13] Their plan was to clear the Circassian coast on the Black Sea from the indigenous population. Those who weren't killed were to be transferred to areas beyond the Kuban River or to be deported to the Ottoman Empire. The Russians' intentions stipulated total elimination of the Circassian national resistance, which aimed to defend the homeland from the invasion of foreign powers that did not have any ethnical, national, religious links or any common goals with the Circassians.

Part of the hundreds of thousands that were deported were transported to the Balkans for protecting the interests of the Ottoman Empire at a time of unrest and local resistance against the Ottoman rule, which led to the Balkan War. Circassians were mobilized and employed to fight with the Turkish Ottoman Army, and they had to face the consequences that resulted from the war, including the redisplacement of many of them to take refuge in other parts of the world.

> However, the tragedy didn't end for those who survived Russia's campaign in the Caucasus Mountains. After their deportation, nearly half were driven from their new homes in the Balkans by Russian troops in the 1870's. They were forced to migrate further to the Middle East and beyond.[14]

The Circassians had gained an influential and precious civilization because of consequential and intermingled elements. They dealt and interrelated through thousands of years, with regional and even cross-regional peoples and nations: "A large body of archeological, cultural, and linguistic evidence points to an ancient culture throughout the North Caucasus dating back to the Paleolithic Era. This population probably served as the substrata from which all the indigenous peoples of the Caucasus emerged. Differentiations between Northwest, Northeast and South Caucasus peoples were the result of influence of later arrivals who superimposed their cultural and linguistic features upon this original population. Further evidence indicates a stable indigenous civilization in the Northwest Caucasus for nearly 5,000 years."[15]

In Heroes and Emperors in Circassian History, authored by Shauket Mufti, his book affirms that in "old times and in different periods of history the Circassians appeared under different names which designated only some of the tribes."[16]

Mufti said in this regard, "The ancient Greeks knew the ancestors of the Circassians under the name Zych and Kerket, which designated two different tribes of the Circassian people. The Georgian chronicles called them Djik (which is the same as Zych), and their country Djiketia. However, the author of the Derbend-nameh called all people dwelling between the Terek River and the Black Sea 'Djuli-and', referring to the Ants, bearing in mind that all those countries have been always inhabited by the different Circassian tribes."[17]

In other details, he said, "The Kerkets occupied the Kabarda region in the time of Strabo, but they lived also on the Black Sea, near the mouth of the Pshat River. There they were good sailors, but a part of the tribe migrated to Byzantium, and it is said that some of them still live in the town of Misrata in Libya under the name of 'Ashirat-el-Sarakissa' (the tribe of Circassians)."[18]

It is noteworthy that some sources mentioned, "The Adyghe people originate in the North Caucasus region, an area they are believed to have occupied as early as the Stone Age period, with traces of them dating back as far as 8000 BC."[19]

There is concrete proof that the Circassians have cultural roots dating from before the fourth millennium BC. It is stated,

> The Maykop culture (3700–2500 BCE), in the North Caucasus, was culturally speaking a sort of southern extension of the Yamna horizon. Although not generally considered part of the Pontic-Caspian steppe culture due to its geography, the North Caucasus had close links with the steppe, as attested by numerous ceramics, gold, copper and bronze weapons and jewelry in the contemporaneous cultures of Mikhaylovka, Sredny Stog, and Kemi Oba.[20]

> The link between the North Pontic and North Caucasus is older than the Maykop period. Its predecessor, the Svobodnoe culture (4400–3700 BCE), already had links to the Suvorovo-Novodanilovka and early Sredny Stog cultures, and the even older Nalchik settlement (5000–4500 BCE) displayed a similar culture as Khvalynsk on the Volga. This may be the period when R1b started interacting and blending with the R1a population of the steppes.[21]

Confirming the facts of Circassian history, the "Circassian Heritage" link has emphasized on the existence of historical proofs:

> The Adygheans (the people's own name for themselves is Adyghe) are an ancient native people of the Northwest Caucasus, better known in historical annals as Circassians

(also Cherkess). An agricultural and cattle-breeding culture arose in the Northwest Caucasus in the early Bronze age. By 3000 B.C., the Dolmen culture, whose name comes from the distinctive megaliths used as grave markers, had arisen here and reached its peak; it lasted until the last quarter of the second millennium B.C. The area where the Caucasian dolmens are found is the ancestral home of the Adyghe-Abkhaz tribes. Today, there are five dolmen fields in the republic with about 200 whole and partly ruined dolmens.[22]

Another source mentions more details:

> The Maykop culture of the Kuban valley coexisted with the Dolmen culture. The first classical monuments of the Maykop culture in the form of large burial mounds (kurgans) containing splendid articles made of precious metals were discovered in the Kuban before the Revolution. They include the well-known kurgan excavated in Maykop in 1897 by Professor N.I. Veselovsky, which gave its name to the culture as whole. The settlements of Meshoko, Skala, Khadzhokh, and Yasenovaya Polyana are other well-known monuments of this period.[23]

The Circassians' ancestors were an integral part of human evolution through all historical ages. There are materialized facts according to compatible evidence provided through archeological excavations of buried material and tools uncovered by specialists:

> The first iron appeared here in the second millennium B.C. and led to major economic and social advances at the end of the 9th and the beginning of the 8th centuries B.C. The economic structure was represented by cattle-breeding, agriculture, metallurgy and metalworking, weaving, and spinning. This period is known in history as the Protomeotic.[24]

The usage of iron in the North Caucasus proves the developments that ancient Circassians were able to achieve:

> The 7th–6th centuries B.C. saw the beginning of widespread use of iron in the Northwest Caucasus, which led to the rapid development of productive forces that transformed the entire

material culture and social life. By this time, the Meotic culture was thriving on the right bank of the Kuban, on the left banks of its tributaries to the northern slopes of the Caucasian range, and along the eastern shore of Lake Meota (the Sea of Azov). The Meots lived in farming settlements, and along with farming, stock-breeding, fishing, metallurgy and metalworking, and crafts (pottery, weaving, jewelry-making, tanning, woodworking, etc.) were also well developed.[25]

All the historical facts retell the names of peoples from the Caucasus, particularly the names of the Circassian tribes and clans that settled in the Circassian homeland since ancient times:

The names of North Caucasian tribes, such as the Meots, Sinds, Akhei, Zikhs, and others that played a major role in the ethno genesis of the Adyghe, first became known in about 1000 B.C. In Greek and Roman sources, they are referred to collectively as Meots, and in 1000 B.C., they occupied the eastern coasts of the Black Sea and the Sea of Azov and the Kuban valley.[26]

Some prominent names of Circassians and their role in forming and developing the nation through the years are as follows:

One of the numerous Taman tribes, they early got separate from the others and lived in the 1st millennium BC—first centuries AD on the Taman peninsula and the nearby Black sea coast up to Novorossiisk. They were first mentioned by logographs, then by the Greek and Roman historians Herodot, Pseudo-Skilak, Pseudo-Scymn, Strabon. The main occupations of Sinds were agriculture, fishing, crafts and trade (in the early period—with Urartu, since the VI century BC—with Greeks). They traded both through their own ports—Sind haven, Korokondama, and through the Greek cities founded on the territory of Sindika. The wars with Scythians caused the strengthening of the power of the military leaders. In the fifth century BC, there appeared a state (Sind state). Since the IV century BC, Sinds lost their political independence and joined the Bosporus kingdom. Sind nobility was part of the ruling Bosporus aristocracy.[27]

Circassia

The names of Circassian tribes and/or entities were used in accordance with the evolving circumstances. They also managed to strengthen and consolidate relations with other ancient nations:

> The 5th century B.C. began with the rise of cities that became craft and trading centers in the lands of one of the Meotic tribes of Sinds. Intercourse with the Greek world, accelerated the process of formation of classes and states among the Sinds. By the end of the 5th century B.C., Sindika had been transformed into a real kingdom. Close political and economic ties were formed with the Bosporus state. Many scientists believe that the Spartacid dynasty that ruled the Bosporus for more than 150 years was Meotic (M.I. Artamonov, E.I. Krupnov) rather than Greek.[28]

The next stage of national convergence necessitated an improvement in different work conducted among the Circassian tribes to unite and to work together:

> The Meots' high level of material and spiritual culture and the influence of neighboring peoples on it are confirmed by the unique discoveries made during the excavation of kurgans near the village of Ulyap in Krasnogvardeysky District, which were first known as the Ulsk kurgans, but after a brilliant analysis by Professor A.M. Peskov in 1981–1982, were renamed the Ulyap kurgans. At the beginning of the Common Era, one of the coastal tribes, the Zikhs, appeared on the historical scene. Being in a more advantageous position than the steppe-dwelling Meats for a number of reasons, the Zikhs began to play an important role in the unification process. By the 6th century A.D., the neighboring tribes had united around the Zikhs to form the Zikh Union. Eighth-century authors refer to Zikhia as a sizable country on the eastern shore of the Black Sea resulting from consolidation of the tribes into a single Adyghe people. Two other unions, namely, the Kasog in the Transkuban region and the Abazg in the southeast, formed along with the Zikh Union.[29]

Relations with the Ancient Greeks

The Circassians were up to a responsible standard regarding their ability to conduct good and fruitful relations that preserved their rights, thus achieving the advancement of bilateral relations with others. This coincided with the foundations of balanced and civilized relations to achieve common interests and mutual relations in all fields:

> In the eighth century BCE, the peoples of Northwest Caucasus unified into the so-called Kuban culture, which stretched from the Taman peninsula to Sochi in the South, and along the left bank of the Kuban as far as western Karachaevo-Cherkessia around the end of the second millennium BCE.
>
> Greek historiographers classified the peoples of this civilization into numerous tribal affiliations. The origin and significance of many of the Greek appellations are problematic and sometimes contradictory, and often the tribes were only known from second- and third-hand reports. These early residents of the Northwest Caucasus were farmers of wheat, barely, and millet, and breeders of cattle, sheep, horses, and pigs. The tribes along the Azov coast engaged in fishing as well.[30]

Seemingly, the Circassians had promoted their relations with the Greeks, which eventually showed coordination and cooperation in all walks of life. Trade was the main concern. They exchanged agricultural products in addition to traditional handcrafted products.

> There appears to have been a well-developed social order, including wealthy families and social stratification throughout society. One tribe, identified by the Greeks as the "Meots," had a ruling class, militias, and a professional military force. After the arrival of the Greeks, the two parties traded extensively, although antagonistic relations and armed conflict ultimately ensued.
>
> Nevertheless, the Greeks adapted to conditions in which they found themselves and began to engage in agriculture as well. By the fourth century BCE large volumes of grain were being shipped from the region to Greece and other locations in the Mediterranean. There is also evidence that the Greek colonies became centers for artisans from among the indigenous population.[31]

The relations resulted in the upswing of cultural exchange and humanitarian relations. Both sides benefited from literary and cultural communications. That gave the relationship impetus for cultural harmony and other associated elements. A focus was made on the establishment of ports and their structures as well as promoting commerce:

> Once the Greeks colonized the northern and eastern shores of the Black Sea in the seventh and six centuries BCE, cities arose in rapid succession, the most important of which was Thanagoria on the Crimean Peninsula. A fusion of Greek and local culture resulted in a unique form of Hellenic civilization which was considered semi-barbaric by the traditional centers of Greek civilization but achieved a relatively high level of cultural development and became active trading centers. These cities functioned as autonomous poleis until around 480 BCE, when they were united by Archaeanactid Dynasty into the Bosporus State. Strategically situated, the Greeks were able to control trade throughout the entire eastern Black Sea. The value of this location would lead to countless wars that repeatedly devastated the Northwest Caucasus.[32]

The Byzantine Contact

Most relationships that took place between the Circassians and other nations had generated positive impacts. Thus, not to underestimate the negative consequences in certain cases. However, reality bites, reveals, and ensures that there is an exception to the Circassian situation. The Circassian nation was subjected to an unprecedented destructive and unmerciful invasion during the Russian-Circassian War.

The Circassians had established distinguished relations with the Byzantines. They gradually embraced the Christian religion. They constructed the churches and monasteries. Also, they commenced practicing Christianity until the time their majority had converted to Islam.

> In the 6th century A.D., Byzantine influence was increasing in the Northwest Caucasus. By this time, the coastal Adyghe had converted to Christianity and a Zikh diocese directly under the Byzantine patriarch had been formed. Contemporary references to the Adyghe as the Zikhs and

Kasogs give reason to believe that the single Adyghe union had split into the western and eastern Adyghe (Kabardians).³³

Mufti says that Circassians

> lived and dwelt in the western Caucasus as well as in the Crim in the same time, from where they were probably expelled by the Tatars under Batu-Khan. Josaphat Barbaro, who was a Venician ambassador to Persia, called the Kabarda region of today already in the year 1474 also Kabarda, Moreover, Strabo knew Kerkets in that region. On the sea map, designed by Freducius of Ancona in the year 1499, appears the name of the Kabardians (written in red ink) at the place where Taganrog lies today.³⁴
>
> Their stay in the Crim did not last long; they left the region under the growing pressure of the Tatars, and they came through the strait of Kertch to settle temporarily on the isle of Taman which lies between the two branches of the Kuban River, named by the Tatars "Kizih-Tash" (Red-stone). But they soon left it too and returned under the leadership of their great Prince Yinal, the ancestor of all Kabardian princes, to the Kuban and settled.³⁵
>
> According to the traditions of the Ossets, the Circassians were referred to by the Mingrelians as "Kazakh" and their princes "Kazakh-mepe" that means "Kings of the Kazakhs", until the arrival of the Kabardian princes from the Crim.³⁶

There was an influential effect of the major players at the time in naming the regional parts: "This statement also coincides with the account of the Emperor Constantinus Porphyrogeneta who called the country of the Circassians on the Black sea 'Zychia' and that adjoining the country of the Alans 'kazakhia.'"³⁷

The author elaborated on the location and influence: "And at the time of George Interiano (about 1502) the Circassians occupied all countries lying about the sea of Azov, and their territories extended from the Don River to Cimmerian Bosphorus."³⁸

Regarding the characteristics of the people, the author said, "If we look into the legends and traditions that have come to us from ancient times, we find that the ancient Adighes had many virtues and admirable qualities including chivalry, self-dignity, sagacity, and intelligence; and that they were known for their bravery and horsemanship. Their national breeding refined their spirits, strengthened their morals and accustomed them to endure fatigue and hardships in war and in long journeys."[39]

The book mentioned the Circassians' persistence and that strategy followed when their country was attacked and occupied by foreign powers: "As a matter of fact our grandfathers were known for their unceasing efforts, diligence, and perseverance, but after being exposed to the attacks of savage people such as the Mongols, the Tatars, the Huns, the Kalmuks, and others they lost most much of their diligence and were forced to leave their homelands and to take refuge in mountains and deep valleys."[40]

Also, it described conditions and circumstances that had affected their social and cultural evolution. They were preoccupied with their concern to defend their very existence as a nation: "Sometimes they had to spend months or even years in the wilderness, which eventually led to their degeneration; and similarly, they did not find sufficient time and tranquility necessary for taking up useful civilian activities or the methods of modern civilization."[41]

Facts about the unique Circassian national character were reaffirmed: "The ancient Adighes were admired by their neighbors for their military prowess, unique horsemanship and neat garments; they were fond of horsemanship and of breeding the finest horses."[42]

The author stated the details of war plans, organizing the ranks, identifying leaders, and sharing the responsibilities by everyone. Also, they determined the style of coordination among them: "When the Adighes went out fighting they chose their leaders from among their ranks and entrusted them with the administration and command of the combat armies according to their traditions." Then he continued, "These leaders were capable, brave and took no heed of caution."[43]

More details were mentioned concerning the impact of the natural terrain on their general conduct. They adapted to the nature of their homeland, giving them self-confidence and helped them to struggle to defend themselves: "Besides their bravery they possessed other characteristic, including the ability to fight at great heights in the mountains and on narrow necks of land, maneuverability and speed in places where others would have had serious difficulties and sensibility in positioning themselves in deep valleys and thick forests."[44]

The book elaborated more on the quality of the people: "Their ambition gave rise to bravery, dauntlessness, and love of adventure; and their extreme self-confidence and self-dignity gave them boundless individual liberty. Nevertheless, they were meek and far from sensuality and base emotions; they boasted of nothing but their bravery and military victories."[45]

He continued on mentioning the Circassians' virtues: "Our traditions indicate that our forefathers knew no deceit or treachery; they bore every sacrifice in keeping their pledges, promises, and mutual friendship; and owing to their simplicity, they have those considerations an importance that is seldom to be found. among their virtues were hospitality and safeguarding the life of and possessions of their guests."[46]

Circassians were known for agriculture in their fertile plains and mountains. They have practiced proper farming that suits them, which demonstrates their progress in this area. They planted crops that they needed for their own consumption and for commercial and trade with others. "The Circassians (i.e. the Adighes) have been used to farming since ancient times; they planted cereal such as maize, barley, wheat and millet together with various vegetables. Our language includes the names of all the cereals, except rice. After harvest and before disposing of the new crop, they performed certain ceremonies, as it was necessary to say some prayers and invocations, after which a person prepared a banquet from the new crop to which he invited his relatives and friends."[47]

Language

The language is an integral element of the culture. It expresses and verifies the Circassians' independent identity and national personality. Attempts to eliminate the language have contributed to making it close to extinction. Through the language, the process of communication had been created between the different individuals and groups of the society. That necessitated the emergence of other important elements, such as literature, poetry, art, music, and others. All this expressed the way that the popular culture had been affected:

> As for our national language, it is an elastic widely in flexional language which can express meanings without having to utilize many foreign words. It is adequate for literature, poetry, and oratory, but it has not been studied carefully by specialized European scholars in order to fully understand its characteristics and origin and to record its literature. Anyhow, it's one of the European languages and resembles the ancient Indian language (Sanskrit) and Lithuanian. It also contains a large number of ancient European roots and words such as Maza (moon) and Gava (cereals). Concerning its construction and riots they are similar to Latin but were greatly influenced by the Caucasian languages.[48]

Religion and Belief

Circassians have always believed in the existence of a supernatural power that controls the whole universe. They drew their own conclusions to get to the spiritual and moral contact with the invisible might. Sometimes they practiced this through natural phenomena or objects like stars, planets, and others. That was derived and inserted within their seasonal customs, traditions, and behaviors, also through literature, ancient epics, and literary texts such as the Nart sagas. Accordingly, they practiced their rituals and offered sacrifices.

> The ancient Circassians attributed all occurrences, worldly affairs and every good or evil which befell a man's life to the will of the Creator who created the skies and the earth; thus they did everything they could to propitiate Him through invocations, prayers, and sacrifices. They slew bulls and gave them as offerings in order to be rewarded with mercy and relief in times of war and disease.[49]

Mufti has categorized the main faiths that the Circassians embraced: "Historically the Circassian religion is confined to three important phases: the pagan, the Christian, and the Moslem. Each of these phases left its effect on Circassian customs and traditions, and many religious teachings eventually became national customs and traditions after the people had forgotten the origin of these customs."[50]

He mentioned two of the prominent gods and what they correspond to the ancient Greek gods: "Their greatest god was Shi-bla, the god of the thunder-bolt who they feared greatly. He corresponds to the Greek god Zeus, and was proverbial for His power and tyranny . . . There was another important god, the god of iron and fire called Leash, who was also the god of the smithy and the maker of the swords of heroes. He corresponded to the Greek god Hephaistos."[51]

The author referred to an approach of one of the stories of Greek mythology: "Again, Prometheus, the titan who stole the Holy Fire, still lives in the memory of our nation. Some old men maintained that on the high mountains there was an old man who had been chained for thousands of years on inaccessible rocks and that his groans could be heard at night when echoed by mountains and deep valleys, as he cried painfully while the horrible eagle ate his liver."[52]

He came to an important fact regarding the Circassian-Greek relationship through mythology and other old ties. It is also confirmed by other scholars: "Under close scrutiny, it appears that these legends we can say without much hesitation that the ancient Greeks took many of their myths from the Caucasians as they knew them and their country well."[53]

At a later stage, and because of their contact with other peoples and regional powers particularly the Byzantine Empire, they were introduced to the divine religions. They converted to Christianity. They practiced that religion, built temples for their religious practice and worship:

> In the 6th century A.D., Byzantine influence was increasing in the Northwest Caucasus. By this time, the coastal Adyghe had converted to Christianity and a Zikh diocese directly under the Byzantine patriarch had been formed.[54]
>
> The Adighes were won over to Christianity during the reign of Emperor Justinian in the 6th century A.D. Consequently, relations were strengthened between our nation and the great Byzantine Empire.[55]

Actions of consolidation are detailed.

> It was during the reign of Justinian that the historic buildings and ancient churches still existing in Circassia were built, a fact which shows that the Circassians had at that time a degree of culture and art and that when the new architectural movement arose they began to work immediately in the fine arts and crafts that accompanied it.[56]
>
> Furthermore St. George is still considered the patron saint of all the Caucasians.[57]

They were introduced by the Ottomans to the religion Islam, which they eventually embraced and espoused. With the passage of time, their majority became Muslims while some of them remained Christians:

> The Adighes did not adopt Islam as one body to at one time, and what has been said applies to the Kabardians only. As to the tribes living in the Kuban and on the eastern coasts of the Black Sea they did not become Moslems until the 19th Century, i.e. till before the exodus of 1864. It seems that they adopted Islam when they despaired of being assisted by the European powers in their fight against the Russians and needed Ottoman assistance.[58]

Some of Christian concepts and practices have been integrated into Circassian daily life, even long after the Circassians had converted to Islam: "Friday is still called Kareem (the day of Our Lady, Mary) and Sunday is called Tha-Mafe (the day of God)."[59]

In this sense, I have witnessed some Circassians in the past who kept an open pair of scissors in a cross shape, placed over a dead body. They do it as a tradition, which explained in different ways and means that this practice keeps the dead body in a good shape until burial, unaware that this was practiced by Christian Circassians by putting a cross on a dead body.

Unprotected Archaeology and Ancient Heritage

On the sixth of October 2016, Paul Goble published a "window" with the title of "Black Archaeology Threatens Cultural Monuments of North Caucasus Peoples," addressing one of the important issues that the North Caucasus in general and Circassians in particular are facing and suffering.[60]

The national archaeological monument's theme of inherited historical heritage and historic cultural collectibles consist of valuable and priceless artistic objects. It is not limited to a specific period of time or certain historical era, but includes all the historical and temporal ages that have passed by this ancient nation. The danger is mentioned as a "threat that up to now has received little attention is that of people who steal the cultural monuments of these peoples to sell them for profit."[61]

The conclusion of dealing and interacting between Circassian culture and civilization and other great cultures and civilizations has positive effects in all aspects. It created a civilization with humanitarian standards and concepts. As a matter of fact, it can be traced back to the "Paleolithic era." Also, "the North Caucasus is a contact zone of three great civilizations, Aleksandr Skakov of Moscow's Primakov Institute on the World Economy and International Relations says, the region is rich in art for which collectors elsewhere are prepared to pay high prices."[62]

Paul Goble continues his analysis, saying, "The situation in this regard is 'especially catastrophic' in Krasnodar kray, Karachayevo-Cherkessia, Kabardino-Balkaria, and Abkhazia. Those who engage in 'black archaeology" use the media and other means to try to convince the local leaders and populations that these 'ruins' can bring them profits."[63]

Goble also mentioned, "According to some estimates, the Moscow scholar says, only about 10 percent of all people involved in searching for artefacts in the North Caucasus are doing so as 'black archaeologists.'"[64]

Selfish behavior that indicates hatred and racism has played negative and destructive consequences to the part of human civilization. It is implemented by those who tried and continue to destroy or tamper with genuine high-valued archaeological ancient culture. Knowing that these irresponsible actions contribute to the loss of cultural and historical legacy, they can't compensate for destroyed or concealed items. The malignant target is to obliterate tangible historical facts.

There are vivid examples of overruling the applicable laws concerning harmful "black" archaeology. The Russian president Vladimir Putin himself has reportedly intervened personally in such exposures. He has unjustifiably fiddled with valuable sites of the Circassian coast on the Black Sea. Archaeological areas and sites have been tampered with[65] in order to cover up what was said in Putin's famous speech in English in Guatemala City. The occasion was the opening of the 2014 Sochi Winter Olympics, where it was stated that "the ancient Greeks lived around Sochi lots of centuries ago," which is located on the Black Sea coast.[66]

Knowing that the Greeks had set up and established strong relations with the Circassians in a particular historical era didn't deter him from deliberately failing to mention Circassians as the rightful owners and inhabitants of the hosting land, where the 2014 Sochi Winter Olympic Games had taken place.

Apparently, those who were guiding that campaign of destroying what is left of the multiple historical and religious heritage of the Circassian nation know what they are doing. They are aiming at the elimination of everything that connects the Circassians with their homeland and their history through the ages.

---

1. https://aheku.net/articles/english/general/1321
2. The Circassian Genocide (Walter Richmond)
3. http://hekupse.livejournal.com/1730.html
4. http://hekupse.livejournal.com/1730.html
5. The Circassian Genocide (Walter Richmond)
6. http://habze.info/publ/what_is_khabze/1-1-0-47
7. The Circassian Genocide (Walter Richmond)
8. John Colarusso, (1994) Encyclopedia of World Cultures, David Levinson (ed.), vol. 6, Inner Eurasia and China, Paul Friedrich and Norma Diamond (eds.), Boston, Massachusetts: G. K. Hall & Co.
9. The Place of the Ottoman Empire in The Russo-Circassian War (1830-1864), by Ibrahim Köremezli

10 Circassian History (Kadir Natho)
11 Muscovite Period, Excerpted from Russia: A Country Study, Glenn E. Curtis, ed. (Washington, DC: Federal Research Division of the Library of Congress, 1996)
12 http://www.encyclopedia.com/topic/Circassians.aspx#1-1G2:3458000968-full
13 The Circassian Genocide (Walter Richmond)
14 The Circassian Genocide (Walter Richmond)
15 The Northwest Caucasus: Past, Present, Future (Walter Richmond)
16 Heroes and Emperors in Circassian History (Shauket Mufti)
17 Heroes and Emperors in Circassian History (Shauket Mufti)
18 Heroes and Emperors in Circassian History (Shauket Mufti)
19 https://sites.google.com/site/narodykavkaza/
20 http://www.eupedia.com/europe/Haplogroup_R1b_Y-DNA.shtml
21 http://www.muturzikin.com/documents/Origins,%20age,%20spread%20and%20ethnic%20association%20of%20European%20haplogroups%20and%20subclades.pdf
22 http://thecircassianheritage2011.webklik.nl/page/history
23 https://aheku.net/stranicza-ajax?id=3941#
24 https://aheku.net/stranicza-ajax?id=3941#
25 https://aheku.net/stranicza-ajax?id=3941#
26 https://aheku.net/stranicza-ajax?id=3941
27 http://www.eng.kavkaz-uzel.eu/articles/556/
28 https://aheku.net/stranicza-ajax?id=3941#
29 https://aheku.net/stranicza-ajax?id=3941#
30 The Northwest Caucasus: Past, Present, Future (Walter Richmond)
31 The Northwest Caucasus: Past, Present, Future (Walter Richmond)
32 The Northwest Caucasus: Past, Present, Future (Walter Richmond)
33 https://aheku.net/stranicza-ajax?id=3941#
34 Heroes and Emperors in Circassian History (Shauket Mufti)
35 Heroes and Emperors in Circassian History (Shauket Mufti)
36 Heroes and Emperors in Circassian History (Shauket Mufti)
37 Heroes and Emperors in Circassian History (Shauket Mufti)
38 Heroes and Emperors in Circassian History (Shauket Mufti)
39 Heroes and Emperors in Circassian History (Shauket Mufti)
40 Heroes and Emperors in Circassian History (Shauket Mufti)
41 Heroes and Emperors in Circassian History (Shauket Mufti)
42 Heroes and Emperors in Circassian History (Shauket Mufti)
43 Heroes and Emperors in Circassian History (Shauket Mufti)
44 Heroes and Emperors in Circassian History (Shauket Mufti)
45 Heroes and Emperors in Circassian History (Shauket Mufti)
46 Heroes and Emperors in Circassian History (Shauket Mufti)

47 Heroes and Emperors in Circassian History (Shauket Mufti)
48 Heroes and Emperors in Circassian History (Shauket Mufti)
49 Heroes and Emperors in Circassian History (Shauket Mufti)
50 Heroes and Emperors in Circassian History (Shauket Mufti)
51 Heroes and Emperors in Circassian History (Shauket Mufti)
52 Heroes and Emperors in Circassian History (Shauket Mufti)
53 Heroes and Emperors in Circassian History (Shauket Mufti)
54 (https://aheku.net/stranicza-ajax?id=3941#)
55 Heroes and Emperors in Circassian History (Shauket Mufti)
56 Heroes and Emperors in Circassian History (Shauket Mufti)
57 Heroes and Emperors in Circassian History (Shauket Mufti)
58 Heroes and Emperors in Circassian History (Shauket Mufti)
59 Heroes and Emperors in Circassian History (Shauket Mufti)
60 http://windowoneurasia2.blogspot.com/2016/10/black-archaeology-threatens-cultural.html
61 http://windowoneurasia2.blogspot.com/2016/10/black-archaeology-threatens-cultural.html
62 http://windowoneurasia2.blogspot.com/2016/10/black-archaeology-threatens-cultural.html
63 http://windowoneurasia2.blogspot.com/2016/10/black-archaeology-threatens-cultural.html
64 http://windowoneurasia2.blogspot.com/2016/10/black-archaeology-threatens-cultural.html
65 https://www.youtube.com/watch?v=LMz_bIzx8HM
66 https://www.youtube.com/watch?v=_aNo3DxWaW4

2

The Circassian Independence

Gathering of the confederated princes of Circassia
on the banks of the Ubin River 1836

Throughout imperial history, occupying and colonizing authorities assumed domination and practices of absolute rule and power to change the realities, features, and landmarks in all walks of life of the colonized nations. Aiming to the furthest extent possible, they wanted to exclude the indigenous people from bearing the responsibility of governing themselves. Unless subjugated nations oppose such authoritarian policies, they will eventually force and compel the greedy and covetous state to comply with their ambitions of freedom to choose their own destiny that necessarily would lead to assume legitimate rights of self-determination, freedom, and independence.

For centuries, since the Greeks and Romans, Circassia had been exposed to continuous foreign attempts and efforts by various foreign imperial, expansionist, and colonialist powers to invade and conquer Circassia. This obliged the Circassians to be engaged in several defensive preparations and operations thought to be of top priority over all other elements. It was not easy for any of the invaders to take advantage of getting through their strength or resilience. They were always eager to defend their freedom and independence.

Even during the Mongol invasion of the Caucasus region in the thirteenth century and their occupation of the territories located north of the Caucasus that was called Russia, it was not possible to occupy and colonize Circassia the way others were occupied for decades to come. In this regard, Geopolitical Club published in January 2017 an article with the title of "Circassia Remained Independent of the Mongol Empire, Founded by Genghis Khan."[67]

Defensive councils were formed whenever they were needed, which consisted of the chiefs of the main Circassian tribes for the purpose of appointing military leaders and commanders to deal with the situation and consequently maintain the independence of the national decision making. The suitable strategy would be agreed upon and followed by all parts of the Circassian fighting units within collective and thorough operations according to a comprehensive plan, which led to the preservation of freedom and independence for hundreds of years until the last Russian-Circassian War that broke out in 1763.

Some known circles persisted to spread malicious tales about Circassia, the motherland, and the nation. They tried to broadcast and circulate news of suspicious objectives that pertained to weak arguments. They stated that the Circassians never had a political entity at all, and they never thought of it before. They forgot that the Circassian tribes were able to coordinate with one another to repel invading attackers throughout their long history; there were national, cultural, and joint defense mechanisms. Accordingly, they managed to fend off their enemies for hundreds of years until the tsarist Russians eventually managed to mobilize hundreds of thousands of military forces and mercenaries. They committed their biggest massacre of perpetrating genocide in the nineteenth century according to reliable historians,[68] which explains the Circassian tragedy without delving into details in this area, although it shows that the Circassian leaders had agreed, as the European newspapers had published in the year 1835, to the "Circassian Declaration of Independence," as stated in the documents, which have been obtained from Russian archives, "V.M. Atalikova Publications" (See Living antiquities. 1992. № 2. Pp 20–23), and has been recently translated into several languages.[69]

> Circassia in the middle of the eighteenth century, prior to tsarist Imperial conquest, occupied an area of 55,663 square kilometres—rather greater than the area of Denmark—and possessed an indigenous population in excess of two million. During much of their history, Circassians existed independently.[70]

After the centuries of military alliance, Russia broke the agreement and attacked Circassia. The Circassians fought against Russian conquest for over a century, from 1763 to 1864—longer than any other people of the Caucasus. Their final defeat in the 1860s led to massacre and forced deportation, mainly across the Black Sea to Turkey.[71]

The Independence is not something never experienced for the Circassians. What you see on this slide is the Declaration of Independence of Circassia, addressed to the courts of Europe in 1837. Europe ignored the brutality of Russia against the Circassian people struggling for survival, and that is the story of how the tolerance supported genocide.

Today the Nations of Europe can fix the mistakes of their ancestors. We, Circassians, around the World call for your attention, and support on our long way to our beloved Homeland. Free Circassia is the only future for our Nation, this is the goal that we, 6 millions of the Circassians, are going to achieve for the holy memory of our ancestors and for the safety of upcoming generations.[72]

There was a response from those who were informed of the declaration of the independence of Circassia. "Lord Palmerston, the redoubtable British Foreign Minister of the 1830s, was an avid Russophobe. He formulated Great Britain's anti-Russian policy with respect to the Eastern Question, considering Russia as a destabilizing force intent on undermining British influence in the East. He sympathized with the plight of the Circassians, covertly sanctioning the dispatch of agents to assess the situation and provide them with help. In 1838, he tacitly recognized Circassia's independence.[73]

Mufti says in his book Heroes and Emperors in Circassian History that the origin of all Circassians is Circassia. Accordingly, the tsarist Russian Empire had intended to destroy the whole country together with eliminating its people: "By oral information about their origin, I came to know from the elders of the Circassians that the progenitor of their princes and of their race came in old times and settled in Shentchir (Shindjir) which is now a heap of ruins of an old city near Anapa in the country of (Nat-Khuadj), from where not only their princes, but the whole of the Circassian nation originated."[74]

The distinct strategic location enjoyed by Circassia, being on the Black Sea with its attractive harbors, had created calamity for its people and other North Caucasus nations because it attracted invaders and imperialists. All that still affects the possibility to enable Circassians, to claim and restore their breached rights and freedom, "three types of decolonization: international, domestic and ideological. The latter is the most relevant with regard to the Circassian context as addresses the context of a totalitarian past where 'liberated peoples' had long-term memories confiscated, destroyed or manipulated."[75]

Interest in considering the history of Russian involvement in the North Caucasus in general and Circassia in particular requires us to be mindful to refer to the history of the major parties involved while it indicates a documented and much more ancient history: "Circassia was referred to as 'Kasaxia' in Byzantine Greek. The native self-designation was first recorded in the fifth century BC. It was explained by some Circassian scholars as a corruption of an older term 'Antixe', the Ants being people thought to be ancestral to the Adiga, and -xe the plural suffix."[76]

Independence and Autonomy in Ancient History

Discussing the Circassian independence requires the need to go back in history to have an idea of where the Circassians have come from. It also requires knowledge of the essence of their relationship with the homeland. Factors of convergence and interdependence between the two must be recognized: "There is not much that is known about the ancient history of the Circassian people which is one of the oldest nations existing today. Our knowledge is mostly based on traditions, legends, old songs and narrations which preserved some of the events of the past."[77]

Homogeneity of population is important to consolidate the coherence of the people: "As the Caucasus was a uniting bridge between Europe and Asia as a route of communication, leading from East to West and from north to South, it won great importance in historical times; this factor also played a big role in the Ethnic composition of the inhabitants. But the most important of those migrating or fleeing peoples were surely the Indo-Arians."[78]

A state was founded thousands of years ago, which the Circassians was its founders: "The Cimmerian Empire was established many centuries before Christ on the Shores of the Azof Sea, as a confederate state and comprised many ethnic elements and different tribes like the Maeots, Sinds, Dandars, Torests, and others. This Empire, after having lasted till 1500 B.C., was finally destroyed by the Scythes. For the Caucasians, this event meant the downfall of a strong line of defense against any possible aggression from the East."[79]

After the destruction of the Cimmerian Empire by the Scythes, the consequences led to division and dispersion that can be traced: "After being defeated, the Cimmerians were scattered and divided into several groups; one of them, the Trers went west, another chose a southern course leading them into Asia Minor. However, the third major group, the Sinds and Kemirgeys, remained as Caucasians in the Caucasus and continued to live as different tribes of the Circassian people under these names."[80]

The information and documents indicate that the Caucasus in general was, through the years and centuries, a crossroad for many parties. Also, it was an in-transit path for passers, in addition to ambitious conquerors and invaders, having the Caucasus a target by itself. That affected the independence of the peoples of the Caucasus from time to time.

> Centuries B.C. this route of communication and migration led the Aryans through the Caucasus as far as Asia Minor, Persia, India, and Turkestan, where they conquered countries and founded empires like the Mitani-Empire in Asia Minor and others, and then disappeared. Not all the migrants left the Caucasus, but some of them remained and settled (r.g. the Sinds).[81]

Homogeneity of population is important to consolidate the coherence of the people: "In this respect, E.D. Phillips (The Royal Hordes) said, 'the name of the Sinds may be the Sanskrit (Sindhava). It is suggested that these Aryans remained in their old home (Kuban) when the majority passed southward (1900–1000 B.C.), along the Caspian coast, to reach the river called Sindhu (Indus).'" Mufti added, "The group that remained in the northern Caucasus became mounted nomads (Cimmerians, Thracians . . .)."[82]

Qualitative and social developments through the ages have combined Circassians' hard work to maintain their national mosaic. "The name Kemirgey means 'Cimmerian' in Circassian and designates one of the important Circassian Tribes" while "the name Temruk for the isle of Taman is especially remarkable and of interest; its original form seems to have been Kemruk which is somehow related to the tribal name Kemirgey, to the name of the 'Strait of Ketch' and, at last, to the name of the Cimmerians."[83]

Thus were the beginnings of Russian manipulation in Circassian fate, in addition to their national status later on: "At the beginning of the 11th century, Mistislav Volodomirowitch conquered the Islae of Taman, which belonged to a prince whose name he did not mention, but of whom he said that he was the 'ruler of the Jasses and Kassogs', that is to say 'Prince of Alania and Kazakhia' (Circassia)."[84]

The sequence of inheriting ruling Circassia was a tangible fact between the ruling families that successively ruled the Circassians at different locations and at varying times.

> Since the 8th century B.C. the Greeks established many colonies on the shores of the Black Sea. Out of these colonies evolved a state called "Bosporus State". As a federal state, it consisted of different ethnic elements including Greeks, Sythes and Sought Caucasians (Circassians). Scholars affirm that the ancient history of the Circassians begins from the period of the Kingdom of Bosporus which was formed soon after the fall of Cimmerian Empire about 720 B.C. under the onslaught of the Scythes.[85]

That is the evidence that unequivocally shows that the Circassians have dwelled in their homeland for thousands of years. They were always eager to preserve their freedom and independence.

> But the dynasty in the period under consideration was formed 438 B.C. by Spartok who was of the same lineage as the former, "Ancient Princes". The Thracian name Spartok was quite normal in view of the Thrace-Cimmerian character of the local population. The power of the Spartok family, however, was not immediately established throughout Circassia.[86]

Ruling the Circassians included all their tribes and regions.

> Levon II (389–349) is called "Ruler" over the Sinds, Torets, Dandars and Psessians. Under Persuades I (344–310 B.C.) the list of the ancient Circassian people subject to the "Ruler" is longer (more complete). His title was "Ruler of the Sinds, the Maeots and Fetayens". Moreover, one inscription in the Taman Peninsula emphasizes that Perisades ruled "all over the lands between the borders of Tauri and those of the Caucasian lands."[87]

When the Huns invaded European territories in the year 374, they also invaded Circassia.

> The Circassians under the leadership of their legendary hero who supposed possessed miraculous qualities, "Tham-Uqa" (Son of God), fought these invaders of their country but they also were defeated at a place called "Gunitey" near Piatigorsk. In Circassian popular tradition, Attila is mentioned and qualified as the "Scourge of God", and when he left, the people rejoiced and said: "God had mercy with us; mountains and valleys belong to us again; the scourge of God has withdrawn his dark shadow from them."[88]

The author continued, "Yet Attila's conquest was only temporary and passed away leaving no notable political or social consequences."[89]

Some of the Circassians were able to maintain their self-governing or maintained their independence, albeit to varying degrees: "Other Circassian tribes also retained their autonomy, having their own princes, such as the Sinds and Dandarians. From the times of Satur I the Greeks in Bosporus enjoyed special exceptions, but the Bosphorians also had their privileges in Athens."[90]

Relations flourished between the Circassians and Greeks in all aspects and developed to a stable level. They founded and maintained mutual respect. The Circassians and their associates in the Bosporus State participated in the prominent and important activities and events that were held in Athens.

> Parallel with commercial relations there developed cultural ties between the two countries. The ancient Circassians took part in Olympic Games, in the Panathemic Festivals and were crowned. The Athenians awarded honorary citizenship to some of the Bosphoric Kings and in public assembles, decrees were accepted concerning the setting up of statues in their honor as well as the award of the gold crown. With such Crowns Levkon I, Spartok II and Perisad were honored. The Greeks placed Levkon and Parisad among their gallery of famous men in government, and their names were mentioned in Greek schools.[91]

Circumstances changed due to the demise of the Bosporus State and the beginning of the Roman control and influence. That extended to areas where the Roman Empire was able to impose its control.

> By the end of the 2nd century B.C. Bosporus faced a series of crisis, inspired by pressure on the part of the Scythians, and to such an extent that Perisad had to give

his crown to Mithridates the Great (114 B.C.). From this moment, the Roman period of the Bosphoric Empire began. The kings of the latter sought the protection of Rome and some Circassian tribes including the Heniokhs, Sanichians and Zichi became dependent on Rome in the time of the Hadrian. As mentioned above, in the year 115 B.C. (or 114 B.C.) Mithridathes inherited this state which lasted until the arrival of the Goths in the 3rd Century.[92]

Matching demographic and cultural data about ancient indigenous people had documented assets in the geographical area of the national territories. They were inhabited for thousands of years, but were exposed to extermination. That lasted until the occurrence of the fierce and barbaric invasion to grab their homelands and for implementation of unholy colonial settlement projects. Those nations have reliable and documented civilized roots and contacts, which benefited mankind.

According to controversial views in the Adyge and Abkhaz historiography, about five thousand years ago ancestors of the mentioned peoples resided on a wide territory that covered the Northwest and Central Caucasus, east and south coasts of the Black Sea and a large part of the Asia Minor. The tribes which were residing on this territory in III–II Millenniums BC belonged to Apkhaz-Adyge languages family or they were speaking the hindered languages of this group (I.Diakonov).[93]

No tyrant may deny that the Circassian homeland is the cradle of a well-known civilization, which is not an arguable or even contradicted reality. For a long time, twisted and crooked policies fabricate and publish incorrect news and undocumented and false information. This leads to develop and pinpoint attempts of the erosion of the colonized peoples and nations.

In view of ethno-genesis of the ancient Circassian tribes, Late Bronze and Early Iron Ages were important stages—the formation of basic cultures of direct ancestors of Adyges took place. By this time, in the Northwest Caucasus Kuban Riverbank and in the Central Caucasus Koban Cultures were being formulated. Each of them was sourced from so called "North Caucasian" culture of II Millennium BC which by originally had linked to Maykop Culture.[94]

Fortunately, professional and unbiased scholars and researchers referred to all available data. The focus was on the human groups and their roots, origin, and developments of the national prospects. They also concentrated on steps that took place, which influenced the formation and distribution of human societies and their civilizations in the region and beyond, particularly the Adyghe Circassian nation.

> Nowadays a large part of archeologists, historians, and linguists consider that the Meotian tribes are the ancient ancestors (anyway, their participation in formation of the Circassian ethnos is undoubted) of Adyges (Kabarians, Adyges and Circassians). In order to prove that the ancestors of Adyges have lived in the Northwest Caucasus, in a settlement areal of Meotianin the mentioned period, they bring numerous and trustworthy data of toponyms and onomastics which can be explained on the basis of Adyge languages.[95]

The Ottoman Negative Effect

The Ottoman Empire established good and friendly relations with the Circassians, especially those located near strategic locations on the Black Sea. Accordingly, they unfortunately misunderstood the friendship and hospitality.

> The Turks had some influence in certain parts of Caucasia, especially in the coastal towns of the Black Sea, such as Anapa, Sodjak and Soukhum Kala, because some of their garrisons were stationed there. Their influence, however, was confined to the strongholds of in which they lived. From this we realize that they did not actually control the Circassians, nor did they know much about their conditions and the long wars that had taken place in their country which were far from Ottoman influence and control.[96]

A vicious and selfish gamble of exchanging interests was conducted between regional powers at the time. That was without worrying about the disastrous consequences that could be caused to the smaller nations: "The Circassians were isolated from civilized world in all directions. Their enemies, the Russians were in the north and the Turks in the south. For a long time this had been an obstacle in the path of Caucasian civilization and progress."[97]

The Ottoman Empire caused real pain and annoyances. With a lack of moral obligation and responsibility, they sacrificed the entire Circassian nation in an irreversible evil manner: "If we look into the history of that area since the beginning of the 18th Century, we will find that the political relations of the Circassians with Turkey were completely stagnant and remained so until the end of that century."[98]

Even though certain Circassian princes permitted the Ottomans to use Circassian ports, the Ottomans didn't return this good gesture with pleasant response to the Circassians' goodwill. They didn't recognize that with gratitude. On the contrary, the Ottomans showed understanding the deal in a completely reverse attitude.

There was a double standard going on at the time. Contrary to the religious values that the Ottomans themselves should have had abided by, they followed the game of self-interest and selfishness.

Regretfully, most of the Circassian nation was on a different track. When they were invited to embrace Islam, they were introduced to different religious foundations and fundamentals.

> None of the inhabitants of those vast territories recognized Ottoman suzerainty, except some groups of Tatars who were Moslems and dwelt on the right bank of the Laba River. These Tatars were, at the time, in constant conflict with the Christian Circassians, and this led them to side with the Turks and recognize their suzerainty, although this was done only nominally.[99]

Eventually, the Ottoman game was contrary to the Circassians' high expectations and trust in their partners in faith.

> Some Ottoman rulers and pashas attempted to penetrate Circassia and gain influence there as a preliminary step towards subjugating it later on. In such attempt, however, they achieved no success. We are not exaggerating when we say that no Ottoman troops ever set foot ever in the regions of the Shapsughs, Abzakhs, or Ubykhs nor were they able to reach any part of Southern Abazia.[100]

They used religion as a trump card to get closer to the nations of the Caucasus in general and the Circassians in particular; the use of religion as a Trojan horse to win the minds, empathy, and influence.

> The utmost they could do was to win over some families living in and around Sohkhum Kala and to convert them to Islam. After one of these families was granted a princely title, the Sublime Porte recognized it and appointed the family to govern Southern Abazia. Needless to say these few 'Secessionists' could not themselves strengthen Ottoman influence in Caucasia.[101]

So those who grabbed the opportunity and moved closer towards the Ottoman Empire ultimately felt that they were gaining glory and fame. They had been granted medals and ranks among their own people. They were requested to carry out the Ottomans' instructions and policies: "The inhabitants considered the Turks as enemies; but they reserved their bitterest contempt for the Russians in whom they had absolutely no confidence at all, especially after the battle of life and death had begun between them."[102]

Circassia was designated as an independent entity, which was shown on the maps as such.

> Notwithstanding the religious differences and the fact that the Circassians had retained their independence and freedom, the Turks in their maps continued to designate Circassian countries subject to the Ottoman Empire under the designation "Circassia". More ridiculous still, the Turks agreed to hand Circassian over to Russia according to the Treaty of Adrianople in 1829.[103]

Circassians were trapped and caught in a dangerous game between two main key players, the Russian and the Ottoman empires. The Circassians, in addition to other peoples and nations of the Caucasus, were victims of colonial greed, exploitation, and control under multiple reasons and titles. "It is well-known that the sublime Porte took no notice of the Circassian protests against considering their country as an integral part of Russia with the assenter Turkey." The Circassians, were cautious dealing with those who worked in secret to have a rotational control, over their homeland. They "were not to be so easily misled. When they realized that the Russians did not honor any of their promises and began to cross their boundaries, they sent their armies to face them. Then they sent delegations to protest the Russian aggressive actions. The Russians replied that by the treaty of Adrianople, in 1829, Turkey had handed Circassia over to Russia and thus they became Russian subjects."[104]

To find out without notification or consultation that a nation is squeezed to be part of a deal between the big powers triggered the reality of exploiting the friendship and confidence to abuse others.

> When Circassians heard this, they were shocked, for they had not contemplated that the Sultan could hand over a country which was not his, and which he had never ruled. They held a general meeting in which it was decided not to recognize the Sultan's action, to resist the Russians by every possible means, and to send a deputation to Constantinople to protest to the Sultan and to ask him to abrogate the treaty with Russia.[105]
>
> All positive outlooks did not yield to a favorable outcome, and did not commensurate with the high expectations in the Ottomans. "Prince Safar Zan was appointed to lead the delegation, had rendered many valuable services to the Turks when they ruled Anapa, the coastal town of his birth, and they believed that he would have some influence and command respect in Constantinople. The Porte, however, received the delegation unofficially and coldly for fear of arousing the Russians.[106]
>
> The Tsar ordered his navy to blockade Circassian and his troops to occupy it by force, so that its occupation might be a matter of 'fait accompli', after the Turks had nominally given up all their claims and alleged rights in it to Russia. That led to a war which lasted for a long time between the Russians and the Circassians.[107]
>
> Circassians showed resistance to the Russian infiltration in all walks of life. They also blocked their areas, where, "the Russians realized that their missionary drive could not benefit them much, nor could it achieve any practical result despite their continuous efforts and financial loss. It became clear, that this screwed nation would not be won over easily.[108]

Antelava specified the course of affairs and active tasks that the "Circassians in the Caucasus War period (1763–1864)" had to face. The Russian Empire was interested in eliminating the actor states and/or empires that were active in the Caucasus region and beyond. Seemingly, Circassia and other nations of the Caucasus, in addition to others, were on an equal footing preys to be obtained when time permits.

Nevertheless, a significant success in the battle against Ottoman-Crimea's aggression and a short peaceful period, an independent status of Kabardo and whole Circassian had been in danger since the start of the last third of the 18th c. In view of the peculiarities of social and political organization, it could be said that Circassian still was in the feudal Middle Ages while its surrounding had been cardinally changed. The Ottoman Empire, Crimean Khanate and Iran appeared within a prolonged crisis.[109]

The Russians imposed their selfish colonial influence against the rights and dignity of others by taking their homelands. Russian authorities, in dealing with the peoples of the Caucasus, considered to act on the grounds that conquering would be a foregone conclusion and take place sooner or later; considering that the geographical proximity and regional contiguity factors were considered important factors for easy accessibility of occupation and annexation.

Political maneuvering era of the states fighting for establishing in the Caucasus was ended for Kabardo. Due to territorial closeness, of the Circassian principalities, Russia's borderline Kabardo was the first which underwent Russia's Caucasian political changes. Moreover, Kabard's domestic disorder enabled a northern neighbor to find pretext to interfere in its interior affairs without any difficulties.[110]

Tsarist Russian plans and policies were continuously enforced in accordance with tactical and even strategic accomplishments in areas of ongoing operations. There was no end or a level of persistence of killing, occupation, and displacement no matter the results on the people. Russia and Turkey didn't even play a positive role to allow people and nations of the North Caucasus to practice their legitimate rights in their historic homelands.

Russian troops under A. Suvorov's command put down an armed protest of Nogais in 1783 spring and autumn. Nomadic population left whole Kuban Region. Only several ten-thousand Nogais moved to other side of Kuban and refuged in Circassia, Laba and the territory of Kuban's middle flow. In 1772–83 the majority of Crimea's Muslim population resettled within the Ottoman Empire in several stages. Crimea and Kuban Region were emptied.[111]

The arrival of any colonial power to in a region or territory, whether during war or at peacetime, was considered as if it were the borders of that imperial state. In all cases, it came at the expense of others. Without the slightest doubt, the great powers at the time had a known aspiration in the Caucasus, the singling out of a people as well as the acquisition of strategic locations and different capabilities, always.

> A border between the Russian Empire and West Circassia was drawn across the Kuban River. Ottomans, who lost all bases in the North Caucasus, began to restore an Anapa fortification. Both states were preparing for a war.[112]

Two imperial empires had bargained and exchanged interests and benefits.

> Treaty of Bucharest, peace agreement signed on May 18, 1812, that ended the Russo-Turkish War, begun in 1806. The terms of the treaty allowed Russia to annex Bessarabia but required it to return Walachia and the remainder of Moldavia, which it had occupied. The Russians also secured amnesty and a promise of autonomy for the Serbs, who had been rebelling against Turkish rule, but Turkish garrisons were given control of the Serbian fortresses. Implementation of the treaty was forestalled by a number of disputes, and Turkish troops invaded Serbia again the following year.[113]

Nevertheless, a strategic borderline was drawn with the absence of Circassians in western Circassia between the Russian and Turkish (Ottoman) empires: "In May 1812 in Bucharest a peace treaty was concluded between Russia and Turkey which defined an international status of western Circassia. A border between two empires again remained along the Kuban River."[114]

The Circassians and other people of the Caucasus had confronted many aggressors, notably in the nineteenth century. The tyrant generals of the tsarist Russian forces did not hesitate to inject their venom and to multiply their evil crimes: "In 1816, General A. Ermolov was appointed as a Caucasus corps commander, who was considered to be a supporter for implementation of radical measures in the struggle for Russia's imperial interests. His appearing in the Caucasus resulted in the escalation of military actions in the whole region."[115]

The instructions issued to the field commanders were to implement the strict orders issued against the Circassians wherever they lived or any part of the Circassians they belong to. And thus, Kabardo became at certain time an important goal for the Russian expansion. There, the Russian invading forces initiated the construction of military facilities and centers for killing and displacing the Circassians from one place to another.

In the winter of 1821 Russian military units were activated in Kabardo. An attempt of Kabardians to start peaceful negotiations had no result. General E. Ermolov demanded unconditional obedience and resettlement of Kabardians on the valley lands. In 1822, he himself commanded the army in Kabardo. Relatively irreconcilable part of rules of Great and Minor Kabardo moved to other side of Kuban, for they had no forces to fight against numerous and well-armed Russian army. In 1822 spring construction of the Kabardo line fortifications began. The line should lock the gorges of Baksan, Chegem, Nalchik, Cherek, Urukh and others. The entire population of Kabardo was concentrated between the left bank of Malqa and Terek and Kabardo line, by what it would be isolated from trans-keban Circassia.[116]

Russian troops were applying what was in their possession to overcome the Circassians for the sake of achieving Russian dreams in domination, colonization, and colonial settlement. The Circassians were employing all their possible capabilities to defend the sovereignty of their homeland and their nation, no matter what this effort might cost them of time, efforts, or potentials.

Kabardians could not get use the obedience for a long time. Their attacks together with Temirgos, Beslens and Abdzakhs on a cordon line became more frequent. In 1823–25 cavalry raids of beyond-Kabardians kept in constant tension a border military administration and Russian population. In 1825 through Karachay they invaded in Kabardo, burned stanista Soldatskaya down and tried to resettle Kabardian auld on the other side of Kuban forcedly. But a retaliatory action on part of the Russian army and the resistance on part of a part of population prevented the full realization of the plan. In 1799–1825 the population of Kabardo so decreased that its number hardly was about 30 thousand people.[117]

Relations between the two empires can be described as bitter foes. Their relationship was exposed at times to surges that indicate selfishness and greed, which led at certain times to devastating wars. Then they reached a truce, followed by peaceful talks that emanate treaties and agreements. Their pledges contained compromises to each other and exchange of influence and pledges, even when betraying other parties and nations.

> On September 1829, an Adrianople peace treaty was signed, that defined an international status of independent Circassia for several decades. According to treaty, Ottoman Empire recognized the Russia's success in Transcaucasia and in the letters' favor gave up its nominal right on Trans-Kuban Circassia.[118]

Many parties, which were unjustly and falsely considered as friends at certain times, pledged to help the Circassians to overcome their difficulties, to overcome the colonial voracious greed, and evil military campaigns to destroy the Circassian nation and the occupation of the homeland and thus the entire Caucasus region. The assistance that the Ottoman Empire had submitted and made available did not differ in the outcome of the desire of the Russian Empire. It was limited to vacating and evacuating Circassia of its indigenous population.

> Having realized their force's inferiority in the struggle with the Russian Empire, Adygean leaders tried to obtain diplomatic and material support from Istanbul. To this end in 1830 a delegation was sent to Turkey's capital. Sultan's government promised Circassians only resettlements on its territory and ships for this process. In 1831, a new Circassian delegation under the leadership of Sefer-Bey Zan arrived in Ottoman. But their visit was again fruitless. Moreover, on Russia's demand, Turkish government arrested Sefer-Bey Zan firstly under house arrest and then in prolonged justified exile.[119]

The peaceful treaty of imperial settlements in 1829 between the Russian and Ottoman empires had become a "road plan" to be implemented, Russia initiated applying its part. Its colonial policy, which was officially protected and supported by false testimony, was signed and stamped by those who had no right to give the property of others to a third party. Even European countries had a paralyzed will, or rather indifference to the fate of a people that had a direct threat to its very survival.

Soon after signing the Adrianople treaty, in order not to be involved external forces in fighting for independence of Circassia, the Circassian coasts were blockaded by the Russian Black Sea fleet, A radical wing of British political elite under the pretext of protecting of England's trade interests, demanded direct involvement in the Caucasian affairs. But fearing the large-scab war with Russia, British government refrained. Nevertheless, in 1834 David Urkart—a devoted supporter for Circassia's independent, arrived in Circassia under direct involvement of English Ambassador in Istanbul Ponsonby and Sefer-BeyZan's recommendation letter. Since that, activities of British political opposition (D. Urkart, L. Longworthy, J. Bell, E. Spencer and others) were directed towards the supporting for an idea of Circassia's independence by real action from the European states. But in vain, Europe had no time to this end.[120]

Applying imperial military projects and strategies, as well as promoting colonial settlement and military incursions, was intended to enhance colonial demographic expansion. Using military forts and garrisons had applied and imposed tight military procedures. Therefore, the entire Circassian coastline on the Black Sea was subjected to a special Russian agenda that could be considered a different phase of the Russian-Circassian War.

In order to strengthen military power in the Black Sea Region, in 1837–39 Russian government established a Black Sea line from Anapa till Sokhumi-Qale. According to the Commander's orders, the forts of a coast line should prohibit contraband trading and besiege coastal settlements of Natukhs, Shapsugs, Ubykhs, and Sadxes. As it is known from the records of a contemporary officer, the garrisons of the mentioned fortifications appeared to be besieged by local population.[121]

Hence, Russia moved a step closer to absolute control of the Circassian coast on the Black Sea. Enforcing new facts on the ground was meant to increase the severity of the noose and the siege of the entire region. Nevertheless, Circassians were able to mobilize their forces and carry out counterattacks with remarkable successes. They were able to break siege and attack the Russian forts, which created noticeable changes in the balance of military strength to a certain extent.

At the start of 1840 Circassians (Natukhs, Shapsugs, and Ubykhs) made a large-scale attack on coastal line fortifications. In February–March they took and ruined the fortifications Lazarev, Veliaminov, Mikhailov, Nikolaev and Navaginski fort. On June 7 Adages attacked Abinsk, but a garrison repelled the attack. By helping of complimentary forces, in November 1840 Caucasus commanding could recapture and restored captured fortifications. After a short break, in April 1841 Circassian unit blockaded Tenginskoe fortification for six days and cause a serious damage to Russians. In November Admiral Serebryakov lost about 3.5 thousand killed and wounded soldiers in the battle against Ubykhs and Shapsugs in Sochi region.[122]

The people of the Caucasus found themselves cornered in a position of self-defense by having to bear a foreign aggressor. Wars that lasted for tens of years led to tragedies, murder, starvation, and siege. It consequently resulted in total occupation and annexation by an irresponsible colonial empire. Revolts occasionally erupted in a sense of refusing the fait accompli. That obliged the colonial authorities to put down national revolts causing human and material losses.

> Active attacks on Russian garrisons in Circassia contributed to the Chechen rebellion in 1840. Already in the 1820' in Dagestan and Chechen a massive anti colonialist movement began. Spiritual leaders of the movement Imams: Gazi-Mahomed (1828–1832), Hamzat Nek (1832–1834), and Shamil (1834–1859) devoted their energies for organizing of anti-colonialist movement.[123]

The proverb "Unity is Power"[124] substantiates the necessity to participate in joint action between all those in the Caucasus. They were exposed to invasion and consequent occupation, which required them to stand together for self-defense and survival. Apparently, the emerging circumstances had persuaded leaders, where possible, to cooperate and coordinate among themselves to oppose and repel any foreign military campaign.

> In 1848 Shamil's third Naib Muhamed-Amin began his activity in other side of Kuban. In order to strengthen the power, firstly Naib based on old Circassian aristocracy and even married a Temirgoan nobleman Bolotoqov'd daughter. But soon he changed priorities and allied with non-privileged layers. During the five years of his reformative activity among Abdzakhs the Naib formulated a united system of administrative governance.[125]

According to Antelava, the countries that were involved were in the regional arena, including some of the European countries. Every country needed its share of the cake, which is the tip of the iceberg. Thus, the Russian and Ottoman empires were exchanging as well as colonial concessions in a deal to acquire and capture the land of Circassia. Some countries benefited from the exchanges, understandings, and the resulting egotistical benefits.

> Despite the fact that in September 1855 Sevastopol was fallen and a coalition of the European states occupied Taman, Anapa, Novorosiisky and Sokhumi-Qale, Russian military commanding maintained its position in the Crimea and Northern Caucasus. Consideration of allies to break Russia's military power with one shot was not realized. In February 1856, a peace negotiation between warring parties began. A Paris peace treaty (March 18, 1856) recognized all achievements of Russia in the Caucasus. Russian state was banned from having a military fleet on the Black Sea and building of coastline fortifications.[126]

Hawks and generals of the tsarist regime in the Caucasus had to meet occasionally to discuss future plans and intentions. All aimed for the occupation of the entire lands and territories of the Caucasus. That would enhance uprooting all the indigenous people utilizing brutal and barbaric methods.

> In October 1860 a higher government meeting, held under A. Bariatinsky's leadership in Vladikavkaz, approved a plan of military operations in trans-Kuban Circassia. The plan was developed by the commander of right flank of the Caucasus line and the army of Black Sea region (since 1861 of Kuban region) General N. Evdokimov. According to the plan, Circassians should have been exiled in Kuban lowlands or in the Ottoman Empire and Cossack stanitses should be founded on their housing territory.[127]

Aggressor forces continued to develop the plans for the completion of the war as soon as possible. After completing the brutal occupation, carrying out murder, torture, ethnic cleansing, and genocide, they wanted to conclude controlling the region geographically and politically. This led to the change of the demographic features and drew a map through forced displacement that eventually reached the extent of deporting the people abroad.

The last stage of fighting for Circassia's independence began. On June 13, 1861, the delegates meeting of Ubykhs, Shapsugs, Natukhs and Abdzakhs in Sochi founded a central government (Mejlisi), declared an introduction of unified tax system, general public mobilization and applied for support to the Ottoman Empire, Great Britain and other states. But the application had no result. In September 1861 Circassian leaders met with the Russian emperor Alexander II who was in inspection trip and agreed to subordination to Russia if they would be left on their dwelling territory. Alexander II's answer was equal to a final verdict for them: "I'm giving you a month period to come to your sense. After a month you should inform Graf Evdokimov what you want—to settle along Kuban or to settle in Turkey." Having received the rejection of the proposal from Circassians, Russians carried out military operations against them more ruthlessly.[128]

Indeed, the steadfastness of the Circassians, and possibly other people in the Caucasus, did not prevent the Russian occupation; but it delayed that to a relatively long period. The invading Russian forces, despite obstacles, managed to systematically grab the land and thus annex it permanently: "Thus a centennial period of fighting of Circassians and Northern Caucasian peoples for independence was ended tragically. A basic ethnic array was finally dissociated from the Circassia who had remained in their historical homeland and was scattered all over the planet."[129]

Russian History

Foreign Policy published on the eighteenth of August 2015 an article titled "Russia's Putin Is Once Again Spending His Summer Riding Submarines," which highlighted one of Putin's hobbies.[130]

In general, this activity is considered as one any president may be scheduled to fulfill, but its significance lies in showing what was published: "Video of Putin's expedition shows him in casual naval uniform and chatting on the radio with Prime Minister Dmitry Medvedev. According to the Associated Press's translation of the two men's radio chatter, Putin told his lieutenant that he hoped his submarine journey would show 'how deep our historical roots are.'"[131]

Occasionally, some people tend to assume the ignorance of others; and it seems that this is an attempt of bluffing and trying to distort, misrepresent, and conceal well-known history. Anyone who wants the search for truth will be able to find facts.

The expression "how deep our historical roots are" is not quite accurate because the Russian state is only 1,100 years old from its establishment from a variety of peoples and origins. Russia was subjugated, whether partially or entirely, to the Mongols for approximately 300 years; and at the same time, Russia destroyed, whether partially or completely, tens of nations in the Caucasus and beyond.

> In the early 9th century Russia was inhabited by Slavic tribes. In the late 9th century Vikings forged them into a nation centered on Kiev. (The Vikings first captured Novgorod in 862 and Kiev in 882). The new nation was called Rus and in time its Viking rulers adopted native customs and language. They were assimilated into Russian society.[132]

This was before they started their imperial and colonial activities against tens of peoples and nations.

The Russian language was founded approximately 1,200 years ago. Russia cannot compare itself with other deep-rooted European nations, and the Russian language is unable to compare its history and importance with other important European languages.

> The evolution of the writing system used by the Eastern Slavs has a history of planned language change and reform. This process of change from the beginnings of written language to the present-day writing system can be explained by citing four important events. These include the 'birth' of the Cyrillic alphabet in 862 A. D., a set of 13th Century reforms known as the Second Southern Slavic Influence, Peter the Great's reforms of the 18th Century and the Communist reforms of 1917.[133]

At the same time, tens of nations, victimized and massacred by Russia, had existed with their languages for thousands of years before Russia even existed as an entity.

Meanwhile, Russia wants the media to focus on other affairs: "The man who fancies himself something of an action movie hero—and doubles as the president of Russia—was in Crimea on Tuesday, where he took another of his summer submarine rides. This time, Vladimir Putin boarded the submarine to check out a newly discovered Black Sea wreck from the 9th or 10th century."[134]

The article also mentioned other voyages: "It's at least the third such underwater journey for Putin, who has previously carried out submarine expeditions in Lake Baikal and the Gulf of Finland. Ostensibly, Putin is in Crimea to promote tourism to the peninsula that he recently annexed."[135]

Circassian Deputies

The Circassian deputies (Hadji Hayden Hassan and Kustar Ogli Ismail) had addressed the Queen of England in London AUGUST 26, 1862, and published in supplement to the Free Press Journal of the Foreign Affairs Committee on January 7, 1863. They summarized their worries about the Russian aggression and foreign intervention in Circassian affairs, specifically the Ottomans.[136]

The collaboration between the two main players was mentioned in brief.

> As Your Majesty is aware, since the world existed, no nation has attempted to conquer our country. Russia only some time ago, under the pretense that she got our country by treaty from the Ottoman Government, invaded us with an overwhelming force, and began against us a war of extermination, which she has waged for forty years, and which she is still waging, at the cost of many thousands of human lives.[137]
>
> The Ottoman Government, never having possessed our country, had no right whatever to give us over to the Russians. There is no other affinity between us and the Ottomans than the similarity of creed and faith which makes us both look upon the Sultan as the successor of our Prophet.[138]

The types of crimes perpetrated were mentioned and listed.

> The tyranny of the Russians was not confined to capturing our cattle, burning our dwellings, and temples, and other unheard-of atrocities, but in order to starve us on the mountains they destroyed all our growing crops in the plain, and captured our land. In fact, they have treated us in an unbearable and barbarous manner, unprecedented in the annals of war. Driven to despair, we resolved to make a last firm stand against our enemies with all the energy we possessed, and the war was carried on with fresh vigour, eight months ago, causing the sacrifice of twenty-five thousand human lives, on both sides, and an immense destruction of property.[139]

They also tackled obstacles placed by the Russian Empire to prevent improving the quality of life for the Circassians. They transformed life into a living hell plus the lack of safety in maritime navigation to and from Circassia.

> While we are on one side repelling our enemies, and on the other trying to improve the government of our country, Russia by brute force, is trying to conquer us; on the neutral Black Sea she is capturing, whenever she can, every ship carrying any of our countrymen, so that we have no home on land, no means of traveling or refuge by sea.[140]
>
> Still we would rather die than submit to the oppression of Russia. If we were to emigrate, abandoning our homes, for ages protected by our forefathers, who shed their blood for them, our poverty would prove a great obstacle to our doing so; in fact, how could we take away our own wives and children, and the widows, orphans, and helpless relations of those slain in this war? Such an undertaking would decimate the emigrants, and blot it\out for ever our Circassian name from the face of the earth.[141]

Testimonies and Comments

The insiders who know what was happening in the Caucasus warned of the dangers faced by Circassians and Circassia because of Russian ambitions and greed: "From the speech of the English Member of Parliament M. Anstey: 'I blame Lord Palmerston for betrayal of Circassia, which is made English-adherent and which is to have trading relations with England. You also betrayed England by surrendering Independent North Caucasia to Russia while you knew about our interests in India.'"[142]

There is a proverb that says, "It is never too late," but for Circassians, there is nothing to be done after all the killing, destruction, and occupation that ended the Circassians' independence: "8 Years later while Lord Palmerston was talking at the same parliament, 'Dear Lords, it is true that we left Circassians alone with their terrible misfortune. Yet we wanted help from them and we used them.'"[143]

The death toll from the deportees was high as victims fell on the way to their final destinations.

Pinson, "The death percentage of Circassians along the Black Sea coasts is about 50%. 53,000 people died just in Trabzon alone. We don't know how many ships, which are "floating graves" had sunk. The number of families exiled from Caucasia to Balkan region is about 70,000. Edirne: 6.000, Silistre-Vidin:

13.000, Niche - Sofia: 12.000, Dobruca-Kosovo-Pristina-Svista: 42.000 families. Total: about 350.000 people. Death percentage is less and is about 15-20%."[144]

Y. Abramov wrote in his book Caucasian Mountaineers,

> There are no words to describe the situation of the mountaineers in those days. Thousands of them died in the roads, thousands of them died due to illness and hunger. The coastal regions were full with people who are dead or on the verge of dying. The babies who are searching for milk in their mother's cold dead body, mothers who didn't leave their kids from their laps even they are already dead from cold, and people who are dead while they got closer just to keep warm, are examples of the scenes that were normal in the coasts of the Black Sea.[145]

Russian I. Dzarov stated, "Half of those who left to go to Ottoman Empire died before they reached there. Such a state of wretchedness is rare in the history of the humankind."[146]

Description of the Situation in the Circassian Capital

Arda Inal-Ipa published an article titled "The Sochi Olympics and the Circassian Question," which pointed to some facts marking a time that characterized the circumstances surrounding the national consolidation during the last stages of the Russian-Circassian War.

She explored the meaning of Sochi for the Russian State and what it means for the Circassians:

> In order to understand why the International Olympic Committee (IOC)'s decision to hold the 2014 Winter Olympics in Sochi has been controversial in relation to the Circassian question, it is necessary to understand some of the historical aspects and episodes from the Caucasian War—a period in the long history of Circassia where tragic events have been intertwined with moments of surprising recovery.[147]
>
> Confronting the expansion of the Russian Empire into the northwest Caucasus and seeking to save its people and defend its land served to consolidate Circassian society and accelerate its development. In June 1861, during the most difficult, final stages of the Caucasian War, a decision was

taken at a Congress of Elders, [2] to create a union for political and military consolidation, to maintain internal order, and to address political and legal issues affecting the whole Circassian nation. A governing body was created for the union—a Mejlis, or Great Free Assembly.[148]

The Circassians launched their efforts to establish links and administrative structures for a government type of entity to address their crucial issues considering the devastating war.

In practice, these decisions meant the creation of a confederal state administered by a permanent collegial authority with both legislative and executive functions. This remarkable event was both a natural result of development within Adygean society, and a response to external threat, which made it necessary to develop and implement a more coherent resistance policy, to prevent conflicting actions and operations by individual sub-ethnic communities.[149]

She articulated the plans that had been developed to inform the world of a Circassian nation and striving for survival as a free nation.

At this stage, the outskirts of modern-day Sochi became home to the Circassian state capital. The newly formed confederation almost immediately began to engage in international diplomacy, leading to international support from civil society organizations established in solidarity with the peoples of Circassia: the Circassian Committees of Istanbul and London.[150]

Circassian interest is demonstrated as they were showing their ability under the imposed war to work on state building.

Thanks to the government's activities, Circassia began to acquire the characteristics of a subject of international law. In September 1861 mountain dwellers expressed their readiness to become Russian subjects, if they would be allowed to remain in their previous places of residence. The Mejlis tried to negotiate with Russian Emperor Aleksandr II, but by that time the Russian government had already finalised its policy and did not intend to cease its military operations and end its harsh measures to conquer the Caucasus.[151]

Seemingly, the Russians had moved to breach what the Circassians wanted to do, which was to intervene as close as possible to change reality.

In June 1862, a Russian fleet organised a landing near Sochi and, following a bloody battle, the Mejlis and other buildings were burned down. Two years later, in May 1864, following the Tsar's government's decision to conduct major military operations in the northwest Caucasus, a Russian military parade was held in the Kbaada plain (modern Krasnaya Polyana, known in Abkhaz as Gubaadey) to mark the end of the hundred-year war with the Circassians.[152]

Analyst Paul Goble stated, "The Circassians recognize that their task is enormously difficult and will take a long time to achieve, but the past year has brought them what may be the most important victory they have won in a long time: they recognize this reality, and they are acting in a step by step way to pursue their goals."[153]

In a conference held in the Parliament of Finland, Fatima Tlisova said, "Seven generations of men in my family died fighting for the Freedom of their Homeland. Seven generations of women in my family became widows at the age of 30, including myself. This pain lives in my heart. The blood of the generations of Freedom fighters runs in my veins as well as in the hearts and veins of millions of Circassians around the globe. We deserve our Freedom, and Independence."[154]

The Issue Is National Freedom and Dignity

All indigenous nations and people of the world wish they have the right to live freely and independently with no foreign intervention in their own national affairs. They also wish to ascend, rise, and flourish as they are morally obligated to preserve their national identity, language, heritage, and culture for national coexistence and survival as respected and dignified nations safeguarding their sovereignty and independence.

This was not considered more than 450 years ago when the Muscovites started their aggressive wars and assaults against all peoples and nations around them, crossing borders, lines of blood, and atrocities until they reached the objectives they wanted to attain, regardless of the high price that they had to pay and the victims had to suffer. Seemingly, it doesn't apply to countries emerging as a result of occupation of the territories of others and illegitimate annexing of other peoples and nations by force and "fait accompli."

The plight of the ancient nations of the North Caucasus with a confirmed history of more than six thousand years was subject to tsarist Russian invasions and crimes. It was mainly based on war, expansion, and murder that consequently occupied the entire North Caucasus territories. They destroyed the homelands, committed atrocities to the degree of genocide and ethnic cleansing, and eliminated a great portion of the population in addition to forced exile, deporting and displacing entire nations. They eventually wrested the freedom and independence of scores of nations and people.

Murder and destruction had continued for centuries, with tsarist Russians occupying all parts of the North Caucasus.

Russia has decided through its present FSB/created and backed leadership[155] to maintain its imperial polices of arming, re-arming, keeping closed society, modernizing in all fields, but to the extent that would keep the authorities in total control of all walks of life, business, and technology, while trying to grasp all what it can from all countries around the hostile state of Russia, which is noticed through the relationship with Georgia, Ukraine, Japan, the three Baltic Republics and others.[156] Not to forget terrorizing Europe with its gas and oil, beside frightening and horrifying all occupied nations in accordance with the Russian imperial well-known policies that had started during the Tsars' era.[157]

The Circassians, Chechens, Daghestanis, Ossetians, Abkhazians, and others had to bear the consequences of crimes committed by the Russians. Many people at different times, after losing their freedom and independence, were affected by exposure to extreme cold in the winter and hot environments during summer. They were forced to live and travel for months on the sand of the coast of the Black Sea. They had to wait for their turn to board the floating "coffin" ships while others consisted of entire families who were gravely ill because of epidemics, let alone the sea and land journeys of agony, suffering, and sometimes inevitable death.

Unfortunately, tragedies faced by the nations of the North Caucasus were never limited to a certain Russian regime. It extended to all successive regimes, reaching the present Russian Federation. When a predominant and capable imperial Russian policy is pursued, it will be free to choose and act, to utilize the ways and means to go on changing the status of its occupied territories. They keep dividing and subdividing the administrative regions of the North Caucasus and elsewhere,[158] being described as "Administrative Divisions of the

Russian Federation" in a stringent way to govern and rule. Let alone, Crimea, Abkhazia, and South Ossetia.

In a "Window on Eurasia," in April 2008, Paul Goble highlighted an example of relentless Russian efforts to implement its domination. He verified, "Moscow's renewed plan to combine regions in the North Caucasus either with neighboring Russian ones or with each other threatens the survival of the national communities there and is leading some of their members to think about independence as the only way to save their peoples from extinction."[159]

He also added, "Magomet Barakhoyev, an Ingush activist, argues that the Russian government's plans to amalgamate regions in the North Caucasus are in fact a plan for the total 'russification' of non-Russian groups there and elsewhere (www.ingushetiya.ru/news/14036. html)."[160]

Referring to the mentioned title, it is worth saying that the whole issue is occupation and colonization performed by a greedy empire on one side and on the other tiny nations that exercised their basic right of self-defense against conquering brutal forces that committed all types of atrocities in addition to full occupation and annexation.

The matter is purely a national one, which is classified and characterized as merely a self-defense of peoples and nations endangered of annihilation and extinction or melting in the multi-Russian crucible. Religion was never a major cause or factor, but from difficult experiences, all those oppressed people believe in "if a thing is worth doing, it's worth doing well."

You cannot balance between those who wanted right but couldn't reach it and those who wanted wrong but attained it. The day will inevitably come when all nations occupied and ruled by imperial Russia will achieve their legitimate rights of freedom and independence. Whatever efforts the KGB had exerted to save the Soviet Union from collapsing and keep control of other nations failed.

The notorious Soviet Union's disintegration occurred, where fifteen independent states had evolved while the so-called Russian Federation kept its prey in the North Caucasus and elsewhere as integral parts of its entity. What had happened with the Soviet Union will be repeated with others, no matter what their action would do to prevent that from occurring, when tens of independent nations will return and be reborn.

Compromising the Circassian Homeland

The importance of a homeland and its fate was never a form of political essay or a subject of bargaining for the Circassians. It has always been and will be an organic topic that will persist, which is the most precious asset that Circassians revere and respect. It is redeemed by hearts and souls, which is considered an identity, affiliation, soil, sky, air, safety, and security. This recalls Nelson Mandela's words: "Man's goodness is a flame that can be hidden but never extinguished."

Various parties have persevered through following intrusive, opportunistic, despicable, and sometimes frantic methods. Jumping on human and national prerogatives that pertain to the Circassian nation and its inalienable rights will never be undisputed. These rights do not tolerate trading, evasiveness, or flattering and consider that the causes for the Circassians' national catastrophe is the interference of greedy countries from all directions, which had meddled in the affairs of Circassia, by selecting blatant and arrogant means.

All that led to determine the fate of a nation that endured bitterness because of a fierce war that destroyed everything. It affected and contributed in exposing the reality and the future of Circassia, the historic homeland of a long-standing and deeply rooted nation in the history of the Caucasus region for more than six thousand years. Consequences consisted of taking the homeland and exposing its people to murder and extermination. Circassians are still deprived of proper civil and political rights.

The inevitable result of bloodshed and loss of innocent lives in a "the end justifies the means" attitude led to assassination, treachery, slaughter, burning, drowning, foreign occupation, and forced deportation, which created a loss of homeland for some time for the benefit of the colonialists' greediness and acquisition; but the truth will prevail.

While most Circassians were deported and deprived of their right to live freely in their own homeland for more than 150 years, the rest had to endure occupation while watching the Circassian homeland being exposed to rupture, division, fragmentation, and a change of identity. The different periods of various successive Russian regimes since the tsarist rule have prevailed. The scene can be shortened as a combination of discrimination, security, colonial, and propaganda forms of chronic control.

The partition was described as for administrative measures, which placed Circassians under the circumstances of a bitter de facto imposed on them. Ten percent of Circassians must live in scattered developed locations and described as autonomous areas and republics in different parts of their homeland of origin. Current landscapes show that not all these so-called administrative regions are adjacent territories and connected with each other!

The Russian authorities have ignored and neglected to find a reasonable and acceptable solution to the Circassian Question. Action is desired in accordance with legitimate international and humanitarian fundamentals. In addition, authorities should stop being blind regarding the case and all its consequences that have resulted with a for-need essential solutions. Tragedies have befallen an ancient nation that is deep rooted in the history of the Caucasus, even though it had reached the extent of genocide, ethnic cleansing, and forced deportation. This led to the elimination of half of the Circassian nation during the unjust Russian war.

Circassians have strived to defend their homeland by limited available capabilities until the war had reached to an end on May 21, 1864. Eventually, numbers prevailed over courage. Circassia and other nations of the Caucasus suffered because of the war that ended with the occupation of the entire North Caucasus. Since the nineteenth century, as an effect, facts and memories still lie in front of us until today.

Nevertheless, there is an important difference between what happened to the Circassian nation and what happened to others. The result is that other nations such as Chechnya, Dagestan, Abkhazia, in addition to others, still exist both demographically and geographically and can be confirmed through the accessible maps. However, Circassia was obliterated and even deleted from the map! Why all this injustice, oppression, intended abuse, and the persistence of denial of rights that fall on them? Nonetheless, rights do not have a statute of limitations.

All reasonable and intellectual people realize that rightness, legitimacy, legality, and justice are natural acquired rights from birth, which are not privileges or awards distributed by selective generous and influential authorities or leaders. However, it must be emphasized that the way to freedom and dignity is not furnished with roses and jasmine. While "God helps those who help themselves," submitting to fait accompli is weakness and escape from reality.

In this context, Tagore said, "Asks the Possible of the Impossible, 'Where is your dwelling-place?' 'In the dreams of the Impotent,' comes the answer."[161] The Circassians' destiny had always been the duty of defending their homeland against greedy invaders. The duty placed on their shoulders requires them to address the civilized world of their concerns and issues, leading to unprecedented unity and solidarity.

They are looking to regain civil and legitimate rights through the implementation of international law, UN Decolonization according to its Charter, the Universal Declaration of Human Rights, the Right of Nations to Self-Determination, and the United Nations Declaration on the Rights of Indigenous Peoples. The prevailing problems that were created by tsarist Russia need to be resolved.

Russia's Chronic Failure in Dealing with Circassians

Russia has consistently adopted an imperial policy of dealing with subordinate peoples and nations that applies in the Circassian model. Being one of the Russian victims, Circassians had endured difficulties because of the findings and implications of the Russian-Circassian War. It has overlapped over the years, and kept ever since, the hostilities and the displacement of the vast majority of the Circassians to accept the status quo and preserve it permanently.

Russians and their mercenaries advanced to rule tens of millions of inhabitants of the nations of the North Caucasus, Circassia being one of them, to prove imperial competitiveness, supremacy, and the ability to access and to reach the strategic seaports of the warm waters of the Black Sea. The purposes were trade and contact with the near and far east ports of the world, thereafter, stretch and widen superior military forces, compete with other major powers, and implement a racist belief in Slavic superiority, which was among those significant incentives.

Stubborn conduct of imperial policies has consistently proven that Russia performed its aggressive and violent methods no matter what the consequences were. Territorial expansion was of ultimate priority for the imperial Russian military forces, which was broadened to commit atrocities such as genocide and ethnic cleansing, followed by displacement and deportation that lead to changing the demographic map.

Purification and cleansing of the territories were performed to control strategic territories such as the Black Sea and its ports and shorelines. They sought to bring Russian settlers for controlling the territories and for the sake of economical assurances after controlling natural resources in the Circassian homeland and beyond.

The awakening of the Circassian sleeping giant is no joke; it's real. Imperialism is bitterly criticized and considered a betrayal to civilization and human values that consist of freedom, equality, and independence. All this must be taken seriously. Circassians have already proven to the world and to the opinionated Russian leadership and beyond any reasonable doubt that ignoring facts continuously and refusing the idea of recognizing the rights of the Circassians will not be accepted in any way.

Circassians who are faithful to their national principles will follow legal and nonviolent working methods. They will not allow anyone to hijack their hopes and aspirations for personal or opportunistic gains. At the same time, it must be clear that such an organizing mechanism should act logically and systematically to assert legitimate rights.

The different issues of the Circassian Question and historical evolution show the origin of the Circassian people as well as the most important, natural, and strategic resources in the region and various links in the North Caucasus that pertain to the Russian occupation and annexation. There must be coordination with the other people of the North Caucasus that are under Russian rule. They ought to obtain backing and support of the Caucasus countries, regional countries, key countries of the world, the European Union, and the United Nations Organization. Providing endeavors and initiatives aim to demand solution in the framework of international legitimacy by applying self-determination on Circassian soil.

The Circassians seek to demand their legitimate rights, as they are entitled to the right to express their thoughts and convictions. Indications necessarily require that if people do not seek to restore their legitimate rights, no one would volunteer to do that on their behalf. Initiative should originate from them, which would stimulate the world to react.

Russians are obliged to recognize the Circassian genocide in accordance with international legitimacy based on international law and the United Nations' Charter, which requires implementing the right of repatriation and returning to their own homeland. The Circassian nation is entitled to regain and enjoy human rights.

Natural rights are inherent to all human beings without discrimination: "Rights must be interrelated, connected and indivisible, the Right to Self-determination in accordance with United Nations 'Declaration on the Granting of Independence to Colonial Countries and Peoples,' and the 'UN Declaration on the Rights of Indigenous Peoples.'"[162]

Circassian Independence in the Belgrade Treaty

The Circassian nation had faced historical and serious challenges for thousands of years. Developments because of foreign greed placed the people either partially or entirely being able to survive or to the brink of extermination. Rather than surrender and accept giving up their freedom and independence, the nation has continued to employ and adapt all surviving conditions and circumstances. The change of names and titles that have described them depended on the change of the names of the groups or different Circassian tribes. In all cases, the ultimate goal for all was to have those entities include everyone.

Aslan Beshto wrote, "277 years ago, on this day, Kabarda was recognized as an independent state. Sound and balanced policy leaders of the country led to the fact that our country has received the official status of the subject's international law."[163]

Beshto has dilated in highlighting the appropriate reference to legal background of the occasion. With no doubt, that is derived from the related international treaties, laws, and norms. Circassians believe that Circassia's independence is not a doubtful prospect or a negotiable subject in any way. That's what the tsarist Russian Empire has worked hard to divert.

Article 6 of the Belgrade peace treaty between the Russian Empire and the Ottoman Empire says, "On both Kabarda's—that is, the Great and Small—and Kabardian people from both parties to the agreement to have Kabarda free and not to be under the possession of either one of the two empires, and now it will be the barrier between the two empires and considered a sovereign nation . . . " 2 days later, on September 20 this text was read at the Great Kabarda Khasa, on the bank of the Baksan River.[164]

Article 6 is mentioned in the same manner as well as in the following: "The History of the Negotiations for the Peace Concluded at Belgrade September 18, 1739: Between the Emperor, Russia, and the Ottoman Porte, by the Mediation and Under the Guarantee of France. Shewing the Grounds of the Present War Between the Russians and the Turks."[165]

The independent decision will be taken and determined by the Circassians themselves. They are entitled to self-determine and to restore their freedom and independence in their homeland, away from dependency of anyone. Instead of grievance or revenge, the Circassian activists continuously function in accordance with international laws and norms.

They follow reason and logic to determine tactics, depending on their legality and civilized methods and manners, highlighting on their nation's legitimate rights and the need to be restored in accordance with the international laws and norms. Mark Twain said, "Action speaks louder than words but not nearly as often."

On the same topic, Eurasia Daily Monitor has elaborated that Circassian independence is still a venerated issue.

> Little by little, modern Circassians have been rediscovering their history, which Russian and Soviet authorities had previously carefully stripped of all their important and proud historical moments. Among such events, Circassian activists have recently pointed to Article 6 of the Belgrade Treaty between the Russian Empire and the Ottoman Empire, signed on September 18, 1739. According to this point in the treaty, the activists argue, the Circassian lands at that time should have been granted independence, as they were formally released from any obligations to either the Ottomans or the Russians for Circassians.[166]

Valery Dzutsati has also drawn attention to "the dynamics of today's Circassian movement and the Russian government's reaction to it indicate that the authorities in Moscow will not be mollified by the Circassians' passivity. Rather, this ethnic minority has learned that activism and collective action is needed to improve its bargaining positions vis-à-vis Moscow. For now, the Circassians have managed to calibrate their activities so as to push for a rejection of the loss of historical memory but without incurring any violent reprisals from the Russian government. It remains to be seen, however, whether growing frustration eventually throws this relationship out of balance."[167]

When invaders occupy the territories and countries of others, they aspire mainly to control the geographical and strategic locations. They also try to eliminate the native nations by utilizing various means. That could not be achieved by successive invaders and occupiers with the Circassians for thousands of years and to the present day. The secret of the survival of the Circassian nation is that its people strived to preserve their national identity in all conditions and circumstances.

Even with most of the nation in exile, that won't change the fact of the ability to restore the usurped rights to their rightful owners by peaceful, civilized, and legal methods.

> Since we know that the Sinds were an important Circassian tribe and they were the same people as the Sindjs, it is obvious that they were not absorbed by the Scyths, as it was supposed by Thumb-Hanschild, but rather survived and continued to live until the present, long after the Scyths themselves had disappeared.[168]

The Circassians were always able to deal with the surrounding circumstances and perils. They exploited the sources of strength and maneuverability that they had enjoyed: "After the fall of the Cammerian Empire the Sends entered the Maeot Federation."[169]

The Circassian Letter to the Queen of England on Independence

A broad sector of the Circassians, especially their leaders, have understood and absorbed the shocks of a malicious game in an irresponsible attitude that was taking place between the Ottoman and Russian empires. On more than one occasion, they eventually exchanged roles and the spoils of the peoples' bounties.

That was followed by sharing the homeland between each other, whether on maps or in actuality, with other major powers' consonance without consulting the Circassians and regardless of their interests and legitimate rights.

Sending a letter to the Queen of England in 1838, the Circassian leaders protested the hazing, isolation, sanctions, and blockade imposed by the Russian Empire. They drew attention that their homeland was targeted. The letter showed resentment for the irresponsible and careless attitude of the Ottoman Empire toward the Circassians.

> In reply to the allegations of the Russians, your humble servants, the Circassians, solemnly protest, that never since its commencement did the Ottoman power conquer us with the sword; never did it bring us succour in our distress; and never at any time did we pay it tribute: on the contrary it took our children and sold them as slaves in its bazars. And such having been the case, how could the Sublime Porte bestow us upon the Russians? If it had friendship for them, it might have given them some of the countries under its sway, but it had not either the power or the right to give them ours.[170]

In the same letter addressing the Queen of England, the Circassians stressed on maintaining their freedom and independence:

> If, however, your Majesty should not deem these arrangements advisable, we trust that your Majesty, and the other Powers, will issue orders that we may continue free and independent like Persia, Afghanistan, and other mountain-countries; and when your Majesty has thus definitively ordered and arranged, we will consider how we shall next proceed. If, however, the above arrangements could be made with the Ottoman government, we should esteem it a special favour, and we should be perfectly satisfied.[171]

Circassia and Abkhazia

Circassia is different from Abkhazia, but both are in the Caucasus region. There should be no match especially with the developments that had occurred in most recent years. They made it impossible to see Abkhazia the way some people wish to see! If Abkhazians want it this way, then it's their choice and decision, even if it is not in favor of the Circassians' very interests.

Circassians do not mind that Abkhazia gets real independence instead of getting all its eggs in one basket. It seems they don't mind doing it on their own. Circassians are working to restore their confiscated rights. They are free to choose the path that makes them reach their national interests. They are the goals that combine most Circassians.

The illusion that Russia is helping anyone is not realistic. If some people would think so, they would sooner or later find out that Russia is in conformity with its own selfish interests. The veto Russia used in February 2012 against the principles of the United Nations, universal declaration of human rights, and against the interests of the Syrian people who are being killed night and day makes it easy to understand what the Russians want out of any conflict.

When the memory of the twenty-first of May 1864 approaches, Russia failed to mention any positive action in respect to solving any element of the Circassian Question. That has implications for any researcher to reach fair conclusions. They even went further in trying to say that the Greeks were in Circassia at one time, but without mentioning the deported Circassians and their homeland. They have achieved their goal, to hold the 2014 Sochi Winter Olympic Games on the land of genocide. Sochi was the last capital city of Circassia.

Common sense makes it imperative to know that the Circassians lost half of their nation and 90 percent of those who lived were deported. They had to endure difficult and tragic circumstances away from their homeland.

Anyone is free to defend any other nation's interest, but not at the expense of Circassian interests because they cannot be mixed together. Let's not undervalue the books and research papers presented by respected academicians such as Let Our Fame Be Great by Oliver Bollough and The Northwest Caucasus: Past, Present, Future by Walter Richmond, which has been translated to Arabic. It's worth mentioning that there are Russian authors who write about Circassians and the Caucasus. They select the way it suits them and according to the way they see things.

If Circassians did not come up with books and information about their past and present, then there are people who are interested to do so with no bias. Humanity is stronger than any prejudice or intolerance. It is hoped that we get to the degree that Circassians do a great job in presenting information about Circassians. There are studies and important information that came about the Circassian Question by many respected scholars in different languages.

No one with common sense would say that we don't need any more books about Circassians because knowledge has no limits or boundaries. Circassian authors write books about other nations in different languages, such as the Circassians living in the North Caucasus, Turkey, or Arab countries. Most Circassians appreciate and value that.

Creative programs are being prepared and applied in Circassian communities, such as presenting lectures and seminars. They are held on the occasions of the Circassian flag, Circassian Memorial Day, and other national and cultural events. Campaigns take place to make the information reach Circassians who are interested to know the different dimensions of the Circassian Question.

Healthy exchange of opinion should not reach the point of creating personal conflicts or to distract Circassians from their fundamental cause.

Post-Tsarist Era

The end of the devastating war was on May 21, 1864. It was associated with a fierce propaganda campaign filled with blatant lies. It all caused ultimate tragedies and disasters, but the torch of freedom does not extinguish:

> The remnants of the Circassian nation who stayed in their homelands in Caucasia after the majority of their kinsmen emigrated to Turkey, remained a source of discomfort to Tsarist Russia. It is true that Russia advanced with its huge forces to the lands lying beyond Caucasia and strengthened its rule in Caucasian for decades, but in spite of that, Russia was not successful in subjugating completely the inhabitants of the mountains of Caucasia or in making them peaceful Russian subjects until the Soviet regime came into power.[172]

Their faith in these postulates made them spare no efforts to sacrifice their souls and the most precious possessions for decades to defend their homeland, which meant freedom and independence and the preservation of dignity.

> The downfall of the Tsarist regime which came about as a result of the Bolshevik Revolution of October 17, 1917, did away with the remnants of six centuries of Tsarist rule. Its downfall was the signal for a number of imprisoned nations in that huge prison called the Russian Tsarist Empire, to liberate themselves from the Tsarist yoke. Subsequently, a number of captive nations became free such as the peoples of Finland, the Baltic states, Poland, the Ukraine, Georgia, Armenia and others.[173]

An important feature of the Circassians is that of their nature: they love and adore justice, freedom, and independence. These virtues are rooted in their hearts and minds as well as their conscience.

> The inhabitants of Northern Caucasia were among those numerous peoples that liberated themselves. They demanded their liberty along with the other nations, and were assisted in this by the chaos which prevailed throughout Russia and by the weakness of the Russian government during interregnum, before the Communist rule known as the Kerenski government. The North Caucasians set up a democratic state on May 11, 1918, under Abdul-Majeed Tchermoy. They were thus able once again to enjoy their liberty having been deprived of it under the despotic Tsarist rule for 54 years.[174]

Circassians participated after the end of World War I to create an independent state, even in participation with other peoples of the North Caucasus. Eventually, they created a union, which they were a part of. They established a correlation between peoples who have been victims of occupation, colonization, and displacement.

> The first to recognize the independence of Northern Caucasia was the Ottoman State, which dispatched an army known as the "Islamic Army" upon the request of the Caucasians under the command of Nuri Pasha, the brother of Anwar Pasha, then Minister of War. The Turks also sent another army under the leadership of some of the high-ranking Circassian officers in the Ottoman Army, including Yousuf Izzat Pasha and Ismael Barkouk charged with the formation of a national army in Northern Caucasia and were to command that army during the anticipated fighting.[175]

The Ottomans welcomed the announcement of some of the peoples of the Caucasus, to establish an independent state after years of Russian occupation. But that was only an exploitation for the new circumstances that had taken place and what the Ottoman state will benefit of. Proof of this is after sending some of its military forces, the focus of the Ottoman occupation was to expand their influence into areas in the South Caucasus such as Azerbaijan, Armenia, and Georgia rather than focus on the North Caucasus or to look at the needs of its people.

Circassia

Within a short time the Fifteenth Brigade under the command of Suleiman Izzat Tsey was able to advance and occupy Baku. After fierce fighting against the Russians on 6 September, 1918, his Brigade occupied Derbend and Petrovsk, from Russian influence. Tsey's advance, however, was short-lived, for the Treaty of Mudros was soon concluded by which the Ottoman Army was obliged to evacuate Caucasia and to hand over to the local Caucasian army which had been set up with Ottoman assistance. In that same treaty the Ottoman state agreed to an armistice with the Allied forces.[176]

Because of imperialist ambitions and the Ottoman betrayal, it was not the first time that the people were left to their unknown fate due to abandonment. Nonetheless, people of the North Caucasus depended on false Ottoman hopes and empty promises that turned out to be not honest at all.

The newly established republic managed to survive only for a short time under the Russian imperial ambitions, which evolved in a Soviet mold and form. The newly established republic had been eliminated and physically reoccupied in a vindictive manner and was renamed the Mountainous Republic of the Northern Caucasus.

In 1918, after the collapse of Tsarist rule, a Mountainous Republic of the Northern Caucasus was established embracing Dagestan, Chechnya, Ingushestia and North Ossetia. The Republic was suppressed by the Soviets in 1920 and Dagestan became an autonomous Soviet Socialist Republic in 1921.[177]

Post-Tsarist Russian Empire

Russian intrigue did not stop against the Circassians and other peoples of the Caucasus at all. Conspiracies were subjected to be practiced against them permanently with intervals during periods of tides and instability. Results of prevailing volatile politics in difficult times had always contributed in the magnitude of Russian pressure experienced on the colonized people.

While the Circassians and the other Caucasians were still rejoicing at attaining their independence again, the Bolsheviks appeared and threatened them, forcing them to make new sacrifices, and to fight the Bolshevists. That fighting lasted six months after which they defeated the Bolsheviks and on November 11, 1919, a truce was arranged between the two parties. At that time General Denikin, Commander of the "White Russians", appeared. The Caucasian Republic made an agreement with him, upon the advice of one of the British commanders. By that agreement an army of Caucasian volunteers was to be formed with the assistance of the European Powers to fight the Bolsheviks. Fighting lasted until January 1920, when the Ingush army succeeded in expelling the invaders from Vladikavkas.[178]

When establishing relationships with others, different countries offer different conditions to meet their interests. Usually, these conditions are incompatible with the fundamental interests of the people. They run counter to the legitimate interests of the people of different nations. Even when having to meet these conditions (or some of them), the other party will not be normally committed while the actual implementation remains subject to the mood and desire.

Britain recognized the Caucasian Republic, but that recognition was accompanied by some heavy conditions, i.e., breaking off the relations with the Ottoman Empire, and opening the country to Gen. Denikin so that the Western Allies might benefit from the strategic position of Caucasia in return for the General's pledge that he would not interfere in the domestic affairs of the Caucasian Republic. The Caucasians were at first unwilling to accept these conditions, but the assurances go General Thomson, the British representative, regarding Gen. Denikin, induced them to assent.[179]

Failure to comply with terms of the agreement held was associated with reluctance of the Whites to work against the Caucasus Republic. Whether the Whites or Bolsheviks, their ultimate objective is well-known: the occupation of the Caucasus in general and Circassia in particular regardless of the circumstances that affect them. They have always pursued various approaches to achieve their goals.

However, it was only when it was too late that the Caucasians realized that their hesitation and distrust of Gen. Denikin had been well-founded and that they had been deceived and led into a trap, for the General soon began to carry out an aggressive policy against their country, aiming at the eradication of the Caucasian Republic. They could do nothing except protest his aggressive acts to the Allied Powers, requesting the withdrawal of the White Russian forces from their country. The Allies however, paid no attention these protests, and considered the Caucasian refusal to obey Gen. Denikin's orders or to enlist in his army as hostile behavior directed against the Allies themselves. Consequently, the Caucasians had to fight Denikin for three months, but in vain, as they were unable to prevent him from occupying their lands, railways, ports and other facilities. However, he was unsuccessful in penetrating deeply into Caucasia, especially into Daghistan, which rose as one man and forced the General to withdraw.[180]

Peoples of the Caucasus were exposed to repeated Russian attacks against their very existence in their own homelands. Experience has proven that the Russians do not respect their commitments and they don't respect conventions and agreements to which they are part of. There was nothing to protect the rights of peoples of the Caucasus in case something went wrong. In case terms of the agreements are not implemented, no penalties will be expected against the side that breaches those terms.

Denikin's control at that time extended from the coasts of the Black Sea in the West to the Terk River in the East (i.e., he ruled the north-western parts of Caucasia). He did not refrain from assaulting the newly-independent local Caucasian governments, which seceded from Russia and declared themselves autonomous states, for he was far from recognizing their independence and sovereignty. Later on he wanted to extend his authority eastwards and to annex independent Chechenia to his new government.[181]

They used their malicious methods that were utilized when they needed to pass some obstacle. To solve some of the dilemmas they faced, they recruited some local indigenous people in local military units as to assist them in many cases to overcome some difficulties. However, this method doesn't always work; it depends on the sensitivity of the mission needed to be implemented as well as the readiness of the members of these units to participate in such missions.

He appointed Gen. Kilich Gerey, a Circassian, as commander of the Circassian troops which he conscripted

> from the Caucasians despite their unwillingness and ordered him to attack the Chechens and to subjugate them. Gerry, however, refused to obey Denikin's orders, saying that he could not think of fighting his brethren and shedding their blood whatever the reasons or dos obligations might be. Consequently Gen. Denikin was obliged to send a brigade of Cossacks to fight the Chechens, but they were unsuccessful and had to retreat after suffering heavy losses.[182]

The priority in the Russians' view, especially the White Russians, was to resist secession of the colonized nations and keep them all under Russian rule. Stopping the communist dilation was not of top priorities, as was to maintain the Caucasus region under Russian control. It was the reason why the military forces belonging to the Whites had conducted military operations against the peoples of the Caucasus.

They condoned the danger posed to them by the Russian Bolshevik forces.

> Though Denikin was a tool in the hands of the allies, he had his own plans and objectives. He considered the independent states which were formed in Caucasia and elsewhere at the expense of a disintegrated Russia, more important and dangerous than Communism itself. Thus he forgot his original duty and neglected the basic task of fighting Communism. Instead he made his supreme objective the combatting the Caucasians whom he fought relentlessly for two years. His wars, however, did not benefit him; on the contrary, they harmed him as he was often obliged to withdraw large units of his forces facing the communists in order to assist him fighting the Caucasians. This weakened his army and was one of the main reasons leading to his defeat in the face of the overwhelming Communist advance.[183]

True Circassians never forgot to preserve their national identity nor their homeland and its independence. They kept looking after their national interests wherever they were, whether in their homeland in the North Caucasus or in diaspora. It was never easy to consolidate all the concerns that lead to improving communication and interdependence. All communities coordinated when possible to reach convergence and to achieve their lofty goals.

> The idea of Caucasian independence and secession from Russia had arisen for the first time at the headquarters of 'The

Circassia

Circassian Co-operation Society' which had been set up in Istanbul after the declaration of the Ottoman Constitution in 1908. The members of that Society asked the Ottoman State to endeavour officially to assist Caucasia, the majority of whose inhabitants were Moslems, to secede from Russia and to become an independent state.[184]

At certain times, Circassian activities did not devoid and even the rest of the people and nations of the Caucasus from attempts of foreign interference, even methods of intrusion that various parties seek to undertake to impose influence on exerted efforts for the sake of reaching a position of having a state of their own.

Thereupon the Ottoman Government decided to set up an official organization of top-ranking officials for that purpose. Marshal Fuad Pasha (Thuga) was appointed Chairman, along with the Georgians Prince Mehaelli and Togridze; Professor Aziz Meker and Dr. Isa Rowhi Pasha, both of whom were Circassians, and Salem Behbudof, an Azerbaijani, as members. The committee was authorized to try to liberate Caucasia. It contacted the great powers and submitted memoranda requesting assistance. However, some of the committee's members withdrew and only its North Caucasian members remained. The withdrawal of the two Georgian members was due to the German promises of assistance, while the Azerbaijanis had good faith in the Turks.[185]

Sadly, the attempts of Turkish intervention did not show innocent and sincere intentions as they were not free at the time of expansionist ambitions. That was compatible with Turkish agenda, which seeks to control the regions that fall between Asia Minor and Central Asia through the Caucasus.

Despite the withdrawals, the Caucasian organization persisted in its work and with the conference of Lausanne which was held in 1916; and actually won wide admiration as an organization that upheld the mottoes and traditions of Shamil and represented his historic mission. A for the Ottoman state, it patronized that organization, since its success would serve the goal of the 'Committee for Union and Progress' which aimed at the formation oft (of) a grand

Trainman State across Caucasian to Turkistan, and at the annexation of Caucasia, which had millions of Moslem inhabitants, to that Empire.[186]

Evolving circumstances sometimes contribute to making influential countries show support for some peoples or nations to enjoy their freedom and independence.

The major European powers, moreover, were seriously interested in Caucasia, for they expected the disintegration of Tsarist Russia, as a result of the First World War, which meant the occurrence of great coups and sudden changes in Russia and in Europe itself. Thus the question of Caucasia became one of the most important world problems. The end of the First World War and the emergence of the Bolsheviks however, changed the course, in a way the European powers found undesirable.[187]

When conflicting interests reach untolerated extents by one of the parties, the matters get more complicated. Accordingly, the small nations become victims and will lose all what had been accomplished to enjoy being independent and not subjects that belong to anyone. Heterogeneity between many partners makes it impossible to save any entity. Due to different influences on participants in the Union, it will be impossible for the continuance of such a union.

During the 1917 Revolution two organizations favoring unity were formed in Caucasia: the first in the North and the other in the South, where on April 19, 1918, the Transacausian Republic was formed, comprising Georgia, Armenia and Azerbaijian (Azerbaijan). That republic did not last long, due to external interference with increased after the strong Tsarist control was removed from that part of the world. The Union was dissolved by a decision taken at a conference held by representatives of these three nations, in which Tserelli, representative of Georgia, frankly announced that union was impossible as each of the three groups believed that their country should live independently. The dissolution was officially declared on May 26, 1918; thus three independent republics emerged: those of Georgia, Armenia, and Azerbaijan.[188]

Perhaps the union of the victims of colonialism makes them feel strong and able to resist subjugation again. Probably part of the former partners who feel the existence of points of accord and aspirations between them would agree to create another manifestation of unification. Seemingly, it will make them feel that they have freedom and independence even with other peoples.

> On May 3, 1917 a conference was held by the Northern Caucasians in Terk Kala in which it was decided to secede from Russia. In the same year it was decided to set up a government known as 'The Provisional Government'. In the following year, on May 2, 1918, they established an entity known as the North Caucasian Republic. The destiny of that government was unlike that of the Southern Union, for it did not disintegrate by itself. Instead the Northern Government was the Victim of external aggression carried out by Gen. Denikin, who had taken upon himself the revival of the Russian Tsarism, fighting everyone who stood in his path, whether Caucasian or not.[189]

Russian policies, and since Russia was founded, would not implement except what matters and what is compatible with its interests. The successive Russian regimes did not consider the rights of the oppressed people except in cases of extreme necessity. Thereafter, the British general did not know about the Russian generals and leaders not having a bond of any agreement to be concluded with any party. They normally sign agreements and make commitments when they are in a position of weakness.

Thus, in regaining their strength, they regain tyranny. They easily flip to achieve their colonial and hegemonic ambitions: "Denikin deceived Gen. Thomson, commander of the British Military Command in Caucasian, into believing that he wanted to conclude an agreement with the Caucasian Republic, which was at war with the Bolsheviks, to assist it on behalf of the Allied Powers, and then to fight the Bolsheviks aided by that Republic."[190]

It is essential that Russian policies reveal their true nature. A struggle for survival and control over what remains of the Russian empire had erupted at the time. The White Russians were tougher in their struggle against the Circassians and other peoples of the Caucasus. They were determined to eliminate any tendency of independence of the peoples of the Caucasus under any circumstances. Although the conflict was between the Bolsheviks and the White Russians, the latter changed their priority. They diverted their struggle to be against the Circassians and other peoples of the Caucasus.

However, instead of fighting the Red Army, their common foe, he massed his troops and concentrated all his effort on fighting on fighting the Caucasians themselves, and sought to wipe out their republic and to set up a new Tsarist regime in Caucasia. By doing that Gen. Denikin gave the Bolsheviks the opportunity to strengthen their hold in Caucasia and to facilitate its occupation, after he failed to defend it, having misused the weapons and military material which he received from the British. Besides, he attempted, on every occasion, to make the Caucasians appear as collaborators with the Communists.[191]

Peoples of the Caucasus had to be the scapegoat in all cases, even when Russian rivals were fighting with each other. As a result, they lost their freedom and independence: "The White Army did not oppose the Bolshevik advance; Denikin and his allies had to evacuate Petrovsk and Dagestan and withdraw to Baku. Thus the Communists over-ran Caucasia whose independence came to an end."[192]

Russian policies in dealing with the colonized peoples and nations are well known to everyone to be advantageous to them.

Not surprisingly, to know that: "On 6 August 1990, Boris Yeltsin, head of the Russian Soviet Federative Socialist Republic, addressed regional leaders: 'Help yourself to as much sovereignty as you can swallow,' he said. So began what Gorbachev called 'the parade of sovereignties' and with it, the slide towards the federalisation of Russia, which became an independent state in December 1991."[193]

An example of Russian failure and retreat at a time of weakness occurred in 1996. The Russian army was surrounded in Chechnya, where the Russians started seeking a way out.

The resulting widespread demoralization of federal forces, and the almost universal opposition of the Russian public to the brutal conflict, led Boris Yeltsin's government to declare a ceasefire in 1996 and sign a peace treaty a year later.[194]

An agreement was reached, which recognizes that Chechens will be independent in the near future. Where their usual practice is to leave then return at a time that suits them, they have met and even exceeded that expectation. It didn't take them long this time, as the conspiracies began forming to create reasoning. Conditions and justifications were prepared and triggered to give an indication for another military campaign for reoccupation: "A virtually unknown ex-KBG officer, Vladimir Putin became Russia's new prime minister in August 1999 and within weeks led a military operation against the Chechen fighters."[195]

The common denominator between all those colonized nations is that they do not share with the Russians their origin, aspirations, or national objectives. The Russians occupied and colonized by force all their neighbors and beyond, the trickery Russian authorities wield when they are forced to abandon any colony during Russian weakness. Immediate preparations and actions begin to overcome the obstacles met in the nearest reasonable opportunity. Revolts or insurgencies are suppressed by deadly and destructive force.

If they must withdraw their forces and even sign a convention that recognizes the freedom and independence of certain nations, it will be ignored and even canceled when the balance of power changes to their benefit. Reoccupation will be executed when conditions are ripe for restoring any colony. There are many examples that occurred with some of the peoples of the Caucasus, the Baltic states, Crimea, and others.

> The Independence of these lands which had been parts of the Russian Empire was an important historical event, but their destiny was not secure. Some great powers actually gave 'de facto' and 'de jure' recognition to that independence. Red Russia, headed by Lenin, was one of the first countries to do so, but when the Moscow Government became stronger it withdrew its recognition and began to assault Caucasian, as had been mentioned.[196]

The successive Russian regimes have complicated the situation. It turned out to be a chronic crisis, where the Russians have placed and crammed the Circassians and others in an unenviable situation. They were rolled into a single entity, under the Russian yoke, tied to be part of Russia no matter what the developments might be. As long as there is an imperial-minded government in Russia, the regime will try to keep grabbing all as long as possible. When the Soviet Union fell apart and fifteen republics got their independence, Russia kept on its colonial policy and kept tens of peoples and nations part of a so-called federation.

When the USSR collapsed what happened was the 15 "republics" declared independence and the Russian Federation was among the first to do so. Yeltsin was elected head of the Russian Federation when it was still a republic of the USSR and when he saw the way things were going, he went ahead and declared Russian independence from the USSR and the Russian Federation's "territorial integrity". This last bit was essentially the reason why Yeltsin and the forces that backed him at the time decided to declare Russian independence in a kind of a preemptive move aimed at arresting further disintegration.[197]

The Circassian nation was considered by the nationalities regulations of the former Soviet Union, one of the peoples and nationalities thoroughbreds, a system that was considered the rightful heir to the Russian Empire, which occupied Circassia.

Minority Rights Group Europe's report on "Protecting the Rights of Minorities and Indigenous Peoples in the Russian Federation: Challenges and Ways Forward" has acknowledged in detail the suffering circumstances of non-Slavic citizens of the indigenous native peoples in Russia. In 1.3 Vulnerable, visible minorities of the report is states,

> For practical purposes, an additional and crucial distinction ought to be made between minorities that are of "Slavic" and "non-Slavic" appearance. While this distinction is not clear-cut, xenophobic sentiments tend to be targeted primarily at darker-skinned people, and particularly those from the Caucasus and Central Asia and Roma people—although at times Africans, Chinese and others are also targeted. Persons, who are also stateless in addition to being of "non-Slavic appearance", are in a position of heightened vulnerability.[198]

The peoples of the North Caucasus are considered citizens of Russia. Their homelands were conquered and annexed by Russia when they were occupied by the tsarist Russian empire. Nevertheless, compatriots from the North Caucasus, when they travel to other parts of the present Russian Federation, are considered immigrants. They get discriminated against and consequently treated in a degrading manner.

In the report published by Minority Rights Group Europe, 1.3.1 Migrant workers, it says,

> Persons from the Caucasus include migrants from the South Caucasus as well as internal migrants (with Russian citizenship and mostly originating from Russia's North Caucasus). These groups are affected by particularly severe forms of mistreatment, and remain for the most part unequipped to end their conditions of vulnerability. The reasons can be found in state policy and the actions of law-enforcement officials, described below, combined with widespread and deeply-ingrained prejudice against particular ethnic groups. The Chechen wars and instances of Islamic fundamentalism have further contributed to creating suspicion towards persons originating from the North Caucasus.[199]

The International Expert Group Meeting for Indigenous Peoples, referred to Development with Culture and Identity Articles 3 and 32 of the United Nations Declaration on the Rights of Indigenous Peoples (New York, 12–14 January 2010), states,

> Russia is one of the polyethnic countries in the world in spite of the fact that about 80% of citizens identify themselves as Russian people. There are 200 ethnic groups residing on the territory of the Russian Federation and apart from the Russian people the population of a million or about this number is reached by buryats, yakuts, bashkirs, kalmyks and others.

It's good that the report is optimistic, which indicates what must be the situation in the Russian Federation, but it is not. Deplorably, the report mentioned,

Lastly:

- historically indigenous peoples have been self-governed with their own languages, cultures, laws and traditions;
- indigenous peoples are independent peoples and communities having the right to self-determination including the right to autonomy, self-government and identity;
- self-government and independent decision making on administrative and economic issues of indigenous peoples are elements of political autonomy;

- the territory of indigenous peoples and resources on it are vital for their subsistence, cultural and spiritual life and for achieving and implementing autonomy and self-government. This territory and resources should be guaranteed to the indigenous peoples in order to ensure their subsistence and sustainable development of their communities and culture.[200]

In a related issue, Paul Goble published a Window in November 2016, titled, Circassians Want to Follow Sakha and Declare Their Nation the Indigenous People of Krasnodar Kray. That is more than six years since the report was published. In the meantime, many of the peoples in the Russian Federation are not able yet to get the right to enjoy adopting such regulations.

Circassian activists have continued demanding to attain their nation's legal rights on an equal footing and similar to others, corresponding to the Russian rules and regulations.

> In September, Circassian activists posted online for signature a declaration to Russian President Vladimir Putin, the government of the Russian Federation, and the administration of Krasnodar Kray calling on them to recognize the Circassians (Adygeys) as the indigenous people of Krasnodar Kray.[201]

Considering Circassian claims, the concerned have mentioned the proven and documented historical facts. Sites, areas, and even the rest of the region have been taken from their legitimate owners. Many of the names of the geographic locations in their homeland still bear witness to that.

> The petition reads in part, "the majority of cities and rivers of the Black Sea coastal region of Krasnodar Kray have Adygey names and the Adygeys have lived there from time immemorial. Up to now, the kray administration has not recognized [the Circassians] as an indigenous one . . . We need nothing except recognition of this fact."[202]

Despite the tragedies caused by the Russian invasion, there are some Circassian activists trying to heal the wounds of the past and to forget about what happened. Nevertheless, the Russian authorities didn't respond positively to their rightful demands. Seemingly, the colonial mentality is still the compass that navigates the current Russian state. The petition continues,

If such recognition is granted, the Circassians "will be able to turn over the page of history and with gratitude go forward! [They] love their country and have promoted its honor both in sports and in military conflicts. Now let our great country meet [the Circassians] half way and recognize this fact. Justice must triumph!"[203]

Circassians referred to legal international declarations, where Goble cited the Russian author as saying, "He bases that conclusion on the terms of the November 2011 Circassian 'declaration on self-determination and statehood of the auto chthonian indigenous Circassian people' that was adopted as the Circassian response to the 2007 UN Declaration 'on the rights of indigenous peoples.'"[204]

Facts cannot be hidden, no matter how hard those with a colonial mentality would try. No one can stop the wheel of time from turning, where it will inevitably lead to the restitution of the usurped rights to their original owners. The Window stated, "Moreover, Priymak suggests, if Russia makes any concessions to the Circassians on this point, the Circassians will then press for recognition of the events of 1864 in which more than half of the Circassians were deported to the Ottoman Empire and which Circassians and their supporters to this day view as an act of genocide."[205]

Justice for Circassia

Circassians, in all their whereabouts, seek to restore their legitimate rights. No matter how long it may take, the usurped rights will be restored. The types of crimes committed against the Circassian nation have no statute of limitation. In the light of developments witnessed by the world, there is an opportunity to demand the restoration of the inalienable rights. The tsarist Russian invasion had violated and seized the Circassian homeland by force and terror. Circassians will adopt peaceful and legal means to restore their rights.

Circassians are continuing their quest to deliver their fair cause to the civilized world. The struggle between good and evil is eternal, and eventually, good will triumph over evil. The Circassian genocide must be recognized. Accordingly, all other associated confiscated and looted rights should be given back to their rightful owners.

Regrettably, different branches of the Russian authorities have ignored the Circassians' legal and legitimate rights. During the past few years, some Russian academicians and scholars intended to issue and publish propagandistic studies and research about the Circassian Question. That was associated with holding meetings, seminars, and conferences for the same purposes of changing and diverting the truth.

Aiming to divert the attention from the real Circassian issues and dilemmas in an academic tone, they followed immense aggressive objectives in recent years. An example of misinformation was published in late 2015 and was analyzed and published earlier this year, under the title, Moscow Disinformation Spreading from Mass Media to Academic Output.[206]

Some Circassians got invited to Russian observatory events. They invited individuals, whether from the North Caucasus or from the Circassian diaspora, to attend such gatherings. They were either invited to attend in person or by utilizing video communication systems.

The most recent seminar took place on December 2, 2016, under the title, "The Circassians and the Circassian Question—the Contemporary Realities."[207]

Unfortunately, such gatherings have the tendency to change facts by concentrating on nonessential issues. They are steering a disinformation campaign to divert and topple the truth. Apparently, to cut it short and to avoid passing propagandistic agendas, projects, and plots against the Circassian Question, Circassians from the North Caucasus have declined to participate in the most recent conferences. However, some members of, or people close to the members of, the International Circassian Association have willingly taken part. Seemingly, they do not see a real threat regarding the Circassian Question because they cooperate blindly with various parties without knowing the extent of the damage they would cause.

Regarding the different Circassian issues, it is not acceptable by most Circassians to waiver any of the nation's rights. This is evidenced by the vigilance and awareness of Circassians who know their status well. Knowledge that deals with national awareness has remarkably improved in recent years, thanks to employed modern technology. It is essential to clarify and protect the identity, elements, foundations, and pillars of the Circassian national character. This is a natural and legitimate right of every people and nation, according to international laws and norms.

Being shallow-minded regarding the national issues can be possibly condoned, but working against the national interests of the people while knowing what damage that may inflict regarding the whole Circassian Question is not acceptable by any standard. Consequences may turn out to be embarrassing for all.

Not to defend terrorism or radicalism in any way, whether coming from groups or states, but matters should be straightened out. The deep Russian involvement in Syria now and the apparent outdated Russian equipment reminds the world of the Soviet involvement and failure in the 1980s in Afghanistan.

Not to intervene in the Russian-Syrian prerogative to do so, but Circassians of Syria are still not permitted to return to their historical Circassian homeland.

Another concern regarding the Circassian Question is the present Russian-Turkish cooperation, which should not cross the Syrian borders' arrangements. Hopefully, it will be positive regarding the different Circassian issues. The recent ongoing agreements and understandings between the two countries should not affect the Circassians negatively or the restoration of their rights, hoping that no disastrous affects would be produced from behind-the-scenes talks, the way they took place between tsarist Russia and the Ottoman Empire, in the absence of those who care for their homeland.

Ancient Circassian Legacies and Antique collectibles

The Circassian nation has been able to have cultural and humanitarian works that reflect the existence of a sound and unprecedented civilization at the time. That was thousands of years ago in the Circassian part of the Caucasus region. They were embodied in and symbolized the ways and means that they lived a long time ago and adopted to their circumstances.

Archaeological remains with documented and incarnated evidence have proven Circassian metallic monetary coins that had been in use even before old Roman and ancient Greek metallic coins were known. Circassians have demonstrated that a money issuance has been evident, whether at the same time of Roman and Greek monetary systems or even earlier. They were ranked aptly beside other ancient nations in the immortal record of mankind, where they were able to be a positive component in the development of human civilization.

Coin minting went along with other positive clues of being constructive starting from their homeland. They managed to maintain their proven sovereignty, where they were able to defend themselves heroically for thousands of years. The most recent of all was in the face of a barbaric and brutal invasion that lasted for decades. Eventually, it affected them tremendously due to genocide, havoc, deportation, and consequent loss of freedom and independence.

While the tsarist Russia Empire had managed to perpetuate or immortalize itself, they wanted to prove that they were negative and even a destructive element in the human civilizations' archives. They were able, in the nineteenth century, to classify themselves in the wicked everlasting records. They commemorated the occasion of the effects of destruction of the Circassian nation by minting medals to be granted to criminal troopers and commanders.

Bearing the image of Emperor Alexander II, the Russian medals showed the ability of committing wars and issuing medals to those who committed mass crimes against an indigenous people. Where "the end justifies the means," the purpose was to celebrate savage invasion campaigns in the west Caucasus. As per their description, that would bear witness to what was committed by their bloodstained hands against innocent human beings.

Odessa Numismatics Museum reveals valuable data and shows images of old coins, which are related to early Circassians. The information showed ancient Circassian coins from ancient historical periods used by different Circassian old forms of states or entities, such as Sinds and Bosporus.[208]

Coins were known in the Caucasus area and the region since they were known by developed and civilized nations:

Six periods can be marked out in the history of the Bosporus state, connected with the events of the political life of Bosporus:

1. Formation of the state—VI BC–480 BC;
2. The government of Archianaktids—480 BC–438/437 years BC;
3. The government of Spartokhids—438/437 years BC–109 BC;
4. Bosporus under the power of Mithradates VI Eupator and Rome—II BC–I AD;
5. Bosporus in the first centuries AD;
6. The decay of the Bosporus state—the middle of III–the end of IV AD.[209]

The coins of the Sindi people shows that Circassians had the coins since the early times:

> Since we know that the Sinds were an important Circassian tribe and they were the same people as the Sindjs, it is obvious that they were not absorbed by the Sychs, as it was supposed by Thumb-Hanschild, but rather survived and continued to live until the present, long after the Scyths themselves had disappeared.[210]

Also, coins were known by the Bosporus. It is important to mention that the Circassian history is well-known and they were an important element at the time: "Scholars affirm that the ancient history of Circassians begins from the period of the Kingdom of Bosporus which was formed soon after the fall of the Cimmerian Empire about 720 B.C. under the onslaught of the Scythes."[211]

Decorations and Medals

Being ideologically biased, proud, and privileged of victorious results of the Russian-Circassian War, the tsarist Russian Empire was able to preserve and locate its ideal position. The world of murder and genocide recognized an eligible member as well, which is not rivaled or competed by any sane party or entity. On top of that, the colonial empire had issued decorations and commemorative medals to honor the commanders, officers, and soldiers of a military structure that took part in crushing a brave nation.

> The Caucasus—for services in the Caucasus between 1859–1864 the Emperor Alexander II granted a small silver medal 1 1/16 in. in diameter bearing on the obverse his bust in profile facing left, and on the reverse across the centre is the date 1859-1864 encircled by an inscription in Russian characters stating that it is awarded for the subjugation of the Western Caucasus.[212]

The medals had variations in their quality and class. Apparently, they memorialized genocide, ethnic cleansing, and forced deportation against the Circassians. An entire nation's fate became hanging in the wind of conflicts to swap interests of a variety of colonial powers. Not to mention the fact that the country of Circassia was eventually annexed by imperial Russia, where it was deleted from the map of the region and the world.

> A bronze Cross, with crossed swords between the arms, to be attached to the uniform by means of a ring and bar attachment, was also awarded for the same campaign. It bears the explanatory inscription across the horizontal arms and Alexander's initial in Russian character surmounted by the Russian Imperial crown in the upper arm, and the date 1864 in the lower arm. In the circle which occupies the centre is the Russian eagle. It is 1 9/10 in. across the arms.[213]

---

67 https://geopolitical.tv/черкесия-оставалась-независимой-от-м/
68 http://unpo.org/demo/article/1639
69 http://adygaabaza.ru/publ/2-1-0-3
70 http://justicefornorthcaucasus.info/?p=1251673688

[71] http://justicefornorthcaucasus.info/?p=1251673688
[72] http://justicefornorthcaucasus.info/?p=1251673688
[73] The Circassians: A Handbook (Amjad Jaimoukha)
[74] Heroes and Emperors in Circassian History (Shauket Mufti)
[75] The Sochi Predicament: Contexts, Characteristics and Challenges of the Olympic Winter Games in 2014 (Bo Petersson, Karina Vamling)
[76] The Circassians: A Handbook (Amjad Jaimoukha)
[77] Heroes and Emperors in Circassian History (Shauket Mufti)
[78] Heroes and Emperors in Circassian History (Shauket Mufti)
[79] Heroes and Emperors in Circassian History (Shauket Mufti)
[80] Heroes and Emperors in Circassian History (Shauket Mufti)
[81] Heroes and Emperors in Circassian History (Shauket Mufti)
[82] Heroes and Emperors in Circassian History (Shauket Mufti)
[83] Heroes and Emperors in Circassian History (Shauket Mufti)
[84] Heroes and Emperors in Circassian History (Shauket Mufti)
[85] Heroes and Emperors in Circassian History (Shauket Mufti)
[86] Heroes and Emperors in Circassian History (Shauket Mufti)
[87] Heroes and Emperors in Circassian History (Shauket Mufti)
[88] Heroes and Emperors in Circassian History (Shauket Mufti)
[89] Heroes and Emperors in Circassian History (Shauket Mufti)
[90] Heroes and Emperors in Circassian History (Shauket Mufti)
[91] Heroes and Emperors in Circassian History (Shauket Mufti)
[92] Heroes and Emperors in Circassian History (Shauket Mufti)
[93] Adygean (Circassian) Culture (Nugzari Antelava)
[94] Adygean (Circassian) Culture (Nugzari Antelava)
[95] Adygean (Circassian) Culture (Nugzari Antelava)
[96] Heroes and Emperors in Circassian History (Shauket Mufti)
[97] Heroes and Emperors in Circassian History (Shauket Mufti)
[98] Heroes and Emperors in Circassian History (Shauket Mufti)
[99] Heroes and Emperors in Circassian History (Shauket Mufti)
[100] Heroes and Emperors in Circassian History (Shauket Mufti)
[101] Heroes and Emperors in Circassian History (Shauket Mufti)
[102] Heroes and Emperors in Circassian History (Shauket Mufti)
[103] Heroes and Emperors in Circassian History (Shauket Mufti)
[104] Heroes and Emperors in Circassian History (Shauket Mufti)
[105] Heroes and Emperors in Circassian History (Shauket Mufti)
[106] Heroes and Emperors in Circassian History (Shauket Mufti)
[107] Heroes and Emperors in Circassian History (Shauket Mufti)
[108] Heroes and Emperors in Circassian History (Shauket Mufti)
[109] Adygean (Circassian) Culture (Nugzari Antelava)
[110] Adygean (Circassian) Culture (Nugzari Antelava)

111 Adygean (Circassian) Culture (Nugzari Antelava)
112 Adygean (Circassian) Culture (Nugzari Antelava)
113 https://www.britannica.com/event/Treaty-of-Bucharest-1812
114 Adygean (Circassian) Culture (Nugzari Antelava)
115 Adygean (Circassian) Culture (Nugzari Antelava)
116 Adygean (Circassian) Culture (Nugzari Antelava)
117 Adygean (Circassian) Culture (Nugzari Antelava)
118 Adygean (Circassian) Culture (Nugzari Antelava)
119 Adygean (Circassian) Culture (Nugzari Antelava)
120 Adygean (Circassian) Culture (Nugzari Antelava)
121 Adygean (Circassian) Culture (Nugzari Antelava)
122 Adygean (Circassian) Culture (Nugzari Antelava)
123 Adygean (Circassian) Culture (Nugzari Antelava)
124 http://www.values.com/inspirational-quotes/3945-unity-is-power
125 Adygean (Circassian) Culture (Nugzari Antelava)
126 Adygean (Circassian) Culture (Nugzari Antelava)
127 Adygean (Circassian) Culture (Nugzari Antelava)
128 Adygean (Circassian) Culture (Nugzari Antelava)
129 Adygean (Circassian) Culture (Nugzari Antelava)
130 http://foreignpolicy.com/2015/08/18/russias-putin-is-once-again-spending-his-summer-riding-submarines/?utm_content=buffer7d090&utm_medium=social&utm_source=twitter.com&utm_campaign=buffer
131 http://foreignpolicy.com/2015/08/18/russias-putin-is-once-again-spending-his-summer-riding-submarines/
132 http://www.localhistories.org/russia.html
133 http://linguistics.byu.edu/classes/ling450ch/reports/russian.html
134 http://foreignpolicy.com/2015/08/18/russias-putin-is-once-again-spending-his-summer-riding-submarines/
135 http://foreignpolicy.com/2015/08/18/russias-putin-is-once-again-spending-his-summer-riding-submarines/
136 https://aheku.net/stranicza-ajax?id=3956
137 https://aheku.net/stranicza-ajax?id=3956
138 https://aheku.net/stranicza-ajax?id=3956
139 https://aheku.net/stranicza-ajax?id=3956
140 https://aheku.net/stranicza-ajax?id=3956
141 https://aheku.net/stranicza-ajax?id=3956
142 http://justicefornorthcaucasus.info/?p=1239745800 and http://www.natpressru.info/index.php?newsid=3850
143 http://justicefornorthcaucasus.info/?p=1239745800 and http://www.natpressru.info/index.php?newsid=3850

144. http://justicefornorthcaucasus.info/?p=1239745800 and http://www.natpressru.info/index.php?newsid=3850
145. http://justicefornorthcaucasus.info/?p=1239745800 and http://www.natpressru.info/index.php?newsid=3850
146. http://justicefornorthcaucasus.info/?p=1239745800 and http://www.natpressru.info/index.php?newsid=3850
147. http://www.international-alert.org/blog/sochi-olympics-and-circassian-question#_ftn1
148. http://www.international-alert.org/blog/sochi-olympics-and-circassian-question#_ftn1
149. http://www.international-alert.org/blog/sochi-olympics-and-circassian-question#_ftn1
150. http://www.international-alert.org/blog/sochi-olympics-and-circassian-question#_ftn1
151. http://www.international-alert.org/blog/sochi-olympics-and-circassian-question#_ftn1
152. http://www.international-alert.org/blog/sochi-olympics-and-circassian-question#_ftn1
153. http://www.interpretermag.com/151-years-after-the-genocide-and-one-year-after-sochi-the-circassian-issue-isnt-going-away/
154. http://justicefornorthcaucasus.info/?p=1251673688
155. http://www.newyorker.com/magazine/2007/01/29/kremlin-inc
156. http://www.rferl.org/content/article/1109598.html
157. http://www.justicefornorthcaucasus.com/eagle_combo/documents/eagle.php?title=north-caucasus-imperial-crisis&entry_id=1214444700
158. http://www.worldstatesmen.org/Russian_republics.htm
159. http://windowoneurasia.blogspot.com/2008/04/window-on-eurasia-kremlins-regional.html
160. http://windowoneurasia.blogspot.com/2008/04/window-on-eurasia-kremlins-regional.html
161. The English Writings of Rabindranath Tagore
162. http://legal.un.org/avl/ha/dicc/dicc.html and http://www.unesco.org/new/en/indigenous-peoples/related-info/undrip/
163. http://justicefornorthcaucasus.info/?p=1251677935
164. http://justicefornorthcaucasus.info/?p=1251677935
165. The History of the Negotiations for the Peace Concluded at Belgrade September 18, 1739: Between the Emperor, Russia, and the Ottoman Porte, by the Mediation and Under the Guarantee of France. Shewing the Grounds of the Present War Between the Russians and the Turks
166. https://jamestown.org/program/circassians-in-predominantly-ethnic-russian-krasnodar-demand-recognition-as-regions-indigenous-population/#.V-L1Q5MrJE4

167 (https://jamestown.org/program/circassians-in-predominantly-ethnic-russian-krasnodar-demand-recognition-as-regions-indigenous-population/#.V-L1Q5MrJE4).
168 Heroes and Emperors in Circassian History (Shauket Mufti)
169 Heroes and Emperors in Circassian History (Shauket Mufti)
170 Journal of a Residence of Circassia During the Years 1837, 1838, and 1839 (James Stanislaus Bell)
171 Journal of a Residence of Circassia During the Years 1837, 1838, and 1839 (James Stanislaus Bell)
172 Heroes and Emperors in Circassian History (Shauket Mufti)
173 Heroes and Emperors in Circassian History (Shauket Mufti)
174 Heroes and Emperors in Circassian History (Shauket Mufti)
175 Heroes and Emperors in Circassian History (Shauket Mufti)
176 Heroes and Emperors in Circassian History (Shauket Mufti)
177 Fields of Fire: An Atlas of Ethnic Conflict (Stuart A. Northolt)
178 Heroes and Emperors in Circassian History (Shauket Mufti)
179 Heroes and Emperors in Circassian History (Shauket Mufti)
180 Heroes and Emperors in Circassian History (Shauket Mufti)
181 Heroes and Emperors in Circassian History (Shauket Mufti)
182 Heroes and Emperors in Circassian History (Shauket Mufti)
183 Heroes and Emperors in Circassian History (Shauket Mufti)
184 Heroes and Emperors in Circassian History (Shauket Mufti)
185 Heroes and Emperors in Circassian History (Shauket Mufti)
186 Heroes and Emperors in Circassian History (Shauket Mufti)
187 Heroes and Emperors in Circassian History (Shauket Mufti)
188 Heroes and Emperors in Circassian History (Shauket Mufti)
189 Heroes and Emperors in Circassian History (Shauket Mufti)
190 Heroes and Emperors in Circassian History (Shauket Mufti)
191 Heroes and Emperors in Circassian History (Shauket Mufti)
192 Heroes and Emperors in Circassian History (Shauket Mufti)
193 https://www.theguardian.com/world/2014/dec/12/-sp-chechnya-russia-war-anniversary
194 http://www.newworldencyclopedia.org/entry/First_Chechen_War
195 http://www.aljazeera.com/indepth/features/2014/12/chechnya-russia-20-years-conflict-2014121161310580523.html
196 Heroes and Emperors in Circassian History (Shauket Mufti)
197 yhttps://www.quora.com/Why-were-the-Northern-Caucasus-retained-by-Russia-when-the-Southern-Caucasus-became-independent-states-after-the-fall-of-the-Soviet-Union
198 http://minorityrights.org/wp-content/uploads/2014/11/mrg-protecting-rights-minorities-indigenous-peoples-russian-federation_English.pdf

[199] http://minorityrights.org/wp-content/uploads/2014/11/mrg-protecting-rights-minorities-indigenous-peoples-russian-federation_English.pdf
[200] http://www.un.org/esa/socdev/unpfii/documents/Paper%20submitted%20by%20Ms%20Anna%20Naikanchina%20(English).doc
[201] http://windowoneurasia2.blogspot.com/2016/11/circassians-want-to-follow-sakha-and.html
[202] http://windowoneurasia2.blogspot.com/2016/11/circassians-want-to-follow-sakha-and.html
[203] http://windowoneurasia2.blogspot.com/2016/11/circassians-want-to-follow-sakha-and.html
[204] http://windowoneurasia2.blogspot.com/2016/11/circassians-want-to-follow-sakha-and.html
[205] http://windowoneurasia2.blogspot.com/2016/11/circassians-want-to-follow-sakha-and.html
[206] http://www.stopfake.org/en/moscow-disinformation-spreading-from-mass-media-to-academic-output/
[207] http://www.pglu.ru/events/?ELEMENT_ID=167777
[208] Heroes and Emperors in Circassian History (Shauket Mufti)
[209] http://www.museum.com.ua/en/istor/sev-vost/sev-vost.htm#3
[210] Heroes and Emperors in Circassian History (Shauket Mufti) and http://www.museum.com.ua/en/istor/sev-vost/sev-vost.htm#3
[211] Heroes and Emperors in Circassian History (Shauket Mufti) and http://www.museum.com.ua/en/istor/sev-vost/sev-vost.htm#3
[212] War Medals and Their History (William Augustus Steward)
[213] War Medals and Their History (William Augustus Steward)

3

The Russian-Circassian War (1763–1864)

Russian-Circassian War Memorial in Maykop, Adygea

Since historical records were found, the ancient native inhabitants of the northwest Caucasus were known in most historical records as the Circassians that existed in their homeland. The Circassian nation had suffered a war of disastrous consequences that included but were not limited to destruction, annihilation, displacement, and deportation. These are elements of mass genocide, used by those who wanted to implement an evil plan of destroying the Circassian nation. During the war, Circassia was subjected to devastation, sanctions, total and strict blockade imposed by sea and land, and eventually total occupation. This consequently resulted in famine, spread of illness, and exposure among those inhabitants who remained alive and had to face severe and extreme circumstances.

Background

The Russian-Circassian War was not an improvised or contingent event, but a predetermined and well-planned project. It was built upon an edifice of tsarist imperialism, a forthcoming entity built upon the ruins of small nations through destructive colonial wars. The Muscovites and their descendants had inherited the desire to control others' homelands from their ancestors who preceded them in this.

> The backdrop of war dates back hundreds of years, which showed old colonial aspirations that fall under the umbrella, were under the command of prince Mstislav of the Princedom of Tamatarkha, invaded Circassian Kasogia, in 1022. The Circassian army, led by Prince Rededey, had faced him. Circassian folklore has preserved the details of this famous encounter and they are recorded in Russian chronicles.[214]
>
> In 1561, Ivan the Terrible, the first Russian sovereign to be crowned as czar, married Princess Goshen, the daughter of Prince Idar Temriuk, in order to place the Kabardians of Eastern Circassia under his control. He hastily built in Kabardia Cossack fortifications: Tumen, Sunja, and Andreevo by 1579. He was well-known for his expansionist policy and cruelty. He was not only trying to lay claim to Eastern Circassia, but in order to expand the boundaries of Russia, he also subdued Kazan, Astrakhan, and annexed Siberia.[215]

Ivan the Terrible had achieved a well-deserved description, being an adventurer ruler who knows neither mercy nor compassion.

> He achieved all that with single-minded perseverance and merciless cruelty, for which he earned the title "Terrible". His cruelty, however, was not limited to the people he conquered. In 1594, the successor of Ivan the Terrible, Czar Feodor Ivanovich, vaingloriously gave to himself the title, "The ruler of the Iberian land, Georgian Czars, Kabarda, Circassians, and mountaineer princes". In other words, the Russian Czars had begun claiming in advance, by title, the plans of expansion they intended to realize.[216]

Russian colonial policies did not emerge from nothing. Predetermined colonial intentions pushed the preliminary steps that led to the occurrence of the Russian-Circassian War, which lasted for 101 years and led to the fall of innocent victims and positioned Circassians in unprecedented disastrous consequences.

> Peter the Great had left a will for his plan: To expand tirelessly the boundaries of Russia north and south, along the Black Sea, and to move nearer to Constantinople and India. Whoever possesses them would own the world.
>
> On May 13, 1711, Czar Peter Alexandrovich I, better known as Peter the Great, ordered Araksin, Governor of Astrakhan, to invade Circassia. Araksin moved with thirty-thousand-strong Russian armed forces and, on August 26, 1711, broke into the lands of the Circassians. 100 km north of the Kuban River, and captured the town of Kopyl (present day Slavianski). From there, heading toward the Black Sea, he seized ports on the Kuban River for 86 km, pillaging villages, devastating the land, and killing the inhabitants. Naturally, this surprise attack had confused the Circassians at first. However, they soon recovered from the shock and sent seven-thousand-strong Circassian cavalry, which engaged the enemy forces at the Chalou River but, having no cannons, they were defeated there on September 6.

Unlike those who have had aggressive intentions and lust to seize others' territories by force and violence, regardless of the human cost and losses, which did not mean anything to them, the Circassians were defending themselves by more conventional means, unlike those who prepared effusive armies, which have been armed and prepared for occupying the land of their neighbors and beyond.

Serious losses in lives, property, and livestock did not discourage the Circassians from defending their homeland by using any available means.

> During this single invasion in Circassia, the Russians killed 43,247 Circassian men and women, drove away 39,200 horses, 190,000 cattle, and 227,000 sheep from Circassia. Russia kept waging this type of warfare against Circassia during the period from 1716 to 1763, but her motif for this mad drive was not material gain alone. This was only the prelude of the terrible war she was to unleash against Circassia for the realization of the secret plan she was trying to conceal from other great powers of the world.[217]

A Look at Russia's Background

> Rus, also spelled Ros, ancient people who gave their name to the lands of Russia and Belarus. Their origin and identity are much in dispute. Traditional Western scholars believe them to be Scandinavian Vikings, an offshoot of the Varangians, who moved southward from the Baltic coast and founded the first consolidated state among the eastern Slavs, centring on Kiev. Russian scholars, along with some Westerners, consider the Rus to be a southeastern Slavic tribe that founded a tribal league; the Kievan state, they affirm, was the creation of Slavs and was attacked and held only briefly by Varangians.[218]

Two other reference books, A History of the Vikings by Gwyn Jones and A History of Russia by John Lawrence, elaborate and explain more:

> The term Rus is a Finnish term for the Swedes, when the Vikings would come down the Dnieper from the Dvina.
> The Viking by the name of Rurik, thought to be Rurik of Jutland, set himself up at Novgorod. Vladimir Prince of Kiev is descended from him.

Here is the passage from A History of the Vikings:[219]

> Rus comes from the Finnish name for Sweden, Ruotsi... The name Ruosti, it is argued, arose from roosmenn, men of the rowing-way, the people of today's Roslagen, the Rowing-Law, the coastal area of Swedish Uppland. Those were the people known to the Finnish, whether the Vikings came from Denmark, Sweden, or Norway.
>
> The formation of a nation with the title of "Rus" or "Russia", "originated from the principality of Muscovy in the 17th century, it expanded later on to become the Russian Empire.[220]

That led to establishing a Russian language that is considered of an Indo-European ethnolinguistic group and relatively a fledgling matter that had taken place approximately 1,100 years ago. The Russian language was founded as such to be a source of culture for the newly born entity (nation), which was assembled, resourced, and collected from different sources and fundamentals.

Human demography shows a combination of many elements of origin including southeastern Slavic tribes, Vikings, Varangians, Norsemen, Germanic, and Asian at later stages.[221] This verifies a difference in origin and deepness from other European nations such as Greek, Italian, French, German, English, Spanish, and others.

> Cyril and Methodius and their missionary work in Greater Moravia 1,100 years ago. It did not join the millennium celebrations of the Christianization of Kievan Rus' in 1988.[222]

Regarding the origin of the Russian language,

> Russian Russki yazyk, principal state, and cultural language of Russia. Together with Ukrainian and Belarusian, the Russian language makes up the eastern branch of the Slavic family of languages. Russian is the primary language of the overwhelming majority of people in Russia and is also used as a second language in other former republics of the Soviet Union.... Russian and the other East Slavic languages (Ukrainian, Belarusian) did not diverge noticeably from one another until the Middle Russian period (the late 13th to the 16th century). The term Old Russian is generally applied to the common East Slavic language in use before that time.[223]

> The evolution of the writing system used by the Eastern Slavs has a history of planned language change and reform. This process of change from the beginnings of written language to the present-day writing system can be explained by citing four important events. These include the 'birth' of the Cyrillic alphabet in 862 A. D., a set of 13th Century reforms known as the Second Southern Slavic Influence, Peter the Great's reforms of the 18th century and the Communist reforms of 1917.[224]

Early Russian history (6th–15th centuries) states,

> In the 6th and 7th century, Viking traders, known as the Varangians, entered the loosely, tribally organized Slavic area that corresponds to present-day Kiev and established an overland trade route that stretched as far south as Constantinople, in the Byzantine Empire. The

Slavs contributed timber, caviar, fish, furs, and amber to this growing trading nexus.[225]

The Mongol invasion of 1236 was considered a "catastrophic event" that brought Russia under direct Mongol rule for the fourteenth and fifteenth centuries: "Russian culture became more influenced by oriental patterns during the Mongol period". As a result, this contributed to "its political fragmentation", which led to the fact that, "Russians lost whatever nationalistic sentiment they may have had."[226]

Romanov tsarism introduced Muscovy, then Russia, to a so-described "modernization and westernization of the army, government, and the nobility; created a Russian navy, controlled the church, and eliminated all opponents" for reforms. They waged colonial and territorial expansion wars against tens of nations in the Caucasus and elsewhere besides "conducting wars against the Ottoman Empire, Persia, and Sweden to expand Russia south and west,"[227] unlike the thousands of years of deep-rootedness, authenticity of the native nations of the Caucasus, and the indigenous Circassians from ancient times being the original inhabitants of the northwestern part of the Caucasus.

> The tsar was known as "Tsar Batushka" or "little father." He knew best and his will was unquestioned and, as such, he had the power of life and death over his subjects without being subject to any laws himself. The present governments continue to rule with the same kind of autocratic absolutism. In addition, in order to fight the Mongols, Ivan had to give total control of the peasantry over to the Boyars, thus establishing the institution of serfdom in Russia at precisely the same time it was going out of style in the west. This would contribute to retarding Russia's economic development well into the 19th and 20th centuries. And finally, since Constantinople had fallen to the Ottoman Turks in 1453, the new Russian state no longer had a Byzantine Empire to emulate. Ivan therefore invented the theory that Russia was heir to Byzantine civilization, which had itself been heir to Roman civilization. Moscow became the "Third Rome," hence Ivan's adoption of the term "Tsar," or "Caesar," and from his time onward, Russians have used their mission to protect Orthodox Christians as an excuse to meddle abroad.[228]
>
> Mongol Invasion: Since the Russian aristocracy, or Boyars, were less powerful than their feudal counterparts

in the west, Kievan Rus was unable to fight off the Mongol invasion of 1236. This catastrophic event brought about the demise of Kievan Rus as the Mongols of the Golden Horde under Batu Khan created their own government and further separated Russia from contacts with the west. All trade and communication with the west ceased for the next two centuries, and Russian culture became more influenced by Oriental patterns during the Mongol period. As a result, Russia missed out on the major advances of the Renaissance and, as the Mongols encouraged its political fragmentation as well, Russians lost whatever nationalistic sentiment they may have had.[229]

The Formation of the Empire of Horror

The tsars' wars and invasions had started more than 450 years ago, right after getting rid of the Mongols' tight control for several hundred years against all the surrounding neighbors in all directions, starting with Novgorod in the year 1478, which got a territory from the Baltic Sea, to the Urals and from the White Sea to Lake Seliger in the present Novgorod Oblast,[230] which resulted in either eliminating those people and nations or subjecting them to subjugation under oppression and tyranny.

A good example of this is provided by Pavel Pryannikov in his Tolkovatel blog, which describes in some detail the political arrangements of the Novgorod Republic, including representation, elections, the existence of parties ("sides"), and various checks and balances that existed until Muscovy destroyed all this in 1478.[231]

Dozens of nations were victims of tsarist Russian wars, invasion, destruction, occupation, maltreatment, atrocities, murder, displacement, ethnic cleansing, and genocide. Colonialism and direct autocracy were always mired with racism that goes in line with apartheid. By use of force and after the total occupation of their homeland in May of 1864, 10 percent of the Circassians ended up as a minority in their own homeland and 90 percent had to emigrate and be deported to the Ottoman Empire, which ended up as minority communities in Turkey, Syria, Jordan, Israel, Europe, the United States, and thirty other countries around the world.

The main law Russia used here was force. General Yermolov, the commander of the Kavkazki Corps, admitted it himself. He claimed, "Fear alone of the Russian arms can keep the mountaineers in submission", and destroyed at will not the mountaineers, but also their habitats, orchards, fields, grain, and hay. He declared cynically, "We need the Circassian lands, but we don't have any need of the Circassians themselves."[232]

Terror, intimidation, and bullying were the well-known means used, along with a propaganda war on the Circassians by the Russian Empire's armed forces and mercenaries.

Russia's Strategic Goal of Eliminating Circassia

The continuous ongoing Russian military campaigns and wars against Circassia and the interests of its people, waged by the Russian State, since its establishment as an entity were crowned and concluded by the last and most subversive one, the Russian-Circassian War,[233] which is described also as the Russian-Caucasian War by some researchers and scholars. Russian sources and decision makers still insist on calling it the Caucasian War; this is apart from mentioning other dates and proceedings of their own, probably to minimize the importance and significance of Russia's competitors and the war itself.[234]

A question about the "purpose of the war" is answered:

> Russia had vigorously entered the international arena, during Peter the Great. This was the period the Ottoman Empire and Iran were weakening and Russia was gaining strength. At that time, Circassia, due to its strategic importance, had become the contending place for these powers. This situation, on the other hand attracted the attention of the major European powers, England, and France that held key positions in the European and world politics and began, regardless of the confrontation they had between them, applying their joint efforts to limit their joint efforts to limit the growing international influence of Russia. The situation had placed Circassia in the circle of the important problems of world politics of the 18th century and her history to a critical stage.[235]

It is imperative to reach a conclusion that the colonial plan implemented by the Russian tsars followed by the consecutive Russian regimes, which apparently turned out to be a vision and a commandment, is at the heart of the Russian state.

Circassia

Peter the Great had left a will for his plan: To expand tirelessly the boundary of Russia north and south, along the Black Sea, and to move nearer to Constantinople and India. Whoever possesses them would own the world. with this aim in mind, to constantly instigate wars, sometimes against the Turks, sometimes against the Persians, and to build shipyards on the Black Sea, which should be taken over gradually as well as the Baltic Sea; both are necessary for the success of the plan—to hasten the fall of Persia, to penetrate to the Persian Gulf, to revive, if possible, the ancient trade of Levant through Syria, and to reach India. This plan of Peter the Great made Iran the gate to India, and the Caucasus the key for that gate.[236]

After the Treaty of Edirne (or the Treaty of Adrianople) on the fourteenth of September 1829, which concluded the Russo-Turkish War of 1828–1829, was signed between the Russian Empire and the Ottoman Empire, where the Britannica Encyclopedia affirms, "the treaty allowed Russia to annex the islands controlling the mouth of the Danube River and the Caucasus coastal strip of the Black Sea, including the fortresses of Anapa and Poti. The Ottomans recognized Russia's title to Georgia and other Caucasian principalities and opened the Straits of the Dardanelles and Bosporus to Russian shipping."[237] Nowadays, Russia's annexation of Crimea and the trend of developing a modern colonial campaign to contain eastern Ukraine and other areas proves the ambition for lust and control of others and to create the "Russian World,"[238] as did the Russian Empire during the eighteenth and nineteenth centuries, as well as the Soviet Union in the twentieth century.

Wanton imperial countries have consistently worked on repeating the nonsense that relates to exchanging waivers between them about areas they consider influence for them. They falsely pretend they are parts of them or within the territorial boundaries of their tyranny, which makes these colonial countries invade and occupy the homelands of others for the purpose of colonizing them and eventual annexation.

In this concept, what does ranting and dictating colonial desires to the Circassians mean? "General Malinowski reminded the Circassians of the Adrianople Treaty and how the sultan conceded the Circassians and the entire Black Sea coastline, from the estuary of Kuban to the pier of St. Nikolay, and to the boundaries of Georgia, Imeretia, and Guria to Russia. One of the Circassians answered, "You are a good General!" Then he pointed at a bird sitting on a tree and added, "For your kind words, I give you this bird for eternity. Take it!" Then he nodded, leaped on his horse, and trotted away. His friends followed him."²³⁹

As General Yermolov was one of those who oversaw the planning and obligated to implement the Russian Empire's plans and policies, he was gathering around him those who were anxious and mentally ready to take part in the task of running a crazy war with evil acts.

> The worthy pupil of "the bloody General" (Yermolov) was General Zass. His candid utterances are practically repeating the words of his tutor: "Russia wants to conquer the Caucasus at any price." He then asked: "How to conquer them, if not by terror?" He also declared, "I am killing the Circassians as my heart pleases."²⁴⁰

It took 101 years to achieve the colonial plans for a dream to come true.

> For the realization of her age-old dream—the drive toward the warm seas—Russia was bent to conquer Circassia and to build the necessary harbors on the Black Sea. Having accomplished that, Russia would seize Bosphorus and Dardanelles with the passage of the Mediterranean Sea, weaken the position of the Ottoman Empire, deal a powerful blow on the trade interests of Great Britain, and gain the upper hand over the European powers in the contest for world supremacy.²⁴¹

After experience, it's not surprising to get across the achieved disastrous results of the war and to read, "Pogodin's report to Czar Alexander II clearly defines the place of Circassia, and of the Caucasus in general, in the foreign policy plans of Russia: The East must belong to us by right. ...We must take over the Black Sea coast, Bosphorus, and Dardanelles. The Black Sea ought to become the place of our maneuvers."²⁴²

The Russian Empire didn't target only the Circassians, but it also aimed at the elimination of freedom and independence of all peoples of the Caucasus with no exception.

> The compliance we displayed at the last meeting proved to be quite sufficient in order "to disarm" the opponent that is ready to oppose us furiously. Regardless of such a state affairs, we have considerable work in store—building fortresses on the Black Sea coast, supplying all the strategic points with

all kinds of armaments. It is imperative to complete the war with the peoples of the Caucasus, which will still demand substantial expenses and a great perseverance. This war must serve for the acquisition of a fitting experience by our armies and become the screen of all our preparatory operations for the mastery on the Black Sea. Our pliancy on signing the Adrianople Treaty served the desired result. By it we staved off the possible future interference of England. We stirred popular unrest in Egypt; we managed to weaken the Porte in the same way. Not far is the day, when our guns "will speak."[243]

The Russian Guns began to "speak" first in Circassia, with unprecedented brutality.[244]

The War of 1763–1864

The Russian-Circassian War takes its starting date as 1763, when the Russians began establishing forts . . . to be used as springboards for conquest.

The tsarist Russian Empire had started its 101-year-long devastating war that is characterized by its disproportionality in troops and weapons used to expand its boundaries into the Black Sea coastline and ports of what used to be called Circassia. It accomplished its long-time dream of reaching and controlling the warm waters so they could control the Caucasus/Circassia's strategic location for control of the Circassian ports that permit freedom of movement and trade to get to the ports on the Mediterranean Sea and from there to be able to reach Southeast Asia, which was previously allowed by the Turkish Ottoman Empire with unrestricted freedom.[245]

The intention of the unjust war formed through attempts of exclusion and cancellation, which have been used to eliminate the existence, survival, and sustainability of the Circassian nation, didn't entirely succeed. Its presence as a reputable nation and its participation in human civilization couldn't be obscured. Information emerged by means of elaborating on the Circassians' historical and heritage significance. In his memoirs on the Caucasus War, General Grigory Filipson discusses St. Petersburg's primary misunderstanding about the Circassian people: "In Petersburg, they did not even suspect that we were dealing with one and a half million valiant, militaristic mountain dwellers who had never recognized any authority over them, and who possessed powerful natural fortresses every step in their forest-covered mountain thickets."[246]

Martin W. Lewis is quoted on Geo Currents as saying,

> Although little known today, the Circassians were once a famous people, celebrated for their military élan, physical mien, and resistance to Russian expansion. In the nineteenth century, 'Circassophilia' spread from Europe to North America, where numerous writers expressed deep admiration for the mountaineers of the eastern Black Sea. Prominent physical anthropologists deemed Circassian bodies the apogee of the human form.[247]

Prezi mentioned the war as follows:

> The Russian-Circassian War was between 1763 and 1864 and it consisted a series of battles and wars in Circassia. Before the genocide, Circassia fought against Russia for over a hundred years, from 1763 to 1864, with the war ending in massacre. Prior to the Russian conquest, the Circassian people numbered up to two million. What was committed by the Russians? The Russians drove the Circassians out of their homes into the Ottoman Empire. Then could have been killed by epidemics. How were they killed?—The Russians killed many inhabitants of these Ottoman lands and expelled the rest to Turkey, Forced out of their homelands.[248]

The Circassian nation used to inhabit the area extending within the northeastern coast of the Black Sea, slopes, and ridges of the northwestern part of the Caucasus. It had to suffer and to defend its homeland and its very survival against Russian tsarist forces that reached numbers, at critical times, in the hundreds of thousands of soldiers and mercenaries.

> Although the Russians were conducting their own raids into Circassia, they found raids against their settlements unacceptable, and so a fortress at Mozdak in modern North Ossetia was established in 1763. A civilian settlement quickly followed. Kabardian peasants began fleeing to the fort to gain their freedom.[249]

Russia made great efforts to fuel a civil war within Circassian society and tribes.

Thus, when the Russians began to attempt to bring the Circassians under their control, the Abadzekhs, Natukhais, and Shapseghs had no aristocracy that could be coerced or enticed into complicity. Furthermore, the peasants of the feudal tribes were equally dissatisfied with their aristocrats and several tribes, including the Kabardians, made their own moves to end the feudal system. Russian support for the aristocrats was interpreted by peasantry as an effort to perpetuate what had for them become an intolerable situation.[250]

The purpose was in the performance of a sinister task—to get rid of the Circassian nation in various available patterns, which had been justified, according to the imperial intentions. Thus, the Russians unwittingly stepped into the middle of a nascent civil war and aggravated tensions. Still, their main problem would be the democratic tribes who represented the overwhelming majority of the Circassian population. On more than one occasion, these tribes offered terms for peaceful coexistence, but their subjugation was essential for the Russian cause as they occupied the most strategic positions, that is, the Black Sea coastline, and some of them collaborated with Turkish and British efforts to undermine St. Petersburg's position in the region. Under these circumstances, war was inevitable. [251]

The Russians kept ongoing and surprise attacks on all parts of Circassia. On the eastern part,

in 1777 Greater Kabarda was invaded by both the Russians and the Crimeans, and the pshis reluctantly accepted Russian suzerainty. That same year Astrakan Governor Grigory Potemkin proposed the construction of a defensive line from Mozdak in Ossetia to the Sea of Azov. Ten fortresses were constructed to serve as a point of departure for the next phase of Russian advancement into the Northwest Caucasus. All ten quickly transformed into Cossack settlements, and by 1779 the line extended to the Kuban River.[252]

Apparently, successive misfortunes have struck Circassians all together at once.

Another tragedy struck the Northwest Caucasus at this time. A plague which continued until the 1830s devastated the population and reduced it to a fraction of its former size.

> Particularly hard hit was Kabarda: the generally accepted estimate is that 90 percent of the Kabardians died as a result of either the plague or Russian military operations in the first quarter the nineteenth century, reducing their number from approximately 200,000 in 1790 to fewer than 30,000 in 1830.[253]

The weakness of the Ottoman Empire as one of the main players on the Caucasus stage has affected the output of the unfair game played by Russia being one of the great powers at the time with the small indigenous peoples and nations.

> At the conclusion of the Russo-Turkish War in 1792 it was clear that Ottoman power in the eastern Black Sea was waning, and Russian Emperor Paul took advantage of the situation, fully incorporating Georgia into the Russian Empire. At the same time the Russians reaffirmed the Porte's Suzerainty of Circassia in the 1792 Treaty of Jassy in an interesting ploy. By acknowledging Ottoman rule over lands they never controlled, St. Petersburg was positioning itself to 'acquire' Circassia from the Porte at some future point.[254]

The colonial mechanism relied on changing the landscape by destroying the Circassian settlements, to build fortresses that allow resettling Russians and Cossacks, thus changing the demographic map.

> Russia seized Taman and the Kuban River delta in 1779, and in 1791 constructed a fortress at the junction of the Laba and Kuban Rivers near Temirgoi territory. On the urging of Field Marshal Gudovich, the Russians constructed six new stanitsas along the Kuban in 1794 and eight smaller fortifications in 1798. The Russian and Cossack populations along the growing line, which now extended from Kizlyar in Dagestan to the Sea of Azov, likewise increased; along the Azov-Mozdak Line the Cossack population in 1793 was nearly 25,000. This line further inhibited Circassian pasturing and provided more places of refuge for indentured laborers fleeing from land owners. Almost immediately after the Russians began creating the line, some Kabardians approached them with their objections, while others opted for military operations against the new fortresses.[255]

Circassians had to face disastrous consequences. The occupying authorities, through coordination with the governments of the Russian Empire and other foreign countries at the time, had brought Cossacks, Russians, and other settlers of different origins to resettle in the area to replace the original oppressed people of Circassia who had either perished or been deported. All that was executed by the Russian Empire could have been due to a lack of safety, self-confidence, and inability to live peacefully with others, which, in turn, made them to be possessive, aggressive, and greedy.

The divide and rule policy[256] had not been excluded from Russian conducts. Included in their military forces were what they described as a "Kabardian regiment"; it tried to show that part of the Circassians were fighting against their countrymen.

> Russian Field Marshal Ivan Gudovich arrived at the North Caucasus Line on 26 January 1791. His army, which included at least one Kabardian regiment, set out on 9 April and faced Natukhai resistance but eventually convinced the local peoples to remain neutral. At Anapa, Gudovich met a combined Ottoman-Circassian force, and after 12 days siege stormed and captured the fort on 21 June, and with it Sheikh Mansour.[257]

For the sake of defending their ancestral homeland, the Circassians had fought courageously, determinedly, and heroically in an unrivaled example; as Mark Twain said, "Courage is resistance to fear, mastery of fear, not absence of fear."[258] But after decades, it came to the conclusion of abundance dominating courage. As a consequence, some of the Circassian tribes had been either partially, completely, or their absolute majorities wiped out like the Ubykh, who had their own distinct dialect/language.

The effect of the tightly predisposing plans intervened in the formation of Circassian society.

> In Kabarda efforts to resist the Russians were impeded by the collaboration of aristocrats with the Tsarist forces in their attempts to defeat the independent tribes. The aristocracy played a two-faced game: on the one hand, they used the Russians to help subjugate the peasantry, and on the other they exploited peasant animosity toward the Russians to minimize Tsarist power.[259]

The results of friction within the society have led, in some cases, for the situation to develop into a situation of struggle between the different classes of the society.

> Occasionally they would take matters into their own hands to secure their peasant's dependence. In 1792 Abaza aristocrats launched a failed assault on peasants who had fled eastward to the Kuma river, followed by similar attacks by Kabardian aristocrats in 1796 and 1798 that were thwarted by Russian forces.[260]

It resulted in the inability of addressing the external invasion due to internal conflicts.

> These efforts by the aristocrats to perpetuate the feudal system led to a dramatic change in the social order of the Abadzekhs, Natukhais, and Shapseghs. Dissatisfaction with the feudal system was widespread among the Circassians, but because their proximity to the Black Sea coast the tfokotl class of these three tribes benefited from trade and developed a level of economic prosperity that allowed to take action against the aristocracy.[261]

Some individuals went out of consensus, where they had made an alliance with the State, which announced its aggressive intentions of grabbing their homeland. An example was noticed "in 1795 Khajimuko led a delegation to St. Petersburg to appeal to Catherine II for assistance. Catherine agreed to send a Cossack regiment. On 29 June 1796, the aristocrats' forces met a combined Abadzekh-Natukhai-Shapsegh army of approximately 8,000 south of Krasnodar on Negid Field in what became known as the Battle of Baziuk (after the Baziuk River which runs through the field)."[262]

Conditions were proper for Russia to implement its expansionist plans and dreams. They had a military force with qualitative superiority in lethal weapons, the artillery in particular being a crucial factor. Conspirators and portability societal disintegration, sometimes, contributed to the imbalance with the Russian Empire.

> Primarily thanks to Cossack artillery, the aristocrats defeated the tfokotl forces, who lost as many as 2000. It turned out to be a pyrrhic victory, however. Khajimuko was killed in the battle, depriving the aristocrats of their most

energetic supporter. The subsequent civil war dragged on for several years, depleting the strength and well of both sides. Negotiations began; at the Pechetniko Zafes of 1803 the aristocrats relinquished their privileges and accepted a new democratic order.[263]

Where the aggressors sowed the seeds of discord between Circassians and other groups living in the North Caucasus, they didn't work as one team to defend their very survival, which proved to be a failure for all. Also, it regrettably prevented them in the long run from deciding their fate and future.

Those who were not killed by the Russians or the plague fled to Circassia, and by the end of the campaign Lesser Kabarda was said to have been completely depopulated. Many Besleneis, Mysylbais, and Kuma Abazas fled to the mountains as well and joined the anti-Russian tribes. A civil war between the pro- and anti-Russian indigenous peoples ensued, and a combination of this and Russian-forced resettlement drove nearly all the remaining Abazas and Nogais into the anti-Russian camp by 1845.[264]

The long war was intervened and punctuated by intensity at intervals and encountered by periods of ups and downs.

The Russian offensive in Kabarda continued until 1826, when war broke out with Persia and then with Turkey in 1828. In the fall of that year the Russians managed to reach the Karachais, who nominally accepted Russian Suzerainty. By the end of the war with Turkey in 1830, the Russians had seized all the Turkish fortresses and gained effective control of the entire Black Sea coast from the Taman Peninsula to Georgia. Furthermore, according to treaty of Adrianople, this stretch of the coast was nominally transferred from Ottoman to Russian control and the Ottomans relinquished their supposed suzerainty over the Circassians. In November 1830, the Natukhais and Shapseghs held a Khase which concluded with an agreement to oppose the Russians militarily and send a delegation to Istanbul to object to the Treaty.[265]

Circassians who discovered the reality of the plans prepared for their homeland and had taken the right decisions at the right time, to side with their nation to defend itself and to carry their concerns everywhere.

> Sefer-Bei Zanoko, who had previously served in and then deserted the Russian army, was selected to head the committee, which was received unofficially and without St. Petersburg's knowledge. Sefer-Bei and his party were told that the Porte abandoned them to St. Petersburg as punishment for their refusal to acknowledge the Porte's complete suzerainty and their failure to convert to Islam. The delegation returned to the Caucasus with small gifts and a small cache of weapons; Sefer-Bei remained in Istanbul.[266]

The Russians always worked in all directions and levels to reach their goals.

> At this same time, the Russians attacked the Natukhais and Shapseghs in order to begin a new line along the Black Sea coast. Four fortifications were built in 1830, and the following year a fortress was constructed at Gelendzhik. Between 1833 and 1835 new expeditions were conducted against the Natukhais that allowed the Russians to construct the first fortress at Novorossiysk in 1838 and a second one the following year. The same year two new fortresses were built in Lesser Kabarda to defend the Georgian Military Highway. Altogether, between 1826 and 1841 14 fortifications were built in Shapsegh territory, six in Abadzekh territory, and two in Kabarda. The Circassians were gradually being hemmed in.[267]

Events proved beyond a reasonable doubt that the superpowers at the time were involved in plotting several forms of genocide against the Circassian nation, including forced deportation from the homeland.

> Before the Treaty of Adrianople, the Porte was able to influence events in Circassia. In July 1826 Haji-Hassan Chechenoglu was appointed Pasha of Anapa. An elderly but vigorous man, Haji-Hassan set out to complete the conversion of the population to Islam and obtain their allegiance to the Porte. Initially targeting the feudal tribes, he had considerable success among the aristocrats, but his efforts among the democratic tribes were met with resistance. In the summer

of 1826 the leaders of the Natukhais and Shapseghs held a Khase where they formulated their reply to Haji-Hassan: "we wish to be Muslims, but of our own free will."[268]

There were no honest intentions by some of the Ottoman high-ranking officials toward the Circassians, regardless of the rhetoric that they tended to use in their speeches.

Haji-Hassan was infuriated and requested 40,000 troops from Turkey to punish the tribes. Upon receiving a refusal, he changed his tactics, first outing for bribery. Having attained modest success through this method, he threw his support behind the tfokotls in their struggle against the aristocrats. By the outbreak of the Russo-Turkish War of 1828-9 he had been recalled to Istanbul, but his efforts had borne fruit. Sharia courts were well established and Islam had taken root throughout Northwest Caucasus society. All the tribes had appointed imams and established Islamic courts. This in turn facilitated further centralization of tribal government; the Circassians were even able to establish a system for storage of provisions for the army.[269]

Sadly, several methods were used to tame an entire nation to satisfy the wishes and desires of some rulers: "Haji-Hassan's success in strengthening Islam among the Circassians might be explained by the clear need for some force to serve as a means of unity. Islamization did in fact lead to greater centralization, increased resolve to resist efforts by any power to subjugate the region, and highlighted animosity towards the Russians."[270]

Those who remained in their homeland and/or were transferred to beyond the Kuban River, stayed under Russian rule and later became Soviet citizens. Most Circassians were resettled in the Ottoman Empire while their descendants are living in Turkey, Jordan, Syria, and other countries of the world today. In addition to annexing Circassia and its deletion from the map as an entity, the Russian authorities worked to change the demographic map and engineered a new ethnic scheme. It worked to change the status and nature of the population that led to reflect different ethnic realities of the region by deporting the Circassian inhabitants away from their original areas.

The tsars and emperors involved in the Russian-Circassian War were as follows: Catherine II (1762–1796), Pavel I (1796–1801), Alexander I (1801–1825), Nicholas I (1825–1855), and Alexander II (1855–1881).[271]

The main tsars, Russian generals, and Circassian leaders are mentioned: "The victor according to details such as casualties, homeland destruction, treaty terms, and land agreements."[272]

Important victor leaders were Catherine II, Tsar Nicholas I, Tsar Alexander I, Tsar Alexander II, Aleksey Yermolov, Mikhail Vorontsov, Aleksandr Baryatinskiy, and Nikolai Evdokimov.

Important opposition leaders were Kazbech Tuguzhoko and the Naibs. The death toll is estimated at 1–1.5 million."[273]

The Cossacks' Role

The Cossack, or Kazak, element is considered an important factor that the Russian invading forces had taken advantage of during the Russian-Circassian War. They committed massive crimes, destruction, arson, and looting. They took advantage of the situation while fighting the Circassians, in addition to the preapproval from the military command for seizing public and private property, as well as the theft of private collections, cattle, horses, grain, and agricultural crops.

In short, they were known for their brutality and blind adherence to implement the colonial policies in Circassia that was entitled to them after occupying Circassia by employing all the negative consequences of eliminating, displacing, and deporting a majority of the population.

Dealing with deceitful state policies has proven that it's easy to retract from any commitment or promise. Promises they make eventually contradict actions they take, and as in all cases, reality sets in. It was never possible to trust the pledges with empty content.

> St Petersburg also saw trade as an effective means of gaining the Circassians' goodwill. Already in the late eighteenth century, vibrant trading relations existed between Circassians and Cossack stanitsas north of the Kuban. However, by 1800 tensions had increased and trade had all but ended. Beginning in 1810 St. Petersburg made efforts to re-establish trade relations between Russia and Circassia. In 1811 six "civilians" and seven "military" trade centers were established in and around Circassia and a formal trade agreement was reached with the Natukhais.[274]

The Cossacks had performed great services to the Russian invading forces by employing their actions in a manner that was unusual and brutal. The "western access along the Black Sea coast was critical for control of the South Caucasus. Therefore, the establishment of Cossack settlements north of the Kuban River, adjacent to Circassia, was accelerated as a preliminary step toward conquest of the Northwest Caucasus."[275]

The gradual increase of the Cossack population made it conceivable to foresee the potential to prepare the proper conditions for future operations against the Circassians to capture their territories.

> Russia seized Taman and the Kuban River delta in 1779, and in 1791 constructed a fortress at the junction of the Laba and Kuban Rivers near the Temirgoi territory. On the urging of Field Marshal Gudovich, the Russians constructed six new stanitsas along the Kuban in 1794 and eight smaller fortifications in 1798.[276]

The Russian-Cossack community in Circassia grew to strengthen and increase its capabilities.

> The Russian and Cossack populations along the growing line, which now extended from Kizlyar in Dagestan to the Sea of Azov, likewise increased; along the Azov-Mozdak Line the Cossack population in 1793 was nearly 25,000. This line further inhibited Circassian pasturing and provided more places of refuge for indentured laborers fleeing from land owners. Almost immediately after the Russians began creating the line, some Kabardians approached them with their objections, while others opted for military operations against the new fortresses.[277]

The extraneous groups that entered Circassia with the invading forces had provided a valuable but clumsy service.

> In spring 1800, Emperor Paul gave permission for the Cossacks to raid Circassia with total impunity. Cossack leader Bursak carried out a series of raids on the Abadzekhs, Bzhedukhs, Natukhais, and Shapseghs between 1800 and 1811 in which the Cossacks burned auls, destroyed crops, and stole cattle and people alike. In 1802, a joint Russian-Nogai-Abaza force invaded the Urup valley in an unsuccessful attack on the Mysylbais. The Caucasus historian Fyodor Shcherbina considers this the actual beginning of the Russo-Circassian

War, preceding the date usually given for the beginning of the Russo-Circassian War, preceding the date usually given for the beginning of the war by decade.[278]

The definition of Cossack is derived "(from Turkic kazak, 'adventurer' or 'free man'), member of a people dwelling in the northern hinterlands of the Black and Caspian seas. They had a tradition of independence and finally received privileges from the Russian government in return for military services."[279] Another source states, "There is hardly a single simple definition for them. They are not a nationality or a religion, they don't represent a political party or movement and there is still no complete agreement among historians and anthropologists on who the Cossacks are."[280] A third source indicates,

> The name Cossack probably originates from Turkic, "Kazakh" meaning either "horseman" or "free man" (i.e. not a serf or noble) depending on context. Both definitions hold true, as Cossack warriors were exclusively cavalry, and actively recruited freed or runaway serfs into their ranks. Going by the Turkic/Mongolian origin of their name, the Cossacks may have originated in Central Asia, and migrated into the Slavic lands as nomads, perhaps on the heels of the Mongol invasions. Historically, the Cossacks were predominantly Russian Orthodox Christian, but there were a few, especially around Crimea, who were Muslim, and some were even Buddhists from Mongolia.[281]

In addition to what is mentioned above, they were brought by the invading Russian forces to carry out the atrocious policies that Russian tsars had planned to execute. They participated in deporting them away from Circassia to resettle with their families in the Circassian land to impose change in the demographic structure. Their presence and actions were decisive factors in the war and the seizure of Circassia.

To combat the "Adyghe galleys," the invading forces tried to use what was in their arsenal.

Russian command established cruises by small rowing boats. To serve on them, Cossacks of Azov Cossack troops were recruited. They consisted of ten crews, each of what included twenty persons. Azov rowing boats were armed with small cannons, sailed by oars and had sails. Cossack boats were allocated in the tsar's fortresses on the Black Sea coast of the Caucasus. Blockhouses were used by Cossacks as barracks. The Russian commander general N. N. Rayevskiy wrote, "Azov rowing-boats would be very useful between the near distanced fortresses against Circassian galleys and contraband ships."[282]

The Russian Intentions of Waging the War

Russia vigorously entered the international arena during the reign of Peter the Great. This was the period the Ottoman Empire and Iran were weakening and Russia was gaining strength. At that time, Circassia, due to its strategic importance, had become the contending place for these powers. This situation, on the other hand, had attracted the attention of major European powers, England and France, which held key positions in European and world politics and began, regardless of the confrontation they had between them, applying their joint efforts to limit the growing international influence of Russia. This situation placed Circassia in the circle of the important problems of world politics of the eighteenth century and her history to a critical stage.[283]

Plans were set to dominate whatever possible territories, nations, and strategic elements that would assist in creating an imperial state.

> With this aim in mind, to constantly instigate wars sometimes against the Turks, sometimes against Persians, and to build shipyards on the Black Sea, which should be taken over as well as Baltic Sea; both are necessary for the success of the plan—to hasten the fall of Persia, to penetrate to the Persian Gulf, to revive, if possible, the ancient trade of Levant through Syria, and to reach India. This plan of Peter the Great made Iran the gate to India, and the Caucasus, the key for that gate.[284]

The situation had initially appeared to deceive the Russian leadership into believing that the enormous numerical and qualitative superiority over the Circassians will guarantee them early and certain success. It has proven that they crashed into a reality and faced solid resistance and made the war go on for over a century.

> They had no idea of the difficulty that would be involved in subduing the Circassians, and as the war progressed they restored to increasingly violent and inhumane tactics, culminating the mass expulsion of the Abazas, Circassians, and Ubykhs to Turkey and the complete destruction of their civilizations.[285]

> For the realization of her age-old dream—the drive toward the warm seas—Russia was bent to conquer Circassia and to build the necessary harbors on the Black Sea. Having accomplished that, Russia would seize Bosphorus and Dardanelles with the passage to the Mediterranean Sea, weaken the position of the Ottoman Empire, deal a powerful blow on the trade interests of Great Britain, and gain the upper hand over the European powers in the contest for world supremacy.[286]

The colonizers' assumed ignorance of others as well as their "superiority" over others that they enjoyed.

> Pogodin's report to Czar Alexander II clearly defines the place of Circassia, and of the Caucasus in general, in the foreign policy plans of Russia: "The East must belong to us by right. We should not relax our activities in that direction for one moment". Constantinople has no knowledge of our real intentions. We must take over the Black Sea coast, Bosporus, and Dardanelles. The Black Sea ought to become the place of our maneuvers. Our pliancy on signing the Adrianople Treaty served the desired result. By it we staved off the possible future interference of England.[287]

Ironically, we find that there were those who thought that they had the right to decide the identity of others.

> The Russians viewed Circassian resistance as rebellion against a recognized sovereign, when in fact the Circassians considered themselves an independent entity and their conflict with Russia a war of national survival. For their part, the Russians not only viewed the Circassians as rebellious subjects but also believed in their own role as "civilizers" of primitive peoples who would abandon their former ways once they saw the superiority of Russian culture.[288]

The Russian objectives consisted of destroying and looting all the pillars of the Circassian homeland, taking advantage of their rich resources, vast territories, plains, and various wealth elements.

The actions of the tsarist command in the northwestern Caucasus were facilitated by the disunity of the Circassian and Abkhazian tribes. The tsarist command took fertile lands from the mountaineers and gave them to Cossack and Russian colonists and carried out a mass expulsion of the mountain peoples. In November 1859, the main forces of the Circassians (up to 2, 000 men) led by Muhammad Emin capitulated and the land of the Circassians was cut by the Belaia River line with the fortress of Maikop. Between 1859 and 1861 trails were made in the forests, roads were built, and the lands seized from the mountaineers were colonized. The resistance to the colonialists intensified in mid-1862.[289]

The Russian Expansion

All through the limited history of its establishment, in comparison with other deep-rooted European nations, terrible and evil war crimes and hostilities were orchestrated and committed with the state's predetermined knowledge and intent against tens of nations in which Circassia and its people were destined to be among those victims.

> The history of Russia has been a series of expansions to the west, the south, and the east, towards the open sea. Each territory occupied was, sooner or later, absorbed into the Empire of which it became in every way an integral part. The fact that Russia was not separated from her colonial possessions by the sea made the process of absorption easier, and the line of demarcation between the mother-country and her colonies is therefore less definite than in the case of Britain or France.[290]

The tsarist Russians had followed a policy of ethnic cleansing and mass murder to capture the land from the indigenous population and to remove them from the Black Sea coastline and the adjacent Caucasus mountain slopes to beyond the River Kuban while replacing them with outsiders.

> The Russians' heavy losses in the Napoleonic War of 1812 impeded their ability to devote economic resources to the Caucasus and led to the appointment of a military strongman in the form of General Alexi Petrovich Yermolov in 1816.

Yermolov chose a brutal military policy. This attitude was reflected in subsequent military regimes the Caucasus, who frowned upon St. Petersburg's occasional efforts at peaceful relations and often undermined them.[291]

The true face and ultimate goal of the unjust war against the Circassians, with all their affiliations, were not hidden or secret to them.

> Kabarda was in the center of the North Caucasus and close to the Georgian Military Highway and a rebellion there, coupled with actions by the Ingush to the east of the Highway, could effectively close the only route to the South Caucasus other than the Daghestani coast. An even greater fear was that the Ingush and Kabardians could unite and create a single anti-Russian front. St. Petersburg took this threat seriously and carried out a campaign aimed at pacifying Kabarda. The original Russian strategy was to destroy as much livestock as possible, but the Kabardians were able to conceal their herds in the mountains, and so in the spring of 1822, Yermolov began a campaign directed against the entire population of Kabarda.[292]

The Imperial Russian military forces and their allies often chose "trigger-happy" policies when engaging militarily with the Circassians. They always ignored causing high losses of life among the Circassian people.

> Once in command, Yermolov initiated a major offensive against the peoples of Dagestan, the Chechens, and the Kabardians. In 1822 seven new fortifications were constructed along the Kabardian portion of the line. Kabardian aristocracy and peasantry joined in a rebellion the same year, but Yermolov managed to play one off against the other and end the uprising. In 1825 and 1826 six more fortifications were built, effectively ending the slave trade conduct through Anapa. In May 1825, a group of Kabardian pchis who were allied with the Porte organized an uprising to coincide with a much larger one in chechnia, and although they were unable to turn the uprising into a mass movement, it caused the Russians a great amount of consternation.[293]

Circassia

After the occupation of Circassia in the nineteenth century, it was divided and subdivided many times. This was in addition to changing the demography, population composition, and names of locations as much as possible without taking the least consideration into account the millions of oppressed Circassians who need to restore their confiscated rights and return to their beloved homeland to live freely in peace like any other nation of the world.

Military Battles

During the war, there were important milestones that were characterized by different periods: "The Russo-Turkish War of 1768-74 marked the beginning of Russia's efforts to fully control the Northwest Caucasus."[294]

"Main military battles" are mentioned according to the following chronology:

"In 1763-1777, near the fort of Mezdagh, the military actions began and then engulfed all the territory along Terek" (River).

Military operations continued during the rule of Catherine II, "but probably increased." She "sent an army of 120,000 soldiers to (the) Caucasus." The article continued that "during the battles Circassians lost 30,000 men" and in 1774 the "Osman Empire sent an army" to help the "Circassians, but it was too late. Russians managed to take over Cuban (Kuban) and Taman peninsula" and Turkey couldn't "win back the native Circassian lands."

The Circassians didn't give up, but they "made several impacts" against the Russians. It mentioned that "part of them tried to get back the seized territories, and other part—attacked Kizlar and Mezdagh," where a "third part undertook military actions on Taman peninsula having out flanked" the Russians. Casualties on the Russian side reported to be "in the course of military actions" that they lost "about 10,000 men."

Military plans continued targeting the Circassian territories.

> In 1776, the Russian army built several forts on Terek (River) to encircle Circassia from the north. Meanwhile Circassians managed to gather 14,000 army and won back several forts having captured a lot of soldiers.

> In 1793, General Suvorov, who could control Noghay tribes, seized the lands of Shapsoughs and Bzedoughs who had lived on Cuban river.

It pointed out that in 1793, the "Noghay tribes" were controlled by General Suvorov and the lands of Shapsoughs and Bzedoughs on the Cuban (Kuban) river" were seized.

The Russian behavior was not accepted by the Circassians: "The Circassian national council addressed to Russia a note of protest against such movements."[295]

The different elements of Circassian society always learned realities the hard way, especially those who had initially trusted the invaders' promises against their people.

> In 1804, a general rebellion occurred among the peasantry nearly all the Northwest Caucasus peoples, who demanded the removal of the Russian military post at Kislovodsk. A major battle took place on 9 May near the Baksan River in Greater Kabarda. The woefully outgunned rebels retreated to the Chegem region of Balkaria and sent out pleas for reinforcements to the Ossetians and Karachais. Negotiations with the Russians failed and on 14 May the decisive battle was fought between the Shalushka and Chegem Rivers. Including both Russian and Caucasian forces, approximately 13,000 combatants took part in the battle.[296]

There is no way that a battle could be won if there aren't any equal types of weapons used by both sides. This affects the impact of one side's strength when they use only old and personal weapons: "Owing to their artillery, the Russians easily defeated the peasant forces, after which the Russians destroyed 12 auls in the region. On 19 May, the peasants surrendered. Discontent continued to simmer, and on 20 September, a Kabardian force of 7,000 engaged the Russians, who again emerged victorious."[297]

Various alliances conducted by the Russians with the various factions made it possible to impose their plans to make life difficult for everyone.

> Russian forces remained in Kabarda until spring 1805, attempting to wipe out resistance, but it became clear that anger, not only with the Russian presence, but also with the feudal system was so great that violence could erupt at any time. Many Kabardians fled to the left bank of the Kuban between the Urup and Zelenchuck Rivers among the Abazas, while Kabardian Pshi Roslambek Misost led a force north to the Kuma and compelled the Abazas there, still loyal to St. Petersburg, to return to Kabarda.[298]

Another Source Describing the War

The war timeline reported by "Prezi" mentions critical war events and describes it in the form of a sequential genocide, in accordance with important proceedings:

> 1859—the Russians began a "scorched-earth" campaign, systematically razing and pillaging entire villages and massacring their inhabitants.

> 1860—The Circassian resettlement plan was eventually agreed upon at a meeting of the Russian Caucasus commanders.

> 1864—the Russians proclaimed an end to what became known as the Caucasian War. Time Line 1763—The Circassian war started.

> 1772—the serious collision between the troops of Peter the Great and Circassian Prince Aslan Kaytouko was taken place.

> 1763–1777 near the fort of Mezdagh the military actions began and then engulfed all the territory along Terek.

> 1817—Russian Tsars started a war in Caucasus in an attempt to conquer the land, but wanted it to be quicker and more efficient. Native Circassians held a good fight.

> 1857—Milyutin and Yevdokimov, leaders in Russia, advocated the expelling of the people in Northern Caucasus.[299]

The Battle of Krasnaya Polyana, May 1864

The final main battle between the Russian Empire and the Circassians took place near Sochi in May 1864. In "The Russo-Circassian Battle of Krasnaya Polyana (Kbaada), May 1864," a summary of the final chapter of the Russian-Circassian War is written and engraved, along with a video that elaborates on the events of the last moments of a brutal defensive war, in which the Circassians lost the last battle of survival as a coherent nation, which made them do what they could to document what happened while the blood flowed on the soil of their homeland.

In The Battle of Krasnaya Polyana (Kbaada), May 1864: The Circassians' Last Stand against the Russian Juggernaut,

> all Circassian fighters (including Abkhazians, Ubykh, and Dzhigets) who refused Russian hegemony amassed at Kbaada in the southwest of Circassia in the spring of 1864. The Russian Army and the Cossacks attacked the Circassians from four different sides in May 1864. The battle lasted for a few days, and both sides suffered heavy casualties. In the end, sheer numbers overcame bravery, and the Circassians were defeated. Many Circassians threw themselves down sheer mountains rather than surrender to the Russians. Russia proclaimed victory in the Circassian-Russian War on 21 May 1864, and a victory parade took place at Krasnaya Polyana on the same day. Most of the Circassians who survived the war were systematically deported in mass to the Ottoman Empire. Thus, came to a tragic end the millennia-old independence of the Circassian nation. The Circassian tragedy of the 19th century constituted the first instance of genocide /ethnic cleansing in the modern era. It remains largely unknown at the global level. "Capturing Kbaade and the End of the Caucasian War in 1864" In the documentary series "Unknown Wars of Russia."[300]

According to Find The Data, the war's end date was June 2, 1864. "The Caucasian War ended with the signing of loyalty oaths by Circassian leaders on 2 June [O.S. 21 May] 1864." [301] The results were Russian victory, annexation of Circassia, mass expulsion, and Circassia was annexed into Russia."

The following is reported and published by Ali, Robert, and Iqbal, which presented the war outcome that led to slaughter, occupation, deportation, and thus enumerating "more than 400,000 Circassians were killed, 497,000 were forced to flee abroad to Turkey, and only 80,000 were left alive in their native area, Circassians died from diseases when they were forced into Turkey" and finally stating, "Sea storms killed some Circassians while on boats looking through the eyes of the Circassians was horrifying, lots of deaths were taking place in front of their family and friends. Circassians suffered from sickness and poverty. They were in oversized groups forced into small boats."[302]

The characterization went on to elaborate on the significance of the results that pertains to deportation: "By 1859, Russians implemented a policy of deporting the Circassian people, by ship, to a choice of Turkey or Anatolia (which is now present-day part of Turkey)."[303]

Displaced Circassians suffered from the horrors of displacement away from their homeland and were subjected to the impact of harsh weather conditions, such as extremely high and low temperatures, rain, snow, storms, exposure to cold, and sunstrokes.

Encirclement and Siege

The invading Russian forces used all available means to achieve their premeditated goals, which were to take complete control of Circassia, slaughter, and disperse its nation. The Russian Empire deemed its success in the fate and destiny of deleting Circassia from the map and to corner Circassians at a difficult time of challenge and controversy, for the sake of eliminating most of the nation.

Before occupation was possible, a tight blockade was imposed beginning on the territories in the mainland, followed by another one at sea, the Circassian coast on the Black Sea. That was followed by building forts and garrisons to be used for troop buildup in locations that can be defended and to be used for raiding villages, towns, and seaports in addition to destroying and stealing crops and livestock. These attacks were unacceptable and unjustified based on the right of people to freedom and independence.

The naval blockade initially decreased the rate of maritime traffic and then entirely prevented ships from getting close to the coast. The blockade wanted to stop contact with the outside world to prevent traveling of delegations, trade, exchange of goods, and importing materials necessary for daily life in order to defend the homeland. Circassian Navy During Russian-Caucasian War, written by A. Y. Chirg, states,

> During Russian-Caucasian War Tsar's Russia did use not just ground forces but also Navy. Tsarism considered blockade of Adyghe (Circassian) sea coast as one of the main measures to conquest the Circassia, thus Russians wanted to stop any kind of connection Adyghe people with the rest world. The active role to fulfil it had assigned to Russian Navy. From the 1830 year along the eastern coast of Black Sea had patrolled especial Russian squadron named "Abkhazian expedition". Battle cruisers did not allow to sail for commercial European and Turkish vessels towards Circassian coast. And on the other hand Tsar's navy fought along the Black Sea coast of Northern Caucasus by landing numerous ground troops. They were occupying the most important places in strategic military

meaning. In 1837–1839 years with the Navy's assistance had been founded such military forts as: Saint Doukh on the Adler cape, Velyaminovskoye on the mouth of Tuapse River, Tenginskoye on the Shapsugh River, Novorossiysk in the Sudjoukh bight, Navaginskoye on the Sochi River, Golovinskoye on the Shakhe River, Lazarevskoye on the mouth of Psishuapa River.[304]

The euphoria of victory made various Russian leaders release hostile and racist statements against the indigenous people: "In the congratulating message Czar II Alexander sent to Earl Yevdokimov: 'You cleaned up and destroyed the rebellious autochthon nations in West Caucasia in the last 3 years. We can recover the cost of this long bloody war from this fertile land in a very short time.'"[305]

One more testimony states,

> A Russian detachment having captured the village of Toobah on the Soobashi river, inhabited by about a hundred Abadzekh (a tribe of Circassians), and after these had surrendered themselves prisoners, they were all massacred by the Russian Troops. Among the victims were two women in an advanced state of pregnancy and five children. The detachment is question belongs to Count Evdokimoff's (Yevdokimov) Army, and is said to have advanced from the Pshish valley. As the Russian troops gain ground on the coast, the natives are not allowed to remain there on any terms, but are compelled either to transfer themselves to the plains of the Kouban or emigrate to Turkey" (F.O. 9-424, no 2, Dickson to Russell, Soukoum Kale, 17 March 1864).[306]

The sequence of occupation is as follows: preparation for the invasion, troop buildup, preparing targets, and a timetable of the battles and executing the offensive. Among the desired results of the invasion is to create a condition of scorched-earth status and mass destruction to destabilize and disable the social, economic, and cultural life of the total population, which helped to terrorize the people and force them to move to areas where the invaders had selected: "Justice Delayed Is Justice Denied."[307]

The article added, "Fighting with aggression of tsarism coastal Adyghes used their Navy, which consisted from small ships, named in European sources of 19 century as 'galley'. Circassians mastered Black Sea navigation from ancient times and therefore they were very experienced navigators and sailors. There is a lot of information about Circassian navigation in ancient (Strabos, Tacitus, etc.) and medieval (Al-Masoudi, D. Interiano, etc.) sources."[308]

They did not neglect the style, but they exploited all potentials to inform the world of what they were facing of injustice and aggression committed against the civilians.

Letter from Circassians to Daoud Bey (DAVID URQUHART)

> The Free Press, Journal of the Foreign Affairs Committees December 2, 1863
>
> The Russians, jeering and deriding us, have begun to be more violent and oppressive, and, hearing of the arrival of the above things, they pushed forward some troops, and surrounded two hundred houses belonging to our people, and even also to our neighbors, by night, and killed the men and took the women and children prisoners; and the number of persons they killed amounted to one thousand and eighty, and those whom they took prisoners to one thousand three hundred.[309]

Russian Domination Policies

Circassia, among others in the North Caucasus and elsewhere, was one of those victims that was not entirely destroyed and eliminated. Resolving its long-lasting plight needs to be taken in consideration. There is a group of Circassians proudly sincere to their Circassian identity and belong to what their conscience and national duty dictate them to do who are performing their utmost to restore the Circassians' rights in their Motherland.

> Throughout history, the North Caucasus remained on the fringes of the Islamic world. The neighboring Ottoman and Persian empires had never succeeded in conquering and annexing the region and remained content with collecting payments in tribute, taxes, and slaves. Thus it was left to the Russians, who since the late eighteenth century had brought in the heavy colonial machinery—the military, bureaucracy, missionaries, settlers, courts, and schools—to begin altering the traditional geographical and social landscape.[310]

Measures should be taken to follow the traces and footsteps of Russian policy makers and promoters who had been the main plotters and dominators in a plan to eliminate any Circassian presence by exterminating half of the population while deporting and displacing the rest with no second thought, mercy, human concern, or fairness towards a nation that believes in freedom and the right to live on its own soil with no foreign intervention.

Apparently, the way they make deals gives them the ability to walk away from any commitment.

> In 1813 Rafael Scassi, a merchant from Genoese descent, was placed in charge of developing commercial ties, and he concluded treaties that increased trade, including the sale of wood for use in shipbuilding at Sevastopol. Scassi also supervised the creation of a major trading center on the Black Sea. In summer 1819 tariffs were removed from the sale of salt, a highly important import in Circassia, and two new trading centers were opened. In 1821 Alexander authorized the 'regulations for commercial relations with Circassians and Abazas', which, in addition to enumerating precise legal procedures for Russian-Circassian trade, established Kerch and Bugaz as the official trade centers. Unfortunately, the regulations were ill-suited to the actual conditions in Circassia and actually impeded trade.[311]

The Russians never respected their obligations toward the Circassians, where Russia preferred its preferences over any other consideration.

> Despite the lucrative potential of expanded trade relations with Russia there were elements on both sides that tried to sabotage them. Many pshis preferred relations with the Ottomans and continued raiding Cossack settlements. On the Russian side, General Alexi Yermolov, commander of the Caucasus from 1816 to 1827, strongly opposed economic relations with Circassia and, having failed to stop trade directly he deliberately attempted to sabotage relations between the Circassians and Russians, destroying auls and massacring peaceful villagers. However, despite these efforts on both sides to poison the situation, trade continued. After the treaty of Adrianople in 1829 trade even increased between the two parties despite the dismissal of Scassi and the termination of the official administration of Russo-Circassian commerce.[312]

The Russian state started from the "rise the Muscovites"[313] more than 450 years ago and was later affirmed, calling itself Russia. It went through eras of "Russia Peter the Great" and the "Russian Empire,"[314] the Soviet Union (dominated entirely by Russia and Russians, beside the Central Committee of the Communist Party),[315] which Circassians and others were not involved in the role of the federation that seemed to be between dominant Russia and tens of nations and different territorial entities. Imperial policies during the tsarist/empire era constituted of establishing large and strong armed forces using mercenaries to carry out wicked policies against tens of nations in the Caucasus and elsewhere.

The Russian military forces and their mercenary allies coordinated to implement the set plan, which included provoking the Circassian natives on the one hand and on abusing and torturing them on the other.

> The increasing scale of colonization in the Northern Caucasus and the cruelty of the policy of conquest pursued by Russian tsarism caused large-scale spontaneous uprisings of the mountaineers. The first of them took place in Chechnya in July 1825: mountaineers headed by Bey-Bulat captured the Amiradzhiiurt post, but their attempts to take GerzeP and Groznaia failed, and the uprising was suppressed in 1826.[316]

To achieve victory with minimal losses, they attempted to impose a blockade on the Circassian coastline.

> On the Black Sea coast the fortifications of Golovinskoe and Lazarevskoe were established in 1839, and the Black Sea shore line, running from the mouth of the Kuban' River to the borders of Megrelia, was created in the same year. The next year the Laba line was created, but the tsarist troops soon suffered several defeats between February and April 1840 when rebellious Circassians captured the fortifications of the Black Sea shore lineLazarevskoe, Vel'iaminovskoe, Mikhailovskoe, and Nikolaevskoe.[317]

Radio Free Europe/Radio Liberty published an article for Paul Goble, which mentions,

> Former Russian President Boris Yeltsin's May 1994 statement admitted that North Caucasian resistance to the tsarist forces was legitimate, but the current appeal notes

that he did not recognize "the guilt of the tsarist government for the genocide committed against the peoples of the North Caucasus."[318]

His successor, President Putin, who assumed the position of prime minister, acting president, and president, introduced the idea of celebrating an unreal event about the so-called "Circassians' 450 years of voluntary association with Russia." It doesn't make sense when a president declares that the defense against the tsarist forces was legitimate while a few years later his successor precludes that a war that lasted for 101 years had never taken place![319]

The Russian-Circassian War Consequences

Circassia was a victim that had to deal with a long-lasting and devastating war waged by the tsarist Russian Empire. The disastrous consequences were felt and sensed by the entire population. The Circassian homeland was destroyed, mass killing inflicted against the Circassian majority, forced deportation for those who managed to stay alive, and oppression for the rest of the population (10 percent), which was the remaining inhabitants who had fled into the mountains and managed to stay alive. (All classes of people had shared and tasted the bitterness of these consequences.)

The situation can be described as a contest of lies and pretending:

> The Russians viewed Circassian resistance as rebellion against a recognized sovereign, when in fact the Circassians considered themselves an independent entity and their conflict with Russia a war of national survival. For their part, the Russians not only viewed the Circassians as rebellious subjects but also believed in their own role as 'civilizers' of primitive peoples who would abandon their former ways once they saw the superiority of Russian culture.[320]

One of the positive consequences that took place during the long-lasting war was the existence of a sense of responsibility for the need of coherence. It provided consistency and solidarity through affirming and announcing the proclamation of their identity, characterized by tangible elements: "In 1834, the Abadzekhs, Natukhais, Shapseghs, and Ubykhs concluded a mutual anti-Russian coalition, followed by a declaration of the Independent Nation of Circassia the following year."[321]

In the meantime, after declaring the independence of Circassia, it was circulated to the major European media at the time. Thus, "by 1836 the Circassians had created their first national flag: three crossed arrows beneath three stars, representing the Zan, Aitek, and Bolotoko clans (considered the most ancient of the Circassians), capped by nine more stars in a semicircle on a green background. The Circassians had begun to develop a sense of national unity at the same time that the Russians, seeing them as rebels who were subject to their authority by the Treaty of Adrianople, were preparing to take control of the Black Sea coast by any means necessary."[322]

The deportations that took place before and after 1864 contributed to inflame the situation of the tragedy when hundreds of thousands of deportees had to be expelled by the tyrant powers involved. They were using worn-out ships, dozens of which had sunk with all their passengers and had great difficulty sailing through the crushing waves and unpleasant weather conditions of the Black Sea. They had brought those who were exiled from their sacred soil to be transferred to new territories, away from the cradle of their hearts, the homeland of their ancestors, until time permits them to return home with dignity and pride.

The spread of infectious diseases, tuberculosis, smallpox, dysentery, cholera, scabies, severe diarrhea, bronchitis, and pneumonia, which had been direct reasons for discrimination when they arrived at the ports of arrival, made the local inhabitants refuse the stay of the arriving refugees in their cities, towns, and communities. They weren't even allowed to settle within the vicinity so that the indigenous people could avoid getting affected or infected with multiple unwanted and hazardous diseases.

From those ports of arrival, Circassians had to later be dispersed to other territories of the Ottoman Empire according to an official plan for the optimal use of those demoralized people who were situated in a position that was orchestrated and intended for them, so as to be employed for defending the Ottoman Empire's territories and interests, especially in the former occupied nations in the Balkan and the Arabic regions.

Generals of Terror

Not to underestimate the importance of the malicious methods and resources used for assuming the control of the Caucasus in general and Circassia in particular, monuments are erected in the memory of the Russian military generals and commanders who committed the evil crimes, such as General Aleksey Petrovich Ermolov: "Aleksey Petrovich Ermolov (also spelled Yermolov) was a Russian general who played a prominent role in the tsar's campaigns into the Caucasus during the early nineteenth century."[323]

Regarding his legacy, it is mentioned that "Ermolov employed a number of brutal techniques to subdue the people of the Caucasus, and as a result he became the face of Russian brutality in the region. The Russian forces entering the Caucasus in the early nineteenth century struggled to compete against the local partisan forces in the mountains."[324]

Another was "Russian General Gregory Zass (1797–1883), one of the most sadistic and bloodthirsty commanders in military history."[325]

Being a Russian army commander, he used to invent unprecedented ways and means to commit crimes against Circassians, depending on his subordinates and mercenaries.

> Dekabrist Lorer: "Zass, near his encampment, on top of a specially prepared small hill, fixed Circassian heads on top of lances, with their beards flying in the air. It was very disturbing to see this scene. One day Zass, agreed to remove the heads from the lances after the request of a guest lady. We were also his guests at the time. When I entered the study room of the General, I was struck by a strong, disgusting smell. Smiling, Zass told us that there were boxes in which the heads were placed under his bed. Then he pulled a big box in which there were couple big-eyed, horribly looking heads. I asked him why he keeps them there. He replied: 'I boil them, clean them, and send them to my professor friends in Berlin for the study of anatomy.'"[326]
>
> Russian-Kazakh women were walking in the battlefields and cutting the heads of Circassian men, after the war was over. Originally German, General Zass was paying them a good amount of money for doing that. Until he was warned by his supervisors to give up this, Zass continued to boil, clean and send many heads to Berlin.[327]

The policy of the Russian Empire was not unknown. It went out of the boundaries and logic in its crimes against the Circassian nation, which was defending itself, including facilitating its simple defensive weapons in the face of enormous offensive capabilities, a huge arsenal of weapons, and tens of thousands of soldiers armed to the teeth on land and sea.

Grand Duke Michael, a member of the then Romanov royal family, was quoted as saying, "We wouldn't leave our duties thinking that Mountaineers are not surrendering. To wipe out the half, the other half needed to be destroyed."[328]

It was also reported about the same commander,

At the end of the war, when Grand Duke Michael came to Caucasia, Circassian Elders visited him and they said that they were defeated, and they demanded to be allowed to live in their lands accepting Russian administration. The answer Grand Duke Michael gave was, "I give you a month. In one month, you either go to the land that will be shown to you beyond Kuban, or you go to the land of the Ottoman Empire. The villagers and mountaineers who are not leaving for the coastal region in one month will be treated as prisoners of war."[329]

The following is reported in the "Reports and the Testimonies" about the war:

Caucasia Armies General Staff Head Milyutin "We should send the Mountaineers by force to the places we want. If we need, we should deport/exile them to Don region. Our main goal is to settle Russians in the regions on the skirts of Caucasian Mountains. But we shouldn't let the Mountaineers know about this."[330]

The "Reports and the Testimonies" about the war also indicated, "In the letter Earl Yevdokimov sent to the Ministry of War in October 1863 he said: 'Now we have to clean the coastal strip as part of our plan for the conquest of West Caucasia' (from the State History Archives)."[331]

Executing evil acts was not the only mission, but it was also adored by others who were following the implementation of genocide.

Russian Historian Sulujiyen: "We wouldn't abandon our cause just because Mountaineers are not surrendering. Half of them needed to be crashed in order to take their weapons. Many tribes were totally annihilated during the bloody war. In addition, many mothers were killing their kids in order not to give them to us."[332]

Russian Historian Zaharyan: "Circassians do not like us. We exiled them from their free meadowlands. We destroyed their houses and many tribes were totally destructed."[333]

The conspiratorial plan with the participation and blessing of the Romanov royal family and the criminal emperors against the Circassians was also against humanity. In the congratulating message Czar Alexander II sent to Earl Yevdokimov, "You cleaned up and destroyed the rebellious autochthon nations in West Caucasia in the last 3 years."[334]

The "Reports and the Testimonies" on the war added,

> A Russian detachment having captured the village of Toobah on the Soobashi river, inhabited by about a hundred Abadzekh (a tribe of Circassians), and after these had surrendered themselves prisoners, they were all massacred by the Russian Troops. Among the victims were two women in an advanced state of pregnancy and five children. The detachment is question belongs to Count Evdokimoff's (Yevdokimov) Army, and is said to have advanced from the Pshish valley.[335]

The descriptions of the evil acts unfold whenever one looks for more information: "As the Russian troops gain ground on the Coast, the natives are not allowed to remain there on any terms, but are compelled either to transfer themselves to the plains of the Kouban or emigrate to Turkey' (F.O. 9-424, no 2, Dickson to Russell, Soukoum Kale,17 March 1864)."[336]

Atrocities and tragedies are mentioned where the deportees were exposed to when being transported across the Black Sea to the Mediterranean. Heavy losses of lives were the result of difficult conditions, such as food shortages, the spread of infectious diseases, and other factors: "English Consul R.H. Lang: 'When 2718 people who left from Samsun to come to Cyprus arrived, 853 of them were dead and the others were not very different from being dead. The daily dead toll is about 30–50.'"[337]

Thousands of deportees are mentioned: "Hakhurat S.Y.- Lichkov L.S in their book entitled Adygheya: 'Czarist administration deported/exiled hundreds of thousands of Circassians from their homeland Caucasia. They expelled Mountaineer nations from their homeland by way of a bloody war.'"[338]

Russian journalists and media were praising the Russian armed forces operations against Circassia: "Russian St. Petersburg Newspaper: 'They started escaping through the coasts which were immortalized by their resistance and defense. There is no more Circassia. Our soldiers will clean out the remainders in the mountains very soon and the war will be over in a short time.'"[339]

The language used did not have any of humanity: "Tercüman-ı Ahval ve Tasvir-i Efkar Newspapers: 'Russians destroyed all of Caucasia. They set the villages on fire. They were exiling the autochthon people from their homelands after the war.'"[340]

Circassia 123

The European correspondents managed to share the news to view the facts and document them: "French reporter A. Fonvill: 'Sailors were acquisitive. They were letting 200–300 people in to the ships that have a capacity of 50–60. The people left with a little bread and water. In 5–6 days, these were all consumed and then they caught epidemic illnesses from starvation, they were dying in the way to Ottoman Empire, and those who die were dumped into the sea. The ship that started the trip with 600 people ended up with only 370 people alive.'"[341]

The specific detailed orders and terms for the evacuation of the dwellers from their homeland were clear:

> As the Russian troops gain ground on the Coast, the natives are not allowed to remain there on any terms, but are compelled either to transfer themselves to the plains of the Kouban or emigrate to Turkey (F.O. 9-424, no 2, Dickson to Russell, Soukoum Kale, 17 March 1864).[342]

> The Ubykh and Fighett tribes are . . . fast embarking for Trabzon. In fact, after their land had been laid waste by fire and sword, migration to Turkey is the only alternative allowed to these mountaineers who refuse to transfer themselves to the Kouban steppes and contribute periodically to the militia (F.O. 881-1259, Dickson to Russell, Soukoum Kale, 13 April 1864).[343]

The ugliest and unprecedented crimes committed by the barbarians are peculiar of their kind.

> A scene of cannibalism has been enacted at the village of Hafifa in the country of the Chapsoughs. The men of that village were at the frontier for the service of the outposts. Taking advantage of their absence, the soldiers of the Czar fell on the rest of the population, which was defenseless, and killed, burnt, and pillage them. Among the number of the victims were eighteen old women, eight children, and six old men. On the back of one of the slaughtered women there was left a board bearing these words: "Go and complain to the Kraalitza (Queen) of England, to whom your Deputies went to demand assistance". On the body of a little boy was found this inscription: "Remain here instead of going to sell yourself to your protectors, the Turks". Finally, on the corpse of an old man, the eyes of which had been put out, was read: "Go

and rejoin your Deputies, you will find some good oculists at Paris." (Courier d'Orient)[344]

Pinson said,

> The death percentage of Circassians along the Black Sea coasts is about 50%. 53,000 people died just in Trabzon alone. We don't know how many ships, which are 'Floating graves' had sunk. The number of families exiled from Caucasia to Balkan region is about 70,000. Edirne: 6,000, Silistre-Vidin: 13,000, Niche - Sofia: 12,000, Dobruca-Kosovo-Pristina-Svista: 42,000 families. Total about 350,000 people. Death percentage is less and is about 15–20%.[345]

Tragic Events and Results of the Devastating War

A series of battles and wars in Circassia, the northwestern part of the Caucasus, which were part of the Russian Empire's conquest of the Caucasus lasting approximately 101 years, starting under the reign of Tsar Peter the Great and being completed in 1864.[346]

The war was described as provocative and brutal and was waged by tsarist Russia. Circassia was totally occupied on May 21, 1864. The military forces and their mercenaries were imposing nothing but death, pain, destruction, disasters, and oppression, which played a great role in totally occupying Circassia and resulted in ethnic cleansing, genocide, and deporting 90 percent of the nation to a compulsory exile. The Circassian nation was deprived of its legitimate rights when it was subjected to catastrophic and devastating consequences as a result of the war and the forced occupation that followed.

The 101 years of war proved to be a long-term project and consisted of and included stages, phases, strategies, tactics, defensive and offensive operational campaigns, and methods that apparently appeared ugly in its entirety and produced serious consequences for the combatants of the two main sides, especially those who showed bravery and courage in defending their own homeland and opposing the invasion.

In 1837, in reply to the Russian Emperor, the leaders of Abadzekh, Natkhuagia, and Shapsugh tribes wrote, "We are fully convinced that . . . friendship and accord between us shall settle when all Your armies and fortifications shall be withdrawn beyond the Kuban River, in that case we all unanimously will be ready to submit". Nevertheless, the official policy of the autocracy was not calculated for a peaceful settlement of the matter, but on forcibly ousting the Circassians from their land and settling on these "freed" lands militarized Cossack stanitsas. The appeal of Circassian leaders to the Russian Emperor remained unanswered. The seizure of the Circassian lands continued.[347]

Results ranged between victories and defeats on both sides that varied between hit-and-run tactics, Circassian territories being occupied, the murder and destruction of the Circassian inhabitants' communities leading to their displacement, where the whole process was executed slowly but surely. One of the periods can be described as follows: "The study will cover the period from 1830 to 1864 when a sanguinary war between Russia and the Circassian tribes took place, ending with the expulsion of the overwhelming majority of the local population and the establishment of the complete Russian control over Circassia."[348]

During the last stages of the long war and its consequences, the Russian military administration went through major changes. The "North Caucasus was redivided in 1860: The Left Flank of the Kavkazski Line was renamed into Terski Region, and the Right Flank, together Chernomoria, became part of the Kubanski Region." Changes introduced to the staff" resulted in appointing General Evdokimov "the commander of the Russian armed forces in the Kuban Region."[349]

> Count Evdokimov submitted in November his proposition about the military operations for the final conquest of the Western Caucasus." The plan offered to settle the Cossacks in the area "between the Shaguasha and Laba rivers and the east coast of the Black Sea, and offering the mountaineers to immigrate to the valleys or to move away to Turkey.[350]

Because of the threat, "the Bashilbeys, Kazilbeks, Tamovs, and a part of the Shakhgireys left their place at the fixed date and moved to Turkey. Only the Besleneys refused to comply with the orders. On June 20, 1860, they were suddenly surrounded and they, about 4,000 families, were forcibly transferred to the Uroup River under the cover of Russian troops and, from there, having received permission, moved away to Turkey."[351]

They decided to utilize available resources to defend their very survival and eventually were persuaded by foreigners "to continue fighting against Russia and convinced them that England, France, and Turkey will take them under their protectorate and declare war against Russia. The Circassians were extremely encouraged by such appeals, and their major tribes, the Abadzekhs, Shapsughs, and Ubykhs, sent their elected elders to Sochi, where on June 13 they reached an understanding to act with united forces."[352]

The Circassian deputies had

> resolved to institute extraordinary union and to preserve internal order in the country. A Mejliss of 15 ulemas and experienced men was established to govern the Union. They called this Mejliss, "The Great Free Conference". The entire region was divided into 12 okrugs (regions, districts), and in each of them they appointed responsible persons. Unsatisfied with these re-organizations, the Ubykhs sought for help in Turkey and England. They turned to Dixon, the English consul in Sukhumi, asking him to inform the English government about the Russian encroachment on their independence, they complained to him that General Evdokimov has surrounded their country from all sides for the subjugation of the Circassians.[353]

> All these efforts of the Circassians could not, however, change the intended systematic plan of conquest of Russia. To begin with Gen. Koliubkin decided to deal a moral blow from the direction of Abkhazia. Having landed at Sochi, the Russian armed forces destroyed by fire the buildings of the Free Conference. In vain, the Circassians came running from all sides and tried to save their sacred building.[354]

> Abadzekh elders came to Count Evdokimov, in Khamketski camp, and requested of him not to march on their land and not to build roads or clear the forests as they have pledged allegiance to the sovereign and wish to live in peace," but Evdokimov has ignored them and continued his hostile operations, and informed the Abadzekh, "that they themselves breached first the submission by concluding union with Shapsughs and Ubykhs.[355]

The Abadzekh endeavor was foiled by Evdokimov. Their efforts were circumvented and procrastinated when they declared their acceptance to the declaration of the conditions put to them in exchange for ending the military operations against them and changing facts on the ground in their own homeland. That shows a trend to make circumstances favorable, to force them either to leave their historic homeland to internal areas designated by the Russian armed forces or to be deported to the Ottoman Empire.

Emperor Alexander II wanted in the "autumn of 1861" to realize for himself the fact that his armed forces are controlling a great and strategic part of the Circassian homeland when he arrived in September, accompanied by his close associates.

He was received on the eleventh of September 1861 at Taman harbor by "Adjutant General Prince Orbeliani, the commander of the Kavkazski Army, with high persons in command, was waiting in the harbor. More than 500 peaceful and refractory Circassians had also come to Taman, to ask the Sovereign not to evict them from the Caucasus. The Emperor at once noticed the Circassian group and, having asked Prince Orbeliani who are they, quickly headed toward them. When the Monarch approached, all the Circassians, like one, took off their weapons, placed them on the ground, and reverentially bowed their heads. After that the eldest of them, having moved a little forward," and articulated a speech promising to accept being subjects of Russia, and to participate in building what needed for the Russians, provided as was put, "only do not evict us from those places, where our fathers and forefathers were born and lived. Henceforward, we will on equal footing with your armed forces defend these places from enemies to the last drop of our blood . . . Only do not evict us and look on us like on the rest of your loyal subjects . . ."[356]

Also, to meet the emperor during his stay at the camp,

> 50 mounted Circassian deputies left their group and headed towards the cam. The Sovereign agreed to receive them. Haji Berzek, the representative of the Ubykhs, appealed to the Emperor, in the name of all the Circassians, to accept them as his subjects. The sovereign said he would be pleased to accept them as his subjects under the following conditions: First of all, they must stop their raids, obey and fulfill all the demands of the Russian authorities and, in order to prove their readiness for it, they must now surrender the prisoners and fugitives. Silence was the answer of the Circassian deputies. It became obvious that the Circassian elders and delegates, who came to the camp, were not the representatives

of the whole people, but only of part of it, who really wanted the cessation of the war.[357]

When the sovereign asked why they are silent, Haji Berzek added that they brought with them a written appeal also. The sovereign ordered to accept the appeal and then declared that he places in the hands of the Russian authorities in the Caucasus the consideration of the appeal of the Circassians and the arrangement of their way of life in general.[358]

The Circassian deputies requested in their appeal the inviolability of their rights to their lands, the cessation of building Russian fortresses, stanitsas, and roads in it. Undoubtedly, such a conditional submission would extend the process of the pacification of the region for many years. Therefore, the sovereign said, "I give you one month. The Abadzekhs must decide, whether they are willing to settle in the Kuban, where they would receive land for ownership in perpetuity and preserve their national arrangement and court, or move to Turkey." This blunt statement of Russian emperor must have shocked the Circassians as they please. The disappointed Circassian delegation returned to their people, and the emperor toured the camp, the Genaderski Rifle Battalion and the seven Rifle Companies of the Line Battalion that guarded the transport.[359]

Apparently, the case was left in the hands of the occupation authorities, whose actions and policies of order and ethnic cleansing towards them and towards their homeland the Circassians had complained of. That was not all what was being plotted against Circassians, as the emperor officially added and authorized one more step of consolidating and implementing the formal Russian plans on the ground.

The main Russian goal is recorded through the imperial order(s).

On June 24, 1861, Alexander II signed the "imperial" rescript on the "Settlement of the North Caucasus". It says, "Now with God's help, the matter of the complete conquest of the Caucasus is near to conclusion. A few years of persistent efforts are remaining in order to utterly force out the hostile mountaineers from the fertile countries they occupy and settle on the latter a Russian Christian population forever. The honor of accomplishing this glorious deed belongs mainly to the Cossacks of the Kubanski armed forces." To encourage the Cossacks and to speed up the process, the emperor promised them monetary compensation and other privileges.[360]

Alexander II came to Ekaterinodar to inspect the districts earmarked for the Russian settlements. On September 11, he arrived in Taman, where a Circassian deputation of 500 persons met him. . . . The Abadzekhs appealed to the Russian Emperor not to send them out of their places . . . His answer was, "I give you one month. The Abadzekhs must decide whether they want to resettle on the places earmarked for them along the Kuban, or to move to Turkey."[361]

The Circassian leaders representing their nation had said their opinion, which ranged from accepting what the enemy was imposing on them and refusing to go voluntarily and into unconditional slavery.

Then spoke Pshimaf, Alanbech Hajemukov. "Now, I see that we do not have sufficient strength to defend our lands with arms. Russians are many. We are only a few. The forces are unequal . . . My opinion is to surrender. God will not blame us." Seeing that the crowd resented the statement, the emperor grew pale.[362]

Then spoke Hatirbay Tsey, "Every nation is born, grows, ages, and dies, exactly like an individual human being. The age of a human being, they say, is one hundred years, but a nation lives for millennia. The Russian Czar liked the Caucasus very much and he is waging a bloody war for more than 60 years and wants to seize it. However, our land, our Motherland, is dear to us too. Sacrificing our blood and our lives, we defended it, we are defending it, and we shall defend it in the future in the name of our fatherland grandfathers, in the name of our children and grandchildren . . . The Czar told us that the Caucasus would be Russian. Perhaps, the Caucasus will be Russian, but the Circassians will not be the slaves of the Russian Czar, while blood runs in them." The Emperor instantly returned to his headquarters.[363]

When the Circassian elders and leaders had reached the conclusion of the ugly truth and became inevitably certain that the Russians were closing in, they gathered in the area around Sochi and appealed to the great powers at the time, mainly the Ottoman Empire and the British Empire. They wanted assistance to stop the advancement of the imperial Russians who got closer and closer to capturing and occupying the whole region. They hoped that they gain their help, but they were faced and met with eternal silence from all sides. Seemingly, some of them even witnessed, with blessings, the occupiers committing crimes. The arrival of two Circassian chiefs (leaders) in England in the year 1862, who represented the national resistance in Circassia, to inform the world about the Russian invasion and imperial plans and seek assistance, didn't help stop the Circassian tragedy.

The profound effect of occupying Circassia, in addition to the geographical and demographical changes implemented by the Russian Empire through its colonial occupation since the year 1864, led to a series of occasions when the successive Russian regimes divided, redivided, then subdivided, and subsequently introduced functions showing their imperial intentions and greed. It demonstrated that those who performed all types of oppression and tyranny, in addition to authoritative imperial rules when dealing with the Circassian inhabitants, wanted to get the Circassian homeland, but without its Circassian people.

The Russians had always entrenched and employed their victory in the war through the years and are still doing so. An extra inhumane step was taken in that direction, which occurred in February of 2014, when the Circassian capital city of Sochi hosted the Russian-accommodated Winter Olympic Games, just shy of commemorating 150 years of its capture by the hands of the invading forces on the twenty-first of May 1864, which will be addressed later in another section. Sochi was the last Circassian stronghold that was lost to the Russians. Accordingly, the Russian Empire imposed administrative colonial control and occupation of the entire Circassian homeland in addition to other parts of the North Caucasus.

> Cossacks have long been at the forefront of the anti-Circassian trend, apparently in accordance with the official Russian Empire's policies of invasion and conquer. The Cossacks—a Slavic-speaking people who had adopted the semi-nomadic lifestyle of the steppes—were instrumental in the expansion process of the Russian Empire, where the northwestern Caucasus was not an exception. The Kuban Cossack Host (Cossack Army), was established on the edge of Circassian territory in the late 1700s, figured prominently in the Russo-Turkish (and Russo-Circassian) wars. During this period, the Cossacks have comprehensively borrowed the Circassian traditional costume from their bitter Circassian enemies.[364]

Russian commanders in the Caucasus wanted to make the Cossacks wear a unified uniform rather than wear what they wished, which acquired the Circassian national outfit.

> In the year 1828, the Commander, Senior Lieutenant Emanuel couldn't bear the Cossacks' random attire, where he ordered all of them to wear the Circassian Costume. The Circassian Costume was called Cherkessia in 27, November 1861, after it was approved by the Defense Ministry.[365]

> On November 27, 1861, he (the Emperor) deigned to issue an imperial decree to call the upper dress of the Kuban and Terek Cossack armed forces "Cherkesska" instead of "uniform". A. Sheen branded this deed of the emperor 'disrobing' the victim, the Circassian nation.[366]

> The uniforms of Kuban (and Terek) Cossacks are a form of the traditional Caucasian garb known as 'chokha.' Historical emulation, however, they didn't entail peaceful coexistence. When the Tsarist government decided to clear out and cleanse the Circassians in the 1860s, the Cossacks were in the vanguard to perform this task. Their assaults usually began with the mass theft of horses—according to a local adage, "a Circassian and a horse together cannot be defeated"—and ended with the burning of villages and the expulsion of the people. As a result, Cossack communities acquired some of the best lands in the northwestern Caucasus.[367]

These were the consequences of the brutal war and the deportation of the Circassian nations.

Humanitarian Reflections

There were still humanitarian thoughts in commenting on the mass killings and the scorched-earth policy: "This was a real and brutal war. Hundreds of Circassian villages were set on fire. We let our horses run over their crops and gardens to destroy them, in the end it turned into a ruin" (Russian historian Y. D. Felisin). [368]

Earl Lev Tolstoy wrote, "To enter the villages in the darkness became our usual thing. Russian soldiers were entering the houses one by one under the darkness of the night. This and following scenes were such horror scenes that none of the reporters were courageous enough to report them."³⁶⁹

Another input is by the oppositional group N. N. Rayevski, "The things we did in Caucasia were very similar to the negative things that Spaniards did during the war in American lands. I wish God almighty would not leave any blood marks in Russian history."³⁷⁰

The long war was also described by Jan Karol: "The Russian conquest of Caucasia is a terrible example of our barbarian times. It took 60 years of military terror and massacre to break the resistance of the Caucasian Mountaineers."³⁷¹

Describing a scenery that is unbearable and unacceptable by human beings, Russian researcher A. P. Berge states,

> I will never forget the 17,000 people I saw at the Novorossisk Bay. I am sure those who saw their situation couldn't bear it and would definitely collapse no matter what religion they belonged to, Christians, Muslims, or atheists. In the cold winter, in the snow, without a house, without food, and without any proper clothing, these people were in the hands of typhoid, typhus, and chicken pox diseases. The babies were searching for milk in their mother's dead body. This terrible black page in the Russian history caused great harm to the Adygean history. The exile caused an interruption in the history of social, economic, and cultural developments and in the process of becoming one political union/confederation.³⁷²

Those who bear the brunt of occupation and colonialism share a sense of humanitarianism and know precisely the calamities imposed by imperialism. Polish colonel Teophil Lapinsky says,

> The situation of the exiled people was turning into a catastrophe. Hunger and epidemics were at their peak. The group who came to Trabzon decreased from 100,000 to 70,000 people. 70,000 people arrived at Samsun. The dead toll per day was about 500 people. This number was about 400 in Trabzon. 300 people in Gerede Camp, the daily death toll in Akcakale and Saridere is about 120–150 people. Italian Dr. Barozzi in his report makes the following important note: People are trying to stay alive for long time with herbs, plant roots and bread crumbs.³⁷³

Human tragedies had exceeded their limits. Y. Abramov wrote in his book entitled Caucasian Mountaineers,

> There are no words to describe the situation of the Mountaineers in those days. Thousands of them died in the roads, thousands of them died due to illness and hunger. The coastal regions were full with people who are dead or on the verge of dying. The babies who are searching for milk in their mother's cold dead body, mothers who didn't leave their kids from their laps even they are already dead from cold, and people who are dead while they got closer just to keep warm, are examples of the scenes that were normal in the coasts of the Black Sea.[374]

Many people who had a conscience talked about the crimes committed against the Circassian people. One is Russian I. Dzarov: "Half of those who left to go to Ottoman Empire died before they reached there. Such a state of wretchedness is rare in the history of the humankind."[375]

Circassian Defense Strength during Russian-Circassian War

Russia had used all its potential, powerful military and demographic structure, which employed all their resources and capabilities in fighting a long and savage war to control Circassia that eventually made the coastline of the Black Sea under Russian control. The entire Circassian homeland was a battlefield, and its citizens were direct targets. To achieve their only goal, the Russian invading forces followed a "scorched-earth warfare" of destroying anything that might be useful to the ordinary people who happened to be on the battlefield.

That policy had badly affected the total population so that the executors of the brutal and hectic campaign could declare "mission accomplished"; the assignment the Russian military commanders had taken on their shoulders and were dreaming to reach for 101 consecutive years was complete.

All types of military ground assault forces, tricks, mercenaries, ammunition, deception, and weapons were utilized. To make sure they attained their list of set targets in their plan, Russian navy vessels and artillery encircled and surrounded the Circassian Black Sea front, ports, strongholds, and shoreline. Initially, it was for imposing a total blockade, sanctions, and preventing the Circassians from trading with the outside world. This prevented European and Turkish ships from sailing to and from the Circassian coast.

Sea navigation during the nineteenth century, the writer describes, had "very serious traditions. According to Swiss scientist F. Dubua de Monpere who observed Circassian galleys personally, the vessels could hold 60–70 persons each. But there was also a type that could hold up to 140 men. Adyghe vessels were sailing ones with the oars and sometimes were armed with light cannons. They could make very long coasting navigation. Russian trade representative in Western Circassia L.Y.Lulye wrote, 'Coastal high-landers sailed very actively. For the transportation of provision from one gorge into another they used the same rowing-ships (galleys) as they did for the sea roads. I saw it by myself, how they were coming on the galleys using oars from very remote places of coast into Sudjouk bight (Novorossiysk) and even to Fortress Anapa.'"[376]

The exceptional quality and performance of the Circassian naval ships was also described by "F.F.Tornau, who served in the Caucasus several years, witnessed about excellent seaworthy qualities of Circassian galleys. The traveler J.Tebu de Marini describes the Circassian vessel in this way, 'Their ship, as all I saw before was flat-bottomed, without keel, casing was fixed to the very fine ship frame by nails and wooden pins. On the nose was image of animal's head. It was hard to figure out what animal that was exactly, but Circassians asserted that it was a head of the he-goat . . .' The oars on their galleys are very short and fixed to rowlocks of enormous length with the transverse cross-bars for the hands of rowers. They used rudder and small square sail."[377]

The described article explained that the Circassians "had not permanent Navy, but they completed galley detachments to take action against Tsar's troops and Navy. The important form of Adyghes' fight was attacks of their galleys onto Tsar's military ships. Quite often on the water of Circassian coast took place very fierce fights. In 1832, year by high-landers was attacked Russian cutter with 12 cannons. Tsar's administration was really afraid to leave vessels in Sudjouk bight even with guard, because Circassians could seize it using galleys during dark night."[378]

The article added, "Circassian Navy from Tebu De Marini's book Three Voyage in Black Sea of Circassia coasts. With sketches of manners, traditions and religion of Circassians." (London 1837) Knight De Marini has been in Circassia three times as ambassador of Holland King: 1818, 1823 and 1824."[379]

They were not able to establish a sophisticated navy during the war imposed on them, but the situation was peculiar. The Circassians "had no permanent Navy, but they completed galley detachments to take action against Tsar's troops and Navy. The important form of Adyghes' fight was attacks of their galleys onto Tsar's military ships. Quite often on the water of Circassian coast took place very fierce fights. In 1832 year by high-landers was attacked Russian cutter with 12 cannons. Tsar's administration was really afraid to leave vessels in

Sudjouk bight even with guard, because Circassians could seize it using galleys during dark night."[380]

Regarding the defending of ports such as Sochi and its importance to Circassians, the Circassian navy, as per the article, was occupied by performing an important duty: "In October of 1836, Tsar's vessel 'Nartsiss' was attacked near to mouth of Sochi River by 7 Circassian galleys. After, the commander of Russian vessel captain Varnitskiy reported that Circassians fought in organized manner, their commander was showing by long pole to each galley its place during attack. After fierce fight Russians escaped."[381]

Despite the Circassians' limited capabilities, "however undertaken measures didn't cause full destroying for Circassian fleet. Adyghes engaged in battles with the Cossacks on the sea many times. What is more clashes with Russian Navy's ships continued. Thus, in February of 1838, took place fierce fight with 4 Circassian galleys from one side and Russian lugger 'Glubokiy' from other."[382]

The article said that the information on the subject is considered extremely scarce despite the significant achievements. "Unfortunately, historical documents and testimonies of eyewitnesses give us very little information about Circassian sea chiefs. In 30 years of 19 century active roads were undertook ships of coastal Circassian, certain Hassan-bey. Other form of using sea fleet by Adyghes in the struggle with tsarism were landings of Circassian troops from the galleys into important places and attacking suddenly points occupied by tsar's troops. Thus, tsar's Command were stupefied by bold and successful landing of Circassian troops close to Bombory in May 1834."[383]

The remarkable role played by the Circassian navy was significant.

> Through the using of galleys, Adyghes adjusted connection between themselves and also for co-action against conqueror. They used their ships on the reconnaissance too. Circassian Navy kept connection with Istanbul and with Turkish ships they conveyed weapon and ammunition into the Caucasus for the struggle. Besides, high-landers sailed towards Ottoman Empire with commercial intentions.[384]
>
> Of course, Circassian attacks on enemy's ships weren't successful in every case. Thus, Vorontsov was an eyewitness of unsuccessful Circassian boarding when brave Adyghes started board Russian ship. They chose position for the attack in front of the vessel's nose, but sailors on the deck cut off the anchor chain and while it was falling down on the light galleys all they sank with the Circassian pirates. Adyghe navigators were based on the most comfortable bays of Black Sea eastern

coast. They had few arranged central points. From the words of Dubua de Monpere: "Mamay bight, which is famous from the ancient times by its sea robbery, was the central spot for all the Circassian corsairs."[385]

The provided testimonies by many parties illustrate the idea of the impact of the Circassian ships and their operators, even though they had limited impact on the conduct of the war in the region.

In the eastern coast of Black Sea Adyghes used to pursue and seize hostile commercial ships. According to words of one Russian sea officer N.N. Sushev, who was an eyewitness of the Circassian assault. During the assault to the hostile trade ship Circassian firstly "knocked by riffle guns all the sailors from the upper deck, after they were boarding with the daggers and then after few moments all was finished . . ." We have to take into consideration that while war time all this also did England, Holland and others. And Circassia was not an exception in this meaning.[386]

The writer concluded, "Adduced facts witnesses about certain contribution of Adyghe military navigators in the war for Freedom and Independence of Circassia. After Russian conquest of the Circassia the navigation of high-landers doesn't exist."[387] As s a result of the 101-year-long war and its consequences, important documents and vital information had been lost, even deleted and destroyed, because the invading forces used to occupy, destroy, murder, loot, confiscate, and deport the remaining population either to beyond the River Kuban or to the Ottoman Empire.

How Circassian Demands Form After the War of Aggression!

A dream that had been dangling in the Russians' mind since the Muscovites, followed by the Tsarist Imperial regime, they had started their conquering wars and invasions against all their neighbors and beyond. They contained the desire of reaching the warm waters and control the coast of the Black Sea to establish a Russian gate from the ports of the Black Sea to the near and far east for territorial extension, trade, and navigational control purposes in the adjacent waterways; no matter how tremendous the cost would be and regardless whether there was any human suffering or not.

Circassia

In the book Circassian History authored by Kadir I. Natkho regarding the Russo-Circassian War, the beginning of the chapter widened the general view, description, and details regarding the war that is referred to, by some historians, as the Russian-Caucasian War.

> Circassian, Russian, and other historians, wrote volumes about this war, the longest and the cruelest in the annals of history, which raged for over one century and a half between two entirely unequal nations, the gigantic Russian Empire and the little gallant Circassia; one, the aggressor, with a mighty military machine, the other, the defender of her land and freedom, without such a thing even as an organized army. The extraordinary stamina, courage, and love for freedom and country, with which this little nation resisted the relentless onslaught of the formidable aggressor for such a long time had fired the imagination of the greatest men of the age, Alexander Pushkin, Count Lev Tolstoy, Mikhail Lermontov, Taras Shevechenko, Karl Marx, and others, yet, strangely enough, the historians did not only misname this war, but most of the information they have furnished to us about it is quite inaccurate and conflicting. In other words, while the works of the great minds idealized the dignity and heroism of the Cherkes (Circassians), the historians ignored the nation against which the Russian aggression was directed and began calling it under two different terms: The Russo-Caucasian War and The Caucasian War. The first term was designed to conceal that Russia, in her drive towards the warm seas, had waged this war to conquer Circassia. The second term, The Caucasian War, which the Russians love to use in referring to this war, was to convey that all the Caucasians had initiated the war and fought it against Russia. Nothing, of course, can be farther from the truth. Some of the Caucasian nations—for example, Armenia and Georgia—did not fight at all against Russia in this war. Neither did the Caucasians ever declare war on Russia as the latter term implies. The fact is Russia had initiated this war and invaded the land of the Circassians—the land of the people that sought for the protection of the Czarist Russia against the aggressions of the Ottoman Empire and the Crimean Khanate in the XV and XVI centuries.[388]

Reality necessitates addressing the following inquiry: do Circassians have the right and legal prerogative to demand a justified solution to the Circassian Question? The Russian state must acknowledge the genocide, brutal polices, and ethnic cleansing as well as apologize, compensate, and allow Circassians to return to their homeland to be able to exercise the right of self-determination!

A Contemporary Opinion

Jacov Gordin's visit to Maikop, the capital city of the Republic of Adygea, in December 2006, was reported on NatPress:

> I'd like to show some aspects of this terrible history that was named the Caucasian war. First, tragedy of the situation on the whole. That tragedy is that Russia could not help to win Caucasus since certain moment. Such plans for Caucasus were made from the end of the XVI century, and even earlier. But the first proved campaign is the campaign of warlord Khvorostinin at Tsar Feodor Ioanovich in 1696. As unsuccessful campaign as many other war expeditions. But from the moment of Georgia's connection—"my destiny is determined"—as Pushkin wrote. The destiny of Russia and Caucasus was determined. They were doomed to be at war",— its author has told after the book's release.[389]

The article continues,

> And here is how the literary critics estimate the writer's work: "the problem as Gordin formulated it, consist of that Caucasus, having the limited natural resources, was not necessary to Russia in itself (unlike Crimea, the Volga region and even Siberia). But connection of Georgia to the Russian empire in 1783–1801 made a war inevitable: on the logic of its existence the empire could not leave between itself and the Christian Transcaucasia 'the boiling with hatred and contempt to wrong-believers Caucasus."[390]

This subject was concluded with a remarkable statement:

> "Gordin represents his position as a search of historical correctness and objectivity. It is reached with division of the

Russian expansion in 'the actions natural and necessary, inherent in any developing state," and "the imperial foolishness," pushed the empire to the actions excessive and in the long term not only unnecessary, but dangerous for the country.[391]

The current Russian involvement, by re-creating its old imperial past by suspicious maneuvers in the Caucasus, Turkey, Baltics, and other former Soviet spheres, especially the annexing of Crimea and interfering in Ukraine's internal affairs especially in the east, reaching to the "Levant through Syria" by involving the Russian military in direct embroilment in Syria and other parts outside the present territorial borders, and getting political and economic influence in Iran and other parts of the world demonstrates a persistence to foster an imperial policy while feeling superior over others both in Europe and in the rest of the world while leaving the Circassian Question unsolved.

FSB persecution of Circassians from Turkey has intensified since the shooting down of the Russian plane, ranging from demands that Circassians give up Turkish citizenship and take part in anti-Turkish demonstrations to arrests and bureaucratic restricts prompted Circassians to hold a protest meeting at the Russian consulate general in Istanbul last Friday (kavkaz-uzel.ru/articles/274672/).[392]

A Quote

If you are neutral in situations of injustice, you have chosen the side of the oppressor. If an elephant has its foot on the tail of a mouse and you say that you are neutral, the mouse will not appreciate your neutrality. (Desmond Tutu)[393]

---

[214] Circassian History (Kadir Natho)
[215] Circassian History (Kadir Natho)
[216] Circassian History (Kadir Natho)
[217] Circassian History (Kadir Natho)
[218] http://www.britannica.com/topic/Rus
[219] A History of the Vikings

220 http://dictionary.reference.com/browse/russia and https://community.dur.ac.uk/a.k.harrington/origirus.html
221 (http://www.carpatho-rusyn.org/where.htm).
222 http://www.carpatho-rusyn.org/where.htm
223 http://www.britannica.com/topic/Russian-language
224 Third section http://linguistics.byu.edu/classes/ling450ch/reports/russian.html
225 . http://www.shsu.edu/~his_ncp/266LecN.html
226 http://www.shsu.edu/~his_ncp/266LecN.html
227 (http://www.shsu.edu/~his_ncp/266LecN.html)
228 http://www.shsu.edu/~his_ncp/266LecN.html
229 http://www.shsu.edu/~his_ncp/266LecN.html
230 http://windowoneurasia2.blogspot.com/2014/07/window-on-eurasia-when-russia-was.html
231 ttolk.ru/?p=21185 and http://windowoneurasia2.blogspot.com/2014/07/window-on-eurasia-when-russia-was.html
232 Circassian History (Kadir Natho)
233 http://www.aheku.net/page.php?id=1068
234 http://www.snipview.com/q/Russian_military_personnel_of_the_Caucasian_War
235 Circassian History (Kadir Natho)
236 Circassian History (Kadir Natho)
237 http://www.britannica.com/event/Treaty-of-Edirne
238 http://www.huffingtonpost.com/news/crimea-annexation/
239 Circassian History (Kadir Natho)
240 Circassian History (Kadir Natho)
241 Circassian History (Kadir Natho)
242 Circassian History (Kadir Natho)
243 Circassian History (Kadir Natho)
244 Circassian History (Kadir Natho)
245 http://wars.findthedata.com/l/99/Russian-Circassian-War
246 The Northwest Caucasus (Walter Richmond)
247 http://www.geocurrents.info/place/russia-ukraine-and-caucasus/the-circassian-mystique-and-its-historical-roots#ixzz419YMi4AB
248 https://prezi.com/ccldra_phmms/circassian-genocide/
249 The Northwest Caucasus: Past, Present, Future (Walter Richmond)
250 The Northwest Caucasus: Past, Present, Future (Walter Richmond)
251 The Northwest Caucasus: Past, Present, Future (Walter Richmond)
252 The Northwest Caucasus: Past, Present, Future (Walter Richmond)
253 The Northwest Caucasus: Past, Present, Future (Walter Richmond)
254 The Northwest Caucasus: Past, Present, Future (Walter Richmond)

255 The Northwest Caucasus: Past, Present, Future (Walter Richmond)
256 https://www.quora.com/What-is-the-historical-origin-of-the-divide-and-rule-policy
257 The Northwest Caucasus: Past, Present, Future (Walter Richmond)
258 http://www.jlhuie.com/2015/02/courage-to-overcome-fear.html
259 The Northwest Caucasus: Past, Present, Future (Walter Richmond)
260 The Northwest Caucasus: Past, Present, Future (Walter Richmond)
261 The Northwest Caucasus: Past, Present, Future (Walter Richmond)
262 The Northwest Caucasus: Past, Present, Future (Walter Richmond)
263 The Northwest Caucasus: Past, Present, Future (Walter Richmond)
264 The Northwest Caucasus: Past, Present, Future (Walter Richmond)
265 The Northwest Caucasus: Past, Present, Future (Walter Richmond)
266 The Northwest Caucasus: Past, Present, Future (Walter Richmond)
267 The Northwest Caucasus: Past, Present, Future (Walter Richmond)
268 The Northwest Caucasus: Past, Present, Future (Walter Richmond)
269 The Northwest Caucasus: Past, Present, Future (Walter Richmond)
270 The Northwest Caucasus: Past, Present, Future (Walter Richmond)
271 http://www.scaruffi.com/politics/russians.html and http://eng.tzar.ru/museums/history/monarchy
272 http://wars.findthedata.com/q/99/2020/Who-was-involved-in-the-Russian-Circassian-War
273 https://www.revolvy.com/main/index.php?s=Genocides%20in%20history&item_type=topic&sr=50
274 The Northwest Caucasus: Past, Present, Future (Walter Richmond)
275 The Northwest Caucasus: Past, Present, Future (Walter Richmond)
276 The Northwest Caucasus: Past, Present, Future (Walter Richmond)
277 The Northwest Caucasus: Past, Present, Future (Walter Richmond)
278 The Northwest Caucasus: Past, Present, Future (Walter Richmond)
279 http://www.britannica.com/topic/Cossack
280 http://russiapedia.rt.com/of-russian-origin/cossacks/
281 http://www.urbandictionary.com/define.php?term=Cossack
282 http://www.aheku.net/page.php?id=1185
283 Circassian History (Kadir Natho)
284 Circassian History (Kadir Natho)
285 The Northwest Caucasus: Past, Present, Future (Walter Richmond)
286 Circassian History (Kadir Natho)
287 Circassian History (Kadir Natho)
288 The Northwest Caucasus (Walter Richmond)
289 http://encyclopedia2.thefreedictionary.com/Caucasian+War+of+1817%E2%80%9364
290 http://www.armenianhouse.org/villari/caucasus/caucasus-history.html

291 The Northwest Caucasus: Past, Present, Future (Walter Richmond)
292 The Northwest Caucasus: Past, Present, Future (Walter Richmond)
293 The Northwest Caucasus: Past, Present, Future (Walter Richmond)
294 The Northwest Caucasus: Past, Present, Future (Walter Richmond)
295 https://aheku.net/stranicza-ajax?id=3943
296 The Northwest Caucasus: Past, Present, Future (Walter Richmond)
297 The Northwest Caucasus: Past, Present, Future (Walter Richmond)
298 The Northwest Caucasus: Past, Present, Future (Walter Richmond)
299 https://prezi.com/ccldra_phmms/circassian-genocide/
300 http://wn.com/russian-circassian_war and https://www.youtube.com/watch?v=MT50djHClkQ
301 http://dictionnaire.sensagent.leparisien.fr/Russian%E2%80%93Circassian%20War/en-en/
302 https://prezi.com/ccldra_phmms/circassian-genocide/
303 https://prezi.com/ccldra_phmms/circassian-genocide/
304 http://adygi.ru/informaci/buxotchit/663-circassian-navy-during-russian-caucasian-war.html
305 http://www.natpressru.info/index.php?newsid=3850
306 http://www.natpressru.info/index.php?newsid=3850
307 http://www.cato.org/blog/four-years-too-long-wait-ruling-constitutional-claim
308 http://www.aheku.net/page.php?id=1185
309 http://www.natpressru.info/index.php?newsid=3850
310 http://www.ucis.pitt.edu/nceeer/2008_821-08g_Khodarkovsky.pdf
311 The Northwest Caucasus: Past, Present, Future (Walter Richmond)
312 The Northwest Caucasus: Past, Present, Future (Walter Richmond)
313 http://workmall.com/wfb2001/russia/russia_history_the_rise_of_muscovy.html
314 http://workmall.com/wfb2001/russia/russia_history_peter_the_great_and_the_russian_empire.html
315 http://www.britannica.com/place/Soviet-Union, and reaching to what presently described to be the Russian Federation and http://www.newworldencyclopedia.org/entry/Russian_Federation
316 http://encyclopedia2.thefreedictionary.com/Caucasian+War+of+1817%E2%80%9364
317 http://encyclopedia2.thefreedictionary.com/Caucasian+War+of+1817%E2%80%9364
318 http://www.rferl.org/content/article/1341730.html
319 Refer to # 14.
320 The Northwest Caucasus: Past, Present, Future (Walter Richmond)
321 The Northwest Caucasus: Past, Present, Future (Walter Richmond)

322 The Northwest Caucasus: Past, Present, Future (Walter Richmond)
323 http://russiasperiphery.blogs.wm.edu/transcaucasia/chechnya/general/ermolov/
324 http://russiasperiphery.blogs.wm.edu/transcaucasia/chechnya/general/ermolov/
325 https://www.facebook.com/permalink.php?story_fbid=978991265478471&id=192171867493752
326 http://www.natpressru.info/index.php?newsid=3850
327 http://www.natpressru.info/index.php?newsid=3850
328 http://www.natpressru.info/index.php?newsid=3850
329 http://www.natpressru.info/index.php?newsid=3850
330 http://www.natpressru.info/index.php?newsid=3850
331 http://www.natpressru.info/index.php?newsid=3850
332 http://www.natpressru.info/index.php?newsid=3850
333 http://www.natpressru.info/index.php?newsid=3850
334 http://www.natpressru.info/index.php?newsid=3850
335 http://www.natpressru.info/index.php?newsid=3850
336 http://www.natpressru.info/index.php?newsid=3850
337 http://www.natpressru.info/index.php?newsid=3850
338 http://www.natpressru.info/index.php?newsid=3850
339 http://www.natpressru.info/index.php?newsid=3850
340 http://www.natpressru.info/index.php?newsid=3850
341 http://www.natpressru.info/index.php?newsid=3850
342 http://www.natpressru.info/index.php?newsid=3850
343 http://www.natpressru.info/index.php?newsid=3850
344 http://www.natpressru.info/index.php?newsid=3850
345 http://www.natpressru.info/index.php?newsid=3850
346 https://www.onwar.com/aced/chrono/c1700s/yr60/russocircassian.htm
347 Circassian History (Kadir Natho)
348 https://aheku.net/fljok/files/3946/1-russo-circassian-war.pdf
349 Circassian History (Kadir Natho)
350 Circassian History (Kadir Natho)
351 Circassian History (Kadir Natho)
352 Circassian History (Kadir Natho)
353 Circassian History (Kadir Natho)
354 Circassian History (Kadir Natho)
355 Circassian History (Kadir Natho)
356 Circassian History (Kadir Natho)
357 Circassian History (Kadir Natho)
358 Circassian History (Kadir Natho)
359 Circassian History (Kadir Natho)

360 Circassian History (Kadir Natho
361 Circassian History (Kadir Natho)
362 Circassian History (Kadir Natho)
363 Circassian History (Kadir Natho)
364 http://www.geocurrents.info/place/russia-ukraine-and-caucasus/caucasus-series/dreams-of-a-circassian-homeland-and-the-sochi-olympics-of-2014
365 http://justicefornorthcaucasus.info/?p=1251676424
366 Circassian History (Kadir Natho)
367 http://www.geocurrents.info/place/russia-ukraine-and-caucasus/caucasus-series/dreams-of-a-circassian-homeland-and-the-sochi-olympics-of-2014
368 http://www.natpressru.info/index.php?newsid=3850
369 http://www.natpressru.info/index.php?newsid=3850
370 http://www.natpressru.info/index.php?newsid=3850
371 http://www.natpressru.info/index.php?newsid=3850
372 http://www.natpressru.info/index.php?newsid=3850
373 http://www.natpressru.info/index.php?newsid=3850
374 http://www.natpressru.info/index.php?newsid=3850
375 http://www.natpressru.info/index.php?newsid=3850
376 https://aheku.net/articles/english/history/1185
377 https://aheku.net/articles/english/history/1185
378 https://aheku.net/articles/english/history/1185
379 https://aheku.net/articles/english/history/1185
380 https://aheku.net/articles/english/history/1185
381 https://aheku.net/articles/english/history/1185
382 https://aheku.net/articles/english/history/1185
383 https://aheku.net/articles/english/history/1185
384 https://aheku.net/articles/english/history/1185
385 https://aheku.net/articles/english/history/1185
386 https://aheku.net/articles/english/history/1185
387 https://aheku.net/articles/english/history/1185
388 Circassian History (Kadir Natho)
389 http://justicefornorthcaucasus.info/?p=1165129260
390 http://justicefornorthcaucasus.info/?p=1165129260
391 http://justicefornorthcaucasus.info/?p=1165129260
392 http://windowoneurasia2.blogspot.com/2015/12/russian-pressure-on-circassians.html
393 http://www.brainyquote.com/quotes/quotes/d/desmondtut106145.html

4

A View on the Circassian Genocide

A Portrait indicating a Scene from the Caucasian war

The invading Russian forces perpetrated crimes of genocide and ethnic cleansing against the Circassian people, which are considered crimes against humanity, punishable under international law, which have no statute of limitations. These tragedies had devastating, serious, and painful repercussions where the effects had impacted the overall population of Circassia. With all its spectra, the urgent component that needs attention and to be addressed is the Adigha language that seems, in light of the current situation, sliding

145

towards the deep hollows of extinction. The language is closely linked with the necessary elements to maintain Circassian culture and what is associated with it, such as literature, prose, poetry, studies, arts, science, archiving, and handicraft and traditional industries. It is of importance for the Russians and the international community to recognize the genocide, the right of return, and the restoration of the legitimate rights, especially those that related to the right of self-determination based on international legitimacy.

On March 15, 2013, Walt Richmond published an article titled "Russia's Forgotten Genocide" on History News Network. The article has shed light on the tragic years of the Russian-Circassian War. He mentioned practices that the criminal Russian military units and commanders had practiced against the Circassians and their homeland. That was part of their evil intent to destroy all elements of a nation that suffered from imperial greed and invasion.

> The most destructive campaign came in the winter of 1822, when Ermolov's troops burned homes and food and rustled cattle, leaving the people to die from starvation and the elements. Often, they massacred entire villages. Ermolov's rampage left the entire district of Lesser Kabardia, which had been perennially loyal to Russia, completely depopulated. Ermolov continued his destruction of Kabardia until 1827. As a result, the Kabardian population dropped from 300,000 in 1790 to 30,000 in 1830.[394]

> The genocide Russia committed against the Circassian nation was unparalleled in the history of man in methods of brutality, in the scope of the military forces she deployed for that purpose, and in the duration of time she persisted to accomplish it. The Russo-Circassian War . . . was a part of the process of that genocide. The eviction of the Circassians from their native lands and the settlement of the Cossacks in them, (which was witnessed) during the Russo-Circassian War, was the beginning of the final stage of the completion of that well planned and systematically executed genocide.[395]

Obstinacy has been shown by the Russians, and it reflects a deep-seated grudge against all what is of the Caucasus and of Circassia. They forget or overlook that justice must be inevitably served, and all sides will regain their rights. What is regrettable, though, is that some people are maintaining strong ties of friendship with those who do not recognize that the Circassians have a Circassian homeland. They are denying them the right to exercise their legitimate rights and their right to their homeland, according to the Universal Declaration of Human Rights,[396] the United Nations Declaration on the Rights of Indigenous Peoples,[397] and even according to Russian laws. To consider the existence of a case that shall be defended by all legitimate ways and means requires hard work, and no one with a heart would condone that because the one who loses his homeland would lose everything; "truth will prevail, and the rest 'with the passage of time' will disappear."

Elaborating on the characteristics of four Circassian tribes (the Natuhay, Shapsug, Abzakh, and Ubykh), it is stated, "As a result, by the nineteenth century they far outnumbered all the other Circassian tribes combined. These were the people who refused to surrender to Russian demands, and in their frustration the Russian military command decided to eliminate them at any cost."[398]

Figures describe the events:

> In this long war attrition, the Circassians suffered heavy losses in terms of human life, as much as 800,000 dead, and their country fell into ruin. Many tribes were completely wiped out and others came close to the edge of extinction. The Shapsugh, who numbered about 300,000 before the war, were almost completely extirpated. The 3,000 survivors, great grandfathers of the present-day inhabitants of the Shapsugh region, either crossed the Kuban in flight or else found refuge in the mountains and forests. The residents of the last Shapsugh village, Tkha-ghapsh about 140 in number, were exiled to Siberia.[399]

It is reported that "all the Ubykhs, numbering about 30,000, chose to immigrate rather than be resettled in the Kuban region." In addition, it is reported that "this is perhaps the harshest and least known episode of genocide in history up to the start of War World I. The number of North Caucasians who left for the Ottoman Empire between 1859 and 1881 is estimated at two million. Conditions were extremely bad and as many as 20% died of malnutrition and disease."[400]

Instead of deportation to the Ottoman Empire, some inhabitants had accepted the bitterness of leaving their place of living to be displaced to the plains north of their original homeland.

> Those who remained in the Caucasus, between 150–200 thousand, were compiled to resettle in the northern plains of the Caucasus where they were easier to control. The mass

expulsion of the Abzakh and Beslanays, who occupied the central part of Circassian, meant that the NW Caucasians were physically separated into three main entities.[401]

The facts assert clearing the coast of the Black Sea of Circassians and to be resettled by others: "The northeast coast of the Black Sea was totally cleared of Circassian presence. The old country was ripe for Slavic and Cossack colonization." That came after either killing or forcing the Circassians away from their historic homeland and, later, dividing the nation: "It was a classic and evil practice of the Machiavellian maxim 'divide and rule'. Its worthy of note that during Soviet rule, four NW Caucasian entities were to be established along these divisions."[402]

Nowadays, attempts are made to divert historical events to a regressive course using the fact that the whole world is closing its eyes and ears, leaving the Circassians and their legitimate rights in a status that can be described as subject to indifference to the freedom of an oppressed nation whose homeland has been occupied now for more than 152 years.

> According to Michael Rothberg, there is a widespread understanding of collective memory as a zero-sum game that promotes the understanding of memory as competitive: "Fundamental to the conception of competitive memory is a notion of the public sphere as a pre-given, limited space in which already-established groups engage in a life-and-death struggle". If not literally a life-and-death struggle, this understanding for competitive memory corresponds in many ways to the wider Russian as well as to the North Caucasian contexts more specifically.[403]

The website Adyghe Hekum and Mak—Voice of Circassia quoted kavkasia. net as an informed source and published that the Georgian News Agency (GHN)[404] reported, "Russia categorically demanded from Georgia in the Georgian-Russian negotiations to repudiate the recognition of the Circassian Genocide and to stop the promotion for the topic." According to other sources, Russia also desires to remove the monument erected on the shore of the Black Sea resort of Anaklia, Georgia, commemorating the victims of the unequal and unfair war that took place between hundreds of thousands of well-trained soldiers and mercenaries of the tsarist Russian Empire against the indigenous nation of Circassia, which led to occupying of the entire Circassian homeland after a brutal war that lasted for almost one hundred years, with all its associated disastrous consequences.

Even if it is true, and Georgians have acquiesced to pressure exercised on them by the Russian state, that would not change facts and realities. Logic obliges the Georgian state to abide by ethical rules by not allowing withdrawal from their promises and covenants, which should be abided out of state self-respect and dignity of the nation, which is under examination in this live example. Not following the ethical principles would make the case look as if giving in to Russian demands; dictating others on what to do and what to say, in a method showing that they are in the lead and on top of events, in a manner giving themselves a "license to disrespect."

The article claimed that former senior Georgian officials have urged Circassians to refuse allowing Georgia to reconsider recognition of the genocide due to Russian pressure imposed on the newly elected party or coalition that formed the present Georgian government. Logic imposes noninterference in the internal affairs of Georgia. Others are trying to interfere in Georgian affairs and policies because the Georgian government and parliament are equally responsible and morally obliged, not only to support the legitimate rights of Circassians, but also to respect Georgian commitments concerning its self-esteem and towards other Caucasian nations.

Different parties have benefited from the disastrous consequences in varying proportions, but absolutely, the Circassians were the losers.

> This tragedy saved well three parties. The Russians conquered the unruly Caucasus and expelled the intractable Circassians. For the next 140 years, they were to face no serious challenge to their domination in the NW Caucasus. Turkey gained martial subjects whom she used to augment her waning military power. The third group that lobbied vigorously to bring the Circassians to Ottoman dominion was some of the exiled Adiga princes who were in dire need of the subjects to rule.[405]

The Circassians were obliged to do whatever was in their power to defend their nation.

> Perhaps Prince Seferbi Zhanoqwe's embassy in Constantinople in the 1830s affords a unique example of an attempt by the Circassians to rally support for their cause for their cause at the Porte. However, the Russians cowed the Turks into removing him from the capital, and he was subsequently of little help to his beleaguered compatriots.[406]

The Circassians being deported was a decision made by the Russian government that was represented by its armed forces and mercenaries. People had no choice but to abide by the instructions or get killed: "Uncompromising and disastrous decision, such as mass exodus, might have shown a tough national character, but the survival of a people on its homeland must at all times remain the first priority of its leaders."[407]

An article titled "The Ethnic Cleansing of the Circassians—A Silent Genocide?" written by Billy Hadaway refers to atrocities suffered by Circassians, which highlighted elements of the Circassian plight:

> Before the end of the wars in 1864, the Circassians (or Adyghe in their own language) that survived the massacres began to be rounded up by the Russian army and driven to ports on the Black Sea, where ships provided by the neighboring Ottoman Empire awaited them. From here the majority of Circassians were expelled, to be resettled away from their homeland to lands within the Ottoman Empire. Historians estimate that around 90% of the Circassian people were killed or exiled during this little-known genocide. Today, the Circassians number around 7 million people spread across the world, with the majority living in exile. Only 750,000 remain in their indigenous regions of the Northern Caucasus.[408]

Senior Russian military commanders and generals in the Caucasus had issued illegal orders. They wanted to resume the war by waging illegal Russian military operations. Their objective was to place a tool of induction of the Circassians against the Russians. Primarily, they wanted to create an atmosphere of instability to provoke the Circassians and other peoples of the Caucasus.

> So it appears that, after being thwarted in his official attempts to stop Russo-Circassian trade, Ermolov instructed Vlasov to carry out an unofficial campaign to reignite the Circassians' hatred of the Russians. His attacks on clans that were well-known Russian supporters-The Hamysh, Bjedukhs, and some Natuhay aristocrats-seem to leave little doubt.[409]

Insecurity was created, and accordingly, the Circassians were pushed again to the front lines to defend their very existence as a dignified nation. As usual, they were again victims of Russian treachery and oppression. They did not withhold any moment to defend themselves and their right to life. Simultaneously, the Russian propaganda campaign was revived again.

> Vlasov's actions succeeded in creating a state of intense hostility between the Circassians and the Russians. As collegial assessor Dmitry Kodinets of the College of Foreign Affairs reported in May 1827 to General Ivan Paskevich, Ermolov's successor: The innocent Circassians have been deprived of their property and have become animated by vengeance, in accordance with their customs, and having assembled in a significant mass have caused damage to our lines.[410]

How funny when any party finds itself in a suspicious situation. It is regrettable to be part of an agreement or treaty without being solicited or consented, especially when it comes to one's own destiny and self-determination. Such situations lead to discontent or embarrassment. This is one example that shows the way how large countries would share or exchange smaller peoples and nations without their prior knowledge.

> The Treaty of Adrianople was the deathblow to Kodinets' hopes; Emperor Nicholas now viewed the Circassians as legally bound subjects and wasted no time preparing for the conquest of Circassia. Already in November 1829 he issued orders for a "change of the system of relations with the mountaineers beyond the Kuban."[411]

All the elements and authorities of the Russian state have not respected their neighbors from all directions. Facts have proven that signed agreements with Russia did not last long. Whether interim or temporary ones, and in most cases, the Russian state has deliberately canceled or revoked any pledge. Circassia was never part of Russia except in colonialists' dreams.

> The first step in this new "system" was the removal of Scassi as director of trade relations in preparation for the complete suspension of Russo-Circassian commerce. The Circassians were no longer to be considered independent tribes to be dealt with through treaties and commercial cooperation but as imperial subjects to be ruled by governmental fiat.[412]

Circassians were, in all cases, in the midst of colonialist greed. The confusion and chaos that was experienced by the management of the Russian

Empire had made its plans for the future with no specific dates to meet: "As eager as the Russians were to bring Circassia under complete imperial control, though, they quite literally had no idea what they were in for."[413]

Russia has always played games regarding their imperial wars. At times, it has ignored facts and realities. When the Russians' plans did not work or were not properly implemented, they would blame anything but their negligence. They assumed the ignorance of others and pretend they did not see or hear. Accordingly, they failed to take certain measures, precautions, and decisions.

> General Grigory Filipson claimed that the emperor and his advisor "didn't even suspect that we were dealing with a one and a half million valiant, militaristic mountain dwellers who had never recognized any authority over them, and who possessed powerful natural fortresses at every step in their forest-covered mountain thickets". Filipson concluded that the emperor truly "thought that the Circassians were nothing more than rebellious Russian subjects, ceded to Russia by their legal sovereign the Sultan in the Treaty of Adrianople."[414]

Confusion of the Russian leadership made it difficult for themselves and their victims as well. It is no excuse to speculate on matters that pertain to a severe and long war that had broken out while they were the ones who started it. The legitimate question remains on who gave them the right to occupy and annex Circassia. Also, who is responsible for giving the Circassians their rights back?

> The projects the Russian government subsequently proposed for incorporating Circassia into the empire are proof that it had no idea what it was up against. Foreign Minister Nesserlode created a committee to establish a "Trans-Kuban Districs", and in early April 1830 the committee drew up a preliminary plan for administration of Circassia.[415]

The approaches of the Russian leadership were always nothing but a way of cunning and deception. They are never straightforward and to the point. They always get their way by twisted methods and tricks. Their twisted attitude is their predominant uniqueness, which is that they cannot be merciful or tolerant, even with the most vulnerable of human beings.

> Under "positive measures", the committee proposed that the "most influential" Circassian leaders should be invited

to an assembly "under the direction of the Caucasus Line Commander", where that they would be informed that Emperor Nicholas, "Generous in kindness and strict in justice, wishes to bring an end to the disorder in the Caucasus", and would be asked their opinions as to how "the Monarch's will" could most effectively to implemented.[416]

Random plans are drafted from bad ideas and pursued to be described as a "coincidence." All that aims to control the indigenous population in any way or form and thus control their homeland to be annexed to an expanding empire. Lies were always composed in a way to show that Russia acts in accordance with a certain criteria or doctrine, but reality proves the opposite.

The rest of the report recommends in great detail how the new district was to be divided and the tribes incorporated into a single administrative unit. Under "negative measures", the committee recommended a complete blockade of the Black Sea coast to stop all Turkish influence in Circassia and to destroy trade: "with the annihilation of the opportunity to market prisoners and other fruits of their thievery, the Caucasus tribes will no longer find any benefit in continuing their rapacious raids into the Russian districts that border them as well as between themselves."[417]

The perceived Russian strategy was to keep implementing their crisis management plan. Russia's comprehensive control and attaching the occupied territories with the Russian Empire was purely a colonial act. Citizens who intend to travel to the Russian regions need a visa. It is clear how the authorities are committing a crime of population screening and ethnic cleansing, in addition to other crimes.

A visa system was to be imposed to prevent free movement of Circassians in the empire, and markets were to be established in urban centers where the Circassians would be able to trade with Russians.[418]

The Circassian Question was neither treated nor solved in a proper way. Nevertheless, to solve the tragedies, the Russian authorities had to provide a solution. The Russian Empire wanted the Circassians to be the scapegoat of any solution or agreement. Of course, they wanted the Circassians to lay down their weapons in the one hand and the Russian authorities to eliminate or deport them away from their homeland on the other.

> If these plans hadn't had such tragic consequences, we could simply dismiss them as ridiculous. Despite three decades of almost nonstop hostilities, Nesselrode somehow believed that the announcement of "the Sovereign Emperor's" will would convince the Circassians to lay down their arms and submit to Russian rule.[419]

The "blame game" was a usual trick of the Russian exaggerators, who harbored hatred and are spiteful by nature towards the Circassians. A prudent observer is capable of exposing their insufficient evidence provided to discredit their victims, who had been invaded in their own homes. Their public policy eventually led to complicating and deterring facts.

> Likewise, the notion that a blockade impeding all trade would stop the Circassians' attacks could only be believed by someone who had not read (or believed) Kodients' report of 1827 that placed the blame for Circassian raids squarely on the shoulders of the Black sea Cossacks, not on any "rapacious" desire for booty.[420]

Anytime the Circassians were confronted, they acted according to the surrounding circumstances. They knew their rights and accordingly acted as such. Seemingly, the general situation and the state of war that was imposed on them had created guidelines and parameters for everyone in a position of responsibility to act without compromising their rights.

> As for the proposal to assemble the "most influential" Circassians in a meeting with the Russian military command, it was fantastic on two counts. First, there were no Circassians who were influential beyond their own tribes—this had always been the central problem with Circassian attempts at self-government. Second, the Abzakhs and Shapsugs still considered themselves at war with Russia and were confident in their ability to defend their homeland. The only "disorder" they wanted an end to was the Cossacks' presence.[421]

Most of the Russian troops and mercenary followers operated and planned in accordance with racist and criminal intentions. Apparently, they were brought up by those who had no problem in doing the "dirty work" to please their leaders and commanders. Human lives were never considered to be an obstacle when they committed any crime.

> In response to the report, Paskevich commissioned General Bekovich-Cherkassky to assess the situation and draw up specific recommendations. Bekovich-Cherkassky, the same former Kabardian Pshi who had slaughtered Kabardian women and children in the 1825 massacre of the Karamuze clan, submitted his report in fall 1830.[422]

They didn't care for human life and were not committed to values, laws, norms, or ethics. In doing what they did, they hoped that their leaders would thankfully approve and accept them. Their main concern was to continue the genocide that had begun earlier, no matter how long it would take.

> Bekovich repeated the Ermolov party line, warning that "by themselves, gentle measures that have not been preceded and supported by the force of arms are insufficient and even harmful', and proposing "the occupation of the locations that serve as the keys to their livelihood," thereby 'depriving them by force of arms of their most important means of survival."[423]

Criminal methods were accompanied by brutal, barbaric, and inhuman doggedness. This was just a stepping-stone to invasion, occupation, destruction, genocide, and forced deportation. They felt that there was no embarrassment in going ahead with their crimes if the end justified the means. They were completely committed to eliminate the Circassians, a top priority.

> In other words, starve the Circassians into submission. In his report to Nesselrode in June1831, Paskevich enthusiastically supported Bekovich's plan and enumerated fourteen measures to enact it, most of which had already been in use for thirty years. The sole innovation was the order that, after 'having caused the mountaineers to fell our might', Russian administration should be rapidly introduced.[424]

Changing and replacing officers and commanders in the Caucasus in general and Circassia in particular was normal Russian procedure. Periodical changes of jobs and command headquarters was a normal practice too.

Typically, they appointed the right people in accordance with the nature of military missions and operations to be planned and prepared for.

> How Paskevich, an experienced commander with intimate knowledge of the intractable situation in the Kuban region, could support a proposal so out of touch with reality is anyone's guess, but in any event he was replaced later that year by Alexei Velyaminov.[425]

William Shakespeare's quote would be consistent with the calamities that befell the Circassians because of colonial greed: "When sorrows come, they come not single spies, but in battalions." The Russian military campaign used terroristic methods with aggressive intentions including murder, destruction, and occupation.

> One very strange detail in military reports that deal with the destruction of homes and food is the absence of any mention of civilians. In the field notes of 1836, rarely does a page go by without mention of at least one aul being burned (forty-four were burned in October alone). Sightings of Circassian parties on horseback are occasionally mentioned, but there are no references to women and children anywhere.[426]

Human lives had no value in tsarist Russian military doctrine. There was not the slightest respect or appreciation of human life. The indigenous people's lives were not considered: "It is clear in some reports that the auls had been abandoned, but occasionally the aul is said to have been taken 'without resistance'. In one case, troops under Colonel Milenty Olshevsky burned two occupied auls, but again there was no mention of what happened to the villagers."[427]

They carried out satanic functions that anyone with a human conscience wouldn't accept: "Though this systematic neglect of the human victims of their campaigns the Russians reduced the war to a bureaucratic procedure. It is also at this time that the term ochishchenie (literally, 'cleansing') begins to appear in field reports in reference to the expeditions into the mountains."[428]

What a silly reason to use to annihilate an entire nation. It is not fair to have such generals and leaders to decide the presence and future of peoples and nations. People don't have to like Russia to be left alone: "The military commanders had already decided that the Circassians hated the Russians too much to ever become subjects of the Empire, so they worked toward their destruction."[429]

The names of the Russian leaders and generals are placed in black history records that they had created for themselves. They have proven to be monsters through their criminal acts against a nation that simply wanted to be free and independent.

> Once they concluded that the Circassians would be eliminated in any event, they began to treat them with increasing levels of brutality. Velyaminov, Zass, Serebryakov, and others were the pioneers who laid the ideological and tactical foundations that Nikolai Evdokimov would employ in the 1860s to commit genocide.[430]

Russian communal chaos and functional improvised acts made it almost impossible to be able to defeat the Circassian forces. That kept going on throughout decades of war, siege, and sanctions, but they couldn't implement their goals. Deadly policies were adopted such as a scorched-earth policy, in addition to the elimination of the entire nation or to be deported away from their homeland. They succeeded when they followed diabolical plans that indicated intense hatred.

> One reason why the Russians turned to genocide as a solution to the Circassian issue was that they could never develop a coherent plan for subjecting them to Russian rule. Although Raevsky's efforts to conquer the Shapsugs in 1838 met with total failure, in January 1839 Russian minister of war Alexander Chernyshev proposed virtually the same plan.[431]

A realistic impression given probably about the first group of Circassians who arrived at a deserted land that was abandoned hundreds of years ago. As expected, the settlers were described to have suffered "physical and psychological damage." It is not unusual to have such an impression about terrified people. This is a testimony about those who witnessed the tragedies of war, endured its horrors, being driven out of their homeland by force of arms and spent a tough time traveling by ship.

> In 1881 British captain Claude Conder arrived in Amman during a campaign against Druze tribesmen. The town had been uninhabited as recently as 1876, and Circassian migrants were just beginning to reclaim the ancient site of Philadelphia.

Conder described the physical and psychological damage the settlers were suffering and painted a less than hopeful portrait.[432]

The Circassians' displacement and deportation, with all its repercussions, did not end in one place; but it was for some of them to move by ships to other places especially from the Balkan areas. They were transferred by the authorities of the Ottoman Empire to the edges and outskirts of the empire. That eventually at the end took them to the Arabic parts of the empire, which Jordan was one of them.

> The Circassian colony at Amman is one of several planted by the Sultan in Peraea. These unhappy people, chased from their homes by the Russians, and again driven from their new settlements in European Turkey by the late war, are now scattered in the wilderness, where land has been assigned them to cultivate.[433]

The British officer continued drawing a bleak picture of the depressing situation that found the Circassians in Amman. He depicted an image that detects how Circassians came out of a furnace of war. A disaster followed, which included death, destruction, displacement, hunger, and disease. They ended up settling in new environments and surroundings, which they had to adapt to and get used to dealing with the demographic dimension.

> They have, however, the listless and dispirited look of exiles who find it impossible to take root in the uninviting district to which they have been sent. Hated by the Arabs and the Fellah, despoiled of money and possessions, and having seen many of their bravest fall or die of starvation, they seem to have no more courage left, and will probably die out by degrees, or become scattered among the indigenous population."[434]

Considering their experiences and difficult times during their voyage of genocide and deportation, they were skeptical of everything. The arrival of the British military pushed them to bear in mind several possibilities.

> Our appearance at Amman at once aroused their apprehensions. They believed us to be the pioneers of a power which was about to seize the country, and anxiously inquired

> whether they would be allowed to remain where they were in case of an English or French occupation.[435]

Through the incidental dialogue with the Circassians, they were introduced to the hanging problems in the region. That witnessed the beginning of the British and French intervention in the region before the end of the Ottoman rule. This is quite different from the Russian invasion and occupation of the Circassian homeland, where they had to bear the consequences of that disaster alone.

> It was in vain that I protested that our work had no connection with politics. The Emir begged to be made the confidant of a secret which, he insisted, we knew, and I was at length obliged, in order to get rid of him, to express the opinion, that whether French or English took Syria, there was no reason to suppose his settlement would be disturbed, or that he would (as he seemed chiefly to fear) be given up to the tender mercies of Russia.[436]

Quoting the British officer's last quoted few lines, he stressed on the first impressions about the people he met; but this time, he mentioned also the ambitious imperialists and colonialists: "It is from such incidents, not less than from the faces of the dead looking skyward on the field of battle, that a man may judge of the sorrow which is brought upon the weak and poor by the restless ambition of conquering races."[437]

Richmond continued elaborating on the same subject (the Circassians of Amman), where he stated that another visitor passed by the area at a later date. It turns out that there is a difference of the situation between what it was like in the region upon the arrival of the Circassians and the situation after two decades. This has proven that always they have been a positive element in any place they lived.

> Despite the overwhelming challenges and the bleak prospects of success, the Circassians survived. Less than twenty years later, Miss A. Goodrich Freer passed through quite a different town: A sudden turning at the ford of a rapid stream revealed the town of Amman, lying in a narrow valley between low but precipitous hills. Most of us were utterly unprepared, after six hours of riding across a lonely tableland, to find an orderly town of 10,000 inhabitants, of an aspect of superior to anything we had seen since leaving

Jerusalem, or even, so far as the actual town is concerned, to Jerusalem itself, that an explanation seemed necessary, and the statement that the population was Circassian was, geographically, an added perplexity. The houses, built partly of mud brick and partly of ancient material like those of Madaba, were well placed, most had porticos and balconies, and some were enclosed with well-swept yards.[438]

It was stated that deportees started adjusting to the new communities that they founded and constructed. Diaspora's pros and cons are mentioned, which included the inevitable dissolving process in the society that the Circassians live in. It eventually led to loss of national contacts.

As time passed, the Circassians who settled in Syria, Palestine, and particularly Transjordan established a good life and even prospered. At the same time, the process of assimilation took its toll and put up barriers between the migrants, their homeland, and each other.[439]

Disasters at sea, as a result of meteorological conditions and an absence of seaworthiness, had contributed to damages and even loss of lives. Ambiguity was always the master of situations, where the conspirators played around with the destiny of the Circassians without their previous knowledge. How could thousands of people board a ship while no one onboard knows their destination?

The voyage of the Austrian streamer Shinx was a grim portent of the coming trials. In March 1878, after having been chased out of Rumelia, about three thousand Shapsugs once again found themselves at sea headed for unknown territory. Intending to land at Latakia, Syria, a storm washed forty people overboard and forced the ship to seek refuge in Cypriot port. There several hundred more were killed when the ship caught fire.[440]

The displaced people were exposed to uncomfortable and inappropriate weather conditions. They were faced with harsh living and health conditions, both on Circassia's coast of the Black Sea before boarding the ships heading to Ottoman ports or at the ports of arrival. Apparently, the coordinating authorities chose where to take the deportees, who had no choice where to go or where to live.

Those who succeeded in making it to Syria were held in the same primitive conditions as they were on the Black Sea coast, the Turkish shores, and the refugee camps in Greece and Istanbul. Utterly disillusioned, many asked if they could return to Rumelia and live under Christian rule.[441]

Circassians were expelled away from their point of origin, just to satisfy the desires of greedy aspirants. Seemingly, they accepted destiny. Reality drove them to a final destination that they didn't know about or even dream of before. They had to restart their entire life from nothing. An example is when the Circassians arrived at Amman and lived in caves and between the Roman ruins.

Some Turks were granted permission, but the European powers refused to allow the Circassians to return. Once assigned a new location, the refugees had to cross desert terrain the likes of which they had never seen to reach the wilderness where they would have to build their new lives.[442]

Sending people as cargo to wild destinations was a way to secure the crumbling empire. The Ottomans intended to send the Circassians who were stripped of their homeland as reason of conspiracy between the beneficiaries. They wanted to grab the land, distribute it to the newly arrived immigrants to cultivate, collect revenues of tax, and at the same time, to strengthen the empire's presence in the region.

As always, the Porte had more than the welfare of the refugees in mind. Shipping them to Syria would have two benefits: the settlers could reclaim barren land and add to the agricultural output of the empire, and perhaps more importantly could serve as a stabilizing force in the region against the Bedouins and Druze.[443]

The Levant was an important part of the Ottoman Empire. It used to have the main overland hajj route that linked between Turkey and the Hijaz, which included Mecca and Medina. It was essential for the Ottomans to have appropriate human elements who can secure the way and to consolidate the empire's domination. The beginning of the twentieth century had witnessed constructing the Hejaz Railway to connect Turkey with Medina. That needed protection from bandits and local rebel groups.

With this in mind, the Porte sent tens of thousands of Circassians to Syria and Transjordan, where they became true pioneers. There was no government and certainly no law enforcement. The lands given to them were technically Ottoman property, but the Bedouins considered the Circassians squatters on their pastures and appropriators of their springs.[444]

The Circassians were not prepared to communicate and deal with other peoples with different languages. That became another task, which they had to speak and deal by mastering other languages such as Turkish and Arabic for people who were finally destined to Arab lands. There was suspension that the Circassians' role would be for the protection of the interests of the Ottoman Empire.

It was also clear that the Circassians had been sent there as agents of the Sultan and were loyal Ottoman subjects. Because Arab nationalism was on the rise, such people could not be met with anything other than suspicion. The Circassians also looked different, dressed strangely, and, like many minorities, kept to themselves. A few may have known some Turkish, but at first none spoke anything but the most rudimentary Arabic.[445]

Despite the difficulties encountered on their way during the deportation process of the agonizing voyage, others didn't comprehend the disastrous details. It wasn't the mistake of the Circassians nor the ignorance of the host peoples to discover differences of habits and traditions of peoples they never met before. This could be described as culture shock due to a cultural gap of peoples living in the nineteenth century at the time. Circassians couldn't visualize or comprehend what had occurred and why they were brought forcibly to this region.

Their traditions frequently conflicted with Arab mores too. For example, traveler Jane Hacker mentioned that the Arabs were horrified when they saw Circassian men and women dancing together at celebrations. Sometimes trouble became too much and the Porte would intervene and even round up particularly aggressive tribes, but for the most part the Circassians were on their own.[446]

> To be fair, the Porte did attempt to settle some refugees in the more hospitable areas near the coast in Lebanon and Palestine, but stories of Circassian 'atrocities' in Bulgaria had reached the Christians of Lebanon, making conflict likely if Circassians were settled there.[447]

Potential political, social, and national problems in multiple magnitudes were possible to erupt in certain areas. That would affect the whole stable situation. Circassians happened to observe that in many areas they had settled in: "Farther south, Palestine was just being claimed by Eastern Europe Jews as a safe place for emigration from Russian chauvinism, and the Sultan thought it wise not to settle more Muslims in that particular region."[448]

Terrorism was imposed as the empire's policy against Circassia and other nations of the Caucasus. Their objective was to conquer all of them to be annexed to tsarist Russia. Horrors were practiced by tyrant military commanders who didn't pay attention to anything except to accomplish their mission of averting decades of failure.

> Ermolov was the quintessential frontier conqueror. He was the first to employ a comprehensive strategy for the subjugation of the Caucasus highlands, and his ruthless methods would be used, in one form or another, by tsarists, Bolsheviks, and Russian generals into the twenty-first century. He was one of the pioneers of Russia's permanent war on its southern periphery, the longest-running conflict in the history of the empire and one that has continued to plague Russian strategists, in rather different forms, up to the present day. His tenure marked the start of long series of wars of conquest in the upland Caucasus, which would come to a close only in 1864.[449]

The offending actions were orchestrated by the military commanders, who did not pay attention to humanitarian standards and the need for leaving the people alone. The worst scenario had struck them when the malicious indulgence of transfiguration in criminal acts created a disaster. That enabled Russian forces to achieve some of their long-awaited dreams. They chased the people away on individual and group bases, depending on the situation.

> For generations of indigenous mountaineers he was the dreaded "Yarmul" who razed villages and slaughtered families. Although he gained the supreme confidence of one

tsar, Alexander I, he was treated with suspicion by another, Nicholas I. He was responsible for implementing a series of policies that were at the time hailed as vehicles for civilizing the benighted Caucasus frontier but that today might well be called state-sponsored terrorism.[450]

Facts have proven that the Russian Empire also contributed in exporting all its corruption and other administrative problems to all entities that eventually became subjects with no rights. The areas that Russia had occupied and controlled in the end consequently attached to a usurper entity. Circassians, like others, had ever since endured the Muscovites' gambles and atrocities for more than 450 years.

Brutal wars were waged against tens of nations: "Enter Ivan the Terrible, the first tsar. He put into practice the concept of attack as defense—consolidating one's position at home and then moving outward. Russia had begun a moderate expansion under Ivan's grandfather, but Ivan accelerated it after he came to power in the 16th century."[451]

He built his fame and glory from his many conquests.

> Russia gained access to the Caspian, and later the Black Sea, thus taking advantage of the Caucasus Mountains as a partial barrier between itself and the Mongols. Ivan built a military base in Chechnya to deter any would-be attacker, be they the Mongol Golden Horde, the Ottoman Empire, or the Persians.[452]

> During Ermolov's decade in the field, Russia became an empire based on the complex policies of bribery, cajoling, and trickery associated with the Muscovites' earliest advances into the north Caucasus but rather on the war-fighting techniques then being developed by other empires around the world: wanton destruction of property, mass deportation, and indiscriminate killing—all committed in the name of bringing true freedom and enlightenment to backward tribal peoples. The political landscape of the Caucasus also began to change.[453]

At the time, the names of the Russian generals and officers no longer indicated any importance. They laid down their landmarks, which in certain cases, had their own fingerprints, styles, and characters. The colonial policy and invasion that drew the evil path pursued by the colonial empire in subsequent years had become landmarks to follow. The evil empire was known by its acts left on dozens of colonized peoples, which were annexed by force and terrorism.

> By the time Ermolov was dismissed from his post in 1827, the Caucasus was no longer an imperial borderland that embraced various forms of autonomy and accommodation. It was quickly becoming a place defined by the full incorporation of outlying regions into a centralized state. Through Ermolov's efforts, Russia's possessions in the Caucasus moved from being part of a premodern imperial order toward becoming, for better or worse, part of a fitfully modern one.[454]

Reckless overconfidence is a way of forfeiture. It will be an involvement of temptation to get inappropriate gains. Imparting extraordinary importance by any individual will lead to bypassing laws, ranks, seniority, and other considerations: "He was not yet forty when he became one of the most highly decorated officers in the empire, a central figure in the transition from the Catherinian wars to the campaigns Tsar Alexander I."[455]

To grant a respect to the word "civilization," it has to be mentioned in the proper view to mean what suits the description. What is the purpose of civilization, which was forced randomly on a person or a state? Human civilization should be based on the proper concept. When "the edge of civilization" description is used, murder, destruction, and genocide should be outside the scope of civilization; and there is no other logical clarification.

> Ermolov saw himself as an imperial commander, one serving on the very edge of civilization, in which the toughness and resolve of the finest Roman generals had to be combined with an unbending will to use barbaric tactics against the barbarians themselves. "I desire that the terror of my name," he once declared, "should guard our frontiers more potently than chains or fortresses." Even more important, Ermolov was an artilleryman, not a cavalry officer like other commanders in the Caucasus theatre. That professional orientation, combined with his self-image as a bearer of enlightenment, contributed to the nature of Russian military planning under his leadership.[456]

At the time, Russian troops and their allies had used lethal weapons against their victims. The Circassians used bayonets, swords, and spears; some of them had managed to get primitive pistols and rifles. Yes, they used their extreme courage, but eventually, abundance had overcome courage. The Russians managed to build barricades, defensive centers, and forts in addition to marine posts to penetrate Circassian territories to controlling them.

> Ermolov appreciated the power of modern weaponry. He had seen it up close during the Napoleonic Wars: the devastating effects of canon on wood, stone, and flesh; and the ability of mobile field guns to decimate infantry and frustrate a cavalry charge. Ermolov's plan involved the construction of a series of new, larger forts that would serve as anchors for military operations in the central Caucasus.[457]

The Circassians had no choice but to resist Russian policies: "This in turn, demanded a clear understanding of highlander tactics, good intelligence, a forward military presence, and above all the stomach to carry the war to the highlanders themselves, including putting aside any scruples about destroying villages, forests, and any other place where raiding parties might seek refuge."[458] The Russian troops proceeded to kill people and to destroy the infrastructure of the Circassian. It included population's settlements, farms, warehouses, and other properties: "Targeted assassinations, kidnappings, the killing of the entire families, and the use of misappropriate force in response to small-scale raids were to become central to Russian operations the opening decades of the nineteenth century."[459]

He was using games and tricks even if they didn't coincide with the laws and norms that state or military establishments recognize: "Ermolov, then commander of the lines, decided to take his own hostages by ordering the arrest of the local notables through whose lands Shvetsov and his captors had passed. The ploy seemed to work, for the ransom was eventually reduced to ten thousand rubles—still an enormous figure at the time—and Shvetsov was released."[460]

Those who were educated of them constantly used provocative expressions in an abusive manner, which was meant to assault, abuse, and change the facts. There was nothing that prevented them from disclosing their intentions and plans that were executed or that were in the process of being implemented. Even if Circassians hated them, didn't they ask themselves why, who brought destruction to the homeland of others?

> The Circassians hate us. We have forced them out of their free and spacious pasturelands; their auls are in ruins, whole tribes have been annihilated. As time goes on, they move

deeper into the mountains, and direct their raids from there
... What can one do with such people?[461]

Misleading was the name of the Russians. Have the Russians forgotten that most Russian citizens had their rights denied, and they lived under harsh conditions? The people reached a deplorable status. Is it enough reason to twist facts if some members of the ruling class and those who are around them visited European countries and accessed knowledge from their institutes? Would it make them feel that their state and their people are at the level of prestigious European countries at the time? Does that give them the right to downgrade or demote other peoples who had a proven civilized history for thousands of years?

> Russia in order to deceive the world, conceals the very object of her continual warfare against us and ours. She diffuses the report amongst the civilized world that she is fighting the Circassians simply because they are a savage, uneducated and unruly people.[462]

It is appropriate to say that this is considered another trick of showing professional but lame excuses. The greedy will of reaching the "warm waters" and conquest of Circassia doesn't mean to follow sleazy provocative methods. Religion was not the reason for all the crimes and misconduct. The boundaries of the Russian's dreams were unlimited. They were unfamiliar with matters when they started their adventures. Development took place during the subsequent years.

When the Russian-Circassian War started in 1763, less than half of the Circassian population were Muslims. While reality indicates that the genuine reasons were race and imperial and colonial intentions, "it is easy to think of north Caucasus as an Islamic wall blocking the expansion of Russia toward Christian populations in the south such as the Georgians and Armenians, as well as toward the warm waters of the Mediterranean and the Persian Gulf, 'the north Caucasus barrier', as it has been called."[463]

The Russian military's cruel behavior was a technique that they decided to follow. Their reckless, but stubborn tactics of military intervention were severely conducted. They made their soldiers and mercenaries prone to inevitable injury or death. They were considered intruders and invaders. As a result, resistance was activated by those who were defending their homes. They were to guard their historic homeland, which successive generations had lived in.

As per the Russian statistics, the counting of their casualties in the Caucasus probably did include the unorganized mercenary groups, which were not considered members of the army. The casualties and death figures between the years 1763–1801 are missing. They must start counting from zero. Even the figures of the indigenous population are not realistic.

> From the annexation of eastern Georgia in 1801 until the end of the Circassian campaigns in 1864, as many as twenty-four thousand Russian soldiers and eight hundred officers were killed in the Caucasus wars, plus perhaps three times that number wounded and captured. (The loss on the native side, while probably far higher, are impossible to calculate.)[464]

The Russian invasion seemingly was taken lightly at the beginning; but as time passed, strategies, tactics, and even objectives were seriously changed, developed, and promoted: "From the late 1820s until the early 1860s conquest meant something entirely different, namely, counter-insurgency, not the older imperial techniques of persuading, cajoling, and redrawing borders, which had worked in Georgia or the Khanates of the southeast."[465]

Out of principle for the right of self-defense, the Circassians were free to defend their territories against the invasion of tsarist Russian forces. They swept the Circassian areas between the coast of the Black Sea, the high mountains, deep valleys, and the interspersed plains. They established military strongholds to enable them to continue their operations. The Circassians never admitted that they approved abandoning their homeland under any title.

> But the real Circassians—the native Adyta peoples of the northwestern Caucasus—proved to be a persistent problem for Russian officialdom. They attacked Russian forts along the Black Sea coast and raided settlements north of the Kuban River. They repeatedly affirmed that their region had long been independent, not a part of the Ottoman Empire, and that the sultan therefore had no right to cede their territory to the tsar as he had done in 1829 under the terms of the Treaty of Adrianople.[466]

Contacts and making alliances with tsarist Russia doesn't mean in any way that the Circassians were incorporated in or attached with such an entity, even if there were a few Circassian chiefs who were friendly or even had family relations and links with the tsar. Those chiefs or clan leaders represented themselves and probably their clans only and not all the Circassian tribes.

The Circassian nation was the last to be entirely subjugated.

The Circassians were both the first and last of the indigenous peoples of the Caucasus to be incorporated into the Russian Empire. The earliest formal contacts between Russia and Circassian communities date to the sixteenth century. The Circassian-speaking Kabardians of the northwest Caucasus lowlands were important allies of the Muscovites in their efforts to counter the depredations of the Crimean Tatars. Yet there were also those who consistently resisted Russian rule, continuing the fight even after the capitulation of Shamil.[467]

Regretfully, Circassia discovered itself in the clutches of predatory monsters that wanted to devour their prey, but only at the right time, in the absence of others: "Throughout the nineteenth century the Circassians were of considerable interest to strategists in western Europe. In the early part of the century the French worked to obtain preferential trading rights with them. Later the Circassian cause came to play a particular role in the overall strategy of Britain, Russia's main rival in the Near East."[468]

The Circassians' reputation and presence had existed in the Western world. Their elegance and decency, in addition to dressing, grooming, and the way they looked, were associated with handsome Circassians. They were described as such while wearing their national costumes. People who met the Circassians were impressed. People that met them had shown appreciation and admiration for their dealings, gentleness, and morals. Thus, how could such people's qualities be as the Russians always try to claim?

It was through the Circassians' place in the grand gambits of the "Great Game" that their reputation as noble freedom fighters first became cemented in the Western imagination. It is no exaggeration to say that for several decades in the middle of the nineteenth century "Circassia" became a household word in many parts of Europe and North America. Correspondents from major newspapers found their way to Circassia or gleaned information from foreign consuls and merchants in Trebizond and Constantinople.[469]

In terms of Circassian affairs, which were met with deaf ears in the nineteenth century, the great powers of the time that had international weight did not utilize their moral duty towards the nation that the Russian Empire deliberately destroyed. Most of the population was annihilated, ethnically cleansed, or deported. All this took place gradually and slowly but surely. The occupation and annexation to the Russian Empire were of top priority.

> The "Circassian Question", the political status of the northwestern highlands of the Caucasus, was debated in parliaments and gentlemen's clubs. For a time in the 1830s British spies crisscrossed the region, seeking to mold the desperate Circassian tribes into a unified military force. In fact, even the Circassian national flag—which bears the stars-and-arrows design that today can be found flying across the northwest Caucasus and among the ethnic Circassian diaspora—was the handiwork of David Urquhart, a querulous Scottish publicist who became the highlanders' chief intercessor in the West and took on their cause as his own.[470]

Despite the appeals and messages sent by the Circassians to the Ottoman Empire and the nations of Europe at the time, they were not heeded. Also, citizens of European countries who had visited Circassia transferred the real image of the situation to their home countries, but there was no response. Consequently, Circassian delegations that were sent to those countries to explain the nature of the crimes that were committed got the message to reach those countries.

> In a plaintive letter to Queen Victoria two Circassian leaders tried to explain the difficulties of coordinated action: "During the Crimean War, we were accused by the Allied Powers of want of sincerity, not having participated with them against our common foe," they wrote a few years after the war's end. "This is true, but it was not the fault of our nation, as it proceeded from want of union and energy between our leaders."[471]

The opportunistic Russian Empire had always acquired the proper moment to clear itself from other tasks in order to place its attention and capabilities in eliminating the Circassians: "The conclusion of the war in Dagestan and Chechnya, followed by the end of the Crimean conflict, allowed Russian planners to turn their full attention to the continuing struggle against the Circassians. The new military offensive that ensued would mark the final chapter in the Caucasus wars the nineteenth century and the beginning of a long history of Circassian exile."[472]

Circassia 171

All abusive military acts carried out by the Russian Empire's troops were intended to terrorize the people. The native people were murdered, and their villages were destroyed. Their eventual plan was the implementation of the tsarist Russians' evil intentions. Chaos in their operations and the multitude of the targets drove them to be elastic, taking their time and repeating the crimes.

> From the earliest days of Russian movement into the Caucasus, the rearrangement of populations was an essential part of the empire's political and military strategy. The burning of crops and destruction of villages, on their own, were imperfect methods of ensuring obedience. Crops could be replanted and houses rebuilt. After any particular campaign season, Russian troops might return to a previously pacified area to find villagers once again providing assistance to the native resistance.[473]

Criminal conclusions indicate that certain inhuman acts against the native inhabitants assisted in carrying out the imperial policies: "In time Russian commanders came to understand that the complete dislocation of populations could ensure that communities conquered during one season did not become rebels during the next."[474]

For people to imagine t an entire ancient nation in the Caucasus that was exposed to genocide: The vast majority of those who survived were deported to an unknown fate—what a unique but evil event in itself. Wartime extrajudicial verdicts were quickly reached and were committed against the biggest people in the Caucasus at the time. Wicked and immoral sentences by a military junta, which represented the emperor, were given against the whole people.

> In a policy memorandum of 1857 Dmitrii Miliutin, chief of staff to Bariatinski, summarized the new thinking on dealing with the northwestern highlanders. The idea, Miliutin claimed, was not to clear the highlands and coastal areas of Circassians so that these regions could be settled by productive farmers, as had happened in other parts of the empire's periphery. Rather eliminating the Circassians was to be an end by itself—to cleanse the land of hostile elements.[475]

The displacement plan, which was at one stage called resettlement, was meant to resettle the land with Russians and Cossacks while deporting the original population without permission. This was colonial invasion and occupation: "Tsar Alexander II formally approved the resettlement plan, with the goal of moving Circassians out of the Caucasus and into the lowlands along the Kuban River. Miliutin who would eventually become minister of war, was to see his plans realized by the early 1860s."[476]

All military commanders who were stationed in various locations were overseeing the brutal operations against the Circassians. They followed vacating the Circassian homeland from its inhabitants in any way possible. In addition to other crimes, odious racism was practiced against one of the most rooted nations in the Caucasus. Using religion as a cause of all the despicable atrocities mentioned above is not a compelling reason. Religion neither incites violence nor murder and usurpation of others' rights.

> In a series of sweeping military campaigns lasting from 1860 to 1864—overseen by Miliutin in St. Petersburg, Bariatinskii in Tiflis, and Nikolai Evdokimov, commander of the right flank, in the highlands—the northwest Caucasus and the Black Sea coast were virtually emptied of Muslim villagers. Columns of the displaced were marched either to the Kuban plains or toward the coast for transport to the Ottoman Empire, which had earlier made provision for resettling Muslim co-religionists.[477]

The unprecedented crimes committed against humanity included all Circassian clans and tribes without exception. The results for those who committed them were impressive. The part of that was inhabited by people was ethnically cleansed and deported. Villages did not survive the inevitable destruction. Soldiers and mercenaries romped and had fun executing Russian command, which required the elimination of the Circassian element.

> One after another, entire Circassian tribal groups were dispersed, resettled, or killed en masse.
> As Russian forces moved farther and farther into the northwest Caucasus uplands, lists of groups targeted for expulsion were drawn up and orders given to move them out of their villages and down to the coast. Russian detachments would march up through river valleys on the north slope, cresting the peaks and then pushing people toward the Black Sea on the other side.[478]

All Russian government authorities and branches had the ability to carry out savage operations of unspeakable cruelty. It is incomprehensible that the invasion and occupation authorities would ruminate then invent their own terminology, which had no legitimacy. How would they describe Circassians that had risen in a rebellion against tsarist Russia while the situation was totally on the contrary? The Circassians and other peoples of the Caucasus were resisting the aggressors who came to take over and dominate their own countries forcibly.

> Russian diplomats repeatedly assured their European colleagues that the expulsions were not meant to be bloody, and that removing the highlanders was the only way to extinguish banditry and organized rebellion. "The war in the Caucasus will not be completely terminated until our soldiers have cross all the mountain ranges and have expelled the last inhabitants," a correspondent for the Journal de St. Petersbourg wrote, "but it is to be hoped, at least, that we will no longer encounter stubborn resistance anywhere and that, because of their numerical weakness, the tribes that remain in the highland gorges will no longer offer us the least bit of danger."[479]

Regrettably, the troops that carried out the repression, killings, and displacement of others did not have human feelings of pity or compassion, but showed spontaneous and automatic treachery and maltreatment and revel. Comprehensive immigration of the whole community had all the categories of Circassian society with no exception. If the Russians had to do something, it is that it should not have involved itself in such criminal mazes.

> The scale of emigration and the suffering experienced by refugees on the coast seem to have taken the Russians by surprise. Circassians not only arrived with their families and their possessions but also with slaves, livestock, and other people and goods. Few provisions had been made for housing them or for safely transporting them either to the Kuban River or, if they desired, to Ottoman ports. It was not until 1862 that a special state commission was established and funding appropriated to organize transport across the seal. While the Russians had long been acquainted with many of the largest and most powerful tribal groupings in the western Caucasus, the final campaign revealed the existence of additional communities about whom the Russians knew little. In one instance, a secretary in the Russian foreign ministry informed Lord Napier, the British Ambassador,

that a previously unknown tribe had been discovered in the mountains. They, too, were scheduled for expulsion.[480]

The voyage of a nation from an original and historic homeland to a new homeland was long and harsh. Unpleasant surprises punctuated throughout the way that was lacking human touches. Harsh and adverse environmental and weather conditions afflicted tens of thousands of displaced people with ailments as a result of physical weakness, as well as the spread of diseases and epidemics and the death of hundreds of people on the way to destination ports.

In the terms of the numbers of individuals and families scrutinized by Russian, Ottoman, and British officials resident in the ports of embarkation or arrival. In December 1863, there were already 7,000 immigrants in Trebizond, with 3,000 more arriving in only three days in February 1864. By May there were 25,000 camped around Trebizond and another 40,000 at Samsun. As many as 150 were dying each day from disease and starvation. In September 4,000 people arrived in Smyrna, with 2,346 arriving in Cyprus in November, all in similarly deplorable conditions. A sense of the scale of death and disease can be gained from the number of people who passed through the Bosphorus—and could therefore be counted by health inspectors—on their way to resettlement in western Anatolia and Balkans.[481]

Physical and mental efforts were given by those who were interested in the development, fate, and destinations of the displaced. The displaced across the Black Sea were sent onboard ships to Ottoman ports in Turkey, Bulgaria, and others as if they were cargo and not people: "In the first nine months of 1864 alone there were just over 74,000. To that number, of course, must be added the many who were shipped directly to Western Black Sea ports, such as Varna, or were dispersed overland from Trebizond."[482]

Deportees were compressed into maritime transport ships that didn't have their seaworthiness tested or certified. They were of various kinds and sizes, but the common factor overall was in the way that the oppressed indigenous people were dealt with. This took place in the light of international conspiracy against their nation and their own destiny, the urgency to transfer the deportees from the Circassian coast of the Black Sea to anywhere.

Conditions during the passage were inhuman. Refugees—as many as 1,800 per ship—were squeezed onto sailing vessels provided by the Ottomans or by the Russian government. Livestock and household goods crowded the decks. Those who could not secure a place on a larger ship took to the sea in small boats, which often foundered during the Black Sea's frequent storms. Even on the more stable vessels, overcrowding led to dehydration and produced outbreaks of disease. The bodies of the dead were thrown overboard and washed up on the beaches along the entire eastern stretch of the Black Sea.[483]

To complete the picture, the passengers were like cargo goods. Such a gloomy atmosphere, there was nowhere to go, except where the ship would navigate to. Ships would make their voyages to where they would lay their worthwhile load. They would head to the coasts and ports that would accept disembarking the displaced deportees. The passengers had left their homeland behind and were forced to travel to places they never thought of before under unfair and discriminatory conditions.

These "floating graveyards", as contemporary observers called them, would sail into Ottoman ports with only a remnant of their original human cargo alive. Once the refugees arrived in the Ottoman lands, there were frequently too few provisions for them. Food, clothing, fuel, and medicine were scarce. Public health was threatened as dead bodies were carelessly buried or abandoned, sometimes even finding their way into freshwater reservoirs in the port cities. "Circassia is gone", concluded a foreign diplomat in a report from May 1864. "What yet remains to save is the Circassians."[484]

The consistent methods of assault had been linked with criminal repercussions. The liquidation, abuse, cleansing, foreigners' settlement, and the uprooting of the indigenous people from their homes is consequently how the situation became. The various Circassian regions and territories were evacuated from their indigenous population. Statistics show the number of tribal people who were in their territories and transported to exile.

By the middle of the 1860s, the traditional lands of the Abzakh, Shapsug, Ubykh, and other Circassian tribal groups had been abandoned. As a local saying had it, even a woman could now travel easily between the harbor cities of Sujuk Kale and Anapa since she could be assured of never meeting a single person on the way. A decade prior to the expulsions, there were perhaps 145,000 people living in the Abkhaz lands and another 315,000 Circassians belonging to various tribes, plus tens of thousands of other coastal and highland peoples.[485]

After the majority of Circassians were dispersed by the mid-1860s, they were settled in the Ottoman Empire as per the Ottoman authorities' requirements. The remaining Circassians in the North Caucasus, apparently, were inhibited in areas imposed by the Russian Empire military units in the Caucasus. That was according to the plan prepared in advance and in accordance with situation changes, due to local conditions in different geographical areas.

Yet at the time of the first general imperial census in 1897, there were only about 60,000 people living on the coasts of Circassia, and of those only 15,000 had been born there. Among these were the last remnants of the populations now exiled across the sea, as well as the offspring of the first generation of Russian settlers who had been sent to take their place. "In the mountains of the Kuban district one can now find bears and wolves", wrote one observer, "but no highlanders."[486]

The Systematic Annihilation in Kabarda

Some suspicious sources had gotten used to spreading lies and driving a wedge between the members of the unified Circassian nation. This organized action has been performed and published irresponsibly many times in different ways, but discovered to be biased and contains unreliable information.

It is an abuse of Circassian self-esteem that someone tries to maliciously differentiate between the Circassians. Ranting of tribal or regional designations will not serve a purpose.

Some wanted to distribute an impression that Kabardians (Eastern Circassians) were never at war with the Russian Empire. They continued to claim that only the Western Circassians were engaged in war with Russia. It included denial and stirring of facts, as well as disclaiming of massacres and genocide against Kabardians as happened with other Circassians. This is pure fabrication.

Some individuals have tried to circulate such deliberate accounts; perhaps they drew misleading information and conclusions from unreliable Russian sources and possibly not qualified to publish historical information, which had already occurred. Still, the effects are still visible and felt by those who have suffered to this day.

The best of what has been mentioned, and it addresses this subject specifically, is found in the book The Circassian Genocide, by Walter Richmond. He referenced the information gleaned from various sources, including Russian ones.

Circassians, in addition to others, have only experienced the Russians through their armies and fighting forces. They have only introduced and provided hostilities and sorrow. Edouard Taitbout de Marigny quoted the following:

"We have never known the Russians," they say, "but with weapons in their hands."[487]

Indications reveal that dealing with the Russians at all levels means that they are the masters and the rest of the people and nationalities are to serve them and comply with the instructions issued by them to be implemented.

> In June 1808 Izmail-Bey Atazhukin, a Kabardian nobleman and colonel in the Russian Imperial Army, asked for permission to cross a quarantine line from Fort Konstantinovskaya into Kabardia with a shipment of desperately needed salt.[488]

There used to be a scale in measuring how good or bad the relations between the Russians and the Kabardian Circassians were. The devious ways which the Russians implemented show ill intentions and distrust, even towards those who ally or befriend themselves with them of Circassians or others.

> Atazhukin and his family were in many ways a microcosm of Kabardia's troubled relationship with Russia. As the son of a powerful pshi, he was sent as a boy to St. Petersburg as an ataman, that is, a hostage, to ensure his clan's loyalty to Russia. Despite his father's strong anti-Russian sentiments, he and his brother Adil-Girey both joined the Russian army and served with distinction. Then in 1795 both Atazhukins were arrested and charged with "unreliability."[489]

It used to be possible that at any time, distrust could come from the Russians regarding questioning credibility or loyalty of anyone. That could include anyone whatever their place within their own people.

> Izmail-Bey believed that anti-Russian forces in Kabardia conspired with Caucasus commander in chief Ivan Gudovich to undermine the brothers' efforts to establish peace between Kabardia and Russia. In 1798 Adil-Girey escaped and became the leader of the anti-Russian movement, but Izmail-Bey still believed Kabardia's future with Russia and repeatedly petitioned for release.[490]

One of the main reasons proven through the bitter experience with the Russians is the fact that Russians show a lack of confidence and trust. The continuation of the confrontation policy would enable tsarist Russia to continue their declared war of hatred and propaganda against Circassia. The main intention was to occupy entire Circassian territories. They didn't intend to leave an area to improve relations with the Circassians.

> When Alexander 1 came to power in 1801, he granted Atazhukin amnesty and in 1803 promoted him to colonel. NOW Atazhukin believed he could contribute to Russo-Circassian relations, so he submitted 'A Note on the Disorder on the Caucasus Line and Methods to End It' to the Russian minister of internal affairs, Viktor Kochubey.[491]

Whatever was said, there were evil methods depending on the deep desires that would be followed when needing a direct cause to act the opposite. Promises, agreements, and even treaties could have been overthrown and cancelled by the generals and their ready-made military plans.

> In it he argued that "We will never pacify the mountain peoples through force", and he proposed developing a working relationship with the Kabardian nobility, who were respected throughout Circassia.[492]

At times, even desired peaceful proposals initiated by Russian senior officials were either ignored or overlooked. All of a sudden, the decision would be taken to resume the violations and to carry on the colonial expansionist plans. The main objective was to occupy the entire Circassian homeland and to annihilate its people. The absence of integrity from the tsarist Russian senior commanders contributed in the reluctance to comply with rational decisions.

In turn, they would influence the other tribes, and peace would gradually be established. In the summer of 1804 Alexander sent Izmail-Bey and his "Note" to the new Caucasus commander in Chief, Pavel Tsitsianov, who called Atazhukin's proposal to remove Cossack stanitsy (fortified villages) from Kabardia "unworkable". The "Note" was forgotten.[493]

Events proved beyond doubt that some Circassians, especially some Kabardians, were wrong in their perception towards the Russians. Some Circassians were betting on a friendship with the Russian state while they were adrift of reality. They were not rewarded with good Russian friendship in return. As a matter of fact, the Russians did not regard them except as a group of people that should be dominated.

The Kabardians, who had been allies with Russia since 1557, had watched their friendly relations with their powerful neighbor deteriorate for some time. Ever since Peter the Great had set the sights on conquest of Iran, Russia's rulers stopped looking at the peoples of the North Caucasus as neighbors and began treating them as subjects wanting to be conquered.[494]

Absence, or rather making Circassians absent from all matters that concern their own future affairs and destiny, proves underrated. Conspiracy against their existence as a nation has demonstrated, unlike all facts, that both the Russian and Ottoman empires had alternatively dictated that the Circassians belong to them. They always seized any opportunity for singling and controlling them and their homeland.

The first clear sign of this new attitude came with the treaty of Belgrade, which concluded the Russo-Turkish War of 1736-1739. Dusting the negotiations—to which the Kabardians were not invited—Kabardia was stripped of its status as Russia's ally and declared a "neutral" buffer state between the two empires.[495]

The intention could have been initially to make Kabarda as a "no-man's land," for both empires to distinguish certain limitations or rather lines. While data shows a possibility of common understanding for the freedom of intervention for both sides in the matters that pertain to each party, still the region under debate is left for consideration for the foreseeable future.

> Furthermore, while neither the Russians nor the Ottomans were permitted under the treaty to meddle in Kabardian affairs, both powers had the authority to take hostages and punish the Kabardians if they had "cause of complaint". The actual effect of the treaty was to leave Kabardia completely defenseless against aggression from either side.[496]

Russian officials and officers did not hesitate, even for a single moment, to continue planning to control the areas adjacent to colonial Russian outskirts. These methods used treachery, oppression, power, and the elimination of the human race when necessary, ignoring the principles, treaties, and laws for such irresponsible moves.

> Accompanying Russia's new attitude toward the Kabardians was a change in administrative style. In 1719 Peter appointed Artemy Volynsky governor of the newly formed Astrakhan Province, east of Kabardia. Historian Michael Khodrakovsky describes Volynsky as "an embodiment of that arrogance of power which reflected the new confidence of an expanding and modernizing Russia."[497]

When the time was appropriate for them, they started building castles, garrisons, and military centers that would serve as a Trojan horse for the entire Caucasus region. After a few years, these colonial outposts would spread across the Caucasus, as well as there being sea garrisons on the coast of the Black Sea. Their functions would be to establish and tighten blockades, surveillance, and sanctions for control of Circassia and the Caucasus.

> Volynsky convinced Peter to construct the Kizlyar fortress on the Terek River in 1735 as a first step toward conquest of the North Caucasus, and this began the military line that would eventually stretch from the Crimean Peninsula to the Caspian Sea.[498]

There was always a lack of trust, suspicion, and a creation of artificial events according to Russian mentality. Their intention was always to evade any agreement, pledge, commitment, or understanding that had been agreed upon with the Circassians.

For example, when the Russians are urged to implement their commitment, and when assistance in accordance with the agreements is needed, and when they are asked to fulfill what is required of them in the event of an attack, they disclaim their pledges.

> Volynsky also ignored Russia's longstanding treaty with Kabardia. Pshi Arslan Kaituke repeatedly asked for assistance in repelling Crimean attacks from 1718 to 1721, but Volynsky refused to send any troops. Realizing the Kabardians' allies had abandoned them, the Khanate launched a major invasion, resulting in devastation of Kabardia.[499]
>
> Volynsky was succeeded by a series of commanders who treated the North Caucasus peoples as rebellious subjects. Rather than wasting resources trying to conquer them one at a time, the Caucasus command opted for a vassal system. In exchange for monetary and material assistance, a local sheikh or chieftain would pledge allegiance to Russia. This arrangement ended with the appointment of Pavel Tsitsianov as Caucasus commander in chief in 1802.[500]

Russian leaders couldn't have changed over time, especially with the method of dealing with the people of the Caucasus. The constant change of commanders and leaders in Russia increased the pace of their inhumane arrogance, according to overwhelming mentality of colonial tyrants. This would suit the prevailing tactics of preference, which consequently harmed dozens of peoples.

> Although he only held the post for four years, he set in motion the brutality that was the hallmark of subsequent Russian efforts to conquer the North Caucasus. Russian historians have nearly unanimously praised Tssitsianov: Speaking of his administration in the South Caucasus, tsarist historian Vasily Potto remarked that with (Tsitsianov's) appointment came better times . . . and a complete transformation of domestic and foreign politics.[501]

The description of what took place is in no way a prejudice against a particular nation or people. It is a description of the people who were at the helm, who did not have anything in their arsenal except ominous arrows, racism, and puny selfishness rampant in the minds of those who did not know a thing except to control other people and nations. Their intention always focused on the annexation of others' homelands as a way of annexing them to their empire using disseminating horror, death, and genocide.

> Writing at the turn of the twentieth century, British traveler John Baddeley praised Tsitsianov for administrative ability of a high order, coupled an aggressive, overbearing spirit that served him admirably in his dealings with the native rulers, Christian as well as Mussulman. American scholar Muriel Atkin holds quite a different position, claiming that Tsitsianov's eloquence was marred by bluster, just as his nobility of character was marred by deceit; the energy he spent was largely other peoples'; and his determination manifested itself in slaughter. While British historian David Lang gives a more nuanced description, calling him "a renegade to his own people, but a man who, in serving Russia, dealt many a crushing blow to Georgia's traditional enemies."[502]

Regretfully, those missing a compass and didn't know the difference between Asia and Europe were entrusted with a task to occupy others' lands and territories and subsequently subdue their peoples at any price. They always tended to defame others' characters with false accusations that is not based on credibility. Their hallmark cannot be described but as vicious.

> Oddly enough, there is truth in all of these statements, but unfortunately only Tsitsianov's negative characteristics were emulated by his successors, particularly his brutality and almost pathological hatred of "Asiatics". Potto reports that Tsitsianov's methods of dealing with the Caucasus peoples were based upon the belief that "the Asiatic people demand that they be treated with exceptional scorn."[503]

Hurting people who had their rights violated had proven a stubborn demeanor. Certain issues reached the point of offending local leaders, which wasn't the only reckless action deliberately carried out. They were instructed and given the task to execute Russia's arrogant policies. They turned a blind eye to the fact that they were strangers to the areas and regions, and they did not have the right to violate their rights and sovereignty.

> Heaping threats and insults upon the local leaders. In letters to various Dagestani sheikhs, which frequently opened with the colorful salutation "untrustworthy bastards,"

> Tsitsianov used stock phrases such as "I thirst to wash my boots with your blood" and regularly promised to burn villages and run entire populations off their land.[504]

Foolish behavior shows ignorance and lack of basic knowledge of the origin of different groups of mankind. Areas of the North Caucasus are the southeastern part of Europe. The plan was to annex the whole area to the haughty empire, even if it meant offending the people and fueling future permanent problems.

> Tsitsianov had no faith in the vassal system, believing that the only effective method of ensuring the 'Asiatics' would remain loyal was conquest and assimilation. Therefore, Yakov Gordin argues, his bombastic style when dealing with the Caucasus peoples was calculated to provoke them to rebellion, and he would use the rebellion as an excuse for military conquest. It was a pattern that would be repeated by nearly all of Tsitsianov's successors.[505]

Groups of Russian officers who had the same racist ideas and principles tended to apply and implement discrimination. There was an unrivaled similarity in the general perception of their concepts. Bullying was practiced because they felt that they were superior creatures.

> Bulgakov was of the same mold as Tsitsianov. a firm believer in Russia's superiority and contemptuous of the peoples of the Caucasus. Even before the June incident, he had targeted Atazhukin for harassment, insisting that he undergo quarantine after his return from Kabardia in March. This turned out to be a house arrest, with Atazhukin being deprived of his weapon and held until his request to return to Kabardia in June.[506]

Colonialists believed that they were entitled to insult others, citing the whims and policies of their empire without paying attention to the possibility of backlash for their acts: "This is why Veryovkin saw no problem in allowing Atazhukin to cross the quarantine line. Bulgakov saw things differently and ordered Veryovkin to hold Atazhukin for an additional twenty days, but the two of them simply ignored him."[507]

Experience has revealed that the Russians were never real friends of the Circassians. No friendship was attained. Aggressive behavior against the

Circassians confirmed that. Russia made the Circassians their bitter enemy and violated the sanctity of their homeland.

> The fact of the matter was that the Kabardians were on the verge of extinction as a result of their former ally's actions. To control the Kabardians more effectively and prepare for eventual conquest, the Russians built the Mozdok Fortress and supporting Stanitsy in Kabardia beginning in 1763. This disrupted and destroyed centuries-old migration routes that were essential for the survival of all the people of the region.[508]

The Russian Empire intended for a long time to give the impression that it was a friend of Circassia, the Kabardians in particular. That turned out to be false and even unrealistic.

> Dozens more stanitsy and fortresses across Kabardia's northern border resulted in more than loss of territory—it created an existential threat to North Caucasus society, whose survival depended on free migration of their herds. After their petitions were repeatedly rejected, the Kabardians had little choice but to fight back. And the war that resulted devastated their society by the beginning of the nineteenth century.[509]

Circassia was not only exposed to colonial ambitions, but also to accompanying effects that exacerbated the impact on the nation. People found themselves in a war and had to defend their survival, freedom, and independence. The infectious diseases exacerbated because of the unjust blockade imposed by the Russian navy on the Black Sea ports that tended to accelerate the eradication of the nation and the occupation of its homeland.

> Compounding the crisis was a plague, possibly malaria or typhus, which struck the North Caucasus in April 1804. It quickly spread throughout the region, and the Kebardians were hit worst of all. Tens of thousands died, including two of their most important leaders, Email-Bey's brother Adil-Girey and Ishak Abuke.[510]

The multiplicity of the insurmountable problems appeared because of imperialist policy. It was orchestrated for the intention of bothering and imposing a fait accompli. A lack of many materials contributed to starvation and outbreak of diseases and epidemics. They founded a quarantine system to protect themselves, but meant to get rid of others.

> The Russian response was predictable: a quarantine line that impeded Kabardian herds further. Disease coupled with starvation drove the entire population to the verge of annihilation. This was why Veryovkin ignored Bulgakov's order and allowed Atazhukin's party across the quarantine line-to save lives. Bulgakov seemed to view the plague differently, however.[511]

The quarantine turned out to be awful because it imposed restrictions on all walks of life. It included, in addition to the health aspect, others such as political, social, economic, and commercial. Severity and impact of military operations had increased. Circassians were trapped due to intensive restrictions and blockades. They were prevented movement, and the Russians had imposed tighter sanctions.

> He turned the quarantine into a complete economic blockade of Kabardia that threatened the tribe with extinction. Weakened from hunger and disease, the Kabardians became victims of their Cossack neighbors, who raided their auls with impunity. "Our people", a group of Kabardian pshis wrote in an appeal to the Emperor, "naked and swollen from lack of salt, have fled into the forests like hungry wild beasts."[512]

Russian generals and commanders acted in an inhumane manner. Their goal was to control the Circassians and their homeland in a step to get rid of them once and for all. That was what the Circassians sensed and felt when dealing with all the savage games and tricks the Russians played.

> Perhaps this is why Bulgakov took such a strong dislike to Atazhukin even before he crossed the quarantine line in June. His blockade of Kabardia wasn't only to stop the spread of the plague but to physically crush the Kabardians into complete submission. This certainly seemed to be the Kabardians' opinion of Bulgakov's quarantine.[513]

Both parties had acknowledged that the Russian Empire had already decided to get rid of the Circassians. That was a result of hostile Russian actions and attitudes. It was no longer hidden, and there was no longer a way to ignore or disregard them. Circassian leaders had to admit that it would not be possible to prevent people from defending themselves.

> Regional commander Ivan Del Pozzo sent him a report in early April 1807 relaying the Kabardians' pleas and quoting the influential aristocrat Kasbulat Kilchuke's accusation that "they want us all to die of starvation". Maybe the Emperor and the administration have decided we're no longer needed? So be it! God knows how this will end! The result of this will be that we won't have the ability to control raids in Kabardia or on the Russian frontier.[514]

The Circassians were short of many basic needs such as food and medicine. The stubborn Russian generals insisted on keeping the quarantine; functioning as a form of preventing the Circassians from getting important access to needed materials.

> We're not asking you and not troubling you to give us free passage everywhere, but at least lift the quarantine enough to allow us to acquire the things we need to survive.
> Despite Del Pozzo's report, Bulgakov made no adjustments to the quarantine. Bulgakov had stumbled upon a strategy that would be used again and again by his successors—conquest through starvation—and Atazhukin's humanitarian efforts ran counter to this goal.[515]

Mixing work and personal matters provoked personal revenge, which also indicated the presence of malicious motives. At the same time, there was a trend of racism, superiority, and heartlessness. Such practices were directed against a person who was considered a Russian loyalist, who happened to be in this case, a Circassian Kabarday individual.

> After Atazhukin crossed the quarantine line, Bulgakov filed a series of petitions demanding that charges be brought against Atazhukin and Veryovkin. Gudovich considered the entire case nonsense, but War Minister Arkcheev took it up with the Interior Ministry. Veryovkin was arrested, but the emperor pardoned Atazhukin in February 1809, citing his "praise-worthy feats and loyalty to Russia."[516]

Circassia 187

Implacability is not an unusual attitude that is taken by bullheaded military officials or commanders who harbored grudges. This kind of stance against political opponents would not be tolerable if there was transparency, sincerity, or honesty. They wanted the Circassians to surrender according to Russian terms.

> He was assigned to duty in Georgia, and that should have been the end of the matter. However, throughout 1809 Bulgakov sent reports about a conference that he has arranged with Kabardian pshis concerning their submission, which he claimed Atazhukin sabotaged.[517]

Falsehood impacts the overall situation and introduces negative consequences. Passive publicity and illogical manipulation of events would not put relations straight. These examples are not to introduce character assassination only, but also to attach with pressing for the elimination of an entire nation and all its viability. False accusations are not based on credibility, but on evil acts.

> Of course, Atazhukin wasn't in Kabardia at the time, but even if he had been, he couldn't have sabotaged the conference because there was none. The entire event was a fabrication Bulgakov created to trick St Petersburg into allowing him to punish his enemy. When this failed, Bulgakov sent Atazhukin a series of letters in spring 1809, demanding pledges of unconditional loyalty from all the pshis of Kabardia. Atazhukin returned home, called a hase to discuss the issue, and told Bulgakov the conditions were unacceptable.[518]

Make the lie big, make it simple, keep saying it, and eventually they will believe it.[519]

This shows similarity in both theory and application of tyrants when dealing with oppressed people, showing that those in the first half of the twentieth century had followed the footsteps of what tsarist Russian commanders had pursued in the early nineteenth century.

> Bulgakov submitted another report, this time to the new Caucasus commander in chief, Alexander Tormasov. Bulgakov now claimed that he called the hase himself and had summoned Atazhukin, who had been evading arrest.

> He reported that the Kabardian pshis had taken an oath of loyalty to the Russian tsar and promised not to engage in "theft or rapaciousness". None of this was true.[520]

Revenge is a cruel practice. Blind hatred would instigate and urge onself to seize the opportunity to get satisfaction. This is a mental illness, which is not easy to overcome. Predetermined and opinionated individuals who assume the responsibility of military commanders would inflict harm or damage against targeted people in any way possible.

> Bulgakov then took his vengeance against the entire Kabardian nation. Accusing them of raiding Cossack settlements in violation of the oath that they never took, Bulgakov arrested Atazhukin and launched a series of attacks on the Kabardians. Potto approvingly reports Bulgakov's campaign.[521]

Reporters of the Russians' actions against the Circassians were showing, even though their reports, their feelings and approval. The reports indicated that there were Russian commanders and officers who had a thirst for blood. They insisted on the burning and destruction of Circassian villages and settlements.

During every military operation, they looted Circassian properties, including grain and food stores. The distribution of spoils to those who participated and supported the criminal and wicked acts proved of a pursued plan by the racist Russian state against people of the Caucasus.

> In order to soothe the disturbed people of the region (Cossacks) and to cheer up the settlers, in the beginning of 1810 Bulgakov himself went into the Kuban and burned villages, destroyed fortifications and penetrated into areas the mountaineers themselves thought impregnable, . . . The energetic Bulgakov, never forgetting the danger, quickly moved his troops into the Kabardian lowlands and seized 25,000 head of livestock, and immediately ordered that they be distributed for the use of the suffering villagers on the line. Deprived of nearly all their means of subsistence, the Kabardians were forced to make peace and accepted the conditions by Bulgakov.[522]

Relentless military and propaganda campaigns inflicted barbaric destruction, ethnic cleansing, and genocide against the people of Circassia. No other description can be given for the uncivil operations. Applied policies against the Circassians were not to take place in isolation of other military plans. They aimed at the occupation of the Circassian territories in the end.

> Such raids were actually common. The Russian military command considered them "punitive expeditions" in retaliation for Circassian khishchnichatvo (rapaciousness), that is, raids on the Cossacks. In fact, in a letter of August 1806 to Gudovich, Del Pozo explained that the Kabardian attacks were retaliation for Cossack raids upon them, adding that when they submitted petitions to the local military authorities asking for justice, they were frequently chased off and even imprisoned.[523]

Hypocrisy triggered clashes that produced fabricated lies, confusion, and misdirection. They evoked images and remembrance to be tizzy over problems that were created by the Russians and their mercenaries. The Russian command embraced the role of acting in a destructive mentality. Moreover, they roused emotions, sowed divisions, and encouraged disputes and conflicts among people.

> Bulgakov took his assault on Kabardia beyond the frontier auls that he accused of "rapaciousness", using as his justification a report submitted by Del Pozzo in early 1810. In it Del Pozzo claimed that the peasants of Kabardia had requested Russian protection from the aristocrats. This was true; a civil war was brewing in Kabardia independent of Russia's actions."[524]

They tend to invent reasons for their intervening in matters not of their concern. Therefore, they built their inhumane, evil, and diabolical plans, which contributed to the worsening of matters to the point of no return. Together with all this, they followed deceit and seized the opportunity to commit murder, theft, and graft. They kept changing the rules of engagement.

> On April 14, under the pretext of protecting the peasants, Bulgakov invaded Kabardia and burned everything in his path. He also stole an enormous amount of livestock. Although Potto mentions twenty-five thousand head were

taken, the Kabardians stated in just one complaint to St. Petersburg that among the goods Bulgakov had absconded with were forty-four thousand sheep, six thousand head of cattle, and more than one hundred tons of honey.[525]

The sky was the limit for their appetite to burn and destroy all the Circassians houses, farms, and public buildings. This included all reachable villages and towns: "The report also claimed that Bulgakov's troops burned nearly ten thousand homes, more than one hundred mosques, and one thousand farmsteads. Even if one assumes this complaint doubles the actual damages, it still represents a crippling loss."[526]

It is not logical to visualize regular military units that abuse the original function assigned to them. On the contrary, they acted like mercenaries. Ethical operational standards were not adhered to. They would not be deterred by the law, and nothing would prevent them from heinous acts. They acted according to a bullying criterion. They don't refrain from carrying out their task to annihilate the indigenous inhabitants.

> As a result of Bulgakov's raids, thousands of people died of starvation, exposure, and the plague (which was certainly exacerbated by lack of food and shelter). Then Bulgakov took his campaign into western Circassia, where he destroyed all the auls he could and blockaded the survivors until they starved or succumbed to the elements.[527]

Events had proven that there were, on the Russian's side, some individuals who assumed senior or junior military positions in the Russian state who had a live conscience. At the same time, they condemned the irresponsible actions that were contrary to the laws, norms, and principles of humanity. However, those who can be described as such could not, through the years of the imposed war, enforce decisive and positive effect.

It was not possible to prevent or stop all the challenges. The crimes and abuses committed against the Circassians and other Caucasians continued to grow and increase like a snowball.

> For this devastation of Kabardia, Tormasov recommended that Bulgakov be decorated. Defense Minister Barclay de Tolly rejected the request, stating that: Various rumors have reached us that cause {The Emperor} to conclude that in pacifying the rebels, General Bulgakov's use exorbitant degrees of brutality and inhumanity went beyond the limits of

> his responsibility. If one believes the reports, the expeditions against the Kabardians and the Kuban mountaineers consisted of the absolute plunder and burning of their homes; these brutal actions, which have driven those people to the brink of despair, have only aroused their hatred for us, and his dealings with the neighboring peoples have served more to create loathing of us than establish peace in that region.[528]

It was an expected consequence that there would be some officials who would change their stance depending on certain circumstances. It could have been the general situation or surrounding official influence. That does not change the fundamental nature of the matter, which were effected by repressive Russian policies. The foregone conclusion shows that the Russians' intended result was to finish off the largest possible number of Circassians and, on top of that, the occupation of their homeland and displacing the remaining outside their homeland.

> Tormasov changed his tune, now claiming that he had always been opposed to Bulgakov's "punitive" raids. For this pillaging of Kabardia, Bulgakov was charged with extortion. After an investigation Atazhukin was released from custody and Bulgakov was relieved of his command for embezzlement, bribery, abuse of authority, and numerous other charges.[529]

Sometimes developments looked like there would be a change of the standards looming. They continued changing the "carrot and stick approach", meaning the flexibility of compliment and punishment criteria. As a result, some of the military officials issued orders to the military units in certain areas to open or close exits to enable Circassians to cross to specific Russian- or Cossack-protected locations for trade or commercial purposes.

That was an easing of the blockade, which was constantly being wavered, eased, or tightened subject to surrounding influence: "Tormasov was replaced by Nikolai Rtishchev, who did all he could to patch over the animosity that Bulgakov had sown, endorsing a Kabardian delegation that traveled to St. Petersburg to negotiate, and facilitating the few concessions that the Russian government had authorized."[530]

Easing of the blockade enters within the occasional Russian policy to execute the methods of modulating pressure on the overall population: "He allowed the Kabardians cross the quarantine line to trade in Cossack towns and reinstated their right to exploit the salt fields in the Caucasus, which had been suspended by Tormasov."[531]

Changing military measures taken against indigenous people were to implement the instructions issued by the Russian military command in the Caucasus. They aimed at passing and implementing instructions that were not implemented except under calm conditions. Once the need was met, further instructions would be issued.

> He worked closely with Kabardian pshi Kuchuk Janhote to establish peaceful relations between the Kabardians and their neighbors the Ossetians, who had been forced by the Russians to migrate to Kabardia (a fate that the Ossetians would suffer repeatedly throughout the nineteenth century). During Rtishchev's rule hostilities slowly decreased, although by no means stopped. Meanwhile Atazhukin continued to work as a mediator between the Kabardians and Russians until his death in 1812.[532]

It is not logically acceptable to believe that a general in the Russian Empire would choose or sponsor policies that contradict the fixed orders issued to a headquarters: "In this one conflict between Atazhukin and Bulgakov, we can see many of the problems that plagued Russo-Circassian relations and led directly to the genocide of 1864. Bulgakov was not the last field commander to deceive administrations in St. Petersburg in order to gain permission to carry out his own agenda."[533]

It is not reliable that a commander gets away with ignoring military instructions or a state policy toward a certain segment of people or a nation. Personalization according to an individual's vision is not suitable. Such discrepancy causes image damage to the state's reputation and standard policies. The generals' arrogance, ignorance, stubbornness, and personal trends are not acceptable by the standard that officers must maintain.

> The mentality of the Caucasus military command was shaped by people who behaved as if they were in charge of their own country, which outsiders couldn't understand. Contemptuous of their superiors in St. Petersburg, they fabricated whatever story suited their needs. Furthermore, the adopted Tsitsianov's view that conquest was the only viable option for control of the region.[534]

These stochastic operations encouraged to consolidate the state of chaos among the ranks of official Russian bodies. They created an atmosphere of distrust between the Russian military units in the Caucasus and the civil employees. This is how they dealt with and treated the people of the Caucasus who had to endure the Russian military units that practiced their atrocities.

> As we'll see, when civilian administrators used peaceful methods, the military commanders undermined them both by petitioning St. Petersburg and by launching raids into Circassia to sow animosity. This continued all the way up the 1860s, when Field Commander Nikolai Evodkimov sabotaged St. Petersburg's final attempt to reach a settlement with the Circassians.[535]

Exercising terrorism and committing crimes against innocent people was an ordinary pursuit and even professional tradition. The question is raised in this context. Who awarded the Russian commanders and generals the prerogative to do all these unpalatable acts against the Circassian nation and other nations in the Caucasus and beyond?

> Bulgakov was also the first Russian commander to use tactics that might today be considered genocidal. His blockade was the beginning of the oft-repeated Russian strategy of starving the population into submission. Likewise, his raids of 1810 weren't intended to punish the Kabardians but to annihilate them.[536]

It's funny to watch the attitude of such supercilious commanders who concentrated their imagination to eliminate others: "Rather than confine his attacks to a handful of auls close to Russian territory, he took his army into the heart of Kabardia and destroyed everything in his path, leaving thousands homeless and starving."[537]

Occupation of peoples' homelands is attached to the usurper entity that had annihilated millions of indigenous people from different nations. Russian leaders and commanders were always applauded and remembered. The invaders considered them deplorable. It is absurd to treat these victims abusively while their homelands were invaded, and reality would visualize and refer to them as victims.

> On the other hand, Bulgakov was the last Caucasus commander to be punished for his atrocities. His successors would not only commit even more egregious acts of terror against the Circassians with impunity, but they would be regularly be decorated and prompted for them.[538]

It is useful and makes sense to draw lessons from Russian hostilities who dealt in a brutal and nasty way, with those who believed in accepting the fait accompli (where Russian laws and norms did not provide the necessary protection for those who submitted to support the occupation). So how would the trespassers deal with those who did not succumb to Russian threats, but insisted on demanding their natural right to freedom and independence?

> The troubles Atazhukin faced were also typical of Circassians who understood the magnitude of the threat posed by Russia and who sought a peaceful solution. The Russian military command disliked all such peacemakers and did all they could to thwart their efforts. Many Circassians likewise distrusted their compatriots who sought peace with Russia, and they worked to undermine their credibility in Circassia.[539]

Fate and destiny necessitated that the Circassians had to deal with what happened to them and what they suffered as a consequence. The misfortunes and tragedies that occurred to them had taken place because of Russian ambitions and clumsy policies: "This would be the fate of all so-called peaceful Circassians-threats from the Russian side and attacks from the Circassian side."[540]

The Russians had turned a deaf ear and exaggerated their aggressiveness. On several occasions, they declared their agenda and published their real intention and ultimate goal. Their real purpose was to occupy the land and to commit genocide or deport the entire nation.

> More importantly, all proposals from figures such as Atazhukin that cut to the heart of the Circassian position—that they wanted to be good neighbors with the Russians, not subjects of the tsar—were dismissed out of hand by both the Caucasus command and St. Petersburg. In this respect, both the civil and military commands were united in the belief that the only acceptable form of peace was the Circassians' unconditional surrender or their elimination.[541]

It is not uncommon to recognize or know one of the criminals who were involved in murdering mankind, but it is not common to come across one who, at the very least, contributed to killing hundreds of thousands. People were slaughtered, and their property was seized. All those who had worked under his command had participated in the crimes, which were perpetrated by "Ermolov, Grandfather of the Genocide."[542]

There are many writers who are interested in reporting the details of the Russian-Circassian War. Professor Walt Richmond deserves tribute for his professional work, research, and dedication to uncover long-hidden information and documents that relate to the Circassian catastrophe: "John Baddeley spends a great deal of time—in his comprehensive English narrative he wrote about Russia's conquest of the Caucasus at the beginning of the 20th century—discussing the tenure of Alexei Ermolov as Caucasus commander in chief."[543]

The Russian authorities showed disgusting behavior that insisted on colonial presence in the occupied areas. They keep constructing a variety of monuments for Russian commanders and generals to substantiate their disgusting behavior that insists on their colonial presence. There are people who keep joking about this hypocrisy by saying that there is a monument between a monument and another monument.[544]

The authorities in the North Caucasus keep propagating this process and keep increasing their adulation and ranting. The authorities do not allow the indigenous people to commemorate their historical heroes and leaders, where it may be understood as a positive element and constitute a cure of the old discrepancies that would encourage reconciliation efforts.

> Circassians, along with other peoples of the North Caucasus, would certainly like to install monuments featuring their own historical heroes. But apparently, Moscow is quietly but effectively discouraging them from doing so. Instead, the North Caucasus is full of monuments celebrating the friendship of Russians and locals, along with Soviet-era monuments of Vladimir Lenin and other Soviet figures.[545]

Narratives focused on one of the unsung Russian commanders, who perpetrated foolish actions against the people of the Caucasus while the Russian Empire deemed the war criminals as distinguished. Commemorating the Russian-Circassian war criminals is a familiar official conduct in the North Caucasus.

> A veteran of the war of 1812 and the greatest hero of the Caucasus wars, Ermolov is eulogized in the poetry of Alexander Pushkin as well as every history written before the Bolshevik Revolution, Monuments to Ermolov can be

found throughout the North Caucasus today, and he is still considered one of Russia's great military figures.[546]

Ermolov wanted to idolize himself and to grant Russian officials an aura of "holiness" that allowed their practices, views, and status to be unchallenged. To act in a ride-roughshod attitude over the natives and even against their religion and their beliefs is not appropriate whatsoever. There is no criterion to allow a clumsy officer in the tsar's army, who is devoid of humanitarian principles, to humiliate those whose homeland was devastated and occupied.

> Just a few paragraphs later. Baddeley describes Ermolov's theory of civil administration. Considered a cornerstone of his famous "system" for pacifying the Caucasus: "Yermoloff was wont to insist that the word of a Russian official should be sacred, so that the natives might be led to believe it more firmly than the Koran itself; and to the extent of his power he enforced good faith on either side."[547]

Needless provocations and controversies ensued abruptly and randomly and would not be tolerated by a civilized society. Such acts cannot be tolerated coming from a general who obviously does not realize the content of humanity. The committed crimes were followed by banishing people from their territories.

> How anyone could expect a people to believe the word of, or have good faith in, a man who led his troops on rampages of pillage, rape, and slaughter against them is a puzzle Baddeley never solves. However, it does give us a glimpse into the incoherence of the Ermolov "system". Such was Ermolov's mentality that he believed that the people he killed, robbed, and kidnapped should have understood he was doing it for their own good and been thankful.[548]

Unbearable behavior is explained in different ways and means by different observers or critics. Satanic acts cannot be justified in any way. The victims must be compensated while their descendants and heirs be restituted for their looted rights in a timely manner, according to international laws and norms.

> As Yakov Gordin explains, Ermolov considered his brutality justified because of his "higher" motivations: "Ermolov and his close associates truly believed themselves to be paladins of 'peace, prosperity and enlightenment.' which

they were bringing to a kingdom of barbarity and cruelty . . . Ermolov could be cruel, but he was cruel in the name of enlightenment and prosperity, he shot and hanged people—sometimes by their feet—in the name of progress for this edge of the empire, for its people". Baddeley ultimately finds the truth beneath this implausible theory:

The Russian General Erckert says Of Yermoloff, "he was at least as cruel as the natives themselves". He himself said: "I desire that the terror of my name should guard our frontiers more potently than chains or fortresses. That my word should be for the natives a law more inevitable than death. Condescension in the eyes of Asiatics is a sign of weakness, and out of pure humanity I am inexorably severe. One execution saves hundreds of Russians from destruction, and thousands of Mussulmans from treason."[549]

The Russian Empire's policy was terrible while its generals' cleansing actions were even worse and terrifying. It is a pity to see an empire follow the footsteps of those who had inspired their leaders to commit crimes of unspeakable cruelty. They devoured anything that came their way with unrivaled atrociousness. Human rights were awfully violated.

A man of the twentieth century, Baddeley ultimately sees through the rationalization of imperialists such as Ermolov and condemns them. Unfortunately, the collective punishment he berates was to become standard operating procedure for the Russians.[550]

People and nations of the Caucasus were targeted by insane military commanders. They took upon themselves to finish off these vulnerable people by adapting brutal methods. Regardless of gross human losses, they clearly never considered the consequences of their criminal operations or whether they would have an impact on overall future generations and environments.

Ermolov reveled in his overwhelming firepower against which his opponents—particularly the mountaineers of Chechnya, Dagestan, and Circassia—were powerless to combat: "It is very interesting to see the first effect of this innocent means [cannons!] on the heart of man, and I learnt how useful it was to be possessed of the one when unable all at once to conquer the other."[551]

There was no reasonable proportion or balance of power used by the superpower at the time against individual weapons. The maximum mode of transport that could be available to those who were defending their homeland was their own horses. They used primitive means for the most part against a repressive military machine that included navy, cannons, and other means of destruction in addition to mercenaries who were not committed to legal standards.

> In his quest for personal glory, Ermolov chose adversaries (victims might be a more appropriate term) who stood no chance against his superior weaponry, and he employed levels of brutality and inhumanity as yet unseen in the Caucasus. It worked, too: Ermolov's officers were decorated and promoted as their tactics became more devastating. Subsequent generations would emulate Ermolov's form of success.[552]

People of the Caucasus didn't go to fight the Russians and occupy their vast land. On the contrary, the Russians coveted to brutally occupy the Caucasus and to get rid of its peoples: "Potto explains Ermolov's attitude toward the peoples of the Caucasus, whom former administrations had (at least theoretically) treated as sovereign nations with whom peaceful relations could be established."[553]

The Russian Empire considered and based its leaders and officials' aspirations and ambitions on subjugating and controlling all its neighbors and beyond. Their intention was to control and annex all regions to make them part of their empire.

> With the appearance of Ermolov in the Caucasus . . . the passive and ineffective politics of palliative methods of giving gifts to our enemies was replaced by active politics which didn't have as its goal a temporary and fragile peace, but rather total victory, complete subjugation of the hostile lands . . . He looked upon all the peaceful and hostile tribes of the Caucasus Mountains, if not as already under Russian rule, then sooner or later destined to be, and in any case, he demanded unconditional obedience from them.[554]

The colonial Russian project was not in any way an event of coincidence, but rather a deliberate policy that was developed by Russian emperors and officials. They did not hesitate to provide support and endorsement for the steps that had been taken and the ones that were scheduled to be completed.

The steps were carried out through a timetable according to possibilities and circumstances that arose from time to time.

> Baddeley summarizes Ermolov's ideology in similar terms: Yermoloff's central idea was that the whole of the Caucasus must, and should, become an integral part of the Russian Empire; that the existence of independent or semi-independent States or communities of any description, whether Christian, Mussulman, or Pagan, in the mountains or on the plains, was incompatible with the dignity and honor of his master, the safety and welfare of his subjects.[555]

Continuing from the previous paragraph, it can be said that the arrangements that had been prepared was as if the work would be carried out in a one-man show profile. All those under his command would be following his instructions to perform the task: "On this idea was based the whole of his policy, every one of his administrative measures, every movement of the troops under his command, and to the end thus clearly set up in his own mind he from the beginning devoted himself heart and soul."[556]

The summary plan showed the main objective and goal to be followed. Occupation and oppression were to be initiated and thus to achieve the final annexation into the Russian Empire under any price.

> In other words, Ermolov's goal was to conquer and assimilate the peoples of the Caucasus, using every weapon at his disposal.[557]
>
> The North Caucasus peoples were of no use to Russia but only stood as an impediment to their free travel to the Christian lands of Georgia and Armenia. As such, the land was valuable but the people themselves were of no consequence; hence, Potto concludes with a justification for genocide.[558]

The brutality used by the invaders to control the Caucasus regions and peoples was unprecedented in its size, upper limits, and brutality. Few individuals have accepted to have their names and titles used as scapegoats in assuming the responsibility of war crimes. However, logic cites otherwise where the empire, and the emperor in particular, bear the official, legal, and moral responsibility.

> In his comprehensive study of Russia's conquest of the northeastern Caucasus, Moshe Gammer notes that "Ermolov

was well within the existing consensus" in his use of violence as the main tool in controlling the Caucasus, and that "if he exceeded it, he did so only in the severity of his measures, in the amount of force he used, and in his brutality and cruelty."[559]

Thus, all those who were described as war hawks are the facades of official black hatred policies. The Russian Empire has shown special resentment towards the Circassians in particular and the other peoples of the Caucasus in general: "In fact, Bulgakov was at least as brutal as Ermolov."[560]

Administrative hypocrisy led to worsening corruption of the authorities' branches. Infamous leaders who showed ferocity of the insidious operations had assumed their responsibilities of all crimes committed during the aggressive war. Legalizing the heavy-handed operations had been carried out against innocent inhabitants whose only fault was being in their homeland.

> Ermolov's significance lay in the prestige he brought as a hero of the war of 1812. He legitimized the barbaric tactics that led to Bulgakov's dismissal. The lack of any meaningful response by the emperor to Ermolov's atrocities assured subsequent commanders and their troops that no acts of cruelty would be punished.[561]

A military commander works on the implementation of the instructions issued to him, whether verbally or in writing, to fulfill all required specifics. It will not be of his concern to question or to bear any responsibility from any action implemented. This is a stain of shame against Russia that will never be erased until the Circassians get their legitimate rights recognized.

> Not that Alexander, and even Nicholas I, didn't try to restrain Ermolov when his brutality exceeded all boundaries of humanity. However, these reproaches never led to the sort of investigation that ended Bulgakov's career. More often, Ermolov's officers received honors for their massacres.[562]

The Russian plan tends to deliberately confuse and embarrass social matters and makes them more complicated. The aboriginals are being situated in unusual circumstances that forced them to choose between two bitter choices when it comes to traditions, especially when they are obliged to accept the application of their national laws to comply with tribal procedures.

Ermolov's encounter with Kabardia began in early May 1818, when five Kabardians assaulted the line and afterward took refuge in the aul of Tram, about seven miles from Fort Kostantinogorskaya. The villagers were ordered to turn the party over, which of course would violate of the custom of hospitality. When the villagers' refusal was communicated to Ermolov, he ordered that the aul be annihilated.[563]

Their plans consisted of quite an extensive amount of cowardliness and treachery. Also, they contained abuse, destruction, murder, slaughter, and all that is contrary to what is acceptable to the human mind. Their tactics were applied as per their typical repressive standard operating procedures, acceptable by their own laws and norms, as if their soldiers and mercenaries are normally briefed in these methods.

The Russians surrounded the aul at night, drove all the inhabitants out with only the shirts on their backs, burned the village, took all of the livestock and distributed it among the Cossacks. Afterward, Ermolov warned the Kabardians that "this time I limited it to [Tram]: in the future, I will show no mercy to convicted bandits: their villages will be annihilated, their property taken, their wives and children slaughtered."[564]

When the Circassians were under attack, it was natural they tended to refer to their own resources. They gathered each other, trying to grab the opportunity for the continuation of their heroic resistance against the aggressors. The assaulters did not have in their project but the desire to achieve victory using every sordid and despicable tactic.

The villagers' response was predictable: they prepared to join the western Circassians and launch raids in reprisal. A series of letters from Ermolov to pshi Tkhamade Kuchuk Janhote followed that reveal Ermolov's failure (or refusal) to understand the Kabardian point of view. In his first letter, written in June 1818, Ermolov takes a belligerent tone.[565]

The Russian troops utilized excessive and unbalanced force while committing genocide. Unlawful murder was both willful and premeditated, which was neither the first nor the last of such crimes. Degrading and humiliating language used by one of the tsarist commanders and generals against the Circassians speaks a lot.

> I ordered [the destruction of Tram] and forewarned you that in more than a year and a half of indulging in the foul and roguish acts of the Kabardian people, I vainly waited for the princes to realize how villainously they betrayed their pledge of loyalty, which they had freely given, and having grown tired of enduring this insult to the authorities representing our great Sovereign, I will now use completely different methods than I have up until now.[566]

This is clearly premeditated ranting, threatening, swearing, and cursing. At the same time, the disillusioned leader allowed himself to continue offending people by crazy revenge. As a result, the barbaric tsarist army wanted to wipe out the people and their homeland.

> A note should be made about the "pledge of loyalty". Whenever there was a skirmish, the Russians insisted the Kabardins deemed to be involved take such a pledge. Because they were too numerous to keep track of, by the time of Ermolov the Kabardians could only have perceived them as a meaningless formality to end Russian hostilities, at best akin to a truce. However, they worked well for the Russians.[567]

The Russians' mentality even wanted to change the rules of nature. It is as if the Russians were allowed to do anything while the Circassians were not allowed to take any reactionary/defensive actions, even on their own soil, even when finding themselves forced to react against a fierce Russian attack.

Attacks against them and against their habitual settlements and properties intensified at the time: "Any hostile act by the Circassians could be labeled a violation of one of the countless 'pledges' and used as justification for a 'punitive campaign'. In any event, by the end of June a nationwide rebellion was brewing in Kabardia, and so in early July Ermolov wrote Janhote again."[568]

It is petty when a frantic person dictates the rules of the game on behalf of his empire. Assuming the official position of commander in chief in the Caucasus had qualified him to so indulge in his obvious threatening. This was an assurance that he was going to implement theories and policies according to his "iron fist" and savage procedures. The intention was to assault the Circassians' villages so they would suffer and lives would be lost.

> After driving the inhabitants of Tram into the woods and threatening to annihilate their villages and slaughter their children, it's difficult to see how the Kabardians could

trust Ermolov when he now promised that he had "no thoughts of causing any harm Whatsoever to the Kabardian people". Not surprisingly, the Kabardians were unimpressed and continued their preparations to migrate into western Circassia. In late August Ermolov wrote Janhote again, now in an almost collegial fashion.[569]

Threatening was employed to retain the Circassians of Kabarda under fear of imminent attacks and psychological warfare. The trick was to oblige them to leave to survive with their children and families. That was one of the methods and steps on the trails deportation: "None of this had any effect, and so in October, Ermolov arranged a meeting with the Kabardian pshis, where he returned to issuing threats, promising that the fate of Tram would be repeated if the Kabardians continued their 'thievery'."[570]

Obviously, when extremist ideas tend to reach a high degree of racism, they are alike for those who embrace them. They look for nests and appropriate incubators, not to mention who share not only in the preaching of these notions, but also in publishing, circulating, and even applying them on the ground. In such a concept, those who dictate the rules of the game are similar and alike and tend to associate with each other.

Believing Del Pozzo to be too conciliatory, Ermolov replaced him as regional commander with General Karl Stahl. Stahl arrived in the regional headquarters of Georgievsk in early 1819 and immediately began a campaign against the residents of Lesser Kabardia, accusing them of concealing fugitive Chechens. The Pshis there denied the charges, pointing out (correctly) that they and their ancestors had considered themselves "forever inclined and loyal to Russia" since the split of Kabardia in the mid sixteenth century.[571]

People with similar views would be comfortable flocking and working together. There are those who keep looking for flimsy reasons to exacerbate problems. There are those who provide good and positive reasons for not going into wicked mazes. This is undoubtedly part of the eternal struggle between good and evil. At the same time, what was going on there was a colonial conflict in its perfect description and formation.

Whether Stahl truly believed that the population of Lesser Kabardia was aiding the Chechens or not (and again, due to the tradition of hospitality, they would have no choice in some cases), he found it a convenient justification for clearing the rest of the fertile right bank of the Terek River. The Chechens had already been driven back from the river and Cossacks were busy colonizing their land, and now it was the Kabardians' turn.[572]

Those who elect to follow specific approaches would normally select what is best for certain circumstances. Only the intention shows if this work is useful or offensive to mankind. Motivation or discouragement is the factor or mechanism that promotes or demotes behavior in any criteria. However, collective punishment and mindless dealing based on arrogance is totally rejected.

After Ermolov annihilated a number of auls in 1820, most of the Lesser Kabardia pshis signed a pledge of loyalty and a promise to inform the Russians of any fugitives in their midst. Despite their surrender, in September Russian troops under the command of Major Taranovsky demanded that the Kabardians living on the Terek leave for the Julat highlands, threatening them with cannons when they hesitated.[573]

Undoubtedly, the Russians created alliances in various forms to apply their malicious aims. They implemented their exclusionary policy against the Circassians with several parties. They had an alliance with herds of Cossack mercenaries and with various countries in order to drive the various tracks through annihilation, destruction, occupation, displacement, and resettlement of strangers.

There was little more that the Kabardians could do after the plague had devastated the entire country. As Ermolov himself mentioned in his memoirs, "The plague was our ally against the Kabardians, for having completely annihilated the population of Lesser Kabardia and devastated Greater Kabardia, it weakened them to the point where they were not able to gather in large numbers as they had previously."[574]

The plague was also their ally, not to mention the siege, starvation, and exposure of the displaced to harsh weather conditions and other evil behaviors. What a feeling, when sensing a victory over small people. They were stripped of their basic and natural rights while that general did not even bat an eye.

Perhaps this is the best testimony to Ermolov's Character: in the face of a disease that nearly wiped out an entire nation that had been a loyal ally of Russia for 250 years, he expressed no sympathy at all. For Ermolov, the plague was a tool, an ally. However, it had only partially destroyed the Kabardians, so Ermolov had to finish the job himself.[575]

They intended to wipe out the people of the Caucasus and control them and their homelands. It was already a relentless and openly declared war against all the peoples of the Caucasus and anyone who demanded freedom: "Ermolov and Stahl became occupied by affairs in Chechnya in 1819 while Kabardian raids increased in size and frequency."[576]

The continuation of hit-and-run operations put the Russian Empire in a constant concern of an ongoing challenge. Hostilities had started hundreds of years ago, but they were not over yet and would not end soon, as per most of the speculations.

The hostilities and raids on the Circassians were intended to eliminate what they owned, in addition to burning and destroying their villages. The driving force behind imperialism and colonialism is greed. Eventually, everything has an end. The old empires disintegrated and ceased to exist. Colonized nations became independent states.

By 1821 the situation was out of Russia's control, forcing Ermolov to return to Kabardia in September. In November, he developed a plan to "pacify" Kabardia once and for all and submitted it to Stahl for execution: The onset of winter has stopped their ability to move on the Line and it will make the punishment more palpable and will be a most certain means of pacifying them... Meanwhile, in order to keep them fearful of our raids and too occupied with their own safety to conduct raids on the Line, I consider it necessary to lead a small force into Kabardia that will not occupy any specific location but rather go quickly from one aul to another, particularly the lowlands where they take their herds of cattle and horses in the winter, where we can ill the cattle and steal the horses.... The primary goal of the expedition commander should not be battles or skirmishes but rather the elimination of the cattle and horses which, of course, they can't hide."[577]

The tsarist Russian Empire's troops were always aiming to continue confronting the Circassians at any time and in any place.

They have always mentioned in their scripts, bulletins, and statements their odd depictions. They ranted expressions like plotting revenge, cleansing, looting, displacing, and punishing. There are other words that a human being would loath recalling. It is strange that they consider themselves a higher class than others, evidently those whose sacred soil was occupied and usurped.

> Russian forces went through Kabardia in December and January, rustling thousands of head of cattle and horses and burning all the auls they came across. Despite Ermolov's order that "the punishment is to be carried out against armed men only", throughout the winter troops led by Colonel Kotsyrev destroyed every aul they came across.[578]

The tsarist Russians couldn't hide their entrenched underlying grudges, portrayed basically on ethnic and religious grounds. They always deviated from any understanding and agreement and even cancelled them. They did not symbolize an empire. Underlying and floating intense malice got to an extent of finding their nation amid a forest of monsters and beasts that ravage their bodies.

> They threw several thousand villagers out of their homes and in least one aul bayoneted all the men, women, and children. The survivors of these assaults were forced to migrate to the lowlands during what turned out to be a very harsh winter and were given no assistance in building shelter. In his orders, Ermolov remarked that "the winter isn't so harsh or enduring in this land that it will be painful for the people to live in the open air for two months."[579]

The Circassians were exposed to disgraceful murder, torture, humiliation, looting, the confiscation of various belongings, and stealing of their horses, herds of cattle, and yields. All this stigmatized the aggressors and offenders by shame. Wise and sane people know the effects in the present and in the future, where rights will not wash away if there are concerned people who call for their retrieval.

Because this statement is so patently false that it borders on the absurd (the average December-January temperature in the Kabardia lowlands is -5 degrees Celsius), one can only assume he meant it as a joke for Stahl. Prisoners captured during battle were either forced into military service or given to the Cossacks as slaves. The livestock was given to the Cossacks and the stolen horses were sent to breeders in central Russia.[580]

Moral bankruptcy had led the tsarist Russian commanders to release specified threats. An example of an ultimatum is indicated as follows: "If you don't do this, you will face that."

> After the conclusion of the operation a major land redistribution project began. Ermolov gave the clans who fled to the mountains an ultimatum to recognize the Russian emperor as their sole sovereign and return to the lowlands.[581]

One cannot help but mention and clarify tragedies that had occurred against the Circassians in all places of their historical presence. Whether in the north, south, east, or west, they were broken and mocked. Offenses originated from multiofficial Russians, particularly the military command and generals in cooperation with the Cossack herds. They were assaulted and uprooted by force from their habitual territories.

> The landowners agreed to accept Russian rule but asked to stay where they were. Ermolov refused, and finally the majority of the clans agreed to be resettled on the left bank of the Terek. The few Kabaridan aristocrats who had remained loyal to Russia throughout the campaign were given huge tracts of land while the winter pastureland of clans who fled to the mountains were given to the Cossacks.[582]

Survivors were moved to places far from their homes, determined by the Russian leadership in advance. People would be forced to walk to where the vicious perpetrators wanted them to. It was an effort to deport them outside the borders of their territories while a large percentage would be deported overseas to the Ottoman Empire.

> As brutal as this campaign was, it was only a preparation for Ermolov's own assault in the spring. Several divisions armed with heavy artillery crossed into Kabardia in late May and followed the river valleys, burning villages and rustling livestock. Little organized resistance was met (there were very few Kabardians left), and the majority of the villagers fled to western Circassia.[583]

Paranoia led them to dwell on the preparations that were made to carry out brutal attacks that would create fatal blows. These operations took place by using lethal weapons and ammunition against lightly armed people and civilians that contained women and children. Aggressors were killing people and destroying and burning their homes, villages, farms, tools, and collectibles that they had gathered during their life.

> At the end of July, the Russians returned to the line, while Ermolov conducted surveys to determine the best places to build a new military line right through the heart of Kabardia. He wasted no time: although he sent his proposal for the new fortress to the emperor only in late July, Baskan Fortress had already been built and others were under construction.[584]

The author has listed acts that are considered genocide according to international laws and norms. Verification of Russian operations did not trigger disagreement on the legal aspect of the interpretation.

> Were Ermolov's actions and orders genocidal? Using definition of genocide in the UN Convention on Genocide, a very strong case against him can be made.[585]

> Ermolov and his men violated all five categories on several occasions. There can be no argument that he killed innocent Kabardians; even Tsarist historian Vasily Potto admits as much. As for points (b) and (c), the wholesale destruction of auls and the vast scale of theft of cattle and other goods necessary for the Kabardians' survival was, Ermolov's own words, intended to terrorize them.[586]

Strategies for unlawful implementation of the provisions and penalties are not accepted by anyone who must respect the military honor. Temperaments and whims are not acceptable when dealing with civilians, especially in adverse weather conditions. Unspeakable criminal acts would haunt the conscience of humanity. That should be incentive to recognize crimes and the Circassian genocide.

> As an experienced officer in the Caucasus, he knew that forcing people into the elements in winter was a death sentence, one more painful than if he had simply massacred them. By destroying entire communities, he disrupted the

Kabardians' social system, forcing them to flee and exit in such conditions that raising families was impossible.[587] Richmond

The Tsarist Russian army in the Caucasus played the role of terrorists who took children as hostages. They followed the methods of fascism stemming from abhorrent racism. Also, mass displacement of people from their place of living is "ethnic cleansing", which was committed against a specific ethnicity.

Finally, when the aristocrats who refused to submit fled to western Circassia, Ermolov sent their children, who had been taken as hostages in 1814, to orphanages or to the army. Because of his actions as well as those of his predecessors, the population of Kabardia was reduced from three hundred thousand in 1709 to only thirty thousand by the 1820s. All of the survivors were in Greater Kabardia, since the entire population of Lesser Kabardia had either died or fled to Western Circassia.[588]

Their reprehensible actions always agreed with their followed agenda. No one can acquit them of their despicable and cowardly predetermined acts. All their military operations were performed in cold blood, undaunted by any laws, values, or sense of ethical responsibility. All age categories from both genders of society were targeted, including the sick and disabled.

Additionally, Ermolov was well aware that the plague had decimated the population of Kabardia. A campaign that did not spare the elderly, women or children and that left thousands of people without shelter in a particularly harsh winter was certainly designed to deal a death blow to the Kabardian nation.[589]

The usual procedure was to keep pushing against soft targets, who were the Circassian people of Kabarda. No truce or rest was taken into consideration. Their task was to complete the conquest, the killing or expulsion of the inhabitants. Tsarist Russian forces were backed by mercenaries, intruders, and thieves who had intensified their repressive operations to get the job done as quickly as possible.

Ermolov's rapid colonization of Lesser Kabardia with Cossacks and Ossetians is clear evidence that he had no

> intention to allow the Kabardians to recover from their losses. Furthermore, as Safar Beituganov has argued, "the punitive expeditions were inescapably accompanied by the mass migration of Kabardian auls across the Kuban-More than sixty settlements between 1821 and 1822.[590]

Circassian families were always targeted. One of the most important Russian milestones in the comprehensive Russian war plan, both strategically and geographically, was the Kuban River. The Russians had already decided to occupy the Circassian homeland, including the coast of the Black Sea, to annihilate its nation or displace them either beyond the Kuban or to the Ottoman Empire.

> The fight of the Kabardians across the Kuban, which was considered the border between the two empires, was in fact the first manifestation of the mass migration of the Circassians to Turkey. Technically, Beituganov is correct: Ermolov's campaign resulted in the first forced migration to the Ottoman Empire. The fact that Circassians considered themselves independent doesn't alter that fact that, from the Russian perspective, the Kabardians were expelled from their homeland.[591]

Many lies had fallen within the fierce propaganda campaign against the Circassians. It continued for the duration of the Russian-Circassian War. It did not cease during the entire period, even to this day. Lies were not limited to place, dates, or certain persons. It was designed as a thorough discrediting process against an entire nation. Invaders utilized psychological warfare, to illogically and unreasonably harm their reputation by spreading their deadly poison.

> Beituganov goes a step further, claiming that the process actually began in 1803 when clans hostile to Russia were forced to migrate from their lands close to the line to the less desirable locations within Kabardia. Forced migrations would follow the Circassians until 1878, when the Russians drove them from the Balkans.[592]

The empire was a foreign occupation force and wanted to have its colonial hegemony imposed on all walks of life. The occupying administration wanted to change the demographic map in any way possible. They wanted to impose their will and even change the laws and the methods used by the indigenous people by force and arrogance.

> Ermolov's actions after the campaign likewise damaged the very fabric of Kabardian society. He abolished the religious courts and created a provisional court in Nalchik, outlawed the custom of pur, required Kabardians to supply information about anti-Russian activities among their compatriots, and restricted the rights of the Islamic clergy while allowing Christian missionaries free access to the peasantry.[593]

They wanted to prove to the Circassians from the beginning that their country had become an affiliate, where restrictive laws were imposed on travel and movement. Consolidation of the forces and military centers in the region were obtained, in addition to Russian and Cossack settlement centers. The entire community started to face daily harassment. Movements were determined even in raising animals while the grazing process of the livestock and land ownership was restricted.

> He Severely Crippled the Kabardians' ability to conduct trade by enacting a strict visa system, and at the same time constructed fortresses and settlements that for them disrupted the feeding of their herds. Although the purposed goal of these measures was to increase security for Russian and Cossack settlers, Ermolov knew very well that the consequences of these new regulations, particularly the restrictions of land use, would be further crippling to Kabardian society.[594]

Evil and aggressive intentions and plans were neither limited nor justified. They couldn't be interpreted except that such commanders did not have anything to offer except destruction and killing in accordance with the goals of their empire.

> Ermolov's destruction of what little remained of Kabardia was total. The reforms he instituted stripped the aristocrats of virtually all their authority and reduced them to subjects of the tsar. The Provisional Court in Nalchik, which dealt with all matters of any substance, was overseen by Russian officers (the first director being Kolsyrev).[595]

Administrative military laws breathed dictatorship and fascism. They were enacted, and the Circassians were forced to deal with them. The Cossacks always performed the role of a perjurer that simultaneously led several tasks that was within the occupation's needs.

They also play the role of policeman, being ready to perform any task assigned to them: "The court also had authority to send Cossack units into Kabardia and western Circassia in 'Police Missions'. One apparently progressive move was the exclusion of the pro-aristocratic Islamic clergy from the courts, which would seem to have been a step toward increasing the rights of the peasantry."[596]

Colonial Russians occupied land that was not owned by them and had no right to conquer. On the other hand, they intervened in the laws of the land.

The Bolsheviks declared that the "October Revolution" (fifty years after the occupation of Circassia) had occurred due to worn Russian laws: "95% of Russia's people were poor peasant farmers who owned no land but paid high rents to the country's landlords. Most of these landlords just happened to be members of the royal family."[597]

Accordingly, Circassians were the only party that cared about their own affairs as well as take care of the laws that affected their nation: "However, this turned out to apply only to major cases in which Russian law held sway; disputes between landowners and the peasantry continued to be decided 'according to ancient [Kabardian] customs and rites', meaning under complete control of the aristocracy and clergy."[598]

The point of no return was passed by the Russian Empire towards destroying and eliminating the Circassians. It is an ancient nation with a proven existence of thousands of years. It was the responsibility, together with the approval and authentication of the supreme bodies in the empire, that started with the emperor in the capital city of St. Petersburg and ended with the tiny Cossack terror units in Circassia.

> One last chapter in this story shows how much the attitude of St. Petersburg had changed since Bulgakov's tenure. In the spring of 1825 the Kabardian aristocracy in exile made a final attempt to break Russian control by the rather extreme method of compelling their countrymen who remained behind to flee to western Circassia as well.[599]

Without a doubt, the Russians had the ability, through their different sources, to get information about the Circassians. They could get knowledge when certain retaliation operations were planned against their terrorist forces. When that was possible, they took the initiative and carried out attacks first. Most of the time, they grabbed the element of surprise to finish off the Circassians in their own homes.

> Hoping to exploit the growing anger at the new regulations, a joint Circassian force of around 500 men prepared for an assault on Russian forces in Kabardia from an aul belonging to the Karamure clan. Line Commander General Alexei Velyaminov learned of the impending assault and crossed the Kuban River into the Besleney lands.[600]

Part of the element of surprise was to attack at night in addition to using proper attack and withdrawal plans, not to mention the methods that were utilized in murder, destruction, arson, and genocide. They did not hide their objectives that they were conducting their operations for, thus eliminating the human element in their destined target. These inhuman acts were committed by herds of monsters.

> Attacking at night, Velyaminov's forces burned the subjected aul to the ground along with most of its inhabitants. Nearly everyone who survived the fire was slaughtered. Afterward the Cossacks counted 570 bodies not including those killed in the fire. All the cattle and houses were stolen and 139 villages who survived were taken prisoners.[601]

It was not a secret that the success of the Russian Empire occupying Circassia and committing heinous genocide was due to the corrupt elements who cooperated and acted with the invading forces against their nation and its existence: "For his participation in the massacre, Ermolov recommended Major General Pydor Bekovich-Cherkassky, a former Kabardian pshi, for the St. George's Cross for 'an exceptionally brave enterprise, fulfilled in the most successful manner.'"[602]

Surprisingly, there are some people, up to the present day, trying to invent explanations and give justifications for offenders. There is a trend to reduce the effects of the crime and tragedy that has befallen one of the oldest nations of the Caucasus. All crime tools, documented confessions, and tragic results prove beyond doubt the magnitude of the tragedy.

> Emperor Alexander rejected the request, stating that "if his behavior at the beginning of the assault merited a reward, he lost his right to it, since the action that was begun sensibly was concluded by the total annihilation of over 300 families,

among which were primarily women and children who were not participating in the battle."[603]

Russian laws and norms are concerned with specific imperial policies. According to facts and realities, good conduct depended on the magnitude of the offenses committed against the victims. Those who were granted pride benefits, decorations, and medals were of a special caliber. They were either Russian or Cossack criminals with no human principles or those who betrayed their homeland and their people.

The emperor could still recognize barbaric behavior for what it was, but his attitude toward it had changed significantly. In 1810, such behavior had led to Bulgakov's dismissal, while in 1825 it was merely cause to withhold honors. It was only a temporary setback as well. Ermolov recommended Bekovich-Cherkassky for the award again in July, and this time Alexander approved the request.[604]

In all circumstances, honest Circassians showed great courage and peerless altruism in defending their homeland. They resisted all attempts to be conquered. They attempted to thwart Russia's aggressive plans, which were designed to eliminate them once and for all.

Despite the death of their leadership, joint Abzakh-Kabardian forces attacked Russian positions throughout the summer and broke into Kabardia. They caused significant damage but were unable to inspire an exodus into western Circassia. The Circassians continued to harass the Russians where they could, but by 1826 Kabardia was firmly under Tsarist control.[605]

The Russians throughout the Russian-Circassian War had their own colonial concepts on the table. Those included demographic engineering, ethnic cleansing, and other evil measures.

Some Circassians swallowed the poison all at once, but some others in batches. Nevertheless, the concluding result was the same: "Thus, ended the first phase of the Russo-Circassian War, the conquest of Kabardia. The aristocrats in exile became known as the 'beglye kabardintsy' : Refugee Kabardians, and remained in western Circassia until they met their fate in 1864."[606]

Although the war had taken a long time, the inevitable result was disastrous. On the impact of the nation's sufferings, the Russian Empire had occupied

Circassia. Vicious leaders did not hesitate to order military units and their supporting Cossacks of committing various crimes of unspeakable cruelty, even if the orders were inconsistent with the formal laws, which were not applied.

> Despite his apparent success in Kabardia, Ermolov's tenure in the North Caucasus was an unqualified failure. His massacres of noncombatants, wholesale plunder of livestock, and dishonesty only inflamed hatred of the Russians in the North Caucasus. Whatever chance there was for a rapprochement was almost totally destroyed.[607]

All people and nations of the Caucasus were targeted because the Russian Empire intended to occupy the entire Caucasus region: "In the east, the Murid movement was a district consequence of his merciless attacks on the indigenous peoples, while in the west the Circassians were so enraged that by 1830 the Shapsugs declared war on Russia."[608]

Serious researchers and scholars have not given up on clearing things up. When following the scientific method of researching through references and sources, they will reach their objectives. Being specific in gathering documented information to be extrapolated will lead to the utilization of the results. Biased information about Russian generals' unprecedented crimes was refuted by respectable researchers.

> As Moshe Gammer concisely states, 'one of [Ermolov's] legacies in particular, to which all Russian sources remained blind, proved to be very detrimental to his successors in their dealings with the mountaineers: his extreme brutality achieved results opposite to his intentions and made the natives immune to terror.[609]

The tsarist Russian Empire's policies imposed terrorism as a means of intimidation and oppression: "Experiencing the worst, they were afraid of the Russians no more'. In a very real sense, Ermolov set in motion the mutual distrust and hatred that would end in genocide."[610]

The tsarist Russian military and propaganda campaigns were launched against the entire Circassian nation. Some Circassians and non-Circassians have claimed that the Russians did not fight the Kabardian Circassians.[611] That turned out to be false and sort of a deception because the Russian Empire at the time was in the process of getting rid of all Circassians.

The destruction of Kabardia remained hidden from the world. When Ermolov conducted the raids that nearly annihilated the kabardians, not a single European newspaper took notice. As the European powers were vying for supremacy in a post-Napoleonic world, there was little interest in an obscure corner of the Russian Empire, far away from any strategic resources or shipping routes.[612]

There might have been priorities to be followed regarding the timing of the deadly military operations against the inhabited Circassian regions and their tribes, but there was a determination to implement the Russians' military plans. One of their most important goals was the overall control of the coast of the Black Sea and the disposal of the residents of coastal areas as appropriate.

Western Circassia was another matter. The Black Sea had been an arena of international competition for centuries, and while in the eighteenth century it was for all intents and purposes an Ottoman lake, Russia continually pressed for control of the northern shore.[613]

No doubt that Russia had followed a timetable drawn by its strategists and military forces' headquarters. Circassia and other areas were in the process to be occupied and annexed. This didn't occur as a coincidence. Wars and conflicts had occurred in the eighteenth and nineteenth centuries among the major powers at the time. The Russian and Ottoman Empires were major players who exchanged concessions.

The first foothold was the Crimean peninsula, which the Russians annexed in 1784. The Circassian occupied two hundred miles of the Black Sea coastline east of the Crimea, and Russia was determined to take this strategic region as well. Once the Black Sea Cossacks settled the north bank of the Kuban River, St. Petersburg looked for an opportunity to expand southward into Circassia.[614]

Regions and countries that were not directly or physically dominated were specified. They were exchanged on the map, between peoples' gamblers, even without the knowledge of the native people. Such unethical actions were going on consistently with the colonial desire to control others' homelands.

At first the other major powers took no notice, but the
Ottomans quickly realized the potentially mortal threat Russia
posed to their troubled empire. They had been manipulating
the Circassians themselves for decades in the vain hope that
they could one day exercise genuine authority over Circassia,
but by 1829 they realized this was never going to happen.[615]

These countries' high-ranking officials used to wear many faces with many different agendas and plans. They used to say one thing and completely do the opposite. False promises were made, irrational and even unrealistic when compared to the facts that occurred on the ground. Common matters had united them. They were partners in decision making and compromises as per surrounding conditions.

In an effort to cut their losses they relinquished their
claims to Circassia in the Treaty of Adrianople. Even this failed
to draw much attention, but when Russia quickly exploited
the weak position of the Porte (as the Ottoman government
was known) to gain special rights in the Dardanelles, Great
Britain saw its own interests in the Black Sea threatened.[616]

Perhaps the most important reason for keeping the Circassians away from the spotlight was the Russian Empire's efforts. They wanted to keep them isolated and under siege of the naval blockade. They wanted to keep the Circassians occupied with the devastating war that kept them busy. Their collective attention was to focus on the way in which they can defend their homeland by using their own resources.

Suddenly European newspapers and politicians took
up the Circassian cause, and some even called for military
intervention. The issue was debated in Parliament, and it
looked at one point as though Britain would go to war with
Russia in order to establish a protectorate over the struggling
nation.[617]

Russia's declaration of war against Circassia was unique of its kind and extension. The Circassians alone had to face the Russian Empire, its invading army and mercenaries. They had to be aware of the conspiracies that existed against them from all directions. Foreign envoys and delegates from different countries were received in Circassia, but there were no positive and tangible results.

Agents lived among Circassians, promising international support and urging them to escalate their war against the Russians. Ultimately, however, the British deserted Circassia. A few politicians continued to press for action, but Parliament wasn't in the mood for a major war. All that British intervention accomplished was to make the Russians determined to conquer Circassia as quickly as possible.[618]

Empty promises by those who promised to help were not honest. At a later stage, the Circassians started realizing the extent of the lack of credibility of the Ottoman Empire. Empty promises were given to them while keeping them unaware of the bilateral agreements that were concluded with the Russian Empire behind their backs.

On September 14, 1829, Russia and Turkey signed the Treaty of Adrianople. Article 4 contained the following stipulation: "All the coast of the Black Sea from the mouth of the Kuban to the wharf of Saint Nikolai inclusive shall enter into the permanent possession of the Russian Empire."[619]

They probably seemed to have paid attention to certain issues by sending agreed-upon signals. Sometimes they might be included or concluded as undeclared items, which were implied or agreed upon in secret. Paying attention to the dissemination of information at a later stage will be too late to know about the hidden conspiracies. In all cases, Russia was occupied with maintaining the war against the Circassians in the absence of the world and the Europeans in particular.

Circassia was never mentioned by name in the treaty, although in the preface Emperor Nicholas I is described, among many other titles, as "the hereditary ruler and possessor of the Circassian and mountain princes". This, of course, was nonsense: the Russian tsars had never been any sort of ruler of Circassian or "mountain" princes, and certainly had no hereditary claim to anything[620]

Exchange of mutual interests and benefits between the dominant forces and powers in the region is an ordinary activity for them where, in fact, from a logical point of view, both powers offend the true owners of the land in a blatant infringement of their rights to sovereignty.

Circassia

> As for transferring the coast of the Black Sea to Russian rule, the Turks did have a series of forts there, but by no means did they control the coast. The forts were trading outposts and places from which the Porte hoped one day to mount an assault on Circassia like the one the Russians were conducting from the north.[621]
>
> Since, according to the treaties of Kucuk Kaynarca and Jassy (1792), all land south of the Kuban River belonged to Turkey, when the Porte ceded the coast in the Treaty of Adrianapole, St. Petersburg took that to mean all land north of the coast was now Russian as well.[622]

Turning events during the eighteenth and nineteenth centuries showed how greedy the Russian Empire was. The Ottoman Empire seemed to be in a weaker position. All those treaties and agreements had placed the Ottoman Empire as low-key. That prepared the scene for the Ottomans to look vulnerable, to be the prey, with all its properties and areas of influence.

> This too was nonsense. Turkey's "possession" of Circassia under Kucuk Kayanacra and Jassy was a de jure declaration that had no connection with reality, so the Russian assumption that Circassia was now under the jurisdiction of St. Petersburg was a fiction built upon a fiction.[623]

The weakness of the Ottoman Empire encouraged the severity of the ambitions expressed by the Russian Empire to seize Ottoman properties. That reflected the nature of the treaties and agreements, to end up all in Russia's favor. Any provisions to the agreements were to satisfy Tsarist Russia.

That is what triggered them to go ahead in implementing the colonial plans to control the regions.

> In his memoirs, Russian officer Fyodor Tornau claims St. Petersburg saw Article 4 for what it really was-the removal of a legal barrier to the conquest of Circassia: [The Turks'] connection had meaning on paper only-in reality, Russia could rule the land ceded to it through force alone. The Caucasus tribes that the Sultan considered his subjects never obeyed him. They recognized him as the successor to Muhammad and the Padishah of all Muslims, their spiritual leader, but they paid no taxes and contributed no soldiers. The mountaineers tolerated the Turks who occupied a few

fortresses on the sea coast because of common religion, but didn't allow them to interfere in their internal affairs and fought with them or, more accurately, attacked them mercilessly for any interference. The Sultan's concession was completely incomprehensible to the mountaineers.[624]

Experience has proven that power, force, strength, and influence can acquire anything. That is what the Russian Empire gained and enjoyed, even though it took them a long time to achieve this. They attained what they wanted slowly but surely. It was the result of the weakness of others.

The Russians were sidestepping another legal barrier. By acquiring Circassia through their interpretation of the Treaty of Adrianople, Russia was violating Article 5 of the 1827 Treaty of London, in which the signatories (England, Russia, and France) agreed not to seek "any augmentation of territory" as a result of the Greek War for Independence.[625]

Greed was at its height, concerning the extent of egoistic gratification. Advancement over the years was earned through thoughtlessness and provocation practiced against the Ottoman Empire being the weak part of this example. Their success was a result of proven willingness. Ottoman wars with Russia were totally different issues from the Russian-Circassian War.

Since this is what caused the Russo-Turkish War of 1828-1829, Russia's acquisition of Circassia was a violation of the Treaty of London-eve Caucasus Archeographical Commission chairman Adolf Berzhe, a staunch defender of the 1864 deportation, admitted as much. In eliminating the Ottoman problem, the Russians had provoked the British.[626]

Any peaceful step taken by the Russian Empire with the Circassians would be temporary at best. Eventually, the war would resume as per a decision or action provoked by Russian military hawks. War always resumed, citing excuses that were invented or provoked. They were dreaming to reach their ultimate goal of occupying Circassian entirely.

By the time of Adrianople, the western Circassians and Russians were on the verge of a workable relationship, but it came about only after decades of fighting. It began in the 1790s, when the Shapsugs unseated their aristocracy. The

Bjedukh and Hamysh aristocrats agreed to help the Shapsug pshis regain power, and after a series of failed attacks, Hamysh pshi Batcheri Hajimuke led a delegation to St. Petersburg to ask Catherine for help. The empress granted his request and ordered Zakhary Chepega, ataman (chief) of the Black Sea Cossack army, so support the aristocrats.[627]

Russia has made itself the enemy of Circassia for hundreds of years. Artillery was used against Circassian cavalry. Vicious acts cannot be obtained except by those who represent evil. Their efforts were exerted to choose suitable criminal methods that enabled them to overcome Circassian resistance. The Russians and Cossacks' persistent killing and murdering to gain victory never yielded.

On July 10, 1796, the Cossacks and their cannons joined the Hamysh and Bjedukh tribes against the Shapsugs in the battle of Bziuk, abut eleven miles south of Ekaterinodar (modern Krasnodar). Although the Shapsug forces numbered perhaps as high as ten thousand and the aristocrats had only one thousand men, the Cossack artillery threw the Shapsug calvary into chaos. After losing as many as two thousand men, the Shapsug infantry retreated.[628]

Evolution of ideas did not discontinue from the Circassians at any given time. They had even broadened involving all strata of society in decision making after constructive dialogue. The Circassians were developing their communities according to social, political, and military needs, even during the raging war.

Seemingly, the imposed genocidal war prevented all the tribes from acknowledging and endorsing the changes at the same time. They were flexible in choosing leaders that could act in the public's interest and even fateful matters according to everyone's participation in the decisions that affected their present and future.

It was a pyrrhic victory for the aristocrats, though, for the civil was continued until the Shapsug aristocracy gave up all their privileges at the Pecheteniko Zafes in 1803. By virtue of their success against the aristocrats, the Shapsugs became the most respected (and feared) tribe in Circassia. Russian intervention in the revolution turned the Shapsugs into the most powerful enemy the Russians had ever confronted in the Caucasus.[629]

Acquired reputation and particularization of misdeeds and wicked acts made the Cossacks possible targets: "The situation deteriorated quickly. In 1798 Catherine's son Paul accepted Shapsug pshi Ali Sheretluke's petition to be accepted as Russian subject, after which Sheretluke moved his villages to the north side of the Kuban River. In response, the Shapsugs increased their attacks on the Cossacks."630

The Cossack Atamans and their subjects and followers had always competed for murder and criminality: "At the end of 1799 Paul suddenly replaced Black Sea Cossack Ataman Kotlyarevky with Fyodor Bursak. This unprecedented move (the Cossacks had always elected their leaders) was immediately followed by Bursak's request to be granted permission to cross the Kuban in order to carry out 'punitive raids'."631

It is probably shameful too in such a tone, as has been described, against the "Cossacks from the past". Nevertheless, their evilness and wrongdoings will never be forgotten. Cossack mercenaries always obeyed what their Russian masters requested them to do and more. They had a thirst for killing and looting.

> Paul granted Bursak's request and, beginning in summer 1800, Bursak led large Cossack parties into Circassia where he burned auls and stole cattle, making no distinction between hostile and pro-Russian tribes. Throughout 1802 and 1803 the Cossacks massacred villages, took prisoners to be sold as slaves, and stole large numbers of livestock.632

The Russians had orders and policies that they implemented in cooperation with all those who fought alongside them. The Cossacks had implemented the orders issued by Russian commanders and officers. They used terror, fear, and intimidation in the Circassian territories. The Circassians had no choice but to act: "The Circassians retaliated in kind. Finally, in December 1804, Bursak led thirteen divisions across the Kuban and, as Cossack historian Fyodor Shcherbina reports, 'having covered the entire land of the bitter enemies of the Black Sea Cossacks in every direction', destroyed their homes, property, and food and forced them to accept Russian suzerainty."633

The Russian Empire always had a lack of respect and appreciation towards the Cossacks. This arrogant Russian opinion was toward all Cossacks alike. But some of them who protected and perpetuated Russian interests were treated differently. During the Soviet era, they were excluded from the scene. In Putin's Russia, they were given back some of their original benefits and powers while those whom the Russians held hatred and racist opinions toward were given lesser status and treatment; they were less desirable. There was no difference between the people and nations of the Caucasus, for example.

That was what the Russians wanted to do. They destroyed everything, even agricultural crops and food storages. They killed everything that moved and looted properties and changed surroundings: "The Russians had never had any problems with the western Circassian tribes until the Black Sea Cossacks settled north of the Kuban. Their predecessors were the Zaporozhian Cossacks, who were exploited by St. Petersburg as defenders of the frontier with Poland. When they rebelled in 1708, Peter the Great decided to eliminate them."[634]

Those who were seduced and fully prepared for implementing the colonial policies of the Russian Empire were ultimately confronted with a bitter truth. They were eventually betrayed by the same authoritarian state that they actively served. Regardless of the consequences, size, or importance, when their masters decided that their mission has ended, their role would be over.

> The fact of the matter was that they were brigands who served a purpose during wartime but whose indiscriminate pillaging ultimately made them a liability. Even pro-Cossack historian Potto admits that "the Zaporozhian Sech . . . caused Russia nothing but misery with their raids on turkey on Poland, which constantly threatened to tie it up in a new war with their neighbors."[635]
>
> By 1775 the Zaporozhians had been split up and scattered around Russia. General Potemkin converted one section of the Zaporozhians into the Black Sea Army during the Russo-Turkish War of 1787–1791, and after the war they petitioned St. Petersburg to settle the land north of the Kuban River. The region was relatively uninhabited after the Russian annihilated the Nogay Turks living there in the 1770s.[636]

Agility helps avoid heavy casualties, especially when facing an army using heavy weaponry against infantry fighters. Hit-and-run tactics were utilized by the Circassians to take the enemy by surprise. The Tsarist Russians were well-known for their deteriorated reputation of integrity and inhumane behavior when they invaded Circassian lands.

> However, the Circassians had relied upon this area to graze their herds for centuries. Even before Catherine granted formal permission, the Cossacks were settling the land directly adjacent to Circassia. The Cossack population

north of the Kuban exploded in the 1790s, exceeding sixty thousand by the end of the eighteenth century.[637]

The Tsarist Russian Empire used everything from reason of differentiation, division, and fooling people in their arsenal. They even used religion as a weapon from their arsenal. They followed this example as an ostrich would think that it is invisible when planting its head in the sand when demonstrating concern for religion or Christianity in particular.

When the war was waged against Circassia, probably more than half of the Circassians were Christians. Even now, many countries that are considered to be targeted by the Russian Federation are Christian, such as Georgia, Ukraine, and the three Baltic republics of Estonia, Latvia, and Lithuania, among others.

> As Thomas Barrett has aptly noted concerning this process: The North Caucasus was a part of the fault line between Christianity and Islam that stretches from the Balkans through Central Asia. The Russian state tried to push that line further south by Christianizing the region, not so much through missionary activity, but by settling Christians there and getting rid of Muslims.[638]

There was friction interspersed by friendly and unfriendly relations between the Circassians and some of the Cossack groups who roamed the remote outskirts of Circassia. Nevertheless, this took a purely local atmosphere. It didn't reach to the extent of hostilities and systematic killing and murder. It didn't indicate territories' occupation or a declaration of war that needed mobilizing their armies.

> The Cossacks had played this role in the northeastern Caucasus for many decades. Of course, some had settled in the northwest as well, but they had relatively peaceful relations with the Circassians. There was a bit of theft here and there: Cossacks raided Circassians and other Cossacks, Circassians raided Cossacks and other Circassians, and Cossacks and Circassians raided Turks together.[639]

It is useful to find out how hostilities and animosity increased between the Circassians and Cossacks. It is important to know how the Russians had a direct impact on creating these reasons of conflicts that extends back decades, even centuries. The Cossacks were enrolled in the ranks of the Russian military forces. They had enrolled themselves in a conflict that is impossible to forget.

The Cossacks fought the Circassians and participated in committing genocide, forced deportation, and the occupation of Circassia. They resettled Circassians and took part in seizing farmland and sea coasts. Circassian properties were seized by force as a result of the devastating war.

> This was life in the North Caucasus, and no one had a problem with it. What escalated the violence was the large influx of settlers after 1792, which cut off the Circassians from some of their traditional pastures. The rapid construction of military outposts certainly didn't encourage trust either: along the 170-mile frontier, the Cossacks constructed sixty posts armed with batteries and more than one hundred pickets.[640]

It is not possible to give these savage conducts a more appropriate description of people who disregard human morality and standards. How could a group of people live with their communities by killing, looting, ransacking rights, and seizing the property of others? It is not logical for a group of people to lack notice of tragedies of an entire nation that suffered from tyranny.

> As Potto notes: With the appearance of Russians all along the banks of Kuban, a wall of Cossack settlements rose before the Circassians; the steppes north of the Kuban were closed off to them, and the Don disappeared into the inaccessible distance. At that point, everything that had nourished the Circassian soul for centuries, all its long martial experience and enterprise, strength and boldness became directed at those who were impending them from spreading out into the Kuban lands, which had at that time became the stronghold of the Russian border and at the same time a bloody arena of countless conflicts.[641]

Frankly, it was the intervention of the Cossacks into Circassians affairs and the Russian war against them that affected the general situation in the Caucasus in general and Circassia in particular: "All of this happened just as the Cossacks interfered in the Shapsug civil war at Bziuk, and it was shortly afterward that violence dramatically escalated."[642]

Banditry, looting, theft, and destruction of peaceful Circassian villages were conducted without mercy or pity. Innocent civilians were not protected. Cossack and Russian forces operated as if they were armed criminal gangs. They deliberately killed people and forced them to flee their homes.

Russian major general Gangeblov was sent to Circassia. He joined Bursak and his forces in the brigandage, where "in May, his and Bursak's combined forces destroyed all the auls along five river valleys, after which Gangeblov ordered a retreat over Bursak's protests. None of these operations served any military purpose; even Potto admits that Bursak's raids of 1807 were of absolutely no use to the Black Sea Province and only provoked the Circassians into further aggressive actions."[643]

Citing the magnitude of the devastation that was inflicted by the invading forces proves the number of Circassian inhabitants who were affected. The direct and indirect loss of life and property were crimes of murder, extermination, and deportation that were carried out as per direct orders given to the Tsarist Russian forces. The main objective was to destroy the Circassian nation once and for all.

> Altogether, almost two hundred auls were destroyed during the period 1807-1810. How many people died as a result of massacres, starvation, and exposure to the elements will never be known, but using KhanGirey's estimate of two hundred persons per aul, at least forty thousand people were displaced by Bursak's raids.[644]

The Russians have never shown goodwill towards the Circassians; it was quite the opposite. They always showed a deep desire for the urgent need to get rid of them, as if they were die-hard competitors to them. Not a single agreement held up for long at any time or at any level between Russia and Circassia. This is evidence of the then existence of spiteful Russians who were filled with hatred and extreme hostility towards the Circassians.

> What was terribly sad about all this was that the Russians could have easily developed a close and lucrative relationship with the Circassians. After Bursak was gone many Russian civilian administrators had great success creating commercial ties between the two peoples. St. Petersburg established thirteen commercial centers in the northwest Caucasus in 1811 and even reached a formal trade agreement with the Natuhays.[645]

Even if the materials that were traded will lead to harm the Circassians in the long run, the obstacles that appeared on the way would subsequently eliminate any future cooperation. It will be the inevitable result; what divides between them is much more than what unites.

In 1813 Rafael Scassi was placed in charge of developing commercial ties; after he arrived in the region, he attended numerous hases and concluded treaties that increased trade. The Circassians even sold the Russians much needed wood for the use in shipbuilding at Sevastopol. Scassi also supervised the creation of a major trading center at the mouth of the Pshad River south of Gelendzhik, which increased economic ties further.[646]

In dealing with the Circassians, Russian behavior showed and indicated that the trade deal is an interim and temporary phase of relations that would eventually end sooner or later: "In the summer of 1819 tariffs were removed from the sale of salt, and new trading posts were opened in Kerch and Bugaze. The Russians, however, had no intention of simply remaining trading partners."[647]

Russia had been working through its malignant scheme since it began preparing to have its soldiers set foot on Circassian land. The plans and policies have never changed, but perhaps there were phases, as well as implementing various methods. The final plans would at last result in control of Circassia in any way possible. They exhausted all available tactics and tricks, leading to revenge from the Circassians.

In 1821 Alexander I authorized "Regulations for Commercial Relations with the Circassians and Abazas," which, in addition to designating Kerch and Bugaze as official trade centers, enumerated precise legal procedures for Russo-Circassian commerce. St. Petersburg's goal was to make the Circassians do dependent upon Russian trade that they could be coerced into incorporation into the empire.[648]

All restrictions on the available possibilities on the table were restricted for Circassian utilization. The decision was, in all cases, to keep their options orbiting in a vicious circle. They were not allowed to have the opportunity to be in a position that enabled them to choose what suited their situation.

Thomas Barrett explains: Russian trade policy with the mountain people was directly connected to attempts to conquer the region through winning over, subduing, killing, or exiling the native inhabitants. Creating a salt dependency was one such tool. Forts or the central government also issued periodic bans on selling weapons or materials used for making weapons such as iron and steel. By the nineteenth century, there was also a fair amount of scheming about how to draw the mountain people into the Russian orbit peacefully, through and expansion of trade.[649]

Russian aspirations and ambitions were not unknown by the Circassians. The preliminary situation indicated the intentions of the Russian and Cossack troops. Attempts to attack and occupy Circassia were apparent.

The Circassians had long understood what the Russians' goal was. The Natuhays expressed their opinion quite clearly when French traveler Edouard Taibout de Marigny visited Circassia in 1813: "The Russians...have always shown the greatest desire to take possession of our territory . . . We nevertheless consented that they should enjoy the sacred right of hospitality, and that one of their vessels should approach Pshad [River] under the direction of Scassi, a merchant known to us for several years, who took a cargo of wood for building, in exchange for salt."[650]

With no doubt, the agreements provided a mix of motivations and rewards, which were enjoyed by both sides at face value. The Circassians, in particular, were at ease for a given time, thus being in a break from sanctions, punishments, and repercussions from the blockade. Probably, benefits were considered motivation to hail bilateral relations, even though if they were to be temporary.

Despite the new regulations and the distrust, trade between the Circassians and Russians was vibrant throughout the 1820s. This attracted the attention of Ermolov, who was interested only in conquest. Responding to Scassi's proposal for direct trade with the Circassians, Ermolov wrote in 1819: "I . . . find that the measures that Scassi proposes will never be of any real use to the administration, but will only result in extreme disconsolation for both the mountaineers and the Russians in their mutual trade, since the mountaineers, being generally untrustworthy, lazy, and uneducated, will remain in ignorance for a long time to come."[651]

Apparently, making peace with the Circassians had prevented or delayed the brutal Russian military operations against the Circassians. They intended to patch up the set military plans. This is what was expected from the start. A Russian commander and general in the Russian army was soliciting to cancel and end the agreements reached, possibly to block the way for possible engagement in joint economic and trade agreements between Russia and Circassia:

> In 1822 Ermolov wrote Foreign Minister Karl Nesserlrode in an attempt to undermine Russo-Circassian commerce, which was now thriving: It's impossible not to feel respect for the government's intention to develop trade relations with the mountain peoples of the Kuban region, and through it to supply them with their essential needs, soften their severity, and moreover convince them of the benefits of ties with us, lessen the exclusive influence over them that the Porte exercises, and finally to bring enlightenment to the half-savage peoples. But the application of this splendid theory is very inconvenient, if not impossible. This project cannot be established among a people hostile to enlightenment, under the power of a foreign government, under an ignorant Muslim government!"[652]

Selective actions, criminal intentions, and preoccupations of revenge all fall under one description: the law of the jungle. This result had placed the Circassians' destiny in the hands of murderers, bandits, and those who ignored the law. It is inconceivable to conclude that those who were obliged to protect the law broke all laws and norms in the empire and even betrayed the principles of humanity.

> Ermolov's warnings couldn't alter reality, however, and trade continued apace. Unable to stop Scassi through official channels, Ermolov took the law into his own hands and sabotaged relations between the Circassians and Russians through the only means at his disposal.[653]

A general who disobeys the law is considered a renegade. Those who betray the law and even positions of leadership that they occupy will be held responsible. They conspired with their superiors and subordinates against their country, which is punishable by law. As result, they attacked people and the countries that they were no part of. This makes their country bear responsibility in the eyes of other nations.

Not surprisingly, they misled national opinion and they did not maintain the truth: "In 1821 Ermolov sent Major General Mikhail Vlasov to take command of the army. At that point the Circassian campaign began to parallel Ermolov's devastation of Kabardia. Vlasov is described by Scherbina as a brigand who 'without doubt was ruled by military vanity and a thirst for rewards."[654]

Junior commanders and officers executed and implemented orders issued by their superiors to satisfy the wishes of their commanders and top command centers. Rogue armies do not take into consideration the law of the land of the state that they belong to. They committed evil military tasks. Various military units would be ordered to execute a variety of crimes and devastation against civilians. People resisting the offenders with individual weapons would be murdered and punished.

> His first engagement with the Circassians was at the battle of Kalaus in October 1821, when the Russians cornered the Circassian force in an estuary and killed perhaps 100 men with cannon fire, while perhaps 1,000 more drowned. Three days later, the Circassians returned to collect the bodies of their comrades and Vlasov ambushed them, using his cannons to kill another 250.[655]

There was a lack of balance and proportionality in the quality, quantity, and intensity of the weapons and ammunition used for destruction and annihilation. Devastation affected inhabitants, villages, cattle, and all properties of importance. The military operations included exposure processes, blitzes, and raids fulfilled indiscriminately with no second thought to any humane or compassionate considerations.

> Nearly all of Vlasov's subsequent actions appeared to serve military purpose at all. Between 1822 and 1824 he burned auls and rustled cattle, making no distinction between peaceful and hostile communities. In two cases Vlasov destroyed the auls of Circassians who were loyal to Russia, and it was the second raid that ended his career.[656]

The quality of the savage officers and commanders are known from their detailed military biography that would reflect an indication of military discipline. Lack of regard for humane conduct and unbalanced character would lead to verify the type of personality of the officer. Not abiding human principles and ethics would give an indication of an unstable personality that should not be in a leadership position.

> The victim, Natuhay pshi Sagat-Girey Kalabatluke, files a formal protest that was supported by Scassi. An investigation

headed by Adjutant-General Strekalov found Vlasov guilty and even prompted a reprimand from Emperor Nicholas I, which was almost unheard of by this point in the war: "It is clear that it was not just a contemptuous desire to gain a reputation for military excellence without real effort that motivated the destruction of the villages of some unfortunate victims, but also unforgivable vanity and a shameful desire for profit."[657]

Apparently, the officers and commanders of the Tsarist Russian imperial army had a confirmed course for future professional progress. There was a possibility to have a guaranteed benefit when attaining higher military ranks. The obvious approach was mass murder, burning, destruction, looting, deportation, and illegal occupation of Circassian villages and territories. This was the best method to attain a leadership position.

Systematic looting was the prerogative of the commanders, officers, and other military ranks. The spoils were distributed to the beneficiaries and participants in military operations against Circassian villages. Circassian personal and household properties were seized; the Circassians have been stripped of all their possessions.

Potto excuses Vlasov for his abuse by noting that everything he stole from the Circassian auls "he gave to the Cossacks to improve their households and support their orphaned children". He blames Vlasov's fall on Strekalov's ignorance of the true state of affairs in the region and the machinations of Vlasov's "enemies."[658]

The Cossacks resettled the territories while the Circassians were being killed or deported. Theorists and strangers have shown their going over of overestimates and underestimates of the proceedings.

Shcherbina, certainly no friend of the Circassians, has a different perspective: "The finale was fitting for the vain general who, in his pursuit of military glory, on the one hand forgot the interests of the people he was sent to defend, and on the other viciously punished the Circassians with unnecessary severity for minor infractions as well as major attacks, and occasionally for no reason whatsoever. The first group, the Cossacks, he destroyed economically, and the second, the Circassians, he drove to the extreme limit of hatred."[659]

They competed in committing their unrivaled barbaric acts. The administrators encouraged military commanders and officers. They showed their heinous acts and crimes while having their hands covered in the blood of innocent people that were massacred.

> Shcherbina also notes that "Vlasov conducted himself in this manner at the pleasure of Ermolov, who was a zealous advocate of a war of devastation against the mountaineers and generously rewarded the executors of his punitive plans."[660]

Convention on the Prevention and Punishment of the Crime of Genocide

Genocide is an organized crime that is committed against a group of people, according to the abbreviation given in the title of "the declaration made by the General Assembly of the United Nations in its resolution 96 (I) dated 11 December 1946." It states that "genocide is a crime under international law, contrary to the spirit and aims of the United Nations and condemned by the civilized world."[661] The international legal definition of genocide is found in articles II and III of the 1948 Convention on the Prevention and Punishment of Genocide.

Article II:

In the present Convention, genocide means any of the following acts committed with intent to destroy, in whole or in part, a national, ethnical, racial or religious group, as such:
 a) Killing members of the group;
 b) Causing serious bodily or mental harm to members of the group;
 c) Deliberately inflicting on the group conditions of life calculated to bring about its physical destruction in whole or in part;
 d) Imposing measures intended to prevent births within the group;
 e) Forcibly transferring children of the group to another group.

Article III:
The following acts shall be punishable:
 a) Genocide;

    b) Conspiracy to commit genocide;
    c) Direct and public incitement to commit genocide;
    d) Attempt to commit genocide;
    e) Complicity in genocide.[662]

The Genocide Watch, the International Campaign to End Genocide, has considered that "genocide is a process that develops in ten stages that are predictable but not inexorable. At each stage, preventive measures can stop it. The process is not linear. Stages may occur simultaneously. Logically, later stages must be preceded by earlier stages. But all stages continue to operate throughout the process."[663]

The Genocide Watch, the International Campaign to End Genocide, stated 10 stages for a genocide, which mentioned that "denial" is the last stage. It "is the final stage that lasts throughout and always follows a genocide. It is among the surest indicators of further genocidal massacres. The perpetrators of genocide dig up the mass graves, burn the bodies, try to cover up the evidence and intimidate the witnesses. They deny that they committed any crimes, and often blame what happened on the victims. They block investigations of the crimes, and continue to govern until driven from power by force, when they flee into exile."[664]

Russian Responsibility

> The Russian Federation, the successor state to the USSR (and the Russian Empire) that has been run for the last 20 years or so by Vladimir Putin.[665]

Non-Applicability of Statutory Limitations to War Crimes and Crimes against Humanity

The preamble to the 1968 UN Convention on the Non-Applicability of Statutory Limitations to War Crimes and Crimes against Humanity recognizes that "it is necessary and timely to affirm in international law, through this Convention, the principle that there is no period of limitation for war crimes and crimes against humanity, and to secure its universal application."[666]

Article 1 of the 1968 UN Convention on the Non-Applicability of Statutory Limitations to War Crimes and Crimes against Humanity provides the following:

No statutory limitation shall apply to the following crimes, irrespective of the date of their commission:

(a) War crimes as they are defined in the Charter of the International Military Tribunal, Nürnberg, of 8 August 1945 and confirmed by resolutions 3(1) of 13 February 1946 and 95(I) of 11 December 1946 of the General Assembly of the United Nations, particularly the "grave breaches" enumerated in the Geneva Conventions of 12 August 1949 for the protection of war victims;

(b) Crimes against humanity whether committed in time of war or in time of peace as they are defined in the Charter of the International Military Tribunal, Nürnberg, of 8 August 1945 and confirmed by resolutions 3(I) of 13 February 1946 and 95(I) of 11 December 1946 of the General Assembly of the United Nations, eviction by armed attack or occupation and inhuman acts resulting from the policy of apartheid, and the crime of genocide as defined in the 1948 Convention on the Prevention and Punishment of the Crime of Genocide, even if such acts do not constitute a violation of the domestic law of the country in which they were committed.[667]

Russian Federation

The Russian Federation's Decree on the Punishment of War Criminals (1965) states, "Nazi criminals, guilty of most serious crimes against peace and humanity and war crimes, are subject to prosecution and punishment, irrespective of the time elapsed after the crimes committed."

The Russian Federation's Criminal Code (1996), with respect to possible release from criminal responsibility owing to the expiry of statutes of limitation, provides,

> The periods of limitation shall not be applied to persons who have committed crimes against peace and the security of mankind, provided for by Articles 353 [planning, preparing, unleashing or waging an aggressive war], 356 [use of banned means and methods of warfare], 357 [genocide] and 358 [ecocide] of this Code.
>
> Limitation periods shall not be applicable to persons convicted for the commission of crimes against peace and the security of mankind, provided for by Articles 353 [planning, preparing, unleashing or waging an aggressive war], 356 [use of banned means and methods of warfare], 357 [genocide] and 358 [ecocide] of this Code.[668]

W. H. Auden said it best:

Acts of injustice done
Between the setting and the rising sun
In history lie like bones, each one.

Deportation Being Part of Devastating War

Heroes and Emperors in Circassian History by Shauket Mufti in 1972 has collected and written major events that took place during the Russian-Circassian war. However, the book has generalized names, descriptions, and expressions rather than particularizing them. For example, the author states the "Caucasian War" instead of "Russian-Circassian War" or even "Russian-Caucasian War" and he uses "Caucasia" instead of Circassia among others, even though he focused on and kept mentioning the expression "Circassian nation." These simple notes do not diminish the importance of his great work, which includes extremely important information and events.

He noted that

> Turkish encouragement of Circassian immigration into Ottoman territories was one of the most important factors that facilitated the permanent Russian occupation of Caucasia.
> It was similar to what happened to the Tatars after the Russians had occupied their homeland in the Crimea. Turkish intervention in Circassian affairs led the Circassians to take more interests in emigrating from their country than continuing to fight. The propaganda that the Sublime Porte spread to that effect and Ottoman stooges and religious leaders helped in that regard.[669]

Displacement of the Circassians from their homeland had relied on both sticks and carrots. On one hand, the Russian Empire was pushing and forcing them to leave their homeland while on the other hand, the Turks really encouraged the Circassians to move to the Ottoman Empire. Instead of presenting prospects of creative innovation for the benefits of human beings, colonial mentality imposed ways and means of violating human rights.

> They made alluring promises to encourage the Circassians to emigrate. That action showed that the Ottoman statesmen of that time did not fully appreciate their situation

vis-a-vis Russia. They likewise did not realize the long-range effect of encouraging the Circassians to migrate from their homelands, which might have served better as both a natural barrier and strong buffer between Turkey and Russia.[670]

Logically speaking, people are honored in their country of origin. It is not reasonable to flee or to leave the homeland and give up dignity, honor, and precious soil for meaningless reasons. Regardless of the reasons and methods of fraud, such allegations are not acceptable. The issue becomes complicated and tangled with evolving interests that grow between empires and major powers, developments in the interests of countries that fabricate dilemmas and problems. Considering this, they can tamper with the security of small nations to manipulate their destinies.

> Needless to say, no one would have encouraged such emigration except completely ignorant, short-sighted people, considering the geographical and military importance of Caucasian to Asia in general and to Turkey in particular. It was impossible at that time to make those responsible in Istanbul understand that they were committing a serious mistake. They believed that by having the Circassians emigrate and by amalgamating them with the Tatars, who had previously emigrated from Crimea, they could settle both parties near the Danube in Bulgaria and in other parts of the Balkans, where they would form a strong bulwark separating Istanbul from Europe and creating a Moslim majority to off-balance the Balkans Christians. Through their rash policy and Turks helped Russia to conquer Caucasia with more ease that had been anticipated, while the Ottomans gained nothing by their erroneous efforts.[671]

The Ottoman Empire had been considered at the time a power that was infected with aging. It had passed the point of no return toward its inevitable fate. Functions of the different elements of the state, particularly the defense, were getting weaker and weaker. That affected the outcome of conflicts that the empire was a major player in.

> As the Ottoman administration was very dilatorily incompetent and inefficient, they completely failed in colonizing the Balkans by emigration. No one benefited from it except some officials who were stooges of both Turkey

and Russia. These feathered their nests at the expense of the inhabitants who either migrated or fought hard. These malevolent stooges brought destruction and woe to the vast majority of those they brought to emigrate. Some emigrants died of hunger, while most fell prey to epidemics and died in deplorable conditions.[672]

Those who encourage and support these malicious ideas are nothing but a group of criminals. They do not even have a minimum of self-esteem and an idea of preserving national identity, which will not be abandoned except by those who lose their mind and senses.

It was said that some Caucasian leaders received a bounty from Russia for every Caucasian family that emigrated. They also were rewarded with ranks and titles for their disgraceful behavior. When the miserable emigrants realized that their conditions in the Balkans were becoming worse and that there was no way out of the dilemma in which they found themselves, they decided to return to their original homelands. Actually many returned despite the severe terms set by the Russians who stipulated that every Caucasian who wanted to return to Russia had to adopt Christianity.[673]

It is permissible, or possible in some cases, that if evil conditions and circumstances are encountered, where people are forcefully displaced from their homes, it should be bearable for a brief period, under the provision that they return to their homeland when the time and situation permit. It is a shame to lose the homeland, which reminds of heritage, culture, history, roots, and the greatness of the nation.

About 6000 families had emigrated from Little Kabardia and Great Kabardia just as the Tatars had left Crimea. Their luck was no better than that of the predecessors. As for free Circassia, only a few fanatic families left it; the vast majority remained in their homes, as they had seen for themselves the calamities that befell the Tatars who had left Crimea, relying on Turkish promises.[674]

All their lies, intimidation, and allegations against the Circassians can be described as the following proverb describes this example: "When the excuse is uglier than the sin."[675] Russian allegations and excuses for their brutal acts and crimes against the Circassians still lie ahead of us to this day. The Russians and their mercenaries did not fight the Circassians for only 101 years, before and after the twenty-first of May 1864, but for hundreds of years. Aggressors and victims are known, and accordingly, it is possible to know who the aggressors are.

> In order to justify its colonial aggression Russia alleged that the Circassians were a people who did not adhere to law or discipline, and that they were always harassing peaceful Russian subjects and invading their villages and fortified positions. Russia, consequently, had to carry out drastic measures to put an end to their incessant raid and invasions. With this justification Russia decided in 1860 to force all the Circassians to move from their mountainous and coastal positions and settle in places located in the plains lying on the left bank of the Kuban. In that way Russia could keep them under strict control. The Russian planned to build Cossack villages and posts in the mountainous regions near the Caucasian chain of mountains in order to maintain security.[676]

This is not emigration, but ethnic cleansing and forced deportation from their own homeland. The Russians demanded that the Circassians leave their original towns, villages, and settlements and move to areas allocated to them beyond River Kuban or to leave for the Ottoman Empire. This was to displace the indigenous people from their country to replace them with Russians, Cossacks, and other settlers. Genocide was part of the committed crimes.

> Despite the fact that the united Circassian nations resisted the Russians obstinately during the final stage of their long war, the Russian armies in 1862 occupied the lands lying between the Laba and Byelaya Rivers and the slopes of the mountains lying between Anapa and Adagum. In this way they obliged all the Abazas and Circassians living on the right bank of the Byelaya to choose either:
> a To accept all the Russian demands in full and to remove to the lands allotted to them, or,
> b To immigrate to the Ottoman territories.[677]

This was that period when Russian generals felt that they were close to victory over the Circassians. Consequently, reaching the implementation of their final goals helped them get rid of the Circassians and made them succeed in occupying the entire Circassian territory. They had implemented heinous crimes with no sense of mercy or regard for humanity.

> On October 15, 1860, General Nikolai Evdokimov proposed what was perhaps the first ethnic cleansing in history. Officially, the Circassians were to be given a choice between settling to the north or immigrating to Turkey. However, eyewitness Mikhail Venyukov reported that Evdokimov stated privately that he planned to drive all the Circassians to Anatolia. The Russians conducted the majority of their ethnic cleansing of Circassia between October 1863 and April 1864. Numerous massacres of unarmed men, women and children ensued. Those the Russians spared were driven to the coast in convoys, even peaceful clans to the coast who were willing to submit to any terms. The Russians refused to allow them to take provisions. Many fled to die in their cherished mountains, and unknown thousands died en route to the shore.[678]

Russian colonialists had imposed their policies and agendas on the Circassians the way they did with others. They were especially driven away from their land and villages to new areas. Evil innovative plans were the master of the situation. The determined residential areas were allocated by the Russian colonial authorities. The Circassians had rebuilt their villages and installations, but they were stuck in a position that they were retained in a besieged and trapped situation.

> The Kabardians living beyond the Laba and numbering 10,000 people, together with a group of Kemirgoi and Besleney, accepted the Russian terms, settled in the lands allocated to them, and built new villages. They were later joined by some emigrants who left the mountainous regions. Those who refused to join them migrated to the south, some moving to the southern slopes of the Caucasus, while others joined the Abzakh tribes, but they didn't enjoy their hospitality for long, and so moved on to the Ottoman territories the same year.[679]

The Circassian people were desperately involved in defending their very survival for nearly one hundred years. They remained under constant Russian military pressure to finish them off and to occupy their homeland, to be annexed to the greedy Russian Empire.

> In 1862 the Circassian defense became weaker as many Abzakhs and Shapsughs agreed to leave the mountains for the plains and the lands allotted to them. It was very likely that others would have followed their example and submitted to Russia had they not always been influenced by the stooges of some foreign states which had private interests and objectives. These states sent messages and leaflets full of enticing promises to encourage the Circassians to go in their fighting whatever the consequences might be.[680]

Some states had pledged to the Circassians empty promises of assistance. On the contrary, some of those countries had conducted with the Russian Empire "under the table" deals, such as agreements and understandings against Circassian national interests.

> They also promised to send reinforcements and military assistance. This renewed the Circassians' hopes daily, so that on the first of each month the Circassians waited for the arrival of a fully-equipped French army or an English navy on their coasts. This excessive reliance on others was one reason for the prolongation of the war and for preventing them from reaching a final decision and from self-determination.[681]

Confusion was generated in some cases where results of empty promises had proven to be fake. Practically, they eventually understood that pledges given to the Circassians by many parties had not come true. No one had assistance in a timely manner. The Circassians had to face the bitter truth alone and swallow the poison that was prepared and delivered by some beneficiaries.

Logic dictated that working hard and effectively, and looking forward to the prospects of a promising future for their future generations, would carry with it salvation, provided that they stayed devoted to the cause of their nation: "That hindered the Abzakhs from defending their homeland effectively and they were obliged in the fall of that year to submit to the Russian military authorities. Many Shapsughs emigrated to the Black Sea coasts."[682]

Stephen Sheffield published an article on his website titled "Special Issue No. 42. May 2008. The Circassians." He detailed substantial Circassian topics. He started by describing who they are.

Almost all of this issue is devoted to the Circassians. (1) The Circassians or—their own name for themselves—Adyg are the descendants of the indigenous inhabitants of the Northwest Caucasus. After an armed resistance to Russian conquest that lasted 101 years (1763 1864) longer than in any other part of the Caucasus almost all of the survivors were deported to the Ottoman Empire.[683]

The author has elaborated from his own experience of a coincidence in coming across the Circassian subject. This enabled him to know and realize the different aspects about their homeland and culture. This also revealed historical events that had occurred and the disastrous consequences that they faced.

I myself came across the Circassian theme pretty much by chance. While browsing in the library of Brown University, I happened to come across some old books by 19th-century travelers describing a country called Circassia and a people called Circassians. Like many others, I had been unaware that there was any such country or people, though perhaps I had seen the words somewhere without understanding them. At about the same time, an antiquarian friend offered me some 18th and 19th century maps of Russia and Europe. From these I learned where Circassia used to be and traced the stages by which the expanding empire of the tsars swallowed it up.[684]

When people are obliged to live away from their original homeland, they will be normally homesick and ready to return to their original homeland whenever possible. There is no doubt that many of the Circassians in diaspora would be ready to return there. They were deported in the nineteenth century after their homeland was occupied by the Tsarist Russian troops, which invaded and occupied Circassia and the Caucasus.

William Safran, in his study of Diasporas in Modern Societies: Myths of Homelands and Return, draws up the general framework of an ideal type of diaspora. He defines diaspora as expatriate minority communities

(1) that are dispersed from an original centre to at least two peripheral places;
(2) that maintain a memory, vision, or myth about their original homeland;
(3) that believe they are not fully accepted by their host country;
(4) that see the ancestral home as a place of eventual return, when the time is right;

(5) that are committed to the maintenance and restoration of this homeland; and

(6) of which the group's consciousness and solidarity are importantly defined by this continuing relationship with the homeland (Safran, 1991: 83–84).[685]

Deportation of the Circassians was an enforcement of ethnic cleansing. This took place through a series of campaigns that eventually represented a mass exodus, which applied several methods ranging from persuasion to threat. The main intention was to replace the Circassians by strangers. Their place of native residence was compromised, where colonial Russian policies were fulfilled, even after the end of the Russian-Circassian War in 1864.

The mass exodus of the early 1860's was preceded by a smaller emigration of war refugees throughout the the late 1850's and followed by a series of further expulsions as late as 1867, when the Muslims of Abkhazia were at last compelled to leave. Additional refugees flooded out of empire during the Russo-Turkish War of 1877–78.[686]

The numbers and statistics of victims published, including those who were deported, are only estimates that do not indicate accurate figures. It is significant to realize that some of the deportees couldn't make it. They were unable to survive the severe conditions during the difficult journey. Accordingly, they were incapable of reaching the ports of their destination safely.

Contemporary Russian figures claimed that, out of estimated 505,000 mountaineers in the northwest Caucasus, between 400,000 and 480,000 left in the early 1860's. Other estimates put the aggregate figure at between 300,000 and 500,000, most of them in the period from 1862 to 1866.[687]

Regardless of the figures given by different parties, there is a constant and well-known fact that cannot be ignored, namely, that the Circassia had endured repressive policies by the Russians. During and after the genocide and ethnic cleansing suffered by the Circassians, the deportation was going on in full swing through successive stages. The inevitable result was to vacate the vast majority from their homes and be deported to the Ottoman Empire. The rest were displaced to places selected by the invading forces.

Besides those who immigrated to Turkey, there were also countless numbers who were resettled in the lowlands, so that the real number of those displaced by the last phase of the Caucasus conquest is probably unknowable. Overall, however, the number of those who left the Caucasus, both highlander and lowlander, from the time of the capture of Shamil until the end of the Russo-Turkish War of 1877–78 may be on the order of two million people, many of whom perished at some point along their journey northward to the plains or across the Black Sea to the Ottoman Empire.[688]

Extermination of Circassians

Throughout history, imperial powers, oppressing states, and tyrants have managed to perform acts of barbarism in order to conquer and occupy others' territories and homelands, with noticeable disastrous consequences that ranged between total elimination of population entities, nations, and countries through bullying and partial elimination that kept enslaving and absorbing the elements of vital resources.

The common factor between the two cases is the commission of genocide that either goes unaccounted for when no one is still alive to raise concern or to demand restoration of rights (no questioning and no accountability) or when those who remained alive would step in with all available resources to restore human rights and privileges in their own homeland.

Known committed crimes of genocide have been announced, proclaimed, or debated and have taken place in recent history in many locations around the world such as Armenia, Bosnia, Cambodia, Darfur, the Holocaust during World War II, and Rwanda.

Unfortunately, the Circassian Genocide is forgotten, and not too many people know about it even though its history is available. The ones who committed this genocide maintain consistent efforts to keep this episode unknown, even for the victims and their descendants, in order to get away with all the atrocities committed.

Regarding the Rwandan Genocide, it took place after ethnic tension had started and developed through the years between the majority Hutus and minority Tutsis, especially during Belgian colonialism towards Rwanda: "Between April and June 1994, an estimated 800,000 Rwandans were killed in the space of 100 days. Most of the dead were Tutsis—and most of those who perpetrated the violence were Hutus."[689]

Ethnic issue took place within a country that can be classified as going through a civil war: "Soldiers and police officers encouraged ordinary citizens to take part. In some cases, Hutu civilians were forced to murder their Tutsi neighbours by military personnel."[690]

The events took a tragic path: "Participants of Hutu ethnic majority (boys being amongst them) were often given incentives, such as money or food, and some were even told they could appropriate the land of the Tutsis they killed"; "during the genocide, the bodies of Tutsis were thrown into rivers, with their killers saying they were being sent back to Ethiopia."[691]

As for the Holocaust, it was genocide carried out by Nazi Germany. It had targeted Jews in Germany and countries occupied by Germany at the time. This means that Germany had executed extermination mainly on its own citizens of a certain origin and religion and similar citizens of countries it occupied during World War II, in addition to members of other tiny minorities and prisoners of war. The millions of Jews were murdered in extermination camps: "The six extermination camps were all situated in former Poland and had mass murder as their purpose. Outside Poland, at least two camps existed that in many ways resembled the six extermination camps in Poland: Jungfernhof (in Latvia) and Maly Trostinets (in Byelorussia)."[692]

The number of victims was "a total of at least 3 million Jews were murdered in the six extermination camps. The precise figure is impossible to estimate, since the Nazis did not calculate the number as individuals but rather as the number of trainloads that arrived to the extermination facilities."[693]

People were driven to their inevitable deaths as per the preset arrangements: "The Jews were herded into the gas chambers, then the camp staff closed the doors, and either exhaust gas (in Belzec, Sobibor and Treblinka) or poison gas in the form of Zyclon B or A (in Majdanek and Auschwitz-Birkenau). Another method was the use of gassing trucks."[694]

Methods were selected according to location and situation: "A third method was mass shooting of Jews and other groups (Soviet POWs, Poles, etc.). After shooting bodies, they were either burnt in the open, in mass graves or in the crematoria."[695]

Victims were misled, and they were lied to: "Most of the victims had been told that they were merely to be moved to the east for new jobs and living places, and most of them had brought their favourite belongings. Later, they were looted and robbed by those who were doing the criminal dirty work themselves."[696]

Details of tyrants' acts were disgusting: "In the 'pure' extermination camps, men were separated from women upon arrival. The first to be gassed were the men—the women had their hair cut off before they went to their death. . . . Those able to work for instance helped carry the bodies to the crematoria or search the bodies for valuables."[697]

The sophisticated methods, equipment, and tools used by the Nazis in the midtwentieth century that were used to eliminate millions of victims in different locations and different methods in the shortest time possible with the least possible traces of a crime (by getting rid of the corpses, "deposits" in the criminals' vocabulary) were learned by reviewing Tsarist Russian methods for accomplishing crimes of genocide against the Circassian nation almost a century earlier. The Russian killing machine in the nineteenth century was well advanced in using the environment's natural substances as a tool of committing a genocide, relatively speaking, as one of the worst in human history. It was clean and green (not to underestimate the hundreds of thousands of oppressed Circassians that were the target of the criminal Tsarist Russian troops), and they were ahead of their time as if reading the future for environmental concerns of the present time, in which they didn't use gas or any other substance that might affect the planet.

Circassians in their homeland were not far away from the sea, and accordingly, the deportation and extermination did not need sophisticated means of land transportation at the time, the way the Nazis had used in the 1940s to transport the victims to remote areas.

Perpetrators will be legally held responsible whether on the state or individual basis.

> While individuals can be prosecuted for genocide, States can be held legally responsible for breaching their obligations under the Genocide Convention. Parties to the convention can bring a case before the International Court of Justice (which handles disputes between States) alleging that another State party has violated the treaty. But no State turned to the ICJ to enforce the treaty against a State said to be responsible for genocide until 1993.[698]

There was no need in most of their evil acts for the Russians to find a way to get rid of the dead. It was performed and processed naturally, by getting rid of batches of people by the following:
- Burying them to enrich the soil of Circassia by using its own people's precious remains that were killed by the invaders. One of the most attractive hobbies for the Russian elite at the time was to keep human body parts, especially heads, to be sent to high-ranking government officials, including the emperor in St. Petersburg.
- Dumping them in the sea to be eaten by the fish.
- Using them for scientific tests and analysis.

Other techniques were used, such as the following:
- Dragging thousands of people to the coastline of the Black Sea and keeping them on the sand, both in winter and summer, for long periods until departure by sea commenced. Many of those waiting for a destiny in poor living conditions were affected by extreme heat in the summer and extreme cold in the winter. They became infected with epidemics with poor or unavailable medical services.
- Taking the difficult trip aboard rickety ships that come to the coast to carry Circassian families to destinations they never dreamed of. Many of those deported travelers did not make it to their destination due to illness or degraded unworthy ships.

To be fair (not in the sense of preferring one over the other), the Tsarist Russians more evil minds than the Nazis, which they had proven to be far more horribly efficient.

Russian State Duma Recognizes the Armenian Genocide

Not surprisingly, the "Russian State Duma" issued a statement on the fourteenth of April 1995, acknowledging the occurrence of the Armenian Genocide.

> Based on irrefutable historic facts which attest to the extermination of Armenians on the territory of Western Armenia from 1915 to 1922 and, in accordance with the following Conventions adopted by the United Nations:
> Convention on the Prevention and Punishment of the Crime of Genocide, December 9, 1948; Convention on the Non-Applicability of Statutory Limitations to War Crimes and Crimes against Humanity, November 26, 1968;
> Aspiring to restore the humanitarian traditions of the Russian State and,
> Emphasizing that through the initiative of Russia, the Great European Powers already in 1915 characterized the actions of the Turkish Empire against the Armenian people as a "Crime Against Humanity" and,
> Noting that the physical extermination of the fraternal Armenian people in its historic homeland aimed at destroying Russia;

The State Duma of the Federal Assembly of the Russian Federation:

Condemns the perpetrators of the extermination of Armenians from 1915 to 1922;

Expresses its deep sympathy to the Armenian people and recognizes April 24 as a day of remembrance for the victims of the Genocide.[699]

Also, it is widely known that the State Duma of the Russian Federation on April 4, 1995, made a statement in which it recognized the fact of genocide committed by Turkey against Armenians in the year 1915.

Archives and Russian Officers' Memoirs

Walter Richmond has participated in the Ninth Biennial Conference of the International Association of Genocide Scholars held in Buenos Aires, dated July 19–22, 2011. He addressed the conference on the Circassian Genocide, where his speech was titled "Evidence of Circassian Genocide from Archives," which included a great deal of information. He presented important results based on his research. Due to its significance, the following is a summary of the most important and highlighted points made on YouTube:[700]

The speech and the conference in Buenos Aires is considered of an important concern because they facilitated to publicize facts that were unknown by lots of people before. It regarded information that was extracted from both the archives and the memoirs of Russian officers and generals. The presentation started by showing a slide that depicted "Debunking the Russian Narrative: The Circassian Genocide in Light of the Georgian State Archives." He also said, "As Circassians always had to depend on official Russian reports because of the absence of their own. . . . but with the archival sources, it was possible to put together the information to complete the picture for exactly what happened."[701]

He explained on the map that Circassians "lived in their homeland located in the eastern shore of the Black Sea, and showed the lines of the Russian military advance." He mentioned that few Circassians are left in the North Caucasus, but the rest were gone either due to massacres or deported away from their homeland, and estimated that the population should have been around 23 million while it's estimated to be 500,000 people.

The following references were used in the presentation:
- Milenty Olshevsky (his memoirs published in 2003)
- Ivan Drozdov (1877)

- Adolf Berzhe (1882)
- Georgian State Archives (1, 2, op. 1, doc 1177; field notes of Field General Nikolai Yevdokimov, dated June 29–December 12, 1863)

Evidence of genocide is presented by mentioning official Russian myths, answered by evidence, which rejects the allegations as follows:

Myth Number 1: The Circassians posed a clear danger to the Russian Empire and had to be moved out of the coastal areas. First postulated by General Rostislav Fadeev, 1880, and repeated as recently as Mark Bliev 2006.

Evidence: "During the 1863 campaign, the Dakhovski Detachment met no organized resistance. The share was completely controlled by Russian troops, and all that remained were unarmed villagers."[702]

By May 1863, the Russians completely occupied the Pshekh Valley. The Russians moved forward and occupied more areas. Circassian elders went to the Russians daily, begging and threatening them not to destroy the forest. There was one last battle on May 20. Five thousand Circassians were rounded by Russian cannon fire; then after that, they began to surrender. That shows no Russian army dealing with unarmed villagers, which means no organized military resistance.

A quote from General Yevdokimov: "The military actions carried out by the Army of Kuban Oblast during the summer of this year (1863) placed the mountaineers of the north face in an inescapable position, and have deprived them of not only the possibility, but also the hope of engaging us in battle."[703]

Myth Number 2: The Circassians were offered fertile lands, better than the land they occupied. Repeated from Adolf Berzhe from the 1880s to Mark Bliev in 2006.

Evidence: "The area north of the Kuban, where they were to be settled, was swampland."[704]

The offered alternative dwelling regions for Circassians were definitely uninhabitable areas, difficult and unbearable living conditions that cannot be overcome easily. The swampland had surrounding insects in addition to suffocating fumes rising from the swamps, causing infectious diseases and an unbearable situation.

Myth Number 3: "The Russians were taken by surprise by the number of Circassians who chose to emigrate. Started by Yevdokimov in his official reports. Repeated by Berzhe, Bliev, and Dana Sherry."[705]

Evidence: "Yevdokimov's private opinion was that the majority would emigrate, and the Russian command also believed this. The Circassians emigrated because they hated and distrusted the Russians."[706]

Myth Number 4: The Russians were concerned about the welfare of the Circassians as they gave them the choice of where they wished to go.

Evidence: "Evdokimov acted in gross disregard and even contempt for the lives of his own men, the settlers and the Circassians."[707]

The Russians wanted to colonize the area quickly, which brought Cossack settlers to replace Circassians, but that placed them under attack by the remaining Circassians. The Russian Empire's political and military leadership had provided nothing but tragedies and death to both parties of the conflict while at the same time the civilians suffered the most.

Between the 24th and 29th of August (OS), 1883 the Dakhosky Detachment burned all auls along the Shekots River, as the Abzakhs watched helplessly. Evdokimov never says what happened to the villagers or exactly where they were. No mention of capturing anyone.[708]

On September, 10th (OS), 1863, the Russians found several recently built at the source of the Pshetsykh River, where they had passed already on the 5th. They burned them.[709]

Myth Number 5: The massive number of deaths of people waiting for ships was the result of bad weather and the intransigence of Turkish skippers.

Evidence: "Evdokimov deliberately forced large numbers of Circassians into small a space, refused to allow them to disperse or return to build shelters, and conducted the action at the worst possible time of the year, regardless of warnings."[710]

The information signaled that "pressing tens of thousands of people in one place to depart to Turkey" has been humiliating and at the same time reflected ruthlessness, recklessness, brutality, and evil intentions as a result of ignoring any human consideration against children, women, and an unarmed population, with all its disastrous consequences.

It is mentioned that Nikolai Evdokimov said while answering questions, "It's a tragedy, but keep it going," encouraging the continuation of the flame of the dirty war policy through speeding up the deportation campaign to achieve its goals of emptying the Circassian homeland from its citizens to be replaced by colonists and imperial land settlers. He concluded with, "Nikolai Evdokimov is the engineer and the main corporate and the Russian army has collaborated" by achieving precision in accomplishing "one of the first modern genocides that ever happened."

The international community and the civilized world are urged to take serious steps for recognizing Russian atrocities and to take the necessary action to implement the proper rules.

Joshua Keating wrote in his article "Did the Age of Genocide Begin in Sochi?" The Russian military commanders and generals did not bear in their consideration the fact that they were carrying out a mass massacre against an entire nation: "Nikolai Evdokimov, the general in charge of the operation, wrote annoyedly, of a subordinate, 'I wrote to Count Sumarokov as to why he keeps reminding me in every report concerning the frozen bodies which cover the roads.'"[711]

The Circassians knew that since the imperial aggression had begun, what could have been done should have been done. They didn't leave anything that can be done without doing it. But eventually, the colonial invaders finished them off from all sides, which submitted to further reprisal acts and repercussions.

When remembering or reminding of the Circassian Genocide, it means that the attention is drawn and concentrated on the past to derive lessons from experiences that can be used to find out the facts of the events that have radically affected an entire nation and because of a devastating war.

Circassians manage their identity and survival at the present, worrying about their future and anticipating what is yet to happen. Recalling their past, with all its glorious and painful details, requires the necessity to follow up effects that show how to find a solution to the issues related to the crimes and atrocities, together with identifying the perpetrators and selecting the proper mechanism of applying the relevant rules for the realization of their legal rights.

Nevertheless, regardless of well-known facts and figures of homeland occupation, genocide, and deportation, there are still some individuals who are ignorant of history. Defeatists, opportunists, and others contribute to hectic propaganda against the Circassian people and its inalienable rights. What do they mean when they say, "Why bother with the past?"

At a time when the exact description of the meaning of genocide reflects the fact of denial, the wordplay, together with illogical explanations and sometimes excuses, lead to confusion and uncertainty.

Logic, ethics, and human obligation require the use of the exact wording to describe the meaning of genocide with what it would reflect of facts on the ground, regardless of contradiction and cross-purposes, together with flimsy excuses and illogical explanations, without addressing the correct definition of genocide, which includes "acts committed for the intent to destroy, in whole or in part, a national, ethnical, racial or religious group,"[712] as there are documents and other proof.

> In 1864, for example, Russian forces carried out what some have deemed "the first modern genocide on European soil" after they seized the lands of the Circassians—which include the area around Sochi where Russia staged last year's Winter Olympics.[713]

The more the facts and realities are known to all concerned, the more positive and assertive acts can be performed in accordance with international law and the Universal Declaration of Human Rights. For those who have perished and those who are still living, we ought to protect the evidence and present it to the world.

Walter Richmond (a professor at Occidental University) wrote his book The Circassian Genocide five generations after the twenty-first of May 1864, which marked the end of 101 years of war. This is the date when the last Circassian defenders signed their surrender to the imperial Russian invaders and mentioned astonishing information mostly extracted from the Tbilisi Archives. The fact turned out to be that "Circassia was a small independent nation on the northeastern shore of the Black Sea. For no reason other than ethnic hatred, over the course of hundreds of raids the Russians drove the Circassians from their homeland and deported them to the Ottoman Empire. At least 600,000 people lost their lives to massacre, starvation, and the elements while hundreds of thousands more were forced to leave their homeland. By 1864, three-fourths of the population was annihilated, and the Circassians had become one of the first stateless peoples in modern history."[714]

In 2015, political analyst Paul Goble published a "Window" about Circassian Memorial Day titled 151 Years after the Genocide and One Year after Sochi, the Circassian Issue Isn't Going Away. He elaborated on the memory and the importance and magnitude of its association with the one hundred and fiftieth commemoration and the Sochi Olympic Games.

> In the past year, the Circassian issue has receded from the front pages of the world's press given that there is no event equivalent to the Sochi Games which were held on the killing fields of 1861. Moreover, unlike the 150th anniversary, the 151st which takes place today is not a "round" one and thus not surprisingly attracts last attention.[715]

Each year on the twenty-first of May, thousands of people gather in front of the Russian embassies and consulates to protest the genocide and deportation.

> Halis Din, Circassian Association Federation Board member has criticized the use of the term 'genocide' referring to the 1915 incidents by Russian President Vladimir Putin. In a written statement, he has said that Putin's use of the word "genocide" and with Putin not participating in the Yerevan programme has caused a backlash in Turkey.[716]

History is a register of series of past events that pertain to individuals and nations. Historical facts and proceedings are studied, evaluated, and processed for planning and piloting in respect to selecting the necessary steps to be taken by those who take human responsibility of continuity and perseverance for the sake of positive change of the society in the present and future, depending on consequences of dangers that affected life, progress, and the advancement of the society and nation.

Many positive and negative developments have occurred during recent years. The yearly commemoration of the twenty-first of May of this year is remarking of the great Circassian catastrophe that befell the Circassians. It reminds of pain and disaster endured by the Circassian people who defended their homeland, identity, and its very survival. They had to fight a fierce defensive war against imperial Russian invaders for 101 years. This included total occupation where Russians committed genocide, destruction, ethnic cleansing, and destruction, followed by deportation of 90 percent of the people. It was a forced exodus to the Ottoman Empire and then dispersion in more than thirty countries of the world of today.

Developments Imposed Themselves on the International Scene

Seemingly, Russian imperialism couldn't hide its real characteristics, but show the continuation of its past imperial practices and nature. To show its true face in the twenty-first century, they occupied and annexed Crimea and continued supporting Russian-backed rebels in parts of Eastern Ukraine. This is a process resumed to destabilize and interfere with other former Soviet Republics.

> Tuesday saw Russian President Vladimir Putin announce the annexation of Crimea, two days after voters in that semiautonomous territory approved a hastily called referendum on separating from Ukraine.[717]
>
> Ukrainian lawmakers believe that Putin wants to control Ukraine in an attempt to reestablish a new version of the former Soviet Union. Ukraine would be an important part of that plan.[718]

What is happening in Southeastern Ukraine at the moment indicates irresponsibility, in addition to a lack of interest and indifference in respecting international law and the right of all nations to maintain their freedom and independence.

The Armenian issue seemed urgent on its hundredth anniversary. The European Parliament "urged Turkey to recognize the Armenian Genocide"[719] as many countries are moving toward recognizing the reality of the "Armenian Genocide."

Openness of talent for regional expansion and the desire of the Russians to control others had not been interrupted over the centuries. It went too far in controlling the homelands of other nations under multiple names and descriptions to this day. Thus, recently, they have annexed Crimea from Ukraine after a quick occupation. Repeated attempts are still under way to support separatist movements in the southeastern part of Ukraine, aimed at the new revival of Russia in the twenty-first century (Novorossiya).

The Circassian Genocide Is the Key Issue

The Circassian Genocide is the matter of focus that needs to be resolved, and accordingly, the Russian state must be held accountable for all its actions, where the criteria for genocide against the Circassians have been met. Others should recognize the Circassians' rights[720] of obtaining a Russian apology, proper compensation, the right of return according to an international protection program, and the restoration of legitimate rights, including the right to self-determination.

The commemoration reminds of the Georgian Parliament's recognition of the Circassian Genocide on the twentieth of May 2011,[721] which indicates the first United Nations member to carry out an academic study of regional and Circassian history by scholars and specialists upon the request of related committees of the Parliament of Georgia that reached the truth of the occurrence of the genocide, ethnic cleansing, and forced deportation committed against the entire Circassian nation. In a related matter, it is of duty and decency to also thank the Georgians who inaugurated an erected monument in Anaklia on the Black Sea on the twenty-first of May 2012, in the memory of Circassian victims.[722]

The Similarities Between the Circassians and the Armenians

The major powers of the nineteenth century had the aspirations and ambitions to consider coordinating among each other to fulfill their selfish benefits. Their purpose was to exchange roles, spheres of influence, and interests targeting to control other people and nations. This shows the extent of their selfishness and greed. They kept looking to pursue self-interests above all other considerations. Those major colonial powers had enforced domination in different ways.

This is a continuation of irreversible colonial policies, similar to, when in the nineteenth century,

> much of the Caucasus coast and portions of historic Armenia and Georgia also came under Russian suzerainty. Russia not only commanded the northern coast but also claimed a right to protect the Christians of the Danubian principalities and formally annexed most of the south Caucasus. Within a little more than a generation, from Küçük Kaynarca treaty (1774) to the treaty of Adrianople (1829), Catherine and her successors had come close to realizing the goal of reaching across the sea to take Constantinople itself. The northern coast and hinterland, far from being a frontier, was made now into a Russian province, a region that tsarist administrators came to call, with all the unabashed optimism of empire-builders everywhere, New Russia (Novorossia).[723]

Still, Russian propaganda and fabrication keep claiming that the successive regimes of the Russian state stand in support of Armenians in all cases and circumstances, particularly in situations where the Armenians were in great strife and bitter dispute with the Ottoman Empire, but the truth is just the opposite. The fact is that Russian positions are limited to the extent that they could've been considered spectacular.

They were exercising and utilizing their intention of controlling, containing, bullying, and implementing policies that benefit the Russian Empire while the gained results had benefited other sides and led to implementing policies and plans, which were prepared in advance.

Double standards and contradictions of the Russian Empire's policies reveal the fact of its real characteristics and consequently narcissistic position. Russians say and declare in private what they hide in public. Irrespective of their declared policy regarding the Armenians and Armenia, they hide fundamental and important issues that would eventually benefit Russia and let others suffer. An example of their opportunistic behavior is revealed through an important and meaningful development: "During the Ottoman era, the Russian Ambassador in Istanbul, Alexey Lobanov-Rostovsky, has said at the Ottoman Foreign Ministry: 'We need Armenia without Armenians. He said those words, when the Turks raised their concerns about the Armenians. Alexey Lobanov-Rostovsky, was the Russian Empire's Ambassador in Turkey. He was appointed by Aleksandr II of Russia from 1878–1879. In 1895, he was appointed by Emperor Nicholas II as Russia's Foreign Minister.'"[724]

Seemingly, "birds of the same feather flock together"; the Armenians and Circassians have had a similar experience that led to great suffering to this day. They were affected by atrocities, planned and implemented by the major powers at the time. Disastrous consequences were unavoidable.

No doubt that intellectuals and serious observers can determine the best way to characterize the events to display their proper classification and description. They must be neutral of bias and away from favoring any party.

> The deportation of the Circassians reminds us of the deportation and dispersal of the Armenians during the First World War. Perhaps the most horrible incident that occurred in Turkey during that war was the extraordinary treatment which the Armenians suffered and which led to their deportation and massacre. That took place, as it is well known, with the full congnizance (cognizance) of the Unionists and in collaboration with the Germans.[725]

Experience has revealed that when ethnic or religious matters arise, the accusations and counteraccusations are exchanged between the different groups and parties in a given country. People should be dealt with humanely and equally with no discrimination. Trending of facts of such events would tend to lean towards creating national calamities. This would lead to unpleasant results that reflect conflicts of interest between the official state policies and certain ethnic and religious groups.

Unfortunately, some countries may behave in denial that is incompatible with laws, norms, and human principles. When following civilized methods in a given society, both national and international concern will be directed to prevent human suffering and at the same time to mitigate the effects of hostile acts at all levels. Civilian and peaceful societies are constructed by all citizens of the nation. This ensures human dignity and relations of harmony among all peoples.

> Some extremist unionists such as Tala'at Pasha have admitted this, although he alleged that the deportation of the Armenians did not take place according to a premeditated plan. The Joint Supreme Command of the Germans and Ottomans, found it necessary, for strategic reasons, to move the Armenians from the borders of Caucasia. At first they wanted to move them to a line thirty kilometers beyond the frontier of the hostile powers, as it is well-known that the Armenians were on the Russian borders and inclined to Russia. They thus constituted a serious danger to Turkey.[726]

Demagoguery and political chaos destroys the present and future of any country, no matter how large or small that state is. Racial and religious discrimination will eventually lead to cracking the state structure and eventually to total collapse. This indicates and shows the narrow-mindedness of those forces that spew toxins, discord, and division in society. This leads to conflicts between the various ethnic groups in the state. Blaming others does not solve any problems. Justice and fairness must be served.

"Tala'at Pasha himself claimed that the Armenians themselves were to blame as they had exerted all their efforts to assist the Russian army in such a way that bands of Armenian outlaws used to hover around the Turkish army and harass its rear in order to enable the Russians to inflict losses on it. Tala'at Pasha stated that after investigation, it was found out that the Armenian churches in the eastern provinces were depots of ammunitions and supplies."[727]

Experience has proven that pressing charges haphazardly without a justified legal reason would create an atmosphere of bickering and accusations that are not based on sound foundations. Excessive hostility leads to imposing unproven accusations.

Tala'at Pasha continued, "Furthermore the Armenians, by their hostile actions, caused the death of more than a quarter of a million Moslem Turks and others. They disrupted communications between Turkish Army in the battle-field and its headquarters Caucasia. He also alleged that the deportation was carried out merely to safeguard the Throne and the Homeland."[728]

It was declared and revealed that administrative and operational chaos had prevailed among the military or semimilitary troops and units. They executed the orders in participation and conspiracy with assigned groups and individuals. Those who carried out massacres and forced deportation, both organizationally and individually, had contributed to increased abuses against Armenian civilians. Innocent people were herded to where the supreme official departments decided.

> He also admitted that deportation was not always carried out according to the regulations in force and with regard to humanitarian precepts, while a number of top-ranking officials misused their authority and deviated from the principles of justice, thus inflicting damage on many innocent people.[729]

Mufti has stressed on the fact that the Circassians were not part of the plan of executing the "genocide" against Armenians. He also mentioned the similarities between Circassians and Armenians regarding their origin and destiny.

> This is what Tala'at himself admitted, but the Circassians did not take part in the hostile actions directed against the Armenians. Many top-ranking Circassian officers and officials who because of their positions were charged with the execution of such actions, used to avoid carrying them out as much as possible, for beside the humanitarian considerations, the Circassians considered the Armenians, despite the difference between their religious beliefs, as brethren and relatives in nationality, being also Caucasians. Thus, they are innocent in this issue.[730]

All signs indicate that the Russian factor was fueling and influencing unfortunate crimes committed at the time. It contributed in aggregating the situation. At certain instances, events looked like they were orchestrated and coordinated events. All this indicated that Russia's desire to control more areas of influence in the cause had produced an outbreak of conflicts and disputes, which evolved into an occurrence of unfortunate events.

> The Armenian massacres of 1915 took place as a result of the victories achieved by the Russians in the Caucasian fronts at the beginning of the First World War and started in the Armenian villages and settlements which had assisted the Russians in their advance in the Turkish territories, and had provided them with men, weapons and supplies.[731]

Deep hatred of the unionists had no limits. They kept up the implementation of their extremist policies and laws that were practiced against all ethnic minorities. They occasionally altered their procedures and priorities due to different surrounding circumstances. The degree of abuse also changed at times when a direct foreign impact on the country was detected, which would have an impact on all minorities.

> During the First World War propaganda increased and reached its maximum intensity; those who opposed the Unionists and had a grudge against them used to say to the Circassians: "Wait a little, we, we will see you a little later; when the Unionists finish with the Eastern provinces, your turn will immediately come!."[732]

Those who were supposed to maintain law and order were the outlaws themselves. Such actions prevent the citizens from feeling reassured and safe. This increases the gap and barrier between different nationalities and ethnicities and thus worsens the relations and ties of trust between them.

> The procedure adopted in those massacres was first to deport groups of un-armed Armenians in caravans. On their way into exile they were attacked by bands of outlaws who had been carefully chosen and assigned to attack them. In most cases these outlaws were disguised bands of Albanians, Kurds, and Turks from the gendarmeries. Many Armenians were able to flee, rescuing themselves from a tragic destiny and taking refuge in Syria and other countries whose peoples treated them hospitably and enabled them to live in security.[733]

A prominent former Ottoman high official had bragged about treating and dealing with the Armenians in the year 1915, which made him face a sad fate: "Tala'at Pasha's confessions, putting the blame on the Armenians, did not benefit him, as he was assassinated by some Armenian commandos in one of the streets of Berlin after the War."[734]

It is true that at times that coincidence or geographic proximity might play a role in the imperial power's priorities. However, in most cases, greed and colonial expansion in addition to economic, political, and geographical reasons were the real causes of the occupation and colonization. This is regardless of origin and religion of the victimized nations. Origin and religion may appear to be sometimes insignificant, but they would appear considerable in all other cases. An example of this is all the Christian nations that were colonized by Russia.

> It is worth mentioning that the misfortunes of the Armenians and the Georgians were brought about because they were neighbors of the Moslem Turks and Iranians; similarly, the Circassians were harassed by their Russian neighbors after they had adopted Islam. This applies to the last phase of the Caucasian—Russian Wars, but does not apply during the first half of those wars, as the Circassians in Western Caucasia were still Christians.[735]

Goals of colonialism are not only limited to occupying and seizing the land, but also to handle it arrogantly according to its whim, to get rid of the indigenous population or to be marginalized, depending on the circumstances created by the occupation. At the same time, it is possible to observe that the colonial and authoritarian powers act with similar barbaric methods against the indigenous peoples. The common factor between these powers is the use of excessive force and the implementation of opportunistic nonhumanitarian plans.

> That, however, did not protect them from hostile Russian actions which aimed at occupying their homelands, through all possible means, in order to safeguard and reinforce their southern borders. The actions of the Tsarist Russians against the Circassians, who were driven out of their homelands, is identical to those which the Turks carried out against the Armenians, as has been mentioned.[736]

> Adolf Hitler infamously observed that he believed that he could get away with killing the Jews of Europe because "nobody talks about the Armenians anymore" and the way that they were killed in 1915 in the Ottoman Empire. If the world forgot that, he reasoned, it would soon forget his actions against the Jews.[737]

He counted some of the tragedies that have either been discussed or been forgotten because of multiple factors and causes. Hopefully, the Circassian Question and genocide will not be overlooked: "Fortunately for the world, almost no one has forgotten or forgiven Hitler's Holocaust; and thanks to Armenians around the world, some people still continue to talk about what happened in 1915."[738]

Tyranny and Ukrainian Holodomor

Intentional brutal acts, nonhumanitarian hunger, and starvation were the circumstances experienced by the Ukrainians. They had endured a tip of the iceberg. Stalin was grabbing Ukraine entirely and intended to change its national character. Genocide was not recognized yet.

> The victims of Stalin's murderous attack by famine on the Ukrainian people which claimed as many as ten million lives, intentionally led to the russification of Ukraine, and thus set the stage for many of today's problems there.[739]

---

[394] http://historynewsnetwork.org/article/151025
[395] Circassian History (Kadir Natho)
[396] http://www.un.org/en/documents/udhr/
[397] http://www.un.org/esa/socdev/unpfii/documents/DRIPS_en.pdf
[398] The Circassian Genocide (Walter Richmond)
[399] The Circassians: A Handbook (Amjad Jaimoukha)
[400] The Circassians: A Handbook (Amjad Jaimoukha)
[401] The Circassians: A Handbook (Amjad Jaimoukha)
[402] The Circassians: A Handbook (Amjad Jaimoukha)
[403] The Sochi Predicament: Contexts, Characteristics and Challenges of the Olympic Winter Games in 2014 (Bo Petersson, Karina Vamling)
[404] http://ghn.ge/news-82836.html
[405] The Circassians: A Handbook (Amjad Jaimoukha)
[406] The Circassians: A Handbook (Amjad Jaimoukha)
[407] The Circassians: A Handbook (Amjad Jaimoukha)
[408] http://www.radioadiga.com/ClosedIndex/artikkk.php?ind=4015
[409] The Circassian Genocide (Walter Richmond)
[410] The Circassian Genocide (Walter Richmond)

411 The Circassian Genocide (Walter Richmond)
412 The Circassian Genocide (Walter Richmond)
413 The Circassian Genocide (Walter Richmond)
414 The Circassian Genocide (Walter Richmond)
415 The Circassian Genocide (Walter Richmond)
416 The Circassian Genocide (Walter Richmond)
417 The Circassian Genocide (Walter Richmond)
418 The Circassian Genocide (Walter Richmond)
419 The Circassian Genocide (Walter Richmond)
420 The Circassian Genocide (Walter Richmond)
421 The Circassian Genocide (Walter Richmond)
422 The Circassian Genocide (Walter Richmond)
423 The Circassian Genocide (Walter Richmond)
424 The Circassian Genocide (Walter Richmond)
425 The Circassian Genocide (Walter Richmond)
426 The Circassian Genocide (Walter Richmond)
427 The Circassian Genocide (Walter Richmond)
428 The Circassian Genocide (Walter Richmond)
429 The Circassian Genocide (Walter Richmond)
430 The Circassian Genocide (Walter Richmond)
431 The Circassian Genocide (Walter Richmond)
432 The Circassian Genocide (Walter Richmond)
433 The Circassian Genocide (Walter Richmond)
434 The Circassian Genocide (Walter Richmond)
435 The Circassian Genocide (Walter Richmond)
436 The Circassian Genocide (Walter Richmond)
437 The Circassian Genocide (Walter Richmond)
438 The Circassian Genocide (Walter Richmond)
439 The Circassian Genocide (Walter Richmond)
440 The Circassian Genocide (Walter Richmond)
441 The Circassian Genocide (Walter Richmond)
442 The Circassian Genocide (Walter Richmond)
443 The Circassian Genocide (Walter Richmond)
444 The Circassian Genocide (Walter Richmond)
445 The Circassian Genocide (Walter Richmond)
446 The Circassian Genocide (Walter Richmond)
447 The Circassian Genocide (Walter Richmond)
448 The Circassian Genocide (Walter Richmond)
449 The Ghost of Freedom: A History of the Caucasus (Charles King)
450 The Ghost of Freedom: A History of the Caucasus (Charles King)
451 http://www.theatlantic.com/international/archive/2015/10/russia-geography-ukraine-syria/413248/

452 http://www.theatlantic.com/international/archive/2015/10/russia-geography-ukraine-syria/413248/
453 The Ghost of Freedom: A History of the Caucasus (Charles King)
454 The Ghost of Freedom: A History of the Caucasus (Charles King)
455 The Ghost of Freedom: A History of the Caucasus (Charles King)
456 The Ghost of Freedom: A History of the Caucasus (Charles King)
457 The Ghost of Freedom: A History of the Caucasus (Charles King)
458 The Ghost of Freedom: A History of the Caucasus (Charles King)
459 The Ghost of Freedom: A History of the Caucasus (Charles King)
460 The Ghost of Freedom: A History of the Caucasus (Charles King)
461 The Ghost of Freedom: A History of the Caucasus (Charles King)
462 The Ghost of Freedom: A History of the Caucasus (Charles King)
463 The Ghost of Freedom: A History of the Caucasus (Charles King)
464 The Ghost of Freedom: A History of the Caucasus (Charles King)
465 The Ghost of Freedom: A History of the Caucasus (Charles King)
466 The Ghost of Freedom: A History of the Caucasus (Charles King)
467 The Ghost of Freedom: A History of the Caucasus (Charles King)
468 The Ghost of Freedom: A History of the Caucasus (Charles King)
469 The Ghost of Freedom: A History of the Caucasus (Charles King)
470 The Ghost of Freedom: A History of the Caucasus (Charles King)
471 The Ghost of Freedom: A History of the Caucasus (Charles King)
472 The Ghost of Freedom: A History of the Caucasus (Charles King)
473 The Ghost of Freedom: A History of the Caucasus (Charles King)
474 The Ghost of Freedom: A History of the Caucasus (Charles King)
475 The Ghost of Freedom: A History of the Caucasus (Charles King)
476 The Ghost of Freedom: A History of the Caucasus (Charles King)
477 The Ghost of Freedom: A History of the Caucasus (Charles King)
478 The Ghost of Freedom: A History of the Caucasus (Charles King)
479 The Ghost of Freedom: A History of the Caucasus (Charles King)
480 The Ghost of Freedom: A History of the Caucasus (Charles King)
481 The Ghost of Freedom: A History of the Caucasus (Charles King)
482 The Ghost of Freedom: A History of the Caucasus (Charles King)
483 The Ghost of Freedom: A History of the Caucasus (Charles King)
484 The Ghost of Freedom: A History of the Caucasus (Charles King)
485 The Ghost of Freedom: A History of the Caucasus (Charles King)
486 The Ghost of Freedom: A History of the Caucasus (Charles King)
487 The Circassian Genocide (Walter Richmond)
488 The Circassian Genocide (Walter Richmond)
489 The Circassian Genocide (Walter Richmond)
490 The Circassian Genocide (Walter Richmond)
491 The Circassian Genocide (Walter Richmond)

492 The Circassian Genocide (Walter Richmond)
493 The Circassian Genocide (Walter Richmond)
494 The Circassian Genocide (Walter Richmond)
495 The Circassian Genocide (Walter Richmond)
496 The Circassian Genocide (Walter Richmond)
497 The Circassian Genocide (Walter Richmond)
498 The Circassian Genocide (Walter Richmond)
499 The Circassian Genocide (Walter Richmond)
500 The Circassian Genocide (Walter Richmond)
501 The Circassian Genocide (Walter Richmond)
502 The Circassian Genocide (Walter Richmond)
503 The Circassian Genocide (Walter Richmond)
504 The Circassian Genocide (Walter Richmond)
505 The Circassian Genocide (Walter Richmond)
506 The Circassian Genocide (Walter Richmond)
507 The Circassian Genocide (Walter Richmond)
508 The Circassian Genocide (Walter Richmond)
509 The Circassian Genocide (Walter Richmond)
510 The Circassian Genocide (Walter Richmond)
511 The Circassian Genocide (Walter Richmond)
512 The Circassian Genocide (Walter Richmond)
513 The Circassian Genocide (Walter Richmond)
514 The Circassian Genocide (Walter Richmond)
515 The Circassian Genocide (Walter Richmond)
516 The Circassian Genocide (Walter Richmond)
517 The Circassian Genocide (Walter Richmond)
518 The Circassian Genocide (Walter Richmond)
519 Mein Kampf (Adolf Hitler)
520 The Circassian Genocide (Walter Richmond)
521 The Circassian Genocide (Walter Richmond)
522 The Circassian Genocide (Walter Richmond)
523 The Circassian Genocide (Walter Richmond)
524 The Circassian Genocide (Walter Richmond)
525 The Circassian Genocide (Walter Richmond)
526 The Circassian Genocide (Walter Richmond)
527 The Circassian Genocide (Walter Richmond)
528 The Circassian Genocide (Walter Richmond)
529 The Circassian Genocide (Walter Richmond)
530 The Circassian Genocide (Walter Richmond)
531 The Circassian Genocide (Walter Richmond)
532 The Circassian Genocide (Walter Richmond)

533 The Circassian Genocide (Walter Richmond)
534 The Circassian Genocide (Walter Richmond)
535 The Circassian Genocide (Walter Richmond)
536 The Circassian Genocide (Walter Richmond)
537 The Circassian Genocide (Walter Richmond)
538 The Circassian Genocide (Walter Richmond)
539 The Circassian Genocide (Walter Richmond)
540 The Circassian Genocide (Walter Richmond)
541 The Circassian Genocide (Walter Richmond)
542 The Circassian Genocide (Walter Richmond)
543 The Circassian Genocide (Walter Richmond)
544 http://russiasperiphery.blogs.wm.edu/transcaucasia/chechnya/general/ermolov/
545 https://jamestown.org/program/new-monuments-russian-heroes-russian-circassian-war-anger-circassians/
546 The Circassian Genocide (Walter Richmond)
547 The Circassian Genocide (Walter Richmond)
548 The Circassian Genocide (Walter Richmond)
549 The Circassian Genocide (Walter Richmond)
550 The Circassian Genocide (Walter Richmond)
551 The Circassian Genocide (Walter Richmond)
552 The Circassian Genocide (Walter Richmond)
553 The Circassian Genocide (Walter Richmond)
554 The Circassian Genocide (Walter Richmond)
555 The Circassian Genocide (Walter Richmond)
556 The Circassian Genocide (Walter Richmond)
557 The Circassian Genocide (Walter Richmond)
558 The Circassian Genocide (Walter Richmond)
559 The Circassian Genocide (Walter Richmond)
560 The Circassian Genocide (Walter Richmond)
561 The Circassian Genocide (Walter Richmond)
562 The Circassian Genocide (Walter Richmond)
563 The Circassian Genocide (Walter Richmond)
564 The Circassian Genocide (Walter Richmond)
565 The Circassian Genocide (Walter Richmond)
566 The Circassian Genocide (Walter Richmond)
567 The Circassian Genocide (Walter Richmond)
568 The Circassian Genocide (Walter Richmond)
569 The Circassian Genocide (Walter Richmond)
570 The Circassian Genocide (Walter Richmond)
571 The Circassian Genocide (Walter Richmond)

572 The Circassian Genocide (Walter Richmond)
573 The Circassian Genocide (Walter Richmond)
574 The Circassian Genocide (Walter Richmond)
575 The Circassian Genocide (Walter Richmond)
576 The Circassian Genocide (Walter Richmond)
577 The Circassian Genocide (Walter Richmond)
578 The Circassian Genocide (Walter Richmond)
579 The Circassian Genocide (Walter Richmond)
580 The Circassian Genocide (Walter Richmond)
581 The Circassian Genocide (Walter Richmond)
582 The Circassian Genocide (Walter Richmond)
583 The Circassian Genocide (Walter Richmond)
584 The Circassian Genocide (Walter Richmond)
585 The Circassian Genocide (Walter Richmond) (Also, see "Convention on the Prevention and Punishment of the Crime of Genocide" in this chapter.)
586 The Circassian Genocide (Walter Richmond)
587 The Circassian Genocide (Walter Richmond)
588 The Circassian Genocide (Walter Richmond)
589 The Circassian Genocide (Walter Richmond)
590 The Circassian Genocide (Walter Richmond)
591 The Circassian Genocide (Walter Richmond)
592 The Circassian Genocide (Walter Richmond)
593 The Circassian Genocide (Walter Richmond)
594 The Circassian Genocide (Walter Richmond)
595 The Circassian Genocide (Walter Richmond)
596 The Circassian Genocide (Walter Richmond)
597 http://www.gohistorygo.com/russian-revolution-of-1917
598 The Circassian Genocide (Walter Richmond)
599 The Circassian Genocide (Walter Richmond)
600 The Circassian Genocide (Walter Richmond)
601 The Circassian Genocide (Walter Richmond)
602 The Circassian Genocide (Walter Richmond)
603 The Circassian Genocide (Walter Richmond)
604 The Circassian Genocide (Walter Richmond)
605 The Circassian Genocide (Walter Richmond)
606 The Circassian Genocide (Walter Richmond)
607 The Circassian Genocide (Walter Richmond)
608 The Circassian Genocide (Walter Richmond)
609 The Circassian Genocide (Walter Richmond)
610 The Circassian Genocide (Walter Richmond)
611 http://justicefornorthcaucasus.info/?p=1251661632

612 The Circassian Genocide (Walter Richmond)
613 The Circassian Genocide (Walter Richmond)
614 The Circassian Genocide (Walter Richmond)
615 The Circassian Genocide (Walter Richmond)
616 The Circassian Genocide (Walter Richmond)
617 The Circassian Genocide (Walter Richmond)
618 The Circassian Genocide (Walter Richmond)
619 The Circassian Genocide (Walter Richmond)
620 The Circassian Genocide (Walter Richmond)
621 The Circassian Genocide (Walter Richmond)
622 The Circassian Genocide (Walter Richmond)
623 The Circassian Genocide (Walter Richmond)
624 The Circassian Genocide (Walter Richmond)
625 The Circassian Genocide (Walter Richmond)
626 The Circassian Genocide (Walter Richmond)
627 The Circassian Genocide (Walter Richmond)
628 The Circassian Genocide (Walter Richmond)
629 The Circassian Genocide (Walter Richmond)
630 The Circassian Genocide (Walter Richmond)
631 The Circassian Genocide (Walter Richmond)
632 The Circassian Genocide (Walter Richmond)
633 The Circassian Genocide (Walter Richmond)
634 The Circassian Genocide (Walter Richmond)
635 The Circassian Genocide (Walter Richmond)
636 The Circassian Genocide (Walter Richmond)
637 The Circassian Genocide (Walter Richmond)
638 The Circassian Genocide (Walter Richmond)
639 The Circassian Genocide (Walter Richmond)
640 The Circassian Genocide (Walter Richmond)
641 The Circassian Genocide (Walter Richmond)
642 The Circassian Genocide (Walter Richmond)
643 The Circassian Genocide (Walter Richmond)
644 The Circassian Genocide (Walter Richmond)
645 The Circassian Genocide (Walter Richmond)
646 The Circassian Genocide (Walter Richmond)
647 The Circassian Genocide (Walter Richmond)
648 The Circassian Genocide (Walter Richmond)
649 The Circassian Genocide (Walter Richmond)
650 The Circassian Genocide (Walter Richmond)
651 The Circassian Genocide (Walter Richmond)
652 The Circassian Genocide (Walter Richmond)

653 The Circassian Genocide (Walter Richmond)
654 The Circassian Genocide (Walter Richmond)
655 The Circassian Genocide (Walter Richmond)
656 The Circassian Genocide (Walter Richmond)
657 The Circassian Genocide (Walter Richmond)
658 The Circassian Genocide (Walter Richmond)
659 The Circassian Genocide (Walter Richmond)
660 The Circassian Genocide (Walter Richmond)
661 http://www.preventgenocide.org/law/convention/text.htm
662 https://treaties.un.org/doc/publication/unts/volume%2078/volume-78-i-1021-english.pdf
663 http://www.genocidewatch.org/genocide/tenstagesofgenocide.html
664 http://www.genocidewatch.org/genocide/tenstagesofgenocide.html
665 http://therightstuff.biz/2015/07/19/the-russian-question/
666 http://www.un.org/en/genocideprevention/documents/atrocity-crimes/Doc.27_convention%20statutory%20limitations%20warcrimes.pdf
667 http://www.un.org/en/genocideprevention/documents/atrocity-crimes/Doc.27_convention%20statutory%20limitations%20warcrimes.pdf
668 https://www.icrc.org/customary-ihl/eng/docs/v2_rul_rule160
669 Heroes and Emperors in Circassian History (Shauket Mufti)
670 Heroes and Emperors in Circassian History (Shauket Mufti)
671 Heroes and Emperors in Circassian History (Shauket Mufti)
672 Heroes and Emperors in Circassian History (Shauket Mufti)
673 Heroes and Emperors in Circassian History (Shauket Mufti)
674 Heroes and Emperors in Circassian History (Shauket Mufti)
675 http://english.alarabiya.net/en/views/news/world/2014/09/03/Rotherham-When-excuse-is-uglier-than-the-sin.html
676 Heroes and Emperors in Circassian History (Shauket Mufti)
677 Heroes and Emperors in Circassian History (Shauket Mufti)
678 http://historynewsnetwork.org/article/151025
679 Heroes and Emperors in Circassian History (Shauket Mufti)
680 Heroes and Emperors in Circassian History (Shauket Mufti)
681 Heroes and Emperors in Circassian History (Shauket Mufti)
682 Heroes and Emperors in Circassian History (Shauket Mufti)
683 http://stephenshenfield.net/archives/research-jrl/96-special-issue-no-42-may-2008-the-circassians
684 http://stephenshenfield.net/archives/research-jrl/96-special-issue-no-42-may-2008-the-circassians
685 https://aheku.net/articles/english/diaspora/1238
686 The Ghost of Freedom: A History of the Caucasus (Charles King)
687 The Ghost of Freedom: A History of the Caucasus (Charles King)

688 The Ghost of Freedom: A History of the Caucasus (Charles King)
689 http://www.bbc.com/news/world-africa-13431486
690 http://www.bbc.com/news/world-africa-13431486
691 http://www.bbc.com/news/world-africa-13431486
692 http://www.projetaladin.org/holocaust/en/history-of-the-holocaust-shoah/the-killing-machine/concentration-camps.html
693 https://berkshireonstage.com/2011/08/31/the-trial-of-fdr-examines-choices-in-time-of-war-genocide-at-pittsfields-new-stage-pac/
694 http://www.projetaladin.org/holocaust/en/history-of-the-holocaust-shoah/the-killing-machine/concentration-camps.html
695 http://www.projetaladin.org/holocaust/en/history-of-the-holocaust-shoah/the-killing-machine/concentration-camps.html
696 http://www.projetaladin.org/holocaust/en/history-of-the-holocaust-shoah/the-killing-machine/concentration-camps.html
697 http://www.projetaladin.org/holocaust/en/history-of-the-holocaust-shoah/the-killing-machine/concentration-camps.html
698 http://www.crimesofwar.org/a-z-guide/genocide/
699 http://www.armeniapedia.org/index.php?title=Recognition_of_Armenian_Genocide_by_Russia and http://www.armenian-genocide.org/Affirmation.151/current_category.7/affirmation_detail.html
700 https://www.youtube.com/watch?v=64vqojH3lRc
701 https://www.youtube.com/watch?v=64vqojH3lRc
702 Drozdov, GSA
703 Georgian State Archives 1, 2, op. 1, doc 1177, p. 111
704 Olshevsk
705 Social Alchemy on the Black Sea Coast, 2009
706 Berzhe, Olshevsky, Drozdov
707 Olshevsky, GSA, Drozdov
708 GSA f. 2, op. 1, doc. 1177 p. 116
709 GSA f. 2, op, 1, doc 1177, p. 157
710 Olshevsky
711 http://www.slate.com/blogs/the_world_/2014/02/05/the_circassians_and_the_olympics_did_the_age_of_genocide_begin_in_sochi.html
712 http://www.preventgenocide.org/law/convention/text.htm
713 https://www.washingtonpost.com/news/worldviews/wp/2015/10/09/how-the-rivalry-between-russians-and-turks-shaped-the-world/
714 The Circassian Genocide (Walter Richmond)
715 http://windowoneurasia2.blogspot.com/2015/05/151-years-after-genocide-and-one-year.html
716 http://www.worldbulletin.net/world/158273/circassia-putin-should-recognise-circassian-genocide

717 http://www.cnn.com/2014/03/18/world/europe/ukraine-crisis/
718 http://www.cnn.com/2014/08/15/world/europe/ukraine-crisis-ripley-explainer/
719 http://www.nytimes.com/2015/04/16/world/europe/european-parliament-urges-turkey-to-recognize-armenian-genocide.html?_r=0
720 http://legal.un.org/avl/ha/cppcg/cppcg.html
721 http://www.nytimes.com/2011/05/21/world/europe/21georgia.html?_r=0
722 http://www.civil.ge/eng/article.php?id=24790
723 The Black Sea: A History (Charles King)
724 http://arm-ge.livejournal.com/13273.html
725 Heroes and Emperors in Circassian History (Shauket Mufti)
726 Heroes and Emperors in Circassian History (Shauket Mufti)
727 Heroes and Emperors in Circassian History (Shauket Mufti)
728 Heroes and Emperors in Circassian History (Shauket Mufti)
729 Heroes and Emperors in Circassian History (Shauket Mufti)
730 Heroes and Emperors in Circassian History (Shauket Mufti)
731 Heroes and Emperors in Circassian History (Shauket Mufti)
732 Heroes and Emperors in Circassian History (Shauket Mufti)
733 Heroes and Emperors in Circassian History (Shauket Mufti)
734 Heroes and Emperors in Circassian History (Shauket Mufti)
735 Heroes and Emperors in Circassian History (Shauket Mufti)
736 Heroes and Emperors in Circassian History (Shauket Mufti)
737 http://windowoneurasia2.blogspot.com/2016/11/nobody-talks-about-armenians-anymore.html
738 http://windowoneurasia2.blogspot.com/2016/11/nobody-talks-about-armenians-anymore.html
739 http://euromaidanpress.com/2016/11/29/its-long-past-time-to-identify-and-shame-holodomor-deniers/

5

The Circassian Flag, the Homeland, the Circassian Identity

The Circassian Flag

There are several reference sources that explain and clarify the history of the Circassian flag. Among those sources is the novel Between the Millstones by the Circassian author Ishac Mashbesh, which states how the Circassians received the news about the Treaty of Edirne (or Treaty of Adrianople) on September 14, 1829.[740]

> The Treaty of Edirne, signed on September 14, 1829, concluded the Russo-Ottoman War of 1828–29.

According to Edirne (ancient Adrianople), Turkey, Russia benefitted out of this treaty as it respectively indicated the weak position of the Ottoman Empire in many locations. The treaty had strengthened the Russian position in Eastern Europe and contributed to the weakening of the Ottoman Empire, which paved the way for eventual prospects that presaged the future for dismantling the Ottoman Empire and the loss of its controlled regions and countries, especially in Europe.[741]

The treaty came to impose the rule of the strong over the weak, which enabled Tsarist Russia to seize the islands controlling the mouth of the Danube River,[742] getting the green light to invade and annex the Circassian coastline on the Black Sea and achieve the old Russian dream of controlling the warm waters of the Circassian Black Sea ports in addition to occupying the northwestern Caucasus region, which contains the northwestern part of the Caucasus Mountains due to its importance by having Mount Ebrus (5,642 meters/18,510 feet high),[743] the highest peak in Europe, in addition to the natural beauty of forests and mountains.

Britannica Encyclopedia affirms, "The treaty allowed Russia to annex the islands controlling the mouth of the Danube River and the Caucasus coastal strip of the Black Sea, including the fortresses of Anapa and Poti. The Ottomans recognized Russia's title to Georgia and other Caucasian principalities and opened the Straits of the Dardanelles and Bosporus to Russian shipping."[744]

The comical effect with such an accord between two opportunist symbols does not lie in the exchange of benefits that characterized the eventual moments of harmony between such wicked partners. This fact shows that the Ottoman Empire had so wavered and given up things, which were neither owned nor occupied by Turkey as to concede influence in the Caucasus according to the convention, which was ultimately acquired by a brutal and merciless war and military force.

In 1830, the Circassians became aware of the agreement signed between the Russians and the Ottomans, where they managed to get a copy of the treaty in Russian, which enabled the delegates to read its articles in their council "Adyga Khasa" to decide during the meeting, on the required next move.

Considering vital circumstances, the meeting was held in Adago Gorge (valley), where the delegates expressed their disbelief over the treaty's contents due to ideas they believed in, such as their belief that Turkey, being a Muslim country, will not abandon the Circassians or Circassia, especially that the said agreement will harm Circassia and its people, which made them send a delegation composed of Circassian leaders to Istanbul to meet the Ottoman sultan, to clarify the situation and to examine the accuracy of the news.

It was confirmed by the Ottoman authorities through minimizing their contacts and relationship with Circassia while the Russians, in turn, started to step up in flexing their strength and exerting attempts to continue manipulating the region with no competition.

Prince Zan, Nour Mohammad Haghur, and Tram were selected to go to Turkey to find the actuality of the issue. The delegates had high hopes in mind during their contact with the Ottomans, but found out the hard way the opposite of what they expected, as the Russians had already informed the Turks about the arrival of the Circassian delegation, requesting to arrest its members until the situation stabilizes in Circassia. Upon arrival at Istanbul, the delegation managed to obtain a Turkish copy of the Adrianople treaty, where a letter from Prince Zan was also sent to Sultan Mahmut, and it was arranged to meet with him.

However, the situation in Circassia worsened during the visit of the Circassian delegation because the Tsarist Russian troops had started an offensive to penetrate deep into Circassian territories, where Prince Zan was informed about the events and forced to remain in Istanbul while the other two delegates returned, having in their possession a Turkish copy of the treaty of Adrianople, where there was a necessity for a Circassian War Preparation Assembly.

While Prince Zan stayed behind in Istanbul trying to defend the Circassian cause in any way possible, he met with David Urquhart, the British embassy's secretary in Istanbul, who had known him for years. Mr. Urquhart, who was impressive for his fluency of the Adyga language, was requested by Prince Zan for Britain's assistance to the Circassians while he replied that the British and French are very much concerned about the situation in Circassia and they were worried about the Circassians.

Urquhart elaborated on the fact that there is no limit to the Russian ambitions that forced Turkey to sacrifice Circassia. He expressed his conviction: England knows that Russia's main interest is to reach the Bosporus while Britain with its allies can stop Russia's ambitions and to offer their assistance to the freedom fighters.

Urquhart also promised to offer much-needed military aid, such as gunpowder, guns, artillery, and ammunition. Prince Zan wanted to know the cost of all that on the Circassians in return for all this promised aid, as Urquhart gave the reassurance that the repayment could be in the form of wheat, corn, honey, animal hide, lumber, etc.

In addition, English engineers could aid in the exploration and extraction of natural resources from Circassia's territories. Zan replied that the Circassians will certainly repay all the expenses of the arms and ammunition Britain will provide; however, what the Circassians hoped for was political (and diplomatic) support in addition to the armaments.

Urquhart stressed that the prince had to seek the unity of the Circassians and, in order to achieve this, he must have professional advisers; so he introduced Zan to Mr. Longworth, a journalist for the Morning Chronicle, and Mr. James Bell, who asked to be introduced to the Circassians as a businessman. Prince Zan promised that he will help accommodate Longworth and Bell who would be arriving in Circassia.

After Prince Zan Seferbi had reconsidered the way, he consulted David Urquhart and included an offer to negotiate future steps. He anticipated tangled concerns and mixed compiled ideas after the rapid and complex considerations, which made him review all the sensations and events and the possibilities of anticipated reactions of his Circassian compatriots when their homeland became prey to the greedy countries, while he "began to realize that the greater tragedy lies in the fact that the Circassians will find themselves being cornered between Europe & Russia which would resemble a mill, and Circassia would be like a seed of wheat that will be crushed into flour".

The following is, in short, the story of the birth of the Circassian flag as told by the Circassian writer Ishac Mashbesh in his book Between the Millstones:

During a demonstration against Russians in Istanbul, which Prince Zan Seferebi had participated in organizing, "he fell down and was trampled on by some protesters causing for him three rib fractures. He was hospitalized for two months." The only persons who visited him at the hospital were three Circassians—Mohamed Selkhur, H'ouri Khanem, and Ismael Bek.

One day when Selkhur visited Prince Zan, the latter presented a folded paper, passed it to Selkhur, and asked him about his opinion about its contents. Selkhur was surprised, and then Zan emotionally replied that it was the Circassian unity flag (Baraq), saying that during his long hospitalization, he thought considerably about a symbol for the Circassian unity and he concluded on the contents of the paper.

It contained twelve gold-colored stars and three crossed arrows.

> Zan explained that each of the twelve stars represents a Circassian tribe and that they are all equally represented without prejudice, they are all equal in the unity. As to the crossed arrows they represent that the Circassians do not seek war, but will defend themselves when attacked.

Zan continued,

> When you lie down in a hospital bed away from your homeland and family, you experience many thoughts, you

can dream with your heart and brain about your homeland, your village, the river, the sky and to clearly hear the birds' songs in the forest, thus the color of the flag should reflect the spring color about the homeland, the color of the meadows and forests, and will have twelve gold stars and three crossed arrows.

Within a few days, H'ouri Khanem brought the readied flag so that it was ready to be sent to Circassia.

Selkhur asked which of these stars represents the Natukhwai, and Shapsough. Prince Zan then got distressed and replied there is no cause to ask such a question, as no one has the right to bring it up and there should be no search for such a star or tribe count, so as to be understood that there is no discrimination or preference of any tribe over the others.

After a period of time, he bade farewell to James Bell and Longworth who traveled to the Caucasus on board the steamer Vixen.

After his arrival, Bill handed over a package to Nour Mohammad Haghur, saying that Prince Zan Seferbi had requested for it to be delivered to him. The package turned out to contain a piece of green silk material, embroidered in gold thread twelve gold stars and three crossed arrows. Nour Mohammad was surprised and wondered, "What is this? Is it what I think?" Bill answered, "Yes, you are right, but I do not want anyone to know that I am who brought it to you."

A general meeting of the Khasa was held in (Psefabe) Valley where representatives of the Circassian tribes met, in which Nour Mohammad Haghur presented the Circassian flag subject by saying, Prince Zan has sent us the Baraq (flag) of the Circassian unity." He asked Tram to unfold the package and present the flag.

When the green-colored silk fabric was unfolded with its golden stars and arrows, the flag began to flap vigorously with the wind, as if it was getting ready to fly in the air. Quietness prevailed in the valley as at that moment hundreds of eyes focused on the flapping green flag with its golden stars and arrows. Then Haghur asked, "Who agrees that this flag is to be the unifying flag for all Circassians?" At that moment, the qamas (swords) were drawn and raised above the heads of those Circassians gathered in the valley.

In other narratives about the construction of the Circassian flag, the green flag contains twelve golden stars and three golden crossed arrows pointing upwards, which was originally created when a number of tribes agreed on a union in the 1830s and the flag was designed and drawn by the Scotsman David Urquhart during that same period. The green color, aquamarine green, a dark bluish green, represents life and freedom and inspired by the spring in the Circassian homeland, enhanced by the color of forests, plains, and mountains, where the stars represent the twelve main Circassian (Adyga) tribes and three crossed arrows, which symbolize union of the tribes in addition to peace. The stars were arranged in two lines, with three placed on a line just above the heads of the arrows and the other nine stars arranged in a longer arching line.

The importance of the Circassian flag was raised in a later date when it was made possible to become a symbol of unity, concord, and positive contact between all Circassians in the world, whether in diaspora or in the homeland in the North Caucasus while the Republic of Adygea adopted this flag to be the flag of the republic.

The British traveler/Orientalist David Urquhart, who is a Scottish scholar, was "sent by the British Government to sustain the Circassian people against Russia."

He gave a speech about the Circassian flag in Glasgow on May 23, 1838.

Circassia and the Circassian Flag in a Speech by Mr. Urquhart

Mr. Urquhart gave a speech in Glasgow on May 23, 1838, which was published by the Circassian committee in 1863, where he pleaded to acknowledge the honor he had observed: "That new-born state, and to thank you for the sympathy you have expressed for its welfare and growth," reminding that until recently, the name of Circassia would only have called forth "thoughts of fable and romance, or visions of manly beauty or female grace."[745]

He added, "Circassia is still the land of poetry and romance, but it has ceased to be that of mystery or of fable; and though the fame of its loveliness has alone hitherto reached the shores of Western Europe, the disciplined thousands and hundreds of thousands of the CZAR have learned to appreciate its manly virtues and heroic deeds."[746]

Mr. Urquhart conversed about Circassia being the "new star of the East" because of its fantasy, romance, fascination, brightness, loveliness, and steadiness, saying, "If you have hailed with enthusiasm the rising of this new star of the east because it is bright, lovely, and poetic, what would not be your calmer satisfaction if, when contemplating this new emblem rising from the Caspian, and shining over Elbrouz, you could but have beheld a real representative of that people, and a sample of the garrison of the Caucasus."[747]

He determined to describe his deep gratitude of what he had seen in Circassia:

> It is utterly impossible for me by words to convey the sentiment of admiration, and the feeling of attachment with which that people has inspired me; but it is not on me alone that such impressions have been made. Two English vessels have touched their shores, and from the captain to the cabin-boy, every Briton who has landed on the coast, has been seized by the fascination of this land of romance, and been filled with enthusiasm for a race, the representatives, in these heartless days, of the moral existence and poetic intercourse of the primeval ages of man. Two of your fellow-countrymen have for a year been resident among these—as Russia informs us—savage bandits and stealers of men; one of these a townsman of your own, and the friend of many who now listen to me. His affection for the Circassians, his estimate of their character as men—of their value to us as a people—has grown with every month of residence among these —.[748]

Sailing away from what his government's attitude, motivation, direction, and favoritism of being closer to accept the Russian agenda against Circassia and its courageous people, who were devoted to defend themselves and their homeland against unprecedented evil invasion methods and scenarios that Circassians had endured, suffered, and experienced silently, quietly, but painfully as a direct result of tremendous, harsh, merciless, and savage assaults and destruction that meant intimidation, insult, and eventual annihilation.

Even though the Circassian population was approximately four million, they were fixated on defending their country and break the cruel blockade and sanctions Russian forces had imposed on Circassia, which left the indigenous nation with no room to look into other options or factors such as founding and organizing a central government and establishing a modern administrative authority to look after education, culture, economy, agriculture, and other fields in addition to establishing a system of foreign relations that would assert contacts and communications with foreign countries, especially the European nations that could have had a positive effect on the war and its objectives and consequences.

Mr. Urquhart questioned how Circassians were able to resist and maintain their independence and freedom against "their aggressors":

> They have been enabled to do so by the value of individual worth, by the strength of single heroism. The child there, like the nursling of Sparta, is considered the property of the community, and educated for the common good, by a discipline alike of the mind and of the frame, giving fortitude and sobriety

to the first, endurance and dexterity to the second. The child, placed under the care of a foster-father, returns not to his home until he has won his rights of manhood by some martial deed.[749]

He continued while simultaneously praising the Circassians:

> Here I beheld the only people from Nova Zembla to Tangier—from the Atlantic to the Indian Ocean—prepared to avenge an insult, or resist an injury from the Czar of Muscovy. Then it was that the involuntary oracle burst from my lips, "You are no longer tribes, but a people; you are Circassians, and this is Circassia."[750]

Here he illustrates,

> But a flag or a colour acquires its power from the past—from association with great men - or with useful principles in times gone by—whose fame or whose memory, as they float down the stream of time, are linked with the feelings of men's infantine years, and become the expression of admiration for what is great, of love for what is good. Circassia, with an ancestry of five thousand years, presented no such associations; no hero had repelled a conqueror—no legislator had given freedom and prosperity by institutes and laws—the arms of no family could be selected as the emblem of noble devotion—the symbol of no institution be adopted as the expression of national unity—from the naked necessities of the moment, therefore, was the colour to be derived—according to the circumstances of the feelings of the day were the devices to be selected.[751]

The story of the Circassian flag goes on in details: "Green, the colour that robes their mountains, and that indicates the faith of Mecca, was that which I chose. On it I placed a bundle of arrows, their peculiar arms and a crown of stars, that in the nightly bivouac they might associate their freedom with the works of their Creator and the glories of the heavens."[752]

Mr. Urquhart expressed in the last paragraphs of his speech an outlook about blockade on the Circassian Black Sea ports:

> Yet it was on that coast, and before the eyes of this people, that an outrage unheard of was perpetrated on the British

flag, and that—I blush as a man, and I tremble as a Briton to record it—England submitted to the outrage, and justified it by a falsehood. An English vessel, the Vixen, was captured by a Russian cruiser while peaceably trading with the independent people, and now bears along these coasts weapons of death and the pennant of Russia.

Had Circassia from time immemorial been a dependency of Russia, the seizure of the Vixen would have equally been an outrage on England, and a violation not only of international law but of peace; but England and Russia have reciprocally bound themselves by the Treaty of the 6th July, entered into for "the pacification of the East," to seek no accession of territory or any exclusive commercial or political advantages. The plea put forward by Russia, and eagerly grasped by England, of the occupation of the coast in question by a Russian force, an assertion which itself is false, is a violation of compact and of treaty; yet this violation is admitted—nay, invented, to justify, the seizure of a vessel which went to that coast under the sanction and patronage of the British Government itself—exhibiting a complication of infamy unheard of amongst mankind, and which must doom the perpetrator to enduring execration. You ask what can be done to maintain the independence of Circassia.[753]

The Homeland Remains in Circassian Memory

Mount Elbrus

The diaspora has suffered difficult circumstances due to being away from their homeland. The people of the Caucasus, particularly the Circassians, have shown considerable interest in issuing printed leaflets and journals and to publish news and matters that concern the various members of the communities.

The following is an article titled "The Close but Far Away Motherland." I sent it to be published in the third addition of the "FREEDOM Bulletin," which used to be published by "the Caucasian Community Center" in New Jersey, USA, dated the first of July 1979. This is to show the feelings toward the situation in the North Caucasus then, during the Soviet era, to reflect the feelings against the imperial power that grabbed the region at the time, not to mention the human suffering of being forced to live away from the homeland.

The Close but Far Away Motherland

I woke up from innocent childhood dreams to be at the center of a painful reality.

A new phase of my life just started by gradual transfer from the home that I was raised at to the life in the society that I found myself living in. Logical Questionnaire started tremendously increasing. Answers started coming and no convincing answers were found at some other times. I know part of my life, which is the personal one; but I couldn't know the most important, which is the national side.

I decided to continuously research and work to obtain what I wanted to know. I studied, asked and dogged deep until I reached painful facts.

I and my people are with no homeland. My people became minorities in all countries of the world. Differences and personal conflicts have occurred within those minorities, and selfishness prevailed. Truth is shone and all my people know it. We were masters in our motherland and now we are slaves for others in the lands of strangers.

We were living on the soil of our Motherland that we inherited from our grandfathers which was irrigated by the heroes with their precious sweat and blood, but now we are living on the soil of foreign and strange lands. Many of my people perished while fighting for those new homelands, defending others' rights and defending themselves and their own honor in some cases.

We used to live in Motherland within our customs and inherited habits and we live now with strangers' customs and habits whether we chose that or we were obliged to do so.

Did those changes alter the fact that we are Circassians? The logical answer which we all know, is that it did not affect our situation or national contents, and even if we stayed away forever, we will always stay as foreigners and minorities with stolen rights, and duties given by others must be fulfilled.

I am addressing all the live conscious individuals of my Circassian People to get all ways and means possible, to renaissance and rise up to the required level and standard of the sense of responsibility and national dignity, and to look for the future to save all those who got lost and misguided.

Let us my brothers and sisters not wait for the saver, which will never arrive. Savior comes through uniting with each other, to return home, to motherland.

We will not steal or rob others' lands or rights, but we want to restore our stolen rights and to return to live with our countrymen who are still living there.

Enough of this mass-homelessness and mass-loss . . . Motherland is calling.

The article has many indications and factors that can be as follows:
- Tough times never last, but tough people do.
- It's a fact of life that the North Caucasus Region is still under colonial rule, but the difference is the change of tyranny from the Soviet umbrella to "Federal Russia."
- The national feelings against imperialism have long been there and long before the "rubber stamp" cliché slogans that were recently invented, such as "religious-influenced radicals," etc. This will not change the fact that nations will struggle for dignity.
- Refugees, deportees, and Caucasian citizens from the North Caucasus Region who are living in diaspora in more than thirty countries of the world did not and will not forget their motherland, and "truth one day will prevail."
- The unseen power that destroyed the colonial empire and the fascist Soviet Union will in turn create conditions for the people to recover their rights, and no tyrant predecessors will be able to change the will of the people to freedom, dignity, and independence.
- Self-determination is a basic human need, which is guaranteed and granted by "human rights" charters of the United Nations and international law.
- Russia has more problems to tackle and worry about than holding on colonies and nations against their will, which requires devoted Russians to release and let go of those nations and make them choose the right of self-determination.[754]

The Need for a Circassian Institutional Work

Winston Churchill said, "There is nothing wrong with change, if it is in the right direction."[755] A common Circassian mechanism will achieve ambitious goals of the Circassian nation if it relies on the basics and perspectives of managing a joint Circassian manner of action currently and in the future by coordinating and consulting through logical and reasonable key elements.

If the Circassians set out in their future work in terms of renouncing selfishness, they will work together to maintain joint collective conduct to help each other, especially to lead the younger generation and encourage them to learn skills and professions necessary to know all that pertains to their existence. They must obtain the necessary academic qualifications that would help focus on the competencies needed by the Circassian communities. They must also be provided by the research institutes themes that will provide useful information on the developments of events in Circassia since the beginning of the Tsarist Russian invasion.

It is necessary for Circassians to know of conspiracies being conducted and arranged against them. A Circassian master's student, during his course of study to receive his thesis, unexpectedly met with a Russian diplomat at his college. The diplomat introduced himself in this capacity in the library of the university. He tried to convince the master's student while claiming false accusations and claims about certain Circassian events to change the subject that pertains to the Circassian part of the North Caucasus that was on his mind. The diplomat had the ability to discuss the matter with the faculty members and at the same time try to convince him to change his mind by trying to impose thoughts about certain facts happening in the North Caucasus and in the Circassian World.

The Russian diplomat started convincing him, with certain claims, to divert the intention of working on such a subject, besides the ability of that diplomat to discuss the matter with the faculty members and at the same time try to convince him to change his mind and impose thoughts about certain facts happening in the North Caucasus and in the Circassian World.

Discussing the thesis was not programed, but this was so as not to let the diplomat know about the time, to avoid his participation. It was coordinated that the thesis would be discussed all of a sudden, on the same day, and within a few hours.

During a presentation about the Circassian subject, and at the time of asking questions, an individual asked a repudiation question: "Where is Circassia?" while coincidently, a map of Circassia, originally published in 1855 was placed on a stand in the same hall; accordingly he was told so.

An individual tried to solicit having documents about the Circassian Genocide, gave a strange remark when she was told that not all the documents available were ready to be given away at the time, but with no second thought, she said in a nasty way that the documents are the property of the Circassian nation.

An individual who acquires information and/or documents to be used for personal gains, in a way, to practice monopolizing a plan or a project.

A person who participates in founding an entity with few others, but when it gets establishes, decides to take over the whole operation.

A person who extract documents from a Circassian Website that is made for Circassians in order to be able to reach the valuable information, while a note is placed in the site, which says:

"All interested are welcome to produce and publish the translated and/or the original information, but with no change to meaning and/or content of the documents in whole or in part. Also Internet Websites are invited to publish, translate, and post the information, but with no change to meaning and/or content of the documents."[756] but decides to stamp the documents in his own name in order to try to blur and ignore the source of the documents or to avoid mentioning "Tbilisi Archives," which creates an infringement on publishing rights, against the indicated source, and in a way to eliminate the idea of team spirit or systematic work.

A person who runs and manages a website looks to be promoting and publishing information, criticizing national Circassian issues, activities and individuals, and at the same time tries to publicize it extensively in social media.

A person said when he saw a photo for a diplomat that he saw him personally, when he was leaving after meeting a friend, while that diplomat was entering the gate of the same multi residence place.

A person says that a diplomat has called him, informing him that he saves a vodka bottle for him in his car's trunk.

A person shows that he believes in actions and procedures taken by certain individuals and entities; but suddenly, he shows a change of position and thoughts, and starts posting articles and/or comments attacking what he used to claim he believed in.

An individual who borrows a book, but he fails to return it, when he is asked to do so.

The Circassian Identity

Personal Family Photo
Elyas Bashqawi, A Circassian Royal Guard in Amman, Jordan in the 1940s

Tunne Kelam, a member of the European Parliament, distributed a statement titled Circassians Standing Up for Their Rights and Cultural Identity Deserve EU Support, which reviews the tragedies faced by the Circassians from the eighteenth to the twentieth century.

> Circassians have been subjected to one of the most severe persecutions among the ethnic Caucasian nations. Since the 18th century, when the authorities of the Russian empire started massive ethnic cleansings and deportations of the native population, more than 1.5 million Circassians are estimated to have been killed. The continuation of Russian colonial policies has had a dramatic impact on today's Circassians. Sadly, their situation has not eased in the 21st century.[757]
>
> The abnormal and tragic situation of the Circassians and other Caucasian native peoples also demands a prompt response from the EU member states based on common European values. The Russian Federation is a strategic partner to the EU; Russia has joined several international conventions and should therefore live up to the commitments and standards stemming from those agreements. If numerous violations of the rights of citizens, native nations and environment are confirmed, the EU should react robustly to the situation.[758]

Associations and individuals incline to protect, strengthen, and fortify the Circassians' identity and unity rather than causing confusion that leads to diverting the diaspora toward assimilation and stagnation.

> A wise man had classified men as five types: The first type serves his homeland by money, the second type by work, the third by his pen, the fourth with his life, and the fifth by silence. All of them would betray their homeland if they fail to do what they must do towards their homeland at the proper time.
>
> According to Hewitt (1999), Circassians have the feeling that their identity is under threat. Circassian organisations have been waging successful campaigns against proposals to merge the autonomous republic of Adygeya with the neighbouring Krasnodar region.[759]
>
> The catastrophe that befell the Circassians in the 1860s put their survival as a people at risk both inside the Russian empire (and later the Soviet Union and its successor states) and in exile. However, among the great majority of Circassians living in exile, the Circassian identity was better able to hold its own against narrower identities. The challenge it faced was of a different kind—that of gradual assimilation into the host societies of Turkey and the Middle East. Over time the exiled "Circassians" tended to become "Turks (or Jordanians, etc.) of Circassian descent."[760]
>
> The effects of the Soviet period on the ethnic identity of the Circassians, as on that of other indigenous peoples, were complex and shifting. Certain aspects of the indigenization policy did serve further to weaken and fragment Circassian identity. In 1927, what had previously been a single Circassian literary language was split into two separate literary languages: Kabard-Cherkess and Adygei. Also Circassian groups were, both in the 1920s and later, arbitrarily put together with the Karachai and Balkar, who speak a Turkic language, to form mixed ethnic territories. The later Soviet period witnessed a return to the policy of Russification.[761]

---

[740] Encyclopedia of the Ottoman Empire (Ga´bor A´goston, Bruce Alan

Masters)
741 Encyclopedia of the Ottoman Empire (Ga´bor A´goston, Bruce Alan Masters)
742 http://www.britannica.com/event/Treaty-of-Edirne
743 http://www.livescience.com/40897-mount-elbrus.html
744 http://www.britannica.com/event/Treaty-of-Edirne
745 https://books.google.com/books?id=lOM_AQAAMAAJ&pg=PP9&lpg=PP9&dq=thoughts+of+fable+and+romance,+or+visions+of+manly+beauty+or+female+grace&source=bl&ots=FcgUTdOadw&sig=h-f-17Hxi16u0ZpM4mocJKtrNJg&hl=en&sa=X&ved=0ahUKEwjyqNTFntbUAhWGSSYKHakvAlsQ6AEIKzAB#v=onepage&q=thoughts%20of%20fable%20and%20romance%2C%20or%20visions%20of%20manly%20beauty%20or%20female%20grace&f=false
746 (End note 6)
747 (End note 6)
748 (End note 6)
749 (End note 6)
750 (End note 6)
751 (End note 6)
752 (End note 6)
753 (End note 6)
754 http://justicefornorthcaucasus.info/?p=1130223780
755 http://www.azquotes.com/quote/531793
756 http://www.circassian-genocide.com/Documents/English.pdf
757 http://www.kelam.ee/in-english/news/circassians-standing-up-for-their-rights-and-cultural-identity-deserve-eu-support
758 http://www.kelam.ee/in-english/news/circassians-standing-up-for-their-rights-and-cultural-identity-deserve-eu-support
759 http://hekupse.livejournal.com/1730.html
760 http://justicefornorthcaucasus.info/?p=1251673688http://justicefornorthcaucasus.info/?p=1251673688
761 http://justicefornorthcaucasus.info/?p=1251673688

6

The So-Called 450-Year Association with Russia

A Portrait of an Adygean strike on a Russian Military Fort, which was built over a Shapsugh village, that aim to free the Circassian Coast from the occupiers in 1840 during the Circassian Resistance.

The historical falsehood, falsification, forgery, and lying is not enough to claim or accept a deal between an individual, whoever it is, that has agreed upon a so-called alliance with Tsar Ivan the Terrible to claim the taking over and the possession of the whole country and impose the exclusion of the whole nation, where "the event being marked took place in 1557, when an alliance was concluded between Kabardin prince Temruk Idarov and Tsar Ivan the Terrible. The deal was sealed when the tsar married the prince's daughter Goshevnai."[762]

Circassia

President "Vladimir Putin has made a new leap forward to the Caucasus. By falsifying history, he has signed three distinct decrees under the topic 'the 450 years Anniversary of Voluntary Unification with Russia' of three republics where Circassians live in; has led the administrations to organize celebration schedules by granting astronomical financing. Dzemikh Kasbolet—the Chairman of ICA—has approved this falsification by making written representations and ICA has become one of the supporters of the Project with 'Forever with Russia...!' slogans."[763]

Obviously, the whole issue appeared to be false and reeks of political hypocrisy for its loss of any realistic content: "An official initiative to celebrate the 450th anniversary of Adygeia's 'unification' with Russia has angered Adygs, also known as Circassians, who accuse the Russian federal and local authorities of distorting history for political gain."[764]

Individuals who live in a fantasy illusion are just anonymous people like a body without an open mind or logical awareness. They can be likened to an ostrich with its head in the sand, leading to loss of vision. They claim false episodes and information with their eyes widely opened while ignoring all facts concerning the victims such as massacres, genocide, and deportation. To celebrate a so-called "450 years" of false and fake association with Russia! This indicates as if the victims of Tsarist Russian crimes have voluntarily associated themselves and their homeland with the invaders and assassins who committed savage aggression and eventually occupied Circassia in a tendency to equalize between the victims and the tyrants.

At the time when the events where to take place, "Rushdi Tuguz, a Syrian-born Circassian who has recently moved to the North Caucasus, remarked that if Adygeia's integration into Russia had been voluntary, his ancestors would not have fled to the Middle East in the 19th century. 'If you add sweet water to bitter water, it won't be good water,' said Tuguz."[765]

Apparently, opportunistic individuals who are organically tied and connected with the Russian authorities were interested in harvesting what they could of Moscow's presents and certificates of good conduct that they would need for future benefits and opportunities, besides spending the financial allowances and gifts lavished on them and their guests, members of the International Circassian Association, and their supporters in both homeland and diaspora, for offering convenient support and legalization.

> Moscow has allocated large sums for the festivities—Kabardino-Balkaria got 600 million roubles (about 24 million US dollars) for events, new buildings and roads repairs, while Adygeia received 200 million roubles.[766]

> There is a significant reluctance to the federal level to accept the ongoing redefinition of the Circassian memory and identity, as illustrated by the celebrations, held in 2007, of the 450-year anniversary of the "voluntary" union between Russia and the Circassians. Ten years earlier, similar celebrations, were cancelled after being rejected as false by a commission of historians from different parts of Russia. In a similar vein, Circassian actors complain that their history as an indigenous people of the area is disregarded in the extensive Sochi Olympic presentation material. This reluctance of the federal center could illustrate the increasing authoritarian tendencies, including attempts to control civil society and ethnic minorities.[767]

Profiteers and those who exploit the advantage of earning personal gains are the type of celebrators who are ready to celebrate anything that might be considered keeping up with the situation, that can be described as de facto even though it ignores the legitimate rights of the Circassian nation; but it is fair to say that the vast majority of Adyga Circassians are characterized by having moral principles, honesty, high values, and good ethics.

> "[Moscow] just wants to tick a box to say that they've carried out work to improve interethnic relations, and local officials just want to make some money," said Aly Tliap, head of Adyge Khase in the town of Adygeisk. "Amin Zekhov, another of the leaders of Adyge Khase, said that Circassians had indeed served the Russian state in the past and had been outstanding military commanders." "However, the truth should also be spoken about the Russian-Caucasian war, during which Adygeia was turned into a colony. How can we talk about voluntarily accession after so much blood was spilt?" he asked.[768]

Circassians are neither robots nor yo-yos. They don't accept being regarded as tools or remote-controlled instruments that can be controlled by proxies. They have human feelings and senses. Accordingly, the Circassian activists have appreciated the support obtained from all peace-loving people, human rights activists, organizations, and all people of goodwill who strive for asserting human dignity.

Over three days of celebrations, Kabardino-Balkaria's capital Nalchik staged concerts and exhibitions, a new theatre was opened, and the president and his team met the people. In Adygeia and Karachai-Cherkessia, the festivities were more modest. Adygeia's president Aslan Tkahkushinov conceded that the date was somewhat controversial, but described the dispute as "insignificant."[769]

Circassians should not have participated in celebrating events that did not occur except in the imagination of those who invented them to capitalize on mobilizing publicity for spreading propaganda against the Circassian activists, who have exerted their efforts to explain the facts about the Circassians to the whole world. They are doing their utmost to verify and define the ways and means to enjoy seized human rights by choosing the correct, positive, nonviolent, and civilized methods to retrieve and recover their legitimate rights in their homeland. Most importantly, they must respond to rumors and lies, to deny and contradict such fake events. Even though people perceive that as a distortion of history and denial of horrific tragedies lived by Circassians, unfortunately, many Circassians were not able to express their thoughts because of the lack of NGOs to voice out their thoughts in the face of an active propaganda machine that keeps twisting the truth.

Zaur Dzeukozhev, deputy chairman of the Circassian Congress, told IWPR, "Adygea was colonized by the Russian Empire in the course of an almost century-long bloody Russian-Caucasian war. All honest historians acknowledge this, and we want the Russian authorities to tell the truth." Murat Berzegov, chairman of the Congress, said, "It's wrong to celebrate an event that never happened historically. Had we joined Russia voluntarily, the Russian-Caucasian war of the 19th century would not have been a popular liberation war but an insurrection by the people against their own tsar. ... This is how a single date—a holiday which should not be celebrated—can change the history of a people, converting them from heroes and champions of liberty into bandits."[770]

Since 2005, a renewed Circassian memorialization process has become a key element of Circassian civil society mobilisation and has increasingly taken the form of a counter-memorialization targeting official Russian historiography, which today prescribes an understanding of the Circassian inclusion into Imperial Russia as voluntary. This is not opposed by most Circassians but is also generally rejected by most international research—including a number of Russian scholars—on the issue.⁷⁷¹

The French historian Pierre Nora has contributed to the discussion on the role of minorities or ethnic groups in relation to the "memory turn"—by referring to this type of memorialization processes as an "emancipator trend" and as part of a "democratization of history". Nora suggests two main reasons behind this outbreak of memory. The first reason is the acceleration of history as reflected in, for example, media books, museums, tourism and historical re-enactments. A second reason . . . is of a social nature," and described "in short, the emergence over a very short period of time, of all those forms of memory bound up with minority groups for whom rehabilitating their past is part and parcel of reaffirming their identity (Nora 2002, 5)."⁷⁷²

Apparently, Russia still evades accepting responsibility for the invasion, occupation, and crimes committed against Circassians by the Russian Empire's armed forces, in accordance with irrefutable evidence. The Russians' stubborn refusal to recognize the genocide inflicted on the Circassians falls within the scope of not only denying their own wrongdoings, but also lying, which overlooked the realities of war, occupation, and their associated consequences and the desire to enjoin Circassians in commemorating a voluntary accession that has never happened!

Paul Goble said,

But in 1990, Circassians across the North Caucasus declared May 21st a national day of mourning, an event they have marked every year since. But this year, not only are more and more Circassians there and across the world celebrating this date, they are stressing different aspects of its meaning (www.kavkaz-uzel.ru/newstext/news/id/1217152.html).⁷⁷³

He continued,

Beyond any doubt, today will feature many wise observations by Circassians and their friends and supporters around the world, but they will have to go a long way to surpass the eloquence of one offered already last week by an unknown Circassian in the Republic of Kabardino-Balkaria (www.runewsweek.ru/rubrics/?rubric=country&rid=2536). Since last year, pro-Moscow officials there have been putting up posters with the legend "450 Years of the Voluntary Joining Together of Kabardino-Balkaria to Russia. Together Forever!" But someone has been periodically crossing out the words 'voluntary joining together' and writing instead "1785–1864."[774]

Russia's celebrations for the so-called "450 years of Circassians' voluntary association with Russia" beside the Russian plans and the International Olympic Committee's (IOC) decision to hold the 2014 Winter Olympic Games in Sochi, which is considered the "Land of Genocide" had sparked anger, dissatisfaction, and a lack of acceptance of the Circassians, which has proven the reality of Russian policies of ignoring the real issues regarding solving the problems and disputes that happened in the past up to the present. The trend has shown that the other side is going deeper in disrespecting the Circassian graveyards of those who perished while defending their own motherland and the unique natural reservation areas in the greater Sochi area that used to be protected by Russian law and the United Nations Educational, Scientific, and Cultural Organization (UNESCO).

Circassians have shown their refusal to participate in such celebrations.

The first demonstration was held in front of the Russian consulate in New York City, while holding signs, banners, and flags of Circassia, to protest the Russian big lie of the so-called 450 years of voluntary association with Russia, which was considered by the demonstrators who represented the majority of the Circassians' who live in the United States as disgusting, antipathetic, unacceptable and naive which will be believed only by primitive and those who lack the tolerance or breadth of vision.[775]

A report titled Circassians, History and Cultural Relations has explained the subject of false allegations in full, which is mentioned in the following:

In the sixteenth century one of the Kabardian noble families, Kemirgoquo (Russian: Temryuk), established close ties with the Russian court (the origin of the Cherkasski family), the Circassians did not see this alliance as an act of submission. Nevertheless, when czarist imperial ambitions brought Russian troops to the Caucasus in force in the late eighteenth and early nineteenth centuries, the Kabardians did not offer prolonged resistance, whereas their kin to the west fought on—at first with Ottoman support and then independently—until 1864.[776]

The evidence proves beyond doubt that there was never any agreement or treaty by a majority of Circassians to accept or to adhere to Circassian voluntary association with Russia as such. The legitimate issue is that supposing there was a so-called voluntary association with Russia for 450 years as the claim states, why all the wars that Russia had waged against Circassia and Circassians with the last war lasting for 101 years?

---

[762] https://iwpr.net/global-voices/outrage-fake-circassian-anniversary
[763] http://justicefornorthcaucasus.info/?p=1251661885
[764] https://iwpr.net/global-voices/circassian-outrage-anniversary-plans
[765] https://iwpr.net/global-voices/circassian-outrage-anniversary-plans
[766] https://iwpr.net/global-voices/outrage-fake-circassian-anniversary
[767] The Sochi Predicament: Contexts, Characteristics and Challenges of the Olympic Winter Games in 2014 (Edited by Bo Petersson and Karina Vamlig)
[768] https://iwpr.net/global-voices/circassian-outrage-anniversary-plans
[769] https://iwpr.net/global-voices/outrage-fake-circassian-anniversary
[770] https://iwpr.net/global-voices/circassian-outrage-anniversary-plans
[771] The Sochi Predicament: Contexts, Characteristics and Challenges of the Olympic Winter Games in 2014 (Edited by Bo Petersson and Karina Vamlig)
[772] The Sochi Predicament: Contexts, Characteristics and Challenges of the Olympic Winter Games in 2014 (Edited by Bo Petersson and Karina Vamlig)
[773] http://windowoneurasia.blogspot.com/2008/05/window-on-eurasia-circassians-remember.html
[774] http://windowoneurasia.blogspot.com/2008/05/window-on-eurasia-circassians-remember.html
[775] http://justicefornorthcaucasus.info/?p=1251669767
[776] http://www.everyculture.com/Russia-Eurasia-China/Circassians-History-and-Cultural-Relations.html

7

Language, Culture, and IT

The Circassian Language and Culture

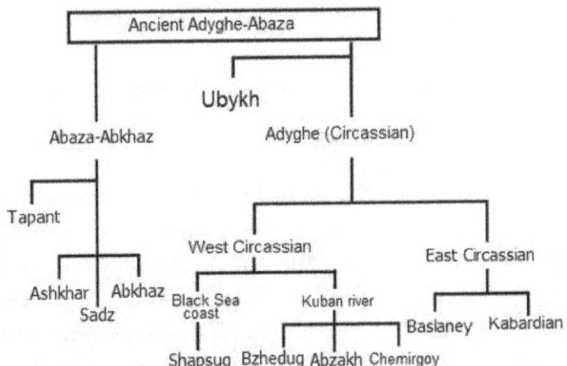

North West Caucasian Family Tree

As I have mentioned in other sections of this book, the development of Circassian culture is an important element of the nation. All aspects of the Circassian culture could be seen through the ages. Language, social behavior, arts, literature, the sciences, music, dance, and other national activities could be traced through Circassian practices.

Songs play an important role in traditional Adyghe society, and each existing genre fulfills its own designated function. Tales of heroes constitute the basis of Circassian folklore. Since the Adyghe people never created their own

293

written literature, they preserve and hand down the history of their people via such songs. Humorous fables, pagan creation tales and Muslim spiritual music exist side by side. The Zachiry genre, for example, is devoted to the foundation of the Muslim faith and praise of the prophet Muhammad. The Adyghe tradition of song relies upon group performance: One person sings the narrative line while the others sing the refrain or "under-ech"—translated into Circassian as "Zhyyu".[777]

The Circassian language and culture would be important pillars in the survival of the Circassian nation. In that concern, Paul Goble published an article titled "Can the Circassian Language and the People Who Speak It Be Saved?" He initiated the article by mentioning, "Two new reports suggest the Circassian language is now at risk of extinction in the coming decades and the North Caucasian nation of those who speak it has entered into a period of demographic decline and could also disappear in the future, prompting their supporters to consider new defenses."[778]

The Minority Rights Group Europe concluded its findings on minorities' languages in Russia:

> While Russia continues to be a diverse country—with schools teaching the languages of national minorities and indigenous peoples, and many representatives of minorities fully integrated in Russian society—numerous, severe problems persist. There has been only limited progress in the implementation of international protection standards, such as the FCNM, and a resistance to ratification of the European Charter for Regional or Minority Languages. The government reports to the Council of Europe on FCNM implementation provide information on numerous programmes to protect minorities and indigenous peoples and promote cultural and linguistic diversity, but they do not include a clear analysis of the practical impact of such programmes.[779]

The Circassian language is one of the languages that are in danger of extinction. It is important to do what is required to stop this from occurring. A necessary reform must be accomplished in accordance with the available resources.

UNESCO has identified Circassian as one of the languages in the North Caucasus at risk of "completely disappearing in the next few decades" given the already low number of people who speak it in that region, the division of the community, and the absence of the use of Circassian in schools and other public spaces (caucasustimes.com/article.asp?id= 21525).[780]

Some proposed methods that could be applied for the possibility of controlling the loss of the language are mentioned. Goble mentioned an important issue, which is the alphabet to be used as a tool to help preserve the language and help in its teaching.

Most in Turkey favor the Latin script while officials in the North Caucasus favor Cyrillic. The Russian Cyrillic is inadequate for the sound system of Circassian, but most textbooks now available are in Cyrillic; and the Turkish government has done very little to develop educational materials in Circassian in the Latin script.[781]

The establishment of a Circassian entity is the best way to protect the language of Circassians in addition to all other cultural and heritage elements. Simultaneously, the foundations and pillars of the nation should be preserved, but it seems that the facts and events show the desire and insistence of the Russian state to ignore the issue entirely, even to the extent of compromising the nation's existence being one of the indigenous nations in the Northwest Caucasus.

Nugzari Antelava mentions in his book Adygean (Circassian) Culture the facts about the status of the language and culture of the Circassians. Deportation took place to Turkey and other parts of the Ottoman Empire, and Circassians continue to live at their destined location to this present day. Being minorities, and due to the continuous change of political systems in the same country or multiple countries, it was not possible to obtain the right to use their own language. As a result, that led to the possibility of language extinction.

The author explored the difficulty of knowing their population in Turkey considering their dispersion all over the country. In the absence of official census and statistics, it is not possible to know the precise number of their population. Therefore, it is not possible to know the percentage of Circassians (Adygha) who utilize and practice either their spoken or written language. Until recently, there were no educational programs for use in teaching the mother tongue.

Exact data on the number of Circassian speakers has not been obtained. During and after the Caucasian War internally displacement of the Adyges to Turkey and other countries has broken not only their language space but it was virtually impossible to determine their number. According to certain reliable sources, more than 3 million Circassians live in Turkey, though in the country the official form of identification is not possible (in 1965 census was ceased considering a native language).[782]

In the introduction of the Adygean (Circassian) Culture, Nugzari Antelava stated,

Caucasian peoples and, of course, the Circassians will have to engage in the development process in world civilization, to find their place in the new world order, to realize future way, to perceive themselves newly in the Caucasus region as well as in the current socio-cultural and geopolitical development processes. Circassians had to bear the cruelty of a century long war and its consequences. It has affected all elements of the nationhood, where the homeland was occupied, half of the people was annihilated and the rest of the citizens were deported or oppressed. All that had necessarily an impact on its presence and future. All that had a negative forcible impinging on the factors that are closely linked to the culture and the language, which needed to be addressed.[783]

Cultural dynamics of ethnic groups living in Russia, including Circassians, is a particular subject of study of various scientific disciplines, mostly of experts of culturology. A goal of culturology is to reveal that inner cultural power of Circassian ethnic group, which led and still has been leading a Circassian cultural dynamics in the past and present, and which suffers its socio-cultural transformation dramatically.[784]

It is beneficial for specialists, whether they are Circassians or not, to seek methods to be followed to facilitate the required action to fix the situation. An integrated program should be provided to study bases that will change the status quo: "In terms of the history of Adygean culture, the issues related to key problems of revival and development of Circassians—at one time united ethnic group and now fragmented culture, residing on different continents and in different countries, are still topical."[785]

Culture is the intellectual heritage that a nation is characterized from others and "refers to the cumulative deposit of knowledge, experience, beliefs, values, attitudes, meanings, hierarchies, religion, notions of time, roles, spatial relations, concepts of the universe, material objects and possessions acquired by a group of people in the course of generations through individual and group striving."[786]

Language is a pattern of signs and symbols, used as a tool of knowledge and understanding between people in all walks of life. It "can be defined as a system of signs (verbal or otherwise) intended for communication. It is a system since its constituent components relate to each other in an intricate and yet organized fashion. But communication is not the only function of language. In fact, language can be used for dreaming, internal monologue, soliloquy, poetry, etc."[787]

Language reflects the reality of a people while culture is an integral element of the actuality, thus reflecting changes and reflection in life, both in culture and language: "The relationship between language and culture is deeply rooted. Language is used to maintain and convey culture and cultural ties. Different ideas stem from differing language use within one's culture and the whole intertwining of these relationships start at one's birth."[788]

It is essential to combine efforts to link both subjects to maintain the most important elements of a nation and to take into account the reality of diaspora difficulties.

> Because language is so closely entwined with culture, language teachers entering a different culture must respect their cultural values. As Englebert (2004) describes: ". . . to teach a foreign language is also to teach a foreign culture, and it is important to be sensitive to the fact that our students, our colleges, our administrators, and, if we live abroad, our neighbours, do not share all of our cultural paradigms."[789]

General Link between Language and Culture

Any nation is naturally interested in taking care of the important elements of its long-term survival: "Language is the principal means whereby we conduct our social lives. When it is used in contexts of communication, it is bound up with culture in multiple and complex ways" while "language expresses cultural reality."[790]

It is useful to know the relationship between language and culture.

> Language is the verbal expression of culture. Culture is the idea, custom and beliefs of a community with a distinct language containing semantics—everything speakers can think about and every way they have of thinking about things as medium of communication. For example, the Latin language has no word for the female friend of a man (the feminine form of amicus is amica, which means mistress, not friend) because the Roman culture could not imagine a male and a female being equals, which they considered necessary for friendship.[791]

Two integrated elements perform the task of giving the nature and the character of a particular nation, and establish necessary inextricable attachments between the two.

> There is a unique tie between culture and language. The languages we speak provide us with the words and concepts to describe the world around us, allowing us to verbalize certain values easily. Anything we as a cultural group value will surely have a known and easily understandable term. The English word "privacy" and the Chinese word "guanxi" both have clear and strong meanings in their respective languages, but are not necessarily found in all other languages. Being a native speaker of our mother tongue brings with it more than just the ability to communicate; it brings with it the ability to understand why someone thinks and acts as they do.[792]

The different elements of culture are expressed through the language.

> Language is heavily influenced by culture—as cultures come up with new ideas, they develop language components to express those ideas. The reverse is also true: the limits of a language can define what is expressible in a culture (that is, the limits of a language can prevent certain concepts from being part of a culture).[793]

A general abbreviation says, "Language is a system of signs that is seen as having itself a cultural value. Speakers identify themselves and others through their use of language; they view their language as a symbol of their social identity."[794]

Language and Culture by Claire Kramsch presents facts about the relationship between different factors and elaborates on "nature, culture and language" that reads,

> One way of thinking about culture is to contrast it with nature. Nature refers to what is born and grows organically (from the Latin nascere: to be born); culture refers to what has been grown and groomed (from the Latin cooler: to cultivate). The word culture evokes the traditional nature/nurture debate: Are human beings mainly what nature determines them to be from birth or what culture enables them to become through socialization and schooling?[795]

Sensible and realistic approaches can be illustrated according to an objective vision regarding "community of language users," which mentions,

> Social conventions, norms of social appropriateness, are the product of communities of language users. As in the Dickinson poem, poets and readers, florists and lovers, horticulturists, rose press manufacturers, perfume makers and users, create meanings through their words and actions. Culture both liberates people from oblivion, anonymity, and the randomness of nature, and constrains them by imposing on them a structure and principles of selection. This double effect of culture on the individual—both liberating and constraining—plays itself out on the social, the historical and metaphorical planes.[796]

The following summary shortens the topic of dealing with the language issue:

> The theory of linguistic relativity does not claim that linguistic structure constrains what people can think or perceive, only that it tends to influence what they routinely do think. In this regard the work of Sapir and Whorf's has led to two important insights:
> 1. There is nowadays a recognition that language, as code, reflects cultural preoccupations and constrains the way people think.
> 2. More than in Whorf's days, however, we recognize how important context is in complementing the meanings encoded in the language.

> The first insight relates to culture as semantically encoded in the language itself; the second concerns culture as expressed through the actual use of the language.[797]

Pursuing to preserve language and culture helps to consecrate and preserve national identity, specifically in diaspora.

> It is widely believed that there is a natural connection between the language spoken by members of a social group and that group's identity. By their accent, their vocabulary, their discourse patterns, speakers identify themselves and are identified as members of this this or that speech and discourse community. From this membership, they draw personal strength and pride, as well as a sense of social importance and historical continuity from using the same language as the group they belong to.[798]

Dealing with originality is an important factor when all the institutions and the qualified specialists, besides other arrangements, to preserve the language and culture available, taking in account the lead of more influenced languages: "Much of the discussion surrounding the native speaker has been focused around two concepts: authenticity and appropriateness. By analogy with the creation of standard languages, nation-states have promoted a standardized notion of cultural authenticity that has served to rally emotional identification both at home and abroad."[799]

It is useful to look at other examples and compare them: Cultures hiding in languages, examines the link between Japanese language and culture. An Insight into Korean Culture through the Korean Language discusses how Korean culture influences the language," where "languages spoken in Ireland, focuses on the status of the Irish language nowadays and how it has changed over time. In our big world every minute is a lesson looks at intercultural communication and examines how it can affect interactions between people from countries and backgrounds."[800]

It is assured that language is necessarily the main instrument that conveys culture and heritage from the past to the future.

> Perhaps. One thing is certain, however. The oral tradition of the Circassian, like that of any other nation, grew inseparably closely linked with the life of her people. It will not be amiss to remember, in relation with this subject, Johnson's words: "There is no tracing the connection of ancient nations but by

language, therefore I am always sorry when any language is lost, for languages are pedigree of nations."[801]

Status

Circassia, being an integral part of the peoples and nations of the North Caucasus, made it the focus of the colonial and expansionist ambitions through the epochs, where the Circassians pose a unique civilization of not less than five thousand years old. They were able, through the centuries, to settle in their homeland and to preserve their civilization, culture, and language, which made them a nation that could survive despite all encountered obstacles and circumstances.

This enabled Circassians to adapt to all types of difficult situations and maintain their national and cultural identity despite all odds, whether in their homeland or in exile. In addressing the Circassian Question with all its details, it is important to realize the various conditions and factors they influenced and continued to effect with all associated developments. Culture and education are important for the future of the Circassians.

Language is considered a key component of national identity and of the essential elements of the culture of any people or nation. Therefore, a closer look should be taken at the conclusion reached regarding the situation of the Adigha language, which seems to be on its way to extinction. This is due to the absence of serious institutional programs or efforts to stop the regression that could eventually lead to the extermination of the language and its total elimination. The situation should not underestimate the fact that 90 percent of the population of the Circassian nation reside in diaspora.

The mother tongue is used infrequently, and there is only 10 percent of the total census that reside in the homeland in the North Caucasus in six areas (enclaves), including three autonomous republics; but unfortunately, the Adigha language is not placed in the level of a main language whether for educational or official use, where the Russian language is the official language and must be used according to the applicable rules and regulations in all walks of life.

Valuable human heritage is one of the pillars of Circassian civilization, which entrenches conformity with reality and highlights the patriotic and national identity and their features while it is circulated and passed over the generations and over the years such as traditions, customs, sciences, and literature, which are linked with horsemanship, chivalry, literary epics, poetry, customs, popular traditions, tales, stories, handicrafts, skills, popular knowledge, fine arts, folklore, and music. This connects the nation with lessons and style comprehended and realized from the past, to be passed down to the present and future younger generations.

Circassians are considered to be on the brink of extinction. Their problems have been little mentioned, despite the tremendous pain and suffering that they had to bear and put up with when their traditional homeland in the North Caucasus was attacked and endangered. Most of them were scattered after being deported to exile by force, out of their homes and territories, to be dispersed at the time, across the Near East and consequently scattered in some parts of the Ottoman Empire.

When they were displaced and settled somewhere else, they often could not use or speak their original language due to inadequate conditions, different and unusual circumstances, and at certain times were discriminated against in many ways. The Circassians who lived in the Russian regions were gradually dissipating and disappearing into a Russian-language society, and even their culture and identity were so little protected.

Yet the Russian government and regional authorities were taking no measures to help them or to protect their basic human rights and cultural requirements. The Russian government had an obligation as per the law that the Russians themselves had instituted—to help Circassians, being one of tens of minorities, and to cooperate in that matter with associations representing the Circassian population and allow those deported more than 150 years ago to return to their original homeland.

Inspired by reality, the "Nafna" (Habza) Association in Maykop published an article titled, "Stone Has Memory. People Do Not," criticizing the general situation and the stage that the Circassian national issue had reached.[802]

The article questioned and wondered over the lack of attention to the pressing issues of the Circassians and mentioned the subject of the establishment of a memorial monument to the victims "in honour of the hundred thousand people, as they lived, they protected the native land. They were the descendants of the Circassians known all over the world who a lot of centuries ago had created the Circassian civilization." [803]

The editor questioned the way the authorities think and propose: "Who can tell, what they think of, when their 'thoughts' do not coincide, even are absolutely inadequate to what people think of?" He debated lack of interest by officials and candidates: "Recollect the last elections: no candidate of the State Soviet-Khase declared in his program any question concerning the survival problems of the Adygs and preservation of their language and culture. Neither about problems of the Russians."[804]

Circumstances and repeated invasion attempts, especially the grinding Russian-Circassian War (1763–1764), made it difficult to preserve the Circassians' cultural and national heritage elements due to the particularities of war and imposed Russian Empire's policies. Many times elements were destroyed, stolen by the invading forces and their mercenaries, or confiscated to be transferred to St. Petersburg as trophies, to be kept in palaces and museums.

The seized items and materials have been messed with by the consecutive Russian administrations and regimes to make them lose their historical importance and value; which participated in the destruction of the pillars of Circassian society, culture, civil social life, economy, and political structure.

A scourged nation was led to be severely punished!

> Three years after the end of the one hundred year war, in the year 1867 the first expedition of the Russian Academy of Science arrived in Circassia, which by that time was completely depopulated. The digs that were undertaken had stunning results. The ecologists discovered incredible and very valuable examples of an ancient culture. For the next 140 years the excavations had continued. Tens of thousands of artifacts had been found over the 140 years were sent and they are now in various museums in Moscow and St. Petersburg.[805]

During the Soviet era, people who participated in Circassian culture and heritage had to face unpleasant endings.

> Not one of the cultural institutes of the 3 republics of Kabardino-Balkaria, Karachaevo-Cherkessia, and Adygea has the right to independently conduct work on these treasures. Again this right belongs to the cultural agencies of Stavropol and Krasnodar Krais (provinces). The cultural inheritance of the Adigas was consistently destroyed during Stalin era. One example: In 1937 simultaneously in all the three republics, about fifty Adiga scientists had been arrested. These linguistics, historians, folklorists, and poets, the majority of them were shot almost instantaneously. All the archives were destroyed and burned. Among those who were shot was a group of scientists who for the first time had collected epos of the Circassian nation. Among the documents that were burned, 20 000 gathered poems, sayings, proverbs, and ethic poems of the Circassians, which had been collected in the thirties of the last Century, and those losses cannot be regained.[806]

A recent development took place on the seventeenth of March 2016, when a group of Circassian activists from Karachay-Cherkessia and Kabardino-Balkaria "voiced a proposal to create a unified interregional organization to be engaged in the protection and development of culture of the Circassian people."[807]

Programs for Preserving Circassian Culture

Circassia is one of the oldest indigenous nations of southeastern Europe and being such must enjoy the preference in the right to demand humane and natural rights to protect its ethnical identity, language, and culture. Resolutions and treaties of the European Union concerning the rights of the peoples to be preserved call for the protection of people and their rights, taking into consideration that Circassia is a nation under occupation and its citizens are denied their basic rights.

Language and Culture Preserved by Charters, Treaties, and Organizations

The first article of the United Nations Declaration on the Rights of Persons Belonging to National or Ethnic, Religious, and Linguistic Minorities indicates, "States shall protect the existence and the national or ethnic, cultural, religious and linguistic identity of minorities within their respective territories and shall encourage conditions for the promotion of that identity."[808]

The PREAMBLE of the CHARTER OF FUNDAMENTAL RIGHTS OF THE EUROPEAN UNION indicates the following in regards to protecting culture and language:

> Conscious of its spiritual and moral heritage, the Union is founded on the indivisible, universal values of human dignity, freedom, equality and solidarity;
>
> The Union contributes to the preservation and to the development of these common values while respecting the diversity of the cultures and traditions of the peoples of Europe

The European Union declared the recognition of "the rights, freedoms and principles set out hereafter," according to the following articles:

Article 1
Human dignity
Human dignity is inviolable. It must be respected and protected.

Article 14
Right to education
1. Everyone has the right to education and to have access to vocational and continuing training.
2. This right includes the possibility to receive free compulsory education.
3. The freedom to found educational establishments with due respect for democratic principles and the right of parents to ensure the education and teaching of their children in conformity with their religious, philosophical and pedagogical convictions shall be respected, in accordance with the national laws governing the exercise of such freedom and right.

Article 21
Non-discrimination
1. Any discrimination based on any ground such as sex, race, colour, ethnic or social origin, genetic features, language, religion or belief, political or any other opinion, membership of a national minority, property, birth, disability, age or sexual orientation shall be prohibited.
2. Within the scope of application of the Treaty establishing the European Community and of the Treaty on European Union, and without prejudice to the special provisions of those Treaties, any discrimination on grounds of nationality shall be prohibited.

Article 22
Cultural, religious and linguistic diversity
The Union shall respect cultural, religious and linguistic diversity."[809]
Council of Europe published Details of Treaty No.148, European Charter for Regional or Minority Languages. It ruled that "Treaty open for signature by the member States and for accession by non-member States."[810]

A Summary of the Treaty

This treaty aims to protect and promote the historical regional or minority languages of Europe. It was adopted, on the one hand, in order to maintain and to develop the Europe's cultural traditions and heritage, and on the other, to respect an inalienable and commonly recognized right to use a regional or minority language in private and public life.

First, it enunciates objectives and principles that Parties undertake to apply to all the regional or minority languages spoken within their territory: respect for the geographical area of each language; the need for promotion; the facilitation and/or encouragement of the use of regional or minority languages in speech and writing, in public and private life (by appropriate measures of teaching and study, by transnational exchanges for languages used in identical or similar form in other States).

Further, the Charter sets out a number of specific measures to promote the use of regional or minority languages in public life. These measures cover the following fields: education, justice, administrative authorities and public services, media, cultural activities and facilities, economic and social activities and transfrontier exchanges. Each Party undertakes to apply a minimum of thirty-five paragraphs or sub-paragraphs chosen from among these measures, including a number of compulsory measures chosen from a "hard core". Moreover, each Party has to specify in its instrument of ratification, acceptance or approval, each regional or minority language, or official language which is less widely used in the whole or part of its territory, to which the paragraphs chosen shall apply.

Enforcement of the Charter is under control of a committee of experts which periodically examines reports presented by the Parties.[811]

The Network to Promote Linguistic Diversity (NPLD) is a European wide network working in the field of language policy & planning for Constitutional, Regional and

Small-State Languages (CRSS) across Europe. NPLD includes Governments both national and regional, Universities and Associations as its members.[812]

The Network executes its experience in language planning and to plan joint funded language projects with participants.

The NPLD's main goal is to raise awareness at a European level on the vital importance of linguistic diversity. NPLD also aims to facilitate the exchange of best practices among governments, policy makers, practitioners, researchers and experts from all over Europe.[813]

NPLD works closely with European Commission, European Union, Parliament and Council of Europe, and during the years the Network has been active it has created strong links and partnerships with individuals, the Commissioner who has responsibility for language and minority language, MEP's and others who are active in promoting minority languages.[814]

Difficulties of Language Teaching

Efforts and measures seeking to guarantee the survival of the Circassian language being under threat of demise both in diaspora and in homeland in the North Caucasus are initiated from committed individuals and entities. There is surely a worthy role to be played in this field by international organizations and bodies such as the United Nations, UNESCO, the European Union, and any competent Western institutions.

Institutional endeavors within the Circassian institutions have not been stopped in both the Circassian homeland in the North Caucasus and in diaspora. A combination of efforts such as conferences, seminars, researches, and meetings have been held, which are still taking place, to survey all possibilities and to come up with decisions. Most people are anxious to reach and provide substantial solutions that guarantee the provision of practical programs and plans to save the Circassians' Adygha language from loss, to provide educational programs at different levels to preserve one of the most key components of the culture.

One of the issues being discussed with great interest and concern is the desire of many Circassians, especially in diaspora to consider the possibility of changing the language's alphabet. The trend is hoped to steer toward using the Latin letters for the Adygha alphabet instead of the currently used Slavic Cyrillic letters. This is considered one of the main obstacles in learning and teaching the language for Circassians who have not learned Russian before. Using the Latin letters will enable more Circassians, especially in Turkey, to learn their mother tongue more easily.

The spread of dealing with publications that pertain to cultural and linguistic issues of the Circassian people has witnessed positive trends. The wide spread of different levels of language teaching is witnessed, but the use of language in schools and colleges in various stages of education has a lack of planning and implementation and has not reached the required level. One trending area, which reportedly has been popular and widely accepted especially by the younger generation, is computerized education programs that disseminated various helpful dictionaries to all those interested. These new means of teaching are available on websites and social media, which can be utilized through computers and smart phones.

An article written by George Hewitt stated, "A Caucasian Cultural Society was founded in Turkey, where estimates place the number of Circassians anywhere between 2 and 4 million, in 1967. Turkey has witnessed in recent years a proliferation of publications dealing with cultural and linguistic problems of (especially N.W.) Caucasian peoples."[815]

The author added, "It can be expected that pressure for measures to guarantee the survival of the Circassian language (under threat of demise both amongst the diaspora and even in the Caucasian homeland) will continue to come from committed individuals, and there is surely a worthy role to be played here by Western organisations such as UNESCO or the EU's cultural fund —recall the much trickier project overseen by the Council of Europe (representative Alison Cardwell) to prepare a common (objective!) textbook to be used in the schools of Georgia, Armenia and Azerbaijan."[816]

The article has mentioned the establishment of a plan to tackle the language issue.

> The Fund is minded to investigate the possibilities of creating a common form of written Circassian not only to bridge the divide caused in the Caucasus by the existence of the two literary languages but to produce a unifying bond between ALL the Circassian peoples, and, in order to make such a form of Circassian attractive to Circassians unfamiliar with the Cyrillic script, the Roman script is envisaged as serving as base for the orthography.[817]

Presence of a safe linguistic and cultural environment is essential to the development of the individual's personality, and no doubt that this environment will be usually available for persons belonging to the majority rather than of persons belonging to the minorities, thus the principle of equality and non-discrimination will not be sufficient alone to ensure that the minority and its members are at the same level that is available to the majority and its members.

There is a need to recognize minorities preferential treatment to ensure maintaining many characteristics and peculiarities, including language, and states that got interest in the minorities subject are obliged to take positive measures to ensure the provision of a safe environment and encouraging for the minorities to develop their own languages and the development of their features and their own identity". The European Charter has reflected in its preamble, the fact that the protection of the regional languages or the minorities' languages in Europe contributes to the preservation of the cultural wealth and its development, which is in resultant a richness of the human heritage (http://www.hrea. org/index.php?doc_id=365). (The scholars and specialists of international law and human rights look to the language and its protection on the basis that the protection of linguistic rights of minorities is presented in ensuring that all individuals enjoy a safe and encouraging linguistic environment. As for the second approach, it can be described as an environmental approach because it looks at the cultural diversity as a value in itself, and it is like the biological diversity that needs protection for what it entails of an intrinsic value that should be preserved. It does not appear that this approach offers anything for the recognition of linguistic rights as rights for human beings because it does not bind these rights to the individual, but by the absolute, that is the language itself.)[818]

The Circassians' Language

Another reference elaborating on the Circassian language and its link to its family of languages is reported by quoting John Colarusso:

> Circassian and Ubykh form two branches of the Northwest Caucasian Language Family, the third being the Abaza-Abkhaz Branch. Ubykh (nearly extinct) formed a transitional language between Circassian and Abaza-Abkhaz. Circassian itself is divided into a conservative Western or Kyakh language, often called Adyghean, and an Eastern one, Kabardian. Besleney, centered in the Karachay-Balkar Republic, is a dialect transitional between the two.[819]

The source also mentioned linguistic technicality features.

> Besleney has strongly influenced Abaza, the Abkhaz language spoken in and around the republic. The languages of this family are remarkable for their complexity—for example, the verb can inflect for all persons in a sentence, and most of the vocabulary is formed from more basic roots by extensive processes of compounding—and for their radical departure from the grammatical patterns that characterize the dominating Turkic and Indo-European languages of this region.[820]

Numerous attempts have been experienced to preserve the language.

> Some attempts were made to formulate a Circassian written language in the nineteenth century, using the Arabic script. In the 1920s two literary languages emerged, Adyghean based on the Chemgwi (Kemirgoy; Russian: Temirgoy) dialect of western Circassians and Kabardian based on the Baksan dialect. The first alphabets were based on the Arabic script, then the Latin was adopted, and finally in the late 1930s the Cyrillic was used. Currently efforts are under way to devise a new Latin-based script.[821]

Sadly, with the unstable conditions and lack of necessary tranquility when dealing with delicate issues, as a result of foreign intervention, devastating wars, and loss of Circassian independence, Circassian linguistic scholars and specialists were unable to choose the alphabet that fits and suits the Circassian nation. This leads to a scientific development that makes it imperative to choose what serves the national interest best and the possibility of interaction with advanced nations in the information technology era, which will contribute in solving chronic problems.

Seemingly, a lack of clarity in the information has made it possible to publish incorrect or incomplete information because there is very limited academic teaching of the Circassians' Adygha language due to limited Circassian schools and cultural institutions due to limited resources: "Folklorists both within and without the Soviet Union have recorded extensive texts in all the Circassian dialects and in Ubykh. In the Middle East, only Israel allows publication of material in Circassian."[822]

Harsh experiences have always taught Circassians to expect the worst. Tough issues have no fundamental solutions, but that does not change the facts of their origin and quality of people: "The Circassians—self-designation Adyge—are the oldest indigenous people of North Caucasus. Their language belongs to the North-West branch of the Caucasian family of languages. Its unusual phonological system—an overabundance of consonants and scarcity of vowels has stimulated much interest among linguists (Kumakhov 1973, Smeets 1984)."[823]

They constantly had close contacts with those around them, and consequently, there used to be exchange in cultures, sciences, trades, and religious beliefs: "In the 6th century, under Georgian and Byzantine influence many Circassians were Christianized, but under the growing influence of the Ottomans, Islam replaced Christianity. However, the process was gradual. Blending with Christian survivals and even pre-Christian folk beliefs, Islam became fully established only in the 18th-19th centuries. "Neither Christianity nor Islam," as Henze points out, "resulted in the creation of a distinctive priestly class who could preserve written literature or encourage literacy" (1986, p. 247)."[824]

The consequences of the devastating war and occupation have lasted through the years, but the fundamentals upon which the nation is rooted persist to this day. Circassians now believe that they must handle and treat the cause and the generating trouble at the source, not the symptoms.

> Attempts at reducing the language to writing in the 19th and early 20th century had also failed. Circassian became a literary language only after the Russian revolution. The Circassians are Sunnis of the Hanafi School who tend to be non-fanatical and among whom the Adat or custom law—the Adyge-Habze—has remained extremely strong (Shami, 1982). It is the language and the custom law that have formed the chief component parts in Circassian self-identity.[825]

The Circassians speak a language that originated in North Caucasus, which can be divided into five different dialects. Two of them are the West

Circassian or Adyghe, mainly spoken by the Circassians in Adygea, and the East Circassian or Kabardian, mainly spoken by the Circassians in Karachay-Cherkessia and Kabardino-Balkaria. These languages are noted for the great number of consonant distinctions and the small number of vowel distinctions in their sound systems. Circassian was first written in its modern forms after the October Revolution of 1917, as the Soviet populist approach to linguistic diversity dictated that the written language was supposed to reflect as closely as possible to the dialect spoken by the people. Therefore, different Latin alphabets were devised for the western Circassians (the Adyghe) and for the central and western Circassians—the Cherkess and Kabardians. During the first two decades of Soviet rule, the Circassian languages were used in almost all domains, including education.

The Russian Empire followed a maddeningly criminal strategy and fooled the world. The whole plot was a preordained outcome, to eliminate the Circassian nation and all its merits, with the language being one of the harmed elements.

> However, in the late 1930s Soviet language policy began to shift away from the emphasis on the mother tongue. In 1938 Russian was officially decreed a compulsory subject in all Soviet schools. In the last decades of the Soviet Union, outright promotion of Russian as the language of a new community— the Soviet People, became the chief goal of Soviet language policy and many non-Russian languages, including Circassian in both its varieties, were phased out of the school system as languages of instruction. (Kreindler 1982, 1989, 1995)[826]

The present Russian regime has dealt with the Circassians suspiciously, even though at the beginning, peoples of the North Caucasus and beyond thought for a while that an era of freedom and prosperity has befallen.

> The collapse of the Soviet Union has heightened Circassian national feeling both in Russia and in the diaspora. Since the collapse, the Circassians have forged links with their brethren all over the world. The International Association of Circassian Peoples has organized world congresses in which Israeli delegations have taken a very active part. Among the issues raised are the need to revive the language in Russia and the diaspora, the desirability of constructing a common literary language and a return to the Latin alphabet (Bram 1994a; Pafova 1992).[827]

An International Circassian Language Conference was held in Amman, Jordan in October 2008, to discuss the status of the Adygha (Circassian) language in Diaspora, and to debate plans to be followed to teach the language to the Circassians who did not have the chance to learn it. "The Circassian community will play the host and organizer of the 1st International Circassian Language Conference, to start Wednesday. Organizers say the first-of-kind gathering has one major mission: To make sure that this language will not die among its children in the Diaspora after generations since the first exodus from the Caucasus, when thousands fled the repression in 19th century Russia.

The effort is coordinated with the Russian Centre for Culture and Science.[828]

It was reported that: "Many points were discussed during the conference time (15–16 October 2008). Some of the most important were the current state of the Circassian language and the ways to teach the language to Circassians who don't speak it."[829]

The Second International Conference on the Adyghe Language was held in Ankara, Turkey, with the presence of the CEO of the Network to Promote Linguistic Diversity (NPLD) in Europe, Meirion Prys Jones. "(www.kaffed.org/index.php) and was aimed at raising awareness of the importance of cultural and linguistic diversity, and in particular, drawing attention to issues regarding the Adyghe language. The conference provided a forum for sharing experiences on Adyghe, especially in the area of education. As part of the three day event, working groups were established to jointly develop new materials, such as an agreed standardized alphabet, text books, dictionaries, and visual materials."[830]

Scholars, specialists, and human rights activists have participated in the conference. Professor Noam Chomsky, the leading linguist and human rights activist, in his message to the conference emphasized the importance of language: "The loss of each language is a tragic event. A language is more than just a way of talking. It is a repository of cultural wealth: of tradition, history, lore, understanding, a source of communal bonds and relations to the past, a perspective on the world and on human life."[831]

The Circassian Alphabet

The exploration on the Circassian alphabet surfaces from time to time. Paul Goble has published an article that elaborated on the issue. The "Window" revealed important information and started by commenting on the arrogant policies executed against the Circassians: "The Soviet regime's divide and rule approach to the Circassian nation not only left them divided among four subjects of the Russian Federation but also gave them different alphabets, an effort to keep the 500,000 Circassians of the North Caucasus from coming together and joining hands with the more than five million co-ethnics in the Middle East."[832]

Unfortunately, the Russians didn't only divide and rip the geographical cohesion between the Circassians, but also intensified all that by shredding the Circassians demographically, socially, culturally and linguistically, administratively, and politically.

The author stated the imposed hostile policies: "The post-Soviet Russian government has made it clear that it will block any effort to unite the Circassian territories into a common homeland, but now Circassians from these four regions and abroad are challenging Russian ethnic management in another way and demanding a common alphabet for the dialects that Moscow has promoted as separate language."[833]

The "Window" mentioned concerns fueled by the usual Russian policies: "Coming up with a common alphabet is no easy task, and there is certain to be opposition both from Moscow, fearful that even this step could empower the Circassians and trigger further instability in the North Caucasus, and from among the Circassians who are far from united on which alphabet should be chosen and whether this is an appropriate next step for the movement."[834]

Developments in the former Soviet Union showed "the need for a common alphabet to help overcome dialect differences, to promote a common Circassian literary language, and on the basis of that alphabet and language to promote a unified Circassian nation that would be in a better position to advance its political goals."[835]

Heavy legacy inherited by years of absence from reality and historical belonging of the nation "have fallen victim not only to internal disagreements over which of several alphabets, Cyrillic, Latin, or traditional Circassian, should be used, whether the dialects are that close, and whether changing alphabets would in fact undermine unity by cutting off Circassian young people from the culture produced in the existing scripts but also by Moscow and by some republic leaders who are concerned about their positions."[836]

The "Window" concluded that "on May 19, the International Circassian Association formed a commission which is supposed to come up with a program for a unified Circassian alphabet based on Cyrillic as well as for a common literary language to be presented in September at the organization's tenths congress (kavkaz-uzel.ru/articles/264019)."[837]

The effects of the current situation enabled "supporters of this idea are enthusiastic and see no insurmountable problems: Petr Ivanov, director of the Kabardino-Balkaria Scientific Center of the Russian Academy of Sciences, says that such a move is 'the normal reaction of a small people seeking to preserve itself' from assimilation (kavkaz-uzel.ru/articles/264071/)." Thus, "'we are a single people, we have a common psychology and a common artistic worldview', Ivanov says, and consequently, it is time to have a common alphabet."[838]

Also, concerned Circassians expressed their opinion of the alphabet unification: "Circassian experts including Khaisha Timizhev of the KBR State University and Kabardin Congress president Aslan Beshto argue that there are no insurmountable obstacles to having a common alphabet and that such a move will not lead to any 'levelling' of the varieties of experience among the various Circassian groups."[839]

The reality that is lived and realized shows an eagerness to describe the bitter truth. The "Window" added, "Commentator Anzor Daur is skeptical, arguing that Moscow will block the move lest alphabet unity lead to political unity in the North Caucasus and expanded ties with Circassians abroad. And he suggests Moscow will play up differences among Circassians about what alphabet they should adopt (onkavkaz.com/news/63-cherkesam-ne-dadut-sozdat-edinyi-alfavit.html)."[840]

Eventually, the alternative to the Cyrillic alphabet is one of the available choices.

> Those most influenced from abroad will likely seek a Latin script, but that is a red flag for Moscow which has refused to allow the Tatars and Bashkirs to shift to the Latin script lest it expand their identification with Turkey. Those more philologically inclined may want to go back to the ancient Circassian alphabet but restoring it would be very difficult. Consequently, Daur says, if any change is going to happen, it almost certainly will have to follow the leader of the International Circassian Association which has made it clear that it seeks a Cyrillic-based script for Circassians in the North Caucasus. It would be truly ironic if the use of this Russian script would promote the national aspirations of the Circassians.[841]

Handling the Language

The situation and circumstances of most Circassians that had to leave and to live in diaspora did not have much better chances of subsistence when compared with their compatriots living in the North Caucasus, and their conditions were not much better in regards to the elements of national survival of the Circassian nation as an entity of their own. For this particular case, Circassians must show greater interest and attention by contacting international and regional bodies specialized in the fields of culture and language in particular.

The Adyga language is the language of all Circassians. The presence of several dialects among the Circassians was exploited as a means of dividing the Adygha language during the Soviet era, where different names, descriptions, and titles were given to them. A Kabardian language[842] for the Kabarday Circassians! The other invented version was kept under the name Adygha language.[843] Also, the Slavic Cyrillic letters were used to write both of them, which turned out to be impractical for Circassians who don't speak Russian to learn their mother tongue, and used fifty-six Slavic letters, which were extracted from the same origin of the Russian language!

This has made it very difficult, and even impossible, for Circassians in diaspora to be able to maintain their mother tongue and to find an easy and logical way for teaching the language to all Circassians who are interested in learning their own language. Similarly, an awkward situation is created among the Circassians living both in their homeland and diaspora, which produced obstacles to preserve and maintain their culture, identity, and language.

According to the current situation, both the federal and regional authorities in the North Caucasus do not use the Adygha language in all phases of education, so they made it an optional language that is taught only to some interested students for a limited time only while all subjects are taught in Russian. This irresponsible practice would lead to circumstances for the language to be on its way to extinction. Circassian linguistics and sociolinguist experts and anthropologists should seek to protect the language in a more serious manner.

The Adyga language is on its way to extinction and may

> be endangered because it is being used for fewer and fewer daily activities and so loses the characteristically close association of the language with particular social or communicative functions. Form follows function and languages which are being used for fewer and fewer domains of life also tend to lose structural complexity, which in turn may affect the perceptions of users regarding the suitability of the language for use in a broader set of functions. This

can lead to a downward spiral which eventually results in the complete loss of the language.[844]

It is the duty of UNESCO, which should be contacted, in addition to the European and international organizations to form a dynamic platform for the linguistic and cultural issues for creating and mobilizing qualified teachers and specialists and to use a program to revive and teach the Adyga language.

An expanded international language conference should be arranged and held for all Circassian communities to save the Adyga language and should be specialized and authorized to discuss all the crucial aspects, such as preparing programs of teaching levels to the Circassian generations, the alphabet, and the feasibility of keeping or changing the present Cyrillic one.

Circassians tend to describe themselves as "Adyghas" in reference to their Adygha language due to their certainty that preserving the language would be the way of preserving their entity and identity as Circassians. The UNESCO Endangered Languages page answered the following question: "What can be done to save a language from disappearing?" UNESCO's answer doesn't apply to the Circassian nation's situation, which should be dealt with in an appropriate way, but the standard answer indicated the following:

> The most important thing that can be done to keep a language from disappearing is to create favourable conditions for its speakers to speak the language and teach it to their children. This often requires national policies that recognize and protect minority languages, education systems that promote mother-tongue instruction, and creative collaboration between community members and linguists to develop a writing system and introduce formal instruction in the language. Since the most crucial factor is the attitude of the speaker community toward its own language, it is essential to create a social and political environment that encourages multilingualism and respect for minority languages so that speaking such a language is an asset rather than a liability. Some languages now have so few speakers that they cannot be maintained, but linguists can, if the community so wishes, record as much of the language as possible so that it does not disappear without a trace.[845]

The UNESCO Endangered Languages page also answered the following question: "What does UNESCO do to prevent the endangerment and disappearance of languages?" The answer stated,

UNESCO acts on many fronts to safeguard endangered languages and prevent their disappearance:

In education, UNESCO supports policies promoting multilingualism and especially mother tongue literacy; it supports the language component of indigenous education; and raises awareness of the importance of language preservation in education.

In culture, UNESCO collects data on endangered and indigenous languages, develops standardized tools and methodologies, and builds capacities of governments and civil society (academic institutions and speaker communities).

In communication and information, UNESCO supports the use of local languages in the media and promotes multilingualism in cyberspace.

In science, UNESCO assists programmes to strengthen the role of local languages in the transmission of local and indigenous knowledge.[846]

Valuable Historic Heritage

Old Circassian traditional house

Ancient Circassian monuments attest to the precious humanitarian heritage.

> Collective dolmen burial of this culture (Early Kuban Culture) appeared in the mountain regions of the North Western Caucasus at the beginning of the second millennium BC. They are found on both the northern and southern slopes of the Caucasus Mountains and along the Black Sea coast. In Laba and Belaya river basins, they are met in large groups, constituting huge tribal cemeteries.[847]

Locations of the sites are specified.

> Over 200 dolmens are located in the Deguakski glade, 300 in Khagiokh, 350 on the "Bolerski road" and so on. Some of the beads found here are supposed to have come here, to the Kuban, through Transcaucasia and by means of intertribal intercourse, from the distant countries of Asia Minor, Mesopotamia, Iran, and China.[848]

The extension of historical eras of stone and pottery industries that preceded the Age of Antiquity and the immersion of the discovery of metals have witnessed an evolution of a civilization: "Widespread use of copper began in Circassia at the end of the third millennium BC. Moreover, the Copper-Bronze Age flourished here during the second and the beginning of the first millennium BC, when the local technique of processing copper, then that of bronze, was mastered."[849]

The northwestern Caucasus region had witnessed the discovery and use of metal tools: "Copper-Bronze Age treasures of the Kuban, and adjacent North Caucasus regions, were divided, in 1929, into chronological: Early Kuban, Mid Kuban and Late-Kuban Cultures." [850]

Specifics of behavior is considered to stay within an acceptable frame where individuals and groups have to follow on different occasions and to act in accordance with the limits and standards that are known to all. Maintaining mutual respect, within "the lofty codes of conducting high moral values of this epic became the norms for the upbringing of all the new Circassian generations through the subsequent centuries, prepared the soil for the breeding ground of the Promethean Spirit and, later on, formed the inviolable Adygha Khabza (Circassian traditions) itself."[851]

The "Nafna" association released its first issue of its publication, Napa newspaper, and the event was published and circulated, where NatPress published the editorial that was written by Nalby Kuiok.

The writer said,

> Khase active workers decided to fix a stone in honour of the defenders of the native land, in honour of tens and hundreds thousand Circassians (Adygs), fallen in the unprecedentedly severe massacre of the imperial army almost in three hundred thousand soldiers against the small people that had never had armies. The action with the stone threatened nobody; it did not call for any illegal actions, did not break up the constitutional bases of the state; it could not cause any nationalist or chauvinistic feelings at all. On the place it was pawned, the monument in memory about the fallen should be constructed. That is a custom all over the world—the dead are buried both in peace times and even on a battlefield.[852]

He continued and demanded to build a monument while remembering the Circassians who perished:

> We, Adygs, have tens and hundred thousand compatriots not buried, and that is immoral, immemorial, it is sinful both for the dead, and for the living. Fascist Germany lost during the last world war some millions soldiers' lives. Now relatives search for their remains in territory of the former USSR and the present Russia, search and find and give them their last honour. We do not search, because our ancestors' bones are in the whole territory of former Circassia. We simply wish to render them a minimum from due: on the native land, on a small part of that Circassia to bury them even symbolically—to fix for them a monument.[853]

Circassian Myths and Legends

Circassia, as part of the North Caucasus, is famous and known for its literature, which contains the myths and legends of the Narts. They are particularly important in understanding the shape of the basic mythology of the people while understanding the old civilization that originated from within the people of the area, which continued to elevate, but which a great part of it was eliminated and eradicated by the devastating war launched against the Circassian nation.

Despite the devastating war, genocide, occupation, looting, and destruction of national and personal holdings and culture, the Circassians have managed to preserve part of their mythology, epos, and myths. The valuable Circassian enlightenment can be indicated by "the Nart Epos"[854] where there is similarity between Circassian and old Greek literature, legends, and epics as well as the literary taste quality, which one of the authors describes as "the influence of Circassian mythology on the old Greek culture."

The Circassian author Shora Begmurzin Nogma collected valuable historical, legendary, innovative, and creative tales called Nart Sagas in the Russian language. He recorded them between 1835–1843, published after he passed away in the year 1861; it was translated into the German language in the year 1866.[855]

In that regard, John Colarusso (a professor at McMaster University in Canada) published a book titled Nart Sagas from the Caucasus [Introduction] that included Circassian myths and legends. Also, he wrote an article on similar subjects in the title of "Myths from the Forest of Circassia, The World & I", dated "December, 1989," which included "two myths from the Circassians of the Caucasus Mountains offer detailed insights into the ancient veneration of trees and sacred groves."[856]

John Colarusso has also written and commented on the history of the Circassian homeland and mentioned the peoples, whom they dealt with at times:

> At a remote period (3000 BC) the Circassian homeland was the site of the Bronze Age Kurgan culture, now identified with the Proto-Indo-Europeans. It is possible that the ancestors of the Circassians may themselves have taken part in this Kurgan culture, for very remote linguistic links between the Proto-Indo-European and Northwest Caucasian languages can be posited. In any event, the Circassians have been in or near their homeland for millennia and have had contacts with the myriad peoples who have passed across the steppes to their north: the Proto-Indo-Europeans; the Kimmerians (from whom the Circassian tribe of the Chemgwi, earlier Kemirgoy,) are descended; the Scythians, Sarmatians, and Alans; the Goths; the Huns; the Khazars; the Turkic peoples; the Mongols; and lastly the Cossacks, Ukrainians, and Russians. During these millennia the Circassians knew

almost constant warfare with these steppe neighbors. More peaceful contacts prevailed between the Circassians and the ancient Greeks in the trading cities along the Black Sea coast, later between them and the Genoese, and then with Venetian traders.[857]

Understanding the history, culture, and language aside from other elements of the nation's heritage would enhance the knowledge and experience of those who are concerned when dealing with such issues, in order to be distributed to scholars, researchers, and others.

The ancient traditional history of the Circassians, like that of any other nation, is recorded and preserved in its folklore and mythology, especially in their Nart Epics. Consisting of twenty-six cycles and seven hundred texts, this epic shows the older members of its pantheon (Narts Nesren, Tlepsh, etc.) entering the historical arena of man larger than life prior to the Copper-Bronze Age. This great epic, perhaps the oldest of its kind in the world, is satiated with symbolism and historical information about the ancestors of Circassians. This epic grew with the nation over absorbing and incorporating new events.[858]

In the process it collected and preserved a rich storehouse of valuable information about the ancestors of the Circassians from the Mesolithic times to the Middle Ages and became the repository of their social laws and moral values. Moreover, these ideal laws of conduct, dignity, and pride of the ancient Adyghas were embodied the Nart heroes of this epic.[859]

The Circassians who participate in the same origin have used a language of understanding among themselves, where it gathered together the different Circassian tribes and communities.

Moreover, in keeping with Johnson's "language is the pedigree of nations," the Adyghabza (Circassian language), in which this epic was composed, was constantly the unifying element for all the Circassian-speaking tribes that have appeared in the historical arena at different times under different tribal names. According to sources, some of the names were the Meots, Sinds, Tauri, Kerkets, Zicks, Geniokhs,

Dandars, Toreats, Agres, Areches, Topets, Obidiakens, Doskhis, and Cholchis.[860]

Contacts between civilizations often were characterized with a documentation feature.

> Ancient Greeks mentioned the Maeotians in the sixth century BC. "The name 'Meote' is a collective term which included in a number of small tribes," wrote N. V. Anfimov. "However, there is archeological proof that their culture took shape much earlier, between the eighth and first half of the seventh centuries BC with roots going back to the Bronze Age." According to A. Sheen, "Hypothesis exists that (pre-Maeotian) Adyghas knew well some distant countries, to which they undertook campaigns." Adygha songs and legends of the epic Narts mention frequently Indyl (Volga) River, Bukhara, and others.[861]

The connection between the Circassians and the Greeks has led to a cultural interaction, which came to fruition in different fields.

> Looking for the details and reasoning would lead to the truth. "The Circassian mythology, like the rich Circassian folklore, reflects much of the history, moral, spiritual, and psychological makeup of the distant ancestors the Adyghas. It has a pantheon of both male and female cosmogonic and chthonic divinities, the former of which are considered to be more archaic and rather formless spirits, whereas the latter are seen allotted with real features. To mention just a few, the cosmogonic gods T'ha (T'hashkho), Psat'ha, Washkho, and Shiba stand nearer to 'natural' religion, while chthonic divinities, Tlepsh, Mezit'ha, and T'hagalege are nearer to his practical activities."[862]

The similarity between the Circassian characters of literature, epics, and mythology, which perform similar roles in different cultures but with different names, has led to the search of the time they emerged. This gives a clear idea of their link with their past.

> Speaking of this epic, many narratologists have expressed their strong conviction that Naty Nesren is the prototype of

Prometheus of the Greek mythology, and that Nart Sausiriko is the prototype of Homer's Achilles, and that the Greeks had borrowed these stories from Caucasus during their early colonization period of the Circassian coast, had polished and written them down as their own, while their true origin remained unknown to the world.[863]

Facts reveal that the tenacity of a nation, its intellectual and heritage liberality and genuineness, have contributed to the facilitation of facts about the Circassians and their association with the seeds of human civilization.

The fact that the ancestors of the Adyghas had created the main embryo of the epic Narts prior to the Copper-Bronze Age in their language Adyghabza in a highly poetical and epic form, with accompanying individual melodies for each. The question is, for how long a time did they exist as an ethnic group before they reached such a highly developed intellectual stage and mastery of language?[864]

This is proof of the link between the output of the Circassians in thought, literature, and epics, and their historic origin: "The existing yardstick for measuring the age of these distant ancestors of Circassians is the information we have about the evolution of man the generally accepted axiom that languages give birth to nations."[865]

The Circassians and IT

Many websites were established since the first Russian-Chechen war in the 1990s, right after the dismantling of the Soviet Union in 1991. At the time, Circassians reviewed their national status, where more of their people around the world participated through the internet to know what was going on. Besides Chechnya, people could follow conflicts in Abkhazia and other parts of the Caucasus.

Circassian identity was a catalyst for the return of national reconciliation, harmony, and communications. New prospects were established between communities, institutions, and individuals across the Circassian world around the globe. World radio, TV, and direct communications prevailed in the most part of the twentieth century, which were controlled and owned by governmental establishments.

From the spread and development of the internet, mainly at the beginning of the twenty-first century, attempts and efforts have brought, enhanced, and consolidated technological information. Typical media outlets were not available for all the public audiences at the international level. Satellite TV channels developed international media, together with radio, local television, and telecommunications.

Internet websites, digital media outlets, and social media have become easily within the reach of more people who could afford and obtain an internet connection for establishing, publishing, and posting programs. Transmitting and receiving data by different means has become available and permissible with red tape procedures, which has led to provide information to all people alike and which has become more affordable.

Progress and development in the communications and internet fields have positively enhanced and impacted Circassian cross talk. The objective is to restore and reestablish coordination between Circassian individuals and communities. Circassian activists in the North Caucasus and the wider Circassian diaspora around the world have utilized technology wisely. They have reinstated contact among one another.

> A new generation aged between 18 and 28 communicates via the internet and is networked with Circassian communities across the world. They provide an example of the phenomenon for which the American political scientist Benedict Anderson coined the term "long-distance nationalism", which has already been identified in the Armenian and other diaspora communities. Although the Circassian case has not produced a coherent, militant or overtly returnee driven national movement liable to burden the problem laden North Caucasus with yet more potentially violent conflict, the revival of interest in their ethnic roots among young people of Circassian origin does represent a challenge for Russia. Moscow finds itself confronted with an unresolved chapter of its colonial history during a phase where President Putin is cultivating a patriotism that leaves little space for self-critical historical reflection.[866]

Circassians could unite over the internet. Use of media, especially its knowledge and means, including modern and advanced communications, the internet, and social media have assisted in paving the way in establishing foundations for addressing the following: teaching the Adigha language, preserving culture, getting eBooks, addressing children concerns, establishing communications, connecting activists, disseminating information on the Circassian Question, sharing petitions, finding research centers, reaching libraries, archives, and bookstores, the merits of knowing the documented Circassian history, and other important matters.

The Journal of Caucasian Studies has published a study titled "iCircassia: Digital Capitalism and New Transnational Identities" by Lars Funch Hansen. Accordingly, the published study touched on the opportunity that opened to Circassians through the use of the internet. In the introduction, the author mentioned the fact of the presence of the "Circassian world" scattered between the Circassian homeland located in the North Caucasus and alienation. It would be appropriate if the peoples of the world would realize the way utilized by Circassians to communicate on the international level in various areas of national interests. Eventually, that would lead to achieve unifying efforts to carry out a comprehensive national renaissance, where efforts will be mobilized to reinstate the rights in accordance with international laws and norms.

> The (almost) wholesale exile of the Circassians from their homeland in 1864 after the final victory of the Russian army resulted in Circassia literally being taken off the map. Nonetheless, countless cartographic representations of Circassia from the preceding centuries exist and have today been digitalised, presented and circulated on the Internet. Circassia has, in this way, little by little begun to come back "on the map"—at least virtually. And to be "on the map" is a strong metaphor, which indicates the importance of recognition in the ongoing Circassian revival.[867]

In October 2014, Lars Funch Hansen defended his PhD thesis titled, The Circassian Revival: A Quest for Recognition.

> Lars Funch Hansen sets out to explore the conditions of this revival and the ways in which Circassians both in the North Caucasus and in the diaspora are being mobilized to participate in it. In the author's own words, the main aim of the thesis is "to unveil, present and discuss the rising transnational revival of the Circassians" (p.9) which emerged in the mid-1990s and continues today.[868]

The Circassian Question is highlighted on multiple issues that if gathered will illustrate the image of the real tragedy that took place, as well as the

Circassians' desire to look forward to acting as a nation where its legal and national rights are violated.

> The thesis focuses on the Circassians, a North Caucasian people that fiercely resisted the conquering of their lands by the Russian Empire in the 19th century. Following their final defeat in 1864, most Circassians were forced into exile and today their descendants live in large diaspora groups in Turkey and neighbouring countries in the Middle East.[869]

In the context of the thread, it is mentioned that switching to digital concepts is practical and does not need to create complications. However, the older technology needed different procedures, equipment, materials and great efforts that require many people to follow a sequence of process. This is performed by coordinated professions of different sides operating for production, printing, and other specialties, not to mention the time and effort it takes to do all that.

> One of the questions, raised by the emergence of "InternetCircassia" and the Circassian digital diaspora, is whether this phenomenon will reduce the desire to repatriate among the diaspora. Repatriation is one of the most difficult issues facing the Circassian diaspora organizations, many of which have formally prioritized repatriation since the 1990s.[870]

An electronic world contributed in bringing a forgotten nation, at least, emotionally closer together. The positive effect of the internet, being a modern technology, has emerged as a positive development of digital potentials. It became a prominent element of a nation that was virtually in a deep sleep after the shock of 1864 and its negative consequences. Accordingly, the thesis has elaborated on features that attributed to web contact in order to achieve national objectives put forward to be accomplished by the Circassians.

> Two main characteristics of the Internet can primarily be emphasized: firstly, the element of convergence of media forms and technologies that is illustrated by, for instance, the integrated use of "older" media forms such as photos and films on social media sites and other parts of the Internet. This is sometimes referred to as "new media" (Manovich 2001). Secondly, the Internet functions as an enormous

digital storehouse, as a media form that is technologically based upon a database model (Manovich 2001, 55). These two twin characteristics of the contemporary Internet—or digital capitalism—to a large extent encapsulate the digital aspects of the ongoing Circassian revival. [871]

---

[777] http://inrussia.com/understanding-circassian-folklore
[778] http://windowoneurasia2.blogspot.com/2016/12/can-circassian-language-and-people-who.html
[779] http://minorityrights.org/wp-content/uploads/2014/11/mrg-protecting-rights-minorities-indigenous-peoples-russian-federation_English.pdf
[780] http://windowoneurasia2.blogspot.com/2016/12/can-circassian-language-and-people-who.html
[781] http://windowoneurasia2.blogspot.com/2016/12/can-circassian-language-and-people-who.html
[782] Adygean (Circassian) Culture (Nugzari Antelava)
[783] Adygean (Circassian) Culture (Nugzari Antelava)
[784] Adygean (Circassian) Culture (Nugzari Antelava)
[785] Adygean (Circassian) Culture (Nugzari Antelava)
[786] http://www.tamu.edu/faculty/choudhury/culture.html
[787] http://africa.peacelink.org/wajibu/articles/art_4485.html
[788] http://edition.tefl.net/articles/teacher-technique/language-culture/
[789] http://edition.tefl.net/articles/teacher-technique/language-culture/
[790] Language and Culture (Claire Kramsch)
[791] http://www.answers.com/Q/What_is_the_relationship_between_language_and_culture
[792] http://languageandculture.com/cultures-languages
[793] http://www.answers.com/Q/What_is_the_relationship_between_language_and_culture
[794] Language and Culture (Claire Kramsch)
[795] Language and Culture (Claire Kramsch)
[796] Language and Culture (Claire Kramsch)
[797] Language and Culture (Claire Kramsch)
[798] Language and Culture (Claire Kramsch)
[799] Language and Culture (Claire Kramsch)
[800] http://www.lexiophiles.com/uncategorized/the-relationship-between-language-and-culture
[801] Circassian History (Kadir Natho)

802 http://justicefornorthcaucasus.info/?p=1161414060 and http://www.natpressru.info/index.php?newsid=2072
803 http://justicefornorthcaucasus.info/?p=1161414060 and http://www.natpressru.info/index.php?newsid=2072
804 http://justicefornorthcaucasus.info/?p=1161414060 and http://www.natpressru.info/index.php?newsid=2072
805 http://justicefornorthcaucasus.info/?p=1251669777
806 http://justicefornorthcaucasus.info/?p=1251669777
807 http://www.kavkaz-uzel.ru/articles/279366/
808 http://www.un-documents.net/a47r135.htm
809 http://www.europarl.europa.eu/charter/pdf/text_en.pdf
810 http://www.coe.int/en/web/conventions/full-list/-/conventions/treaty/148
811 http://conventions.coe.int/Treaty/en/Treaties/Html/148.htm
812 http://www.npld.eu/about-us/
813 http://www.npld.eu/about-us/
814 http://www.npld.eu/about-us/
815 https://aheku.net/articles/english/ethnography/1119?pn=71
816 https://aheku.net/articles/english/ethnography/1119?pn=71
817 https://aheku.net/articles/english/ethnography/1119?pn=71
818 http://conventions.coe.int/Treaty/en/Treaties/Html/148.htm
819 http://www.encyclopedia.com/topic/Circassians.aspx
820 http://www.encyclopedia.com/topic/Circassians.aspx
821 http://www.encyclopedia.com/topic/Circassians.aspx
822 http://www.encyclopedia.com/topic/Circassians.aspx
823 https://www.researchgate.net/publication/233241208_Circassian_Israelis_Multilingualism_as_a_way_of_life
824 https://www.researchgate.net/publication/233241208_Circassian_Israelis_Multilingualism_as_a_way_of_life
825 https://www.researchgate.net/publication/233241208_Circassian_Israelis_Multilingualism_as_a_way_of_life
826 https://www.researchgate.net/publication/233241208_Circassian_Israelis_Multilingualism_as_a_way_of_life
827 https://www.researchgate.net/publication/233241208_Circassian_Israelis_Multilingualism_as_a_way_of_life
828 http://circassianworld.blogspot.com/2008/10/keeping-ancestors-tongue-alive.html
829 https://jansait.wordpress.com/2008/10/17/international-circassian-language-conference-amman/
830 http://www.npld.eu/news/latest-news/74/second-international-conference-on-the-adyghe-language-in-ankara/

831 http://www.npld.eu/news/latest-news/74/second-international-conference-on-the-adyghe-language-in-ankara/
832 http://windowoneurasia2.blogspot.fr/2015/06/challenging-moscow-circassians-seek-to.html
833 http://windowoneurasia2.blogspot.fr/2015/06/challenging-moscow-circassians-seek-to.html
834 http://windowoneurasia2.blogspot.fr/2015/06/challenging-moscow-circassians-seek-to.html
835 http://windowoneurasia2.blogspot.fr/2015/06/challenging-moscow-circassians-seek-to.html
836 http://windowoneurasia2.blogspot.fr/2015/06/challenging-moscow-circassians-seek-to.html
837 http://windowoneurasia2.blogspot.fr/2015/06/challenging-moscow-circassians-seek-to.html
838 http://windowoneurasia2.blogspot.fr/2015/06/challenging-moscow-circassians-seek-to.html
839 http://windowoneurasia2.blogspot.fr/2015/06/challenging-moscow-circassians-seek-to.html
840 http://windowoneurasia2.blogspot.fr/2015/06/challenging-moscow-circassians-seek-to.html
841 http://windowoneurasia2.blogspot.fr/2015/06/challenging-moscow-circassians-seek-to.html
842 http://www.ethnologue.com/language/kbd
843 http://www.ethnologue.com/language/ady
844 http://www.ethnologue.com/endangered-languages
845 http://www.unesco.org/new/en/culture/themes/endangered-languages/faq-on-endangered-languages/
846 http://www.unesco.org/new/en/culture/themes/endangered-languages/faq-on-endangered-languages/
847 Circassian History (Kadir Natho)
848 Circassian History (Kadir Natho)
849 Circassian History (Kadir Natho)
850 Circassian History (Kadir Natho)
851 Circassian History (Kadir Natho)
852 http://www.natpressru.info/index.php?newsid=2072 and http://justicefornorthcaucasus.info/?p=1161414060
853 http://www.natpressru.info/index.php?newsid=2072 and http://justicefornorthcaucasus.info/?p=1161414060
854 http://iccs.synthasite.com/nart-epos.php
855 http://www.liquisearch.com/nart_saga/study_and_significance
856 http://aheku.net/articles/english/epos_en/1165

857 http://www.everyculture.com/Russia-Eurasia-China/Circassians-History-and-Cultural-Relations.html
858 Circassian History (Kadir Natho)
859 Circassian History (Kadir Natho)
860 Circassian History (Kadir Natho)
861 Circassian History (Kadir Natho)
862 Circassian History (Kadir Natho)
863 Circassian History (Kadir Natho)
864 Circassian History (Kadir Natho)
865 Circassian History (Kadir Natho)
866 https://www.swp-berlin.org/fileadmin/contents/products/comments/2014C37_hlb.pdf
867 https://dspace.mah.se/bitstream/handle/2043/20181/icrassia.pdf;sequence=2
868 http://blogg.mah.se/caucasusstudies/2014/10/24/lars-funch-hansen-defended-his-phd-thesis-on-the-circassians/
869 https://blogg.mah.se/caucasusstudies/2014/10/24/lars-funch-hansen-defended-his-phd-thesis-on-the-circassians/
870 https://dspace.mah.se/bitstream/handle/2043/20181/icrassia.pdf;sequence=2
871 https://dspace.mah.se/bitstream/handle/2043/20181/icrassia.pdf;sequence=2

8

Commemoration of the Twenty-First of May

Photo By: Imad Shabsough
"Circassia forever in our Hearts", May 21 Demonstration in
front of the Russian Embassy in Amman, Jordan

History is a register of series of past events that pertain to individuals and nations. Historical facts and proceedings are studied, evaluated, and processed for planning and piloting with respect to selecting the necessary steps to be taken by those who take human responsibility and perseverance for the continuity of positive change in society in the present and future, depending on consequences of dangers that affected life, progress, and advancement of the society and nation.

Commemoration of the twenty-first of May, or other important events, is always attributed to the memory of the victims of Circassia and the Caucasus and supplicate for the sacred souls to rest eternally in peace, all those souls who fought the fight in defending their homeland with personal weapons against a well-equipped military consisting of criminals and mercenaries. The civilians had no means of self-defense, but had to face their inevitable fate of hunger, exposure to harsh weather conditions, having infectious diseases, getting killed, or pushed for displacement and deportation.

A yearly commemoration to remember the genocide is performed by Circassians: "Each year on the 21st May, thousands of people gather in front of the Russian consulate to protest, with this year's organization already under way to object to the genocide reference."[872]

Many positive and negative developments have occurred during the previous years, as the yearly commemoration of the twenty-first of May of every year keeps reminding of the great Circassian catastrophe that befell the Circassian nation, that recalls the pain and disaster endured by the Circassian people who defended their homeland, identity, and its very survival when it had to fight a defensive fierce war against the imperial Russian invaders for 101 years. It included total occupation while Russian forces committed genocide, ethnic cleansing, and destruction followed by the deportation of 90 percent of the people, which can be described as a great forced exodus toward exile in the Ottoman Empire then the dispersion in more than thirty countries around the world today.

The Circassians have considered a day of memory.

> The NW Caucasians have assigned 21 May as the National Day of Mourning, commemorating the tragedy of the nation. Ceremonies are held by all communities in the Caucasus and the diaspora. In addition, a cenotaph to the martyrs and those expelled was erected in the Freedom Park in Nalchik near the statue of the Circassian sage Zhebaghi Qezenoqwe. On this date in 1914, tsarist Russia celebrated the fiftieth anniversary of the formal conclusion of the War, considering it as one of her greatest national victories. In stark contrast, the luckless Circassians had to wait 70 more years to observe the bleak day.[873]

No event can be compared with its predecessor. The differences between the consecutive Circassian Memorial Day commemoration have shown an improvement in the number of participating people and the activities practiced compared to the previous years. Positive differences and developments have been noticed by all observers while more awareness and concern are prevailing and more people are becoming increasingly aware of the Circassian plight due to the available information published in books and other means, especially social media.

The gathering that takes place on the twenty-first of May in a meaningful memorial is to pay admiration and respect to all of those who perished as victims of a predetermined aggression that had colonial and imperial intentions and deeds by performing their directives, which led to creating disastrous impacts on Circassia as a prominent North Caucasus nation, with all what the expression would mean and indicate.

This painful occasion in the history of the Circassians, the peoples of the North Caucasians, and mankind alike unfortunately have different types of commemoration by individuals, citizens, and human rights activists, in addition to officials, agents, and puppets that have different directions, ambitions, desires, and agendas to observe this day of remembering humans who were subjected genocide, forced deportation, ethnic cleansing, apartheid, extrajudicial measures, torture, rape, and kidnapping; beside destroying all constituents, elements, and ingredients of the homeland.

> Since 2005, a renewed Circassian memorialization process has become a key element of Circassian civil society mobilization and has increasingly taken the form of counter-memorialization targeting official Russia historiography, which today prescribes an understanding of Circassian inclusion into imperial Russia as voluntary. This is not only opposed by most Circassians but is also generally rejected by most international research—including a number of Russian scholars—on the issue.[874]

The unilateral style of functioning has shown Russian operating agenda trying to ignore the facts and figures as much as possible: "Operating on the principle that if 'there is no publication, there is no problem,' the FSB has sought to reduce to a minimum coverage of the Circassian issue both in Russia and abroad, efforts that reflect Moscow's concerns about it and unfortunately point to more trouble ahead in the North Caucasus."[875]

Paul Goble's article titled "FSB Seeks to Suppress Coverage of Circassian Issue" mentioned the following:

> Abroad, he points out, the FSB "is working among the Circassian diaspora", urging its leaders not to raise the issue

lest the situation for their co-ethnics inside the Russian Federation deteriorate, a classical Soviet-era strategy that traces its roots back to the "Trust" Feliks Dzerzhinsky set up under Lenin to work against the first Russian emigration. While the FSB has had some success among the older generation, its efforts have proved to be "a Pyrrhic victory" at most, because others in the diaspora and especially its younger members recognize that the Russian security services would not be making these efforts if they were not afraid.[876]

This remembrance links Circassians, whether in the North Caucasus or in diaspora, to ascertain that they will never forget their homeland, as long as they have arteries that pulse and eyelids that blink. They also confirm that their native land is loved as much as they respect and admire their courageous forefathers who sacrificed dearly and preciously with blood, sweat, and tears. Dignity has led them not to give in easily, while they refused to surrender for dozens of years, but sadly resulted in an obnoxious Russian occupation.

The Circassian Genocide Memorial

Photo By: Imad Shabsough
A Commemoration of Circassian Memorial Day on 21 May 2012, in Anaklia, Georgia, on the Black Sea Coast

On the twenty-first of May 2012, exactly one year after Georgia had recognized the Circassian Genocide, ethnic cleansing, and deportation from their homeland, Georgia inaugurated a memorial in Anaklia on the Black Sea, in the memory of the Circassian victims perished during the implementation of a hyper brutal method in the nineteenth century, intended to sterilize the Circassian homeland from its own people by evacuating all those who stayed alive: "'Memorial for the Victims of the Circassian Genocide' was opened in Anaklia, close to the Abkhaz administrative border, in presence of Georgian minister in charge of diaspora issues Papuna Davitaia."[877]

The importance and significance of Anaklya lies in the fact that it was a sea port for the Georgian Principality of Mingrelia, which

> in 1723, the town was captured by the Ottoman Empire and converted into its maritime outpost and slave-trading locale. Western Georgian kingdom of Imereti regained control over Anaklia in 1770, seizing the opportunity of Ottoman Empire being at war with Russia (Russo-Turkish War (1768–1774)). Solomon I, the king of Imereti, was supposed to be supported in this endeavor by a small Russian contingent under General Totleben, but the Russian troops retreated before a clash against the Turks.[878]

The developments showed an eventual Russian control of the area.

> In 1802, Kelesh-Bey Sharvashidze, the pro-Turkish ruler of the neighboring Principality of Abkhazia, capitalized on the internecine feuds in Mingrelia, and forced Prince Grigol Dadiani of Mingrelia into surrendering Anaklia, taking Grigol's son and heir, Levan, as a hostage. When Mingrelia accepted the Russian protectorate in 1803, the Russian commander in Georgia, Prince Tsitsianov, demanded that Kelesh-Bey release Levan. On his refusal, Tsitsianov sent Major General Ion Rykgof into Abkhazia. In March 1805, the Russians took hold of Anaklia and threatened to march against Sukhum-Kaleh, forcing the Abkhazian prince to release Dadiani.[879]

"Civil Georgia" reported on that date: "May 21, the day when in 1864 the Russian Empire declared victory in the Caucasus war, is marked to commemorate victims of deportation of Circassians and other North Caucasus peoples. On May 21–22 number of events is planned in Anaklia to mark that day, including a conference to discuss results of recognition of the Circassians genocide by Georgia," and reported that Papuna Davitaia, the Georgian Minister in Charge of Diaspora Issues has said, "This [monument] is an important step towards the Caucasian solidarity," adding that the Georgian state was now capable to carry out its Caucasian policy and engage with the peoples of the North Caucasus.[880]

It is of no coincidence that thousands of Circassians gather every year in Nalchik, KBR, like other places in the Circassian homeland and in diaspora to perpetuate the memory of the victims who perished in the massacres of the nineteenth century.[881]

In a move aimed to minimize the impact of demonstrations and sit-ins, usually in front of Russian embassies and consulates organized by the Circassians on this day of grief, the Russian authorities (to follow different tactics to stop these activities or at least to reduce the number of participants), invited some activists to be in the Caucasus on the twenty-first of May 2015.

The Russian government's response to Circassian activism has been quite nuanced. Moscow appears to have chosen a low-key containment strategy. The authorities are afraid to crack down on Circassian activists with full force, fearing a backlash from Circassians in the North Caucasus and abroad. Instead, small obstacles are put in the way of the activists to halt their activities and prevent them from operating effectively. At the same time, Moscow has successfully tried to engage the Circassian diaspora abroad in an attempt to show that the Circassians in the North Caucasus are well treated.

On May 20, a large international delegation of Circassians arrived in the North Caucasus. Most of the members of the delegation came from Turkey, but some came from Germany. The delegation toured the three North Caucasian republics with large Circassian populations—Adygea, Kabardino-Balkaria and Karachaevo-Cherkessia. Even though the participants attended mourning ceremonies in these three republics, for some reason they did not visit the Sochi area, or the Krasnodar region in general, from which the Circassians were completely and forcibly removed by the Russians 150 years ago (Natpressru.info, May 24).[882]

The articled added, "It is unclear who sponsored the visit of the Circassian delegation to the North Caucasus, but it was certainly financially supported in one way or another by the Russian government."[883]

Developments Imposed Themselves on the International Scene

Seemingly, Russian imperialism couldn't hide its real characteristics and show the continuation of their past imperial practices to show its true face in the twenty-first century, through the occupation and annexation of Crimea, and parts of Eastern Ukraine; resuming motion to destabilize and interfere with other former Soviet republics. What is happening so far in Southeastern Ukraine now, indicates irresponsibility in addition to lack of interest and indifference in respecting international law and the right of all nations to maintain their freedom and independence. All these actions remind of the Circassian nation that wished to live freely with no foreign intervention or colonial tutelage; but faced with devastating war that destroyed everything and impacted everyone in one way or other.

The Armenian issue seemed urgent on its hundredth anniversary of the tragedies that occurred in the year 1915, during the Ottoman era, where the European Parliament "Urged Turkey to Recognize Armenian Genocide,"[884] as many countries are moving toward recognizing the reality of the Armenian Genocide.

Regarding this, I coauthored an article titled "Sochi and Yerevan Analysis," with my friend Garegin Nalbandian, member of the Geopolitical Club in Los Angeles, which was translated to Arabic and Turkish. It was mentioned that May 21 for Circassians is like April 24 for Armenians. The following was mentioned in the article:

Putin's visit to Ankara in 2014, and his visit to Ataturk's tomb during his visit, was a preparation and cover-up for his visit to Armenia, instead of Turkey on April 24, 2015, but of course, that was probably the start of Erdogan's politics with Putin and Turkey's cautious relations with Russia.

Putin wanted to rant-show Armenians his support and protection, in order to keep that country hostage to his regional plans and deals, in order to keep Armenia under Russia's control and Armenians assimilated, as per his preferences, and at the same time, prevent any Circassian-Armenian direct contacts, the same way it happened between the Circassians and Georgians.

Last April, when the world was commemorating the 100 years of the Armenian Genocide, many Circassians have felt with the Armenians, and many Circassians expressed their positive feelings about that; however, Vladimir Putin poisoned the atmosphere when he travelled to Yerevan and played a cunning role. So many Circassians were annoyed to see Putin push his agenda using the Armenian Genocide.

Putin went to Armenia in April 2015; however, his visit was to meet with the presidents and the elites of other countries who also went to Armenia. It was a political networking event for him. In his speech, Putin mentioned the word genocide, not as Armenian Genocide, but as Russia's involvement to "prevent genocides".

There was and there is genocide everywhere Russia was involved in. Russians passed through here, where there used to be a village, is a common phrase in the Caucasus. Armenians have the same saying about the Turks.

Russia announced celebrating the Den' Krasnoi Polyany (Red Prairie Day) on May 21 this year. For those who know nothing about May 21, it is an important day for the Circassian people. May 21 is the day all Circassians mourn the deaths of the Circassian Genocide victims. The terms Krasnaya Polyana, Krasnodar, and anything that is associated with the color red is associated with blood—in this case, Circassian blood.

In conclusion, the recent "rivalry" between Russia and Turkey demonstrates a theatrical written by the same "screenwriter" to cover up the main agenda, which is the transfer of power and control from Russia (the Muscovite Golden Horde) to Turkey (Byzantium). Let's not give in to emotions, and let's analyze the facts. If we allow evil to win, the entire Caucasus, the Middle East, and possibly the entire world, will be in war, World War III, which may have already started, does not have to spread. Together we can put out the fire. It's not about religion. It's about good and evil. Please side with good by preventing wars and by promoting peace. Stop future genocides because it's the right thing to do.[885]

An article titled "One Year Less of 'Russian Colonialism' Countdown" stated,

> Many episodes and proceedings had passed by, while the large audience and spectators had watched and witnessed conflicts, crisis, wars, and events that some of them had turned out tragically and/or dreadfully.
>
> One of those important occurrences was the devastated war that had erupted last August in the Caucasus Region, and was mainly a struggle for imperial and colonial gains which showed the violent competition for controlling the land of others under different ways and means of description and deception.[886]

The article gave an idea of the situation, not only about Circassia, but about the North Caucasus in general.

> This yearly "turn of time-disk" occasion had passed before, for more than 140 times, while many nations in the North Caucasus had suffered of brutal foreign occupation that had lasted all that time-counts, while the occupants had enjoyed being sadists that had occupied the land.
>
> And grabbed the opportunity to control the destiny and fate of millions of dominated, subjugated, and exiled Human Beings, that their guilt remained being members of tiny nations, but the gluttony of the greedy ambitious and blood-thirsty neighbors that had the guts to make them the victims that had to bear the misery under the conditions of loss of hope and civil liberties that yet to be justified and their rights to be recaptured and recovered.[887]

The article concluded, "The dream of yesterday is the hope of today and the reality of tomorrow. The following were said about impossibility: Nothing is impossible; there are ways that lead to everything, and if we had sufficient will we should always have sufficient means. It is often merely for an excuse that we say things are impossible."[888]

The Circassian Genocide Is Linked with the "May 21" Key Issue

Photo By: Imad Shabsough
The Inauguration of The Circassian Genocide Memorial
on 21 May 2012, in Anaklia, Goergia

The Circassian Genocide is the matter of focus that needs to be resolved, and accordingly the Russian state must be held accountable for all consequences, where the crime of genocide against Circassians has met "the two elements: intent and action" where the definition says, "It is a crime to plan or incite genocide, even before killing starts, and to aid or abet genocide"[889] and others should recognize the Circassian rights[890] of obtaining proper reparations.

The commemoration, since the twentieth of May 2011, reminds of the Georgian Parliament's recognition of the Circassian Genocide,[891] which indicates the first country member of the United Nations to carry out an academic study of regional and Circassian history. It was performed by scholars and specialists upon the request of related specialized committees of the Parliament of Georgia that reached the bitter and ugly truth of the occurrence of the genocide, ethnic cleansing, and forced deportation. The entire Circassian nation was targeted. In a related matter, it is of duty and decency to thank the Georgians who inaugurated and erected a monument in Anaklia on the Black Sea[892] on the twenty-first of May 2012, in the memory of the Circassian victims.

Referring to the commemoration on the twenty-first of May, Joshua Keating wrote,

> Today there are about 3 million to 5 million Circassians living abroad and about 700,000 in the Caucasus. The post-Soviet Russian government has been slow to recognize the extent of what happened to the group and has strongly resisted attempts to label it as genocide—the anti-Russian government of nearby Georgia did so in 2011 portraying Circassian nationalism as merely an outgrowth of the region's Islamic radicalism. The global community commemorates Circassian Genocide Memorial Day every May 21.[893]
>
> On this day, May 21, 1864, Russia declares an end to the Russo-Circassian War after the scorched earth campaign initiated in 1862 under General Yevdokimov. When the Circassian people refused to convert to Christianity from Islam, almost the entire population was forced into exile from their North Caucasus homeland. More than 1.5 million Circassians were expelled—90% of the total population at the time. Most of them perished en route, victims of disease, hunger, and exhaustion. The day is designated the Circassian Day of Mourning and the event is known as The Circassian Genocide. The Sochi Olympics were held on former Circassian land.[894]

Activities and Positive Efforts

Circassian activists try their best to manage collective coordination of Circassian communities in all their whereabouts. They established working and coordinating with each other to fulfill the spirit of sharing in all the places of the Circassian diaspora. This issue is deemed of great importance in the Circassians' aspirations and endeavors. Commemoration of the Circassian tragedy on the twenty-first of May every year is one of those matters that almost everyone agrees upon.

Knowing that some parties and individuals deal with this topic as if it is a transient event that is not linked to the survival and extermination question of the Circassian nation.

> On May 21, 2011, Circassians protested at the Russian embassies and consulates in the United States, Turkey, Germany, Israel, and Jordan. Since then the Circassian anti-Sochi movement had gradually gained attention, including an article by Reuters in October 2011, and a mention in Time magazine. Using social media tools such as Facebook and Twitter, Circassians have also created a network of anti-Sochi activists numbering in the thousands who continue to hold and plan protests, meetings, and discussions on regular basis. Websites in English, Turkish, Arabic, Russian, German, and other languages publicize the Circassian campaign to stop, or at least discredit, the Sochi Games.[895]

Circassians showed and proved persistence in asserting their very survival and continuity in order to be an admired and dignified nation and in order to maintain their status as civilized and respected. The usurped and confiscated rights must be observed and restored according to the documented information, counting on connections and good relations with friendly peoples and nations to reclaim and restore their rights in accordance with the relevant international resolutions and regulations:

—The Universal Declaration of Human Rights Preamble says, "Whereas recognition of the inherent dignity and of the equal and inalienable rights of all members of the human family is the foundation of freedom, justice and peace in the world."[896]

Circassia 343

— The United Nations Rights of the indigenous peoples and Nations indicates, The {States "welcome[d] the adoption of the UN Declaration on the rights of indigenous peoples which has a positive impact on the protection of victims {urge[d] States to take all necessary measures to implement the rights of indigenous peoples in accordance with international human rights instruments without discrimination . . ."}.[897]

— Declaration on the Granting of Independence to Colonial Countries and Peoples states, "Conscious of the need for the creation of conditions of stability and well-being and peaceful and friendly relations based on respect for the principles of equal rights and self-determination of all peoples, and of universal respect for, and observance of, human rights and fundamental freedoms for all without distinction as to race, sex, language or religion."[898]

— International Law says, "International Law defines the legal responsibilities of States in their conduct with each other, and their treatment of individuals within State boundaries. Its domain encompasses a wide range of issues of international concern such as human rights, disarmament, international crime, refugees, migration, problems of nationality, the treatment of prisoners, the use of force, and the conduct of war, among others. It also regulates the global commons, such as the environment, sustainable development, international waters, outer space, global communications and world trade."[899]

Institutionalization of Ideological Invasion

Of the risks facing Circassians is hostile propaganda that remains in denial of the Circassians' sacred rights regarding their homeland by the use of different techniques and tools. The intent is reflected in their homeland and in Diaspora in accordance with an effective systematic method of diverting the Circassians' attention and concerns to insignificant matters; but continuity and persistence of the Circassian nation requires it to assert its survival by expressing crucial concerns in the present and future.

The Circassians should take this positively, by being firm in their demands and seeking recognition by maintaining self-confidence to claim their legitimate rights in accordance with legal and lawful means. This should be observed with maintaining gratitude to their ancestors, speaking up about the atrocities that faced their nation, and coordinating among Circassians of the world to cooperate between all sincere active associations and to focus on contributions for the needs of the people within a team-like structure in everything that contributes in consolidation of the necessary means to operate issues such as the media.

Circassians, to assert their existence, continuity and persistence, should oppose and reject the approach of the imposition of the occupation's dominance and the de facto concepts meant to contaminate the Circassians' efforts of maintaining their national identity in their whereabouts. They also should pay heed to what matters to them, and avoid distorting their image by depending on individuals or structures that behave in subservient manners, acting as "social climbers" by fawning opportunists or greedy individuals, and try to implicate the Circassians as weak, unwanted, and unenviable.

After all dreadful and disastrous outcomes that infected the Circassian scene, there is always hope as there is something worth struggling and aiming for. Circassia is the homeland of the Circassians, and no one can change that.

The Twenty-First of May, Circassian Memorial Day, and Loyalty to Circassia

May 21, 2012, marked a reminiscence of the yearly memory of the Circassian Genocide, ethnic cleansing, and forced deportation of 90 percent of those who remained alive. They were deserted to the wider world in over forty countries of the world today, after 101 years of devastating war waged against Circassia and its very survival as an entity of the Circassian nation in the midst of harsh circumstances and situations, associated with enormous risks.

This anniversary links with the ancestral homeland, which will never be forgotten as long as Circassians have a vein pulsing and an eyelid blinking. They love their homeland as much as they respect and admire their courageous forefathers who sacrificed dearly and preciously. They utilized what they had in their power to defend themselves, dignity, and homeland, while refusing surrender, humiliation, and ignominy under obnoxious Tsarist Russian obnoxious occupation.

Despite multiple appeals sent to Russian leadership and the Russian State Duma for the recognition of genocide against the Circassian nation as well as the responsibility for the forced deportation caused by war in the Caucasus, the Russian leaders have not responded, despite the historical evidence and hundreds of official documents obtained from official Russian archives as well as the Tbilisi archives, that had retained the official Russian military documents kept after the Russian occupation of Georgia, as Tbilisi, later became on a center for the southern military command of Russian forces that were operating in the Caucasus in general and in Circassia in particular.

We cannot, in this scope, but to recall the International Olympic Committee's decision to convene the 2014 Winter Olympic Games in the city of Sochi. It is the location that has a special place in human and Circassian memory alike, due to the particularity of the site being the last capital city of Circassia when the Russian Tsarist occupation had taken place. In the area are the scattered grave yards of those who perished while they were defending their homeland. Also, the significance of the event links what memorizes of the provocative military parade of the victorious forces at the end of the Russian-Circassian War.

The Russian military authorities in charge of the war against the Circassians have concluded the mission: "On May 21, 1864, Great Prince Michail—the commander in chief of the Kavkzski Army (Russian army in the Caucasus)—ascertained in the order of the day the final 'conquest of the Western Caucasus and the end of the Caucasian War.'"[900]

The important event at the end of the Russian-Circassian War is remembered in a form that shows what happened: "Sochi is considered by the Circassians as the last capital of independent Circassia. Its port was the place from which the Circassians were deported to the Ottoman Empire. Moreover, Krasnaya Polyana (Kbaada in Circassian), the area that will be the center of the 2014 Olympic Games, was the place where, on May 21, 1864, a parade of Russian troops celebrated the end of the war against the Circassians."[901]

Circassians recall their painful past with all its disasters and implications as lessons, where factors of evil, tyranny, and brutal war worked on the consecration of oppression. The main objective should be a bright, promising, and prosperous future with hope and optimism to attain friendship, fraternity, and peace among all nations of the world of the twenty-first century that hopefully, will prevail with stability, progress and mutual respect among peoples.

It would be highly appreciated if the appeal of the mind reaches the government of the Russian Federation to take a positive step towards solving the Circassian Question and its related problems, which have not yet been resolved. Results will be better off by establishing reconciliation with the Circassians; that leads to recognition of the Circassian Genocide, official apology to the Circassian nation, moral and material compensation, the right of return to their homeland and self-determination on Circassian soil.

Memorial Day and Sharing the Pain

In May 2014, on the Circassian Memorial Day, the (then)

> Turkish Prime Minister Recep Tayyip Erdogan, sent a "Letter of Sympathy" to the Circassians of Turkey. He said in his letter:

Mr. Recep Tayyip Erdogan has sent the letter to the "President of the Federation of Caucasian Associations (KAFFED)" on the 150th commemoration of the "Great Circassian Exile" which stated, "We share your pain heartily."

He said in his letter: "The Great Circassian Exodus in its 150-year memorial, remind our Circassian brothers once again of the great pain, suffered once again, where we share wholeheartedly."[902]

Many thanks are sent to Mr. Erdogan for his letter of sympathy to the Circassians of Turkey, and the statement saying: "We deeply share your pain."

This comment is not meant to downplay the positive words, but rather to focus on acts that remind us of the proverb: 'Deeds, Not Words.'[903]

This statement doesn't delete or hide Erdogan's support to Sochi Olympic Games on the land of the "Circassian Genocide" and his preference of strengthening economic ties with the Russian state!

Even if we consider that Erdogan didn't consider Circassians as close ethnicity to the Turkish race; but that doesn't relieve him from the duty and responsibility to support the Crimean Tatars who are ethnically closer to the Turks, and the Russian Federation annexed their homeland in March 2014. Also, if he remembers, or his advisers would remind him, of the Crimean Peninsula was lost by the Ottoman Empire in favor of the Russian Empire a result of the "Treaty of Adrianople" of September 14, 1829, signed between the Russian Empire and the Ottoman Empire, which gave Russia rights that was not enjoyed by the Ottoman Empire itself!

Without the slightest doubt, the letter comes as a strong supportive position that rang a bell, which presents embodiment of highlighting the significance of the facts that were not mentioned by any Turkish senior official before.

This Turkish initiative is highly appreciated by Circassians, wishing that more tangible steps would be taken in the near future, in order to offer duty of solidarity with the Circassian nation. The great majority of Circassians reside in Turkey, accordingly the Circassian Genocide should be recognized. Retrieval of usurped rights, it is good to remind Turkey that the Russian Federation is one of the countries that have recognized the Armenian genocide. Where there's a will there's a way . . .[904]

Comparing Cruelties

Paul Goble published an article titled "Crimean Tatars No Longer Alone in Remembering Stalin's Crimes Against Their Nation." It consisted of a comparison made between the eighteenth of May for the Crimean Tatars and the twenty-first of May for the Circassians.

> Seventy-two years ago today, the Soviet state deported the Crimean Tatars from their homeland to Central Asia, a tragedy that resulted in the death of many and the wounding of all. And in the years since, the Crimean Tatars have marked this horrific event every May 18. They are doing so today.[905]

Goble matched the Crimean Tatars, Circassians, and Ukrainians' disasters being perpetrated by the same tyrant.

> But this year, far more than at any time in the past, the tragedy of the Crimean Tatars is being remembered not only by them but by others, some of whom like the Circassians who were also subject to deportation, by others like the Ukrainians who were harmed by the genocidal policies of the Soviet regime, and by people of good will throughout the world.[906]

He continued,

> Given Russia's invasion and occupation of part of Ukraine, this is perhaps no surprise, although especially for the Crimean Tatars, it is welcome. But there has been another development this year: other groups who were victimized by Russian governments are joining with the Crimean Tatars to mark their common tragedy.
> The clearest and best example of this is provided by the Circassians, who three days from now will mark the 152nd anniversary of their expulsion from their historical homeland by tsarist forces. The Federation of Circassian Organizations in Istanbul have issued a statement on the Crimean Tatar deportation (qha.com.ua/ru/obschestvo/cherkesi-razdelyayut-gore-krimskotatarskogo-naroda/159642/).[907]

The statement proclaimed,

"We share the pain of the Crimean Tatar people which was subjected to genocide and deportation from its own Motherland on the order of the harsh ruler Stalin in 1944. We as a people who suffered a similar grief express our solidarity with the Crimean Tatar nation", the declaration says.[908]

The Crimean Tatars declared their appreciation for the Circassians: "In reporting this statement, the Crimean Tatar QHA news agency says that 'such a declaration of solidarity from a nation which in its history saw the cruelty of the Russian government is extremely significant for the Crimean Tatar people.' But in fact it is even more than that."[909]

The Unforgotten Circassian Dilemma 152 Years On

The twenty-first of May 2016 coincided with the commemoration of the 152 years of the end of the Russian-Circassian War. It is a reminder of the Tsarist Russian Empire's devastating war against Circassia, the foreign occupation of the Circassian homeland, the physical liquidation, genocide, forced displacement and deportation, and all the other disastrous consequences that befell the Circassian nation.

It does not matter how long it takes the Circassian nation to restore its usurped rights; time is on their side. The proper time will come, since Circassian rights have no statute of limitations. They are protected by international laws and norms.

The cooperation and coordination between all Circassians is the key for success. A peaceful, nonviolent future move will lead to achieving the objectives. The Circassians ought to use the documented evidence and international legal terms. The wise move could be to follow the example of Mahatma Gandhi, Martin Luther King, or Nelson Mandela.

It's not surprising that when Circassian activism was revived and became active, different ways and means were utilized to go around the achievements. Since the Sochi Olympic Games, Russian methods were revised, and the Russian propaganda machine started spreading rumors in different media outlets, including social media on the Internet. They utilized pro-Russian agents, journalists and academicians to use methods of psychological warfare, including intimidation and enticement.

Generally speaking, media outlets have a constructive role in reporting what is going on in many parts of the world. Unfortunately, some of them, with the help of some writers, tend to paint a misleading and deceiving image, spread wrong information, or even mix facts with confabulations, resulting in the production of wrong impressions about the subject discussed.

The commemoration of the Circassian Memorial Day should concentrate on the brutal behavior conducted against Circassians. Hibernation, in a matter of the size of the Circassian Question, is neither logical nor realistic. It is also not acceptable. The path is known and the objectives will not change. No matter what forces are pushing against the current are trying to do, in the end, the truth will prevail.

An article titled "Circassia the Beautiful Homeland" stated meanings of the Circassian Memorial Grief Day. The article started by saying,

> The sad memory knocks the door again. The evil events of the massacres and other crimes against Circassians and other nations of the Caucasus have been revised and inspected. They showed the world the real face of the Russian Tsarist Empire. Facts have shown that the consecutive Russian regimes were not any different from their evil predecessors. At the same time, no review of the criminal policies perpetrated by the Russian state had been conducted in order to carry out corrective actions for the crimes committed against innocent people.
>
> The Circassian Memorial Day, which recalls the 21st of May, 1864, is a reminder of the Circassian Genocide. Remembering the past doesn't mean living in it. On the contrary, it guides and steers the way that should be followed for the sake of reclaiming the Circassian legitimate rights. It asserts the achievements accomplished in recent years, especially in regard to recognizing the Circassian legal rights and recognition of the Circassian Genocide, which will be built upon in the future.[910]

A comparison is carried out with a similar Crimean Tatars situation.

> There is a similarity between the crimes committed against victims, regardless of the identity of the aggressors. Part of the song in the title of "1944", which won the Eurovision Song Festival competition, performed by Crimean Tatar singer, Jamala, says:

"When strangers are coming . . .
They come to your house,

They kill you all;
And say,
We're not guilt, not guilty.'⁹¹¹

The article stated,

> Last year's developments showed further violations against the Circassian activists in the North Caucasus. The Russian authorities have continued preventing the Circassians of Syria from returning to their historical homeland. They have exceeded the reasonable human limits through the harassment and detention of Circassian citizens who have returned from Turkey to their homeland in the North Caucasus because of the aftermath of the shooting down of a Russian Sukhoi Su-24 fighter jet on the Turkish border. They were asked to leave the North Caucasus and return to Turkey.

Then it continued,

> The Circassians do not accept the Russian apathy and stubbornness toward restoring their rights. The international developments, especially with regard to the occupation of Russian troops to the Crimea, the continuity in what they call support for rebel forces in south-eastern Ukraine, and attempts to interfere in the republics of the Baltic region, show the extent of disregard for others and international laws by the Russians.

The conclusion was as follows: "The usurped rights must be given back to their owners. They will never stop working on restoring them no matter how long." ⁹¹²

Moscow's Attempts to Block Circassians

"Moscow Seeks to Block Circassians in Russian Capital from Marking Genocide Anniversary" was an article by Paul Goble that explained what he described as Moscow's attempts to muzzle the mouths and prevent activists from commemorating the end of the Russian-Circassian War.⁹¹³

An introduction included a portrait and an explanation.

"Highlanders Leaving Their Village" by Petr Gruzinsky shows the deportation of Circassians, the indigenous peoples of the region from their homeland at the end of the Russo-Circassian War by victorious Russia. The expulsion was launched before the end of the war in 1864 and it was mostly completed by 1867. The peoples involved were mainly the Circassians (Adyghe), Ubykhs, Abkhaz, and Abaza. (Image: Wikimedia)[914]

The article illustrated,

> For decades, Circassians have marked May 21 as a Day of Sorrow, the anniversary of their expulsion from Russia in 1864 and an event many view as an act of genocide. Until recently, they did so only privately but beginning in 1989, they have held public ceremonies in the North Caucasus, and three years ago, began to do so in Moscow as well.[915]

Goble stated,

> But unlike in 2014 and 2015, this year the Moscow authorities have turned them down, refusing several requests and explain in some that this is because of scheduling conflicts. The Circassians are uncertain whether they believe what they are being told, but they are upset and fear this points to even more neglect of their issues and more repression of their activists.[916]

He continued,

> However, it is entirely possible that Moscow will regret its action because it is likely to energize Circassians. As one pointed out, when officials in the North Caucasus tried to block such demonstrations, that only led more Circassians to take part in informal ones and to demand that their issues be addressed.[917]

The article concluded,

> That Circassian pointedly added that the Circassians have carefully played by the rules in seeking permission for ceremonies and that "prohibitions on the carrying out of such

measures will have just the opposite effect," especially given that the Russian authorities now refuse to address Circassian issues as legitimate but instead cast them as the work of foreign forces.[918]

Adyghe Heku published an article about the refusal of the Russian authorities to hold the Circassian commemoration on the twenty-first of May 2016. Experts have linked the refusal to hold the Day of Remembrance of the Circassians to ignoring the effects of the Caucasian War.[919]

Furthermore, the Russian authorities in Moscow have detained eight Circassian activists in a Metro Station for distributing memory ribbons for the Circassian Day of Memory and Grief. The tape is made available to memorialize the victims of the devastating war that ended on the twenty-first of May 1864. After few hours, they were released.

> Beslan Teuvezh (Teuvazhev) and the other activists were distributing ribbons among their friends and acquaintances, but they were accused of participating in unsanctioned rally. Earlier, the Metropolitan Interior Ministry denied Beslan Teuvezhu and his friends of bid to host mourning rally on the Day of Memory and Grief for remembering the Circassian victims.[920]

The Statement by the Turkish Foreign Ministry

The Turkish Ministry of Foreign Affairs website published "Statement of the Spokesman of the Ministry of Foreign Affairs, Tanju Bilgiç, in Response to a Question Regarding the Anniversary of the Circassian Exile." This shows a positive Turkish change in dealing with the Circassian Question, even though it is not yet addressing the real issues of the Circassian Question.

The spokesman has said, "During the fights that occurred in the invasion of the Caucasus by the Tsarist Russia throughout the 19th century and as a result of the oppression and persecutions that followed afterwards, hundreds of thousands of Caucasian people lost their lives and most of the survivors migrated to Anatolia."[921]

He continued, "This great catastrophe, known as the 'Circassian Exile' in history and commemorated every year on May 21, has been etched on the memory of Caucasian people, who were exiled from their homeland, and opened deep wounds in their hearts. We respectfully commemorate those who lost their lives in this atrocity, which constitutes one of the greatest massacres in the history of humanity."[922]

In a related matter, the Turkish Daily Sabah published on its website, that "Turkish Foreign Ministry commemorates 'Great Circassian Exile.'" The Daily Sabah mentioned, "The Foreign Ministry commemorated the 152nd anniversary of the 'Great Circassian Exile,' as remembered on May 21 every year." The described "written statement" has mentioned the statement issued by the Foreign Ministry Website.[923]

Commemoration Attempts

An article titled "21 Circassians Denied Entry by Russian Land Border Authorities After 12 Hours Delay" reported an event that seemingly wouldn't be considered unexpected by the Russian authorities. Similar incidents have occurred in the past and will happen again.

It started by saying,

> Another intended Russian provocation against Circassians, has taken place this time in land border. On the Georgian-Russian land entrance border on the eve of the Circassian Memorial Day, a group of Circassians were denied entry. Last night a group of 21 Circassians from Turkey, were not admitted to cross the Georgian Russian land border. After 12 hours delay, they were denied entrance through the border. They were obliged to return to where they came from.[924]

The article added, "The group wanted to travel by bus from Ankara, Turkey, to cross the Black Sea on ship to Batumi, Georgia, then continue on the same bus to Nalchik, the Republic of Karabardino-Blakaria. They wanted to be in Nalchik on the Circassian Memorial Day, on the 21st of May."[925]

When entry was not possible, they had to return to where they came from: "All passengers had their travel documents properly prepared for the trip, which presented at the border check point. Valid Visas were stamped on the passports. After holding them for 12 hours, they were told that they are not allowed to proceed to their homeland."[926]

The 2016 Circassian commemoration witnessed a participation by Japanese friends in front of the Russian Embassy in Tokyo, Japan. The event included raising the Circassian flags and banners with pictures that represent symbols of the Circassian Question.

Circassians have participated in commemorating the Circassian Memorial Day, in Cherkessk, Maykop, Nalchik, and other places of the North Caucasus. They also did so in diaspora in many locations such as Ankara, Istanbul, Amman, Rehanye, Munich, London, Helsinki, and other locations.

Circassian Memorial Day Anniversary in Jordan

The Circassian community in Jordan has proceeded for years to organize a yearly event of meaningful Pause for Remembrance of victims and homeland. On Memorial Day, they started to execute a standing in front of the Russian Embassy in Amman. This took place since it became possible to express their opinion in a peaceful and nonviolent way. The Circassians gather to protest the outcome of the Russian Empire's atrocities against the Circassian nation.

JFNC has published an article on the twenty-first of May 2016 that the "Circassians in Jordan have shared the world Circassians to commemorate, the Circassian Day of Grief and Memory, which is commemorated by Circassians every year. It links the past with the present, where it gives the resolve and fortitude in order to consider the future of the coming generations."[927]

The article stated,

> Despite the ban imposed by the Jordanian Ministry of the Interior to conduct the annual vigil in front of the Russian Embassy in Amman on the Day of the Circassian grief, the Circassians commemorated the memory of the victims of the devastating war, foreign occupation, genocide and forced deportation, that is commemorated by the Circassians in the world every year, on the twenty first of May.[928]

A surprising event has erupted.

> The young men in the afternoon, went to the Russian Embassy location in Amman, and lined up in front of the main entrance of the embassy, while holding Circassian and Jordanian flags, as well as they raised banners denouncing the crimes committed against the Circassian nation, calling for the recognition of genocide and all its repercussions. Some of the participants wore Circassian clothes and hats, where it imposed a Circassian character.[929]

Narration has continued to stress on the fact that the commemoration has taken place in an ordinary form, which usually occurs every year.

> On the other hand, the main Circassian Charity Association has commemorated the annual memory. They invited members and concerned people, where speeches were given, including the speech of the Head of the Association, and the speech of the Circassian Tribal Council of Jordan. Also commemoration included other paragraphs devoted to shed light on the themes of culture, arts and social matters, linking the present with the past, which states all matters relating to Motherland.[930]

The article concluded that this time it has interspersed with the surprising participation of the young people who participated in the vigil in front of the Russian Embassy in Amman. They raised Circassian flags in addition to the banners.

> Also, a group of young men came to the place of commemoration, while waving Circassian flags and banners such as those raised during the vigil that took place in front of the Russian Embassy in Amman; they stood in front of the audience and on the stage prepared for this occasion. When the program prepared for the occasion has started, they withdrew and dispersed in the place.[931]

---

[872] http://www.worldbulletin.net/world/158273/circassia-putin-should-recognise-circassian-genocide

[873] The Sochi Predicament: Contexts, Characteristics and Challenges of the Olympic Winter Games in 2014 (Edited by Bo Petersson and Karina Vamlig)

[874] The Sochi Predicament: Contexts, Characteristics and Challenges of the Olympic Winter Games in 2014 (Edited by Bo Petersson and Karina Vamlig)

[875] http://windowoneurasia.blogspot.com/2009/05/window-on-eurasia-fsb-seeks-to-suppress.html

[876] https://windowoneurasia.blogspot.com/2009/05/window-on-eurasia-fsb-seeks-to-suppress.html

877 http://www.civil.ge/eng/article.php?id=24790
878 https://en.wikipedia.org/wiki/Anaklia
879 https://en.wikipedia.org/wiki/Anaklia
880 http://www.civil.ge/eng/article.php?id=24790
881 http://www.kavkaz-uzel.ru/articles/224505/
882 http://www.jamestown.org/programs/edm/single/?tx_ttnews%5Btt_news%5D=43982&cHash=a5a3746b9118d10f0e383b10df2e3f8c#.Vm8LkRorJE7
883 http://www.jamestown.org/programs/edm/single/?tx_ttnews%5Btt_news%5D=43982&cHash=a5a3746b9118d10f0e383b10df2e3f8c#.Vm8LkRorJE7
884 http://www.nytimes.com/2015/04/16/world/europe/european-parliament-urges-turkey-to-recognize-armenian-genocide.html?_r=0
885 http://justicefornorthcaucasus.info/?p=1251677132 and http://www.lragir.am/index/eng/0/politics/view/35260
886 http://justicefornorthcaucasus.info/?p=1230735300
887 http://justicefornorthcaucasus.info/?p=1230735300
888 http://justicefornorthcaucasus.info/?p=1230735300
889 http://www.preventgenocide.org/genocide/officialtext.htm
890 http://legal.un.org/avl/ha/cppcg/cppcg.html
891 http://www.nytimes.com/2011/05/21/world/europe/21georgia.html?_r=0
892 http://www.civil.ge/eng/article.php?id=24790
893 http://www.slate.com/blogs/the_world_/2014/02/05/the_circassians_and_the_olympics_did_the_age_of_genocide_begin_in_sochi.html
894 http://www.thisdaygenocide.org/this-day-in-genocide/category/caucasus-region#/
895 The Circassian Genocide (Walter Richmond)
896 http://www.un.org/en/documents/udhr/
897 http://www.un.org/esa/socdev/unpfii/documents/DRIPS_en.pdf
898 http://www.un.org/en/decolonization/declaration.shtml
899 http://www.un.org/en/sections/what-we-do/uphold-international-law/
900 Circassian History (Kadir Natho)
901 http://www.ponarseurasia.org/article/circassian-memorial-day-sochi-and-syria
902 http://www.kaffed.org/haberler/federasyondan/item/2203-ba%C5%9Fbakan-erdo%C4%9Fan-ac%C4%B1lar%C4%B1n%C4%B1z%C4%B1-y%C3%BCrekten-payla%C5%9F%C4%B1yoruz.html
903 http://www.definition-of.com/deeds+not+words
904 http://justicefornorthcaucasus.info/?p=1251672777
905 http://windowoneurasia2.blogspot.com/2016/05/crimean-tatars-no-longer-alone-in.html

906 http://windowoneurasia2.blogspot.com/2016/05/crimean-tatars-no-longer-alone-in.html
907 http://windowoneurasia2.blogspot.com/2016/05/crimean-tatars-no-longer-alone-in.html
908 http://windowoneurasia2.blogspot.com/2016/05/crimean-tatars-no-longer-alone-in.html
909 http://windowoneurasia2.blogspot.com/2016/05/crimean-tatars-no-longer-alone-in.html
910 http://justicefornorthcaucasus.info/?p=1251677517
911 http://justicefornorthcaucasus.info/?p=1251677517
912 http://justicefornorthcaucasus.info/?p=1251677517
913 http://euromaidanpress.com/2016/05/19/moscow-seeks-to-block-circassians-in-russian-capital-from-marking-genocide-anniversary/#arvlbdata
914 http://euromaidanpress.com/2016/05/19/moscow-seeks-to-block-circassians-in-russian-capital-from-marking-genocide-anniversary/#arvlbdata
915 http://euromaidanpress.com/2016/05/19/moscow-seeks-to-block-circassians-in-russian-capital-from-marking-genocide-anniversary/#arvlbdata
916 http://euromaidanpress.com/2016/05/19/moscow-seeks-to-block-circassians-in-russian-capital-from-marking-genocide-anniversary/#arvlbdata
917 http://euromaidanpress.com/2016/05/19/moscow-seeks-to-block-circassians-in-russian-capital-from-marking-genocide-anniversary/#arvlbdata
918 http://euromaidanpress.com/2016/05/19/moscow-seeks-to-block-circassians-in-russian-capital-from-marking-genocide-anniversary/#arvlbdata
919 https://aheku.net/news/society/ekspertyi-svyazali-otkaz-v-provedenii-dnya-pamyati-cherkesov-s-ignorirovaniem-posledstvij-kavkazskoj-vojnyi?_utl_t=fb
920 http://www.natpressru.info/index.php?newsid=10444
921 http://www.mfa.gov.tr/qa_16_-20-may-2016_-statement-of-the-spokesman-of-the-ministry-of-foreign-affairs_-tanju-bilgi%C3%A7_-in-response-to-a-question-regarding-the-anniversary-of-the-circassian-exile.en.mfa
922 http://www.mfa.gov.tr/qa_16_-20-may-2016_-statement-of-the-spokesman-of-the-ministry-of-foreign-affairs_-tanju-bilgi%C3%A7_-in-response-to-a-question-regarding-the-anniversary-of-the-circassian-exile.en.mfa
923 http://www.dailysabah.com/politics/2016/05/21/turkish-foreign-ministry-commemorates-great-circassian-exile

[924] http://justicefornorthcaucasus.info/?p=1251677545
[925] http://justicefornorthcaucasus.info/?p=1251677545
[926] http://justicefornorthcaucasus.info/?p=1251677545
[927] http://justicefornorthcaucasus.info/?p=1251677573
[928] http://justicefornorthcaucasus.info/?p=1251677573
[929] http://justicefornorthcaucasus.info/?p=1251677573
[930] http://justicefornorthcaucasus.info/?p=1251677573
[931] http://justicefornorthcaucasus.info/?p=1251677573

9

The Circassian Legal Status and the Right to Self-Determination

19th-century postcard of Mount Elbrus in the Caucasus Mountains

-The Circassian Legal Status

It is established beyond any reasonable doubt that Tsarist Russia has committed in the nineteenth century terrifying crimes of genocide, ethnic cleansing, deportation, and other associated evil acts.

The Circassian homeland has witnessed, over the years, invaders and colonizers' greedy attempts to control Circassia through campaigns and wars of aggression that had pervaded in many different ways and means. But the Circassians, through exercising their natural right to freedom and national dignity, managed every time, they were subjected to aggressive acts, to deal with the situation until they eventually were able to maintain their freedom and reliance on themselves in saving their homeland, which they inherited from their ancestors. The last example turned out to be the Russian Empire proclaiming an uncompromising aggressive 101-year-long war for the control of Circassia at any cost and to eliminate the presence of the Circassian nation as an entity, nation, or homeland.

Matching reality with results and their implications, the Circassian nation's inalienable, non- waived, and non-forgotten rights cannot and should not be neglected or aborted, because the Circassians have confirmed that they are eager to live in their own homeland like any other nation and to regain their usurped rights that are dear to their hearts and consciences than has been obtained so far. There is nothing more precious than their homeland, especially since the quest for that is a noble goal in itself, cannot be achieved except through dedication, honesty, and altruism to reach the desired objective, and anyone who forgets or overlooks their homeland or thinks to waive their legitimate national rights, whether individual or collective, they would be considered hypocrites, opportunists, or careless for every lurk against their own nation, whether in their homeland or in the whereabouts of Circassian societies and communities throughout the world.

Regarding the above, logic imposes to investigate the rules and statutes pertaining to the various areas of human perception in various fields of existence to solving problems: "There are several stages to solving a problem: Evaluating the problem, managing the problem, decision-making, resolving the problem and examining the results."[932] At this point, accordingly, it is inferred through knowledge and reasoning that correcting thinking processes and matching logic with reality will necessarily lead to reach the truth ahead.

In a related development, at a time after the Russian-Circassian War came to an end (which did not apply to the Circassian case at a time the Circassians had endured murder, genocide, and ethnic cleansing that led to forced deportation of ninety percent of those who remained alive in harsh and brutal conditions), International Humanitarian Laws had been developed and approved during the last 150 years under the auspices of the International Committee of the Red Cross, which was released later in the form of international rules, "were unanimous on one fact that the goal of this law is to protect people who suffer from the scourge of war", and "includes in its broadest sense the entire international legal texts, of which provide protection and rights for the individual"; which is "the set of international rules laid down by treaties or norms, which is specifically designated for solving the problems of human character arising directly from international or non-international armed conflicts, which limit '—for human considerations—from the privilege of the conflict parties choice of choosing fighting methods or means, and they protect individuals and properties.'"[933]

Natural and legal rights are widely affected by the authoritarian regimes that decide on the form of government that eventually would practice the acquisition and usurpation of power. "'Natural law theory' is a label that has been applied to theories of ethics, theories of politics, theories of civil law, and theories of religious morality," and "it is a participation in the eternal law." Natural rights are considered of the true and justified human values being enjoyed by the people, and it is palatable for the human race since birth, such as the right to life, to enjoy human dignity, and the freedom to choose of what suits and fits to reach and preserve self-determination. It also determines that every human being, regardless of gender, origin, religion, age, place of residence, color, and ideological affiliation an inalienable right as a human being. Inalienable rights are the right of property (ownership rights) that is not like acquired rights, so "no one can dispose such as despoil, abandon or replace," and "the natural rights are closely related to human rights." These rights are considered eternal and not interim, all of them belong entirely to the set of basic rights and no human authority can intervene or even affect them.[934]

It is axiomatic that the "Ottoman Turkey" also bears part of the responsibility for the consequences of the Circassian ordeal. Ottomans played a role in a numerous of its elements, whether negatively or positively that ultimately led to the deportation of displaced Circassians to locations decided upon and endorsed by the Ottoman Empire's authorities. It aimed at securing its interests regarding the protection of borders and boundaries on the outskirts of the sprawling parts of the empire, which were in a state of weakness and disintegration. From this perspective comes the duty of the Turkish state in supporting human rights issues that relate to the Circassian nation, and to extend assistance and advocacy to the stranded Circassians in the midst of civil war taking place nowadays in Syria, to get them to a safe haven, which has happened on a limited scale when aircrafts flew several groups of displaced Circassians of Syria from Beirut, Lebanon to Gaziantep, Turkey to accommodate them in a compound that was initially allocated for the Circassians of Syria. Secondly, to support the Circassian nation in order to obtain its ultimate goal, namely the restoration of the Circassians' legitimate rights to return to their Motherland and the recovery of their usurped rights, according to applicable international laws and norms.

The ordeal suffered by the Circassian nation was, and still is, a result of the policy of tyranny and the autocracy of imperial Russia and the continuation of successive Russian governments on the same arrogant and sadistic approach in dealing with the Circassians and their cause. It has not been dealt with as required, as it is imperative to shed light on tyranny based regimes for the sake of approximation and comparison, which consist of fascism, racism, and Nazism that do not pay any interest to high human values and always intervenes in the lives of individuals and groups based on oppression and the policy of acquisition and bullying to impose a fait accompli which will not be in all cases in line with the interests of those to be suppressed, but to have an impact on their morale and the course of their lives. Thus, the cited regimes can be described as follows:

* Fascist regime: "Under fascism, the state, through official cartels, controlled all aspects of manufacturing, commerce, finance, and agriculture." "Fascism embodied corporatism, in which political representation was based on trade and industry rather than on geography. In this, fascism revealed its roots in syndicalism, a form of socialism originating on the left." The individuals in the fascist regimes are transferred to tools that don't receive except initial rights (such as breathing). Natural rights in a fascist regime are wasted because the regime intends to build a social core of one color, and they do not hesitate in that notion. They try to break the backbone of the individuals and to forcibly intervene in the formation of the individuals' core to go in parallel with the regimes' principles, because their goals at the end are deemed elevated and dignified, and to be the goodness for all, or the protection of the entity that it is keen to promote and strengthen. Often hypocrisy becomes the most important means of human horizontal interaction. At the end of the fascist regimes, the authorities would merge into a single authority that does not hesitate to exclude all the individuals who differ with its opinion and to deprive them even of primary rights such as the right to life.[935]

* Nazi regime: "Nazism is defined as a form of socialism featuring racism and expansionism and obedience to a strong leader," and according to Bertrand Russell, Nazism comes from a different tradition than that of either liberal capitalism or communism. Thus, to understand values of Nazism, it is necessary to explore this connection, without trivializing the movement as it was in its peak years in the 1930s and dismissing it as a little more than racism," and "the Nazi regime rejects the existence of a race or color beside the race, which considers the best of all races," as it "tries to intervene with individuals in form and substance way."[936]

* The Apartheid regime: Based on the laws of the rule of the minority over the majority, as was the case in South Africa, as the goal of the race division regime (apartheid) to create a legal framework that maintains the economic and political domination of the minority. Individuals are divided

into ethnic and class groups. "The practice of apartheid existed in South Africa for more than forty years and came to an end when Nelson Mandela (see also African National Congress) was elected president in 1994. During those forty years' control of the power and wealth by the white minority was systematically increased through laws enforced with enthusiasm, resulting in the extreme repression of the majority native African population. As the world community became more aware of the abhorrent practices of the white oligarchy, a chorus of condemnation and approbation resulted in local and international actions designed to force change. Chief among these measures were economic sanctions."[937]

Natural rights: They are the "rights that all men possess, because of which they may be obligated to act, or to refrain from acting, in certain ways. According to the teaching developed primarily by Hobbes and Locke, there are many natural rights, but all of them are inferences from one original right, the right that each man has to preserve his life. All other natural rights, like the right to liberty and the right to property, are necessary inferences from the right of self-preservation, or are conceived as implicit in the exercise of that primary right." The excessive in bragging and egotism, which controls and haunts some people, makes it necessarily holding to own and selfish interests regardless of the circumstances, results and the ways chosen, and tries to pursue and enforce to achieve own ambitions and objectives. It is no secret that most wars occur to satisfy the expansionist ambitions of the lands of others and to control the destinies, fortunes, and fate of nations and peoples. History bears witness to injustice, murder, destruction, occupation, and deportation through violations practiced by tyrants to attack the freedoms of others, deprive them of their natural rights, and the occupation of their homelands through the cruelty that does not pay any attention to limits or restrictions to satisfy colonial desires.[938]

Attempts of Falsification

Russians have permanently and consistently pursued a marginalization and even a "deletion from existence" policy against the Circassians. Apparently, Russia is a crow playing a pigeon's role while at the same time, the consecutive Russian regimes have ignored the different crimes committed against a nation that had its homeland occupied, its rights violated, and its people murdered, displaced, or deported.

Fatima Tlis published an article titled "Moscow Uses Commission on 'Historical Falsification' to Deny Circassian Rights." The article elaborated on the so-called "special presidential commission" for the purpose of declaring innocence of moral and legal responsibility, which seemed to be false testimonies.[939]

Circassians hang on hope despite the pain, while obvious indications reveal aggressive attitudes and suspicious behaviors. It is mentioned that "the 'Special Presidential Commission against falsifications of the history of the Russian Federation causing harm to Russian national interests' is to identify and fight against conscious, imprudent falsifications, aimed on the political results."[940]

That is proclaimed by "Sergei Markov, the deputy head of the State Duma's committee on public associations and religious organizations and a member of the special presidential commission (Vechernyaya Moskva, December 29, 2009)."[941]

It is reported that Sergei Markov mentioned "the Golodomor" committed against the Ukrainian people in 1932–1933, as one of the "falsifications that damage Russia's national interests." That is "according to Ukrainian claims, the famine did not have a natural cause, but was organized by the Russian state in order to reduce the number of Ukrainians."

The article added, "A second example of such historical falsification, said Markov, is related to the Sochi 2014 Olympic Games and aimed at falsifying the history of the Russian-Caucasian war from 1817–1864. 'Yes, the war was bloody', said Markov, adding, 'However, it was only thanks to Russia that the Adygs-Circassians received their own state. Those who left for the Middle Eastern countries are in an incomparably worse situation today than those who remain in the Caucasus'. He underscored that those 'extremists' who use the slogan, 'No Olympic games on the land of genocide', are not worried about the 'historical truth', but rather are trying to call the whole world to boycott the Sochi games (Vechernyaya Moskva, December 29, 2009)."[942]

Those statements had preceded the Russian occupation and annexation of the Crimea, which stressed on events happening at the time. The article continued, "The two main targets of the special commission as indicated by Sergei Markov (the Ukrainians and the Circassians) are becoming more of a headache for the Kremlin not because those two issues are falsifications of history, but because there is in fact unbeatable historical evidence behind the genocide claims."[943]

Legally, Circassians have the ways and means to prove the crimes committed against their ancestors, where

> the Circassian Congress NGO claims that the genocide committed by Russia against the Circassians can be easily proven based solely on the official documents from the Russian Imperial archives. According to the Circassian Congress, approximately 1,500,000 people were massacred

and partly deported from the Caucasus, and the Circassians lost 99 percent of their population during the war and deportation (www.circassiangenocide.org).[944]

The article mentioned the success of Circassians in diaspora playing an active role in the countries they live in, but added that

> they have suffered from losing their identity, traditions, language, culture and ties with their homeland. Repatriation is one of the possibilities for restoring their homeland in the Caucasus, but the process implies appealing to the Russian Federation for permanent resident status and then, if such status is granted, living in the Caucasus for seven years and then applying for citizenship. And while the process itself is already complicated, those repatriated often face additional impracticable requirements.[945]

The author has reminded of the difficulties faced with the Russian authorities by Haci Bairam Polat (mentioned in another chapter): "However, even those who have fulfilled all the requirements still cannot be sure that their status in their homeland is secure. The case of one Circassian repatriated to Nalchik (Kabardino-Balkaria), Turkish citizen Bolat Haci Bairam, is one of the clear examples of Circassians lacking the right to freely return to their country."[946]

Discriminative policies have proven that "the government of Kabardino-Balkaria (KBR) has not only denied the same collective appeal to receive and resettle Circassians from Turkey, but even appealed to Russian Prime Minister Vladimir Putin, demanding that he exclude KBR from the 'Sootechestvennik' federal program aimed at bringing ethnic Russians from all over the world back to Russia (www.elot.ru, January 6)."[947]

Circassian republic authorities have repeatedly failed to meet the optimistic high expectations of the individuals and parties who are eager to realize their dreams of hope for Russian authorities' response of goodwill: "The Circassian Diaspora in Jordan had made a special effort to convince the Russian government to include Circassians in the program. However, the news from KBR suggests that their success was, at best, temporary."[948] However, reality has proven that both Russia and its local authorities in the North Caucasus are pairing their execution of the Center's decisions.

The declared and open propaganda war incompatible with reality is lived by members of the Circassian nation.

Sergei Markov's attempt to present the situation as the Circassians enjoying 'their own state' in the Caucasus is, in fact, a major and deliberate effort to falsify history. In reality, while approximately five million Circassians live in exile in more than 50 countries, today only less than one million Circassians remain in their homeland. The majority of them live in three republics in the North Caucasus separated by artificial boundaries and officially identified as Kabardins, Cherkess, Adygs, Shapsugs—that is, not by their ethnic names but by their geographical locations.[949]

The indigenous people are targeted in their unity and territorial integrity of their fragmented homeland since it was occupied by the Russian imperial forces, which led to the denial of legal status of the Circassians: "By cutting Circassia's territory into separate pieces and giving them different names, Russia effectively achieves the aim of eradicating the national identity of Circassians, as well as visually erasing Circassia from the geopolitical map of the region."[950]

A change has occurred toward counterfeit labels that were known with, including ethnic denomination and subregions. The Circassians have taken their own initiative to launch a uniting name, where "recently came up with an initiative which, if successful, can return them their single ethnic name and geopolitical position (Window to Eurasia, January 8). The Circassians are calling on their compatriots to identify their ethnicity as a Circassian in the upcoming Russian census, not as Adyg, Kabardin or Cherkess, as required from Soviet times until recently."[951]

The article added, "For propaganda purposes, the Circassians have developed a special website, www.perepis2010.org, where they post excerpts from the Russian constitution regarding their rights of ethnic identification, news about the census and propaganda materials that they plan to circulate in a printed form among non-internet users."[952]

Legal Status Contradicts Repeated Denials

The intensification of the merciless war in Syria has led to prevailing catastrophic circumstances affecting the Circassians of Syria. All that did not convince the decision makers to provide the necessary support and assistance: "In the early 1990s Russian Caucasian republics with residual Circassian populations established ties to the diaspora and supported returnee programmes. But aside from a few thousand returnees the contact remained largely restricted to tourism by diaspora Circassians in the historic homeland."[953]

The right of return to their homeland has been categorically denied, according to firm decisions.

> The current exception is Syria, where the escalating civil war represents an acute threat to ethnic and confessional minorities. Circassian organisations worldwide are now calling upon Russia, which in 1999 gave refuge to Circassian families from the war zone in Kosovo, to accept Syrian Circassian "returnees". While several hundred have already arrived in Maykop and Nalchik, Moscow is generally wary of returnee movements of non-Russian nationalities in the North Caucasus.[954]

The International Circassian Association failed to address the real interests and concerns of the Circassian communities in the Circassian homeland and in diaspora: "ICA sees its main task as coordinating cultural relations between Circassian communities across the world. It has, however, not pursued that goal with great vigour."[955]

The reality of the association indicates,

> Its offices are staffed largely with members of the bureaucratic elites of the three Caucasian republics, who were concerned to avoid confrontation with Moscow and practically failed to respond to Russian repression against activists who raised the 'Circassian question' in connection with Sochi 2014. Such activists increasingly organise in small autonomous groups outside the ICA, which also missed the transition to the internet age and for a long time did not even have its own website.[956]

In characterizing recent developments of Circassian youth across the world,

> a new generation aged between 18 and 28 communicates via the internet and is networked with Circassian communities across the world. They provide an example of the phenomenon for which the American political scientist Benedict Anderson coined the term "long-distance nationalism", which has already been identified in the Armenian and other diaspora communities.[957]

Furthermore, legal rights are in the midst of commonness of hostile conditions.

> Although the Circassian case has not produced a coherent, militant or overtly returnee-driven national movement liable to burden the problem laden North Caucasus with yet more potentially violent conflict, the revival of interest in their ethnic roots among young people of Circassian origin does represent a challenge for Russia. Moscow finds itself confronted with an unresolved chapter of its colonial history—during a phase where President Putin is cultivating a patriotism that leaves little space for self-critical historical reflection.[958]

Slavery in Modern Time

There are many concerned people who fear increasing concerns of human rights issues relating to the Russia Federation. Many people within present Russia are seeking the possibility to attain the right to self-determination guaranteed by international law. However, the facts mentioned in the report on slavery in Russia suggests that the issue of restoring rights will not be easy and will take time and sustained efforts.

The Globalist published a report titled, The New Russian Empire: Modern Slavery in Russia. This current study comes "154 years after the abolition of serfdom, Russia is Europe's most slave-holding nation, in modern terms."

The brief report elaborates on the entire situation in modern Russia and lists five points that sum up the human rights issue of being a slaveholding nation:

1. Russia has the largest incidence of modern slavery of any European or Eurasian nation.

2. This figure is according to the Walk Free Foundation's 2014 Global Slavery Index, which defines modern slavery as any practice that traps people in modern servitude, including human trafficking and forced labor.

3. Estimated at just over one million, the number of modern slaves in Russia represents 0.7% of the country's 143 million people.

4. Many of the victims of slavery in Russia come from former provinces of the Russian Empire (and former republics of the Soviet Union), such as Tajikistan, Kyrgyzstan and Uzbekistan.

5. The U.S. State Department has reported that, in 2013, thousands of North Korean citizens were being forced to work in the timber industry in Russia's Far East—apparently with the approval of both governments."[959]

Russian Intervention and Ensuring Russians' Immunity from Syrian Law

"Details of Moscow's Deal With Syria Reveal Extent of Russian Dominance" was the article of the Washington Free Beacon that detailed the Russian intervention in Syria, which stated, "The Washington Post's Michael Birnbaum wrote on Friday that the open-ended agreement between the Russian and Syrian Ministries of Defense gives Moscow a virtual 'carte blanche' in Syria. The agreement allows for the unrestricted passage of Russian men and material into Syria, allows Russia to direct its own military operations without Syrian input, and gives Russia immunity from Syrian law and an exemption for any damage incurred by Russian actions in Syria."[960]

The Russia-Syrian military agreement reminds of the 1939 Soviet-Baltic deals: "The Baltic experience is a good example of how open-ended, broad access rights for Russian military forces in times of crisis can be used to first erode, and then erase, national sovereignty', says Eerik-Niiles Kross, an Estonian historian who is now a member of parliament. 'Russia is obsessed with these types of treaties and agreements. They are paper shields—vague reassurances to national hosts and the international order while they plan the next move in a revanchist game.'"[961]

It concluded, "It's clear Russia has broad, game-changing ambitions in the Middle East," says Kross. "Their land grabs—like Crimea—have often left allies and opponents alike reeling ... The Syrian agreement must be interpreted through that lens." The article concluded "It's just paper—but paper is important to Putin."[962]

The Right to Self-Determination

The definition derives the concept.

> The principle of self-determination refers to the right of a people to determine its own political destiny. Beyond

this broad definition, however, no legal criteria determine which groups may legitimately claim this right in particular cases. The right to self-determination has become one of the most complex issues facing policymakers in the United States and the international community at large. At the close of the twentieth century, it could mean the right of people to choose their form of government within existing borders or by achieving independence from a colonial power."[963]

Freedom to choose one's own destiny is one of the fundamental human rights: "The principle of self-determination fared considerably better in other areas of the world. In effect, what World War I did for Eastern Europe, World War II accomplished in Asia and Africa. Between 1946 and 1960, thirty-seven new nations emerged from colonial status in Asia, Africa, and the Middle East."[964]

The reference and practice of self-determination is obvious, where "the United Nations Charter reflected both the triumph of Wilson's concept of self-determination and the change in international relations that had occurred during the intervening years. Whereas the Covenant of the League of Nations ultimately had no references to the concept of national self-determination, the charter of the United Nations mentioned it three times. However, the charter did not insist on independence, but spoke only of self-government."[965]

For small nations, options were provided to keep national identity and dignity while linked with other nations. Nevertheless, the realistic implementation made this trend a way of domination under false and decorated descriptions: "The principle of federation was more promising than that of national independence. What was essential in the democratic tradition—and here the charter drew largely from Wilsonian thought—was not national independence but self-government, government based upon the consent of the governed, and respect for the equality of the peoples involved. After 1960 the right of colonial peoples to self-determination and independence was reaffirmed almost annually by the General Assembly of the United Nations."[966]

It is the right of all the oppressed people that live under oppression and injustice of colonialism to secession and the formation of their independent states. It should protect people from the cancellation of their advantages and restrictions of ethnic, national, and religious character. All minorities and ethnic groups must restore their full freedom. Also, minorities, racial groups, indigenous peoples and nations should be protected and respected.

> Three types of decolonization: international, domestic and ideological. The latter is the most relevant with regard

to the Circassian context as addresses the context of a totalitarian past where "liberated peoples" had 'long-term memories confiscated, destroyed or manipulated.'⁹⁶⁷

Self-Determination Followed the Fall of the Russian Empire

Colonial powers have always tried, to the last moment, to hold control and rule other peoples and nations.

> The disintegration of the Russian Empire began after the February Revolution of 1917. Although of the taking of power by the Bolsheviks accelerated this process, it was not the root cause. By 1917 the Russian Empire, which as member of the Entente was technically undefeated in the world war, had in fact, suffered defeat. In the course of military hostilities it had lost Poland and significant part of the Baltic territory. Having overthrown the autocracy, the February Revolution of 1917 greatly weakened the imperial center, and the October coup dealt it a fresh blow.⁹⁶⁸

Even when countries restore their freedom and independence, colonial powers would reoccupy these countries when time permitted.

> In the period from 1917 to 1920, national independence was proclaimed by such countries as Poland, Finland, Estonia, Latvia, Lithuania, Ukraine, Belarus, Georgia, Armenia, Azerbaijan and other colonies of the Russian Empire. Russia also lost real power over Turkestan. As a result of, at the height of the Civil War the Soviet Republic incorporated only 25 provinces of Central Russia. Nevertheless, by the end of the Civil War and Bolsheviks had managed to win back the majority of former colonies of the Russian Empire, with the exception of Poland, Lithuania, Latvia, Estonia, Finland and Bessarabia.⁹⁶⁹

The principle of self-determination was linked to the Bolshevik Revolution from its inception in 1917. This application appeared in the Declaration of Rights of the people of Russia, issued in 1917. It stated that the right to self-determination is summarized in respecting the national characteristics of every people and based on equality in all rights among nations. It led to the achievement of the proletarian system, which means the solidarity of all workers of the world.

The right of self-determination in the Bolshevik Revolution in the year 1917 was granted.

> The Sovnarkom issued a series of decrees concerning peace, land, the establishment of workers' control, and the nationalization of all heavy industry. It also issued the Declaration on the Rights of the Peoples of Russia on 15 November 1917, in which the equality of all peoples was proclaimed, and in which the 'right of self-determination, even unto separation' was formally recognized.[970]

On this basis did the right of self-determination of peoples who lived under the rule of the tsars apply, and among the peoples who won the right are the peoples of the Baltic states "Estonia, Lithuania, Latvia and the people of Ukraine"; the result of the application of this principle is that the proportion of the regions that have been abandoned were 62 percent of Russia's population (Saad-Allah, 38: 1986). Thus, we conclude that the Russian Bolshevik Revolution had recognized and applied the right of self-determination since birth and considered it as a fundamental principle for any peaceful settlement after the end of the First World War.[971]

> Nevertheless, international decolonization is also relevant in the Circassian context; international decolonization, which has allowed societies previously stagnating in the ethnological inertia of colonial oppression access to historical consciousness and the rehabilitation (or fabrication) of memories.[972]

The observer of the Circassian Question notes that there is a wide gap between each of the "political and legal handling" concerning the Circassian Question and its main elements, as what is recognized by law (the provisions of the law and/or the Constitution of Russia). Some parties try to make it empty of its contents through policies of broken promises, passive connections, and cultural activities limited to purely technical matters and most importantly to institutionalize a social nature of activities, meetings, exchange of visits and various contacts, which transpires premeditated intents (with premeditation) by inspiring everybody to stay in diaspora because of its positive repercussions for them; coordination remains among them whether with the authorities that belong to the Russian State in the North Caucasus, its official parties, and the International Circassian Association on the one hand, or directly with the

Russian authorities through its embassies and the Russian cultural centers linked directly to the Russian Foreign Ministry on the other hand, in order to impose a policy of fait accompli that ignores the axiomatical in order to blur the core issues.[973] Thus, relevant international laws must be noted and understood and, as a minimum, should not accept less when dealing with everyone who wants to cooperate and to engage in dialogue and may not waive the inalienable legitimate national rights, which must take into account the United Nations Declaration on the Rights of Indigenous Peoples."[974]

> This links to the pre-Soviet era of the Russian Empire as addressed by the documentation and research efforts prioritized by many Circassian organizations and their partners. A revised "domestic decolonization" is in many ways what Circassian actors are asking for. On the one hand, these types of decolonization frame the Circassian memorialization efforts as parts of a redefinition of minority memories in a democratization and emancipation perspective. On the other hand, they also illustrate that this struggle for "decolonization" continues in the case of Circassian revival.[975]

Therefore, logic imposes us to find a working kernel to represent the partnership between the Circassians, in all their whereabouts and all those who are interested in their cause, human rights organizations, and legal organizations to activate international resolutions and regulations and to explain the Circassian Question to the world in an ample form, and in line with the right of unconditional return, compensation, and self-determination without outbidding by any party, and to work on the rejection of the possibility of relinquishment of any kind in regard to the Circassians' rights. In addition to that, attention must be paid to disseminate knowledge and documented information that relate to the Circassian Question for the Circassian nation to be aware of what has happened and what will happen, and must maintain contact and communication consistently for that purpose, using modern communications technology.[976]

> It is the first time in contemporary History that Circassians called for Freedom in their collective statements, using the slogan "Free Circassia Now."[977]

JFNC's website published an article signed by Eagle, titled "Circassians More Determined and More Resolute," which addressed a prospect about the Circassian determination for restoring Circassian legitimate rights.

Nations will not rebirth and homelands will not be built by submission, weakness, subordination, selfishness, degradation and humiliation, that lead ultimately to slavery, but by dignity, pride, magnanimity and altruism, as if the great ancestors wanted to live humiliated under the Tsarist Russian occupation forces, they could have done so, but authentic Circassian will not allow injustice and humiliation on himself.[978]

Self-Determination (International Law) and Independence of Colonized Nations

Sovereign states should adhere to international law, where they should observe legitimacy of other nations and their compatibility with the international community. They have the obligation to share moral values and to respect peoples' and nations' right to choose their own destiny.

Self-determination denotes the legal right of people to decide their own destiny in the international order. Self-determination is a core principle of international law, arising from customary international law[979], but also recognized as a general principle of law and enshrined in a number of international treaties[980]. For instance, self-determination is protected in the United Nations Charter and the International Covenant on Civil and Political Rights[981] as a right of "all peoples."[982]

Practically, decolonization and self-determination are paired together: "While self-determination is a cardinal principle of international law, its meaning is often obscure. Yet international law clearly recognizes decolonization as a central application of the principle. Most ordinary people also agree that the liberation of colonial peoples was a moral triumph."[983]

Human rights were considered with respect to peoples' freedom.

Mindful of the determination proclaimed by the peoples of the world in the Charter of the United Nations to reaffirm faith in fundamental human rights, in the dignity and worth of the human person, in the equal rights of men and women and of nations large and small and to promote social progress and better standards of life in larger freedom. Conscious of the need for the creation of conditions of stability and well-being and peaceful and friendly relations based on respect for the principles of equal rights and self-determination of all peoples, and of universal respect for, and observance of, human rights and fundamental freedoms for all without distinction as to race, sex, language or religion.[984]

The stricken Circassian nation does not consider, after most of the nation was compulsorily expelled away from their homeland, their issue resolved. Quite the contrary, deportation was the initial step toward returning to Circassia, no matter how long it takes.

> Our grand-grand parents did not untie their bales for the first fifty years with the expectation of return to the homeland sooner or later; I, myself, haven't yet untied the bale in my soul.[985]

The homeland is deemed, in Circassian heritage and culture as basically the mother that is embraced. The mother symbolizes kindness, generosity, sacrifice, and is an inexhaustible source of cordiality, kindness, loyalty, and liberality. Without getting tired, love is unconditional, watching over all worries and troubles. The human being does not dispense his own country easily, which is like his own beloved mother.

The Circassians have always considered that they have a special link with their valuable and precious homeland. It is deemed to be their own mother, being full of love, compassion, honesty, warm-heartedness, self-sacrifice, devotion, fulfilling, and virtuous. Over all, she takes care of all her children, with no exception. A Circassian song mentioned the motherland that is compared with the mother. "We are abandoning our Motherland, but she will never abandon our hearts."[986]

The United Nations INTERNATIONAL COVENANT ON CIVIL AND POLITICAL RIGHTS

PART 1, Article 1:

1. All peoples have the right of self-determination. By virtue of that right they freely determine their political status and freely pursue their economic, social and cultural development.

2. All peoples may, for their own ends, freely dispose of their natural wealth and resources without prejudice to any obligations arising out of international economic co-operation, based upon the principle of mutual benefit, and international law. In no case may a people be deprived of its own means of subsistence.
3. The States Parties to the present Covenant, including those having responsibility for the administration of Non-Self-Governing and Trust Territories, shall promote the realization of the right of self-determination, and shall respect that right, in conformity with the provisions of the Charter of the United Nations.

Art. 1 (2) UN Charter

All peoples have the right to self-determination. By virtue of that right they freely determine their political status and freely pursue their economic, social and cultural development. All peoples have the right to self-determination.[987]

Restoring Indigenous Self-Determination: Theoretical and Practical Approaches

Who are Indigenous Peoples? People who inhabited a land before it was conquered by colonial societies and who consider themselves distinct from the societies currently governing those territories are called Indigenous Peoples. As defined by the United Nations Special Rapporteur to the Sub-Commission on Prevention of Discrimination and Protection of Minorities, Indigenous communities, peoples and nations are . . . "those which having a historical continuity with pre-invasion and pre-colonial societies that developed on their territories, consider themselves distinct from other sectors of societies now prevailing in those territories, or parts of them. They form at present non-dominant sectors of society and are determined to preserve, develop, and transmit to future generations their ancestral territories, and their ethnic identity, as the basis of their continued existence as peoples, in accordance with their own cultural patterns, social institutions and legal systems (Martinez-Cobo, 1984).[988]

- Indigenous peoples all over the world find themselves locked in power struggles with dominant states and transnational actors who resist their claims to land, culture, political recognition and other key factors associated with the idea of national self-determination. In the vast majority of cases, states and transnational corporations see such claims as barriers to the state-building projects that depend heavily on accessing and extracting resources from traditional Indigenous lands. In 2007, the importance of Indigenous self-determination alongside that of nation-states was significantly enhanced when, on September 13, the United Nations General Assembly adopted the Declaration of Indigenous Peoples – suggesting that an important attitudinal shift might now be taking place internationally. Yet, as this volume's contributors suggest, much more work is needed in terms of, on the one hand, what Indigenous self-determination means in theory and, on the other hand, how it is to be achieved in practice.[989]

If Circassians Do Not Seek the Restoration of Their Confiscated Rights, Then Who Would?

On the 19th of January 2012, an interview that was conducted with me was published and titled, If Circassians Do Not Seek the Restoration of Their Confiscated Rights, Then Who would? The following is the detailed interview:

> J.T.: Hello Adel. Thank you for giving me an interview. First I would like to give our readers some information about you, your profession and your activities for the Circassian topics. Can you tell us something about your background?
>
> Adel: Thank you Jinal for allowing me to speak through "CHERKSSIA.NET" which would make me glad to appear on your Website to talk about what wanders in my mind through answering your questions. I was born in Amman, Jordan in a Circassian family of Shapsough father's side and Hatuqwai mother's side. I am married and I have the privilege to be a father and a grandfather. I worked for few years in the Jordanian Armed Forces, and then continued in Aviation profession.
> I started since I was young to search and examine through referring to books and asking the elderly about the whereabouts of the Circassians, what happened to the nation and what caused that dispersion. I started writing, translating,

researching, investigating and posting on the Circassian issues and other topics of the North Caucasus as there is similarity between Circassians' fate and other peoples of the North Caucasus.

There was also an interest to follow activities on the international level which made me attend conferences at Harvard and William Paterson Universities in April, 2008, when I had moderated part of the one day event, and in another part I had given a speech in Arabic in the title of Circassia The Homeland, Where To, and the Circassian Day in the European Parliament in October 2008.

I also participated in March 2010, in the first international conference held in Tbilisi, Georgia, in the title of Hidden Nations, Enduring Crimes: The North Caucasus Between Past and Future, and I gave a speech in the title of Circassia Our Motherland. I had the opportunity to attend in 20, May 2011, the Georgian Parliament's session when the Circassian Genocide was officially recognized by Georgia.

In between, I attended some activities in Jordan, among them was a speech at the main Khasa in Amman in the year 2008, about the activities took place at Harvard University in April 2008, in regard to the Circassian Question, and another one a speech in 20, May 2009, in the title of The Circassian Mobility Between the North Caucasus and Diaspora, which was given in Arabic language but was translated to English language as well.

J.T.: You are active in Jordan. What are the topics, you are working on?

Adel: When time permits, I attend certain activities held at the Khasa, and that is why I have limited activity in that level; but I try as much as possible to follow what is going on, and I would always advise Circassians to give the necessary importance in the direction of self-preservation which is the first law of nature.

J.T.: What can you tell us about the situation of the Circassian Diaspora in Jordan? How are you living there? What are the main targets and outcomes of the Circassian there?

Adel: Circassians in Jordan are well respected as a distinguished community due to their positive and keen roll in the social and daily life of the country, as they participated in the foundation of modern Jordan since the Jordanian Monarch arrived to Jordan from Hejaz, who was welcomed and supported by Circassians and other Jordanians as well. Circassians are open towards others and they are not introverted, they are active in all walks of life and they keep their characteristic and particularity as a recognized minority.

Circassians are well known among Jordanians of their honesty, loyalty, devotion and truthfulness; also there is mutual respect and trust with all factions of the Jordanian society. Being living in Jordan for more than 140 years, Circassians are interactive with the environment that they found themselves in after they had to leave homeland, which the majority of them are engaged to get access to decent living and to educate their children, while asserting the fact that they are proud Circassians, and at the same time to get linked to Motherland, but with difference of depth, methods and priorities.

J.T.: Is there any support from the government towards Circassians?

Adel: According to the Jordanian constitution all citizens are equal under the law, and accordingly Circassians are getting their rights the way others should and they getting the benefits of the Jordanian citizens which is evidenced by allowing Circassians to work in the government and the army, and Circassians had reached the highest official positions such as the positions of Prime Minister, Ministers, Senators, Members of Parliament, Judges, High Ranking Officers in the Armed Forces, Security Department and the Intelligence Department.

- J.T.: On the 20th of May, this year, the Georgian parliament confirmed, that Tsarist Russia conducted crimes against humanity against the Circassian nation – genocide and extreme ethnic cleansing. What do you think about this conclusion? What does it mean for our nation's future?

Adel: Circassians had never given up hope, because hope springs eternal. I had the honor to attend and watch that important event at the Georgian Parliament. I observed the representatives of the Georgian people commenting on the Draft Resolution then the Members of Parliament voting by absolute majority of the attending members for the recognition of the "Circassian Genocide and Ethnic Cleansing" that had been committed against the Circassian nation by the Russian Tsarist Empire in the Nineteenth Century.

The conclusion is unprecedented and it is the most important recognition and/or positive gain that the Circassian nation has ever gotten since the end of the Russian-Circassian (Caucasian) War that had ended in 21, May, 1864, which will open closed doors in order to retrieve Circassians' rights. Truth will prevail.

J.T.: You had been there in Tbilisi. What happened there? What is the attitude, Georgia has for the Circassians and our genocide? Do you think, they just want to make their politics with us and use us for their own?

Adel: True, fortunately I was there to observe an important event that would affect solving out the Circassian Question later on. The Georgian nation as one of the nations of the Caucasus and a member of the United Nations, has shown a sensible attitude and a degree of moral responsibility by uncovering the overwhelming documented proof presented by specialized committees, scientists, historians, academic institutions, university professors and experts from many countries even from Russia itself and had in earlier stages testified to the dedicated Parliament Committees about the scientific findings, which made the committees reach a resolution in order to be submitted to the Parliament for voting, which had occurred and the world was informed that Circassians were oppressed and had been subjected to Genocide and Ethnic Cleansing with all its consequences, based on irrefutable evidence.

All that showed Georgian willingness to recognize the injustice suffered by Circassians, "Example is better than precept". Circassians are not naive to look at facts in a different angle than they actually are. There are mutual interests between peoples and nations, each working to ensure their basic rights to freedom and human dignity.

When Circassians know what they want and consequently they can distinguish between good and evil, they will be able to see and select their path and choose a way that makes them take what is appropriate for them and leave what is wrong and mischievous. The principle of reciprocity should be the dominant. I would comment on suspicions in that regard by saying: None are so blind and so deaf than those who neither want to see nor hear.

There is no way that the perpetrators would get away from the penalty of crimes committed against the Circassian nation and humanity. That is the law and that is a moral obligation towards civilization, that no crime goes unpunished and/or without accountability.

– J.T.: There are many Circassian organizations, like KAF-FED, Kafkasya Forumu, the Circassian head organization of Europe – FDTKV and others, who are against this conclusion or at least try to ignore it. What do you think about this?

Adel: Being exiled away from homeland is no sin, but forgetting homeland is evil. With respect to all associations and organization that called either Circassians or Caucasians, the rule or the most important issue should be how serious and effective these particular parties are in serving the very essential concerns of "Adiga Circassians" and to adopt and implement fateful commitments; but the query arises about what are the principles that those organizations and associations were created for!

Are their objectives sports, culture, social, business, professional, interethnic or national? People tend to talk in subjects of their interest or specialty. The answer would determine the specialty, therefore it is possible to judge, and they should practice what they preach. Real "Adiga Circassians" will be the ones who are supposed to give their opinion, because they are the real victims of hostilities that ended in deportation and exile away from Motherland.

I believe the answer of who is with and who is against the conclusion of Genocide recognition cannot be answered without real scientific method of research, but it is absent from some minds that "still waters run deep"! "Adiga Circassians" who are not under the influence of "Self-Ego" or other Non-Circassian sides should have an organized conference or collateral activities to cover all topics that pertain to Circassians, and accordingly they will come up with the real Circassian decision.

At the end what is useful for Circassians will remain and what is bad will end. Georgia as a good gesture towards the Circassian nation has announced adopting a project for respecting Immortal Memory of Victims of the Circassians' Genocide, Carried out by Russian Empire, on the basis of which the Georgian Government would frame a plan in memory of the victims of Circassians' genocide and the framework will compose a victims' memorial.

Anyone is welcome to recognize the Circassian Genocide even Russia itself.

J.T.: Here in Germany we often heard phrases like:

"If you want to make politics, than go to homeland and make it there, but not here, where you are sitting in your warm and safe place!"

"If we start making politics here, our sisters and brothers in the homeland will suffer from it, so be quiet!"

"We should do nothing, to make Russia angry; otherwise they will stop the ability of contact to homeland!"

"Our xases cannot do politics, because we were established, just to keep our culture; and it is against the laws of Germany, to do political work with such organizations!" (Which is not true)!

Or they are manipulating xase-votings, in order to hamper open political discussions. (Which goes against the democratic laws of Germany)!

From my point of view, the deeper meaning of these sayings and actions are just, to keep us silent and inactive and to hold our new generations stupid in relation to politics. What is your opinion about it? Do you have similar experiences in your Xases there?

Adel: Being away from Motherland for more than 147 years didn't make Circassians forget their precious homeland. If we look at extinct civilizations and nations and we compare them with our nation, we find out that our nation's history is rooted in the human history for more than 6000 years, and the Circassian nation being subjected to the disastrous and grave circumstances of oppression, genocide, expulsion & deportation, oppression and disguise in addition to destroying its cultural heritage did not extinct and still exist but on the contrary, the Circassians still more determined to preserve their distinctive identity and to adhere to its unique culture, values, customs, traditions and ethics, which have distinguished them from others, gives hope because Almighty God helps those who help themselves.

Sometimes "Speech is silver, but silence is gold". Your question has reminded me with an important statement that Mr. Paul Goble had said in an event on Circassians that had taken place in Harvard University in April, 2008, when he said that based on facts remembered from the Soviet era that relate to Polish and citizens of the Baltic Republics at the time, the strength of Circassians lies in the number of Circassians living in exile (90% live outside homeland) which gives them freedom of movement in terms of the dimension of pressure placed on those who live at homeland.

Those who issue rumors and who try to drop morale should know that ill-gotten gains never prosper and bullying policy they are adopting will not succeed. Good citizen will serve own country wherever he/she lives, as long as Motherland is not forgotten, and preserving the national identity is the real compass for exploring and choosing the way that leads to the objectives.

No matter what is done in Diaspora, how that would make our brothers and sisters suffer in homeland, while the occupation had already committed the Genocide, deported 90% of Circassians in difficult and tragic circumstances, resettled settlers from different origins instead of the Circassians who were uprooted from their Motherland, Circassia was totally deleted from the map, and the remaining

10% of Circassians in the North Caucasus were scattered in different autonomous republics and enclaves.

Russia looks at its own interests and if Circassians do not seek the restoration of their confiscated rights, then who would? Russia wants to keep Circassians wherever they are through vague promises and assurances that are with empty contents. How could we whip ourselves and ignore our rights for a mirage of "presumed good faith" of the descendants of those who committed hostilities against the Circassian nation by offending the nation with tight sanctions that affected its existence, present and future.

You don't have to be involved in politics to claim your right of your very existence! Khasas are not asked to proclaim a state, a political existence or to declare war against anyone. They must have a little respect to their ancestors who had perished with the weapons of treachery. Being Circassians does not mean that we are members of an international dance, sport or social club. It is much deeper than that. Culture is part of integrated elements that would form a nation or a people.

Manipulating voting will one day end when kidnapped institutions regain their status and opportunists stop their dirty games of falsification, and a good example about this is what is called now the "Arab Spring" when we see that peoples and nations were ignored for decades, elections fraud had been the common factor, abuse of power was in force, and peoples' rights were not respected; but when the peoples woke up, in matter of no time circumstances have changed completely.

People do not hear from a silent individual, and at the same time "beggars cannot be choosers". When Circassians demand to restore their legitimate rights, they must do it properly and to be addressed to the right side which can be done in a non-violent and peaceful way that reflects the level of civilization that Circassians had reached even during the defensive wars that they had to face for defending their existence as they were pioneers in the enrichment of others' cultures. The people should be united because "union is strength".

J.T.: What is your attitude toward the International Circassian Association? There are some organizations that have no hope about the ICA and are not a part of it? What should they do, in order to promote their politics?

Adel: Unfortunately, Circassians have bad experience with ICA in the form that the association was transferred and kept in Nalchik after it was considered sanctuary and people held high expectations which had meant hope for all Circassians around the world. The organizations that have no hope built on the ICA which are not part of it as you mentioned in your question, are mostly in obvious conflict with its current policies and objectives.

They must individually and collectively meet and revise the Circassian disastrous consequences that had followed the genocide and the exodus of the majority of the nation and to contact the Circassian public to spread and circulate information to explain the task and the way needed to decide on, to be able to build an agenda and a Circassian national plan in order to address the world, starting from the Republics of the Caucasus, to the European Union and even the Russian Federation in a civilized way to request the recognition of the Circassian Genocide and to end up all hostilities against the Circassian nation.

In addition to recognition of the Circassian Genocide, Russia is obligated to present apology, compensation, rehabilitation, and to assure legitimate rights in self-determination on own soil.

J.T.: How do you see the Diaspora in Jordan in the worldwide Circassian political movement? What can you contribute to the whole?

Adel: From my point of view, there is a contact between the Diaspora in Jordan and worldwide Circassian political movement on individual bases, apart from the organic link between Jordan's main Khasa and the ICA, which are in direct contact in accordance with the rules that pertain to their going on contact due to the fact of well-known membership.

It is worth to mention that Circassians of Jordan had demonstrated for the first time ever in front of the Russian

Embassy in Amman, Jordan on the 21st of May 2011, and they held signs that were similar to signs held in Turkey, Europe and USA, such as "NO FOR SOCHI 2014, SOCHI LAND OF THE CIRCASSIAN GENOCIDE".

J.T.: And what about those, living in Europe?

Adel: It is obvious that Circassians living in Europe are experiencing high ceiling of freedom and free movement; but there is no tangible and positive result to their activities in regard to the Circassian issues, most probably due to the multiplicity of the number of associations and organizations, beside their contacts and loyalty to well established ones in other countries of origin especially Turkey.

Unity between associations would contribute in strengthening the Circassian communities and would enhance the awareness of contacting all branches of the European Union especially the European Court of Human Rights, the European Parliament and the European High Court, in addition to Non-Government Organizations.

That would lead to opening new horizons to explain the Circassian Question and all its issues to a majority that had not heard of before. Circassians in Europe and their friends should mobilize their efforts to oppose the 2014 Sochi Winter Olympic Games which are meant to erase the memory of what Sochi had meant when it was the last capital city of Circassia.

The darkest hour is that before dawn.

J.T.: Thank you very much, for sharing your viewpoints with us.

Adel: You're quite welcome.

This interview was performed by Jinal Tamszuqo for Cherkessia.net and has been sent by Adel Bashqawi to be published in "Radio Adiga".[990]

---

[932] http://www.kent.ac.uk/careers/sk/problem-solving-skills.htm
[933] http://www.icrc.org/eng/war-and-law/index.jsp

934 http://plato.stanford.edu/entries/natural-law-ethics/ and http://plato.stanford.edu/entries/rights/
935 http://www.econlib.org/library/Enc/Fascism.html
936 http://sitemaker.umich.edu/rememberingnazism/what_is_nazism_and http://www.nazism.net/about/nazi_ideology/
937 http://www-cs-students.stanford.edu/~cale/cs201/apartheid.hist.html
938 http://www.encyclopedia.com/topic/natural_rights.aspx
939 http://www.jamestown.org/programs/nc/single/?tx_ttnews%5Btt_news%5D=35942&tx_ttnews%5BbackPid%5D=24&cHash=0256175191
940 http://www.jamestown.org/programs/nc/single/?tx_ttnews%5Btt_news%5D=35942&tx_ttnews%5BbackPid%5D=24&cHash=0256175191
941 http://www.jamestown.org/programs/nc/single/?tx_ttnews%5Btt_news%5D=35942&tx_ttnews%5BbackPid%5D=24&cHash=0256175191
942 http://www.jamestown.org/programs/nc/single/?tx_ttnews%5Btt_news%5D=35942&tx_ttnews%5BbackPid%5D=24&cHash=0256175191
943 http://www.jamestown.org/programs/nc/single/?tx_ttnews%5Btt_news%5D=35942&tx_ttnews%5BbackPid%5D=24&cHash=0256175191
944 http://www.jamestown.org/programs/nc/single/?tx_ttnews%5Btt_news%5D=35942&tx_ttnews%5BbackPid%5D=24&cHash=0256175191
945 http://www.jamestown.org/programs/nc/single/?tx_ttnews%5Btt_news%5D=35942&tx_ttnews%5BbackPid%5D=24&cHash=0256175191
946 http://www.jamestown.org/programs/nc/single/?tx_ttnews%5Btt_news%5D=35942&tx_ttnews%5BbackPid%5D=24&cHash=0256175191
947 http://www.jamestown.org/programs/nc/single/?tx_ttnews%5Btt_news%5D=35942&tx_ttnews%5BbackPid%5D=24&cHash=0256175191
948 http://www.jamestown.org/programs/nc/single/?tx_ttnews%5Btt_news%5D=35942&tx_ttnews%5BbackPid%5D=24&cHash=0256175191
949 http://www.jamestown.org/programs/nc/single/?tx_ttnews%5Btt_news%5D=35942&tx_ttnews%5BbackPid%5D=24&cHash=0256175191
950 http://www.jamestown.org/programs/nc/single/?tx_ttnews%5Btt_news%5D=35942&tx_ttnews%5BbackPid%5D=24&cHash=0256175191
951 http://www.jamestown.org/programs/nc/single/?tx_ttnews%5Btt_news%5D=35942&tx_ttnews%5BbackPid%5D=24&cHash=0256175191
952 http://www.jamestown.org/programs/nc/single/?tx_ttnews%5Btt_news%5D=35942&tx_ttnews%5BbackPid%5D=24&cHash=0256175191
953 http://www.css.ethz.ch/en/services/digital-library/articles/article.html/183019/pdf
954 http://www.css.ethz.ch/en/services/digital-library/articles/article.html/183019/pdf
955 http://www.css.ethz.ch/en/services/digital-library/articles/article.html/183019/pdf

956 http://www.css.ethz.ch/en/services/digital-library/articles/article.html/183019/pdf
957 http://www.css.ethz.ch/en/services/digital-library/articles/article.html/183019/pdf
958 http://www.css.ethz.ch/en/services/digital-library/articles/article.html/183019/pdf
959 http://www.theglobalist.com/the-new-russian-empire-modern-slavery-in-russia/#.WF7XrNfS9jM.facebook
960 http://freebeacon.com/national-security/details-of-moscows-deal-with-syria-reveal-extent-of-russian-dominance/
961 http://freebeacon.com/national-security/details-of-moscows-deal-with-syria-reveal-extent-of-russian-dominance/
962 http://freebeacon.com/national-security/details-of-moscows-deal-with-syria-reveal-extent-of-russian-dominance/
963 http://www.encyclopedia.com/topic/Self-Determination.aspx
964 http://www.encyclopedia.com/topic/Self-Determination.aspx
965 http://www.encyclopedia.com/topic/Self-Determination.aspx
966 http://www.encyclopedia.com/topic/Self-Determination.aspx
967 The Sochi Predicament: Contexts, Characteristics and Challenges of the Olympic Winter Games in 2014 (Edited by Bo Petersson and Karina Vamlig)
968 **The New Russian Diaspora: Russian Minorities in the Former Soviet Republics (Edited by Vladimir Shlapentokh, Munir Sendich, and Emil Payin)**
969 The New Russian Diaspora: Russian Minorities in the Former Soviet Republics (Edited by Vladimir Shlapentokh, Munir Sendich, and Emil Payin)
970 http://www.encyclopediaofukraine.com/display.asp?linkpath=pages%5CO%5CC%5COctoberRevolutionof1917.htm
971 http://www.encyclopediaofukraine.com/display.asp?linkpath=pages%5CO%5CC%5COctoberRevolutionof1917.htm
972 The Sochi Predicament: Contexts, Characteristics and Challenges of the Olympic Winter Games in 2014 (Edited by Bo Petersson and Karina Vamlig)
973 http://www.unpo.org/article/4957
974 http://www.ohchr.org/EN/Issues/IPeoples/Pages/Declaration.aspx
975 The Sochi Predicament: Contexts, Characteristics and Challenges of the Olympic Winter Games in 2014 (Edited by Bo Petersson and Karina Vamlig)
976 http://www.un.org/News/Press/docs/2012/gashc4051.doc.htm
977 http://justicefornorthcaucasus.info/?p=1251673688
978 http://justicefornorthcaucasus.info/?p=1251661212

[979] https://www.law.cornell.edu/wex/Customary_international_law
[980] https://www.law.cornell.edu/wex/international_conventions
[981] http://www.ohchr.org/en/professionalinterest/pages/ccpr.aspx
[982] https://www.law.cornell.edu/wex/self_determination_international_law
[983] http://journals.cambridge.org/action/displayAbstract?fromPage=online&aid=10020478&fileId=S0265052515000059
[984] http://www.un.org/en/decolonization/declaration.shtml
[985] https://aheku.net/articles/english/diaspora/1238
[986] The Circassian Genocide (Walter Richmond)
[987] http://www.hrweb.org/legal/cpr.html
[988] http://www1.umn.edu/humanrts/edumat/studyguides/indigenous.html
[989] http://www.e-ir.info/wp-content/uploads/2014/05/Restoring-Indigenous-Self-Determination-E-IR.pdf
[990] http://www.radioadiga.com/ClosedIndex/artikkk.php?ind=3855

10

Circassian Political Activism

Estonian parliament (riigikogu), Tallinn (Photo by: Stephen Colebourne - Flickr) Where the Circassian Diaspora representatives met with Estonian Parliament members on June 4, 2015

The International Circassian Association

The International Circassian Association was founded when the Soviet Union started to collapse. It was the first Circassian entity which managed to connect the Circassian people across international borders. At the same time, its national principles united the Circassians of the diaspora with their compatriots who still live in the homeland, that is, the North Caucasus. The national goals prescribed were unprecedented.

The nascent organization attracted the attention of Circassians all over the world. This is because Circassians seek to achieve their rights and save their homeland. The organization discussed the methods to be followed to restore the natural and respectable status of Circassia as a dignified nation among other nations of the world. Regrettably, the conditions were not appropriate to accomplish those goals then as it was a newly established organization, which was founded to address crucial issues.

Background

The Circassians found themselves in an unenviable position since most them were forced to leave their homeland following the end of the Russian-Circassian War on the 21st of May 1864, and during which the Russian Empire implemented its colonial policies of terrorism, genocide, and ethnic cleansing in all Circassian territories overlooking the Black Sea. They gathered all those who survived and forcibly made the Circassians leave their places of residence either to areas beyond the Kuban River or to the Ottoman Empire. This was for the sake of establishing government-sponsored settlements for resettling Russians and mercenaries who contributed to the military operations, occupation, and destruction of the Circassian homeland.

Circassians have never accepted the language of force and the fait accompli policy and what Russians wanted to impose on them; on the contrary, they kept with them their dignity, freedom, concerns, and aspirations. Being denied of their homeland, they watched the demise of the Romanov family alongside their evil Russian empire, they observed the establishment of the Soviet Union with all its brutal and savage practices including the "iron curtain," then its disintegration 70 years later to witness the emanation of the Russian Federation without any Russian officials that are ready to recognize the plight of the Circassian nation and restoring the Circassians' confiscated rights.

Founding and Functions

From the 1970s, with the start of the disintegration of the Soviet Union in the 1980s, Circassian nationalists, both at homeland and in diaspora, have worked for establishing a common entity aimed to address the Circassian Question. In the North Caucasus, it started in culture and history by establishing "Ashemez," developed to "Khase," then kept a window-open to seek discussing other aspects such as: "native language, the return of the Diaspora, true aspects of the Caucasian Wars, and culture sustainability."[991]

As of direct result of ICA objectives, Circassians took into consideration to "adopt a unified Circassian alphabet and literary language, the usage of native language in education and official matters, the recognition of the Circassian Genocide and Circassians' deportation by the Russian Empire with the assistance of international organizations, obtaining the right of dual citizenship, and establishing an independent Circassian radio, television and a satellite channel service." [992]

The lifespan of the International Circassian Association (ICA), from its establishment until now, shows the following operational phases:

> Founding and establishing the association in addition to approval of the agenda of Circassian national principles & objectives.
>
> Working for a relatively short period of time, in line of duty and the implementation of programs of tasks according to priorities, considering lack of confidentiality due to information leakage especially when addressing significant Circassian national issues.
>
> Recruiting and installing staff with Russian governmental backgrounds contributed to hijacking and then absorption of the association and to dictate its operations by transferring its center and central management from Diaspora to Nalchik, the capital city of the Republic of Kabbardino-Balkaria, where they eventually imposed the reality of controlling the administration to steer all functions through repudiating real Circassian demands.
>
> Since the change that took place in the leadership and management of the International Circassian Association, it embarked on a path parallel and identical to what Russian policies have dictated by refusing to listen to fair Circassian demands, calling for the restoration of Circassian rights.

The Fact of Indifference in the Circassian Situation

The following list leads to a realistic evaluation that is intended to be objective; but are unforgivable improvisational steps that were taken against the Circassians' national interests:

Unclear and vague procedures followed all the associations' proceedings, which affected the association's elections, method of conducting the elections, and appointing members and functionaries.

In September of 2007, the ICA was part of a farce celebration of a so called "450 years of voluntary association with Russia," an event that has never taken place. It was intended "to mislead, misinform, deceive, and cheat the general public, the international community and even the victims themselves!"[993] Some ICA members in the North Caucasus and in Diaspora played the godfather roll of the Russian authorities' festivities linked to the false celebrations. Some travelled to the North Caucasus and some others sent letters of congratulations to both the Russian authorities and the local Circassian republics' leaders.

When the Circassian activists and organizations in the three Circassian republics in the North Caucasus have called for uniting Circassians in a unified Circassian republic, the ICA officials and their supporters have stood against even thinking in this matter.[994]

Even though the ICA has failed to convince its Russian allies to help the Circassians of Syria in any way possible (to exit the Syrian war zone); and on the contrary to this demand, the Russian embassies and consulates in response to the Russian government's instructions, have stopped granting permission to Circassians of Syria to return to their original homeland.

Ironically, the "President of the Union of Veterans of Abkhazia" sent a criticizing letter to the ICA, which stated: "Neither the President of the International Circassian Association, Khauti Sokhrokov, nor the ICA, nor any other Circassian Association are entitled to deny the genocide of the Circassian people." The letter confirmed that Sokhrokov "does not consider that the killing of the Circassian people is a crime." The letter added: "Information was received that he sent a letter to the Parliament of Georgia on his behalf and on behalf of the International Circassian Association requesting from the Georgian Parliament to cancel its decision of recognizing the Circassian Genocide," even though "he is not authorized" to do so.[995]

Referring to the previous paragraph, the former ICA President, Kanshobi Azhakhov, sent a letter to the Circassian Conference held in Tbilisi in March 2010, showing desire of becoming part of consultations, in a way trying to relay a typical sadist message in order to suit ICA policies based on ignoring and contradicting the real interests of the Circassian nation; and trying to impose certain tactics thinking that all Circassians are ruled by those who accepted the duty of implementing of clumsy policies, seemingly in an attempt to steer the conference to the wrong direction.[996]

"Bureaucratic elite" members of the International Circassian Association have joined, whether intentionally or unintentionally, a Russian propaganda campaign against their own nation. They consider any criticism to its way of handling the Circassian issues, as an interference with internal Russian affairs or a so-called "Western conspiracy behind it,"[997] which is contrary to the ICA title and principles. The clear majority of Circassians, both in Diaspora and in homeland, know where the answer of their agony is.

It's worth mentioning that some Circassian contractors who are linked to some Circassian organizations in Turkey, and consequently with ICA, were involved in building some constructions in Sochi in preparation for 2014 Winter Olympic Games.[998]

In December 2013, ICA resident Sokhrokov was planning to travel to London to encounter the Circassian activists' activities to boycott the Sochi Winter Olympics, but eventually he didn't because he couldn't obtain a British visa; but "his intention of helping the Russian government to suppress the Circassian subject in marked contrast to the majority of Circassian activists, who sought to make their plight known to the general public." In a related context, the ICA was in favor of accepting the idea of holding a project called "Circassiada," thought to be a sporting project aimed to make Circassian communities gather in the year 2012, almost two years ahead of 2014 Sochi Olympic Games as a bridge to make Circassians accept the fact of Sochi Olympics, but the widely rejected idea prevented holding such project after an active campaign by the promoters of the project in several locations including Diaspora.[999]

Cooperation with the Russian authorities to invite some Circassian associates from Diaspora and their homeland to visit the site of the Sochi Olympic Games' facilities construction sites before the games took place, ignoring the fact of arresting Circassian activists in their homeland in the North Caucasus;[1000] but it is fair to say that two Circassians from Kfar Kama have left the tour when they knew that the tour organizers' intention was to take the group to Sochi. Some of those associates were also re-invited to attend on the opening ceremonies of 2014 Sochi Winter Olympic Games, and other events connected with the games in a stubborn attempt to challenge the Circassian national sentiment, but in all cases they do not represent the Circassian Diaspora.[1001]

Ignoring the Russian authorities' deliberate indifference about the challenge taken by the Russian authorities when dealing unjustifiably at airports and government centers[1002] with visiting Diaspora Circassians who are members of organizations considered part of the ICA.

- "Russia still treats them as 'blackheads'. Last year, Cihan CANDEMIR – the Chairman of Kaf-Fed which combines 56 associations and represents Turkey at ICA – had been kept waiting in airport and two days later deported. Also, the Deputy Chairman of ICA Orhan OZMEN had met with a refusal for entry on the border. Yet, Cengiz GUL – the delegate of ICA and a businessman – was remanded from Rostov on Don Airport."[1003]

The unpleased majority of Circassian Diaspora organizations with the ICA's performance has created the conditions of change in the ICA. Controversies made KAFFED, the largest Circassian organization in Turkey to think to withdraw from ICA.[1004]

Asker Sokht, the Krasnodar "Circassian Khase," said that in recent years the Krasnodar regional organization "Adyghe Khase" did not participate in the activities of the ICA, and added that ICA should prepare for a meeting which involves different Circassian organizations for a dialogue, but complained about the refusal of the association to agree on such an idea.[1005]

Recent Vacuum of Administrative Structure

Recent events indicate a vacuum in the administration's structure of the ICA, and gives an idea of a one-man-show pattern performed by the higher management of the ICA, particularly the head of the ICA, which has highlighted the issues that were dealt with according to Russian policies' requirements; but a significant part of the bases and lower ranks do not agree on the denial of the Circassian nation's common interests and aspirations.

Adam Bogus, the vice president of the International Circassian Association, "announced that he was suspending his membership in the organization until its next leadership elections, and "'Adyghe Khase' of Adygeya has suspended participation in the International Circassian Association."[1006] Bogus, who is from the Republic of Adygea, also refused to take part in an ICA conference that was held on June 12. According to Bogus, also Khakuz Adam, a member of the ICA executive committee from the Republic of Adygea, has suspended his membership in the ICA. "Both Circassian leaders cited their disagreement with the policies of the organization's president, Khauti Sokhrokov, as the reason for their demarche."[1007]

Delegates of the "Adyge-Khase" of the Republic of Karachaevo-Cherkessia met on the twenty-seventh of June 2015 to discuss "state authorities' inaction in addressing Circassians' problems," and they "decided to convene an extraordinary congress for the Circassian people."[1008]

Circassian identity and unity should be strengthened and fortified instead of the confusion that leads to directing Diaspora associations toward assimilation and stagnation. A wise man had classified men as five types:

The first type serves his homeland by money, the second type by work, the third by his pen, the fourth with his life, and the fifth by silence. All of them would betray their homeland if they fail to do what they must do towards their homeland at the proper time.

Unstable Relations with the International Circassian Association

When the Russian authorities consider the Circassians who live in their homeland, an interest to Russian benefits, they are treated nicely. In case of any doubt or suspicion, a crack-down will be imposed on them. Russia practices courting the diaspora Circassians, to attempt getting closer with them for certain advantages. When matters over turn, these policies can be turned upside down, without the slightest concern of its effect on the relations between the two sides.

Russia has always set up deals, whether directly or indirectly, with people and organizations dedicated to implementing Russian policies. In a related issue, Paul Goble has published FSB Overplays Its Hand in Circassian Affairs, Freezing Out Diaspora but Weakening Moscow's Influence Abroad.

Seemingly, the game had a dimension of intelligence: "That is especially the case with the FSB's involvement with groups involving the Circassian nation, one numbering more than a half a million in the North Caucasus and more than five million in the countries of the Middle East and one that has challenged Moscow over the 1864 genocide and the right of Circassians from Syria to return to their historical homeland."[1009]

During the past years, and after the disintegration of the Soviet Union, the Circassian associations were the right place for polarization. They attracted and passed different policies in multiple directions and magnitudes: "This complex game is described by Inal Kardnov on the Caucasus Times portal yesterday (caucasustimes.com/article.asp?id=21535). Because of FSB actions, he says, Nalchik, the capital of Kabardino-Balkaria has ceased to be the heart of the international Circassian movement and the International Circassian Association (ICA) near dissolution."[1010]

Regrettably, the Russian authority's airport entry and exit control in the Circassian part of the North Caucasus moved towards stepping on the toes of the president of one of the most prominent Circassian associations in the Turkish diaspora: "Last month, KAFFED, the Federation of Turkish Circassians, decided to withdraw from the ICA after Russian border guards deported Yashar Aslankay, the vice president of the ICA and the president of KAFFED, and prohibited him from entering the Russian Federation until 2020."[1011]

Goble concluded that a gap has been established between Circassians and the International Circassian Association while it will not be corrected in the short term. "This complex game is described by Inal Kardnov on the Caucasus Times portal yesterday (caucasustimes.com/article.asp?id=21535). Because of FSB actions, he says, Nalchik, the capital of Kabardino-Balkaria has ceased to be the heart of the international Circassian movement and the International Circassian Association (ICA) near dissolution."[1012]

Judicial Proceedings to Forbid Dealing with Political Issues

Very well-known parties have launched a feverish campaign using individuals who were not the real Circassian founders of the International Circassian Association and other national establishments, for the purpose of changing the fundamentals of operations and activities.

Those who do not like to hear the voice of reason try also to believe possessing the absolute truth in order to crack down on the national ranks both in the Circassian homeland and diaspora. Circassians have always proven to maintain a continuous and developing contact between parts of the widely extended and dispersed geopolitical and social Circassian communities, whether in their homeland or in diaspora.

> Adyga Khase activists had been facing oppressions like sacking from job and school, financial suppression, harming relatives, arrogation of properties and threatening with a view to block Adyga Khase.[1013]

People who have connections with the Russian authorities have used the carrot and stick technique to participate in gagging freedom of opinion and expression, in addition to introducing indoctrination as a way of life to deal with public opinion. The practice of misinformation, deceptive information, suppression of public opinion, and civil rights has an impact on the objective reality and is an insult of human values.

> In 1999, the Minister of Justice of Kabardino-Balkaria Republic has taken judicial proceedings in order to forbid Adyga Khase from dealing with political issues. The Court has rejected this appeal. Opposition of Adyga Khase (the founder member) executives to the efforts in order to make Valerie KOKOV the Chairman of ICA which is the highest representative body of Circassians internationally was the straw that broke the camel's back.

The article continued.

> At this, they attempted to 'buy' the executives of Adyga Khase. According to Russian media, employment at the Ministry of Sports and Tourism was offered to the members of the executive board of Adyga Khase in return of the ruler

ship of Adyga Khase. Despite the oppressions, Adyga Khase executives have stood firm."[1014]

An ICA member called "veteran," made a statement to Radio Free Europe/Radio Liberty and said,

> The statutes of Republics in the Caucasus ought to be eliminated and the peoples should confine themselves with making use of only cultural rights. This phrase proves how He's loyal to Russian imperialism.

Domestication of the ICA as an independent Circassian entity has been unfortunately activated, by people who were not of the founders of the association and its basic principles have diverted from its original course of defending the Circassian nation and the restoration of its legitimate rights, which ended up to, "the operations of 'nationalizing' NGOs in Russian Federation have begun with ICA and Adyga Khase operations in 2000. Communist surplus Nomenclature has guaranteed their posts by the operations in Adyga Khase and ICA, and they have given the message below to 'iron hand' V. PUTIN: 'The NGOs both in the Diaspora and the Caucasus are under 'control' ..!"

It's described:

> ICA that could not perform crucial task has become thoroughly dysfunctional, discursive and flippant organization. For instance, according to the work program dated with 17.08.2003, ICA does not deal with political activities; "Today, it's frankly predicated that ICA does not take place in political activities . . . If a member of ICA in any part of the world wants to enter politics, this ICA member should finish with his/her membership to ICA and establish a political party and then join political struggle.'[1015]

Activities and Positive Efforts

Seemingly, the Circassians have gotten to the point of what Mahatma Gandhi said, "You must be the change you want to see in the world,"[1016] and started taking the initiative in recent years to get their long-lasting "frozen dilemma" solved by enabling the demands and fair claims raised by the Circassians and reach the Russian authorities and the international arena by explaining and elaborating on the suffering that resulted from evil elements and factors that impacted the Circassians both in their motherland and diaspora that is as large and as far as more than forty countries in the world.

The cold response towards the initiative of sending letters to the Russian president and to other Russian officials, including the Russian state duma, did not lower their morals nor discourage them from sending an important letter to the European Parliament, which was sent by Adygeyan (Circassian) public organizations of Russia, Turkey, Israel, Jordan, Syria, USA, Belgium, Canada, and Germany to the president of the European Parliament Mr. Joseph Borrell Fontelles, calling for recognition of the genocide that took place against the Adygeyan (Circassian) people during and after the Russian-Caucasian War of the eighteenth and nineteenth centuries.

The letter received signatures from twenty Circassian organizations. In addition, a compact disc with archival documents, mostly written during that period of time by Russian imperial war commanders and generals, was enclosed with the letter. The archival documents included in the compact disc were sent as well. They were kept in Russian, just as they are in the Russian archives. A group of diaspora Circassians have translated the documents to English, Arabic, and a part of them to Turkish.

The Circassians do not utilize any instigation campaigns against anyone in any way. Quite the contrary, they tend to criticize and analyze the careless colonial attitude and mentality that was adopted against them due to selfish and unilateral policies. This type of imperial behavior has no room in the sensible civilized world.

Circassia, like any other small nation of Eastern Europe and elsewhere, is considered a part of the Unrepresented Nations and Peoples Organization (UNPO), and its representatives took part and participated in meetings and conferences, which some of them are listed in the following:

> Resolution on the Situation of the Circassian Nation, issued by the UNPO General Assembly dated July 15–19, 1997, which called for
>
> > * Russia and the international community to acknowledge the genocide of the Circassian Nation that took place in the nineteenth century and to grant the Circassian people status of an exile nation;
> > * Russia to grant the Circassian people dual citizenship, both that of Russia and their respective countries; and
> > * Russia to ensure the possibility of the Circassian people to return to their native land.[1017]

UNPO Sixth General Assembly in Tallinn, Estonia: February 14–18, 2001[1018]

As an example of knowing the blunt Russian official policies against the aspirations and hopes of the Circassian people, made Russia sense that

the "Circassian Congress" is a truly dangerous organization since its stated goal is the recognition of the genocide of the Circassians by the Russian state. The "Congress" has chapters in twenty countries around the globe, with those located in Russia subject to harassment by the authorities. The leader of the Cherkessk chapter, Beslan Makhov, told this author that he is regularly called in for questioning by the local office of the FSB and that he has even been forced to cease the publication of a free youth newspaper.[1019]

"We only published archival documents about the war between Circassia and Russia", Makhov explains, "but that was enough to have our newspaper labeled as 'extremist' by the FSB and shut down."[1020]

The Writer and Historian from St. Petersburg

The Russian writer and historian from St. Petersburg Jacov Gordin arrived at Maykop on December 4, 2006, according to the Russian REGNUM news agency and said, "Russian society knows too little about Circassians' tragedy." He was described as a specialist in the Caucasus affairs and the Circassian matter in particular.

He was interviewed by "IA REGNUM" news agency's correspondent and was asked to explain the purpose of his visit. [1021]

It was presumed that Gordin's visit would be used for "gathering of materials for his new book about Caucasus. However, as others argue, if to consider some circumstances it would be possible to assume that the received information can be used by the visitor for some other needs."[1022]

Gordin, as a public figure, considered the person from St. Petersburg with "outlook that almost completely corresponds to Putin's one" and thought that his "gathering of materials for his new book about Caucasus. However, as others argue, if to consider some circumstances it would be possible to assume that the received information can be used by the visitor for some other needs."[1023]

This subject was concluded with a remarkable statement: "Gordin represents his position as a search of historical correctness and objectivity. It is reached with division of the Russian expansion in 'the actions natural and necessary, inherent in any developing state', and 'the imperial foolishness', pushed the empire to the actions excessive and in the long term not only unnecessary, but dangerous for the country."[1024]

The question arises to the reason for committing genocide against all Circassians alike, in addition to the forced deportation of most Circassians, which furthermore led to hundreds of thousands of Circassians to perish during the inhumane war. Why is the name of Circassia eliminated from all Russian maps, and why did all those geopolitical and demographic changes take place in Circassia?

If the deportation process was a friendly initiative and gesture towards the Circassians from their Russian associates (who claimed that the Circassians had voluntarily associated their nation and fate with them), then why were most Circassians deported?

Acts of Protest

The measures imposed by Russian authorities drove those despairing people (when they realized they're heading into the unknown) into taking fatal decisions; they tend to consider that desperate cases require desperate remedies. When average citizens are treated badly and recklessly, their logical expectation is to feel unsafe and unsecured. The following, include, but are not limited to, some Circassian protests in different locations of Diaspora and in their homeland.

As a result of tough circumstances in their homeland, some of the desperate citizens tend to hurt themselves to the extent of committing suicide to protest the violations of the "Law Enforcement Agencies" against them and against their existence, such as the Kabardino-Balakaria resident who tried to commit suicide by burning himself in the "Lobnoe Mesto" (Ancient Execution Place) in the Red Square in Moscow, "having explained the attempt by his discontent with the work of law enforcement agents at investigating his brother's murder."[1025]

Another occurrence: "Soslan Zhigunov, a witness to the death of Murat Borlakov, a detained resident of Karachay-Cherkessia in the Ust-Djeguta ROVD (District Interior Division), who was questioned at the trial in the case against five policemen, has changed his testimony given at the preliminary investigation stage. Advocate Merzakulov, who represents his interests, claimed pressure on his client."[1026]

"An advocate jumped out of the window of a Cherkessk hospital, in an apparent suicide attempt," and the advocate's father said, "We will appeal to all authorities. Now, we have a weekend, and this makes it difficult to act. We will investigate how a perfectly healthy man suddenly wanted to jump out of a hospital window and why that happened."[1027]

On March 17, 2008, in the Province of Krasnodar, "Anatoli Malyshev, resident of Tuapse, tried to burn himself in protest against his family eviction from the dormitory."[1028]

A picket was held in Adygeya's capital city of Maykop on the 5th of July, 2007 against holding the "2014 Winter Olympic Games" in Sochi. With their slogans: 'No to the mendacious Olympic propaganda!', 'The woods to the oligarchs, and tree stumps to descendants?' and 'No to the privatization of the woods!', public organizations and parties, including the Union of Slavs of Adygeya, the republican branch of the Communist Party of the Russian Federation and others, expressed their discontent with the decision of the International Olympic Committee [to make Sochi host of the 2014 Olympics] which came despite the fact that public environmental organizations had for a long time been reporting to the International Olympic Committee serious environmental threats that the holding of the Olympic Games in Sochi carries."[1029]

In October, 2007, Circassians held two demonstrations in New York City, one "in front of the Russian Consulate" and the second one "in front of the United Nations building" ... "Both demonstrations showed their remarkable enthusiastic feelings about the planned Sochi winter Olympic Games of the year 2014, which are going to be held on the cemeteries that contain the bones and the remains of those who perished while defending their Homeland against Russian Tsarists' invaders who terrorized, killed, displaced, deported and exiled the entire brave Circassian Nation."[1030]

Also, "Circassians in Turkey held a demonstration in Istanbul which came at the same date while holding the same protest demands and signs."[1031]

The demonstrations that took place in Circassian communities' reflected remarkable enthusiastic feelings about the planned 2014 Sochi Winter Olympic Games, which were held on the remains of those who perished while defending their precious homeland against Russian Tsarists' invaders who terrorized, killed, displaced, deported, and exiled the entire brave Circassian Nation. Genocide and the claims of voluntary association were condemned and denounced.

On May 21, 2014, "Descendants of the Circassian community which was sent into exile after Russia defeated an army of Caucasian peoples, gathered in Istanbul at an event organized by Federation of Circassian Associations, holding banners and 'Circassian' flags. They chanted slogans 'Circassia will not be Russian territory,' 'Russia will pay for genocide' and held torches as they marched.'"[1032]

How can the so-called Russian Federation consider itself as such, while it differentiates in its treatment between Russian citizens, and those who are regarded in Moscow as people of the Caucasus or Circassians. "In the early morning of December 6, 2010, a group of young Russian men got into a fight with a few young men from the Caucasus. During the clash Yegor Sviridov, a Russian, was shot and killed. An investigation identified Aslan Cherkesov, a twenty-six-year-old Circassian, as the trigger man. A drunken brawl ending in a homicide was really nothing unusual in Moscow and shouldn't have attracted any particular attention, but on December 11 several thousand protesters marched from the site of the shooting to Manezh Square across from the Kremlin, shouting nationalist slogans and making Nazi salutes."[1033]

How could the two highest ranking officials of the so-called federation take sides? How could they stand alongside one of the parties against the other, all while the court has yet to decide who is responsible for the murder?

Eventually it consequently affected the course of the investigation and its outcome, as well as it imposed influence on the judges and court. The trial results had been affected because of the official prejudice against the defendant.

> The riot was the result of this propaganda campaign. Afterward, the "football clubs" promised more violence if the government didn't crack down on Caucasians in Moscow. Russian president (Prime Minister now) Dmitry Medvedev condemned the nationalists' actions and tried to patch up the quickly deteriorating relations between ethnic Russians and Caucasians. Prime Minister (president now) Vladimir Putin, on the other hand, visited Sviridov's grave and placed a bouquet of flowers there, an act that was widely viewed as a defense of the ultranationalist.[1034]

It is quite clear that Circassians and other nations ruled by Russia are not treated the way the so-described ethnic Russians are treated. Circassians are dealt with according to this example, like third-class citizens, according to the racial segregation that is conducted by the current Russian state, and its officials.

> The subsequent investigation was conducted like a celebrity trial. Politicians and journalists alike turned Sviridov into a martyr, murdered in cold blood by Circassian

criminal—most conveniently named Cherkesov—who had come to Moscow to terrorize the citizens there. The Kabardino-Balkaria Human Rights Center issued a statement on December 15 that summarized the Circassian perception of the event:

> We cannot but be disturbed and indignant at the anti-Caucasian hysteria fomented by some Russian media outlets and certain politicians in connection with the murder of Yegor Sviridov and the events on Manege Square. Over the past two years we have registered at least five cases of murder of people from our republic in large Russian cities for reasons of racial and ethnic hatred. No significant publications on any of these cases have appeared in the Russian press. In none of these cases has an objective investigation been conducted or charges been brought against the murderers.[1035]

Positive Freedom Development for Nations and Individuals

Awareness should be increased and intensified, which will be attained through relaying the information of the truth of what had happened in Circassia and what the results were, which had led to the forced exile of most Circassians. In that regard, a recent study published established that the Circassians are living in 52 countries of the world today.

Independent media is essential to be found, especially to have an active news agency. Satellite radio and television, websites, and even social media outlets that deal with written and published scripts, audio, and video should be established, which must be run by those who are devoted to the Circassian Question.

Transparent, fair, and dependable information that reflects reality should be posted, published, and televised to keep informing all those who are interested to know and understand whatever pertains to Circassia and the Circassians.

The establishment of a unified national center for research and studies is a necessity to gather, collect, and publish all available information from all the different sources available to avail the necessary references. This center should produce in print and digital sources.

The Circassian culture, in all its derivatives, should be preserved and proper archiving should be established. The attention should be paid to the Adyghe language in all its dialects and components, in addition to adopting interested and professional scholars and researchers to communicate and cross-talk with all the Circassian communities, to develop plans and programs to revive and teach the language. There should also be study and research conducted on the alphabet, for the potential of using a Latin alphabet, if it is seen appropriate.

Irina Bokova, UNESCO Director General has said on the occasion of "International Mother Language Day," which falls on February 21, "Mother languages in a multilingual approach are essential components of quality education, which is itself the foundation for empowering women and men and their societies."[1036] The late Nelson Mandela has said, "The rights of every citizen to his or her language, culture and religion must also be guaranteed."[1037]

The examples of Kosovo and East Timor can be considered symbolic for the North Caucasus, where Circassia should not be excluded, in the sense of allowing the different nations to practice the right of self-determination and to choose their way of life and government. Murat Berzegov, the Circassian Congress leader, said, "In our opinion, the authorities wrongly try to solve the problems of Caucasus in break, forgetting that Caucasus is the one organism." He added, "It is impossible to solve, for example, the Abkhazian question separately from the Circassian one."[1038]

A Statement Issued by the ICC

The International Circassian Council has issued a statement titled, "The Circassians' Sacred Duty," dated June 2, 2014, which addressed certain issues that exist in Circassian communities.

The statement reminded that "defending dignity, truth and honor is always the duty of those highly dignified and honorable people, and those who don't know the meaning of dignity, do not appreciate freedom, self-respect and national pride. As dignity is one of the most important elements of the Circassian personality, politeness is a sign of dignity and respect. Albert Einstein said: 'If I were to remain silent, I'd be guilty of complicity.'"[1039]

It recounted different sides concerning the troubles and difficulties faced, while it stressed on the consequences of the Russian-Circassian War. It considered, "Sharing and raising the Circassian concerns is not limited to and/or manipulated by certain individuals, groups, Diaspora communities or homeland communities!" The odds are reminded as: "Those who want to stay in a deep dormant, would apply to them what Norman Peale has said: 'Don't take tomorrow to bed with you!'"[1040]

As per the statement, the momentum suggested, "the only allowed move should have only one direction to proceed, which makes Circassians exert their efforts to end all the negative consequences of the tragedies of their catastrophic circumstances with a solid Circassian framework that depends on confirming the Circassian identity within a self-denial and transparent national agenda that precludes accepting any ambitious 'proxy', and type of propaganda."[1041]

A firm statement is added: "Navigation and steering against the Circassian interests is not acceptable in any way, and the insistence of anyone to continue on scattering and puffing aggressive and poisonous propaganda, lies and rumors here or there will not be tolerated." Then pointed at those people opposing restoring the Circassian rights, "who are maintaining the same imperial interests and policies of denial, intimidation, neglect, assimilation, harassment, and maintaining the status quo."[1042]

A conclusion is offered: "The spontaneous commemoration of the end of the Russian-Circassian war on the 21st of May of every year, which reminds of the past to manage the present and plan for the future, is an obligation that the majority of Circassians will not stop doing whether Russia and its allies like it or not. Circassians knew after experience that: 'If You Want Something Done Right, Do it yourself.'"[1043]

Condemnation of the Boris Nemtsov Assassination

On February 28, 2015, a statement was issued on behalf of the Circassians, to condemn the murder of Russian opposition leader, Boris Nemtsov. The statement has shown the commitment to sanctity of human life and their rejection to violence to achieve political expediency purposes. The statement assured their rejection to repressive tactics and their respect to international law, in addition to human rights, whatever race, origin, or religion.[1044]

The following is the statement which was signed by me and Iyad Youghar, President of the International Circassian Council:

> The International Circassian Council (ICC) is shocked and saddened, and strongly condemns the cold-blooded murder of the leading Russian opposition politician Boris Nemtsov. The murder occurred on Bolshoy Kamenny Bridge near the Kremlin in central Moscow. The deceased was an economic reformer while governor of one of Russia's biggest cities, Nizhny Novgorod, and a former Deputy Prime Minister under the late President Boris Yeltsin in the 1990s, also a sharp critic of the present situation in Russia. While walking on the sidewalk, Mr. Boris Nemtsov, was shot four times in

the back and faced inevitable tragic death on the evening of the 27th of February, said in a recent interview that he feared he would be killed because of his opposition to the war in Ukraine.

As it appears that the horrible crime came to confuse the scene in the ranks of the Russian opposition, the International Circassian Council and its associates and supporters both at homeland and in Diaspora, offer their sincere condolences and sympathies to Mr. Nemtsov's wife, his four children, family, friends and colleagues, wishing that the perpetrators will be brought to justice, appropriate punishment will be implemented, democratic procedures and values will be followed and the main task will remain accomplishing peaceful and civilized ways and means throughout the civil society.

Late Mr. Nemtsov always believed Russia could change from the inside and without violence, he had spoken few hours before the crime on Ekho Moskvy Radio calling on Muscovites to attend an opposition march, which was planned to take place on Sunday, and seems that the murder took place in anticipation to prevent people from expressing public opinion freely in a peaceful and democratic way. He was a man of peace as he died just before a Moscow march against the war in Ukraine which he was actively promoting.

This brutal heinous murder should attract the attention to human sufferings endured by many peoples and nations ruled directly from Moscow, where the Circassian nation is one of them, unable to attain their confiscated rights and looking forward to be treated according to proper human rights values, laws and norms. It is a sad episode that reminds of the tragedies of hundreds of journalists, lawyers, intellectuals, politicians and human rights activists such as Anna Politkovskaya, Anastasiya Baburova, Natalya Estemirova, Akhmednabi Akhmednabiyev, and all victims who perished for their lofty principles they had embraced, while in most times the real perpetrators where not caught and/or punished.

The International Circassian Council joins the voices of democratic and peace-loving activists, forces and entities for calling upon the Russian society to act within the voice of reason, hoping that the international community, will intervene to enhance the efforts of respecting the human life, which should be taken in account against murder, oppression and the crimes still going on, both in the center or in the regions, whether against individuals, people's or nations.[1045]

Nations of Similar Destiny

Friendly people and nations did not hesitate to help the Circassians and to lend them a helping hand in the midst of the ominous crisis that they had to face. Both at the individual and national level, that help included assisting them before, during and after deportation. "The Poles bore the cruelty of their oppressors until 1830; when they could not bear it no longer, they revolted.

The Russians, however, did not hesitate to use the severest disciplinary measures against the mutineers and rebels. The result of that insurrection was that many Poles had to flee, leaving behind their possessions and effects, and take refuge in other countries that would shelter and protect them from the cruelty of their pursuers."[1046]

Oppressed peoples and nations react similarly to tyranny and authoritarianism. They don't stand being exposed to the occupation and arrogance of imperialism and colonialism. When the voice of reason is lost, the authorities deal with these people with a sense of superiority, brutality, humiliation, and disrespect. These very authorities tend to offend the occupied and oppressed peoples to implement inadequate, short-sighted, and foolish policies.

> Many of those who could not flee were exiled by the Russian government to the various parts of Russia, including Caucasia, where their number rose in time to 30,000 persons. That number comprised officers, soldiers, politicians, rebels, and others. In their exile they were treated most harshly, a fact which caused many of them to desert from the Russian lines and camps to the Circassian side in order to join the ranks of their friends in fighting their mutual enemy, the Russians.[1047]

There are dozens of these friendly people, whether in the Caucasus or other afflicted nations as a result of the Russian occupation or other regional and international countries. "The Poles, who had been for a long time watching the Caucasians' fight with the Russians, wished them success. We are sure that their intentions were good and their sympathetic feelings undoubtedly resulted from the pains and bleeding wounds they had suffered under the torture of

Russian rule. We also believe that their feelings are noble and genuine and as such, they deserve our extreme appreciation and admiration."[1048]

An Event in Polonezköy to Articulate the Circassian Question

On the anniversary of the Independence of Poland, the Patriots of Circassia Group in Turkey proposed an initiative to call for the gathering of Circassians in Polonezköy, east of Istanbul. They intended to memorize the Polish Independence, which was commemorated on November 11, 2014. Both the Poles and Circassians were honored.

That was at a time when Poland was occupied by the Russian Empire. The Russian army was recruiting Polish people in the ranks of the units, fighting in the Caucasus. Many of those polish soldiers were sent to the fronts in Circassia during the Russian-Circassian War. Many of them preferred to runaway via the Caucasus to the Ottoman Empire. While some of them preferred to switch to the Circassian side, knowing that the Circassians were absolutely fighting the invading forces, defending their homeland, and their freedom.

Background of Polonezköy

"Polonezköy or Adampol, is a small village east of Istanbul, and it is within the boundaries of the Beykoz district. "The history of the Polish village Adampol - Polonezköy begun in the year 1842 when duke Adam Czartoryski founded a settlement for Polish immigrants to Turkey.

Today's Polonezköy, "was founded by Adam Czartoryski in 1842. He was the chairman of National Uprising Government and the leader of a political emigration party. Because of the name of the founder that place was named Adam-koj, which means "Village of Adam" (abbreviation form Adampol)." [1049]

Polonia Ottomanica mentioned: "In the early 1830s Prince Adam Czartoryski, a key patron of the Wielka Emigracja (Great Emigration) of polish intelligentsia and nationalists from the defunct Polish-Lithuanian Commonwealth to the cultural and political centers of Paris, London, and Istanbul, sent the first Polish agents to meet with Circassian leaders in their alpine redoubts in the north Caucasus."[1050]

In an article titled Polish-Circassian cooperation against Russia in the 19th century, dated March 18, 2014, it stated: "Although Poles and members of the Circassian diaspora may seem as though they have little in common today, it was not always so. Perhaps one of the most unusual partnerships of the 19th century was born of the intense collaborative efforts of Poles and Circassians to free themselves from Russian domination."[1051]

It continued that the Poles, "In their continued fight for national independence following the partition and dissolution of the Polish-Lithuanian Commonwealth at the end of the 18th century by Russia, Prussia, and Austria, Polish nationalists perceived that they were quite alone amongst the various minority populations of the Romanov Empire in their efforts to stage large-scale uprisings against Russian rule. In the early 1830s, however, Polish insurrectionists recognized that they shared common goals with the Circassian population of the Caucasus, which was in the throes of a prolonged armed resistance against Romanov expansion."[1052]

The article concluded: "The overall effect that the Polish émigré community had on the Circassians' struggle for survival may not have been monumental in scope, but the personal sacrifice of combatants and the political influence wielded by their Polish patrons abroad provided new lines of communication through which Circassians could forge relationships with the governments of the Western Powers. The result of these efforts was to keep the 'Polish Question' alive amongst the Great Powers of Europe; the Circassians were not as fortunate."[1053]

Press Release

A press release was read in front of those who attended the event, which stated:

> Just as the Berlin Wall literally moved several hundred kilometers to the east since it collapsed 25 years ago, situation on the ground deteriorated for Circassians too.
> Winter Olympics in 2014 were held in Sochi, the ancestral land of Circassians, despite a global campaign to remove it, Syrian Circassians caught in the civil war were not allowed to return to their homeland, and Moscow ignored demands to recognize Circassian Genocide, to name just a few grievances.
> All Russian President Vladimir Putin had to say was that Circassians were an "atavism of the Cold War."
> Circassian Question dating back to 1864 was abruptly reduced to the Cold War in Mr. Putin's words.
> Georgia was the first nation to recognize Circassian Genocide in 2011.
> Then we appealed to brotherly Ukraine hoping it would be next.

On November 11, on her national day, we formally requested Poland to recognize the Circassian Genocide.

Circassian and Polish peoples have collaborated on several occasions in history.

First, several thousand Polish volunteers have fought with Circassians in the nineteenth century struggle for freedom against advancing Russian forces.

Second, following Bolshevik Revolution Pilsudski's Poland sponsored Prome the movement bringing together non-Russian emigres in 1920's and 1930's.

Third, Poland has served as a bridge between former Communist countries and the West since 1989.

Under the Polish motto of "za nasza i wasza wolnosc" (for your and our freedom) Circassians and Poles share a common vision of a Europe whole, free and at peace.

Recognition of the Circassian Genocide is the first step to a peaceful resolution of the Circassian Question.

Appeal to Poland will be the final act in 2014, the 150th anniversary of the Circassian Genocide.

So let us hail the world from the symbolic venue of Adampol, named after late Prince Adam Czartoryski who was a friend of the Circassian people:

ZA NASZA I WASZA WOLNOSC!
FOR YOUR AND OUR FREEDOM!
RECOGNIZE THE CIRCASSIAN GENOCIDE!
"Never Again" Circassian Initiative[1054]

Delivering a Speech

I was one of the participants, and I delivered the following speech:

> Respected Ladies and Gentlemen
> On the occasion of the Polish Independence which was commemorated on the 11th of November, I am proud and honored to be among my Circassian colleagues to pray for our deceased ancestors, and to greet our brothers and sisters, the inhabitants of Polonezköy who are the descendants of the Polish heroes who exerted their blessed efforts to help their brethren Circassians during their legitimate struggle

against Tsarist Russian imperial invasion against the country of Circassia.

The letter that was sent to the Polish leadership, which was an initiative taken by the "Patriots of Circassia", and was signed by 52 Circassians from 10 different countries that represent more than 50 countries that the Circassian Diaspora is located at.

The noble idea often needs to be sensed, and thats exactly what those great people did when they decided to stand on the side of right, justice and distinguished human values fighting with their fellow Circassians in their ordeal, who fought a defensive war for 101 years, against savage and criminal military armies, which eventually implemented the plans of committing Destruction that lead to Genocide, Ethnic Cleansing and Deportation of the entire Circassian nation. Hopes, aspirations and faith of the entire human race are eternal and "truth will prevail". Those facts remind us of what Mahatma Gandhi had once said: "Truth never damages a cause that is just."

It's worth mentioning though that just after the Sochi Olympics, the Russian president in a rare comment on the subject, he criticized the West being trying to exploit the Circassian Question to discredit or harm Russia! It's good that eventually a Russian high ranking official (the Russian president in this exclusive case) has confirmed that there is such a problem that is not yet been solved, and Russia in obliged to solve it out.

Poland and other victims of Russian oppression and colonialism can create cooperation and coordination between all concerned and across the civilized world to assist circassians by recognizing the circassian ethnic cleansing and genocide in order to restore legitimate rights in accordance with the International Law and the United Nations Charters.

Who said that Circassians got no memory? On the contrary, Circassians remember "the good, the bad and the ugly"; that means: (Read my lips)... They will never forget any of them! The Circassians must thank and highly value the true, courageous, sincere, and unforgettable action taken by the Parliament of the Caucasian Republic of Georgia for recognizing the genocide and ethnic cleansing inflicted on the Circassian nation. Thanks to the former Georgian President

Mikhail Saakashvili's speech in the General Assembly of the United Nation in September, 2013, when he mentioned the genocide: (That's why the Georgian Parliament has recognized [in May, 2011] genocide of Circassian people – one of the most unknown and tragic pages of history of the world, when the whole nation was wiped out because their land was needed by the Russian Empire.)!

Nevertheless, recent and still going on developments in Southeastern Ukraine, which followed annexing the Crimea in a way that recalls the Tsarist Russian Empires' way of annexation of Circassia, Chechnya and other nations whether in the North Caucasus or elsewhere.

As of our aim is to protect the Circassian nation through legal, nonviolent and civilized ways and means, and looking forward to protect the Circassians' identity, language, culture and homeland, besides enjoying their rights of being a respected indigenous nation, I call on all Circassians whether at homeland or at the Diaspora to unite for these sacred purposes.

God Bless you all.

Long Live Circassia, Long Live Poland, and Long Live Freedom and Independence.[1055]

Armenian-Circassian Synergy

An article titled "Armenian-Circassian Synergy," dated February 3, 2016, by Garegin Nalbandian from Geopolitical TV elaborated on two indigenous nations: "The synergy between the Armenians and the Circassians has always been present since ancient times. Many historians of Armenian and non-Armenian descend have written about it in their works."[1056]

A briefing about Russia from 1721 onward indicated that the tips Russian rulers got from certain advisers and generals caused them to continue their predecessors' adventures. They eventually "conquered Crimea, Circassia and the rest of the Caucasus, partitioned the Polish-Lithuanian Commonwealth, and started to colonize Alaska."[1057]

The author introduced the situation realistically.

> Russia's greatness; unfortunately, was built on the suffering of the nations who were conquered by the Russians. Specifically, what Russians called it a war, was in

reality an ethnic cleansing, a genocide. The term genocide was developed much later to describe the Holocaust. The Circassian Genocide took place during the 1763–1864. For 101 years, the Russians continued the ethnic cleansing against the Circassians by killing and displacing millions of Circassians.[1058]

The article mentioned that the Russian plan necessitated categorically changing the demographic map of its victim nations; a mass transfer of population from different peoples to live in places of other peoples to apply their imperial goals.

> Thus, the Russian Empire took the Armenians and Udins from the Baku Gubernia and resettled them in Circassian lands. Decades later Russia filled the Baku Gubernia with Tatars. In 1905, there were clashes between the Turkic speaking invaders and the native Christians (Armenians and Udins) of the Baku Gubernia. The relationship of the Armenians and the Circassians recorded an adverse turn when the Circassians, who found refuge in the Ottoman Empire, were used by the Ottomans in the Balkans and in the Armenian Highlands to kill Christians, who were portrayed by the Ottomans as Russia's allies.

Nalbandian showed approaches between the Circassians and Armenians, and links between their communities, even in their diasporas.

> Despite the fact that both the Russians and the Turks used the Armenians and the Circassians against each other, both nations lived as neighbors in many communities in Iraq, Syria, Jordan, and Lebanon. Presently 1.5 million Armenians live in Circassian lands and millions of Circassians live in Western Armenia, and both nations maintain a great relationship living in the same communities. Naturally, the synergy between the Armenians and the Circassians is developing from past to present in order to prepare both nations for all present and future challenges and opportunities.

The author mentioned,

On January 28, 2016, a representative of the Geopolitical Club's Circassian Desk, Adel Bashqawi, was our guest speaker on Geopolitical TV. He was interviewed by a representative of the Armenian Desk, Eduard Enfiajyan. The main topic of the interview was the causes of the Circassian Genocide and how it affected the Circassians as a nation. The current events in the Russia, the war in Ukraine, the war in the Middle East and in Asia Minor (Turkey) were also discussed because both Armenians and Circassians have diaspora communities in all those war zones. Here is the link https://youtu.be/9gu2jCC0jdc for those who are interested to watch the interview.[1059]

Then there was an advice for long-time foes.

The theatrical that Russia and Turkey try to establish is that there is a religious war in the region (in the Caucasus and in the Middle East) when in reality Armenians and other Christians lived well with their Muslim neighbors in all communities of the same region. If the Russians and the Turks can work together, the indigenous people of the region, who have history of commerce, trade, and at times of war, military alliances together, can definitely work together once the isolating barriers break and new opportunities allow such synergy.[1060]

Sochi and Yerevan Analysis

On February 14, 2016, an article titled, Sochi and Yerevan Analysis, by Adel Bashqawi and Garegin Nalbandian, which is mentioned in the following:

Many people probably remember the 2014 Winter Olympics, and have seen the Olympic Complex in Sochi, where the Winter Olympic Games took place. However, not many people know about the fact that Russia specifically chose that part of Sochi, where the Circassians regard as a sacred place because many Circassians, who were fleeing from the ethnic cleansing, were killed there by the Russian Army.

Turkey did not oppose the Winter Olympics in Sochi, where many Turkish investors and construction companies participated in building the Olympic structures, and saw it as an opportunity to make money. Erdogan personally attended the opening ceremony and part of the games, just to keep warm relations between Russia and Turkey. Unfortunately, some pro-Russian Circassian businessmen from Turkey also participated in the construction of the resorts, hotels, and other facilities for the Sochi Olympics. One of those hotels was the Marriott Hotel in Sochi.

At that time Erdogan had no problems with Putin or with Russia, and as "Money Talks", they announced that they had mutual business deals worth tens of billions of Dollars.

Putin's visit to Ankara in 2014, and his visit to Ataturk's tomb during his visit, was a preparation and cover-up for his visit to Armenia, instead of Turkey on April 24, 2015, but of course, that was probably the start of Erdogan's politics with Putin and Turkey's cautious relations with Russia.

Putin wanted to rant-show Armenians his support and protection, in order to keep that country hostage to his regional plans and deals, in order to keep Armenia under Russia's control and Armenians assimilated, as per his preferences, and at the same time, prevent any Circassian-Armenian direct contacts, the same way it happened between the Circassians and Georgians.

Last April, when the world was commemorating the 100 years of the Armenian Genocide, many Circassians have felt with the Armenians, and many Circassians expressed their positive feelings about that; however, Vladimir Putin poisoned the atmosphere when he travelled to Yerevan and played a cunning role. So many Circassians were annoyed to see Putin push his agenda using the Armenian Genocide.

Putin went to Armenia in April, 2015; however, his visit was to meet with the Presidents and the elites of other countries who also went to Armenia. It was a political networking event for him. In his speech Putin mentioned the word genocide, not as Armenian Genocide, but as Russia's involvement to "prevent genocides."

There was and there is genocide everywhere Russia was involved in. Russians passed through here, where used to be a village, is a common phrase in the Caucasus. Armenians have the same saying about the Turks.

Russia announced celebrating the Den' Krasnoi Polyany (Red Prairie Day) on May 21st this year. For those, who know nothing about the May 21st, it is an important day for the Circassian people. May 21st is the day all Circassians mourn the deaths of the Circassian Genocide victims. The terms Krasnaya Polyana, Krasnodar, and anything that is associated with the color red is associated with blood; in this case, the Circassian blood.

May 21st for Circassians is like the April 24th for Armenians.

Ironically, the Turks changed their celebration of Gallipoli to April 24th in 2015.

The same way we find similarities when comparing the Armenians and the Circassians, we can also find similarities when comparing the Russians and the Turks.

Both Russians and Turks are mix of Tatars. Russians are Muscovites mixed with Tatars, who in the past attacked and destroyed the Russian kingdoms of Novgorod, Suzdal, Yaroslavl, Kiev, Tver' and others. The term Russian did not exist until 1547. They chose the name Russia and Russians to pose themselves as natives of the land. The first Muscovite Royal Dynasty were the Rurik Dynasty. Rurik was the leader of the Byzantine Varangian (Vayrag) Guards. The population in Turkey is also a mix of Byzantines and Tatars. Thus, it is only natural that Russia, Byzantium, and the Golden Horde, all used the double headed eagle as their symbol.

In conclusion, the recent "rivalry" between Russia and Turkey demonstrates a theatrical written by the same "screenwriter" to cover-up the main agenda, which is the transfer of power and control from Russia (the Muscovite Golden Horde) to Turkey (Byzantium). Let's not give in to emotions, and let's analyze the facts. If we allow the evil win, the entire Caucasus, the Middle East, and possibly the entire world, will be in war, World War III, which may have already started, does not have to spread. Together we can put off the fire. It's not about religion. It's about good and evil. Please side with the good by preventing wars and by promoting peace. Stop future genocides because it's the right thing to do.[1061]

Russia's Falsification Dares to Attack Circassian Activism

Patriots of Circassia Organization had sent complaints to international human rights organizations, in regard to the Circassian activist, Adnan Khuade. He was arrested, and charges were fabricated against him by the Russian police and the FSB to detain him for the purpose of oppressing and humiliating him.

It is not surprising for Circassians to be offended and ill treated by the Russian authorities. There is no end in sight to slow down or to stop the series of human rights abuses and infringes; on the contrary, they increase and become more complicated and repressive. The patriots of Circassian has issued a statement mentioning "unlawful suppressing by Russia against Adnan Khuade who is a human rights defender for circassians."[1062]

The statement stated,

> As it is known by public, Russian security forces, including FSB, permanently maintain a campaign of harassment against Adnan Khuade who is repatriated inhabitant of Maykop city, Circassian public figure and activist defending human rights and minority rights of Circassians. Adnan Khuade is continually prosecuted, investigated and detained by Russian authorities to intimidate aiming to divest him of struggle for Circassian rights before the public opinion of Russia. Said tools veiled by so-called legal forms are completely based on fictitious incriminations such as breaching of consumer law.[1063]

It added that "previously, Adnan Khuade was detained and sentenced many times because of political reasons, for instance, to pressurize protests against Sochi Olympics where taken place historical Circassian capital city, a group of Circassian activists including Adnan Khuade was detained (https://www.hrw.org/news/2013/12/18/russia-new-harassment-olympic-critics)."[1064]

Then it continued,

> One of the examples of suppressions and false charges was occured on 15.12.2015, FSB officers came to carpet store, belonging Adnan Khuade, under cover of investigation for consumer rights, committed violence on him and his daughter and employee but then oficers accused that Adnan Khuade, his daughter and employee beat member of security forces. In virtue of this intriguing accusation, court handed down prison sentences upon them and sent to jail.[1065]

Following the statement, a summary of the Circassian Question has been mentioned to give a brief idea about the series of events that took place when the Russian Empire invaded Circassia. It recalled that Russia had performed genocide and deportation against most Circassians, reaching today's Russian refusal to allow Circassians of Syria to rehabilitate to their historic homeland.

Writing to Human Rights Organizations

An example of modern tyranny is observed through an open autocratic detention conducted by the local police and FSB in the Republic of Adygea. There are persistent arbitrary actions against members of the indigenous people by following fraudulent means.

PATRIOTS OF CIRCASSIA website has published copies of documents that were sent to prominent international human rights organizations. They were regarded unlawful suppression against the Circassian activist Adnan Khuade by the Russian local authorities. The organizations were listed to be "Amnesty International, Human Rights Watch, Human Rights Foundation, and FIDH (Worldwide Movement for Human Rights)."[1066]

The related applications sent in respect to Khuade's arbitrary arrest and mock trial hearings were based on fundamentally false allegations and legally unproven.

> As it is known by public, Russian security forces, including FSB, permanently maintain a campaign of harassment against Adnan Khuade who is repatriated inhabitant of Maykop city, Circassian public figure and activist defending human rights and minority rights of Circassians. Adnan Khuade is continually prosecuted, investigated and detained by Russian authorities to intimidate aiming to divest him of struggle for Circassian rights before the public opinion of Russia. Said tools veiled by so-called legal forms are completely based on fictitious incriminations such as breaching of consumer law.[1067]

Also, the local office of the Federal Security Service (FSB) has coprosecuted Khuade on its part in addition to the charges that were initially cited. Basically, he was also falsely accused, which was intended to keep the defendant in prison as well as get the court to issue a ruling to keep him in prison as long as possible.

On the eve of May 21, 2016, 152nd day of mourning for Circassian Genocide and Exile, he has been detained on the pretext of old traffic ticket and passing over red traffic light, but according to eyewitnesses coming from Finland as guests of him said that this was not happened.

On 05.05.2016, traffic policeman stopped his car in which eyewitnesses there, then additional police units attended, 8 police cars in toto, took Adnan Khuade into custody, then court has sentenced him 15 days prison on 06.05.2016. However, Russian FSB is conspiratorially about to charge him with offering bribery to policeman. Its penalty is at least six months prison additional to said 15 days.[1068]

The letters addressed to human rights organizations have mentioned an antagonistic article published in the Sovetskaya Adige Journal. They mentioned that Khuade was attacked and criticized "in its issue published on 02.02.2016 (http://советская-адыгея.рф/index.php/bezopasnost/6064-po-kovrovoj-dorozhke-vrazhdy)." The accusations were inconsistent with basic human rights.[1069]

The title of hostile article was "Enmity on Red Carpets" referring Adnan Khuade's carpet store. In said article, 'Circassian Genocide' and applications for recognizing Circassian Genocide to parliaments of Ukraine, Poland, Estonia, Moldova and Latvia are considered an order of Western countries, USA, Jamestown Foundation, Paul Goble, Paul Henze and Zionism. Thus, it can be said that Adnan Khuade is officially deemed an enemy by Russia.[1070]

After the text of Patriots of Circassia's statement, it mentioned a realistic historical overview summary about the Circassian Question that confirms related linkage with Adnan Khuade's matter altogether.

The summary elaborated on the genocide inflicted upon the "Circassian (Adygean) people" in the eighteenth and nineteenth centuries. It mentioned that "significant majority of Circassians were exterminated by the Russian Empire to take over Circassia, the Circassian (Adygean) homeland." It added, "The ones who survived were forced to leave their homeland and were deported and exiled as a whole, and as the Russian Empire planned, hundreds of thousands of people died during the exile process."

The summary also mentioned, "According to a motto belonged to Russian generals and Russian authorities, the Russian Empire needed 'the land that belonged to the Circassians, not the Circassians themselves'." It continued, "Exile continued also after 1864 with different excuses and different disguises, all kinds of pressure was implemented to make a handful of Circassians left behind by some means to leave their homeland as well. Relevant documents are in the archives in addition to published documents by eyewitnesses in propria persona."[1071]

Circassian Activism and Related Conferences

Nations and people rise, grow, and prosper as a result of the devoted who feel that they are morally obligated to provide assistance at times when contribution is needed to maintain a dedicated guidance for the sake of saving their very existence and survival as a respected and dignified nation that is wants to maintain its perpetuation, sovereignty, and identity; which are necessary for national survival.

History is the interaction of people and nations with direct and indirect effects of occurrences that happened because of events and circumstances, depending on documented information and the human factor, which has led to constant change, whether rapidly or slowly, and which are recorded according to the scientific method, to research and access accurate information, and impartially and without bias, in order to reach the truth. Past events and proceedings are studied, evaluated, and processed for planning to choose the necessary steps to be taken by those who bear human responsibility of continuity and perseverance for the sake of positive change of their society in the present and future, depending on consequences of dangers that affected life, survival, progress, and advancement of their society and nation. Propaganda is always a main tool that greedy imperial powers have adopted and maintained since they decided to intervene in the affairs of others and control the destinies of nations and peoples, apart from occupation and colonization.

Regarding the Circassian situation, Circassian activist organizations and individuals advocate vigorously and lively the different issues of the Circassian Question and they are opposing to surrender to despair. Their special status is no less important and serious than their nation, which suffers from serious consequences as a result of the occupation of their homeland and the fact that Circassians are scattered between their homeland and wide Diaspora. Hopes are pinned on the intellectuals and the educated generation, who are aware of the Circassians' legitimate rights.

Not so many activities are known about their role in the Circassian homeland, but their established associations and organizations are considered influential in among the scattered Circassian communities both in the Circassian republics and enclaves in the North Caucasus or in Russian cities such as Moscow and St. Petersburg. They emerged during the time of the disintegration of the Soviet Union at the end of the 1980s or the beginning of the Russian Federation. The most important of them is the International Circassian Association, which is based in Nalchik, KBR, which has veered away from its goals and why it was established for.[1072]

The efforts executed by the Circassians, both in the North Caucasus or in Diaspora, should not be underestimated or overlooked. They have proven that all activities have shown to be in harmony and uniformity in the work and efforts made by the Circassians in the various places of residence, and have continuously exerted their relentless efforts to work on what pertains to the different Circassian issues. They felt that the situation of the Circassians of Syria has necessitated to extend a helping hand to them, to be able to leave the battlefield of the grinding civil war, and to enable them to return to the Circassian homeland, which they have received a deaf ear from the Russian government to their justified demands.

The following are some activities that represent certain periods:

The issuance and sending of a message with a non-surprising gesture taken by some Circassian leaders in the North Caucasus, which reviewed all important events that took place recently in the Circassian homeland in the North Caucasus and in Diaspora, was sent to the Russian President Vladimir Putin and the Deputies of the Federal Assembly of the Russian Federation.[1073] The letter clearly demanded the recognition of the Circassian Genocide and the firm rights of the Circassian nation. The letter proved beyond any reasonable doubt the common destiny that brings all Circassians together regardless the time and distance away from their homeland. This gesture has shown to everyone that skeptics and doubters who always tried to influence the Circassian communities that any work related to claiming the Circassian rights would negatively affect our people in the North Caucasus, which always has proven to be false and untrue.

Numerous proceedings have occurred since then, which include but not limited to, continuous Circassian activities on the way to achieving and reclaiming the Circassians' rights whether in the North Caucasus or in Diaspora. Important conferences and events have taken place in various countries such as Tbilisi, Kfar Kama, Istanbul, the United States, and Jordan. Some of the events and activities occurred on the Circassian scene are mentioned for example, but not limited to the following:

* On the 21st of May 2007, a conference titled, The Circassians: Past, Present and Future, was held by Jamestown Foundation, in Washington DC.[1074]

* On the 8th of April 2008, a Circassian conference was held by Jamestown Foundation titled, The Circassians: Past, Present And Future, RUSSIA AND THE CIRCASSIANS: An Internal Problem or an International Matter?[1075]

* On the 13th of April 2008, and in cooperation between William Paterson University, the Department of Languages, and the Circassian Cultural held a conference titled, Embracing Circassia, Building our Future.[1076]

* "The Jamestown Foundation with Georgia's Ilia State University held two landmark conferences on issues connected to the Circassians and other North Caucasian peoples in Tbilisi in 2010."[1077] The two conferences were in the titled, Hidden Nations and Enduring Crimes in the months of March and November.

* "On May 16, 2011, members of the Russian State's Duma committee on foreign affairs met with a group of Circassian activists from the North Caucasus and the overseas diasporas. The short, one-hour meeting, which was the highest level Russian government meeting with Circassian activists to date, was allegedly driven by the ongoing debates in the Georgian parliament that are expected to culminate in a resolution on the Circassian issue by May 20."[1078]

* In 2011, Circassian activists from the North Caucasus and Diaspora attended an important event at the Georgian Parliament in Tbilisi, as "Georgia on May 20 became the first country to recognize as genocide Tsarist Russia's massive slaughter of ethnic Circassians in the mid-19th century."[1079]

* On the 21st of May 2012, Circassian activists from different parts of the world attended in Anaklia, Georgia, the inauguration of the Circassian Genocide Monument and participated in a conference on the Circassian Genocide and other Circassian issues.[1080]

* The Seventh Circassian Day in the European Parliament, June 2012.[1081]

* A gathering in Kfar Kama included a paper titled, The Circassian Mobility During the Past Few Years in July 2012.[1082]

* Tbilisi Symposium Conference, July 2012.[1083]

* During the 2012 London Summer Olympic Games, Circassians protested in East London against the plight of Circassians and the (then) planned Sochi Winter Olympic games, July 2012.[1084]

* Solo and group demonstrations to bring the attention to the Circassians of Syria,[1085] which were held in the North Caucasus, Turkey, and Moscow.

* In November 2012, the Russian police suppressed a peaceful Circassian sit-in in Nalchik, the capital city of KBR demanding to extend a helping hand to Circassians caught in the midst of the civil war in Syria.[1086]

* In December 2012, a hostile workshop against Circassians held in Rostov.[1087]

* In December 2012, Circassians of Turkey demonstrated in Istanbul against Vladimir Putin's state visit.[1088]

* The leader of Nalchik Adigha khasa in KBR, Ibrahim Yaganov, who is called the Hero of Abkhazia, stated in December 2012, that he does not understand "why the Abkhazian leadership voluntarily took on the mission to prove that there was no Circassian genocide."[1089]

* In January 2013, the Committee of Nationalities of the Russian State Duma and Ministry of Regional Development of the Russian Federation stated that "Syrian Circassians are descendants of families of Adyghe people from the North and West Caucasus that have not adopted the Russian citizenship and made a voluntary choice to leave the region after the Caucasus War (1817 – 1864). Thus, ancestors of the Syrian Circassians living in the territories, until their resettlement in 1864 in the Ottoman Empire were not part of the Russian State."[1090]

* In March 2013, rain washed out part of a dam in Krasnaya Polyana near Sochi,[1091] and created floods and mudslides.[1092]

* In March 2013, Veterans Federation of Abkhazia condemned statements made by the Head of the International Circassian Association on the recognition of the Circassian Genocide crime committed by Tsarist Russia[1093]

* The Jordanian Circassian Political Movement on the 24th of March 2013, held its "Third Workshop" in cooperation with the "Circassian House" and "Al Jeel Al Jadeed Club" at Al Jeel Al Jadeed Club's Hall, which came in three main axes.[1094]

* The establishment of the Circassian National Movement emanating from the Jordan Association of Circassian Caucasus Friends.[1095]

* A new Circassian center is established in Latvia called "The Circassian Culture and Human Rights Center."[1096]

* Window on Eurasia issued a special weekly Sochi Count-down feature published by political analyst Paul Goble, which lists all information that pertains to the 2014 Sochi Olympic Games.[1097]

* A letter is sent to Beslan Kopakhia, the Coordinator of the International Movement for the Protection of the Rights of Peoples, about his statements against Circassians.[1098]

* A fund raising event was held by the International Circassians Council in N.J., USA, on the 27th April 2012, which Circassians from the USA, Turkey, Syria, and Jordan participated in and gave speeches.[1099]

* The establishment of a new organization in the Republic of Adygea called Adigha Khasa of Maykop,[1100] which doesn't belong to the Adigha Khasa of the Republic of Adygea.

One of the most important issues tackled is the Circassians of Syria regarding their safety and security, which showed real Circassian solidarity regarding fund raising and to provide, whether directly or through third parties, food, cash, in-kind materials, and medical assistance, not to mention housing. Many of the Circassians of Syria once again became refugees as they had to flee the fighting after their places of residence were destroyed, to safer areas within Syria or to neighboring countries such as Jordan, Lebanon, and Turkey. Circassians were able to help their brethren Circassians in Jordan and Turkey, and the Solidarity Committee of World Circassians'[1101] help was not limited only to raise funds to offer mentioned types of assistance, but also managed to get the Turkish government's assistance to recognize documents and identification cards for the refugees, to establish a special camp for Circassians, and on top of that, the establishment of an air bridge[1102] to transport Circassians of Syria from Beirut to Gaziantep.

The Circassians Encounter Russian Propaganda Campaign

Circassian grass roots activism in Russia appears to be maturing as the Russian authorities ignore the plight of the Syrian Circassians. The rise of activism among previously unknown Circassian figures also shows a certain degree of failure of the existing civil organizations to represent Circassian interests. Moscow's position has not changed much, as Russian authorities for now pretend that they do not notice the Circassian issue.[1103]

Systematical Promotion of Misinformation

An example of a misinformation campaign is an article that was published on "kavkazoved's" website known by its hostile orientations towards Circassians and other peoples of the North Caucasus, which published the events of a hostile "workshop" against Circassians, and was held in the city of Rostov to elaborate on the "Circassian Question" in accordance with prejudiced and intolerant outlines and directives. It attracted the participation of "experts" from Rostov, Moscow, St. Petersburg, Cherkessk, and Pyatigorsk in the presence of several representatives of the Russian media, educational institutions, and social organizations. The theme of the meeting was the so-called "Circassian Question" which has become the subject of different speculations with then, the approach of the Olympic Games in Sochi.[1104]

The meeting was organized, commenced, and held by Edward Popov, the director of the Center for Information and Analysis for the Black Sea and the Caspian Sea of the Russian Institute for Strategic Studies, pointing out that the "Circassian Question" had received wide attention and reactions both on the interior and exterior levels, and its related "attempts of some external actors (some Circassian communities and non-governmental foreign institutions) to politicize the issue of the Caucasian war that had taken place in the period between 1817–1864 and the resulting adverse consequences for the peoples of the two regions of northwestern and southwestern Caucasus such as Kabardians" ignoring that the Russian-Circassian War had taken place between 1763 and 1864, and the fact that Kabardians are an integral part of the Circassian nation![1105]

Circassia Is a Nation Denied by Genocide

The different described Circassian entities, with no exception, should feel and act like human beings. Yes, what happened in 1864 is genocide. The description given by the ICA, President: 'According to Sokhrokov, some Circassians consider what happened in 1864 to be a genocide, but "contemporary Circassian society recognizes that the Caucasus war was the result of the policy of tsarist Russia and do not shift the blame for the tragedy of the Adygs [Circassians] onto contemporary Russia."[1106] This is not acceptable, because the definition of the word genocide is: "Crimes against Humanity and War Crimes; also extermination, atrocities, massacre, killing fields, ethnic cleansing or bloodbath."[1107] If Russia is honest and truthful in solving out the problems created for Circassians, present Russia should recognize the Circassian Genocide.

It must be known that "objective discussion" is a two-way street, and doesn't work if only one side accepts anything that is offered while everybody knows that nothing is offered or proposed to the Circassians. Obvious facts cannot be ignored as what Russia is doing is completely ignoring Circassians and their status and legitimate rights. The proof that the truth cannot be flipped is the reaction and backfire triggered by Adygs in the North Caucasus and Diaspora to Russia's efforts to tame Circassians in order to convince and even force them to(then) accept holding Sochi Winter Olympic Games on the Circassians' graves.[1108]

An exception to this, is some Circassian activists have observed that occasion by raising Circassian flags and anti-Sochi Olympics signs in Nalchik.[1109] A proverb says, "The history of a people is found in its songs" which complies with the occurrence reported when tens of Circassians who were detained in Nalchik in February 2013, for opposing the Sochi Olympic Games, were singing well-known Circassian patriotic songs.

In January 2013, the Russian Duma replied to the Head of the Adigha Khasa, the Circassian Association in the Republic of Adygea, Adam Boghos, in regard to helping Circassians of Syria to return to their original homeland, and the response was: "Committee for Nationalities in the Russian Duma would inform you that your request to help the Circassians of Syria to return to the Russian Federation has been transferred to the Ministry of Regional Development of the Russian Federation, and sending you this reduplication of the Ministry's response!" The response declared: "Circassians of Syria are the descendants of immigrants of Adigha origins, from the Northern and Western Caucasus, who did not accept the Russian citizenship, and chose voluntary migration from the region after the end of military operations of the Caucasian War. Thus, the ancestors of the existing Circassians of Syria had resided in the territories that have not yet been within the Russian Federation until their migration in the year 1864 to the Ottoman Empire, which they cannot be considered as immigrants from the Russian State."[1110]

The above-mentioned statement reflects the Russian State Duma's recognition that Circassians have never joined Russia voluntarily, which was officially claimed that Circassians had voluntarily joined the Russian Empire 450 years ago that was officially celebrated in September, 2007, by the Russian government and its administrative staff including the International Circassian Association, in the Circassian enclaves in the North Caucasus.

The Head of the Adigha Khasa of the twenty-first century, Amin Zekhizv, commented on the response and described it as

> it is true and means the following:
>
> – Circassians are occupied people,
>
> – Circassian territories are colonized by the Russian State,
>
> – We are the descendants of the occupied people,
>
> – As long as Circassia is within the Russian Federation, Circassians got no way to return home,
>
> – The rulers of the North Caucasus region are the colonial administrative rulers in the Caucasus,
>
> – Maria's status, the Russian Tsar's wife, in the city of Nalchik must be removed,
>
> These are some of the issues that you have opened the Circassians and other Caucasian peoples' eyes on.[1111]

Activists who have true loyalty to their homeland reject injustice, while Circassians believe in what Nelson Mandela has said: "Difficulties break some men but make others. No axe is sharp enough to cut the soul of a sinner who keeps on trying, one armed with the hope that he will rise even in the end."[1112] After all the atrocities befallen them, it is not fair to be given the choice between the devil and the deep sea! It is felt that Mount Elbruz is warmer to Adigha Circassians than the hearts of some individuals who pretend to be Circassians.

Andzor Akhokhov, an embattled Circassian activist, told Kavpolit.com about the police crackdown on civil activists. On February 7, when the Winter Olympics opened in Sochi, dozens of Circassians staged a protest in the central part of Nalchik, Kabardino-Balkaria, but they were quickly dispersed by police. According to Akhokhov, about 50 people were detained—more than initially reported. Many of the detained demonstrators were released, but some, including Akhokhov, were placed under administrative arrest. Moreover, according to Akhokhov, the police used torture and threats of force against the young people to make them confess to crimes they did not commit. The police reportedly used electric shocks and plastic bags to simulate suffocation. They forced us to confess to carrying out some acts and cooperating with the American side, which cannot be in principle, in front of video recorders. The police officers also repeatedly threatened to launch a criminal investigation against us on the grounds of extremism if we did not admit to cooperation with organizations that we had not known previously.[1113]

In an interview with Gazeta Yuga, a weekly newspaper published in Nalchik, Akhokhov said,

I was prepared to being beaten up, also assumed plastic bags on the head would be likely, but did not expect electric shocks. In the 6th Department [police department responsible for fighting extremism and organized crime] I confessed to everything they wanted—an attempt to overthrow the government and so on, although I did not aim to overthrow anything. We only paid tribute to the memories of our ancestors.[1114]

On February 10, at a meeting with the Civil Council for Holding the Winter Olympics in Sochi, Russian President Vladimir Putin said that foreign powers were using the Circassian issue to hold back the development of Russia. Even though Putin did not name the foreign countries that were behind this clever plan, he referred to the Cold War mentality that prompted those countries to act against Russia, thereby hinting at the United States and at the West in general.[1115] The information that police extracted from the arrested Circassians in Nalchik through threats and torture was probably some of the "proof" of the foreign involvement in the North Caucasus.[1116]

The Blessed Circassian Youth Efforts

Thanks to self-motivation and some internal values core of Circassian youths, which witnesses a genuine high awareness and performance regarding their crucial and important task, contrary to what some are trying to impose. It is appreciated to notice the way of participation in dealing with the relevant matters of the Circassian Question. The young Circassian generation showed in recent years, sincere and marvelous interaction that was stimulated with interests to be aware of all matters related to their just cause, and thus work for highlighting important Circassian elements for the international community, in addition to stick to future's ambitions and assurances of asserting and restoring the Circassian confiscated rights. Use of media, technology, modern communications, internet, and social media, assisted in teaching the Adigha language, culture, the merits of the documented Circassian history, and other matters.

Praise should not be limited to a certain Circassian community, whether at homeland or in the wide Diaspora, but for Circassians everywhere. Gratitude is owed to those who exercise extraordinary work for great Circassian benefits in a difficult situation, especially for those who are living in their homeland, and bear extraordinary rules dictated by the laws of the strangers who set the terms and conditions that stripped them of their human rights as an indigenous people, living in six different non-contiguous administrative areas of historic Circassia.

Circassian youth, supported by the Circassian people, together with activists have increasingly shown in recent years tremendous and unprecedented concern that proved and established resolve, determination, dedication, and altruism in many different fields and activities in many countries including their homeland. They demonstrated drawing attention to the Circassian Question, which combines disastrous consequences, contemporary developments, and related updates. Important subjects were addressed such as the Circassian Genocide, ethnic cleansing, deportation, Sochi Olympic Games, and stubborn Russian policies of ignoring the Circassian nation. Activities included demonstrations, commemorations, meetings, conferences, exhibitions, media interviews, and multiple activities in countries such as Turkey, Jordan, the USA, and some European countries beside the North Caucasus.

The following are highlights mentioned, as examples and not limited to the overall scene, which include excerpts of some events and activities that took place and related to the North Caucasus in recent years, which are linked with what happened in the past and still is happening in the Circassian homeland:

— In Nalchik on February 7, 2014, more than 50 peaceful Circassian picketers against the Sochi Olympics were arrested by the Russian police. The Circassian activists were detained in the capital of Kabardino – Balkaria after "which they formed a convoy of dozens of automobiles and headed to the center of town. They hung Circassian flags out of the windows, and also waved a banner with the words, 'Sochi – Land of Genocide' in English." As usual, the picketers who were released were subjected to beating and torture. In particular, "eye-witnesses report that police were forced to carry Anzor Akhokhov into the courtroom for the reading of his sentence, since he was not in condition to move independently as a result of beatings at the police station." "His entire body is covered with bruises – his face, hands, legs, everywhere there are the marks of hard blows," said his brother Aslanbek Akhokhov.[1117]

For the first time ever, the Russian President has mentioned the Circassians, by claiming that the West is exploiting the Circassian Question to its advantage, where he automatically admitted that there is a Circassian issue, which Russia has proven that it refrains from offering a fair settlement for! "With this statement, Vladimir Putin made the Circassians a subject of relations between Russia and the West," American political analyst Paul Goble, author of the blog Windows on Eurasia, told VOA. "Instead of putting out the fire, he only poured oil over the flames."[1118]

— Circassians loyal to their nation, who are eager to address the Circassian Question in all possible ways, have opposed lies Russia tried to implement through its propaganda a misleading claim of so-called commemorating[1119] with some Circassians and Caucasian bureaucrats who are loyalists and collaborators with the Russian authorities, that is still ruling the North Caucasus, to celebrate the memory of the "so-called" 450 years of voluntary association with Russia, which was "formally" celebrated between the September 7–9, 2007.

— That was with the participation of individuals from the Circassian Diaspora, who had special relations with the Russian-backed International Circassian Association, and who accepted invitations to participate in the Russian festivals. Such false allegations have never occurred except in the imagination of those who tried to impose such unrealistic ideas, while assuming the ignorance of all those involved in such a big lie, which intended to deceive public opinion. All that in contradiction with the reality of imperial Russian occupation of the Circassian homeland and disregarding all considerations, ethical or moral obligations towards the

Circassian nation that had lost half of its population during a 101 yearlong "Russian-Circassian War" when Circassians were exposed to murder, genocide, extermination, deportation, torture, and humiliation by hordes of invading forces.

— "That indicates that those who got their own occasions to mark and celebrate irrespective of what was the title of their celebrations which they were pushed to decide to rush madly upon and to perform regardless of what were the results and consequences, even the main reason was to consolidate and hallow the control, occupation, colonization, imperial accomplished facts, and fait accompli."[1120]

—"The chairman of 'Circassian congress' Murat Berzegov informed "Caucasian unit" correspondent: "Our position concerned this question is unequivocal – it is impossible to celebrate the date which did not exist in the history. We have already sounded this idea before singing of the decree of the president of Russian Federation "About celebrating the 450th anniversary of voluntary association of Adygeya to the Russian state" at the joint meeting of public organizations of Adygeya."[1121]

— "The Circassian Congress added: "On what basis is it possible to speak about 'voluntary association' if there is no document confirming that? Even if some delegation of separate princes addressed to the Russian tsar in 1557 for support as to an ally, it could not speak about its voluntary integration to the Russian state. But if we by all means would like to have such holiday and the 450th anniversary let it be the anniversary of creation of the allied relations with Russia. We could agree with such formulation."[1122]

— The Russian contradiction didn't take long to surface after the false Russian celebrations, and to prove that they occupied Circassia through military intervention, and Circassians had never associated voluntarily with the tyrant Russian Empire! Aleksandr Zhuravsky, the head of the International Department of the Russian Ministry of Regional Development responded in December 2012, to a letter sent by Adam Bogus, the head of the Circassian Adyge Khase in the Republic of Adegea to Sergey Naryshkin, the State Duma Speaker, requesting that Moscow provide assistance for Circassians of Syria to return to their homeland, which was transferred to the Russian Regional Development Ministry for consideration.

The Ministry's letter provoked anger after it was widely disseminated, because it stated, "the Syrian Circassians are the descendants of refugees from among the Adyge peoples of the North and West Caucasus who did not accept Russian citizenship and made a voluntary choice to leave the region after the completion of military operations in the course of the Caucasus War!"[1123]

— A strong example of true loyalty and attachment to the motherland was expressed by those who participated and reached magnificent results after a one-day forum during a significant event that was held on the 12th of September 2009, in Cherkessk, the capital of the Republic of Karachay-Cherkessia, titled Circassian Youth Forum, which was attended by active Circassian youths who are members of the Circassian (Adigha) Khasa (association) branches, Circassian Congress, and other active organizations from the Circassian republics and enclaves, beside the Republic of Abkhazia in the north Caucasus region, to discuss the important issues that concern the Circassian nation both in their homeland and Diaspora.

The eight-point Resolution of Circassian (Adygeyan) Youth Forum contained declarations. Following the meeting, it appeared to be as a "genie erupting out of the bottle" after 145 years of "deep-sleep", which is considered in all measures, a very successful attempt for the efforts exerted by all of those courageous young Circassians who seemed that they had never forgotten their duties towards their nation.

The following is a summary of the eight points:

1. To establish a "Coordination Council of Circassian Youth",

2. To support the decision of unifying the name of the purposefully divided Adygeyan subethnoses: Kabardians, Adygs, Circassians and Shapsugs and to recognize the name "Circassian" as a one nation

3. To call on ICA to create "World Day of Circassian Flag".

4. To address the Adygeyan International Academy of Sciences and the Ministry of Education of the Republics of Kabardino-Balkaria, Karachaevo-Circassia and Adygeya to reform the methodology of teaching of the native language.

5. To request from the Russian Academy of Sciences to organize a scientifically-practical conference to commemorate: "The 180th Anniversary of the First Military-Scientific Expeditions on Mount Elbrus of general Emmanuel, the Feat of Kabardian Kilar Khashirov".

6. To authorize delegates of the forum at the next congress of the ICA to act on behalf of Circassian youth and to have youth representatives in the executive committee of the association.

7. To demand from the ICA to create a committee to counteract the historical falsifications.

8. To address the President of the Russian Federation in regard to falsification of history and with the offer of adopting the Law of Return of Circassians to their homeland.[1124]

Faithful Circassians would prove that no one will be able, in any way, seize the capabilities and conclusions gained by Circassian activists for personal or opportunist gains, and at the same time, it is obvious now that vision, mechanism, and coordination, which linked all sincere Circassians together, would pave the way and lead for a fruitful output, and success will be inevitable.

---

[991] http://justicefornorthcaucasus.info/?p=1251661885
[992] http://justicefornorthcaucasus.info/?p=1251661885
[993] http://www.justicefornorthcaucasus.com/eagle_combo/documents/eagle.php?entry_id=1158227100
[994] http://windowoneurasia.blogspot.com/2009/05/window-on-eurasia-circassians-reaffirm.html
[995] http://www.natpressru.info/index.php?newsid=8108
[996] http://justicefornorthcaucasus.info/?p=1251676013
[997] https://aheku.net/news/policy/5958?pn=455
[998] http://justicefornorthcaucasus.info/?p=1251675380%2035th%20paragraph
[999] http://www.justicefornorthcaucasus.com/jfnc_message_boards/conferences.php?entry_id=1271198474
[1000] http://america.aljazeera.com/articles/2014/2/17/russia-detains-circassianleaderprotestingsochiolympics.html and http://www.refworld.org/docid/52cfed024.html
[1001] http://eng.kavkaz-uzel.ru/articles/27210/#.UwFYJCLXNKo.facebook
[1002] http://www.thedailybeast.com/articles/2014/02/09/the-lost-tribe-of-sochi-russia-s-circassian-diaspora.html
[1003] http://justicefornorthcaucasus.info/?p=1251661885
[1004] http://aheku.net/news/policy/5892

[1005] http://www.kavkaz-uzel.ru/articles/264918/
[1006] http://www.natpressru.info/index.php?newsid=9692
[1007] http://www.jamestown.org/regions/thecaucasus/single/?tx_ttnews%5Btt_news%5D=44131&tx_ttnews%5BbackPid%5D=54&cHash=4db9d6027c62b4827ae921f7accf2127#.VaB7hpOqqkp
[1008] http://eng.kavkaz-uzel.ru/articles/32192/
[1009] http://windowoneurasia2.blogspot.com/2017/01/fsb-overplays-its-hand-in-circassian.html
[1010] http://windowoneurasia2.blogspot.com/2017/01/fsb-overplays-its-hand-in-circassian.html
[1011] http://windowoneurasia2.blogspot.com/2017/01/fsb-overplays-its-hand-in-circassian.html
[1012] http://windowoneurasia2.blogspot.com/2017/01/fsb-overplays-its-hand-in-circassian.html
[1013] http://www.justicefornorthcaucasus.com/jfnc_message_boards/circassia_adiga.php?entry_id=1289349161&title=the-institutional-face-of-collaborationism%3A-international-circassian-association
[1014] http://justicefornorthcaucasus.info/?p=1251661885
[1015] http://justicefornorthcaucasus.info/?p=1251661885
[1016] http://www.wildmind.org/blogs/quote-of-the-month/quote-gandhi
[1017] http://www.21mayis.org/content/pdf/recognition/UNPO_1997.pdf
[1018] http://www.unpo.org/content/view/249/259/
[1019] http://www.jamestown.org/single/?tx_ttnews%5Btt_news%5D=32501&no_cache=1#.VpnjEZMrJE5
[1020] http://www.jamestown.org/single/?tx_ttnews%5Btt_news%5D=32501&no_cache=1#.VpnjEZMrJE5
[1021] http://justicefornorthcaucasus.info/?p=1165388580
[1022] http://justicefornorthcaucasus.info/?p=1165129260
[1023] http://justicefornorthcaucasus.info/?p=1165129260
[1024] http://justicefornorthcaucasus.info/?p=1165129260
[1025] http://eng.kavkaz-uzel.ru/articles/6679/
[1026] http://eng.kavkaz-uzel.ru/articles/31372/
[1027] http://eng.kavkaz-uzel.ru/articles/34171/
[1028] http://eng.kavkaz-uzel.ru/articles/7249/
[1029] http://www.caucasustimes.com/article.asp?id=12900
[1030] http://justicefornorthcaucasus.info/?p=1251669767
[1031] http://adigasilk.blogspot.com/
[1032] http://www.dailysabah.com/nation/2014/05/22/circassians-march-to-russian-consulate-on-the-anniversary-of-exile
[1033] The Circassian Genocide (Walter Richmond)
[1034] The Circassian Genocide (Walter Richmond)

1035 The Circassian Genocide (Walter Richmond)
1036 http://unesdoc.unesco.org/images/0024/002435/243531E.pdf
1037 https://twitter.com/UNESCO/status/701463849745195008
1038 http://justicefornorthcaucasus.info/?p=1165388580
1039 http://justicefornorthcaucasus.info/?p=1251672814
1040 http://justicefornorthcaucasus.info/?p=1251672814
1041 http://justicefornorthcaucasus.info/?p=1251672814
1042 http://justicefornorthcaucasus.info/?p=1251672814
1043 http://justicefornorthcaucasus.info/?p=1251672814
1044 http://justicefornorthcaucasus.info/?p=1251674340
1045 http://justicefornorthcaucasus.info/?p=1251674340
1046 Heroes and Emperors in Circassian History (Shaukat Mufti)
1047 Heroes and Emperors in Circassian History (Shaukat Mufti)
1048 Heroes and Emperors in Circassian History (Shaukat Mufti)
1049 http://www.stambul.msz.gov.pl/en/polish_community_in_turkey/adampol_polonezkoy/
1050 http://poloniaottomanica.blogspot.com/2014/03/eagles-in-caucasus-polish-circassian.html
1051 http://poloniaottomanica.blogspot.com/2014/03/eagles-in-caucasus-polish-circassian.html
1052 http://poloniaottomanica.blogspot.com/2014/03/eagles-in-caucasus-polish-circassian.html
1053 http://poloniaottomanica.blogspot.com/2014/03/eagles-in-caucasus-polish-circassian.html
1054 http://www.cherkessia.net/news_detail.php?id=6462 and https://www.youtube.com/watch?v=-HNe5opssIc
1055 http://www.cherkessia.net/author_article_detail.php?article_id=3987 and https://www.youtube.com/watch?v=-HNe5opssIc
1056 http://www.lragir.am/index/eng/0/politics/view/35230
1057 http://www.lragir.am/index/eng/0/politics/view/35230
1058 http://www.lragir.am/index/eng/0/politics/view/35230
1059 http://www.lragir.am/index/eng/0/politics/view/35230
1060 http://www.lragir.am/index/eng/0/politics/view/35230
1061 http://www.lragir.am/index/eng/0/politics/view/35260
1062 http://www.cherkessia.net/news_detail.php?id=6948
1063 http://www.cherkessia.net/news_detail.php?id=6948
1064 http://www.cherkessia.net/news_detail.php?id=6948
1065 http://www.cherkessia.net/news_detail.php?id=6948
1066 http://www.cherkessia.net/bakisacimiz.php?id=3402
1067 http://www.cherkessia.net/bakisacimiz.php?id=3402
1068 http://www.cherkessia.net/bakisacimiz.php?id=3402

1069 http://www.cherkessia.net/bakisacimiz.php?id=3402
1070 http://www.cherkessia.net/bakisacimiz.php?id=3402
1071 http://www.cherkessia.net/bakisacimiz.php?id=3402
1072 Please refer to the ICA Section in this book
1073 http://www.natpress.ru/index.php?newsid=8234
1074 http://justicefornorthcaucasus.info/?p=1209963600 and https://www.youtube.com/watch?v=Xxxxd_0TGZ8&feature=share
1075 http://justicefornorthcaucasus.info/?p=1206667800
1076 http://justicefornorthcaucasus.info/?p=1251676736
1077 http://www.jamestown.org/single/?tx_ttnews%5Btt_news%5D=37942#.VndoEpMrJE4
1078 http://www.jamestown.org/single/?tx_ttnews%5Btt_news%5D=37942#.VndoEpMrJE4
1079 http://www.eurasianet.org/node/63530
1080 http://www.unpo.org/article/14338
1081 http://www.natpressru.info/index.php?newsid=7314
1082 http://justicefornorthcaucasus.info/?p=1251670398
1083 http://www.justicefornorthcaucasus.com/jfnc_message_boards/circassia_adiga.php?entry_id=1343449150
1084 http://www.natpress.ru/index.php?newsid=7736
1085 http://www.eng.kavkaz-uzel.ru/articles/22997/
1086 http://www.youtube.com/watch?feature=player_embedded&v=e_wqocupAMs#!
1087 http://justicefornorthcaucasus.info/?p=1251662272
1088 http://www.caucasusforum.org/we-are-welcoming-a-dictator/
1089 http://eng.expertclub.ge/portal/cnid__13078/alias__Expertclub/lang__en/tabid__2546/dfault.aspx
1090 http://justicefornorthcaucasus.info/?p=1251662840
1091 http://www.itar-tass.com/en/c154/674268.html
1092 http://www.itar-tass.com/en/c154/674383.html
1093 http://www.natpress.ru/index.php?newsid=8108
1094 http://justicefornorthcaucasus.info/?p=1251670015
1095 http://justicefornorthcaucasus.info/?p=1251671166
1096 https://www.youtube.com/watch?v=ZkSWJUGUtGY
1097 http://windowoneurasia2.blogspot.com/2013/05/window-on-eurasia-sochi-countdown-38.html
1098 http://justicefornorthcaucasus.info/?p=1251670294
1099 http://www.circassianews.com/2013/04/27/%D8%A7%D8%B3%D8%AA%D8%B6%D8%A7%D9%81%D8%A9-%D8%B4%D8%B1%D8%A7%D9%83%D8%B3%D8%A9-%D8%B3%D9%88%D8%B1%D9%8A%D8%A7-%D9%81%D9%8A-%D8%A7%D9%84%D8%A3%D

8%B1%D8%AF%D9%86/
1100 http://www.radioadiga.com/ClosedIndex/artikkk.php?ind=4170
1101 http://www.unpo.org/article/15757
1102 http://www.radioadiga.com/ClosedIndex/artikkk.php?ind=4058
1103 http://www.jamestown.org/single/?tx_ttnews%5Btt_news%5D=40201#.Vm-PfxorJE4
1104 http://justicefornorthcaucasus.info/?p=1251662272
1105 http://justicefornorthcaucasus.info/?p=1251662272
1106 http://windowoneurasia2.blogspot.com/2014/07/window-on-eurasia-moscow-works-to.html
1107 http://www.preventgenocide.org/genocide/languages.htm
1108 http://www.kavkaz-uzel.ru/articles/237791/
1109 http://www.kavkaz-uzel.ru/articles/237828/ and http://www.kavkaz-uzel.ru/articles/237908
1110 http://justicefornorthcaucasus.info/?p=1251662840
1111 http://justicefornorthcaucasus.info/?p=1251666942
1112 http://www.usatoday.com/story/news/nation-now/2013/12/05/nelson-mandela-quotes/3775255/
1113 http://www.jamestown.org/single/?tx_ttnews%5Btt_news%5D=42010#.VnNzL5MrJE4
1114 http://www.jamestown.org/single/?tx_ttnews%5Btt_news%5D=42010#.VnNzL5MrJE4
1115 http://news.kremlin.ru/news/20203
1116 http://www.jamestown.org/single/?tx_ttnews%5Btt_news%5D=42010#.VnNzL5MrJE4
1117 http://www.interpretermag.com/putin-blames-circassian-protests-on-the-west-amid-arrests/?utm_source=rss&utm_medium=rss&utm_campaign=putin-blames-circassian-protests-on-the-west-amid-arrests
1118 http://www.interpretermag.com/putin-blames-circassian-protests-on-the-west-amid-arrests/?utm_source=rss&utm_medium=rss&utm_campaign=putin-blames-circassian-protests-on-the-west-amid-arrests
1119 http://www.cherkessia.net/author_article_detail.php?article_id=4020
1120 http://www.justicefornorthcaucasus.com/eagle_combo/documents/eagle.php?entry_id=1158227100
1121 http://justicefornorthcaucasus.info/?p=1251673996
1122 http://justicefornorthcaucasus.info/?p=1251673996
1123 http://justicefornorthcaucasus.info/?p=1251672464
1124 http://www.natpress.net/engine/print.php?newsid=3693

11

Recognizing the Circassian Genocide

A Portrait of the mountaineers leaving the aul

Circassians have constantly shown honesty and patience. They always hope for the best, but prepare for the worst. They have often confronted different parties practicing covenant denunciation or backing out from promises and assurances, which they always have the daring to withstand consequences, courageously and persistently. They do not wait for good things to happen to them; they instead, work hard and smart to achieve their objectives.

Genocide is considered the main issue out of many others of the Circassian Question. Therefore, emphasizing on this issue is considered substantial to solving others, based on the "Elements of the Crime of Genocide"[1125] agreed upon by the "Preparatory Commission for the International Criminal Court in New York on June 30, 2000,"[1126] and the "Explanatory note: The elements of the crime of genocide follows the corresponding provisions of Articles 6 of the Rome Statute of the International Criminal Court of 1998 and Article II of the Convention for the Prevention and Punishment of Genocide of 1948."[1127]

There are Circassian organizations and activists who do all they can and are working both separately and collectively in reaching many parties around the world to present all related facts about the Circassian atrocities. They included countries, organizations, and individuals to explain and illustrate all aspects of the Circassian tragedy. Circassians work hard and actively in order to stay alive as a nation and insist on the restoration of Circassia's rights, with an important motivation in mind:

> Admission of a genocide would result in the recreation of Circassia within its historical borders. As the Caucasus scholar Yakov Gordin told this author, this could lead to Russia's loss of the entire Caucasus. This is why the Russian media occasionally features stories regarding the 'dangerous plans of re-creating a {Greater Circassia} stretching from sea to sea'. The ostensible backer of this plan is the exiled Russian oligarch Boris Berezovsky. Such articles indicate that the Kremlin takes the Circassian problem seriously and is willing to implement harsh steps to crush the smallest demands by the Circassians for recognition of their rights.[1128]

As a good gesture towards Circassians was that one of the Caucasus region's states that the Republic of Georgia has hosted a conference held between the 20th and 21st of March 2010, in Tbilisi, which was held by Jamestown Foundation, Elia University, and the International School for Caucasus Studies. It was titled Hidden Nations, Enduring Crimes: The Circassians and the Peoples of the North Caucasus Between Past and Future, which presented a chance of direct contact between Georgians and many other nations of the North Caucasus, particularly the Circassians, which paved the way for further steps taken later.[1129]

The next special event that is directly connected to May 21, 1864, has legally evolved through legislative channels from Tbilisi, the capital city of the Republic of Georgia, after more than a year of study and scrutiny of information that was requested by the Circassians in March 2010, calling for recognizing the

Circassian Genocide, which took place against the Circassian nation in the 19th century. To conclude, the Parliament of Georgia has formed bodies through several committees assisted by scholars, historians and scientists who referred to dependable and legal deeds beyond doubt such as the Tbilisi Archives that contain original and legitimate documents written, issued and addressed by the perpetrating leaders and commanders concerned in the Imperial Russian military campaign against the Circassians. Those professionals and specialists who testified about their findings were from different countries, including Russia.

On the 19th of May 2011, the Parliament of Georgia's concerned committees have adopted a draft. The Georgian Parliament passed on May 20 with 90 votes to 0 a resolution saying that "pre-planned" mass killings of the Circassians by the Tsarist Russia in second half of 19th century, accompanied by "deliberate famine and epidemics," should be recognized as "genocide" and those deported during those events from their homeland, should be recognized as "refugees."[1130]

As a spontaneous show of appreciation to the Georgian people, the Circassians participating in the Circassian Memorial Day in Nalchik, the capital city of KBR, on the twenty-first of May 2011, raised the Georgian flag beside the Circassian flags during the yearly event, and even the Georgian flag was laid on the Circassian Memorial Stone.

An important study has taken place in Tbilisi, Georgia, by Professor Merab Chukhua about the Circassian Genocide titled, The Circassian Genocide-The History of Problems, Chronicles of Events, a Scientific Conclusion,[1131] which provided important scientific evidence and reference to prove the atrocities committed by the Russian Empire against the Circassians. It was presented to the Georgian Parliament, which created a basis for recognizing the Circassian Genocide.[1132]

The Georgian Recognition of the Genocide

The Georgian recognition progression went through the following stages:

— It started with contact and interaction between Circassian activists and Georgian leaders.

Circassia 443

— Two Circassian conferences were held in Tbilisi in the year 2010, in March and November titled, Hidden Nations, Enduring Crimes: The Circassians and the People of the North Caucasus Between Past and Future.

— In March 2010,[1133] Circassian activists participating in the first Circassian conference in Tbilisi, and in the presence of some members of the Georgian Parliament, signed an official letter that was and handed to the Georgian Parliament appealing to recognize the Circassian Genocide based on the testimonies, documented facts, and evidence.

— The Georgian authorities made it possible for Circassians to access documents kept in Georgian Archives in Tbilisi, which were written and kept by the Tsarist Russian military leaders and officers of the Southern Russian Command, where Tbilisi was occupied and ruled by the Russian Empire, as Russia continued attacking Circassia from the Southeastern side.[1134]

— The Georgian Parliament within its committees,[1135] studied the Circassians' fair demands, and formed specialized scientific committees consisted of scholars, historians, specialists, and academicians from different origins, even from Russia itself, which they attended special hearings, scientific presentations, and legitimate documents proving the occurrence of the genocide and ethnic cleansing inflicted on the Circassians.

— On the 11th of June 2010, public hearings took place in the Georgian Parliament about the Circassian Question. It was broadcasted live and publicly on Georgian national TV, which was viewed by many Georgians. Two famous Georgian historians, Bejan Chorava and Merab Chukhua, spoke and testified in front of the Georgian Parliament about historic facts. It was shocking to listen to their testimonies and the evidence presented.[1136]

— Fourteen months after presenting the Circassian letter, the Georgian parliamentary committees endorsed on May 19, 2011,[1137] a draft resolution recognizing the 19th century massacre and deportation of Circassians, which the Georgian Parliament held a session on May 20, 2011,[1138] and voted on a draft resolution that resulted in the approval of recognizing the genocide and ethnic cleansing[1139] inflicted on the Circassian nation in the 19th century.[1140]

— On May 21, 2012,[1141] the Circassian Genocide Monument was inaugurated after it was erected on the shore of the Black Sea resort of Anaklia, Georgia, one of the sea ports used to deport the Circassians to the Ottoman Empire, in order to commemorate the Circassian victims and others.[1142] The inauguration of the Circassian Genocide Memorial was part of the Circassian Culture Days, which lasted between May 20–23, 2012.[1143]

— "Papuna Davitaia, the Georgian state minister for diaspora issues, said: This [monument] is an important step towards the Caucasian solidarity, adding that the Georgian state was now capable to carry out its Caucasian policy and engage with the peoples of the North Caucasus."[1144]

Regarding the Southern Russian Command Center in Tbilisi, Georgia, it is worth mentioning the following:

> On 12 April 1802, the Russian commander-in-chief in the Caucasus, General Karl Knorring, published in Tbilisi the imperial proclamation of September 1801, confirming Tsar Paul's earlier decree, and affirming Kartlo-Kakheti to be an integral part of the Russian dominions. The general then administered to the princes and notables of Georgia the oath of allegiance to the Tsar. The effect was somewhat marred by the presence of armed Russian guards around the audience hall, making it clear that any attempt to avoid due compliance would provoke reprisals. A few Georgians who voiced disapproval were taken into custody. This made a poor impression on Russia's new subjects, deemed to have placed themselves voluntarily under the Tsar's benevolent protection."

In light of the disintegration of the Soviet Union, the Georgian Parliament declared "secession from the Soviet Union after independence is overwhelmingly supported in a referendum."[1145]

The Importance of Recognition

Lars Funch Hansen, from the University of Copenhagen, has said in a speech at the Seventh Circassian Day in the European Parliament, Bruxelles, June 18, 2012, titled "Genocide Recognition as a Key Issue in the Circassian Revival," as he questioned, "How the issue of genocide recognition has been reinforced as a key Circassian issue that has been strongly enhanced by 2014

Sochi Winter Olympics as a mega sports event taking place at key locations in the historical Circassian homeland."[1146]

He intended to affirm that the Circassian Genocide recognition is one of the most important pillars of the Circassian renaissance:

> In this presentation I will argue that "genocide recognition" has become a key headline of the Circassian revival—a type of catch-phrase that can encompass most of the aims of the Circassian revival. Genocide recognition has in this way become the 'What' of the Circassian revival—supplementing the 'Where' of 'Sochi'—that has been promoted through the 2014 Winter Olympics—and the already established creation of the 'When' of 1864—especially through the May 21 commemorations of the last twenty years. "Genocide Recognition" through the latter years has become the new headline for the Circassian revival to a much larger degree than earlier. I suggest that these three issues—the "What", the "When" and the "Where"—together can be seen as linked in a triangle where each of the three issues constantly and mutually reinforce each other.[1147]

All related issues were mentioned such as "documentation," and suggested ways and means to consider elements of solution depending on the "Genocide Recognition" as it he stated that: "Circassian civil society actors have managed to enlarge and develop a new space for action – both among the diaspora and in Russia. It is important to stress that this is not just a virtual space. It includes the use of the internet as both a means of publication of and campaigning for counter-versions of the Circassian identity and history – as seen in the case of promoting the understanding of the exile as an act of genocide – and as a means of communication, coordination and cooperation between the Circassian organisations. The arrival and increased outreach of the social media of Web 2.0 has resulted in new forms of youth activism and has further resulted in a large number of discussions on the definition and understanding of Circassian history and identity on sites such as Facebook, YouTube etc."[1148]

Russian scholar VM Mikhailov, who is a senior research fellow at the Center for the Caucasus and Regions, says Moscow's mistakes opened the way for the Circassians abroad to raise genocide issues.[1149]

A. Bogus, M. Cherkesov, and A. Sokht, the presidents of the Circassian associations called "Adyghe Hase," in the Republic of Adygea, the Karachay-Cherkess Republic, and the Province of Krasnodar, sent a letter in May 2013 to the President of the Russian Federation Putin V.V. and to the Federal

Assembly of the Russian Federation, urging the Russian leadership to consider the Circassian situation realistically and to work on the recognition of the Circassian Genocide, in accordance with available data, and they concluded their call in the last paragraph: "We find that the infinite ignoring this complex of problems is counterproductive. We hope that our appeal will be treated with due care, and the raised complex of problems will be effectively solved."[1150]

In May 2013, the leader of the Kurdish Peace and Democracy Party (BDP) in Turkey, Selahattin Demirtaş, has addressed the public about the Circassian Day of Remembrance, and he expressed his desire to demand from parliament to recognize the Circassian Genocide. Selahattin Demirtaş said:

> This morning, Circassian associations held protest actions in front of the Russian Embassy. In our turn, we intend to propose that parliament recognize the Circassian genocide and promote publicity for this issue in the international political arena.[1151]

> Moreover, on May 18, the Circassian diaspora in Istanbul unveiled a monument dedicated to the genocide and exile of the Circassians. The organizers of the event invited Turkish Prime Minister Recep Tayyip Erdo?an to attend, and even though the prime minister did not find time to visit the site, he sent a sympathetic letter stating: "I reckon that such events possess special importance for both, receiving international acclaim and strengthening our unity and brotherhood that is held together by honoring the memory of those who died in exile."[1152]

The developments that accompanied shooting down the Sukhoi-24 Russian warplane in November 2015, on the Turkish-Syrian borders, including the media war of words, will probably affect the course of events with regard to the Circassian Question. The recognition of the Circassian Genocide as far as Turkey is concerned will be inevitable, especially that Russia has already recognized the Armenian Genocide, would be at hand at any time if the Turkish State considers taking this step. "The 'genocide' issue is especially sensitive for Turkey, because of Armenians' claims that Turkey should recognize the atrocities committed in 1915 as 'genocide' by the Ottoman Empire. The Russian Federation officially recognized the Armenian 'genocide' in 1995 (http://ria.ru/spravka/20100305/212370444.html), so if Turkey were to recognize the Circassian 'genocide' by the Russian Empire in 19th century, it would be only a belated tit-for-tat move."[1153]

Georgia is thus far the only country in the world to have officially recognized the Circassian "genocide": it did so in 2011. Turkey may want to avoid negative repercussions, as it has relatively warm relations with Russia. At the same time, Turkey is certainly trying to establish itself as a regional power that has its own views on the countries that border it. This means that Ankara will have to make some decisions that strengthen its identity and show its leadership role. Therefore, the issue of recognizing the Circassian "genocide" appears to be growing as part of the widening public debate inside Turkey.[1154]

Under constant Circassian demands, to this day, and on each occasion, they look to the subject of their exposure of their people to genocide, which lead to heavy casualties, as the foundation to be taken to remove the sorrow as well as for the restoration of the Circassians' rights in accordance with international laws and norms. "On May 21 (2014), Circassian communities worldwide commemorated the 150th anniversary of the end of the Russian-Circassian war."[1155]

The voice of Turkish officials, where the majority of Circassians reside, was also unusually strong. The deputy speaker of the Turkish parliament, Sadik Yakut, said: "The right of return of peoples who were expelled from their homeland should be considered from the point of view of human rights. Circassians have the natural right to be granted dual citizenship in countries where they reside, and for May 21 to be recognized as the day of the genocide and expulsion of Circassians." (http://www.aheku.org/news/society/5822)[1156]

The Russian authorities have not only ignored the call of logic and reason, which calls for dealing with the Circassians' issues in tactics of humanity for solving all overdue and unsolved problems, but it even went beyond that to create excuses leading to new heresies purposely to falsify the facts altogether.

Russian historians pretend that history is free from government intervention despite the fact that President Putin himself has urged the government to produce a single view of Russian history to avoid stirring doubts and controversy within the younger generation. Many Russian historians still use outdated concepts, describing the deportation of the Circassians to the Ottoman Empire as a "voluntary resettlement" and even denying the very fact of the Russian-Circassian wars. The language used by Russian professional historians is often quite biased. For example, instead of saying that the Russian Empire conquered the North Caucasus, they say "after many military campaigns between the Russian armies and the mountaineers, the region entered the Russian Empire." (http://georgia.kavkaz-uzel.ru/articles/242940/)[1157]

Circassian Activists for Genocide Recognition

An article by Eurasia Daily Monitor listed several events and facts that occurred with Circassian activists in the North Caucasus, which showed the insistence of the Russian authorities using police tactics to downplay the activities carried out by the Circassians. The article added,

> Khuade, for his part, told Natpress: "They said that the reason for the investigation was my possible involvement in another case against five immigrants from Turkey, who, in the opinion of investigators, acquired land illegally in the village of Khamyshki in Maikop district." He said investigators confiscated cell phones, a computer hard drive and other digital devices to sift through and try to find at least something that would allow them to connect Khuade to the alleged land fraud. Khuade said the real reason for the government pressure on him was that he repeatedly signed petitions initiated by Circassian activists asking foreign governments, including the Ukrainian, Polish, Lithuanian and Estonian governments, to officially recognize the Russian "genocide" of the Circassians in the 19th century (Natpressru.info, May 26).[1158]

The Circassian Representatives Meet with Members of the Riigikogu

There was an initiative by Patriots of Circassia, with the participation of Circassians from both the diaspora and the homeland, where they sent letters in several languages to several countries. They sent letters to Ukraine, Poland, Latvia, Estonia, Finland, Moldavia, and Turkey. The letters were signed by the participants to inform those countries of Russia's denial of its own doings.

The letters explained the Circassian catastrophe and requested to recognize the difficulties and obstacles that the Circassians have faced. They explained the crimes committed by the Russian Empire against the people of Circassia, such as genocide and forced exile.

On the eighth of May 2015, the Circassians sent a letter to the Estonian president, the prime minister and the president of the Parliament. On the fourth of June, Circassian envoys met the Foreign Committee of the Estonian Parliament. They handed a letter from the Circassians and explained the plight endured by the Circassian nation.

The letter explained the Circassians' concerns and concluded, "We call upon the people of Estonia represented by its Parliament to follow similar approach made by the Parliament of the people of Georgia in recognizing the Circassian Genocide and the ethnic cleansing of our people as a Genocide and a crime against humanity."[1159]

In a press release issued by the Riigikogu of Estonia, the "chairman of the Foreign Affairs Committee of the Riigikogu Hannes Hanso said that the fate of the Circassians is a historical issue that by today has acquired a clearly international character. In Hanso's opinion, the Circassians support the European values."[1160]

In addition, "member of the Riigikogu Eerik-Niiles Kross said that Estonians have a certain debt of honour to the Circassians, because the Estonian settlers near the Black Sea, for example, in Krasnaya Polyana, were settled on the Circassian lands. Kross noted that during the 150 years of living in exile, this North-Caucasian nation has preserved both its language and its culture, and added that today the communication of the Circassians with their historic homeland is hindered, several hundreds of thousands of Circassians live as refugees as a result of the Syrian War."[1161]

....

Publication: Eurasia Daily Monitor Volume: 11 Issue: 98
May 27, 2014
By: Valery Dzutsev
Circassians Want Russia to Recognize 19th Century Conquest as "Genocide"
Ribbons commemorating the 150th anniversary of the end of the Russian-Circassian War[1162]

On May 21, Circassian communities worldwide commemorated the 150th anniversary of the end of the Russian-Circassian war. According to some accounts, the war lasted for a hundred years—from 1763, when Russian armies invaded Eastern

Kabarda, to 1864 when the Russian military paraded at the place Krasnaya Polyana near the modern-day city of Sochi. The Russian Empire killed or deported to the Ottoman Empire an estimated 90 percent of the Circassian population of the Caucasus. As a result of the large-scale deportation of the Circassians, the majority of them now reside outside their North Caucasus homeland. To mark the anniversary, Circassians held demonstrations in Turkey, Germany, the United States, the North Caucasus and elsewhere.

The Circassian-Russian war of the 19th century has been a matter of great controversy in the North Caucasus. The tensions derive from the Circassian belief that Moscow should recognize what the Russian Empire did to the Circassians as "an act of genocide." The Russian government, in turn, tries to ignore the issue or deny its importance, quietly putting pressure on the regional authorities in the North Caucasus to alter the discourse. In the run-up to the 150th anniversary of the conclusion of the Russian-Circassian war, Circassian organizations in Adygea, Karachaevo-Cherkessia and the Krasnodar region addressed President Vladimir Putin once again, asking him to recognize the "Circassian genocide" (http://www.aheku.net/news/society/3542). More importantly, a group of activists from the North Caucasus, led by Israeli activist Avrom Shmulevich, addressed Ukraine's acting president, Oleksandr Turchynov, asking him to recognize the "Circassian genocide" (http://www.natpress.info/index.php?newsid=8989). The activists apparently expect the Ukrainian government to be especially sympathetic to the plight of the Circassians in the North Caucasus, given Russia's aggressive policies against Ukraine. Shmulevich predicted that Ukraine would recognize the "Circassian genocide" before the end of 2014 (http://avrom-caucasus.livejournal.com/359996.html). The voice of Turkish officials, where the majority of Circassians reside, was also unusually strong. The deputy speaker of the Turkish parliament, Sadik Yakut, said: "The right of return of peoples who were expelled from their homeland should be considered from the point of view of human rights. Circassians have the natural right to be granted dual citizenship in countries where they reside, and for May 21 to be recognized as the day of the genocide and expulsion of Circassians" (http://www. aheku.org/news/society/5822). The authorities in republics with titular Circassian populations have remained relatively timid. For example, several years ago, Circassian activists in Adygea asked the authorities to build a monument dedicated to the Circassian victims of the Russian-Circassian war. The government instead built a monument called Unity and Accord that included both those who fought on the Russian side and on their home country's side. A Circassian activist from Adygea, Aslan Shazzo, told Ekho Kavkaza radio: "We want a monument for our fallen. Only defenders of the homeland should be among them, but not the tsarist soldiers who died in the war." In Nalchik, Kabardino-Balkaria, republican officials oversaw the celebrations this year. Republican Deputy Prime Minister Ruslan Firov practically chaired the commission on celebrations. An estimated 3,000–4,000 people participated in the events in Nalchik. The Russian authorities' pressure manifested itself most vividly in Moscow. Police arrested Circassian activist Beslan Teuvazhev on May 19, and law enforcement agents confiscated 71,000 Circassian ribbons, which depicted Circassian symbols and dates of the Russian-Circassian war. Teuvazhev was soon released, but the police did not return the ribbons, saying they were being checked "for extremism" (http://www.ekhokavkaza.com/content/article/25393637.html). On May 20, Circassian activists in the village of Akhintam, in the Sochi area, held a night vigil, lighting 101 candles—representing the number of years the Russian-Circassian war lasted. A Circassian leader from Krasnodar region, Aslan Gvashev, told Kavkazsky Uzel that Circassians perceive the Black Sea as a big grave for all the Circassians deported in the 1860s. "The majority of the coastal Circassian villages do not fish and do not even swim in the sea. This sea is full of our ancestors' bones and we cannot allow ourselves any other attitude," Gvashev said (http://www.kavkaz-uzel.ru/articles/242975/). Sergei Arutyunov, a well-known Russian historian and member of the Russian Academy of Sciences, told Kavkazsky Uzel that in order to resolve the controversy around the Russian-Circassian war, the Russian government should recognize the Circassian "genocide." Moreover, Arutyunov suggested that the government remove monuments dedicated to Russian heroes who fought in the North Caucasus and return the original names of the settlements. Referring to a town in the Sochi area named after General Ivan Lazarev—who was known, especially among the Circassians, for his brutality during the Russian conquest of the Caucasus in the 18th–19th centuries—Arutyunov said: "Lazarev was a person of great accomplishments in Russian history and no one is prepared to forget about that. However, the settlement called Lazarevsky should be somewhere where he was born or some other place that is connected to his biography, not in the place where he fought and where his role was controversial" (http://www.kavkaz-uzel.ru/articles/242980/). The Russian authorities installed monuments dedicated to controversial Russian generals in the historical Circassians lands, further antagonizing the Circassian population. Russian historians pretend that history is free from government intervention despite the fact that President Putin himself has urged the government to produce a single view of Russian history to avoid stirring doubts and controversy within the younger generation. Many Russian historians still use outdated concepts, describing the deportation of the Circassians to the Ottoman Empire as a "voluntary resettlement" and even denying the very fact of the Russian-Circassian wars. The language used by Russian professional historians is often quite biased. For example, instead of saying that the Russian Empire conquered the North Caucasus, they say "after many military campaigns between the Russian armies and the mountaineers, the region entered the Russian Empire" (http://georgia.kavkaz-uzel.ru/articles/242940/). In using such wording, Russian historians and politicians are attempting to put the conquerors and their victims on the same footing and depersonalize the conquest of the North Caucasus by Russia as a kind of process of accession of the region into the Russian state that progressed almost on its own. Circassians have become remarkably united around the tragic events of the past and Russian authorities will have to take this into account sooner or later.[1163]

....

Circassians Want Genocide to be Recognized by Russia, Turkey

Saturday May 24, 2014.

Circassians in Turkey have called on Russia to recognize what they call a genocide against their ancestors, most of whom were killed or expelled from their homeland in the North Caucasus in the 19th century, and have appealed to the international community to bring them justice.

"The genocide against the Circassians was a crime against humanity and we urge Russia to recognize it as such, even though we know that these atrocities will not see justice," Erdoğan Boz, a board member of the Ankara-based Circassian Foundation, said in an interview with Sunday's Zaman. Boz also said steps need to be taken to secure justice for Circassians, such as securing unconditional recognition from Russia of their right to return from around the world to their homeland, building up the status of the Circassian language in the modern sub-national republics in Russia with large Circassian populations and providing greater political rights to Circassians in their homeland.

Almost all Circassians were expelled from their native lands in the northwestern Caucasus in the aftermath of the 1817–1864 Caucasian War. Those remaining were later scattered, and mostly live in three semi-autonomous republics in Russia: the Republic of Adygea, the Karachay-Cherkess Republic and the Kabardino-Balkar Republic. Their homeland is now home to only 700,000 Circassians—a fraction of the total community. Over 90 percent of Circassians were killed or forcibly deported to the Ottoman Empire or other parts of Russia. More than half of the exiled and deported people died of hunger and illness within a few years. The Unrepresented Nations and Peoples Organization (UNPO) estimates that the Circassian diaspora is 3 million strong, of whom an estimated 2 million live in Turkey, about 150,000 in Syria, Jordan and Israel and about 50,000 in Europe and the United States.

Calling the historical experiences of the Circassians "a battle waged to maintain their population in their native lands," Boz says the mass atrocities against the Circassians fit well with the concept of genocide as defined by Raphael Lemkin in

1948, and the international community should put pressure on Moscow, which is "responsible for the painful past of the Circassians and should recognize the genocide."

"However, despite 150 years having passed since then, Russia has not taken any steps in the direction of recognizing the genocide," Boz said, adding that there have actually been changes for the worse, with Moscow not only refusing to listen to their demands but continuing to increase oppression, especially amid the recent Sochi Olympics controversy.

A tragic history

The Circassians, a largely Muslim population of the North Caucasus, argued before the Sochi Olympics held in February of this year that holding the Winter Olympics in Sochi—a city located on the site of Circassian massacres—on the eve of the 150th anniversary of the alleged genocide is at odds with the Olympic spirit of peace and fair play. Moscow clamped down heavily on Circassian activists across the country, and President Vladimir Putin said in a statement on Feb. 10 that the Circassian issue is being artificially stoked to divide Russia and the West and aims to damage the country's image in the world.

Ethnic cleansing was not only led against Circassians in North Caucasus early 19th century. Russia waged a series of military actions against Caucasian ethnic groups including Chechens, the Abkhaz people, the Ubykh people and many ethnicities in Dagestan as Russia sought to expand southward into territories in geographically important places between Russia, Iran and the Ottoman Empire.

On May 21 of each year, Circassians living in different parts of the world, including Turkey, mark the anniversary of the massacre carried out against their ancestors in 1864. This year, it was commemorated more solemnly as 2014 is the 150th anniversary of the Circassian ethnic cleansing.

The ethnic cleansing of Circassians by Russia and their expulsion from their homeland constitute the most essential elements of the national identity of the Circassians, binding together groups scattered around the globe.

"No matter whether you call it the Great Circassian Exile, the mass ethnic cleansing of Circassians or a genocide, it forms a basis of Circassian identity, a nation forced to leave its homeland. Without this, it is impossible to talk about the Circassian identity," Boz said.

Turkey needs to recognize Circassian genocide.
The Ottoman Empire was one of the first stops for the deported Circassians.

Upon arrival in the Ottoman Empire, the Circassians did not know Turkish but after 150 years, they are on the brink of losing their native language, says Murat Yalçın, co-founder of the İstanbul Circassian Foundation, who told Sunday's Zaman that the Circassians are losing their own culture in Turkey.

"We have no TV stations that broadcast in the Circassian language seven days a week, 24 hours a day. Elective Circassian language courses in school are inadequate. We want our native language to be taught in schools. In history textbooks, there are statements that hurt Circassians and that need to be changed," Yalçın said.

"In addition, the Turkish Republic, where hundreds of thousands of Circassians are now living, has to recognize the Circassian genocide. Turkey should support the study of the Circassian genocide and assist attempts to establish a museum of the genocide," he continued.

Turkey maintains very close economic ties with Russia and has never issued an official statement on the Circassian genocide. On the eve of the 2014 Sochi Winter Olympics, Circassians in Turkey called on Prime Minister Recep Tayyip Erdoğan not to attend the Winter Olympics, claiming that his attendance would show that the Turkish government is insensitive to the feelings of its Circassian minority. Nevertheless, Erdoğan visited Sochi and met with President Putin before the opening ceremony of the 2014 Winter Olympics.[1164]

....

About Circassian Genocide Perpetrated by Russian State in 1861–1864

9, February, 2014

- Based upon irrefutable historical facts testifying to the crimes committed by the

Russian officials against the Circassian population, within their ancient Motherland, Circassia, during the years of 1861–1864;

Being aware of the resembling destinies of Circassian and Armenian nations, which experienced similar tragedies,

Being aware that part of the Armenian population of Western Armenia had resulted to live within the territories of Circassia in the course of the Armenian Genocide of 1915–1923.

Acknowledging the annihilation of Circassians in Circassia according to the plans of Russian Administration, which further initiated "peoples' exchange" between Russia and Turkey, triggering the reasons for the tragedy of Armenian nation.

Sharing with the brotherly Circassian nation, mutual Caucasian values and moralities.

Remembering about the equality of the identities of Circassians and Armenian community of Circassia, known in history under the name of Cherkeso-Ghay.

We, the representatives of Armenian communities of USA, united into organizations and associations,

1. Condemn policies of Russian State, which organized the annihilation and deportation of the Circassians in 1861-1864, resulting into the drastic changes of the demographic situation in the Caucasus, and consider May 21st as a day of the Circassian Genocide.

2. Urge the Governments of the Republic of Armenian, Nagorno-Karabakh Republic, and all the Armenian organizations worldwide join to and undersign our statement.[1165]

The Dimensions of Designing and Building a Genocide Monument

After the Parliament of Georgia recognized the Circassian Genocide and ethnic cleansing inflicted on the Circassian nation in the nineteenth century, the Georgian government decided to construct a monument in Anaklia, in memory of the perished victims and those who had been deported to the Ottoman Empire.

The victims' descendants did not forget their homeland, even after the elapse of approximately a century and a half from the end of the war imposed on the Circassian nation and the occurrence of genocide and deportation. That even increased the bonds of brotherhood and belonging among the Circassian people, whether they are in their homeland in the North Caucasus or in Diaspora.

A competition for designing a memorial had been declared: "29 competitors had participated in the contest from Georgia, USA, Turkey, Jordan and the North Caucasus." Circassian and non-Circassian competitors from different countries presented their diligent symbolic efforts to commemorate the important event. In December 2011, the top three winners won rewards presented by the committee commissioned by the Georgian government while four additional symbolic prizes were presented by the International Circassian Council.[1166]

The top winning project had been utilized to construct a memorial in Anaklia, Georgia, on the Black Sea. It was designed by Hussein Kochesokov, a Circassian artist from Lower Kurkuzhin, Republic of Kabardino-Balkaria. The Circassian Genocide Memorial on the Black Sea coastal resort of Anaklia was constructed and subsequently inaugurated on the 21st of May 2012, in the presence of Circassians from several countries including the Circassian homeland in the North Caucasus. In addition, their friends and supporters from Georgia and various Diaspora countries were invited as well. The exceptional inaugural ceremonies coincided with the yearly remembrance of the postponement of the Russian-Circassian War.[1167]

Circassian flags were raised, and red roses were thrown in the Black Sea by the participants, dedicated to the Circassian victims annihilated and forced into exile by the Tsarist Russian Empire; to add to that, Anaklia in the nineteenth century was occupied by Russia and was a marine garrison on the Black Sea, which is a Georgian territorial entity.

During their long journey of exodus and deportation, some of the Circassians were gathered in Anaklia. It was one of the ports used by the Russian authorities to deport the Circassians to the Ottoman Empire.

In an interview with Hussein Kochesokov, the winner of the first prize for his design published by NatPress, quoting Gazeta Yuga, gives an important indication that the sons and daughters of the Circassian nation are associated and linked with indissoluble strong bonds, despite the prolonged time after the tragedy, geographical distribution and remoteness, and the fact that the Circassians live in many countries of the world including their fragmented historical homeland.[1168]

Kochesokov knew about the competition through his son, who is a historian, and read about it on the internet: "I thought to myself 'Maybe I'll be lucky?' and said to my son that I would make the sculpture. And I worked over it for two months: after classes with children in school—as I have classes of sculpturing—I came home, sculpted from clay for 2–3 hours."[1169]

He explained what he felt and reflected that in his meaningful artistic work: "I find it hard to express the whole meaning, which I had put in my sculpture. But I was very upset. Circassia was a big country. And now it's not. This is the genocide. On the pedestal of my sculpture in a circle there is a figure: a Russian soldier facing a Circassian Wark on a horseback near—dying women and children, old plates with inscriptions, emblems, dolmens, a century-old oak tree—the symbol of Circassians and an old man, stretching his hands to the sky. Under an oak tree—the inscription 'Praise be to Allah.' And then—the sea, a ship with Circassians, sailing to a strange land . . . On the pedestal there is a weeping woman, hugged by a girl, and a boy standing proudly and looking hard far away. Their father is not with them—all the men were killed."[1170]

He was asked about the political dimension of his participation, but answered: "At first I did not fear, and when I finished my sculpture I started thinking. But I do not care. I love my people. I know what we have experienced. I want at least something to do for him. I think I'm a patriot. I read a lot, I know a lot about our history, I worry about it... Let something happen to me, but all this is for my people."[1171]

The Circassian Question and the Ukrainian Factor

According to facts, proceedings, and documents it is mandatory for the Russian State to recognize the Circassian Genocide. In that regard, Paul Goble published an article titled, Russians Won't Admit Expulsion of Circassians was Genocide—But Ukrainians Should.

Goble has started by mentioning the commemoration of the Circassian Memorial Day. "One hundred fifty-two years ago today, tsarist forces defeated the Circassians in the North Caucasus after the latter had successfully resisted the Russian advance for 101 years and then the Russian government expelled most of them to the Ottoman Empire, completing the genocidal policy that St. Petersburg had decided upon early on."[1172]

The article recalled the intransigence of denying the invasion's outcome: "Russian officials to this day can't admit this not only because to do so would allow many of the five million Circassians in the diaspora to return home, changing the ethnic balance in the North Caucasus away from Moscow, and because such honesty would inevitably provoke more questions about Russia's imperial policies elsewhere."[1173]

The article pointed out, "But on this anniversary in particular, one that pro-Moscow groups even more in the past are seeking to limit the commemoration of within Russia and beyond and to confuse the issue in the minds of many, Ukrainians should take the lead in recognizing what Russia did as genocide not only on moral grounds but because of the role Circassians have played in Ukrainian history."[1174]

Goble addressed and quoted a viewpoint that is related to the Circassian Question: "That is the thrust of an article by Avraam Shmulyevich, an Israeli expert on the Caucasus, in a message to Ukrainians on the TSN news portal (ru.tsn.ua/blogi/themes/politics/genocid-cherkesov-esche-odno-prestuplenie-rossii-634709.html). It is one with which people of good will in Ukraine, Russia and around the world can only agree."[1175]

The article continued, "The Israeli scholar points out that the Circassians resisted the expansion of Russian power in the Caucasus longer than anyone else, from 1763 to 1864, thus earning the grudging respect of those who took part in the battles against them but also the undying hatred of the Russian state which decided that it could only hold the region by getting rid of its residents."[1176]

Goble verifies the Russians' plans and intentions: "Already in September 1829, Shmulyevich says, Nicholas I wrote that 'having finished one glorious task [the war with Turkey], we now have another, just as complicated and in terms of direct benefit to us much more important the suppression of all the mountain peoples and the destruction of the disobedient.'" Then he added, "Nicholas I did not live to see that day; and Russia's greatest poet, Aleksandr Pushkin in his 'Passage to Arzrum' put the Russian 'task' even more clearly: 'The Circassians', he wrote, 'hate us. We have driven them out of their customary fields, their auls have been burned, whole tribes have been destroyed.'"[1177]

The so-described greatest Russian poet, playwright, novelist, and the founder of modern Russian literature, showed no regard for humanity or to the fact that the Russian Empire invaded and occupied the Circassian nation while killing and deporting its people. The article reveals, "As a result, the poet continued, 'there is almost no way to pacify [the Circassians] even after they are disarmed as were disarmed the Crimean Tatars.'"[1178]

The article elaborated on figures: "At the end of the 101-year war, the Russian army in the North Caucasus numbered some 300,000 men and was suffering annual losses of 30,000. The Russian state was spending a sixth of its budget on the task of defeating the Circassians and their allies, and it was prepared to be brutal, Shmulyevich says."[1179]

It stated the actions of the invading forces and their similarity with the criminal actions after decades against the Ukrainians: "'In the course of military operations', he writes, 'the Russian army burned auls together with their residents', and it 'widely applied the tactic of the terror famine [holodomor] by destroying crops and reserves of food, condemning the mountaineers to hunger'. And not least, 'the tsarist government took the decision to completely cleanse the Caucasus from its indigenous residents, the Circassians, to physically destroy an entire people.'"[1180] Then he explained more of the plans: "Those it couldn't destroy in this way, the tsarist authorities decided, must be expelled beyond the borders of the empire. As one Russian general put it, the Russian state needs the lands of the Circassians, but it has no need for the Circassian people and so they must be killed or expelled."[1181]

The article clarified some figures of casualties, fatalities, deportees, and for those who managed to stay behind.

> Tsarist historians had no problem talking about this and about the losses involved. According to Russian government accounts of those times, more than 400,000 Circassians were killed and 497,000 forced to leave the empire. From what had been an autochthonian nation in the region of more than a million remained "about 80,000" Circassians . . . A large number of Circassians who were expelled to the Ottoman Empire, Shmulyevich says, never made it to their destination. Only about a third of those who were put on ships in Sochi arrived alive on the other side of the Black Sea. The rest died from hunger, disease, and drowning.[1182]

Referring to Article II of the Convention on the Prevention and Punishment of the Crime of Genocide, it states,

In the present Convention, genocide means any of the following acts committed with intent to destroy, in whole or in part, a national, ethnical, racial or religious group, as such:

(a) Killing members of the group;
(b) Causing serious bodily or mental harm to members of the group;
(c) Deliberately inflicting on the group conditions of life calculated to bring about its physical destruction in whole or in part;
(d) Imposing measures intended to prevent births within the group;
(e) Forcibly transferring children of the group to another group.[1183]

Goble stressed, "This was an obvious case of genocide, the physical destruction of a people on the basis of its identity alone. Unfortunately, the Russian authorities continue to deny that their predecessors committed a genocide and have gone further by dividing up the Circassian nation into five parts in five different administrative districts."[1184]

The article also mentioned the Circassian demographic dimensions: "Circassians—and they number more than 500,000 in the North Caucasus and five million in the diaspora—Shmulyevich notes, are 'struggling for unity, for the right to return to their historical Motherland, for the preservation of their culture and historical memory and for recognition of the most horrible crimes committed against them—genocide and a terror famine.'" It then continued to elucidate, "For a variety of reasons, the Israeli analyst continues, 'the much suffering Ukrainian people as no one else can with sympathy and understanding relate to the tragedy of the Circassian people which has been deprived of its rights to return to its Motherland and even to the right of historical memory.'"[1185]

The article listed several factors that combine, compose, and reconcile Circassians and Ukrainians from a long time ago. With no doubt, the hopes that were held on achieving tangible results will encourage coordination and dialogue. This will synchronize bilateral work to recognize the Circassians' legitimate rights.

Goble stated, "In 2011, Georgia became the first country to officially recognize what the Russians did to the Circassians as genocide. Now, Ukrainians should become the second, the Israeli analyst argues, not only on moral grounds but also for deeply practical ones." In addition, he added, "'A country battling foreign aggression needs to find new friends', he writes, 'and the Caucasus can become an ally of Ukraine against imperial Moscow'. The Ukrainian parliament should recognize this reality and adopt a resolution recognizing the Russian treatment of the Circassians as genocide."[1186]

The article concluded, "'May 21', he concludes, 'is a day of sorry and memory not only of the Circassian people but of all peoples who have become victims of the pitiless and destructive Russian colonialism, victims of Russian aggression.'"[1187]

Recognizing the Circassians' Rights

The Daily Sabah (Turkish newspaper) published an article titled, "Circassians Seek Recognition of Genocide by Russia." It started with its introduction by saying, "The Circassian community in Turkey hopes the expulsion and genocide of their ancestors by Russia will be recognized both by Ankara and the Kremlin on the 152nd anniversary of their exile from the Caucasus."[1188]

The article stated, "Ahead of the 152nd anniversary of its expulsion and ethnic cleansing by the Russian Empire in the 19th century, Turkey's Circassian community is demanding international recognition for what they term genocide at the hands of the now-defunct empire." The article continued, "Turkey has a sizable community of Circassians, a Caucasian ethnic group many of whom left their homeland due to Russian policies to drive out minorities. Every year, they mark the anniversary of their expulsion, which landed many Circassians in Turkey and other countries in the region, by staging events across the country and rallies outside Russian diplomatic missions. This year, demonstrations are scheduled for May 21, or Circassian Genocide and Exile Day as the community calls it."[1189]

The newspaper added, "Nusret Baş, head of the Federation of Circassian Associations, a prominent nonprofit representing the community, told the state-run Anadolu Agency (AA) that they seek recognition of the genocide around the world, especially in Turkey, and urge Parliament to launch an inquiry into the genocide and recognize it. Baş said 1864 was a year when their community was 'destroyed, oppressed, driven out of their homes and their rights were trampled on' and was "a year of heartbreak and unforgettable suffering.'" [1190]

Russian ambitions are mentioned to be against other peoples of the Caucasus beside the Adyghe Circassians: "The expulsion of Circassians, who call themselves Adyghe, happened toward the end of the decline of the Ottoman Empire, whose clout spread to the Caucasus, and at a time of an ambitious campaign by the Russian Empire to extend its borders despite tough resistance locals in the region—Circassians, Abkhazians, Chechens and others. The resistance, which gained prominence through the leadership of Sheikh Shamil, was brutally quashed with massacres of local populations and subsequent exile. Most Circassians were herded onto ships to be transferred from the northeastern shores of the Black Sea to Anatolia. Thousands perished due to hunger and thirst, and many others died when their ships sank. Estimates range from 300,000 to 4 million deaths as a result."[1191]

The Daily Sabah clarified the intentions of the colonial Russian ambitions:

> "Caucasia was a place where Circassians lived freely for centuries, but they were an obstacle for Russia's plans to expand to the south. Circassians defended their lands for more than a century, but they were a meager force compared to the vast army of Russia. In the end, the community was destroyed, forced to surrender as a result of disproportionate Russian attacks that included killing innocent civilians. This was genocide in the true meaning of the word and fits the genocide description of the United Nations", Baş said. He said Circassians who still live in the Caucasus are still deemed a threat by present-day Russia and are under constant surveillance by Moscow. "[Russian President Vladimir] Putin pursues the same policy on Circassians as the policies he executed in Crimea, Ukraine and Syria", he said.

The article stated, "'The Circassian genocide is currently only recognized by Georgia, a foe of the Kremlin since the collapse of Soviet Union. But Turkey has the largest Circassian population, and this is why we want Turkey to recognize it, too', Baş said. A Cabinet minister attended last year's commemoration ceremony of the Circassian exile." In addition, "Foreign Ministry spokesman Tanju Bilgiç said on Friday in a statement in response to a question that the Circassian exile was 'a great disaster etched into the memory of Caucasian people expelled from their homeland.'"[1192]

The newspaper continued, "Baş said their demand is not 'revenge' but rather to 'reveal a historical truth'. 'We are not aiming to raise a political matter, and we are not enemies of the Russian people. Russia has a responsibility to recognize the genocide', he said. Baş said their calls have not drawn attention from the international community, as it involves Russia, a global superpower. 'Other than that, our cause is not championed because Circassians are Muslims', he claimed."

The article concluded, "Turkey has a well-integrated Circassian community of about 1.5 million to 3 million people, mainly concentrated in the northern provinces of Samsun, Amasya, Tokat and the northwestern provinces of Sakarya, Kocaeli, Balıkesir and Kütahya. There are currently about 750,000 in Caucasian republics currently located in the Russian Federation. High estimates of Circassian communities in Jordan and Syria are about 180,000 and 120,000, respectively, although the latter has suffered from civil war in the last five years."[1193]

Circassians and Crimean Tatars and the Risk of Repression

On the fourteenth of May 2016, Window on Eurasia published an article titled "Under Putin, Circassians and Crimean Tatars at Greatest Risk of Repression – and for Same Reasons" by the respected analyst Paul Goble. He started by saying, "For most of Soviet times, Western commentators, to the extent they dealt with the issue at all, assumed that those ethnic communities inside the USSR which the West ignored were most at risk of repression because Moscow could act without fear of international repercussions."[1194]

Brevity is given about the attention from the West toward peoples under Russian control. The article clarified that "under Vladimir Putin, those which have attracted a large amount of attention in the West and then lost it are most at risk because the Kremlin leader views them as 'agents' of the West and thus prime candidates for repression."[1195]

Paying attention to the repressed peoples is evident: "Among all the nations inside the borders of the Russian Federation or occupied by Russian forces, the two that fall into the category of having attracted enormous attention at one point and then less attention after a time are the Circassians in the North Caucasus and the Crimean Tatars whose homeland is on the Ukrainian peninsula."[1196]

Goble illustrated the lack of knowledge about the demographic distribution of Circassians: "Prior to the Sochi Olympics, few beyond the specialist community paid much attention to the large Circassian population in the North Caucasus (500,000) and in the Middle East (more than five million); but thanks to the work of Circassian activists in both the homeland and the diaspora, the world came to know the history of this proud people."[1197]

He stated that "the Circassians resist Russian aggression far longer than any other people eventually absorbed into the empire" and continued "Putin was anything but pleased with the attention they attracted during the run-up to the Sochi Games, but he was constrained by it from acting against this nation. Indeed, in order to muddy the waters in his best 'hybrid' fashion, the Kremlin leader even made certain concessions to them and promised more."[1198]

The article showed the weakness of the media and political attention received: "But unfortunately and despite new and compelling reasons for paying attention to this nation—many of its members are attempting to flee from war-torn Syria and have been blocked from returning to their ancestral homeland—international attention has flagged. Circassian activists continue to speak out, but they no longer have the 'peg' the Olympics represented to tie stories about them to and thus are getting less and less media and political attention."[1199]

The analysis has demonstrated how the Circassians are still targeted and suppressed: "Because of that and because of their actions earlier, Circassians appear to have become a target for Putin's increasing repression. And his crackdown on them is likely to increase because he believes they deserve punishment for what they did earlier and he is convinced that they will see that this time around the West will ignore them—and feel compelled to turn to him." [1200]

Goble's explanation struck a nerve. He mentioned that there is a lack of interest to comprehend the plagued outcomes for oppressed peoples and nations due to invasion and colonial occupation: "But now, while Western outlets still talk about the need for Russia to return Crimea to Ukraine, they speak less and less about the Crimean Tatars—and Moscow has responded in the same way it has to the Circassians after the West began to ignore them against after the Sochi Games were over."[1201]

The objective analysis has uncovered the importance of presenting the information. This explains that the Circassians still lack the ability of presenting well-prepared documentation about their plight: "Russian repression of the Crimean Tatars has been far better documented than has Russian repression against the Circassians, thanks to the work of a remarkable group of Crimean Tatar and Ukrainian journalists and activists and the fact that Russian repressions in Crimea have been so outlandish and brutal."[1202]

Nevertheless, the article emphasizes that the information is mostly circulated in local Ukrainian media outlets. It emphasizes that the Russian State takes advantage of the shortage and the lack of dissemination of information. The fewer stories about the Circassians and the Crimean Tatars that appear, the more confident he will be that he can get away with his authoritarian actions. The only way he can be stopped is for the West to begin paying more attention to both these peoples and others in the new Russian empire. Goble concluded, "Western media outlets and governments have a double obligation for doing so: On the one hand, it is a simple matter of morality to defend the weak victims against the often vicious strong. And on the other, earlier Western coverage helped make these people targets of Russian repression. Only more coverage of them has a chance of stopping Putin's moves against them."[1203]

Commemorating Genocide

Georgia's leading independent English-language newspaper, Georgia Today, published an article titled "Circassians Around the World Commemorate

Genocide" by Nicholas Waller. It dealt with the Circassians' commemoration of the genocide and its consequences.

The author started with an introduction quoting the Russian military command: "In this year of 1864, a deed has been accomplished that is almost without precedent in human history: not one of the mountaineer inhabitants remains on their former places of residence, and measures are being taken to cleanse the region to prepare it for the new Russian population."—General Staff of Imperial Russian Army in the Caucasus."[1204]

Waller has stated, "Russia's century-long conquest of the Caucasus was a gruesomely bloody affair that was often characterized by acts of unspeakable cruelty and a particular macabre obsession by the tsar's armies to inflict the type of pain on their victims that would leave generations of local nationalities burning with a deep-rooted hatred for their Slavic conquerors."[1205]

The article illustrated tragic events: "Decades of brutal guerrilla warfare in the isolated mountains left whole swathes of the region in ruins as the Russians attempted to deny the warlike indigenous populations any safe haven from their marauding armies. Five years after capturing Imam Shamil—the legendary fighter who led Chechen and Dagestani forces in an epic 25-year war of resistance against the Russians—the Russians finally subjugated the last remaining Caucasus people to resist tsarist rule in May 1864."[1206]

The author stated, "Collectively known as Circassians—or Cherkess—they were the North Caucasus' largest ethnic group, stretching across southern Russia and the mountain regions of Adygea, Kabardino-Balkaria, Karachay-Cherkessia and Georgia's Black Sea region of Abkhazia. They put up stiff resistance to the far better equipped Imperial Russian Army. Like the Chechens under Shamil, the predominantly Muslim Circassians were master guerrilla fighters who used their knowledge of the terrain, superior skills with blades and legendary riding abilities to keep the Russians at bay for nearly 100 years."[1207]

Tsarist Russian propaganda has relentlessly been publishing and spreading lies and exaggerated inaccurate figures: "Following their defeat, however, the entire population was either dispatched or deported en masse to the Ottoman Empire. According to official tsarist documents of the time, just over 400,000 Circassians were killed and 497,000 more were deported to modern-day Turkey and the Near East."[1208]

Waller continued,

> The survivors scattered across Anatolia and parts of the Levant, many of whom were welcomed by local authorities as fierce, loyal fighters. To this day, the royal guard of the Hashemite Dynasty of Jordan consists entirely of Circassians, all of who are direct descendants of those who survived

Russia's brutal ethnic cleansing campaign in the middle of the 19th century. Russian officials and the overwhelming majority of academics in the country vehemently reject any claims that genocidal policies were ever a part of the strategy of the Imperial Russian Army when it conquered the Caucasus.[1209]

The author said, "Much in the same vein as Turkey's denial of the Armenian Genocide of 1915, the issue over the history of the Circassians remains a highly contentious political issue in Russia. Vladimir Putin's Russia has consistently tried to hide the scale of its cruelty towards groups like the Circassians by creating a wall of silence and denial about the 19th century Caucasus Wars." [1210]

Waller touched the reality of what is going on regarding the freedoms in today's Russia and the legality of the Circassians' status within Russia.

Open discussions by Russian scholars are suppressed; no specific state commemorates the Circassian Genocide and Kremlin-loyalists in academia continue to invent new reasons that explain why the Circassians "voluntarily" joined the tsarist empire. This is all done while Russian officials continue to push their state-sponsored denial that Russia's military leaders carried out against the peoples of the Caucasus.[1211]

He also clarified that "Circassian activists were outraged that Putin's government chose to build most of the 2014 Sochi Winter Olympics venues in Krasnaya Polyana, the site of a major massacre of Circassians in what was once the village of Atquaj on May 21, 1864. The Russian government predictably ignored the Circassians' demands to respect the memory of the site, but the six million-strong diaspora's goal of drawing more attention to their cause was, by and large, successful."[1212]

The article has mentioned the Circassians' demands and their cultural demeanor: "Large-scale annual demonstrations demanding that Russia take responsibility for their actions grow with each passing year in Turkey, Jordan and Israel. Georgian officials are now expected to follow standard protocol by making a pilgrimage to the Circassian Cultural Center in Tbilisi to pay their respects."[1213]

Waller pointed out the fact that "Georgia was the first, and to-date, the only country in the world to officially declare the ethnic cleansing of Circassians an act of genocide." Also, he referred to the fact to creating distraction on the date of the Circassian Memorial Day. Apparently, "Abkhazia, Georgia's Moscow-backed separatist region on the Black Sea, has named May 21, a day of remembrance for the victims of the Caucasian War."[1214]

The author concluded by focusing on Moscow's deteriorating relationship with the KBR:"Even in Russia, a rare crack in the Kremlin's usual rhetoric appeared in the North Caucasus republic of Kabardino-Balkaria. The region's governor declared May 21 Circassian Day and publically acknowledged that "certain hardships were endured" by the region's previous inhabitants." [1215]

[1125] http://www.preventgenocide.org/genocide/elements.htm
[1126] https://www.iccnow.org/documents/Report_inf3e.pdf
[1127] http://www.preventgenocide.org/law/icc/statute/ and http://www.preventgenocide.org/law/convention/text.htm
[1128] http://www.jamestown.org/single/?tx_ttnews%5Btt_news%5D=32501&no_cache=1#.VpnjEZMrJE5
[1129] http://worldlibrary.in/articles/2010_circassian_genocide_conference_in_tbilisi
[1130] http://www.civil.ge/eng/article.php?id=23472
[1131] http://justicefornorthcaucasus.info/?p=1251657594
[1132] http://www.parliament.ge/files/1544_32742_536746_genocidi-en.pdf
[1133] http://www.unpo.org/article/10925
[1134] http://www.circassian-genocide.com/TbilisiIndex.php
[1135] http://www.civil.ge/eng/article.php?id=22961
[1136] http://www.civil.ge/eng/article.php?id=22231
[1137] http://www.civil.ge/eng/article.php?id=23466
[1138] http://www.civil.ge/eng/article.php?id=23472
[1139] http://justicefornorthcaucasus.info/?p=1251656096
[1140] http://www.eurasianet.org/node/63530
[1141] http://www.civil.ge/eng/article.php?id=24790
[1142] http://diaspora.gov.ge/index.php?lang_id=ENG&sec_id=124&info_id=2698
[1143] http://justicefornorthcaucasus.info/?p=1251660700
[1144] http://www.civil.ge/eng/article.php?id=24790
[1145] http://www.conflicts.rem33.com/images/Georgia/Lang_3.htm and http://news.bbc.co.uk/2/hi/europe/country_profiles/1102575.stm
[1146] http://justicefornorthcaucasus.info/?p=1251661330
[1147] http://justicefornorthcaucasus.info/?p=1251661330
[1148] http://justicefornorthcaucasus.info/?p=1251661330
[1149] http://www.mgimo.ru/files2/y08_2012/226157/Zak446_Ejeg12_9.pdf
[1150] http://www.natpress.ru/index.php?newsid=8234
[1151] http://www.jamestown.org/single/?tx_ttnews%5Btt_news%5D=40935#.Vm8LkBorJE4

1152 http://www.jamestown.org/single/?tx_ttnews%5Btt_news%5D=40935#.Vm8LkBorJE4
1153 http://www.jamestown.org/single/?tx_ttnews%5Btt_news%5D=40935#.Vm8LkBorJE4
1154 http://www.jamestown.org/single/?tx_ttnews%5Btt_news%5D=40935#.Vm8LkBorJE4
1155 http://www.jamestown.org/single/?tx_ttnews%5Btt_news%5D=42427&tx_ttnews%5BbackPid%5D=7&cHash=570704968c9153226238e4e264d17fce#.Vm82BRorJE7
1156 http://www.jamestown.org/single/?tx_ttnews%5Btt_news%5D=42427&tx_ttnews%5BbackPid%5D=7&cHash=570704968c9153226238e4e264d17fce#.Vm82BRorJE7
1157 http://www.jamestown.org/single/?tx_ttnews%5Btt_news%5D=42427&tx_ttnews%5BbackPid%5D=7&cHash=570704968c9153226238e4e264d17fce#.Vm82BRorJE7
1158 http://www.jamestown.org/programs/edm/single/?tx_ttnews%5Btt_news%5D=43982&cHash=a5a3746b9118d10f0e383b10df2e3f8c#.Vm8LkRorJE7
1159 http://justicefornorthcaucasus.info/?p=1251675400
1160 http://www.riigikogu.ee/en/press-releases/others/members-of-the-riigikogu-met-with-the-representatives-of-the-circassian-community/
1161 http://www.riigikogu.ee/en/press-releases/others/members-of-the-riigikogu-met-with-the-representatives-of-the-circassian-community/
1162 Caucasian Knot
1163 http://www.jamestown.org/single/?tx_ttnews%5Btt_news%5D=42427&tx_ttnews%5BbackPid%5D=7&cHash=570704968c9153226238e4e264d17fce#.U4W-xvmSyn_
1164 http://justicefornorthcaucasus.info/?p=1251674960
1165 http://justicefornorthcaucasus.info/?p=1251674700
1166 http://justicefornorthcaucasus.info/?p=1251658770
1167 http://natpress.net/index.php?newsid=7957
1168 http://natpress.net/index.php?newsid=8074
1169 http://natpress.net/index.php?newsid=8074
1170 http://natpress.net/index.php?newsid=8074
1171 http://natpress.net/index.php?newsid=8074
1172 http://windowoneurasia2.blogspot.com/2016/05/russians-wont-admit-expulsion-of.html
1173 http://windowoneurasia2.blogspot.com/2016/05/russians-wont-admit-expulsion-of.html
1174 http://windowoneurasia2.blogspot.com/2016/05/russians-wont-admit-expulsion-of.html

1175 http://windowoneurasia2.blogspot.com/2016/05/russians-wont-admit-expulsion-of.html
1176 http://windowoneurasia2.blogspot.com/2016/05/russians-wont-admit-expulsion-of.html
1177 http://windowoneurasia2.blogspot.com/2016/05/russians-wont-admit-expulsion-of.html
1178 http://windowoneurasia2.blogspot.com/2016/05/russians-wont-admit-expulsion-of.html
1179 http://windowoneurasia2.blogspot.com/2016/05/russians-wont-admit-expulsion-of.html
1180 http://windowoneurasia2.blogspot.com/2016/05/russians-wont-admit-expulsion-of.html
1181 http://windowoneurasia2.blogspot.com/2016/05/russians-wont-admit-expulsion-of.html
1182 http://windowoneurasia2.blogspot.com/2016/05/russians-wont-admit-expulsion-of.html
1183 http://www.preventgenocide.org/law/convention/text.htm
1184 http://windowoneurasia2.blogspot.com/2016/05/russians-wont-admit-expulsion-of.html
1185 http://windowoneurasia2.blogspot.com/2016/05/russians-wont-admit-expulsion-of.html
1186 http://windowoneurasia2.blogspot.com/2016/05/russians-wont-admit-expulsion-of.html
1187 http://windowoneurasia2.blogspot.com/2016/05/russians-wont-admit-expulsion-of.html
1188 http://www.dailysabah.com/nation/2016/05/21/circassians-seek-recognition-of-genocide-by-russia
1189 http://www.dailysabah.com/nation/2016/05/21/circassians-seek-recognition-of-genocide-by-russia
1190 http://www.dailysabah.com/nation/2016/05/21/circassians-seek-recognition-of-genocide-by-russia
1191 http://www.dailysabah.com/nation/2016/05/21/circassians-seek-recognition-of-genocide-by-russia
1192 http://www.dailysabah.com/nation/2016/05/21/circassians-seek-recognition-of-genocide-by-russia
1193 http://www.dailysabah.com/nation/2016/05/21/circassians-seek-recognition-of-genocide-by-russia
1194 http://windowoneurasia2.blogspot.com/2016/05/under-putin-circassians-and-crimean.html
1195 http://windowoneurasia2.blogspot.com/2016/05/under-putin-circassians-and-crimean.html

1196 http://windowoneurasia2.blogspot.com/2016/05/under-putin-circassians-and-crimean.html
1197 http://windowoneurasia2.blogspot.com/2016/05/under-putin-circassians-and-crimean.html
1198 http://windowoneurasia2.blogspot.com/2016/05/under-putin-circassians-and-crimean.html
1199 http://windowoneurasia2.blogspot.com/2016/05/under-putin-circassians-and-crimean.html
1200 http://windowoneurasia2.blogspot.com/2016/05/under-putin-circassians-and-crimean.html
1201 http://windowoneurasia2.blogspot.com/2016/05/under-putin-circassians-and-crimean.html
1202 http://windowoneurasia2.blogspot.com/2016/05/under-putin-circassians-and-crimean.html
1203 http://windowoneurasia2.blogspot.com/2016/05/under-putin-circassians-and-crimean.html
1204 http://georgiatoday.ge/news/3868/Circassians-Around-the-World-Commemorate-Genocide
1205 http://georgiatoday.ge/news/3868/Circassians-Around-the-World-Commemorate-Genocide
1206 http://georgiatoday.ge/news/3868/Circassians-Around-the-World-Commemorate-Genocide
1207 http://georgiatoday.ge/news/3868/Circassians-Around-the-World-Commemorate-Genocide
1208 http://georgiatoday.ge/news/3868/Circassians-Around-the-World-Commemorate-Genocide
1209 http://georgiatoday.ge/news/3868/Circassians-Around-the-World-Commemorate-Genocide
1210 http://georgiatoday.ge/news/3868/Circassians-Around-the-World-Commemorate-Genocide
1211 http://georgiatoday.ge/news/3868/Circassians-Around-the-World-Commemorate-Genocide
1212 http://georgiatoday.ge/news/3868/Circassians-Around-the-World-Commemorate-Genocide
1213 http://georgiatoday.ge/news/3868/Circassians-Around-the-World-Commemorate-Genocide
1214 http://georgiatoday.ge/news/3868/Circassians-Around-the-World-Commemorate-Genocide
1215 http://georgiatoday.ge/news/3868/Circassians-Around-the-World-Commemorate-Genocide

12

Institutionalization of Ideological Invasion

Circassian Children

One of the risks facing the Circassians is hostile propaganda by the same side that wanted and still remains in a situation of denying the Circassians' sacred rights in their homeland, by the use of different techniques and tools. The intent is reflected in their homeland and in Diaspora in accordance with an effective systematic method for the sake of diverting the Circassians' attention and concerns to be directed to insignificant matters; but continuity and persistence of the Circassian nation requires that it assert its survival by expressing its current concerns and for the future. This reminds me of Roland Reagan's saying, "We maintain peace through our strength; weakness only invites aggression".

The Circassians should take this positively by being firm in their demands, seeking recognition by maintaining self-confidence in their claim to their legitimate rights in accordance with the law. This should be observed while maintaining gratitude to their ancestors. They need to educate people about the atrocities that faced their nation through coordinating with other Circassians of the world. Cooperation is necessary between all sincere active associations and to focus on contributions towards the needs of the people within a team-like structure in everything that contributes in strengthening the necessary means to operate such as the media.

To assert their existence, the Circassians should oppose and reject the approach of the imposition of the occupation's dominance and the de facto concepts meant to contaminate the Circassians' efforts of maintaining their national identity in their whereabouts. They also should pay heed to what matters to them, and to avoid distorting their image by depending on individuals or structures that behave in accordance with a groveling and subservient manner. They must act as "social climbers" by shunning greedy opportunists that try to implicate the Circassians in weak, unwanted, and unenviable situations, which would affect them in the present and future.

The Circassians have suffered, either self-appointed or delegated, by certain parties who have a common objective aiming to steer the Circassian Question toward the unknown. After the International Circassian Association (ICA) has shown its phases of activities and developments that has currently reached a "point of no return" regarding stubbornness and exaggeration of the support and endorsement for the official positions of the Russian authorities, which are mainly against the Circassian national interests and even indifferent in the face of colonial arrogance, is well known to all.

Unfortunately, Circassians, whether they reside in their homeland or in Diaspora, are dealt with in a way as if they must accept what they are offered but nothing earnest or tangible. The ICA has proven weakness in presenting any legitimate Circassian project to those who have imposed their influence on the fate of an entire nation, and went further in uncalculated steps to disregard legitimate rights, dignity, and human suffering regardless of any consequences to show egoism and to please others.

After setbacks that were suffered by the International Circassian Association's leadership and the restlessness dissatisfaction of individuals and associations' members of the ICA in Krasnodar, the two Republics of Adygea and Karachay-Cherkessia, in addition to Turkey and elsewhere, a PR tactic was introduced by higher management trying to eliminate the effects that resulted from recent protests in response to their opponents' escalatory steps. The President of the ICA, Khauti Sokhrokov and two of his associates travelled to Turkey and Jordan, a step taken to campaign for the agenda, and in arrangement for their next elections, (they usually know the results in advance), to continue serving their mission of steering the ICA according to their ineffective agendas.

It was not a simple task; the members of the delegation had to meet with people and members of the Circassian institutions to convince them of their views. It was easy for them sometimes but difficult at other times. The members of the delegation had to face, in the places they visited, unwelcome attitudes when they had to listen to what the attendants told them, to reach to an inevitable result to be told that the deviation from the basic principles that have been overlooked and even bypassed and changed over the past years would not be useful because the Circassians, whether in their homeland or in Diaspora, will never be satisfied that their legitimate rights to be underestimated.

The Jordanian Association of Caucasus Circassians' Friends (JACCF) prepared a brief statement signed by the President of the Association. It was translated into Russian and addressed to the delegation of the International Circassian Association that visited Jordan and all the participating audience by the President of the JACCF, Dr. Rouhi Sh'haltough, at a reception held by the Circassian Charity Association for the delegation in its courtyard in Amman. The President of the International Circassian Association, Khauti Sokhrokov, and the members of the delegation were given written copies of the proposals in Russian. Some of them stated,

> The interest to gain the recognition of the Genocide that befell on the Circassian nation", "issuing a statement by the International Circassian Association to denounce the visit of what the (Russian Federation has described, the visit of tribal leaders of the Circassian Diaspora and their statements for holding the Olympic Games on the occupied Circassian territories)," and "the commitment to the Statute of the International Circassian Association, which calls for the observance and implementation of international laws and treaties.[1216]

Having the Circassians unequal relationship with the Russian side taken into account, due to the fact that they are considered followers and cannot be otherwise, makes it look like a relationship between "tyranny" and "weakness," becoming between "sadism" and "masochism," which practically makes the two sides of the equation.

Stockholm syndrome can be seen as a form of traumatic bonding, which describes strong emotional ties that develop between two sides where one side harasses, beats, threatens, abuses, or intimidates the other side. The hypothesis is based on a Freudian theory, as it suggests that the bonding is the individual or group's response to trauma in becoming a victim. Identifying with the aggressor is one way that the ego defends itself. When a victim believes the same values as the aggressor, they cease to be perceived as a threat.

In an identical example, the distinguished analyst Paul Goble published a "window" on Window on Eurasia's blog titled "Russians Continue to Suffer from Stockholm Syndrome, Kirillova Says," which highlighted a situation that shows the same arrogant party controlling different victims in a comparatively similar scenario, that in this example, "associate themselves as close as possible with the authorities", but with different players and/or implementers of the measures and policies aimed to control the whole country. It concludes, "As long as economic problems do not become truly catastrophic, the majority of Russians will to the last hold on to the appearance of state defense and propaganda surrogates and this means that they will continue to show their loyalty to those in power."[1217]

After all the dreadful and disastrous outcomes that infected the Circassians, there is always hope that there is something worth working and aiming for, as the bright stars can be seen in dark nights. Circassia is the homeland of the Circassians, which no one can change that.

Deciding on the Circassian nation's destiny should be taken by those who are eligible to do so without any psychological effect, foreign pressure, or polarization of power centers, which should depend on rules set by the Circassians themselves according to the conditions and circumstances of all the Circassian communities and granting their rights.

The Circassians Refuse Hostile Attitude

Circassians, especially their activists and national movements, are accustomed to rumors and lies implemented by the devices and the arms of systematical propaganda. This affects any call for the restoration of legal rights, and to reclaim the legitimate rights and self-determination in accordance with international laws and norms.

In response to the malicious propaganda, lies, and misrepresentations made by the parties that deliberately publish twisted facts and disseminating false information committed against the Circassian nation, the International Circassian Council has published a statement refuting the allegations and condemning unilateral actions carried out by various Russian entities.

The statement titled "The Circassians Refuse the Hostile Attitude" states, "In a publicity stunt, an article was published in 2015, by Sochi State University, funded by the Ministry of Education and Science of the Russian Federation, with the title 'Circassian Question: Transformation of Content and Perception.'"[1218]

Analyzing Misleading Disinformation

Paul Goble elaborated on the Russian propaganda that commented on the ICC's statement through a "window," titled Moscow Disinformation Spreading from Mass Media to Academic Output. The Window mentioned that, "When most people think about Russian disinformation now, they think almost exclusively about stories directed to a mass audience, be it via the print media or the Internet. That is a certainly a serious problem, but attention to it has kept many from focusing on what may be an even more serious development."[1219]

The "window" addressed the tainted atmosphere that pervaded much of the destructive propaganda against the Circassians and their issues. "That problem is the spread of propaganda and disinformation from these mass media outlets to what are ostensibly scholarly publications, a development that represents a return to some of the worst excesses of Soviet times when scholars were forced to follow the party line on issues of importance to the Kremlin."[1220]

The article revealed that, "this development threatens both Russian scholars who, while they may not have to cite Lenin as their parents and grandparents did, have to hew the Putin line on such issues and Western scholars who may not recognize the way in which this new "party" line has infected nominally "academic" research."[1221]

It also mentioned biased information, whether quoted or published. "The challenge of identifying and countering such propaganda and disinformation in ostensibly academic articles is far more difficult than pointing up the latest lies, misrepresentations and distortions in the statements of Russian officials or commentators. It requires more time, more expertise, and more effort."[1222]

The author brought attention to misleading information, "weave together misrepresentations with real facts in order to lead astray both Russian and Western audiences by promoting the Kremlin's ideology." Paul Goble added that, "A remarkable example of this is provided this weekend by two members of the International Circassian Council, Iyad Youghar and Adel Bashqawi who analyze one such example of Russian disinformation and in so doing highlight both the insidious nature of such things and the reasons it has to be done (justicefornorthcaucasus.info/?p=1251676982)."[1223]

Then he moved to pinpoint a particular example. "They focus on an article by two researchers at Russia's Southern Federal University entitled 'The

Circassian Question: Transformation of Content and Perception' that has been published in Bylye gody, vol. 36, no. 2 (2015): 450-460 (academia.edu/15285565/Circassian_Question_Transformation_of_Content_and_Perception).[1224]

The analysis added, "Among the distortions this brief work contains, Youghar and Bashqawi point out, are the following, each of which reflects Russian efforts at disinformation cast in terms that make the article sound less like propaganda than like scholarship and that as a result are likely to be accepted by many and inform the thinking of those less attuned to the issues involved."[1225]

Goble analyzed five propaganda distortions, where "each of which reflects Russian efforts at disinformation cast in terms that make the article sound less like propaganda than like scholarship and that as a result are likely to be accepted by many and inform the thinking of those less attuned to the issues involved."[1226]

First, they note, the article not only falsifies dates of the Russian-Circassian War which lasted from 1763 to 1864 but rechristens that conflict as "the Caucasian War," a Russian innovation which ignores what really happened in the western North Caucasus.

Second, the article suggests that "the so-called Circassian question" only became "hot" in the run-up to the 2014 Sochi Olympiad. In fact, Circassians have been protesting Russian actions in their homeland for a long time, most prominently in recent times in 2007 when Moscow invented the idea that the Circassians had been "voluntarily" associated with Russia for 450 years.

Third, the article presents as fact Vladimir Putin's mistake about the history of the Sochi coastal area. He talked about the Greeks settling there in antiquity without making reference to the fact that it was already populated by Circassians.

Fourth, the article says that the rise of the Internet has allowed Russia to expose Circassian falsifications and overcome Circassian resistance. In fact, Youghar and Bashqawi say, the worldwide web has led to greater Circassian activism and greater attention to the real history of the Circassians.

And fifth, the article blames outside powers for everything bad that has occurred in the North Caucasus and presents Russia as being an invariably positive force, a misrepresentation that falls on its face if one examines any of the records of the conflict and the genocidal expulsion of the Circassians by Russian forces.[1227]

The analysis added an important fact of misleading information: "In Western academic life, any article that got so much wrong would be the subject of intense criticism by other scholars. But Russian articles of this kind often seem to get a pass, with those who read them forgetting to do the basic fact checking that they would insist upon if the article were published anywhere else."[1228]

Goble concluded, "It is time for that to stop, not only for the benefit of those in the West who need to know the truth about what Moscow has been doing but also for the benefit of scholars and others within the borders of the Russian Federation who once again are being spoon fed the kind of propaganda that many had hoped had ended with the demise of the USSR."[1229]

CIRCASSIANS WILL NOT ALLOW "THEIR HOMELAND" TO BE STOLEN

May 21 is linked to the Circassian Genocide that marks the date the Russian-Circassian War ended in 1864 and resulted in disastrous repercussions that accompanied and followed the criminal and savage war waged by the Russian Empire against the Circassian nation to occupy their homeland and deport all those who remained alive outside the borders of Circassia to areas beyond the Kuban River, away from the Circassian coastline on the Black Sea, on board rickety ships to the Ottoman Empire.

Every time an important Circassian event is approaching, such as "Circassian Memorial Day," the usual aggressive Russian propaganda intensifies against Circassian existence and survival through the usage of proxies and agents who are working within an organized network to distribute and circulate lies and false information. In this regard, a fishy article signed by someone who claims that he "lives and works" in Moscow, titled "Dear Circassians Don't Let Them Steal Our Homeland on May 21," indicates contradiction, bluffing, and wandering.[1230]

The writer or publisher of the article appears to have no identity. He apparently doesn't know who he is since in his pursuit to attain the mission as the title in his article states, he is definitely lost between being a Circassian sometimes and being an outsider at other times.

The impolite way that is used in criticism shows the worsening of the crisis of those who are worried about the "Circassian genie that came out of the bottle." It is disgusting, though, to observe ignorant intruders' scheming plots and machinations behind the scenes while at the same time applying outdated police and intelligence methods, which range between yawping, clowning, defamation, and shaming in a series of lies that turned up in aligned words and sentences according to malignancy and suspicion.

The first paragraph commenced with mentioning "victims of the Caucasus War", which is the categorically untrue usual Russian propaganda because the right description is the Russian-Circassian War.

Commenting on the second paragraph of said article, it's not unusual to see at this time of the year all Circassians commemorate the atrocities committed by the Russian Empire, which caused pain and deportation. This does not only happen in Jordan, but in all Circassian communities and associations around the world including those in the motherland in a civilized manner.

In the third paragraph, the so-described article shows lack of codes of conduct together with a shortcoming of the slightest tact and civility:

— The proxies who wage unethical antagonistic campaign in an evil method of personalizing an important matter such as the Circassian Question which shows a ridiculous approach to shortcut the whole affair to look as if it is limiting all the consequences of the Circassian Genocide, ethnic cleansing, deportation in few persons and only in one country (http://www.interpretermag.com/putin-blames-circassian-protests-on-the-west-amid-arrests/).

— Those who assume the ignorance of others are trying to minimize Circassian realization and block wide horizons and visions besides turning a blind eye on the ongoing atrocities Circassians still suffering to this day since imperial Russia had occupied and colonized their homeland.

— Misleading public opinion by spotting a few people who call for the implementation of all related international laws and norms to restore Circassian stolen rights.

— When the Circassians in Jordan count approximately 100,000 people, their percentage is approximately less than 2 percent of the total Circassians, where approximately 6 million live in Diaspora and 800,000 of them living in the Circassian Homeland in the North Caucasus, but divided in six different administrative enclaves.

— Circassians from all ages, in all their whereabouts, are using all available means and seeking to regain their confiscated rights by following peaceful and civilized methods. Since the collapse of the Soviet Union, Circassians sent letters and appeals to both the executive and legislative branches of the Russian government to recognize the Circassian Genocide, but the Russian authorities neglected in doing its moral duty. Circassians also sent similar appeals to many sides, such as the European Parliament and other parliaments and other parties of concern (http://www.cherkessia.net/news_detail.php?id=6664).

— Although individuals have importance in the delivery of what aspires to their own people, the importance of the issue they seek to achieve makes them in self-denial, indifferent to praise and flattery, where they prioritize the public interest instead of achieving a narrow individual benefit.

— Circassians demand the unification all the Circassian territories in one geographical entity and to restore a "single Circassian Republic" (http://www.moldova.org/circassians-reaffirm-common-identity-on-deportation-anniversary-200774-eng/).

— Who performs a duty, "luxury" will not be of concern to him, but it is a well-established fact when Circassians get their demands implemented, Circassians will restore their national identity, and dignity to live freely in their own homeland.

— Circassians remember and know their homeland very well more than any loudmouthed so-called writer and/or journalist while they understand that their homeland is hijacked. At the same time, news are available everywhere through known and dependable media outlets that don't spin in the orbit of the Russian propaganda headed by Russia Today.

— Published false news about the Circassian different issues of the Circassian Question will not deter Circassians from raising their demands to stop all kinds of systematic lies. Mentioning Jamestown Foundation doesn't mean more than what is shown by Russia as a narrow-minded matter, where Jamestown is one of hundreds of research and study centers in the United States that focus on regular studies, seminars, and conferences on various issues in the world, including the Circassians and their plight.

The following are comments on the fourth paragraph:

— "Who are you to pass judgment on others?" Circassians know what they want better than anybody else, and at the same time, they refuse to allow anyone trying to dictate what they should and what they shouldn't.

— If intruders want to make Circassians happy, they should leave them alone. Circassians believe in the saying, "A friend in need is a friend indeed".

— Intruders should abide by minding their own business: "Never worry about what I'm doing. Only worry about why you're worried about what I'm doing".

— Russia has consistently failed to prove anything other than its adopted imperial policy of dealing with the Circassians as a subordinate nation (https://www.youtube.com/watch?v=uh8FXIW5NbY).

— Circassians had no other hostile enemy in this world besides the Russian imperial tyrants, which are still taking advantage over denying Circassians from retrieving their rights.

Commenting on the fifth paragraph, Circassians are free to move and to return to their homeland whether to live or to establish business whenever possible while they don't approve any guardianship of those who are playing the parrot's role. Of course, the Circassian Genocide should be recognized, and one day it will be acknowledged with all its consequences.

The sixth paragraph shows unified reaping goals:

— Such propaganda neglects stating a reason for the fact that "the Circassian community in Turkey is considered one of the largest diaspora communities of Circassians in the world" and why those people are not living in their historic homeland.

— Circassians do not have to review their attitude as far as Russia is required to reconsider and cancel its hostile policies toward them.

— Yes, Circassians both in Turkey and other diaspora locations have reviewed the Russian position and apparently knew the hard way how aggressive the Russian policies are towards Circassians especially in regard to refusing Circassians of Syria's repatriation to their Circassian homeland in light of the ongoing civil war in their place of residence in diaspora.

— The method used in this propaganda absolutely ignores clumsy actions of the Russian authorities about the detention and dealing with the Circassian activists living in their homeland such as Andzor Akhokhov (http://eng.kavkaz-uzel.ru/articles/31318/); Ibrahim Yaganov (https://sg.news.yahoo.com/russia-detains-caucasus-activists-ahead-olympics-190701010.html); Ruslan Kish; Adnan Khuade (http://caucasreview.com/2015/05/v-rf-nachalis-repressii-protiv-cherkesskih-aktivstov/); Asker Sokt (http://

edition.cnn.com/2014/02/16/world/europe/russia-arrest/); Chermit Mahmoud; and others.

That is called development of police methods against the indigenous Circassian people. The latest example of a Circassian solid demand is the action taken by Circassians in Karachay-Cherkessia for demanding from Russia to recognize the Circassian Genocide plus their complaint of "discrimination in the implementation of constitutional rights" (http://www.kavkaz-uzel.ru/articles/262696/).

— Russian authorities have always succeeded in destroying bridges of love and links with the Circassian homeland. The Russians must revise their outdated policies.

— The Republic of Adygea is not mentioned in this paragraph besides the other Circassian republics showing no respect to the intelligence of the readers (http://eng.kavkaz-uzel.ru/articles/12942/)!

The seventh paragraph shows the author's own ideas about investment at homeland:

— Ranting about the Circassian diaspora business community in Turkey and holding a business conference in the presence of officials from the Republic of Adygea is a good idea, but it is useful to mention that some Circassian businessmen from Turkey have already assumed business in Sochi as one of the construction companies built one of the major hotels (Marriott Hotel) in Krasnaya Polyana.

— The Russian authorities didn't provide facilities for Circassian businessmen to establish business of their choice in their homeland.

—Realities have proven ill treatment of individual Circassians who repatriated to homeland with police and immigration officials maltreating Circassian returnees.

— "Federation of the Caucasian Associations" (KAFFED) may represent some Circassians but not all of them, especially in recent years that many Circassians have founded new Circassian associations.

Finally, comments on the eighth paragraph are as follows:

— The article continues with hypothetical image of wallowing through the embodiment of a conspiratorial role in the affairs of others on behalf of the party that the so-called "writer/publisher" works for, is trying to market delusions and lies seemingly in coordination and cooperation with others who took on their shoulders an opportunist task that can be described as following the victims and their descendants not only to their homeland, but to the large diaspora locations around the world.

— The so-called "political utilization" does not mean in any way that would discourage those who work in order to restore the usurped rights from the legitimate goal, which they advocate to achieve.

— Only cheap and low-class individuals are those who mention and accuse the sincere people of receiving bribes or wages while working in a sacred and inviolable matter for the elevation, dignity, and freedom of an oppressed nation, plagued by occupation and rights denial.

— The 2014 Sochi Winter Olympic Games contributed in unifying Circassians and understanding the real Russian policies against their survival as a respected nation, regardless of a handful of Circassians who were satisfied in accepting attending the controversial games by an invitation received from the Russian authorities. Sochi made it possible for more people to know about the Circassian plight, and even more media outlets around the world have published reports about Sochi and the Circassian Genocide in many different languages.

— Features of Sochi, the capital city of Circassia and its surroundings, have been changed (http://www.onislam.net/english/health-and-science/nature/479647-gazprom-destroys-the-circassian-capital-sochi.html).

— Definitely, Circassians are looking for the future as "strong people don't give up when they come across challenges. They just work harder".

"If You're Not Part of the Solution, You're Part of the Problem."[1231]

History Falsification

Russian falsification indicates neither limit nor ceiling to keep the present situation of imposing and extending the influence, totally and absolutely, of controlling the homelands of vulnerable peoples and nations, including the Circassian people, which led to the change of the natural features and marks, according to the whims, lies, and forgery refuted by the facts that depend on evidence and documents.

Fatima Tlis wrote an article titled Moscow Uses Commission on "Historical Falsification" to Deny Circassian Rights. It was elaborated on "'the main goal of the 'Special Presidential Commission against falsifications of the history of the Russian Federation causing harm to Russian national interests' is to identify and fight against conscious, imprudent falsifications, aimed on the political results', declared Sergei Markov, the deputy head of the State Duma's committee on public associations and religious organizations and a member of the special presidential commission (Vechernyaya Moskva, December 29, 2009)."[1232]

Markov inserted himself and his country in a subject that a neutral observer cannot help but notice and wonder the extent of a relentless media campaign, spreading information that cannot be characterized except as questionable in its accuracy and validity, leading to stigmatization of the role of the media as unfair and irresponsible. Not to neglect mentioning the destruction of protected areas and matters related to human rights and the infringement on the duties of specialists and workers who carry out their duties in the field of environmental protection and nature conservation. As well as the historical facts concerning the eviction of Circassians from their original residential and agricultural areas of origin, and the few who managed to stay in their homeland.

Baseless allegations were pressed against anyone who calls for rights, even though they are violated by the Russian State: "In his statement, Markov gave two examples of what he called 'purely politically-aimed' falsifications that damage Russia's national interests. The first, he said, is the Golodomor (the Ukrainian accusation that the Soviet Union committed genocide against the Ukrainian people in 1932–1933, when thousands of Ukrainians died of hunger). According to Ukrainian claims, the famine did not have a natural cause, but was organized by the Russian state in order to reduce the number of Ukrainians."[1233]

Apparently, it wasn't a coincidence that Markov mentioned Ukraine, as if looking beyond the horizon towards the present problems with Ukraine, where holding the Olympic Games was the main reason behind delaying to implement the Russian plans both in Ukraine and the Crimea.

- It wasn't a surprise that Markov targets the Circassians because he has been brought up in an ivory tower environment, where he lived and operated in an isolated world that is separate from reality.
- Where the end justifies the means, political and entertainment publicity have beaten fairness and justice.
- Irrational talk is indicated by a clumsy way of recalling wrong dates, which reverse truth, contradicting facts.
- Mentioning that "the Adygs-Circassians received their own state" is kind of political heresy.

Saying that "those who left to the Middle East" proves his ignorance that the so-called "those" are the vast majority of Circassians who were forced to leave their homeland and deported to the Ottoman Empire, which they didn't go for a tour around the world.

- Those who said "No Olympic Games on the Land of Genocide," both in the Circassian whether at homeland or in Diaspora, didn't pay 50 billion dollars to make their point, but they were doing that out of their conscience and national duty to notify the world that the so-called Olympic Games have taken place on the Circassian soil and graveyards in the last Circassian capital city of Sochi.
- While the Russian State and in order to celebrate 150 years of euphoria a military parade was performed in Sochi when Circassia was entirely occupied, Russia was able to create a large fund to pay 50 billion dollars in order to achieve political, propagandist, and promotional objectives.
- Circassians are worried and at the same time concerned of the absent but documented "historical truth."
- Yes, Circassians called on the "whole world to boycott the Sochi games," and at the same time they were able to make the world know for the first time that the Circassian nation was denied of its rights by genocide.

A second example of such historical falsification, said Markov, is related to the Sochi 2014 Olympic Games and aimed at falsifying the history of the Russian-Caucasian war from 1817–1864. "Yes, the war was bloody," said Markov, adding, "However, it was only thanks to Russia that the Adygs-Circassians received their own state. Those who left for the Middle Eastern countries are in an incomparably worse situation today than those who remain in the Caucasus." He underscored that those "extremists" who use the slogan, "No Olympic games on the land of genocide," are not worried about the "historical truth," but rather are trying to call the whole world to boycott the Sochi games (Vechernyaya Moskva, December 29, 2009).[1234]

It was sensed and proven that "the two main targets of the special commission as indicated by Sergei Markov (the Ukrainians and the Circassians) are becoming more of a headache for the Kremlin not because those two issues are falsifications of history, but because there is in fact unbeatable historical evidence behind the genocide claims."[1235]

The article tackled the Circassian rights claims: "Focusing on the Circassian issue, the Circassian Congress NGO claims that the genocide committed by Russia against the Circassians can be easily proven based solely on the official documents from the Russian Imperial archives. According to the Circassian Congress, approximately 1,500,000 people were massacred and partly deported from the Caucasus, and the Circassians lost 99 percent of their population during the war and deportation (www.circassiangenocide.org)."[1236]

With respect to the right to return, taking into account the crippling conditions issued, are in the trend of tightening the process over the time to discourage Circassians from thinking about settling in their homeland and make it a more difficult task:

> Every problem that befalls a separated nation applies to the Circassian Diaspora living in exile. Although Circassians traditionally played a significant role in the government, military and diplomatic fields of the host countries, they have suffered from losing their identity, traditions, language, culture and ties with their homeland. Repatriation is one of the possibilities for restoring their homeland in the Caucasus, but the process implies appealing to the Russian Federation for permanent resident status and then, if such status is granted, living in the Caucasus for seven years and then applying for citizenship. And while the process itself is already complicated, those repatriated often face additional impracticable requirements.[1237]

An example about a Circassian from Turkey reveals that

> Haci Bairam had been deported from Nalchik to Istanbul in his pajamas without money and documents just a few days prior to receiving Russian citizenship, for "violating the registration regime"—that is, for spending one night in his friend's house. Although Haci Bairam appealed to the

European Court for Human Rights and has won the case against the Russian Federal Security Service (FSB), he has not been allowed to set foot on Circassian land ever since. The FSB paid Haci Bairam a fee of 8,000 Euros, but when he arrived back to Nalchik, he was kept for 24 hours and then was deported back to Turkey without any explanation (Radio Free Europe, October 16, 2003).[1238]

An assertion is made that "what is exceptional about Haci Bairam's case is not that he was deported—deportations of repatriated Circassians happen on a monthly basis—but the fact that he made it public and stood up for his rights, while the traditional way is to find a police or FSB official who, for a certain fee, will help you to regain your permanent resident status until the next deportation."[1239]

Seemingly, when Markov says that "Circassians enjoying 'their own state'," either he is trying to play smart or he doesn't know the actual situation in the Caucasus since Circassia was deleted from the map. Circassia was divided and subdivided on different occasions. Circassians don't have their own state as claimed, but on the contrary, their homeland is detached to several enclaves including the so-called Circassian republics, which have different features while they have noncontiguous borders.

In reality, while approximately five million Circassians live in exile in more than 50 countries, today only less than one million Circassians remain in their homeland. The majority of them live in three republics in the North Caucasus separated by artificial boundaries and officially identified as Kabardins, Cherkess, Adygs, Shapsugs—that is, not by their ethnic names but by their geographical locations. By cutting Circassia's territory into separate pieces and giving them different names, Russia effectively achieves the aim of eradicating the national identity of Circassians, as well as visually erasing Circassia from the geopolitical map of the region.[1240]

The Institutional Trend

It is no secret that the Circassian nation has suffered greatly, and it is still trying hard to defend its national dignity, survival, and identity in the face of evil ambitions and exterior invasions, which it was exposed over tens of years for murder, genocide, occupation, exclusion, displacement, forced deportation, and exile abroad and away from the Circassian homeland located in the North Caucasus.

More than 150 years have elapsed since the end of the devastating war waged by the Tsarist Russian Empire against Circassia. It is the duty of Circassian individuals, associations, and establishments, whether in their homeland or in diaspora, to do what their national and humanitarian imperative duty dictates them to do. Everyone must work in cooperation and coordination among themselves to take into account the requisites that require the development of a partnership mechanism with international organizations.

They should oppose racism, incitement, denial of rights, racial superiority, and hatred. The goal must be to demand the application of the United Nations bodies, especially the United Nations High Commissioner for Human Rights, and in respect to the United Nations Declaration on the Rights of Indigenous Peoples, as well as government and nongovernment institutions and organizations of the world, especially in the member states of the European Union and its affiliated organs, which are interested in human rights and issues of oppressed people.

The invading Russian Empire's forces had perpetrated crimes of genocide and ethnic cleansing against the Circassian people. They are not other than crimes against humanity, punishable under international law, and they are no statute of limitations regardless of the elapse of time. The tragedies had devastating, serious, and painful repercussions where the effects had an impact on the overall population of Circassia from all spectra that need attention to be addressed in a proper form.

Of the urgent matters to focus on is the Adygha language that seems, considering the current situation, to be sliding towards the deep hollows of extinction, which is closely linked to the necessary elements to maintain the Circassian culture and all its associated elements. The importance of the need for the perpetrators and the international community to recognize the Circassian's legitimate rights, especially what is related to the right of self-determination based on international legitimacy.

The Circassian people are required to stand united against the exclusionary projects and plans related to the liquidation of the Circassian Question. They must object the dispersion and division of the Circassian regions in the North Caucasus or through the Russian authorities' attempt of trying to maintain the status quo. Denial of the Circassian rights, neglecting the subject of Circassian Diaspora, and dwarfing Circassians should not be accepted. They should avoid promoting and maintaining their present status, in a way that coincide with ICA objectives.

The Circassian Action Common Mechanism

The ambitious crucial goals of the Circassians urge them to rely on the basics and perspectives of managing a joint Circassian mechanism of conduct. The present and future should be established by coordination and consultation according to the following key elements:

— The formation of constituent committees to coordinate and oversee the establishment of Circassian organizations. This will ensure achieving the goals of the Circassian nation concerning the restoration of its legitimate rights. It is important to establish permanent institutions through democratically elected members and administrations in addition to interaction from all members.

— To induce sub-committees with clear terms of reference which operate in accordance with established goals in the whereabouts of the Circassians. Field of operation, whether at home or in Diaspora, would operate within local communities as dictated by the surrounding circumstances and events for the purpose of emphasizing on the unity and integrity of the Circassian territories.

— Develop an integrated program that embodies both horizontal and vertical organizational structures, by the consistent with its duties, and what needs to be done in all walks of life. To raise awareness on different levels and multiple forms, Circassian national duty should expand its efforts to include many segments of society for the sake of participating in all related activities.

— Clarify the methods that will be followed for harmony and collaboration to be adopted in the revitalization of the direct and indirect contact with members of the Circassian communities. The joint links between all Circassians living in the Circassian homeland and their peers in Diaspora should be strengthened.

— Work on the establishment of an independent Circassian media system using all means available. It must work on addressing the Circassians and the world alike, to expose racialism, ethnocentrism, and fascist methods pursued in the past, and still by the same parties.

— Holding seminars, meetings, and conferences addressing the "Circassian Question." Also, demand from the United Nations, the European

Union countries, the United States of America, and all human rights organizations to perform their humanitarian duty to recognize the right of self-determination and the restoration of Circassian confiscated rights.

— Press for promoting social, cultural, civil, economic, and political activities to support the various paths of the "Circassian Question" wherever and whenever possible.

— Most importantly, act within a pattern of allowing anyone who can provide the required efforts according to mutual respect. Self-confidence and creative opinions are important away from the effect of ill-motivated individuals. No selfishness or self-ego behavior is accepted. No one should be allowed to make the subject tied to a certain individual or any particular party!

Foreign and Intruders' Interventions

The contradictions associated with the developments of the Circassian Question in recent years and holding the Olympic Winter Games in Sochi in February 2014 have created a lack of trust between several parties. That trend flourished among some of the associates of the Abkhazian government, which due to its proximity to Russian policies, it has taken a hostile attitude toward the Circassians, and the pursuit of Circassians to demand asserting and restoring their nation's legitimate rights.

In this context, criticism came through a letter directed to Beslan Kobakhia, the described "Coordinator of the International Movement for the Protection of the Rights of Peoples." The original letter was initiated in Russian. On the April 22, 2013, the Circassian National Movement translated and published the letter into Arabic.[1241] On April 23, 2013, I translated and published the letter in English.[1242]

Future Expectations

The criminals have gone, but the repercussions of their crimes have remained. The intransigence has been shown by the Russians and still, shows grudges towards the Circassians and other peoples and nations of the Caucasus. Forgetting or overlooking that justice will be inevitably done is not realistic or acceptable.

Everyone will regain their rights. What is regrettable, though, is that some people are maintaining strong ties of friendship with those who do not recognize that the Circassians have a homeland in the first place. However, they are denying them the right to exercise their legitimate rights and their right to their homeland, according to the "UNIVERSAL DECLARATION OF HUMAN RIGHTS," the United Nations Declaration on the Rights of Indigenous Peoples, and even according to Russian laws.[1243]

To consider the existence of an issue that shall be defended by all legitimate ways and means requires hard work. No one with a heart would condone losing their homeland. Truth will prevail, and the rest, with the passage of time will disappear.

Propaganda as a Way of Existence

Ordinary Circassian men and women are those who are entitled to choose the future of their dispersed nation. They were, and still are, targets of the Russian army's invasion along with groups working in its favor. Circassians believe in what Nelson Mandela said, "Those who conduct themselves with morality, integrity and consistency need not fear the forces of inhumanity and cruelty."[1244]

No logic is followed when national and emotional tones are utilized. Sometimes even religious dimensions are used. Appealing to people's sentiments and emotions is a way to reach different segments of society. As violence and force were and still used as methods to grab people and nations against their will, the authorities always turn their backs on listening to ongoing claims and demands or restoring the colonized nations' rights.

The fifteen points:

— A black and white division of the world into "ours" and the "alien" other;
— Epithets that imply more than they describe;
— Constant assertions that those supporting Putin not only are numerous but united;
— Empty declarations that mean nothing but that appear to promise or justify everything;
— Playing games with cause and effect, often reversing their true order;
— A vicious circle or tautology in which the second part of an assertion is simply a repetition of the first;
— Confusing the part and the whole by focusing on only one part of something such as liberals within the opposition;

— Creating false dilemmas that don't exist;
— Careful preparation of headlines which are the only thing most people pay attention to;
— Citations to experts, often false and even more often out of context;
— Claiming the media say when in fact only one media outlet does;
— Using weasel words like "so-called" or "it would appear" to give the appearance of objectivity;
— Outright falsification; and
— Conspiracy theories and suggestion of hidden motives.[1245]

Dimensions of Russian Duma's Reply to Circassians' Return to Their Motherland

The intensification of battles between the parties of the war that erupted in Syria is clearly seen and has affected all walks of life of the Syrian people. The Circassians living in Syria, who were expelled from their original homeland in the North Caucasus in the second half of the nineteenth century, have been exposed to the implications of the intensification of the battles and its extension to the areas of their residence as well as to all parts of Syria.

The circumstances have helped to find an incubator environment to the risk of killing, displacing and exhaustion of citizens' capabilities in the midst of the lack of possibility to reach results that would lead to stopping the armed conflict between the parties in the foreseeable future. It is obvious that in order to solve any problem, it must be specified; what its nature is, to analyze its tensioned status, and then seek solutions and alternatives that provide an expanse of hope.

There is a growing desire from Syrian Circassians that there is an urgent requirement for their return to their ancestors' homeland in these difficult circumstances. Due to the result of their suffering, there is an urgent need to move to a haven to protect them from the evils of civil war and its negative effects for a decent living in the present and future. All expectations should be considered to avoiding a dark future that awaits them and their children. Serious attempts of Circassians living in Syria have emerged to move from the existing crisis.

Unfortunately, Russian-published news concerning the Circassians of Syria is not quite correct. Even though some Russian media outlets rant aiding Circassians to return to their homeland. Russia Today's website published information that contrasts with real Russian intentions and policy applications: "Syria's 18-month war has generated a massive wave of refugees, with some coming to Russia. Many are rediscovering their historic links to their new surroundings and mourning the peace and prosperity they once enjoyed in their former home."[1246]

Nevertheless, several hundred of them have managed to be displaced and have reached the cities of Nalchik and Maykop. However, everybody was surprised by the decision of the Russian authorities to stop granting visas for families to travel back to their original homeland. The situation seemed to be in crisis, marred with provoking excitement and suspicion, especially since the official Russian decision came at a critical time. Those stranded amid a raging armed conflict were trapped in the midst of imposed aggravated circumstances that blocked providing a reasonable space to move due to the limited options.

An Al-Monitor's article titled "Turkey's Circassians Jangle Russian Nerves" stated, "The outbreak of the Syrian war rekindled the issue of repatriation. Adige Khase, a civic group in Russia's autonomous Republic of Adygea, petitioned the Kremlin, the Foreign Ministry, the Duma and the Federation Council in a bid to pave the way for Syrian Circassians' return to their homeland, but all its applications were rejected."[1247]

The freedom of Circassians to return to their homeland was impeded by the Soviet State's stringent laws until the end of the twentieth century. The then presence of the "Iron Curtain" used to be in the real tyrant sense of the term. The curtain continued where it was founded and sustained by the Soviet Union from the end of World War II in 1945, until the end of the Cold War in 1990, by the collapse of the Soviet Union.

As soon as the winds of change started blowing, the enforcement of laws relating to human rights and the rights of indigenous people has prevailed. A temporary improvement has occurred for the personal and cultural freedoms, liberties and the right to return. Slight segments of the Circassian Diaspora had started a shy return to their homeland. After the disintegration of the Soviet Union, the Russian Federation has emerged as an independent state, consisting of more than one hundred different peoples and nations.

The late Russian president Boris Yeltsin sent a telegram in 1994, on the anniversary of the end of the Russian-Circassian (Caucasian) War in May 1996. He said, "Russia is aware of those mistakes that were made during that period."[1248] On the impact of that rational statement, the return of Kosovo Circassians to their homeland and their residence in the Republic of Adygea in 1998 arose after the Kosovo War in the Balkans. In January 2012, the Caucasian Knot published an article on repatriations titled "Repatriation Experience to Homeland in the Nineties of the Last Century."[1249]

Al-Monitor's website published an article that elaborated on Yasar Aslankaya's case, when he traveled to the North Caucasus to attend a meeting: "As head of KAFFED, the umbrella organization of Turkey's largest Circassian groups, Aslankaya attended the ICA board meeting on March 29, held in

Nalchik, the capital of Russia's Kabardino-Balkaria autonomous republic. During his stay there, he faced warnings he might not be allowed to the Caucasus again and was followed throughout Nalchik, with intelligence services on watch even at the door of his hotel room."[1250]

The article added, "It should be noted that KAFFED has been criticized for going too far in accommodating Russia's sensitivities and for shying away from advocacy that could irritate Moscow. A significant part of the diaspora is strongly critical even of KAFFED's membership in the ICA, which has been accused of operating as Moscow's puppet ever since its independent Circassian leaders were purged in 1999."[1251]

Changing ways of dealing and communication has become the status quo, which cannot be ignored: "Yet, even KAFFED was crossed out earlier this year when it dared to hold a put-out-the-Olympic-torch demonstration outside the Russian Embassy in Ankara. KAFFED officials who used to be in direct contact with the ambassador tried for some time to get appointments."[1252]

Covert forces kept working behind the scenes to impose certain effects on the Circassian issues: "Meanwhile, plans to hold an international conference in Istanbul either in May or September under the auspices of the Circassian Associations Federation, another umbrella group, came to naught as ICA threw spanners into the works."[1253]

The article continued,

> Murat Yalcin from the Istanbul Circassian Association, which is part of the federation, complained of persisting Russian interference. "We are under Russia's indirect pressure. They take every opportunity to convey their discontent over our activities," Yalcin told Al-Monitor. "We use a very measured language.
>
> We demand the recognition of the exile and genocide. Yet, certain attempts were made via influential diaspora figures to end especially the demonstrations we hold outside the Russian consulate in Istanbul on the 21st of each month to call for the recognition of the exile and genocide". Despite the pressure, a large crowd gathered outside the consulate on May 21 for the latest commemoration event.[1254]

In a subtitle entitled "Grassroots Pressure," it stated, "Erdogan Boz, a board member of the Ankara-based Circassian Association, is irked by KAFFED's policy of accommodating Russia, even though his group is a driving force within KAFFED. In remarks to Al-Monitor, he complained of Russian manipulations, saying, 'Manipulative attempts have been on the rise, especially since opposition mounted against the Sochi Olympics. ICA and KAFFED have become a vessel for those attempts.'"[1255]

Then it continued, "In contrast to KAFFED, the Circassian Association is lifting its voice, willing to heed diaspora sensibilities, Boz said. Their key demands include recognition of the 19th century events as genocide, recognition of the right to repatriation and concrete measures to facilitate the return. Back in July 1997, at the general assembly of the Unrepresented Nations and Peoples Organization (UNPO), the ICA called for the acknowledgment of the genocide, the Circassian people's recognition as a nation in exile and a guarantee of repatriation to their historical homeland. Yet, the ICA not only failed to pursue its demands, but turned into an organization seeking to quiet anti-Russian sentiments in the diaspora."[1256]

At the time of publishing the article, the KAFFED official, "Aslankaya told Al-Monitor he relayed the following message to the Russian envoy at their latest meeting: {Not only have you failed to deliver your promises, but now we face threats and bullying in the Caucasus. Russia is unable to tolerate any criticism. And when we keep silent, we lose our support base. If you are not going to address our problems, we'll take our demands to international platforms. Even the students we sent to the Caucasus have had their scholarships cut. This can no longer go on like this. Russia has to acknowledge the historical tragedy and remove barriers to reconnections with the homeland. [Turkish] Prime Minister Recep Tayyip Erdogan's condolence message to Armenians generated a very positive response.}"

Russian leader Vladimir Putin could take a similar step. The diaspora had welcomed former president Boris Yeltsin's statement on May 18, 1994, when he said, "the problems we inherited from the Caucasian War, and in particular the return of the descendants of emigrants from the Caucasus to their historical homeland, should be resolved'. Twenty years have passed with no progress at all. We believe that recognizing the Circassians' suffering, sharing their pain and resolving historical problems can be possible through direct dialogue at the 150th anniversary of the end of the Caucasian-Russian wars. The acceptance of these demands will boost our people's trust in the Russian Federation."[1257]

The Russian Contradictions

Since the outbreak of fighting in Syria in the spring of 2011, the issue of the Circassians of Syria has surfaced, in addition to other Caucasian communities, which led to the aggravation of this issue steadily because of the events. On the January 17, 2012, an Abkhazian official delegation had suddenly visited Syria and discussed what had been described as: "Checking the status of the Abkhaz and Circassian population there".

On March 16, 2012, a Russian parliamentary delegation visited Syria. Upon its tasks was to discuss[1258] the plight of Circassians in Syria and the possibility to return them to their homeland in the North Caucasus. The delegation included members of the Federation Council, which is the Senate of the Russian parliament, regional officials and activists from Adygea, Karashivo – Cherkessia and Kabardino – Balkaria, which they numbered 11 people. According to "Caucasian Knot"[1259], some participants said that the delegation would strive to enhance opportunities for migration of the Circassians living in Syria.

Following that visit, one of the participants in the delegation, Askar Sukht, said, "Circassians of Syria should consult the Russian Consulates in the locations they reside at (Syria, Jordan or Lebanon) to submit "applications to be able to obtain refugees status three months after submitting the application, initially for three years entry to the Russian territories to attain the citizenship of the Russian Federation within a special mechanism to speed up the process."[1260]

With the approach of the Winter Olympic Games of 2014 in Sochi, the "Caucasian Knot"[1261] has published that Circassian activists spotted a children's game so as to indicate the "good" Cossacks fighting the "bad" Mountaineers—in other words, people from the North Caucasus.

On the ninth of January, the Russian Duma replied to the Head of the Adigha Khasa, the Circassian Association in the Republic of Adygea, Adam Shoaib Boghos[1262] in regard to helping Circassians of Syria to return to their historical homeland, where the response stated, "Committee for Nationalities in the Russian Duma would inform you that your request to help the Circassians of Syria to return to the Russian Federation has been transferred to the Ministry of Regional Development of the Russian Federation, and sending you this reduplication of the Ministry's response!" The response declared, "Circassians of Syria are the descendants of immigrants of Adigha origins, from the Northern and Western Caucasus, who did not accept the Russian citizenship, and chose voluntary migration from the region after the end of military operations of the Caucasian War (1817–1864). Thus, accordingly, the ancestors of the existing Circassians of Syria had resided in the territories that were not by then within the Russian Empire. Their migration in the year 1864 to the Ottoman Empire cannot be considered as immigrants from the Russian State, in accordance with "paragraph 3 of Article 1 of the Federal Law." In addition to details regarding the considerations formulated by what was called the Russian Federal Law, as well as "the implementation of the governmental program for supporting the citizens residing abroad for their return to homeland, which is established in its new format with the Presidential Law No. 1289 of 14, September, 2012."

The "director of Nationalities Relations Department, A. F. Joravsky" concluded the reply in the following: "Based on the above mentioned, we believe that the issue of reunion of Circassians of Syria and the citizens living abroad needs a comprehensive study in cooperation with the Russian Foreign Ministry and the Immigration Service Department in the Russian Federation." Seemingly, till now, the comprehensive study is still ongoing.

Symbolic Letter

A symbolic letter was sent on January 18, 2013, by Amin Zekhizv, the president of the Social Movement "Adygeya Khasa – The Twenty-First Century" to the Russian state duma and to the Russian Ministry of Regional Development, which stated the following:

> The Honorable Georavsky!
>
> On behalf of the members of the social movement, on my own behalf and on behalf of Circassians of the Northern and Western Caucasus, I thank you for your response No. 31 368/04 dated 21/12/2012, as you are the only person who placed the point on the ongoing historical lie since 500 years ago on the so-called Circassia's voluntary accession to Russia.
>
> The response is true and means the following:
>
> – Circassians are occupied people,
> – Our territories are colonized by the Russian State,
> – We are the descendants of the occupied people,
> – As long as Circassia is within the Russian Federation, Circassians got no way to return,
> – The rulers of the North Caucasus region are the colonial administrative rulers in the Caucasus,
> – Maria's status, the Russian Tsar's wife, in the city of Nalchik must be removed,
>
> These are some of the issues that you have opened the Circassians and other Caucasian peoples' eyes on.
>
> With my regards, wishing you blessing and prosperity to you and all the Russian people,

- President of the Social Movement "Adygeya Khasa – the XXI Century.[1263]

Regarding these controversial responses, the following must be noted:

– The Committee for Nationalities' Affairs, of the Federal Council of the Russian Federation / Sixth Session in the State Duma is transferring the response of another party (formal response) as if it acknowledges information and the positions of a high degree of importance. That reaches to the extent of contradiction with the historical facts and realities on one hand, and with the Constitution and Russian laws in force on the other one. What came in the response, does not only allude to ignore the rights of the Circassian people (Circassian nation) as one of the indigenous and authentic nations in the North Caucasus, but even ignores its human rights, the UN principles and legislations of Human Rights, and the International Law. Ref. to (No. 10).

– There is insistence by the Russian side on labeling the Russian-Circassian (Caucasian) War as the Caucasus War, which leads to ignore the real designation, and to divert attentions and interests towards reading between the lines in order to try to distort reality and to change facts. Ref. to (No. 2)

– The Russian-Circassian War, which lasted for a period of one hundred and one years (101) between 1763–1864, is reported in this scope: "The military operations of the Caucasian War (1817–1864)", which is inconsistent with the correctness of the description and the accuracy of the history, that raises confusion in meaning and desire. Ref. to (No. 2)

– There is a contradiction in the documented and verbal Russian policies and assurances, which did not see the light in serious and balanced form. Starting from remarks by former Russian President, Boris Yeltsin, in the year 1996, what followed of Russian authorities dealing with the Nalchik-based International Circassian Association, ICA, and concluding with the dead end which the humanitarian plight had reached. The Circassians of Syria faced difficulties as a result of the ongoing violence in Syria, and the unwillingness of the Russian authorities to cooperate in these tragic and repeated circumstances and developments!

— The unprecedented ratification by the "Ministry of Regional Development of the Russian Federation," supported by the "Committee for Nationalities' Affairs in the Russian Duma," shows beyond any reasonable doubt that the

Circassians of Adigha origin who are 90% of half of those who survived after systematical genocide, ethnic cleansing and deportation in tragic circumstances away from Motherland. They were forced to take refuge to a safe haven shielding them from evil organized crimes. They were described as the existing Circassians of Syria who had stayed in the territories at the time, were not within the Russian Federation until their migration in the year 1864 to the Ottoman Empire.

— Also, they cannot be considered as immigrants from the Russian State, in accordance with paragraph 3 of article 1 of the Federal Law, and this is an unprecedented Russian recognition, which proves and declares that Russia had occupied their homeland in the year 1864. Thus, how it can be that citizens of occupied territories would hold the citizenship of the state that had occupied their homeland!

— Notwithstanding all the foregoing contradictions, the Russian State Duma has dared to announce the recognition of a so-called voluntary joining of the Circassian nation to the Russian Empire, 450 years ago. In contrast to what the Ministry of Regional Development of the Russian Federation, the Russian official claims, where the Russian government celebrated accordingly in September, 2007. Ref. to (No. 14)

The anniversary of that event was supposed to be with the participation of Circassian parties considered part of the Russian official administration in the North Caucasus and some other Diaspora Circassians associated with the Nalchik-based International Circassian Association. That would mean that the Russian state duma has thankfully acknowledged that the Circassian homeland was not at any time among the properties of the Russian Empire, but the Tsarist Russian Empire had occupied it in the nineteenth century after a brutal and devastating war.

Ref. to (No. 14)

John Colarusso of McMaster University and Walter Richmond of Occidental College, are quoted on "THE DEPORTATION / THE CONQUEST AND DEPORTATION OF THE CIRCASSIANS," by Stephen D. Shenfield (ed.) Johnson's Russia List, Research and Analytical Supplement, Special Issue: The Circassians, Issue No. 43 - May 2008. They stated in the following, Russia's overall plan, characterized by hooliganism, to get rid of the Circassian nation:

> At a meeting in October 1860, Prince Bariatinksy and General Fadeev called for "the unconditional expulsion of the Circassians from their mountain refuges." General

Yevdokimov wanted to "compel them either to resettle in the open lowlands or leave for Turkey". The tribes that had already submitted were to be deported as well as those still resisting, such as the Shapsegh, Natukhay, Ubykh, Abaza, and Abkhaz.[1264]

Arbitrary Titles

In the same context, a "window" was published by Paul Goble titled "Moscow Not West Keeping Circassian Issue Very Much Alive." The concept has shed light on the developments of the Circassian activities. While authoritarian scramble has submitted clumsy means and methods executed by propaganda linked with certain Russian parties closely attached to the decision-making centers in Moscow and the Kremlin. Due to its importance, it will be mentioned in the following:

Goble started, "Many in both Russia and the West assumed that the Circassian issue, one that involves recognition of the 1864 genocide and the restoration of the rights of the Circassian people in their North Caucasus homeland, would fade after the end of the Sochi Olympiad, an event Circassians around the world used to highlight their plight."[1265]

He continued by elaborating on the reality of the course of events: "But while news coverage of the Circassians has certainly slipped in many places, their issues have not gone away—and not because of some Western conspiracy against Russia as some pro-Kremlin writers think but rather because of Moscow's continuing oppression of Circassians in their North Caucasus homeland."[1266]

The logic of the Circassian population's distribution is stated, "These issues are not going to disappear not only for the more than a half million people in the North Caucasus and more than five million in the diaspora but also for all those who care about justice. And as a result of Moscow's clumsy and repressive policies, they are likely to become even more prominent in the coming months."[1267]

Contrary to "how most Russian commentators see it. Instead, they use the standard Soviet-style methods of blaming the victims of Moscow's policies, or presenting anything they don't like as being the result of a Western conspiracy against Russia in which this or that group is encouraged to recognize that it is only a pawn in the hands of others."[1268]

Goble has mentioned the recent typical Russian propaganda policies: "A classical new example of this approach is an article by Yana Amelina of the Caucasus Geopolitical Club in 'Russkaya planeta' entitled 'The Galvanized Corpse of {the Circassian Question}'" (rusplt.ru/views/views_158.html)."[1269]

The "window" stated, "That of course is not how most Russian commentators see it. Instead, they use the standard Soviet-style methods of blaming the victims of Moscow's policies or presenting anything they don't like as being the result of a Western conspiracy against Russia in which this or that group is encouraged to recognize that it is only a pawn in the hands of others."[1270]

The article continued, "She argues that 'the events of the last few months show that someone is trying to give new life to the so-called 'Circassian question' which it appeared had finally been buried in the period of the preparation for the Sochi Winter Olympics in 2014' and that standing behind the Circassians who are asking it again are 'foreign forces' in Britain and Turkey."[1271]

Goble added that they envy Circassians for celebrating "for the sixth year in a row of the Day of the Circassian Flag in Adygeya, Kabardino-Balkaria and Karachayevo-Cherkessia with car processions, meetings and concerts, Amelina says, is simply the latest example of efforts by the special services of Britain, Turkey and their friends in Georgia to cause trouble for Russia."[1272]

The article quoted Amelina commenting on events intended to attract the attention of the young people on one hand. On the other hand, "they were designed to attract international attention and politicize an issue that shouldn't be, the Russian commentator continues. They had nothing to do with promoting national self-identification."[1273]

The analysis once more indicates what the Russians pretend, which they are claiming at all times. When the evils of their deeds are shown to be crystal clear, they twist the truth to blame others: "According to Amelina, both Britain and Turkey 'have brought the Circassians only misfortunes—Britain by pushing Circassian leaders into a hopeless struggle with the Russian Empire and Turkey by using them exclusively in their interests and in fact wiping out their national identity'. Unfortunately, she suggests, not all Circassians recognize this."[1274]

Goble continues that Amelina mentions that there is "a new Circassian organization" that has been established in the United States. She claims that the organization "encouraged by Western money and special services, are increasingly making aggressive toward Russia." She continues while assuming ignorance of others, for seeking "to promote Circassian refugee flows the resettlement of Circassians in the West now that Moscow has largely blocked the return of this community to its historical homeland."[1275]

To rant saying the "truth" in its absence, while conducting an anti-Circassian smear campaign, needs to be totally condemned, where the analysis continues, "(For those who need what she considers the truth on this, Amelina suggests that they read the highly tendentious report prepared by the Russia Institute for Strategic Studies (RISI) in advance of the Sochi Olympics entitled '{The Circassian Question} and the Foreign Factor' (riss.ru/events/2031/) and widely used by pro-Kremlin commentators at the time.)"[1276]

The article stated, "In brief, Amelina blames the usual suspects—Western intelligence services—for re-animating the Circassian question. But in fact, Moscow's actions against the Circassians are playing a much larger role. Among them in recent months are the following:

- Fears in Adygeya that Moscow if it restarts its regional amalgamation campaign will do away with that Circassian "matryoshka" republic and the only one that bears the common name of all Circassians, whose self-designator is Adygey.

- Anger that Moscow will now allow more Circassians from war-torn Syria to return to their ancestral lands in the North Caucasus and that the Russian government has overseen the worsening of economic conditions in Circassian lands.

- A wave of arrests of Circassian activists who came from other countries, including Adnan Khade, against whom the Russian authorities have fabricated charges and about whom Circassians in the North Caucasus and the diaspora are now speaking out.[1277]

- And most recently the refusal of authorities in Nalchik to open a criminal case against persons unknown who desecrated a statue there devoted to the memory of the victims of the Caucasus war, among whom the Circassians were the most prominent."[1278]

Goble concluded, "If Russian officials continue to act in this way, they and not any mythical hand of 'Western special services' will ensure that 'the Circassian question' is going to remain open and important for a long time to come."[1279]

In a similar concept, Eurasia Daily Monitor has published an article titled "Circassian Activism Appears to Be Thorn in Russia's Side, Despite Its Moderation" by Valery Dzutsati. The article has dealt with the Russian propaganda campaign and mentioned Yana Amelina in particular and with what she had written and published.

Dzutsati has stated that Amelina "unexpectedly lashed out at Circassian activists for their attempts to 'revive' the Circassian question. According to Amelina, the Circassian question was already 'over' at the time of the 2014 Sochi Olympics, but recently, some in the United Kingdom, Georgia, and Turkey have tried to revitalize the Circassian movement. The expert scorned Circassian Flag Day, which Circassians celebrate at the end of April, denigrating it as an insignificant event."[1280]

The article stated that "Russian experts like Amelina have increasingly used threats to convince Circassian activists to give up on their attempts to defend their interests. Once again, Amelina warned that Circassians should not rely on the UK and Turkey as allies, because they previously used them in a 'futile war against Russia' and eventually abandoned them (Rusplt.ru, May 4)."[1281]

Dzutsati has elaborated on the Circassian activists' objectives and careless Russian manners.

> Circassian activists have tried to attract the world's attention to the plight of their people in the past years. The Russian empire used military force, famine and disease to expel the majority of the Circassian population from their homeland in the North Caucasus in the 19th century. About 90 percent of the Circassian population ended up outside their homeland. The Russian government, however, has refused to recognize its negative impact on the Circassian nation or to alleviate its consequences. Many Circassians campaigned against the Sochi Olympics, claiming that Sochi was the "land of genocide." But Russia refused to recognize the conquest and ethnic cleansing of Circassians from the Black Sea coast as "genocide." The Russian authorities did not even offer significant incentives for the Moscow loyalists among the Circassians. Moscow did not rescue the Syrian Circassians, which would have allowed it to pose as their savior and win over some Circassians.[1282]

Eurasia Daily Monitor's article showed how Amelina belittles and mitigates the impact of the Circassian activists' motion. She tries to publish false news about the Circassian institutions: "According to Amelina, Circassian leaders rejected the idea as "virtual and stillborn." The expert also noticed the recent spike in activities of the Circassian cultural center in Tbilisi, Georgia. The head of that center, Merab Chukhua, reportedly received support from Circassians in Turkey and from Swedish academic circles (Rusplt.ru, May 4)."[1283]

Dzutsati mentioned that seemingly there is a Russian-backed writer who is pretending to be Georgian. His purpose is to offend the sincere Georgian humane motives toward the Circassians: "Irakly Gogoberidze, a pro-Russian writer who poses as a Georgian, warns that Georgia should abandon its efforts to support the Circassians or face a backlash from Russia. Gogoberidze claims foreign powers send 'thousands of dollars' for 'further incitement of ethnic hatred, and unleashing a new fratricidal war' (Worldandwe.com, May 5)."[1284]

The new verbal attacks on Circassians come at a time when Circassian activists are fairly reticent about their further actions, although Circassian Flag Day and the Day of Remembrance usually take place in April–May. Meanwhile, the attacks on Circassians were not limited to verbal assaults. A well-known Circassian activist, Adnan Khuade, was sentenced to 15 days in detention for driving his car without a license. In addition, the road police, who are notorious throughout Russia for corruption, accused him of trying to bribe road police officers. Khuade is known for holding multiple protests demanding that Russia repatriate Circassians from war-torn Syria (Natpressru.info, May 6).[1285]

Prejudice, intolerance, injustice, and pressing accusations are usual and familiar Russian practices.

In March, unidentified individuals vandalized a Circassian monument in Nalchik, Kabardino-Balkaria, specifically dedicated to the memory of those who died during the Russian invasion of Circassian land in the 18th and 19th centuries. A Circassian activist, Astemir Shebzukhov, made a formal appeal to the authorities asking them to investigate the incident. However, the police, who usually handle such investigations, rejected Shebzukhov's appeal (Natpressru.info, May 6).[1286]

Russian policies are prepared and coordinated, where the officials and their tools and proxies are concerned with urging allegations against Circassian activists "whether or not they were part of a campaign by Russian authorities remains to be seen, but the series of incidents and accusations by Russian experts against Circassian activists demonstrate that Moscow is worried not only about Circassians taking actions against the government but also about Circassians simply having their own days of remembrance and strengthening their identity."[1287]

Falsification of history and getting rid of evidence are well-known instruments used against the Circassians and other oppressed nations.

The Russian government at the highest level has said numerous times that it is determined to fight falsifications of history. Moscow regards all interpretations of history except those that are officially approved as "false". The Circassians' consistent narrative about their destruction by the Russian empire and subsequent exile poses a general challenge to the

Russian government. Circassians have largely become aware of their history and rocky relations with Russians, and Moscow finds it hard to fight against that.[1288]

Circassians know what their rights are, and they will never give up on their rights.

> The Russian authorities are thus nervous because they cannot force the Circassians to forget what they learned. The Circassian question undermines the "correct" version of Russian history, which traditionally portrays territorial conquests by the Russian Empire as benign for the people who were conquered.
>
> In many cases, Russian historians completely deny that these were conquests at all, referring to conquered areas as having "voluntarily joined Russia". Circassians are now aware of having been both conquered and destroyed by Russia. This self-awareness concerns Russian experts and shows the limits of Russian state propaganda.[1289]

Russian-Turkish Cooperation to Produce Joint TV Series

It is of no coincidence that the Russians and the Turks agree to cooperate and work for certain objectives to implement joint projects, which is normal practice between mutual partners. However, after a period of stagnation in relations that came to the point of hostility after "Turkey's downing of Russian warplane"[1290] on the Syrian-Turkish border in November 2015, the two sides have resumed relations in many fields.

After a consensus was reached between the two countries, the two parties have declared to work on joint projects to produce historical works and "to shoot joint historical TV series."[1291] This TV project regarding historical aspects of the region may lead to falsifying history more than it has been if no one would envisage the accuracy and truth.

[1216] http://justicefornorthcaucasus.info/?p=1251676204
[1217] http://windowoneurasia2.blogspot.com/2015/08/russians-continue-to-suffer-from.html

1218 Appendix (g)
1219 http://windowoneurasia2.blogspot.com/2016/01/moscow-disinformation-spreading-from.html
1220 http://windowoneurasia2.blogspot.com/2016/01/moscow-disinformation-spreading-from.html
1221 http://windowoneurasia2.blogspot.com/2016/01/moscow-disinformation-spreading-from.html
1222 http://windowoneurasia2.blogspot.com/2016/01/moscow-disinformation-spreading-from.html
1223 http://windowoneurasia2.blogspot.com/2016/01/moscow-disinformation-spreading-from.html
1224 http://windowoneurasia2.blogspot.com/2016/01/moscow-disinformation-spreading-from.html
1225 http://windowoneurasia2.blogspot.com/2016/01/moscow-disinformation-spreading-from.html
1226 http://windowoneurasia2.blogspot.com/2016/01/moscow-disinformation-spreading-from.html
1227 http://windowoneurasia2.blogspot.com/2016/01/moscow-disinformation-spreading-from.html
1228 http://windowoneurasia2.blogspot.com/2016/01/moscow-disinformation-spreading-from.html
1229 http://windowoneurasia2.blogspot.com/2016/01/moscow-disinformation-spreading-from.html
1230 http://justicefornorthcaucasus.info/?p=1251675380
1231 http://justicefornorthcaucasus.info/?p=1251675380
1232 http://www.jamestown.org/single/?tx_ttnews%5Bany_of_the_words%5D=circassian&tx_ttnews%5Bpointer%5D=2&tx_ttnews%5Btt_news%5D=36941&tx_ttnews%5BbackPid%5D=7#.VqCKxVMrJE4
1233 http://www.jamestown.org/programs/nc/single/?tx_ttnews%5Btt_news%5D=35942&tx_ttnews%5BbackPid%5D=24&cHash=0256175191
1234 http://www.jamestown.org/programs/nc/single/?tx_ttnews%5Btt_news%5D=35942&tx_ttnews%5BbackPid%5D=24&cHash=0256175191
1235 http://www.jamestown.org/programs/nc/single/?tx_ttnews%5Btt_news%5D=35942&tx_ttnews%5BbackPid%5D=24&cHash=0256175191
1236 http://www.jamestown.org/programs/nc/single/?tx_ttnews%5Btt_news%5D=35942&tx_ttnews%5BbackPid%5D=24&cHash=0256175191
1237 http://www.jamestown.org/programs/nc/single/?tx_ttnews%5Btt_news%5D=35942&tx_ttnews%5BbackPid%5D=24&cHash=0256175191
1238 http://www.jamestown.org/programs/nc/single/?tx_ttnews%5Btt_news%5D=35942&tx_ttnews%5BbackPid%5D=24&cHash=0256175191
1239 http://www.jamestown.org/programs/nc/single/?tx_ttnews%5Btt_

1240 news%5D=35942&tx_ttnews%5BbackPid%5D=24&cHash=0256175191
http://www.jamestown.org/programs/nc/single/?tx_ttnews%5Btt_news%5D=35942&tx_ttnews%5BbackPid%5D=24&cHash=0256175191
1241 http://news.circassianews.com/2013/04/22/%D8%B1%D8%B3%D8%A7%D9%84%D8%A9-%D8%A5%D9%84%D9%89-%D8%A8%D8%B3%D9%84%D8%A7%D9%86-%D9%83%D9%88%D8%A8%D8%A7%D8%AE%D9%8A%D8%A7%D8%8C-%D9%85%D9%86%D8%B3%D9%82-%D8%A7%D9%84%D8%AD%D8%B1%D9%83%D8%A9-%D8%A7/
1242 http://justicefornorthcaucasus.info/?p=1251670294
1243 http://www.un.org/en/documents/udhr/ and http://www.un.org/esa/socdev/unpfii/documents/DRIPS_en.pdf
1244 http://www.theguardian.com/world/2013/dec/06/nelson-mandela-life-quotes
1245 http://windowoneurasia2.blogspot.com/2016/04/15-characteristics-of-russian-propaganda.html
1246 http://rt.com/news/syrian-refugees-russia-kevorkova-751/
1247 http://www.al-monitor.com/pulse/originals/2014/05/turkey-circassian-tragedy-commemoration-strain-diaspora.html
1248 http://justicefornorthcaucasus.info/?p=1251660991
1249 http://www.windowoneurasia2.blogspot.com/2012/01/window-on-eurasia-syrias-circassians.html
1250 http://www.al-monitor.com/pulse/originals/2014/05/turkey-circassian-tragedy-commemoration-strain-diaspora.html
1251 http://www.al-monitor.com/pulse/originals/2014/05/turkey-circassian-tragedy-commemoration-strain-diaspora.html
1252 http://www.al-monitor.com/pulse/originals/2014/05/turkey-circassian-tragedy-commemoration-strain-diaspora.html
1253 http://www.al-monitor.com/pulse/originals/2014/05/turkey-circassian-tragedy-commemoration-strain-diaspora.html
1254 http://www.al-monitor.com/pulse/originals/2014/05/turkey-circassian-tragedy-commemoration-strain-diaspora.html
1255 http://www.al-monitor.com/pulse/originals/2014/05/turkey-circassian-tragedy-commemoration-strain-diaspora.html
1256 http://www.al-monitor.com/pulse/originals/2014/05/turkey-circassian-tragedy-commemoration-strain-diaspora.html
1257 http://www.al-monitor.com/pulse/originals/2014/05/turkey-circassian-tragedy-commemoration-strain-diaspora.html
1258 http://kabardino-balkaria.kavkaz-uzel.ru/articles/203163/
1259 http://www.kavkaz-uzel.eu/blogs/1927/posts/10025
1260 http://www.kavkaz-uzel.eu/blogs/1927/posts/10025

1261 http://www.kavkaz-uzel.ru/blogs/1927/posts/10025
1262 http://kavpolit.com/otvet-aleksandra-zhuravskogo-na-obrashhenie-po-voprosu-vozvrashheniya-sirijskix-cherkesov-v-rossijskuyu-federaciyu/
1263 http://justicefornorthcaucasus.info/?p=1251666942
1264 http://johncolarusso.net/pdf/the_deportation.pdf
1265 http://windowoneurasia2.blogspot.com/2016/05/moscow-not-west-keeping-circassian.html
1266 http://windowoneurasia2.blogspot.com/2016/05/moscow-not-west-keeping-circassian.html
1267 http://windowoneurasia2.blogspot.com/2016/05/moscow-not-west-keeping-circassian.html
1268 paragraph http://windowoneurasia2.blogspot.com/2016/05/moscow-not-west-keeping-circassian.html
1269 http://windowoneurasia2.blogspot.com/2016/05/moscow-not-west-keeping-circassian.html
1270 http://windowoneurasia2.blogspot.com/2016/05/moscow-not-west-keeping-circassian.html
1271 http://windowoneurasia2.blogspot.com/2016/05/moscow-not-west-keeping-circassian.html
1272 http://windowoneurasia2.blogspot.com/2016/05/moscow-not-west-keeping-circassian.html
1273 http://windowoneurasia2.blogspot.com/2016/05/moscow-not-west-keeping-circassian.html
1274 http://windowoneurasia2.blogspot.com/2016/05/moscow-not-west-keeping-circassian.html
1275 http://windowoneurasia2.blogspot.com/2016/05/moscow-not-west-keeping-circassian.html
1276 http://windowoneurasia2.blogspot.com/2016/05/moscow-not-west-keeping-circassian.html
1277 natpressru.info/index.php?newsid=10391 and cherkessia.net/news_detail.php?id=6948
1278 nazaccent.ru/content/20583-policiya-nalchika-ne-budet-rassledovat-oskvernenie.html
1279 http://windowoneurasia2.blogspot.com/2016/05/moscow-not-west-keeping-circassian.html
1280 http://www.jamestown.org/programs/edm/single/?tx_ttnews%5Btt_news%5D=45412&tx_ttnews%5BbackPid%5D=27&cHash=f0373fee9bb8b6c04d26be5f7050be8f#.VzNFfqNcSkp
1281 http://www.jamestown.org/programs/edm/single/?tx_ttnews%5Btt_news%5D=45412&tx_ttnews%5BbackPid%5D=27&cHash=f0373fee9bb8b6c04d26be5f7050be8f#.VzNFfqNcSkp

[1282] http://www.jamestown.org/programs/edm/single/?tx_ttnews%5Btt_news%5D=45412&tx_ttnews%5BbackPid%5D=27&cHash=f0373fee9bb8b6c04d26be5f7050be8f#.VzNFfqNcSkp
[1283] http://www.jamestown.org/programs/edm/single/?tx_ttnews%5Btt_news%5D=45412&tx_ttnews%5BbackPid%5D=27&cHash=f0373fee9bb8b6c04d26be5f7050be8f#.VzNFfqNcSkp
[1284] http://www.jamestown.org/programs/edm/single/?tx_ttnews%5Btt_news%5D=45412&tx_ttnews%5BbackPid%5D=27&cHash=f0373fee9bb8b6c04d26be5f7050be8f#.VzNFfqNcSkp
[1285] http://www.jamestown.org/programs/edm/single/?tx_ttnews%5Btt_news%5D=45412&tx_ttnews%5BbackPid%5D=27&cHash=f0373fee9bb8b6c04d26be5f7050be8f#.VzNFfqNcSkp
[1286] http://www.jamestown.org/programs/edm/single/?tx_ttnews%5Btt_news%5D=45412&tx_ttnews%5BbackPid%5D=27&cHash=f0373fee9bb8b6c04d26be5f7050be8f#.VzNFfqNcSkp
[1287] http://www.jamestown.org/programs/edm/single/?tx_ttnews%5Btt_news%5D=45412&tx_ttnews%5BbackPid%5D=27&cHash=f0373fee9bb8b6c04d26be5f7050be8f#.VzNFfqNcSkp
[1288] http://www.jamestown.org/programs/edm/single/?tx_ttnews%5Btt_news%5D=45412&tx_ttnews%5BbackPid%5D=27&cHash=f0373fee9bb8b6c04d26be5f7050be8f#.VzNFfqNcSkp
[1289] http://www.jamestown.org/programs/edm/single/?tx_ttnews%5Btt_news%5D=45412&tx_ttnews%5BbackPid%5D=27&cHash=f0373fee9bb8b6c04d26be5f7050be8f#.VzNFfqNcSkp
[1290] http://www.bbc.com/news/world-middle-east-34912581
[1291] http://www.dailysabah.com/arts-culture/2017/01/20/turkey-russia-ready-to-shoot-joint-historical-tv-series

13

Developments that Imposed Themselves on the International Scene

Statue of Satanaya in the Circassian village of Beer
Ajam, in the Golan Heights region of Syria

Proxies such as Russian local employees and officials are apparently
behind the reputation that shows Russia using old practices with new dreams

to show others that the FSB is able to control Caucasian/Muslim fighters. The evidence is contrary to the real policies regarding the use of Islam (Islamophobia) for its selfish benefits!

The Focus on the Chechen and Ukrainian Factor

Various reports from Ukraine, Russia, and Chechnya indicate that there is Chechen involvement in the military operations in Eastern Ukraine[1292] supporting the pro-Russians. At the same time, there is no confirmed number of Chechens in Ukraine defending the so-called "Russian-backed rebels" who are trying to secede from Ukraine in a similar way to what has happened in Crimea.[1293]

Russia wants to get support on religious bases and plans to win Western sympathy; the problem for Russia and for the West is shown as if it is coming from Muslims or Islam, even though there is a long Russian history of political murders against politicians, journalists, and human rights activists both inside and outside of Russia.[1294]

The media has reported that Chechen fighters are interfering in Eastern Ukraine for the sake of supporting both the Ukrainian government and the Russian-backed rebels.

> The Chechens arrived at about the same time on both sides of the war in eastern Ukraine. On the side of the Russians, they came last spring with no insignia on their uniforms, crossing the border into the rebel-held territory of Ukraine and taking up positions around the city of Donetsk. General Isa Munaev, by contrast, arrived on the opposite side of the front lines with a suitcase full of insignia—military berets, pins and flags bearing the symbol of Chechen independence: a wolf in repose above nine stars, each representing one of the major clans, or teips, of Chechnya.[1295]

Russian propaganda publishes that Muslim fighters would be deployed in battles to Russia's side, but it is a well-known fact that Russian military forces have committed crimes against the Chechen and Ingush people, as was published on "Prague Watchdog" in regards to Russian tradition of immoral "ritual behaviors" consisting of barbarian practices that had been common since the Tsarist military campaigns against the Caucasian nations, including the Circassian people, such as burning and destroying homes, whether partially or completely, total military occupation, genocide, ethnic cleansing, deportation, and beheadings of victims that had been eventually sent to museums and research centers to be performed by the criminal General Zass during the Tsarist era.[1296] They would take relatives hostage, compelling fathers and mothers to repudiate their children publicly, and when they killed those children, they fanatically danced around their corpses and pulled them by military vehicles, showing it all on television for greater effect—often for the eyes of the world to see.[1297]

When Russia declared that it was fighting Islam in Chechnya, Muslims were accused of causing explosions in certain Russian cities while according to confirmed sources, the FSB managed to blow up residential buildings and apartments in certain locations in September 1999, according to former KGB agent Litvinenko (who was later assassinated in London). The second Russian-Chechen War had begun with Russian forces being redeployed in Chechnya in a campaign that was led by then Russian prime minister Vladimir Putin, but human rights organizations had "expressed concern about human rights violations in Chechnya, including alleged torture and widespread detentions at the hands of Russian troops; concerns were fueled by the discovery of a mass grave filled with Chechen mutilated bodies."[1298]

In reference to the first Russian-Chechen War (December 1994 to August 1996), it resulted in a surprise Chechen victory against the invading Russian military forces; regardless of the devastating Russian military operations that almost destroyed Grozny and other cities and towns, along with crimes committed against prisoners of war.[1299] The war couldn't be won in Chechnya by Russia without the support from the West, and now it is using Islam as a monster in its imperial war in Ukraine, the same way when Russia proclaimed in its colonial expansion and genocidal wars[1300] against the Circassians and other Caucasian nations, that it was fighting a religious war against Muslims. They were given nasty names by its criminal generals while the same imperial Russia is now fighting Christians in Eastern Ukraine and had fought Christians in Georgia in the summer of 2008, not including the deportation of millions[1301] from the Caucasus and the Crimea by the Soviet communist authorities.

Memorial Human Rights Center's report on "disturbing parallels between the Crimea and Chechnya" focuses on similarity between crimes committed by Russian troops between 1994 and 2014 in Chechnya and Crimea, which indicates the meaningful proverb: "By their fruits ye shall know them."[1302]

The Significance of a Research Paper Titled "Blowing Up Russia"

A research paper titled "Blowing Up Russia" was made by Yuri Felshtinsky (a Moscow-born scholar who immigrated and earned a PhD in history in the United States) and Alexander Litvinenko (who worked in the counterintelligence agencies of the Soviet KGB and from 1991 in the Central Staff of the MB-FSK-FSB of Russia, specializing in counterterrorist activities and the struggle against organized crime). The topic contained eleven chapters,[1303] which described the FSB/KGB methods as "alien to the qualities of pity and mercy".

The paper was published as a book in the same title about the 1999 Russian cities' explosions, which was banned in Russia and contained the statements of ex-KGB/FSB agent Alexander Litvinenko regarding the described events and the leadership's decision to follow old KGB methods.

It listed tasks such as follows:

— The "special services foment war in Chechnya" seemingly had created conspiracies to prepare appropriate conditions for Russian military intervention again in Chechnya.

— The "security services run riot" include fabrication of news and charges.

— The "Moscow detectives take on the FSB" explaining how "the Moscow Department of the FSB had been transformed into a gang of criminals".

— "The political goals of the second Chechen war were far more serious: besmirched by the genocide of one of the nations of the Caucasus, Russia would be excluded for decades from the community of civilized nations by her own actions".

— The "FSB fiasco in Ryazan" elaborates on how "Ryazan FSB operatives were spotted planting sugar sacks containing hexogene in the dormitory district of Dashkovo-Pesochnya".

— The "perpetrators of the terrorist attacks in Buinaksk, Moscow and Volgodonsk were never found, and we can only guess at who was behind the attacks by analogy with the events in Ryazan,"[1304] stating that "on September 24, like a chorus in some well-planned stage performance, Russian politicians begin demanding war," reaching to the conclusion that "when the guns roar, the public prosecutors fall silent".

— Showing another way of dealing with the situation, "the FSB sets up freelance special operations groups" that could be from the mafias and gangsters, radical groups, former and current special armed forces.

— The "FSB organizes contract killings" in supervising operations of required physical liquidations.

—When it is considered appropriate to apply their policies against any individual or party, they manage "special services felony and abductions".

— Another example is "the well-known civil rights activist and Duma deputy Sergei Kovalev," mentioning that well-known criminals turned to be "KGB agents".

— For the conclusion, a statement was made by the coauthor Litvinenko[1305] who knew that his fate would be at the hands of those he mentioned,[1306] saying, "Russia, however, is an unpredictable country – which is the only thing which we know for certain about it. It is no longer possible to pull the wool over the Russian people's eyes, and perhaps that may prove to be a source of strength more powerful than the clenched fist of the special services."

The facts are accessible to those who want to know the details and intricacies, but this would reveal the contradictions and felonies of those who are interested in the domination of others.

The Developing Events in the North Caucasus

It seems that the typical trick of putting the blame on others by claiming repudiation is the usual Russian officials' nonrecognition of the facts that are known to everyone.

> On October 26, the Russian president's envoy to the North Caucasus Federal District, Aleksandr Khloponin, held his first live TV press conference. Khloponin expressly blamed instability in the region on the security services of Western countries, stating that the situation in the North Caucasus was aggravated "artificially." According to Khloponin, Western security services and various "provocateurs" are inflaming interethnic tensions in the region in the run up to the 2014 Olympic Games in Sochi on the Black Sea coast. In particular, Khloponin pointed to the Circassian question and the Ossetian-Ingush conflict—which, he said, are drawing the attention of the Russian government's "opponents" abroad (www.kavkaz-uzel.ru, October 27).[1307]

Standard procedures and official policies operate under the obligation of double standards (they show that they are criticizing a certain party in a certain area, but deal with the same party in other areas).

Khloponin's accusations are especially ironic given that only in May he came up with the plan to develop tourism in the North Caucasus and is expecting assistance from a number of Western banks—Morgan Stanley, J.P. Morgan, City Bank and Allianz (Kommersant-Daily, May 17). It is peculiar how Moscow reconciles its suspicions of the West's meddling in the North Caucasus (never even attempting to prove it) with seeking support from Western financial institutions for its high-flying plans in the region.[1308]

Developments that cannot be ignored are the Slavic Russians and Cossacks' practice of bullying and being arrogant towards the people and nations of the North Caucasus.

Khloponin periodically reiterates his support for the ethnic Russian population of the North Caucasus, including the Cossacks, who were the backbone of the Russian empire's dominance of this conquered region. On October 30, Khloponin officially became a member of the so-called Terek Cossack army (www.kp.ru, October 30). The Terek Cossacks celebrated the 20th anniversary of their post-Soviet rebirth with a monument to the nineteenth century Russian general, Yermolov, in Pyatigorsk (www.kavkaz-uzel.ru, October 31). Yermolov was known for his unchecked cruelty to the North Caucasians during the initial stages of the Russian conquest of the North Caucasus and is still denounced by many North Caucasians. Khloponin's willingness to rely on Cossack paramilitary forces is a reminder of Russia's imperial past in the North Caucasus.[1309]

Annexation of Crimea

In a sudden move in early 2015, which astonished the world but was not surprising if the involved parties and regions background are known, unidentified armed soldiers invaded the Crimean Peninsula and eventually occupied all the strategic and sensitive areas and locations in it, which neutralized the Ukrainian police and armed forces. Subsequently, Russian political steps and decisions were taken, which paved the way to the announcement and declaration of the annexation of Crimea and its being part of the Russian Federation without the consent of Ukraine or the Crimean Tatars, knowing that Ukraine, after the collapse of the Soviet Union, had abandoned its nuclear weapons that were in its possession in exchange for "Great Powers" commitment to the protection of its territorial integrity and its international borders.

The event is still in memory as the attendants, including Russia and a selection of Western countries, are responsible for imposing binding commitments on everyone, which were not yet respected as they should be.

> Who remembers that in 1994, the country gave up the world's third-largest nuclear arsenal in exchange for guarantees of its sovereignty and territorial integrity? Certainly, not the signatories of the Budapest Memorandum: Russia has just annexed part of its territory, for which the United States responded with laughable sanctions while Great Britain did nothing at all. Its hands are tied . . . to the coffers of British banks loaded with Putin's dirty money. The European Union, too, shows great reluctance to impose economic sanctions against Russia—after all, Russian gas, like Russian money, does not stink. The result: Putin gets free reign.[1310]
>
> On February 27th, four days after the end of the Sochi Olympics, Russia in effect occupied Crimea, part of the sovereign territory of Ukraine, under the pretence of protecting its Russian-speaking population. Russian forces based at various installations on the peninsula seized airports, government buildings and broadcasters within hours, and blockaded Ukrainian military bases. In Sebastopol, home to Russia's Black Sea fleet, local people celebrated their liberation in the central square, waving Russian flags to the accompaniment of Cossack songs, a Soviet-era pop group, and the fleet's choir.[1311]

Thugs have supported the undeclared invasion and started to do what is possible to embarrass the Ukrainian troops stationed in various parts, such as circling and seizing those locations.

> President Vladimir Putin has signed a law formalising Russia's takeover of Crimea from Ukraine, despite fresh sanctions from the EU and the US.[1312]
>
> President Vladimir V. Putin of Russia has publicly indicated for the first time that the planning to reclaim Crimea from Ukraine started weeks before the Crimean

referendum on the issue, which he had cited repeatedly as the main reason for Russia's annexation. Mr. Putin said he made the decision around 7 a.m. on Feb. 23, 2014, after an all-night emergency meeting with his security chiefs on the crisis in Ukraine. Viktor F. Yanukovych had just been deposed as the president of Ukraine, and the meeting was called to discuss his rescue, Mr. Putin said.[1313]

President Vladimir Putin completed the annexation of Crimea on Friday, signing the peninsula into Russia at nearly the same time his Ukrainian counterpart sealed a deal pulling his country closer into Europe's orbit. Putin said he saw no need to further retaliate against U.S. sanctions, a newly conciliatory tone reflecting an apparent attempt to contain one of the worst crises in Russia's relations with the West since the Cold War.[1314]

Abkhazia, South Ossetia, and Transnistria

The Russian-Georgian War in the summer of 2008 has apparently been devoted to the separation of the two republics from the Republic of Georgia, in addition to expanding and strengthening cooperation with Russia in all walks of life, including the fields of military and defense.

> Russian President Dmitry Medvedev says Russia recognizes Georgia's breakaway regions of Abkhazia and South Ossetia as independent.[1315]
>
> The Russian pledge came after a resolution calling on President Medvedev to recognize the independence of South Ossetia and Abkhazia sailed through both houses of the Russian parliament on August 25. Medvedev said his decision to recognize the independence of South Ossetia and Abkhazia, which he called on other countries to do, as well, "was not an easy choice, but it is the only possibility to save the lives of the people."[1316]

In August 2013, during the eve of the Sochi Winter Olympic Games, "the Russian President has congratulated the leaders of the two republics on the fifth anniversary of international recognition of independence, and promised future aid and support from Russia's side. On the eve of the holiday, Vladimir Putin paid a working visit to Abkhazia's resort town of Pitsunda where he held a meeting with the country's President, Aleksandr Ankvab."[1317]

Also, for relations to look more intimate,

> the Russian President sent addresses to Ankvab and to the South Ossetian President, Leonid Tibilov. In the messages the Russian leader wrote that the decision to support the two nations' struggle for independence, made in 2008, was not easy but it was the only right option. Such a move was crucial for the young states because it allowed them to take independent decisions on their future, Vladimir Putin added in his message. Russia will continue to provide comprehensive help and support to the republics, Vladimir Putin emphasized.[1318]

Transnistria is a strip of territories located east of Moldova adjacent to the Ukrainian borders.

> U.S. Air Force Gen. Philip M. Breedlove was voicing fears that the small country of Moldova will very soon become Europe's next crisis point . . . A Russian army base in Transnistria, with 1,200 soldiers, has helped ensure the region's invulnerability.
> After brief and inconclusive fighting broke out, the Russian army imposed a truce on both sides in 1992. Russian Lt. Gen. Alexander Lebed, a profane and charismatic officer, had little use for either the Moldovans or the Transnistrians, who began to devote sectors of their economy to human trafficking, drug running and arms smuggling. But he successfully separated the two warring parties, and they've stayed that way ever since.[1319]

Is It Going To Be a Conditional Recognition of Different Dimensions?

Based on events that have occurred in the past and according to experts' predictions, other surprises might be in the horizon, but probably waiting for the appropriate time for change.

> In the wake of the brazen yet choreographed annexation of Crimea by the Russian Federation, many are wondering who is next on Russian President Vladimir Putin's list?[1320] Beyond the worrying prospect of Russian irredentism in eastern and

southern Ukraine, speculation inevitably falls upon three post-Soviet de facto states that have long been propped up by financial subventions from Moscow. The Kremlin recognized two of these separatist entities as independent states in August 2008, following the short Russo-Georgian War: the Republic of South Ossetia and the Republic of Abkhazia, both in Georgia. The third, the Pridnestrovian Moldavian Republic (PMR), commonly known as Transnistria to English-speakers, remains unrecognized by Moscow. (This week its Supreme Soviet sent an official note asking if, in the light of Crimea, it, too, could join the Russian Federation).[1321]

Why the Double Standards?

Let's assume that the annexation came because of a request, initiated in part by the inhabitants who had Russian connections, without taking the opinion or the consent of the rest of the population, especially the indigenous people (who in this case happen to be the Crimean Tatars). Concerning the recognition of the independence of the republics of Abkhazia, South Ossetia, and Transnistria, it is appropriate to also recall that Russia doesn't bother listening to the voice of reason of the people and nations of the North Caucasus who demand freedom and self-determination while Russia says that those nations are part of its federation. This is in total contradiction to what has happened in the East Timor[1322] and Kosovo;[1323] they are examples of who were granted by the United Nations the right to decide their own self-determination and future.

[1292] http://www.npr.org/2014/05/20/314087662/the-secret-players-in-the-russia-ukraine-game
[1293] http://www.youtube.com/watch?v=qFeFNjc-0yE
[1294] http://larussophobe.wordpress.com/putinmurders/ and https://cpj.org/killed/europe/russia/
[1295] http://time.com/3893066/chechens-ukraine-war/
[1296] http://www.justicefornorthcaucasus.com/jfnc_message_boards/genocide_crime.php?entry_id=1307174818
[1297] http://www.watchdog.cz/?show=000000-000024-000005-000008&lang=1
[1298] http://www.refworld.org/docid/3ae6a86d8.html

1299 http://www.radioadiga.com/ClosedIndex/artikkk.php?ind=4263
1300 http://www.circassian-genocide.com/
1301 http://www.red-channel.de/the_real_stalin_deportation.htm
1302 http://hro.rightsinrussia.info/hro-org/ukraine-13
1303 file:///Users/adel/Downloads/Blowing%20Up%20Russia.pdf
1304 http://felshtinsky.livejournal.com/707.html
1305 http://www.theguardian.com/world/alexander-litvinenko
1306 http://www.cbsnews.com/news/who-killed-alexander-litvinenko/
1307 http://www.jamestown.org/programs/nc/single/?tx_ttnews%5Btt_news%5D=37111&tx_ttnews%5BbackPid%5D=24&cHash=3e40b701ee
1308 http://www.jamestown.org/programs/nc/single/?tx_ttnews%5Btt_news%5D=37111&tx_ttnews%5BbackPid%5D=24&cHash=3e40b701ee
1309 http://www.jamestown.org/programs/nc/single/?tx_ttnews%5Btt_news%5D=37111&tx_ttnews%5BbackPid%5D=24&cHash=3e40b701ee
1310 http://www.northjersey.com/opinion/opinion-guest-writers/the-price-ukraine-paid-for-giving-up-nuclear-arms-1.753757
1311 http://www.economist.com/news/briefing/21598744-having-occupied-crimea-russia-stirring-up-trouble-eastern-ukraine-end
1312 http://www.bbc.com/news/world-europe-26686949
1313 http://www.nytimes.com/2015/03/10/world/europe/putin-contrary-to-earlier-assertions-suggests-planning-to-seize-crimea-started-in-early-2014.html?_r=0
1314 http://www.telegram.com/article/20140321/NEWS/303219786
1315 http://www.rferl.org/content/Russia_Recognizes_Abkhazia_South_Ossetia/1193932.html
1316 http://www.rferl.org/content/Russia_Recognizes_Abkhazia_South_Ossetia/1193932.html
1317 https://www.rt.com/politics/putin-ossetia-abkhazia-independence-005/
1318 https://www.rt.com/politics/putin-ossetia-abkhazia-independence-005/
1319 https://www.washingtonpost.com/world/europe/transnistria-the-breakaway-region-of-moldova-could-be-russias-next-target/2014/03/24/c68c50a4-be46-4042-a192-6813e93380bc_story.html
1320 https://www.opendemocracy.net/od-russia/agnia-grigas/who%E2%80%99s-next-on-putin%E2%80%99s-list-Ukraine-Putin
1321 https://www.washingtonpost.com/blogs/monkey-cage/wp/2014/03/20/how-people-in-south-ossetia-abkhazia-and-transnistria-feel-about-annexation-by-russia
1322 http://www.un.org/en/peacekeeping/missions/past/unmiset/
1323 http://www.un.org/en/peacekeeping/missions/unmik/

14

Humanitarian Issues

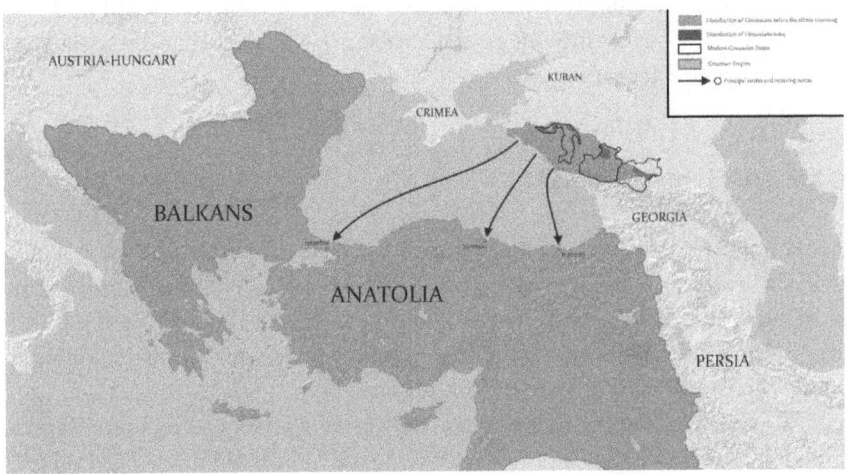

Resettlement of Circassians Into Ottoman Empire

The Human Dimension of the Circassian Question

If the Circassians are to maintain their demands, they need to stand united in the face of exclusionary projects and plans related to the liquidation of the "Circassian Question" whether through dispersion and division of the Circassian regions in the North Caucasus or through the Russian authorities' attempts of trying to maintain the status quo that consists of imposing denial of the Circassian rights, neglecting the Circassian diaspora subject, and dwarfing Circassians by promoting and maintaining their present status permanently in their current places of residence through cooperation with some of the heads and members of the boards of certain Circassian entities linked, whether directly or indirectly, with Russian interests.

Under an unequal relationship, the Circassians don't receive anything from the Russians (who fought and invaded them in their own homeland), except for murder, destruction, injustice, persecution, expulsion, and deportation into exile. Those who survived and could reach safety, in many cases, were able to reach places where there are bighearted people, with magnanimity and chivalry. They went to countries with people of good qualities who are known for their ethics, prudence, good judgement, and don't hesitate to do good or afford to provide hope and encounter trustworthiness, as well as honesty, kindness and fairness, and honesty in taking responsibility according to the noble values.

Circassians in return, have kept their values of fixed loyalty, courage, kindness, honesty, integrity, patience, and satisfaction in God's will and the search for a way out of difficulties and hardships without losing the basic goal of restoring their legitimate rights.

What Are Human Rights?

Human rights are considered a primary element and a necessity of the civilized world as humans regardless of their origin, religion, language, or race, individually and collectively, as they are entitled to respect, freedom, and privileges: "Fundamental assumption is that each person is a moral and rational being who deserves to be treated with dignity."[1324]

Proceeding from the fact that the Circassian Question is a humanitarian issue par excellence that is linked with the issue of humanitarian high values, it assumes to request applying human rights, which can be linked with what the Circassians must demand for the implementation of international laws concerning the Circassian tragedy in accordance with the thirty rights listed in the Universal Declaration of Human Rights proclamation.

The rights that should be enjoyed by all people alike, no matter where they live, will enjoy the following:

> Human rights are rights inherent to all human beings, whatever our nationality, place of residence, sex, national or ethnic origin, color, religion, language, or any other status. We are all equally entitled to our human rights without discrimination. These rights are all interrelated, interdependent and indivisible.

Universal human rights are often expressed and guaranteed by law, in the forms of treaties, customary international law, general principles and other sources of international law. International human rights law lays down obligations of Governments to act in certain ways or to refrain from certain acts, in order to promote and protect human rights and fundamental freedoms of individuals or groups.[1325]

The mentioned rights' articles are depicted as "the Universal Declaration of Human Rights (UDHR) is a milestone document in the history of human rights. Drafted by representatives with different legal and cultural backgrounds from all regions of the world, the Declaration was proclaimed by the United Nations General Assembly in Paris on 10 December 1948 General Assembly resolution 217 A[1326] as a common standard of achievements for all peoples and all nations. It sets out, for the first time, fundamental human rights to be universally protected.[1327]

The described "achievement for all peoples and all nations" is valuable for serving and preserving human dignity. The following is enumerated for the approximation, which mentions a few articles that have immediate relationship with the Circassians' confiscated rights, without minimizing the importance of the rest of the articles, which all of them mention, without exception, important human rights:

> Article 7. "All are equal before the law and are entitled without any discrimination to equal protection of the law. All are entitled to equal protection against any discrimination in violation of this Declaration and against any incitement to such discrimination."
>
> Article 9. "No one shall be subjected to arbitrary arrest, detention or exile."
>
> Article 13.
> "(1) Everyone has the right to freedom of movement and residence within the borders of each state.
> (2) Everyone has the right to leave any country, including his own, and to return to his country."
>
> Article 15.
> "(1) Everyone has the right to a nationality.

(2) No one shall be arbitrarily deprived of his nationality nor denied the right to change his nationality."

Article 28. "Everyone is entitled to a social and international order in which the rights and freedoms set forth in this Declaration can be fully realized."

Article 30. "Nothing in this Declaration may be interpreted as implying for any State, group or person any right to engage in any activity or to perform any act aimed at the destruction of any of the rights and freedoms set forth herein."[1328]

Democracy, Imperialism, and Human Rights

The term democracy is used by anyone who fancies attacking others, even when it is seen as a result that leads to the whims of selective binding to mismatches between theoretical scheme and its real contents leading to a lack of implementation of its essential elements. In this concept, and in the light of Western leaders accusing "Mr. Putin of backsliding on democracy," the BBC published an article titled "Putin Rebuffs 'Colonialist' West," which is started by "Russian President Vladimir Putin has accused Western critics of Russia's record on democracy of using 'colonialist' rhetoric. In TV interviews, he said it was unacceptable for the West to use the issue to interfere in Russia's affairs."[1329]

The Russian president, through an interview with France's LCI television, said, "If you look at newspapers of 100 years ago, you see how, at the time, colonialist states justified their policies in Africa or in Asia. They talked of their civilising role, of the white man's mission."[1330] He acted as if no one has witnessed how his words are embodied in the role of Russia in dealing with the people and nations invaded and occupied by the Russian Empire in the past, and still are, in addition to annexing Crimea from Ukraine, and the negative role Russia plays in Eastern Ukraine and Syria, which led to the deterioration of relations with many countries, including Turkey.

Reality shows that Russia is not granting human rights, legitimate rights, self-determination, and freedom to choose for many of the people and nations that are considered to be part of the Russian Federation! Commenting on the BBC article, a logical question was asked by one of the articles on the internet: Who are the colonists, Mr. Putin?

The article commenced, "Those who live in glass houses should not throw stones at others, and it seems that you are totally assuming the ignorance of others, and you are at the same time ignoring the fact that the state called

'Federal Republic Of Russia' which is a member state in the United Nations and supposing this dignified United Nations Security Council Member had already signed, certified and approved all the Universal Declaration Of Human Rights and Geneva Conventions relative to treatment of Prisoners of War. Knowledge is power, and none are as blind as those who will not see."[1331]

The article added, "The well-known colonial powers, that Mr. Putin meant, had already recognized their colonies to be independent states and those independent countries had joined the United Nations and other international and regional agencies and organizations."[1332]

A Tree Is Known by Its Fruit

A human initiative and touching story was performed by King Abdullah I of Jordan, who took a humanitarian step, which is not surprising coming from him. On the sixth of January 2011, the Jordanian Ad-Dustour newspaper published an article that took place sixty years ago, which gives an idea about the Circassian migration to Jordan in the midtwentieth century, which is a reminder to the migration of Circassians in the nineteenth century and the first years of the twentieth century, which was about a young Circassian who travelled to Amman for a specific human issue.

> In 1948, in the midst of Jordanian government's preoccupation with the reception of Palestinian refugees after the Palestinian Catastrophe.[1333]
>
> The late King received the young Circassian who informed His Majesty of the presence of a number of Circassians who are refugees in Rome in the wake of the defeat of Hitler's Germany, where they are exposed to hand them over to Soviet Russia, under the "Yalta" Agreement on the ground that they are Soviet subjects, who joined Germany's forces during its occupation of the Caucasus territories in World War II.[1334]

It was an important human step to deal with in order to save the Circassians:

> Those people had taken refuge in the Vatican seeking protection, which they were welcomed, and were refused to be covered by the exchange of prisoners between the Allies and Soviet Russia, and Mr. Shwabzouqa sought from the late King the acceptance of these Muslims Circassians as Jordanian subjects like their brethren living in Jordan, where His Majesty

has responded, and immediately ordered to take measures to transport them from Rome to Jordan.[1335]

The step was followed by another.

> After the elapse of another period, Mr. Jangeri Habjouqa arrived to Amman from Rome, and sought from the late King, to accept the second group, which consisted of 86 people of the Kabarday immigrants, where the King has responded to his request, and orders were given to receive them.

Circassians were requested and still to adapt by what one of the websites has sarcastically published in the title of "Survive in Hell and Do Not Dream About Heaven," which described the situation and the circumstances that Circassians have encountered and featured in their homeland.[1336]

Unfortunately, they are targeted for racism, racial discrimination, intolerance, xenophobia, and all forms of bias while victorious Russian and Soviet statues and monuments commemorating genocide, imperialism, and occupation are still erected in all parts of their homeland: "On November 21, the authorities in the Black Sea resort town of Sochi erected a monument to Russian Tsar Alexander II."[1337]

Prince Ali's Trip to the North Caucasus

An article titled "Journey to the History of the North Caucasus" was published on JFNC's website, which shows a meaningful event that awakens feelings of confluence of thoughts that has originated and inspired descendants, where the path of goodness is illuminated by their great-grandfathers.

> The title reminds the reader of a mixture of the present and the past that mix the painful realities of the past—which made the blood shed—leads to the loss of homeland, becoming genocide and ethnic cleansing victims and eventually part of the population were living under occupation and the vast majority were brutally killed by the Tsarist Russian aggressors' army, killed during the deportation process while transported by sea and land, killed because of illness, disease and severe effects of the rough living circumstances, or who ended up living as refugees in diaspora.[1338]

Unprecedented motion led to the opening of a bright page for the future of the Circassians by reminding the world of a forgotten people.

> Prince Ali Ibn Al-Hussein decided to set up a historical journey after the traces and the incoming footsteps of the devastated deported Circassians and Caucasians who had to depart their motherland in the year 1864. He accompanied the descendants and grandchildren of the Circassian diaspora in Jordan to take a historical and meaningful trip to the heart of the North Caucasus, to historical Circassia.[1339]

The route back to the Caucasus was selected by going from Jordan via Syria and Turkey, then from the Black Sea port of Trabzon across the Black Sea by boat to landing in Sochi, then going to the present Circassian republics of Adygea, Kabardino-Balkaria, and Karachaevo-Circassia, which has attracted the attention of Circassians all the way to the Circassian homeland in the North Caucasus, and to be greeted warmly by the Circassians there.

Prince Ali Ibn Al-Hussein organized a trip to the Caucasus with "a team of 14 Circassian riders" and was interviewed with Sigma News Agency, which was published in the Jordan Times newspaper, about his historical trip and in which he explained his opinion on why he had undertaken this mission, along with "the motives behind the trip, his interest in the Circassian culture."[1340]

He referred to the Circassian mythology:

> According to legend, when God was creating the earth He carried all the mountains in a bag in order to distribute them across the land. The devil seeing his chance slit a hole in the bottom of the bag and all the mountains fell in one area between the Black Sea and the Caspian. So God made that land the one place in the world where the devil would not be able to penetrate and make its people evil, since life would be hard enough for them as it is.[1341]

Prince Ali said that the North Caucasus

> is described by many visitors as Eden itself, with warm rich lowlands followed by majestic forests and alpine pastures, abandoned rivers and lakes, superimposed by eternally snow-capped peaks. These are the Frosty Caucasus of which Shakespeare sang, and which dwarf the Alps. Mount Elbrus, the tallest mountain in Europe, where legend has it, between

its two peaks the Ark rested on its way to Ararat. Kazbek, where Prometheus was chained, known in ancient Greek legend as the Land of The Golden Fleece, the land of fables and dreams, from which Tolstoy, Lermontov and Pushkin drew their inspiration.[1342]

In addition, I hope to bring the Circassian issue to the world's attention, so that they can no longer be used as pawns in a chess game, and future bloodshed in the Caucasus, caused by ignorance and neglect, can be avoided.

He called for "setting up a Circassian Culture Fund with branches in Israel, Turkey, the United States and the Caucasus, in order to work on and achieve international recognition for Circassians as displaced people and to implement their rights under international law to automatic citizenship in their homeland, as well as the preservation and revival of the Circassian language and to research and write the common and entire history of the Circassian nation."[1343]

Describing the response of the Circassians in the North Caucasus about the historical trip, he said,

> It was immensely spiritual and emotional, and their reaction seemed mostly to be of shock and disbelief especially among the elder people, with tears in their eyes as they never dreamt that such a thing could really happen. There was always tremendous joy and pride among the younger generation and the children and much celebration. All of it was immensely satisfying and gave me a sense of euphoria and inner peace. What was really most touching was when members of our team met their relatives and families, whom they had never seen or knew existed, in villages and cities along the way.[1344]

Among other points, Prince Ali said in his answers the following:

The Circassians are an ancient race, composed of twelve tribes, who have been dwelling in the mountains of the North Caucasus and along the Black Sea coast since time immemorial.

Many would-be invaders had found them a terrible foe, Roman Legions, Attila, Gengis Khan, Arabs, Temirlane and the Persians, who called the Caucasus "Sedi Iskender," or the barrier of Alexander. The mighty conqueror had set out to possess the world and met his first check here.

Having never been conquered, the Circassians have managed to preserve their ancient culture without outside influences up until the time of the Russian invasion, that began in the late 18th century and which flamed into a terrible war, which lasted over a hundred years.

The Circassians, freedom-loving and bold, fought desperately and fiercely, earning themselves legendary status and respect throughout Europe and the Middle East.

For one hundred years they held all the might of the Czar's armies at bay, preventing them from colonial expansion and the long-cherished Russian dream of an over-land route to India.

It was said that one Circassian is worth ten of anyone else, and their struggle is best described by the great Russian poet Mikhail Lermonotov, who wrote in the times of the Russo-Caucasus wars: "Circassian treasure rueful dreams, Circassian hearth is their supreme, but freedom, freedom for the man is more than peace and motherland."

The war lasted until 1864 resulting in the death of over half of the entire Circassian population, and the two great powers of the time, Russia and Turkey, collaborated to cause the forced migration of over half the entire remaining population to the Ottoman Empire.

Russia wanted the Circassian land for its emancipated peasants, and Turkey needed fresh blood for its armies in the Balkans. The Circassian expulsion was the largest mass exodus in modern times and another third of them perished along the way from disease and starvation.

It is estimated that if not for the war, Circassians today would number over 25 million or more, instead of less than six million spread out in countries all over the world.

Yet, wherever the Circassians went they contributed tremendously to the countries that they now live in.

They were the first people to settle in revived modern Amman. When Prince, later King Abdullah, arrived in Trans-Jordan, they welcomed him, and during a rebellion in the early days of the Emirate they camped around his palace to protect him and were then given the honour of being the King's personal guards.

Nowadays, they can still be seen guarding the palaces and the Royal Court in their fabulous and romantic costumes. The Circassians have served in every government and military office, and are well-known for their honesty and loyalty.

Today there are roughly one hundred thousand Circassians in Jordan, five million in Turkey, 700 hundred thousand in the Caucasus and smaller communities in Israel, Syria, and U.S. and Western Europe.

The Circassians practiced civilized behavior at a time when Europeans were still cave-dwellers. Their culture is extremely rich in poetry, myth, legend, song, dance and music. Their social structure is governed by the "Adygha Khabza," or Circassian etiquette, a set of unwritten rules which emphasize perfect manners, hospitality, honesty, chivalry and respect for elders.

They esteem their women and grant them full public freedom and they never practice polygamy or marry anyone even distantly related to them, as all Circassian relatives and neighbors are considered brothers and sisters. Indeed the Circassian's greatest achievement has been the perfection of their own culture.

Nevertheless, due to the fact that they have been separated for nearly one hundred and thirty years, Circassians are finding it increasingly difficult to preserve their language, cultural heritage and are at risk of large scale assimilation, that threatens their very existence as a people.

Circassia 531

My interest, therefore, comes from a want to reverse this process and give the Circassians the basic human rights, granted to all peoples of the world; to live together in peace and happiness, practicing their own culture, speaking their own language and respected and known by the rest of the world we live in.

This campaign is a symbolic beginning of the work to come. The horse-ride is in essence a reverse of the mass exodus that brought the Circassians to Jordan and the diaspora.

Circassians of the Caucasus and the diaspora are part of a single ethnic and cultural entity, and uniting these parts is a natural human right.

My goals are, therefore, to open the door for any Circassians wishing to return to their homeland, to be able to do so freely, without the complications and problems that they are presently facing due to lack of organization and barriers posed by people who wish to prevent the spiritual and physical unity of the Circassian nation.[1345]

Chauvinism Mixed with Religious Exclusivity

Regrettably, Slavic chauvinist lies against other nationalities, within the described federation ligament including the Circassians, and the fishy religious feelings and sentiments led to continuously building monuments that remind of such thoughts and occurrences. Acts such as building the monument of Nicolay "Miracle-Maker" in Maykop in 2007 has led only to one single score, which is the increase of mistrust and doubt between peoples, who are supposed to be fellow citizens within the state.[1346]

Maykop township administration has issued a statement on its website, which stated, "Perpetuating of the memory of the outstanding defenders of Fatherland,—it was spoken in the reference,—becomes the next step to revival of the traditions of the civil and patriotic education. In Maykop's history another—significant for all the generations—page will be written. The monument to the Heroes will become a portraying of courage demonstrated by Maykop citizens during both the Great Domestic war, and the peaceful time." [1347]

The single-minded administration's wording tried to defend the imperialism mentality regarding questioning the will of the peoples for national independence, who decided to get rid of the dependency and colonialism symbols in their homeland.[1348]

The statement showed defending the right of erecting Russian monuments, even if the described "heroes of Russia" have committed crimes or the idea was not accepted by others: "Since we found ourselves witnesses of an orgy of nationalism and vandal acts against the monuments of history in a number of republics of the former USSR, in particular, in Baltic countries,—it was told in the document further,—construction of a monument to the Heroes of Russia in Maykop becomes one more example of preservation of peace and the interethnic consent."[1349]

The article continued, "Let's remind, the new place of the Heroes' monument's construction is the square on the joint of the two main micro-districts of the town—'Centre' and 'Cheremushki'. That is the place where in the summer of 2005 the picketing then organizations 'Adyghe Khase' and 'Circassian congress' stopped construction of the monument devoted to Nicolay Miracle-maker. Let's remind, that monument is now in the territory of the military unit, situated in Maykop."[1350]

Cossacks' Influence

A report titled "Russia: Cossacks and Their Role in Sochi (Krasnodar Krai)" explained the situation in Sochi and the Krasnodar region then concluded,

> Angela Charlton writes, "When five uniformed Cossacks boarded the tram, conversations hushed mid-sentence, passengers' backs stiffened and the air seemed to chill". (Charlton, 1999) In Krasnodar, the Kuban' Cossacks now have government authority to conduct passport checks jointly with the police as well as perform quasi-military duties. Unfortunately, there have been numerous accounts in newspapers, academic journals, and NGO publications, reporting that Cossack units abuse this power regularly by harassing and targeting ethnic minorities.
>
> No information could be found on the Sevan Organization despite extensive research using the Internet, Westlaw and Lexis-Nexis, as well as consultation with representatives from the State Department and Doctors Without Borders. The rest of this response was prepared after researching publicly

accessible information currently available to the RIC and on the World Wide Web.[1351]

The Cossacks' behavior has been aggressive ever since as they have the green light to act accordingly. Eagle's Editorial published an article titled "Guards of Evil" in regard to "an earlier report on 'Institute for War & Peace Reporting' IWPR about Cossacks behavior against minorities in Krasnodar and because they were given the necessary support and they had been effectively given the go-ahead to bully and harrass all minority groups with no exception, including the original inhabitants, since the report was made, which was 18-Jan-02! 'Why have a dog and bark yourself?' (With all due respect)."[1352]

The article started with the following:

> When the 'Federal President' Putin made the main racist and anti-Semitic force in southern Russia (The Cossacks) as legal group, after signing the official documents, that triggered an earlier event which proves the fact that this policy had been implemented long time ago and this signing ceremony was for psychological influential effect by the security/police state policy, to make people more afraid and scared, and to make people fear approaching the point of requesting and/or demanding any change or their human rights of self-determination, freedom, and independence.[1353]

The Cossacks' demagoguery conduct was described:

> They antagonize, whip, kick, spot-check, attack, harass, torture and kill any one that they feel they wanted to harm and/or humiliate! Those Cossacks had started their duties in "smart red, white and blue uniforms trailing swords or cracking whips", while going on patrols harassing and bothering people in the Black Sea region, that used to be called Shapsugia, which is a name of one of the Circassian main tribes that was changed on May, 24th, 1945 according to the Decree of Presidium of the Supreme body of RSFSR about renaming area 'Shapsugskogo' to be Lazareevsky (after Admiral Lazarev) had been signed; but it seems that the name was changed again to "Krasnodar Region."[1354]

The article resumed,

Guess what they are wearing while performing their new but old duties? The answer comes straight away. They liked their victims' suits and clothes and they are wearing the Circassian clothes as a uniform now! They even had on Circassian coats and clothes, which there is nothing wrong with that if we think about it in a simple way; but the problem is that they are wearing the national clothes and uniform of the Circassians who got slaughtered, massacred, and brutally killed with acts of genocide when they were the servants of the tyrant Tsars, and now in the 21st century they are renewing the criminal killing of peoples and nations contract with the change of the boss and uniform![1355]

Some of the benefits offered to the Cossacks in exchange for the evil services provided are as follows:

Cossack units have signed agreements with the local authorities which gives them tax exemptions and better land leasing rights in exchange for patrolling the border and other duties. They acted like a mafia that takes to the streets to act as gangsters with the authorities turned blind eye on their savage attacks and brutalities.[1356]

To increase their influence,

the Cossack organization of Adygea is pushing for the introduction of Cossack patrols in the republic like those in neighboring Krasnodar region. Circassians in Adygea, however, are against the move, fearing the Cossacks will gain disproportionate power in the republic. "When a Cossack patrol steps onto the territory of Adygea, it will be the start of a catastrophe without an end," said Zaurbiy Chundyshko, chairman of the Circassian organization Adyge Khase in Maikop, Adygea's capital (Kavkazskaya Politika, August 11).[1357]

The fact is that "Circassians associate the Cossacks with the bloody conquest of their homeland by Russia in the 19th century." There are "several Circassian organizations appealed to Adygea's parliament not to pass the law on Voluntary People's Squads (Dobrovolnaya Narodnaya Druzhina). Even though the law is general, only the Cossacks are expected to benefit from it."[1358]

Another Circassian activist, Arambiy Khapai, who is a member of Adyge Khase in Maikop, said in an interview with the Kavkazskaya Politika news agency that budget resources should not be spent on additional volunteer forces. The police in Adygea already have 5,000 servicemen under their command, which is a sufficient number for carrying out their duties, according to Khapai. Another Circassian leader in Adygea, Adam Bogus, advocated for a more lenient approach that envisaged setting up Circassian groups of volunteers that would patrol the streets alongside the Cossacks.[1359]

Distribution of Tyranny Roles with Parallel Groups and Organizations

Where the end result will be only to achieve the hopes and aspirations of peoples to freedom and national dignity, "the arc of the moral universe is long, but it bends toward justice."[1360]

The existence of semiofficial organizations composed of veterans from the special services is barely acknowledged and considered standard policies within the Russian Federation, where they say in an example, "We're veterans of the security services, professionals and Russian patriots." It is mentioned in another paragraph: "The existence of semi-official organizations composed of Soviet and Russian veterans of the special services is barely acknowledged within the Russian Federation."[1361]

There is an "unknown fate" that some people face in the North Caucasus: "At least two men famous in the Northern Caucasus have suffered this grizzly fate in the recent past. One of them was Rashid Ozdoev, an investigator from the Ingush attorney general's office. He disappeared two years ago following his investigation into the FSB's kidnapping of civilians and community leaders. Ozdoev had assembled materials proving the FSB's crimes in Ingushetia, but the information disappeared along with the investigator."[1362]

The article also mentioned that

> the second man was Ruslan Nakhushev, a former KGB major who simply vanished in early November 2005 after being questioned in the FSB office in Nalchik. This distinguished graduate of the Academy of Internal Security was linked to attacks against security officers committed on October 13, 2005 and accused of terrorism by the local prosecutor's office. A month before Nakhushev disappeared, certain government-controlled newspapers published articles detailing the

supposed betrayal committed by the former KGB officer who had sided with the separatists.

A week before he vanished, Nakhushev told this author that he would be killed—"They'll get rid of me. They don't let you go once you've been part of the organization". Nakhushev became a "traitor" after he founded the "Institute of Islamic Studies" in Nalchik. His deputies were Anzor Astemirov, Musa Mukozhev and Rasul Kudaev, all three of whom were leaders of the Kabardino-Balkaria dzhamaat and two of whom subsequently took up arms and organized the 2005 attack on the Russian security forces in Nalchik.[1363]

Besides being a writer, the author is also a witness relaying to the world the terrible testimonies from those who were directly involved in the events, which shows the extent of arbitrary actions that go on while the perpetrators hide behind and coordinate with formal security parties: "These two cases pose unanswerable questions. As they like to say in Russia these days—'without a body there is no crime'. Nevertheless, there are other cases. Suspicious and unexpected deaths have claimed three of today's most famous Circassian leaders."[1364]

Brutal and inhuman conduct never was extraordinary behavior in the Russian dictionary of conduct.

> Police in Maikop detained six men on the night of 22 October as they left the city's Cathedral Mosque after prayers, regnum.ru and islam.ru reported on 24–25 October. The believers, who included the imam of the mosque and his deputy, were taken to Maikop police headquarters where they were stripped and beaten in an attempt to induce them to confess to being religious extremists, islam.ru reported. They were taken the following morning to the city court, where the judge ruled there was no reason to charge them with any administrative offense. The police who arrested them admitted that they were "acting on orders from above" in the aftermath of the 13 October attacks by militants in Nalchik, islam.ru reported. LF[1365]

This is not to underestimate the Slav unions and movements that follow a chauvinist line against other nationalities including the Circassians. On the sixteenth of January 2006, "4 public organizations of Adygeya had signed a joint statement and sent it to the Office of Public Prosecutor of Adygeya.

The organizations were concerned with chauvinistic statements of the social movement 'Union of Slavs of Adygeya', sounded at the congress of the organization on December, 18th of the last year."[1366]

On the nineteenth of May 2008, "Rashid Gurzhiev and Anatoly Dursunov, members of the Kurmanch community, were beaten by employees of law enforcement bodies of the Krasnodar Territory. Hasan Gurdji, chairman of the community, has informed the 'Caucasian Knot' correspondent about it."[1367]

The article continued, "Persons in civil clothes sat into their car, planted a package with drugs into Rashid's pocket, and tried to force the guys to work on them," Hasan Gurdji told later. "They gave money to Rashid and asked him to visit the crack house as a buyer of drugs. Then, they asked to rehearse a number of phrases. Rashid began to repeat the phrases, and militiamen recorded them to a dictaphone. Other employees soon drove up and started beating Rashid and Anatoly."[1368]

The organizations of Adygeya stated that "the statements sounded at this congress, were penetrated by xenofobia, chauvinism, national hatred, we cannot regard in any other way but a display of fascism. Similar things took place in Germany in relation to Jews, Slavs, and gypsies before coming to power of fascism. The right for existence of the entire people had been put under doubt."[1369]

On the twentieth of May 2008, Caucasian Knot published that Rashid Gurzhiev was kidnapped on the proceeding day, "about a dozen of persons in civilian clothes appeared in ward No. 14, Surgery Division, of the Central District Hospital of the city of Apsheronsk, Krasnodar Territory, and forced" him away after being beaten. His mother was handcuffed "to the bed and I lost consciousness. When I regained consciousness, Rashid was no longer there, only his slippers were left on the floor."[1370]

On the twenty-sixth of June 2008, "10 Kurmanch nationals have held a picket in Krasnodar against tortures applied to Rashid Gurzhiev, Anatoly Dursunov and Ruslan Kelosmanov. The picketers grouped in the mini-park opposite the administration of the Krasnodar Territory and demanded that law-enforcement and judicial bodies treat the detainees objectively."[1371]

Systematical tyranny and humiliation are considered the daily practice of the security elements supported by militias and illegal gangsters:

"Public prosecutors, judges and other power bodies would not react to violations of the rights of the members of our community", Hasan Gurji, head of the Kurmanch community told the "Caucasian Knot" correspondent. "The reason is in our nationality and in general attitude of the Russian state to all its citizens."[1372]

"Every fifth Russian was tortured by the militia. And only citizens themselves can resist to it", said Tatiana Rudakova.[1373]

Cemetery Vandalism

There were acts of vandalism committed on the Adygeyan cemetery of aul Aguy-Shapsug (Krasnodar territory) on June 26, 2005.

"Adygeanatpress" published on the web that on the seventeenth of May 2005,

> an act of vandalism above the body of Rashid Natkho buried on November 9th the last year has been committed. This vandalism is a handwork not hooligans or fascist swells, but investigatory bodies of Tuapsinsky interdistrict Office of Public Prosecutor. 1973 by birth, father of two juvenile children, Rashid Natkho died because of knife wound.
>
> To give a legal estimation to the actions of "the guards of the law" is just a matter of the nearest future—the father of the victim, Madin Natkho, has already addressed with the application to the public prosecutor of Tuapsinsky interdistrict Office of Public Prosecutor V.J. Kruglov in which he demanded to punish guilty persons in violation of remains of his son. In lawyers' opinion, there is an obvious infringement of some clauses criminally-remedial Code (CRC) of Russian Federation, which define the order of preparation and carrying out of post-mortem examination (autopsy).[1374]

The savage way the tomb was dealt with is explained as

> under a pretext of carrying out of autopsy an investigatory group headed by the senior inspector of Tuapsinsky interdistrict Office of Public Prosecutor, the 3rd class-lawyer A.S. Janovsky, has made opening a tomb on the aul cemetery, and then autopsy of the victim. The whole process—since arrival of officials till their departure from the settlement had been carefully hidden. The father and relatives of the buried have learned that the tomb was destroyed only the next day. Having arrived at the place, they saw a monstrous picture: the sepulchral hill was completely leveled, the stones framed a tomb, were scattered in disorder around it, stone columns on which on Adygeyan cemeteries the floor of buried is established, have appeared to be buried in the ground hastily, incorrectly.[1375]

When the family asked the village elders, responsible people went to check what wrong had gone there. They were astonished to find that the body seemed to have been thrown and displaced besides being damaged and the dislocation of body parts was carried out in a barbaric way.

> Moreover the scalp of the dead man was completely shaved away, one leg (left) was near to the trunk lying separately, and on the back of the body there was no skin. Boards which had been sloped in the tomb above the body laid in the hole in the full disorder.[1376]

Another incident mentioned is the authorities didn't inform the relatives in advance; falsification tricks were used on the correspondence dates:

> By the way, the elder of the aul Salim Mafagel some time ago too went through the similar insult himself. Without any notice of relatives and himself the investigatory organs opened a tomb and made autopsy of body of his daughter who have lost several months ago in an automobile crash. Only three days later the father absolutely casually learned about this illegal action of the law enforcement bodies and managed, as that is demanded by the national and religious traditions, to make reburying of his relative.[1377]

The article concluded,

> His point of view on the problem was stated also by the chairman of Adyghe Khase—public parliament of Shapsugs Madjid Chachuh. As he said, the scandalous fact which has amazed everybody with its cynicism, will become a subject of serious consideration at the nearest session of Khase. In this occasion they planned to pass a special application, references to the authorities and the Offices of Public Prosecutor as well as to address of legal expert organizations and the Plenipotentiary on human rights in Krasnodar territory.[1378]

Chasing the Activists

On the fifteenth of February 2007, North Caucasus Analysis Publication published an article titled "The FSB's Campaign to Eradicate Circassian

Nationalism" and mentioned one of the irresponsible actions that was carried out by the following: "Three Russian men pressed a pistol muzzle against the back of Murat Berzegov's head. Earlier that evening, they had abducted the leader of the Circassian National Movement of Adygea right in front of his house." They told Berzegov, "We're veterans of the security services, professionals and Russian patriots. You won't be able to die a national hero. If you don't stop shaming Russia with your talk of 'genocide', we'll discredit you and you'll lose your kids."[1379]

> As Murat Berzegov's story shows, such "veterans" are even active in the Caucasus, where Berzegov was targeted for appealing to the President and Congress of the United States to recognize Russia's genocide of the Circassian people.[1380]

The article explained that the groups and individuals working behind the scenes were serving the purpose of doing "the dirty work," which is not normally performed by official security branches, and verified that

> the existence of semi-official organizations composed of Soviet and Russian veterans of the special services is barely acknowledged within the Russian Federation. The subject is taboo in the media, with the prohibition only recently broken by the opposition Novaya Gazyeta newspaper. In a three-page article entitled, "The Backup Services", the paper describes the existence of secret divisions of the Russian security establishment functioning under the guise of social organizations or private security firms. These organizations of "veterans" are well structured, organized along hierarchies and closely connected with the official security services of the state. Remaining outside the official structures, such "veterans" are able to carry out the dirty work of disposing those whom the chiefs of the security apparatus deem inconvenient.[1381]

The Circassians' destiny and fate made the Circassian Question have different dimensions, but mostly it is dominated by conspiracies, harassment, procrastination, and assimilation.

> Yuri Kalmykov, a Circassian who held the post of Minister of Justice under President Yeltsin, died from acute heart failure while exiting an airplane. Kalmykov was the only

member of the Russian cabinet to resign as a sign of protest against the war in Chechnya, and after leaving his government post, he dedicated himself to the idea of reuniting the Circassian people. A man with an extensive understanding of Russian law, he worked on creating a foundation for a new Circassian state. For example, in accordance with his plans, an "Inter-Parliamentary Council" of three republics (Adygea, Karachaevo-Cherkessia and Kabardino-Balkaria) was formed. In accordance with the decisions of this council, a single executive authority and even a unified budget were created. The next step would have been the ratification of a new constitution, but when Kalmykov died, so did his project.[1382]

The unenviable situation that the Circassians have reached has made them a fragmented nation, that any Circassian who wants to review what has happened find ways and means to ensure unity, to restore their usurped rights, which were forcibly taken when the Circassian homeland was occupied.

A similar cardiac disorder claimed the life of Boris Akbashev, Kalmykov's successor to the presidency of the "International Circassian Association" in Cherkessk. The third such death was the sudden and unexpected demise of Stanislav Derev, an important businessman and widely acknowledged leader of the Circassian national movement in Karachaevo-Cherkessia. These deaths could, of course, have been completely natural. However, the doctors of all three men were completely surprised by the autopsy results, which revealed that the hearts in all three were almost entirely shredded and destroyed. Two of the deceased—Akbashev and Derev—had no histories of cardiac problems. In fact, Derev was a competitive tennis player and ran ten kilometers every morning. The funerals of all three men were accompanied by widespread demonstrations across Cherkessk, with many people speaking openly about the assassination of their leaders. A meaningful conclusion is a sign of the true picture of the situation in the North Caucasus. "It is true that all of these undertakings of Russia's unofficial security services are quite effective in keeping Russia's influence in the Northern Caucasus alive. The Russian government continues to sacrifice tens of thousands of victims on the altar of its geopolitical interests, multiplying the violence within the North Caucasus and thus furthering the spread of dangerous global instability."[1383]

Security Services Encroachment

Human rights abuses in Russia against individuals and families are considered to be a common practice. According to what happened with Zukhra Tsipinova and her nine-year-old son, who was married for five years to her ex-husband, Anzor Astemirov (Amir Seyfullah) is an example. She complained "that starting from spring of 2005, she—Zukhra Tsipinova—and her son of 6, have been exposed to prosecution by employees of power agencies of Kabardino-Balkaria." Her human suffering continued as she "has addressed her complaint to President of the Russian Federation (RF) V. Putin, General Public Prosecutor of the RF Yu. Chaika, and Chair of the Human Rights Commission under the RF President E. Pamfilova."[1384]

The social services didn't leave her alone, even after she moved to live in another republic.

> On May 27, 2007, Zukhra Tsipinova got married anew and left for the Republic of Adygea. Hardly had she lived for five days only with the new husband when he was arrested. According to Zukhra's version, the employees of special agencies suggested to release her new husband in exchange for information about whereabouts of Anzor Astemirov.[1385]

Targeting Circassians and Others in Moscow

RIA Novosti reported,

> A suspect has been arrested in Moscow in connection with the attack on a minister of a North Caucasus republic, police said Monday. Zaur Tutov, the culture minister of Kabardino-Balkaria, was attacked by a group of 12–15 people Saturday night and hospitalized with a broken jawbone and concussion.[1386]
> Zaut Tutov is the minister of culture for the autonomous republic of Kabardino-Balkaria in the northern Caucasus. He was taking his daughter home from dance classes when

Circassia 543

fifteen skinheads surrounded him, shouting "Russia for the Russians", and beat him up.[1387]

The BBC reported,

> Zaur Tutov, a singer and culture minister for the republic of Kabardino-Balkaria was attacked in Moscow on Saturday by a group of up to 20 young men said to have been shouting racist slogans. He was treated for concussion and a fractured jaw.[1388]
>
> Moscow prosecutors have given their go-ahead to a criminal investigation into an attack on Kabardino-Balkaria Culture Minister Zaur Tutov under charges of inflicting body injuries. "Nothing suggests thus far that the attack was motivated by ethnic enmity, but all theories will be checked", an official with Moscow's Eastern District Prosecutor's Office told Interfax.[1389]

In a related link, Eagle's Editorial Collection published on April 2, 2006,

> The Kabardino-Balkaria president's press service said Tutov, also a famed baritone, had been attacked by 15 people who had shouted "Russia for Russians". The prosecutors said other versions, except ethnically motivated violence, would be investigated! The government of the Republic Of Kabardino-Balkaria accused police that had arrived at the scene of reluctance to capture the attackers and demanded a thorough investigation.[1390]

On April 19, 2006, Yulia Latynina published an article titled "Official Silence." She questioned,

> For the past two weeks, the state television stations have given blanket coverage to the growing threat of skinheads. Mindless nationalism is obviously a very bad thing. Yet something prevents me from joining in the chorus of indignation on the television news. The main reason is that the Kremlin is exploiting the issue of nationalism as part of a blatant political strategy. In the run-up to the presidential election in 2008, the specter of rising nationalism will be used to frighten us into voting for the incumbent.

She added,

> There is also a disturbing discrepancy between the official indignation about skinheads and the official silence about so much else. Take the case of Zaur Tutov, the culture minister from the North Caucasus republic of Kabardino-Balkaria, who was attacked by a gang of skinheads earlier this month. The attack, which left Tutov with a broken jaw, set off the current spate of official concern about hate crimes.[1391]

On April 14, 2008, while fifteen meters away from his residence in Moscow, the knife-cut corpse of a forty-three-year-old man was found for the "inhabitant of village Karagach of Prohladnensky area of Kabardino-Balkaria. As they informed IA REGNUM in the Ministry of inner affairs of Russian Federation, on his body there were revealed twelve pricked and snipped knife wounds in breast, stomach, back, neck and hands." Apparently that has happened after the occurrence of a series of similar crimes: "The man became the eighteenth victim from the beginning of the current year from among the natives of Kabardino-Balkaria, murdered by unknown criminals in Moscow. Let's remind, the most notorious crime of such kind was the attack on the minister of culture of the same republic Zaur Tutov on April 1, 2006 in Moscow."[1392]

Faith in Humankind

After more than 150 years since the end of the devastating war waged by the Tsarist Russian Empire against Circassia, it is the duty of Circassian individuals and institutions to do what their national and humanitarian imperative dictate them to do. Where everyone works in cooperation and coordination among themselves to take into account the requisites that require the development of a partnership mechanism with international organizations that follow the United Nations bodies especially the United Nations High Commissioner for Human Rights, and in respect to the United Nations Declaration on the Rights of Indigenous Peoples, as well as government and non-government institutions and organizations in the world, especially in the States of the European Union and its affiliated organs, which are interested in human rights and oppressed peoples' issues.

Elaborating on human rights breaches, a writer stated,

> In the Caucasus, the most apparent evidence of "service veterans" activity is the mysterious disappearance of thousands

of people. One officer of a so-called "death squadron" from the region provided this author with information on condition of anonymity. According to him, there are many ways of making an individual vanish without a trace with different methods being used depending on whether information is needed or only assassination is required.[1393]

According to the officer, those men that need to be questioned are abducted using a well-rehearsed plan. A special group will drive to any city of the Caucasus fully prepared with a full knowledge of the victim's schedule and movements. The actual abduction can be carried out with little to no trace, even on a crowded street. The victim is driven outside the city limits and is then placed in a waiting helicopter that takes the man to a special base in Khankala (Chechnya) or a secret prison in Mineralnyi Vody. Interrogations are then performed using both chemicals and torture (such as electroshock). After the necessary information is obtained, the body is driven to remote locations and dumped into specially prepared chemical-filled pits. Over the course of several days, the body simply dissolves and the man in question vanishes without a trace.[1394]

In illustrating a short-sighted policy pursued by the Russian authorities, it was described as "the evidence that the Human rights policies of the Russian state are obviously not less violent on the territories that are not announced as the zone of war or co-called counter-terror operations."[1395]

Even though the Russian demographic situation is worsening, "one month does not make a conclusive trend, but Rosstat just released its preliminary demographic data for January 2015 and the results are ugly. Compared to the previous year, deaths were up and births were down by 2 and 4% respectively. This means that the overall natural movement in population for the month was -25,000, compared to only -15,000 the year before,"[1396] "where the escalating civil war represents an acute threat to ethnic and confessional minorities. . . . the Russian leadership has no interest in immigration increasing the Caucasian population in the region, after most of the ethnic Russians left during the course of the past twenty years. The Ukraine crisis has heightened contradictions in Russian immigration policy. After annexing the Crimea, the Kremlin offered all citizens of the former Soviet Union Russian citizenship as long as they were able to speak Russian. The language restriction naturally excludes diaspora Circassians. At the same time, Russian speakers from eastern

Ukraine are currently being resettled in the North Caucasus, despite concerns about the security situation there."[1397]

Typical Russian authorities' dealing with Circassians had no limits in respect to trampling on human rights; thus the fundamental rights of citizens are dealt with rudely and in ways that could be inhumane and provocative through directing haphazardly ready-made accusations without regard to the age and dignity of people.

The Circassian activists Aslan Shazzo, Adnan Khuade, Evgeny Tashu and Ilyas Soobtsokov, who live in Adygea, were summoned to the Centre for Combating Extremism (known as "E." Centre) of the republic's Ministry of Internal Affairs (MIA). According to their story, the talks there concerned the appeal to the authorities of Ukraine urging to recognize the genocide of Circassians, which was signed by them.[1398]

Notes of Importance

With pride and appreciation, it is possible to say that many people are doing what they can without any hesitation.

Efforts should be exerted to respect good and noble values and at the same time, apart from any kind of sensitivity or narrow-minded personal considerations, use straightforward facts and figures to address Circassian issues. To maintain continuity, they must know what is going on from related events and developments to draw attention of the younger generation to look at Circassian public interests, with proper dimensions and urgency to avoid any negative practices that may arise.

Those who intend to place barriers and obstacles on the way of proper peaceful and nonviolent activism must be properly watched and monitored, and they must be identified and verified. Matters should be dealt with an open-minded attitude that is required to raise awareness, address the proper issues, and follow the means of interlacing sincere efforts to seek using the principles of selecting the right action to follow to avoid deviation from the right path that leads to national objectives.

Interaction between Circassians is vital in both personal and systematical coherence. Regrettably, there are certain individuals that show egoism and even excessive selfishness when dealing with their fellow Circassians in the field of working on important Circassian issues.

Cremation as a Tool of Punishment and Revenge

According to news agencies, authorities have cremated the bodies[1399] of dozens of suspected "militants" killed on the October 13, 2005, attack on government buildings in Nalchik, according to a document obtained, adding to controversy over a law that allows the government to withhold the remains of terror suspects.

The authorities reacted "in response to that perceived threat, immediately after the multiple attacks by militants on police targets in Nalchik last October, police in Adygeya began checking the identity of young men who regularly attend prayers at several Adygeya mosques (see "RFE/RL Newsline," October 25, 2005) (Liz Fuller)."[1400]

More human rights breaches and violations were committed when the parents and the relatives of the suspected militants who fell victim during the 2005 autumn attack on the capital city of Kabardino-Balkaria when parents and relatives presented a complaint to the European Court[1401] against the refusal to give the bodies back for a basic human right of a dignified burial.

> Dozens of relatives of the deceased rebels gathered outside the republican prosecutor's office in Nalchik late yesterday morning. They had been trying to obtain the bodies of their dead relatives for a year and a half. "I have some bad news for you", lawyer Larisa Dorogova, who represented their interests in court, began. When told that the bodies were cremated on June 22, 2006, one woman fainted and several others began to wail. The crowd then proceeded to the headquarters of the republic's administration to ask President Arsen Kanokov why authorities had cremated the bodies. Cremation is against the precepts of Islam. Kanokov was in Makhachkala at a conference on religious and political extremism.[1402]
>
> The relatives of the militants who fell victim during the 2005 autumn attack on the capital of Kabardino-Balkaria are convinced that cremation of the militants' bodies that became known on June 6 was nothing else but an attempt of the authorities to destroy the traces of tortures applied to them and lawless executions, writes the Polish Gazeta Wyborcza."

The parents and relatives who were shocked for the news said,

"When collisions were over and the militants completely defeated, we learnt from official messages that the perished militants were 37 in number. And later, in the course of time, the number started to grow—up to 95 victims", the Polish edition quotes calculations of human rights activist Lev Ponomaryov, Chairman of the organization "For Human Rights."[1403]

The brutal police behavior was witnessed:

Thus, militiamen came home to Boris Dzagalov on October 14, 2005, already after the fight was over in Nalchik. Boris' father—Betan—saw his son next time on the following afternoon—in the city's morgue. Boris' face was disfigured by a monstrous blow. However, father heard that his son was killed on October 13 as an armed terrorist during attack on the militia post, the journalist of the Gazeta Wyborcza wrote about the events in Nalchik, adding that "such cases were in plenty in Kabardino-Balkaria in those days."[1404]

It took a heavy toll on the relatives, where the Polish newspaper quoted a human rights activist: "'When collisions were over and the militants completely defeated, we learnt from official messages that the perished militants were 37 in number. And later, in the course of time, the number started to grow—up to 95 victims', the Polish edition quotes calculations of human rights activist Lev Ponomaryov, Chairman of the organization 'For Human Rights.'"[1405]

The relatives of the suspected militants who perished in Kabardino-Balkaria Republic (KBR) indicated that no criminal liability was proven, taking into consideration that none of those that were killed had ever been convicted on any count.

Moreover, even if those victims were convicted after a fair prosecution of legitimate accusations in accordance with the law, and if the verdict proved that they were guilty, then executing the penalty should also be in accordance with the law, which was not followed in any way in this case. In case of the death penalty, a dignified human way of burial should have been adopted in accordance with the religious beliefs of those individuals.

On June 10, 2007, "Eagle's Editorial Collection" website summarized and described the bitter experience through an article in the title of "Fascists & Modern Gas Ovens Prove the Circassian Holocaust" about the crimes committed, "which are considered a continuation of their everlasting crimes against individuals, citizens peoples and nations," when the fascists decided to burn and cremate the individuals' bodies who were killed and their families were prevented to get their bodies for a dignified burial. Instead of giving the bodies and corpses of people who were not tried or convicted, they were burnt apparently in the modern ovens that came to prove the Circassian holocaust in the twenty-first century after it had started and continued in the eighteenth, nineteenth, and twentieth centuries. Unfortunately, the state policy is not only turning the table around, but seems to be in an "upside-down" position, with the usage of bluffing extremism and terrorism expressions!

The article continued,

> This time the crime is of different angle, caliber, size, magnitude, and meaning; but at the same time it is of considered premeditation, willfulness, and with forethought. It is not only a normal or accidental crime, but war crime, murder, assassination, homicide, manslaughter, and killing, against the remains and corpses of dead innocent people who had been physically kidnapped, confiscated, and seized by the Russian authorities and their security enforcement fascist forces, since the year 2005.[1406]

The article concluded with,

> The World should move positively in accordance with the International Law and Human Rights Charters. Russians must be held accountable for all crimes, and atrocities committed against the oppressed nations that used to be and/or still under brutal imperial rule.[1407]

Regardless of the militants' political parties and religious beliefs, or how they are described by their warders who held the bodies of the dead persons, so-called militants, the occurrence can be linked to the brutal way the so-called Islamic State (IS) has executed the Jordanian military pilot, Moath al-Kasasbeh, in 2015, near Raqqa, Syria, who was burned alive, and even his ashes were not given to his family.[1408]

The following is a timeline of some media titles that gives a brief indication of the developments until the Russian authorities announced the tragic news:

–20, January 2007
L. Dorogova: refusal to give out bodies of the militants perished on October 13, 2005, aggravates the situation in Kabardino-Balkaria[1409]

–14, March 2007
Strasburg has responded to appeals from Kabardino-Balkaria to give out militants' bodies to relatives[1410]

–28, May 2007
Russian CC to consider the complaint of the relatives of the militants who perished in Kabardino-Balkaria;
"The Constitutional Court of the Russian Federation (RF) has made a decision to consider, with participation of representatives of the parties, the appeal of the parents of the militants who died on October 13, 2005, in Nalchik."[1411]

–06, June 2007
Russia responds to European Court on the case of not giving out the militants' bodies for burial in Kabardino-Balkaria
"The bodies of 95 militants who perished in the events on October 13, 2005, in Kabardino-Balkaria were cremated on June 22, 2006," runs the answer of V. Milinchuk, Representative of the Russian Federation at the European Court for Human Rights, to the Memorandum of the European Court on the complaint "Sabanchieva et al versus Russian Federation."[1412]

–14, March 2007
Strasburg responded to appeals from Kabardino-Balkaria to give out militants' bodies to relatives[1413]

–27, April 2007
Russia asks extra time to answer European Court's questions[1414]

–06, June 2007
Russia responds to European Court on the case of non-giving out militants' bodies for burial in Kabardino-Balkaria[1415]

–07, June 2007
Prosecutor-General's Office has investigated the attack on capital of Kabardino-Balkaria in 2005[1416]

–07, June 2007
People in Kabardino-Balkaria condemn cremation of militants' bodies[1417]

–19, June 2007

Relatives of the militants who perished in Kabardino-Balkaria intend to complain to the European Court[1418]

–28, June 2007
The RF Constitutional Court upholds the decision not to give the militants' bodies out[1419]

–29, June 2007
Persons on trial in Kabardino-Balkaria voice protest against cremation of militants' bodies
"13 detainees kept in the Nalchik pre-trial facility (SIZO) refused from their further participation in investigatory actions in protest against cremation of the bodies of the victims of the events on October 13, 2005. The 'Caucasian Knot' correspondent learnt about it from informal sources."[1420]

–07, July 2007
Relatives of those perished in Nalchik: they burnt torture traces in crematorium[1421]

"In response to that perceived threat, immediately after the multiple attacks by militants on police targets in Nalchik last October, police in Adygeya began checking the identity of young men who regularly attend prayers at several Adygeya mosques (see 'RFE/RL Newsline', October 25, 2005). (Liz Fuller)"[1422]

[1324] http://www.humanrights.com/what-are-human-rights.html
[1325] http://www.ohchr.org/EN/Issues/Pages/WhatareHumanRights.aspx
[1326] http://www.un-documents.net/a3r217a.htm
[1327] http://www.un.org/en/universal-declaration-human-rights/
[1328] http://www.un-documents.net/a3r217a.htm
[1329] http://news.bbc.co.uk/2/hi/europe/5172794.stm
[1330] http://news.bbc.co.uk/2/hi/europe/5172794.stm
[1331] http://justicefornorthcaucasus.info/?p=1251677018
[1332] http://justicefornorthcaucasus.info/?p=1251677018
[1333] http://justicefornorthcaucasus.info/?p=1251676762 and https://www.youtube.com/watch?v=W0NzudbT5LU
[1334] http://justicefornorthcaucasus.info/?p=1251676762
[1335] http://justicefornorthcaucasus.info/?p=1251676762
[1336] http://justicefornorthcaucasus.info/?p=1166943660

1337 http://www.jamestown.org/single/?tx_ttnews%5Btt_news%5D=44878&tx_ttnews%5BbackPid%5D=7#.VoCqUJMrJE4
1338 http://justicefornorthcaucasus.info/?p=1251676063
1339 http://justicefornorthcaucasus.info/?p=1251676063
1340 http://www.angelfire.com/hi2/Royaltyandstuff2/Ali2.html
1341 http://www.angelfire.com/hi2/Royaltyandstuff2/Ali2.html
1342 http://www.angelfire.com/hi2/Royaltyandstuff2/Ali2.html
1343 http://www.angelfire.com/hi2/Royaltyandstuff2/Ali2.html
1344 http://www.angelfire.com/hi2/Royaltyandstuff2/Ali2.html
1345 http://www.angelfire.com/hi2/Royaltyandstuff2/Ali2.html
1346 http://justicefornorthcaucasus.info/?p=1172559840
1347 http://justicefornorthcaucasus.info/?p=1172559840
1348 http://justicefornorthcaucasus.info/?p=1172559840
1349 http://justicefornorthcaucasus.info/?p=1172559840
1350 http://justicefornorthcaucasus.info/?p=1172559840
1351 http://www.refworld.org/docid/3ae6a6b57.html
1352 http://www.justicefornorthcaucasus.com/eagle_combo/documents/blog.php?entry_id=1134664800
1353 http://www.justicefornorthcaucasus.com/eagle_combo/documents/blog.php?entry_id=1134664800
1354 http://www.justicefornorthcaucasus.com/eagle_combo/documents/blog.php?entry_id=1134664800
1355 http://www.justicefornorthcaucasus.com/eagle_combo/documents/blog.php?entry_id=1134664800
1356 http://www.justicefornorthcaucasus.com/eagle_combo/documents/blog.php?entry_id=1134664800
1357 http://www.jamestown.org/single/?tx_ttnews%5Btt_news%5D=44321&tx_ttnews%5BbackPid%5D=7#.VqCGzFMrJE4
1358 http://www.jamestown.org/single/?tx_ttnews%5Btt_news%5D=44321&tx_ttnews%5BbackPid%5D=7#.VqCGzFMrJE4
1359 http://www.jamestown.org/single/?tx_ttnews%5Btt_news%5D=44321&tx_ttnews%5BbackPid%5D=7#.VqCGzFMrJE4
1360 http://www.npr.org/templates/story/story.php?storyId=129609461
1361 http://www.jamestown.org/single/?tx_ttnews%5Btt_news%5D=32501&no_cache=1#.VphPDpMrJE5
1362 http://www.jamestown.org/single/?tx_ttnews%5Btt_news%5D=32501&no_cache=1#.VpnjEZMrJE5
1363 http://www.jamestown.org/single/?tx_ttnews%5Btt_news%5D=32501&no_cache=1#.VpnjEZMrJE5
1364 http://www.jamestown.org/single/?tx_ttnews%5Btt_news%5D=32501&no_cache=1#.VpnjEZMrJE5

1365 http://www.rferl.org/content/article/1143507.html
1366 http://justicefornorthcaucasus.info/?p=1251676958
1367 http://eng.kavkaz-uzel.ru/articles/7580/
1368 http://eng.kavkaz-uzel.ru/articles/7580/
1369 http://justicefornorthcaucasus.info/?p=1251676958
1370 http://eng.kavkaz-uzel.ru/articles/7584/
1371 http://eng.kavkaz-uzel.ru/articles/7799/
1372 http://eng.kavkaz-uzel.ru/articles/7799/
1373 http://eng.kavkaz-uzel.ru/articles/7799/
1374 http://justicefornorthcaucasus.info/?p=1251676775
1375 http://justicefornorthcaucasus.info/?p=1251676775
1376 http://justicefornorthcaucasus.info/?p=1251676775
1377 http://justicefornorthcaucasus.info/?p=1251676775
1378 http://justicefornorthcaucasus.info/?p=1251676775
1379 http://www.jamestown.org/single/?tx_ttnews%5Btt_news%5D=32501&no_cache=1#.VpnjEZMrJE5
1380 http://www.jamestown.org/single/?tx_ttnews%5Btt_news%5D=32501&no_cache=1#.VpnjEZMrJE5
1381 http://www.jamestown.org/single/?tx_ttnews%5Btt_news%5D=32501&no_cache=1#.VpnjEZMrJE5
1382 http://www.jamestown.org/single/?tx_ttnews%5Btt_news%5D=32501&no_cache=1#.VpnjEZMrJE5
1383 http://www.jamestown.org/single/?tx_ttnews%5Btt_news%5D=32501&no_cache=1#.VpnjEZMrJE5
1384 http://eng.kavkaz-uzel.ru/articles/6159/
1385 http://eng.kavkaz-uzel.ru/articles/6159/
1386 http://sputniknews.com/russia/20060403/45136468.html
1387 https://www.opendemocracy.net/globalization-institutions_government/racism_3482.jsp
1388 http://news.bbc.co.uk/2/hi/europe/4871816.stm
1389 http://justicefornorthcaucasus.info/?p=1251676972
1390 http://www.justicefornorthcaucasus.com/eagle_combo/documents/eagle.php?title=ill-gotten-gains-never-prosper&entry_id=1143987900
1391 http://justicefornorthcaucasus.info/?p=1251676976
1392 http://justicefornorthcaucasus.info/?p=1251676974
1393 http://www.jamestown.org/single/?tx_ttnews%5Btt_news%5D=32501&no_cache=1#.VpnjEZMrJE5
1394 http://www.jamestown.org/single/?tx_ttnews%5Btt_news%5D=32501&no_cache=1#.VpnjEZMrJE5
1395 http://justicefornorthcaucasus.info/?p=1251673688
1396 http://lingualeo.com/ru/jungle/russias-demography-just-took-a-

significant-turn-for-the-worse-381125#/page/1
[1397] http://www.css.ethz.ch/en/services/digital-library/articles/article.html/183019/pdf
[1398] http://eng.kavkaz-uzel.ru/articles/28279/
[1399] http://slideplayer.com/slide/1659065/
[1400] http://www.rferl.org/content/article/1066530.html
[1401] http://eng.kavkaz-uzel.ru/articles/6055/
[1402] http://slideplayer.com/slide/1659065/
[1403] http://eng.kavkaz-uzel.ru/articles/6013/
[1404] http://eng.kavkaz-uzel.ru/articles/6013/
[1405] http://eng.kavkaz-uzel.ru/articles/6013/
[1406] http://www.justicefornorthcaucasus.com/eagle_combo/documents/eagle.php?title=fascists-%26-modern-gas-ovens-prove-the-circassian-holocaust&entry_id=1181484600
[1407] http://www.justicefornorthcaucasus.com/eagle_combo/documents/eagle.php?title=fascists-%26-modern-gas-ovens-prove-the-circassian-holocaust&entry_id=1181484600
[1408] http://www.bbc.com/news/world-middle-east-31121160
[1409] http://eng.kavkaz-uzel.ru/articles/5311/
[1410] http://eng.kavkaz-uzel.ru/articles/5311/
[1411] http://eng.kavkaz-uzel.ru/articles/5872/
[1412] http://eng.kavkaz-uzel.ru/articles/5912/
[1413] http://eng.kavkaz-uzel.ru/articles/5531/
[1414] http://eng.kavkaz-uzel.ru/articles/5852/
[1415] http://eng.kavkaz-uzel.ru/articles/5912/
[1416] http://eng.kavkaz-uzel.ru/articles/5917/
[1417] http://eng.kavkaz-uzel.ru/articles/5918/
[1418] http://eng.kavkaz-uzel.ru/articles/6055/
[1419] http://eng.kavkaz-uzel.ru/articles/5959/
[1420] http://eng.kavkaz-uzel.ru/articles/5969/
[1421] http://eng.kavkaz-uzel.ru/articles/6013/
[1422] http://www.rferl.org/content/article/1341673.html

15

The 2014 Sochi Winter Olympic Games

Photo By: Imad Shabsough
No Sochi Demonstration in Amman, Jordan

The 2014 Sochi Winter Olympic Games, regardless of all the objections and concerns, eventually took place on February 7, 2014. Adler, which includes Sochi International Airport, and is situated twenty-five kilometers away to the southeast of Sochi, was nominated to host the skating events while ski events took place in the Caucasus slopes of Krasnaya Polyana, which is sited against the scenic backdrop of the Caucasus Mountains with an elevation of 6,600 feet

(2,000 meters) above sea level. It is located sixty-seven kilometers away to the northeast from Sochi and forty kilometers away from Adler.

Also, to coincide with Imperial Russian pride that is related to drawing the attention to Russian dominance of the area, "the event is intended to be the culmination of the achievements of Putin, a leader who many Russians believe was dispatched by God to guide Russia away from its defeats and ignominies. The seed of these games was planted in his mind more than a decade ago."[1423]

We cannot help in this scope but recall the International Olympic Committee's decision to convene the 2014 Winter Olympic Games in the city of Sochi, which has a special place in human and Circassian memory alike due to the particularity of the site's being the last capital city of Circassia when the Tsarist Russian occupation took place because of the scattered graves of those who perished in that location and adjacent places while they were defending their homeland. Also, the significance of the event connected with the memories of the provocative military occupation of Sochi, the last Circassian capital city.

Facts mentioned in The Fire Below: How the Caucus Shaped Russia include the following:

> As time passed, however, the complexity of the project began to overwhelm the government. When Moscow began to address the problems that arose, it revealed its limited ability to deal with such a major endeavor. Finances were fraught with waste and corruption, efforts to minimize ecological damage were amateurish at best, and despite some attempts to address local concerns federal authorities were either uninterested in or oblivious to methods of dealing with citizen groups. In fact, rather than face the challenges the Olympics posed in the manner of a representatives democracy, Moscow has adopted strategies reminiscent of its Soviet and Imperial predecessors.[1424]

Eventually, a total occupation of Sochi and its surroundings was not enough. Accordingly after 150 years, a more subtle plan of continuity was the master of the situation. A drastic change of the nature of the place had been fulfilled: "Sochi is a renewed site of memory within the Circassian memorialization process has increasingly become part of the rituals and performances carried out by Circassians in relation to the annual May 21 events."[1425]

The book continued,

> Sochi also presented major challenges. First and foremost was the issue of the municipal infrastructure. The soviets

developed Sochi as a resort city for the Party elite and designed it to accommodate 250,000 residents. Sochi is now a city of over 400,000 but the infrastructure has remained unchanged since the 1930. A plan for the development of Sochi was proposed at the beginning of the decade, but once the city became candidate for the Winter Olympics it was put on hold, and the infrastructure became even more overtaxed. Water systems are inadequate even for the current population, much less the increased population expected during the Olympics. Trash dumps are overfilled, and owing to the fragile environment locations for new dumps are limited. A recycling plant was planned, but it was delayed due to lack of expert analysis.

It added,

> The terrain itself presented two other fundamental problems. First, the entire greater Sochi area is environmentally fragile and unique. A nature preserve established by the Bucharest Convention in 1994 is adjacent to Sochi and actually overlaps some of the land Moscow included in the construction projects. Second, the location selected for main Olympic complex is the Imereti Lowlands, a swampy and geologically unstable area that has presented serious challenges for construction.[1426]

Selecting Sochi for the Winter Olympics was not an ordinary matter for Circassians.

> In addition to political, infrastructural, and ecological problems, there are also ethnic and historical issues centering on the reaction of the Circassian community to the selection of Sochi as the Olympic host city. Sochi was one of the departure points for the Circassian deportation of 1864, an event that many Circassians and many scholars consider genocide. Furthermore, the Olympics will take place on the one-hundred-and-fiftieth anniversary of the deportation, and Krasnaya Polyana (Red Meadow), the location of many Olympic events, is precisely where the Russians held their victory celebration. Circassians activists saw this as an attempt

by the Russian government to erase the memory of their people and the genocide.[1427]

The Russian authorities have always used all means to perform their plans.

> This chapter suggests that, while the federal government has been very aggressive in confronting individuals and organizations that threaten to slow down the project, it has wasted enormous amounts of money while falling behind schedule in nearly every sector of construction. Construction of building, ports, power stations, roads and waste dumps have suffered from serious delays. There is concern in the Russian government that some may not be ready for the start of the Olympic Games, and all have consumed resources that might better have been allocated to other parts of the Russian economy. On May 13, 2012, Russian President Vladimir Putin visited Sochi to find that delays and price increases were "unacceptable". He warned contractors of stiff fines if deadlines continued to be disregarded.[1428]

To facilitate all possibilities to hold the games on time, the Russian authorities were ready to do anything, even modifying the related rules and regulations.

> December 3, 2016, nearly three years after the Games are scheduled. There is speculation that this has to do with the law's reference to "the development of Sochi is a mountain resort" in addition to preparations for the Games. If this is the case, Moscow is apparently using an extraordinary situation to suspend federal law for a regular development project.[1429]

Reality shows a stubborn policy and proceedings: "Sochi 2014 confronted the world with the hitherto largely neglected 'Circassian Question'. Although the Olympic city and its North Caucasian neighborhood had been the Circassians' historical homeland until 1864, the host nation neglected to include them in the planning of the Games."[1430]

Obviously, instead of solving the Circassian Question and address the issue of genocide and forced deportation of the Circassian nation, the Olympiad was considered an important victorious event for the Russian state, especially focusing on Sochi, where 150 years earlier, it was occupied by the Russian Empire's invading forces. They had conducted a provocative military parade on May 21, 1864, of the victorious forces dedicated to the memory of subduing the entire North Caucasus region. Seemingly, the political system glorified the status of the Russian state and even focused on personifying the success of holding the games as such in one individual that is the current Russian president Vladimir Putin.

This also reminds of previous regimes, where the influential media is used as a tool for the oriented public opinion to support the undisputed leader of the regime. Exploring a prelude of what was coming in February of 2014, all media propaganda outlets focused on one charismatic individual who represents the whole regime.

> When President Vladimir Putin presented Sochi's bid in 2007, his speech to the IOC mentioned numerous nations and cultures that had shaped the Caucasian Black Sea coast since classical antiquity, but not the Circassians. The first time he spoke of the original inhabitants of the area was shortly before the Games opened, to complain that forces hostile to Russia were exploiting the "Circassian card." [1431]

As part of a public relations campaign waged on the global scene, to get more attention and backup from foreign friends and supporters, the Russian president has shown a friendly initiative, when "in January 6, 2013; he was in Sochi, granting Gerard Depardieu a passport (so the actor could avoid paying taxes in France) and skiing at the newly groomed Olympic slopes."[1432]

Exploring a prelude of what was coming in February of 2014, all media propaganda outlets focused on one charismatic individual who represents the whole regime.

> Putin's sixtieth birthday on October 7, 2012, was celebrated across the nation in a manner befitting a cult of personality, something he always professed to find distasteful. No more, it seemed. In the days leading up to it, an exhibition of paintings was held in Moscow entitled, without irony, Putin: The Most Kind-Hearted Man in the World.[1433]

In an interview with Dmitry Chernyshenko, the president and chief executive of the 2014 Winter Olympics in Sochi, Russia, said to TIME magazine about the preparations for the Sochi Games: "[The Olympics] is a showcase. It's a display of the new, modern Russia. We are developing awareness that Russia has changed a lot, and that we are democratic, we are friendly, we are transparent, and we are welcoming the world to Sochi in 2014."[1434]

The authorities in Russia were able to bestow certain status describing the characteristics of the undisputed leader: "Putin's sixtieth came with no medals, and there was something hollow in the fanfare. Despite the official adulation, the was an intangible sense of trepidation, among both his supporters and his critics, a realization of his age and mortality, a feeling that he had become indispensable but that no one could be forever." [1435]

Sochi and the Focus on Inspirational Leaders

In a related subject, the book The New Tsar: The Rise and Reign of Vladimir Putin by Steven Lee Myers elaborated on President Putin's curriculum vitae. The author "coherently, comprehensively and evenhandedly tells the story not only of Putin's glory years, but also of his hardscrabble childhood in Leningrad, his checkered academic career, his undistinguished work as a KGB agent in East Germany, his remarkably loyal service to the mayor of post-Soviet St. Petersburg, and his reluctant but speedy climb through President Yeltin's ministries in the late 1990s." [1436]

The book mentioned that "a youth group affiliated with United Russia produced a four minute, sexually charged video of beautiful women reenacting his most famous exploits: from riding a horde in the mountains to flying in a fighter jet to driving a yellow Lada in Siberia. There were poetry readings and essay contests for schoolchildren. The milestone had special political resonance in Soviet history, where the fate of the leader and the country seemed inexorably intertwined." Then he clarifies the way the former Soviet leader was honored.

> Stalin's sixtieth birthday 1939 had been treated as a national holiday that overshadowed the Winter War with Finland. He was awarded the Order of Lenin medal. Adolf Hitler even sent a telegram with his best wishes "for the prosperous future of the peoples of the friendly Soviet Union." Nikita Khrushchev received the same award on his sixtieth birthday in 1954, while Leonid Brezhnev was given the honor of Hero of the Soviet Union upon his.[1437]

Putin's birthday is addressed, which was characterized as a different style from that of the former Soviet leaders: "Putin's sixtieth came with no medals, and there was something hollow in the fanfare. Despite the official adulation, there was an intangible sense of trepidation, among both his supporters and his cities, a realization of his age and mortality, a feeling that he had become

Circassia 561

indispensable but that no one could be forever." The birthday was celebrated in ways that glorify and magnify various abilities and skills.

> Putin had charmed his supporters with various encounters with wild animals (some of them sedated), but his choreographed stunts no longer seemed convincing. He had stopped during the upheaval around his election, perhaps embarrassed by his "discovery" of the planted amphorae in the Black Sea. It is mentioned that in order to join a glider's pilot to: "lead cranes raised in captivity," he "dressed in a willowy white jumpsuit . . ." Putin had reportedly paid for the glider and spent hours training for the flight, but the event was ridiculed as a twenty-first-century for of Soviet hagiography.[1438]

The book mentioned that matters are not linked or related to each other, when he insisted that only Russia had a strategic nuclear parity with the United Stated: "Putin's answer ignored the daily humiliation and anger of Russians forced to pay bribes for virtually any public service, the high graft that Navally made a specialty of exposing, the dismal rankings of Transparency International that place Russia 133rd out of 176 countries."[1439]

Eventually it was proven that the results of spending the huge amounts of money for holding an international sports contest was for the sake of political objectives. Apparently, Sochi constructions and business packages with different parties didn't promote the Russian economy any better; on the contrary, the conditions did not improve. Transparency International published a list in December 2012, ranking countries of the world: "Russia ranked 133rd of 174 countries in the latest Corruption Perceptions Index by the Transparency International watchdog."[1440]

The book explained how Lyudmila was "conspicuously absent at Easter Services that year, when Putin appeared with Medvedev and his wife, accompanied with the mayor of Moscow, Sergei Sobyanin. Putin also avoided her fifty-fifth birthday on the eve of Orthodox Christmas in January, 6, 2013; he was in Sochi, granting Gerard Depardieu a passport (so the actor could avoid paying taxes in France) and skiing at the newly groomed Olympic slopes."[1441]

Under the title of Putingrad, the author started to shed light on the preparations for holding the 2014 Sochi Olympics: "In February 2013, Putin led a large entourage of Russian officials and members of the International Olympic Committee to Sochi for two days of meetings exactly a year ahead of the planned Opening Ceremony. He did not appear pleased."[1442]

He explained, "From the start, Putin had been intimately, obsessively, involved in the Olympic project, awarding contracts (often without competitive bidding), approving designs, and policing construction schedules. He visited Sochi repeatedly, on official visits as well as private ones to his dacha at Bocharov Ruchei, or to a new one built by Gazprom in the mountains."[1443]

The author specified some Russian concerns: "For Putin, the Olympics had a purpose deeper than the merely political. He believed them to be a palliative for a country that had suffered so much over the previous decades. 'After the collapse of the Soviet Union, after the dark and, let us be honest, bloody events in the Caucasus, the public attitude in Russia became very negative and pessimistic."[1444]

Activists and dissidents were prosecuted for opposing illegal development and abuses committed by the authorities.

> However, these environmental victories eventually forced Gazaryan into exile. In 2012 he was sentenced to three years' probation for taking part in a public rally against a land grab for a mansion for regional governor, Tkachev. Just months later, Russian officials charged Gazaryan with making death threats against security guards while the scientist protested outside a lavish mansion linked to Vladimir Putin.[1445]

The repressive Russian police tactics did not discourage those who were inspired by their conscience, but the unbearable humiliating harassment and ill treatment in detention centers and prisons made them seek asylum.

> This work came at a great personal cost and risk for Gazaryan, yet he refused to abandon his environmental activism. In June 2012, he was sentenced to a three-year probation for a public rally against the illegal seizure of protected forestland around the regional governor's mansion.
>
> In August 2012, the Russian authorities charged him with a second criminal case for allegedly threatening to kill security guards at an illegal construction site. Facing a harsh prison sentence in a corrupt justice system, Gazaryan was forced to flee to Estonia where he received political asylum.[1446]

Astronomical Costs and Crisis

An article titled "One Year Less of 'Russian Colonialism' Countdown" mentioned the international economic crisis and its effect of the Russian economy: "A Reader Poll on Oppositionist 'The Other Russia Site' asked: When will Russia have a truly democratic government? The answers came as follow: Between the years 2009–2010 6%, between the years 2011–2015 7%, between the years 2016–2025 16%, and last but not least 71% voted 'Not until the oil and gas run out.'"[1447]

The article added,

> When the most recent international economic crises struck the markets of the world, the Russian government disparaged and underestimated the consequences on the Russian economy and said at the time that the Russian economy is strong and went to the extent that they started giving lessons in the economy, before they found out that their case if not worse than the others, it is as bad, having the Russian industrial production falling down with the "oil and gas" revenues had fallen sharply, and even though the Russian media kept quiet and was paralyzed to provide any useful information.[1448]

High costs did not have a logical justification.

> Nearly every venue for the games has been built from scratch—the ice rinks in Adler, the bobsled run and facsimile alpine villages of Krasnaya Polyana, the rail and infrastructure that connect and enable. The current official price tag, $50 billion, is probably lowballed. Even so, the Sochi Olympics have cost more than any games before them. With many billions of dollars conjured up and carried away, this is not the tightest business plan ever designed. But this is not business.[1449]

Russia spent a record $50+ billion to put on the Sochi Games, effectively building sports venues, hotels, transportation infrastructure, and housing from scratch. There were questions before the Olympics about what these buildings would be used as after the Games, and now some of those fears are coming to pass. The "apartment units looted and vandalized. Residents in the area say that the owners are nowhere to be found."[1450]

The Olympic Games on the Land of Genocide

The Winter Olympic Games are considered an international winter sporting event that takes place once every four years. Hosting an international event in Sochi was a priority of the Russian state and wanted to achieve it at any price.

> The first talks about Sochi hosting the winter Olympics happened in the '80s. In 1990, the Krasnaya Pollyanna area [the area that became the Olympic ski village] was surveyed by experts from international winter sports federations and the International Olympic Committee (IOC). An official bid to host the 2002 Olympics in Sochi was submitted in 1994, but the Black Sea resort town did not make it to the shortlist of candidate cities. The IOC concluded that Sochi did not meet the technical criteria.[1451]

It is documented that Leonid Tyagachev, the head of the Russian Olympic Committee, has said in an interview,

> The 2014 Olympics project started [in 2000] when we visited Krasnaya Pollyanna with Russia's President. We looked at the mountains and got to thinking, "How can we have a world-class resort here? Of course, we need the Olympics." And then this idea captivated the President. Of course, if he wasn't an avid skier himself, he would have understood the "charm of Krasnaya Polyana." There were just three supporters of the Olympics. Others didn't believe that this miracle was possible. For me it was important to convince the President that this was necessary not for me, not for him, but it was necessary for the country. It was time for our country to have at least one real resort. It was important for our people, for sport.[1452]

The Russian government seemingly created its own workshop and plans to pursue and implement its project, regardless of all the legal obstacles and laws that had been violated, and thus eliminating irreplaceable places, areas, and natural phenomena that cannot be compensated or returned to their natural status.

In February 2003, the Chairman of the Russian Government, Mikhail Kasyanov, signed Decree No. 238-r: "The description of the boundaries of Sochi National Park that can be leased for construction of sport and tourism resort Krasnaya Polyana." This document actually became the starting point for all subsequent Olympic lawlessness. Kasyanov ordered valuable natural areas, such as the mountain ridges of Aibga, Psekhako, Gryshevui, and the area of Hmelevskih Lakes, to be earmarked for construction.[1453]

Holding the 2014 Winter Olympic Games in Sochi raised questions, doubts, and issues, revealed their implications and consequences as well as their effects, particularly on the environmental, construction, and material sectors: "The decision was taken after considering the materials submitted by Greenpeace of Russia. Ecologists inform the Committee members about the large-scale construction planned in the buffer zone of the 'Western Caucasus' (which was recently prohibited by Russian laws, however, the legislation has been changed in order to legalize the occupation of unique nature reserve territories)."[1454]

The Russian authorities have dropped from their accounts the possibility of adherence to the laws relating to restrict the construction and change of landmarks of the Northwest Caucasus, but they continued the infringement of protected sites despite all caveats and precautions.

On October 4, 2004, a group of high ranking officials pompously poured the symbolic "first square cube" of concrete, beginning construction of the ski lift for the new resort "Gornaya Karusel" on the Aibga Ridge near Sochi. The event was covered in the media as a "major breakthrough" and a "new milestone in the history of Sochi". But the media did not mention another "milestone"—an act of lawlessness: contractors or Gornaya Karusel did not complete an environmental impact assessment. Exactly in the same manner, violating various legislative norms, subsequent Olympic structures were built.[1455]

Violations were intentional and were considered as ordinary and usual conduct.

The Sochi Olympics have created an extremely dangerous precedent for our country: federal laws being amended to allow for megaproject construction. Another shameful aspect was the role of international institutions such as National Olympic Committees and the United Nations Environment Programme in monitoring and enforcing environmental standards in preparation for the Games. They failed to fulfill their responsibilities; they closed their eyes to numerous violations.[1456]

One should not forget the role of some international parties that were involved in the politicization of such a sporting event and other consequential decisions while hurting many things for the sake of satisfying and pleasing certain agendas, celebrities, and officials.

International complacency allowed the Russian government to implement a large scale construction project that destroyed a unique ecosystem and caused environmental damage unheard of since the industrialization era over a century ago. We really do not want this analysis of mistakes to turn into a blame game, but rather to be used as a serious lesson for all of us.[1457]

The International Olympic Committee accepted the Russian offer while at the same time all the concerned officials engaged in this suspicious choice ignored all the facts and precautions while they chose the Circassian city of Sochi to host the 2014 Winter Olympic Games: "The International Olympic Committee has accepted the Russian offer, while at the same time all the concerned in this suspicious choice have ignored all facts and precautions, while they chose the Circassian city of Sochi to host the '2014 Winter Olympic Games.'"[1458]

National Geographic magazine published an article titled "Putin's Party," a detailed report on the Winter Olympic Games and the facilities constructed in Sochi and Krasnaya Ployana. The article included interviews, photos, information, and facts about the Circassians, including the map of Circassia that was published in 1855. The article pointed out,

Ultimately, Russian military capability proved too much for the warriors of the mountains, who refused to accept the tsar's offer to live in Siberia or emigrate to the Ottoman Empire. The Circassians made their last stand in the small canyon that is now called Krasnaya Polyana, or red glade, a name some erroneously attribute to the bloodshed of the battle. After their surrender in 1864 the Circassians were expelled, and refugees died by the thousands on their way to Sochi. Survivors were shipped to various corners of the Ottoman Empire. Some of them died aboard the Turkish vessels, cast overboard into the Black Sea.[1459]

One year before the Sochi Winter Olympic Games, Paul Goble published the following:

> Each Friday over the coming months, I will prepare a special Window on Eurasia about the meaning and impact of the planned Olympiad on the nations in the surrounding region. These WOEs will not aim at being comprehensive but rather will consist of a series of bullet points about such developments. I would like to invite anyone with special knowledge or information about this subject to send me references to the materials involved.[1460]

Ecologists, historians, and human rights groups and organizations have totally rejected the move to contaminate a protected sight by UNESCO. It was possible to observe a breach of the integrity of maintaining one of the world's protected ancient forests, natural native plant habitats, wildlife species and animals, and natural reserves.

> "The Committee final decision is not very strict. This seems to be connected with the fact that the experts do not wish to exert influence on the International Olympic Committee in the process of passing a decision on the venue of the 2014 Olympics," says Roman Vazhenkov, program manager on specially protected natural territories, Russian Greenpeace.[1461]

An initiative was taken by the Russian authorities to invite Circassian individuals to Sochi, according to a deliberate and well preprared plan to organize and execute a tour of the construction areas and especially to visit the region that had witnessed a sweeping change in its landmarks, just shortly before the games took place: "Recently, a delegation of Circassians traveled to their ancestral home to visit historic sites ahead of the games."[1462] It is appropriate to say that only two out of the group, Zoher Thawcho and Nalchik Ashmoz, who are Circassians from Kfar Kama, Israel, have refused to continue the tour the moment they found out that they were going to Sochi. They refused to proceed in the tour and left the area right away, back to Kfar Kama.

The Memory of Mass Murder and Deportation

A decision was taken to hold the 2014 winter Olympic Games in Sochi, which was opposed by Greenpeace of Russia. Ecologists informed the IOC members about the large-scale construction planned in the buffer zone of the "Western Caucasus" (which was recently prohibited by Russian laws and was changed in order to legalize the occupation of unique nature reserve territories). Ecologists, historians, and human rights groups and organizations had rejected the move to contaminate a protected site by UNESCO.

Matthew Light gave an interview and stated, "On the challenges and opportunities for the Sochi 2014 Winter Olympics," where he spoke about the Circassian genocide, human rights issues, invasion, occupation, and the Olympic structures being placed on the Circassian graves, and its attachment with the Russian policies and present administrative issues in the North Caucasus, where he also presented his elaboration on specific details and facts that would pertain at the time to holding Sochi Olympic Games, on the land of the Circassian Genocide.[1463]

Russia had dropped all available winter sports sites in its vast and spacious land that is available, then offered, and the International Olympic Committee accepted Sochi. But at the same time, all those who were involved in this suspicious choice ignored all facts and precautions that had do with choosing the Circassian city of Sochi to host the 2014 Winter Olympic Games.

Circassians issued a letter in six languages and sent it to the International Olympic Committee, condemning and denouncing holding the games. The reason was not only the environment, but the plans of holding the Olympics on the cemeteries of those who perished while defending their homeland against invaders who terrorized, killed, displaced, deported, and exiled the entire oppressed Circassian nation. In the explanatory letter, two main questions were asked:

> Do you know that those beautiful highlands are now banned to the local population? Only tourists having gotten a special permit from the FSB can have access there to admire the beauty of the blue mountain lakes, the green pine forests and to breathe the pure mountain air.
>
> Today, the few native Caucasians who remained in their motherland are forced once more to quit their mountains. Is it on those mountains, "cleaned up" from their native population, which the Olympic sportsmen are going to ski? Are the bobsleigh tracks going to be constructed on the bones

of people annihilated by bloodful wars for the conquest of the Caucasus?[1464]

Valery Brinikh, head of the Maikop City Public Organization of All-Russia Wildlife Protection Society and a member of the Board of the Ecological Watch for North Caucasus, showed disapproval and condemnation for planning to create damage to a valuable area that cannot be restored. He voiced his opinion and said,

> Sochi will become a huge all-Russian construction site and cease to exist as a balneo therapeutic health resort. For example, for the sake of the Olympiad, they are "developing" the Imereti Lowland. But this is the unique source of therapeutic muds. That is, by drying the Lowland to launch their large-scale construction, the Olympiad organizers will liquidate the Matsesta medical resorts. In this sense, our protest ceases to be just ecological, it acquires a social aspect.[1465]

Shortly before the opening ceremony of the 2014 Winter Olympic Games and to circumvent the objections and rejections of the majority of Circassians to hold such games in Sochi, without solving the Circassian Question, in accordance with "the declaration made by the General Assembly of the United Nations in its resolution 96 (I) dated 11 December 1946 that genocide is a crime under international law, contrary to the spirit and aims of the United Nations and condemned by the civilized world."[1466]

In Did the Age of Genocide Begin in Sochi? by Joshua Keating, it stated in regards to the objectives of the Russian Empire and other major powers: "With the fairly cynical encouragement of the Ottomans, many Circassians resisted, but the 'Caucasus War' was a one-sided affair and Russia declared victory after a last stand by the Circassians at Sochi in 1864, after which the formal evacuation of the group by ship from the Black Sea coast to Turkey began." He continued,

> Despite a horrific humanitarian catastrophe taking place along the coast, with those waiting for boats to take them away dying in massive numbers from typhus and smallpox amid a brutal winter, Russian troops continued their campaign of destroying Circassian villages in the mountains, creating thousands more refugees. Turkish ship owners did not help the situation by overcrowding their boats and charging exorbitant fees to the refugees.[1467]

Russian media outlets couldn't blur facts anymore. They are unable to publicly influence people of the world to access facts of the Circassian tragedy and how much the Circassians have endured and still suffer as a result.

> The Russian reaction has been a combination of hardline policies to silence opposition in Russia and a multifaceted propaganda campaign.
> One part of this effort is designed to portray the opponents of the Sochi Games, and indeed all Circassian activists who have adopted a confrontational attitude toward Moscow, as part of a U.S.-driven effort to increase instability in the North Caucasus and perhaps even wrest it away from Russia altogether.[1468]

It is not possible to underestimate the influence of the effect of Russian strength used against Circassian activists, especially those who are still clinging to their homeland's soil. It is well-known what can be done by the Russian local security authorities against anyone who may think of using the correct vocabulary regarding basic human rights: "The Russian government itself continues to portray Circassian activists as extremists, and has gone so far as to file criminal charges against people who discuss the genocide of 1864. On September 23rd, the Russian Ministry of Justice made the policy official, issuing a warning to the Circassian Congress in Adygeia that discussion of the 'Russo-Circassian War' or 'genocide' against the Circassians by the Russian Empire would be considered an extremist act."[1469]

Russian authorities have imparted an atmosphere of fear and terror against Circassian citizens in their own homeland. This gives them the feeling that their families and properties are not safe: "At this same time, assassinations of Circassian activists began. Well-known Circassian activist Suadin Pshukov was murdered in Nalchik less than two weeks after the Ministry of Justice's announcements. In addition to its efforts to silence Circassian activism, the Russian government began to campaign to undermine claims that the genocide of 1864 was intact genocide."[1470]

Scientific integrity requires utilizing the scientific method, especially that the subject here deals with human and legal rights issue. Truth cannot be condoned or changed in any way. Unfortunately, Russian research centers are supported by an imperialist policy of disseminating outcomes. Their information reflects irrelevant truth and completely defies reality. They turn facts upside down and at the same time publish exposed lies that can be challenged and proven invalid.

Much of this was predictable and has been going on since 2001, when the Russian Institute of Sciences published Fasikh Baderkhan's Severokavkazskaya Diaspora v Turtsii, siriii Iordanii (The North Caucasus Diaspora in Turkey, Syria, and Jordan). Baderkhan conflates the genocide into the entire process of Muslim out-migration from Russia and omits the details of the 1864 campaign to portray it as voluntary. A more comprehensive effort was Mark Bliev's 2004 publication, Rossiia i Gortsy Bol'shogo Kavkaza: Na Puti K Tsivilizatsii (Russia and the Mountaineers of the Great Caucasus: On the Road to Civilization). Believe repeats nearly every justification used for the genocide since the time of the Caucasus wars, from the myth of the Circassian "raiding culture" as cause of the war to the claim that the Circassians were hostile to Russian aggression only because of British and Ottoman agents.[1471]

Misleading Russian policies never stopped from the time it started when the Russian Empire decided to occupy Circassia. They have always attempted to harm the Circassians in any way possible. Russia always tried to delude others, presenting the aggressive nature of Circassians, and they do not believe in peace as their inherent features dictate so. They lied that the reason of the Russian aggressive policy towards them is due to their bellicosity and ill temperament. In addition, they claimed that they left their homeland voluntarily and because of the religion that they espouse. Trying to give this picture, they forget the fact that the Russian Empire had invaded and occupied their homeland to uproot them and deport them.

Multiple television programs, conferences, and roundtables have echoed the claims of Baderkhan and Bliev, inciting public opinion against the Circassians. Moscow couldn't even leave a good deed unsullied while conducting this campaign. On November 16, 2011, Russian journalist Sergei Kholoshevsky reported on the nationally televised "Today Results" that the Kosovo Circassians who immigrated to Adygeia in 1998 were 'the descendants of soldiers and officers in the Tsarist army who were based in Yugoslavia after the revolution. Of course this was utter nonsense: the Circassians in Kosovo were the remnants of the diaspora population in the Balkans that the Russians failed to kill or chase out in 1878. Not only was Kholoshevsky's fabrication viewed by the Circassian community as another attempt to conceal the results of Russia's genocide against the Circassians, it was seen as an attempt to distort Russia's role in the Balkans during the Russo-Turkish War of 1877–1878.[1472]

The Steps Taken to Seek Sochi Olympics Nomination and Execution

In February 2003, the prime minister of Russia, Mikhail Kasyanov, signed Decree No. 238-r: "The description of the boundaries of Sochi National Park that can be leased for construction of sport and tourism resort Krasnaya Polyana. This document actually became the starting point for all subsequent Olympic lawlessness. Kasyanov ordered valuable natural areas, such as the mountain ridges of Aibga, Psekhako, Gryshevui, and the area of Hmelevskih Lakes, to be earmarked for construction."[1473]

The sequential series of events regarding consolidating project elements have proven, beyond doubt, a breach of the law. All applicable laws were blatantly broken, which shows recklessness and challenges by government officials, who were well aware and assured that they will not be touched or prosecuted.

> Year 2004, the construction of the gas pipeline to Krasnaya Pollyanna was the first legal violation during infrastructure development. The beginning section of the gas pipeline cut through the natural protected area "Kudepstinskij Canyon", in which, based on our estimates, about 2,000 rare, mature boxwood trees were cut down. There were alternative routes that would bypass the Canyon and minimize the tree clearing; however, it would have slowed down the construction. In May, the LLC Krasnaya Pollyanna received 1,920 hectares [about 4,700 acres] of Sochi National Park land for Gornaya Karusel ski resort construction. The same year, it was decided to build Roza Hytor ski complex, and another 541.5 hectares [about 1,340 acres] of Sochi National Park were allocated for construction."[1474]

Waivers, concessions, sharing, and exchanging of benefits and interests were made between all administrative entities and those who took it upon themselves to move forward in achieving their desire to change the entire area's landmarks regardless of the damages. This opened the way for entrepreneurs and contractors to earn money fast.

Favorable and obtainable conditions made it profitable for all those who wanted to initiate and achieve harmonization between projects in progress and the burning desire to attain commercial ambitions, regardless of another important aspect, which is the human element.

> Year 2006. In June, Sochi was among the three cities competing for the bid to host Winter Olympics. Immediately following, the Russian Government initiated the change in zoning of the Sochi National Park. The greatest environmental threat at that time was construction in the virgin forests on the Psekhako Ridge. In June, the Russian Government approved the "Sochi Development Strategy for 2006–2015". According to this plan, 10 sport complexes would be built in Sochi National Park. To provide electricity to all these facilities, a thermal power plant would be built in the Adler District. It soon became clear that not enough land was set aside for construction. The process of forcing residents in the Imeretinskaya Lowland to give up their homes and land began.[1475]

To control both the north and south parts of the Caucasus region, the Russian authorities moved in several directions for organizing the different pressing matters. All attempts made by the Circassians and environmentalists did not produce anything but stubbornness, obduracy, and arrogance, in addition to ignoring all the facts on the ground.

> Year 2007. On the eve of the vote for the Olympic Games venue, a coalition of 47 Russian environmental organizations made an appeal to the International Olympic Committee to "make a responsible decision." Russian environmentalists drew the attention of the IOC to the fact that in the history of the Olympic movement, never had all Olympic venues been placed in valuable natural areas. For the first time, the vote to hold Winter Olympic Games was given to a city where all of the structures would need to be built from scratch.[1476]

On July 4, 2007, the International Olympic Committee in Guatemala City chose Sochi as a host city for holding the 2014 Winter Olympic Games. Russian president Vladimir Putin made the proposal. The controversial content of the speech was seemingly intended to change and distort historical facts and realities when he mentioned, "The ancient Greeks lived around Sochi lots of centuries ago. I also saw the rock near Sochi, to which, as legend has it, Prometheus was chained. It was Prometheus who gave people fire, fire which ultimately is the Olympic flame."[1477]

Mentioning the Greeks, Prometheus, and the rock near Sochi doesn't prevent the honesty and transparency from recalling historical facts, including the home of the Circassian nation and the fact about Sochi in 1864, in addition to Krasnaya Polyana. Contradicting truth creates a gap between people who watch things happen and people who make things happen.

Some individuals used to own and run a business in provincial Krasnaya Polyana, but had to give it up.

> "Pyotr Fedin sits at his desk, a dissatisfied success, a mere landowner instead of the alpine entrepreneur he once was, and he tells the story of how government power made it so." His time has come! "The calendar turned to 2008, and a Gazprom plane arrived from Moscow. As Fedin recalls it, the men from Russia's largest company, the state-controlled gas monopoly, suggested that he join them for a ride. And in veiled language that anyone could understand, while the Gazprom plane flew north over Rostov, then Voronezh and Tula, the men looked at Fedin and said, 'We respect you'. They offered a figure to buy him out. Fedin knew there was nothing he could do. At the darkly prismatic Gazprom tower in Moscow, Fedin signed the papers placed before him. 'I can see your face', the man with the contracts said to Fedin. 'You are sad. The money isn't what's interesting for you'. Fedin received fair value, he says, but the business he had built was no longer his. 'Money is only paper', Fedin said, spelling out his name on the contract. (A spokesperson for Gazprom said in an email that the company 'was acquired on commercial terms'.)"[1478]

Changing the rules had reached multiple dimensions such as switching property ownership and permitted utilization.

> The Federal government's first use of 310-F3 was to acquire land owned by locals for construction. Initially the authorities failed to consider their impact upon the residents, but quickly learned that angry civic groups can be disruptive. They modified their approach but still seemed incapable of considering the residents as partners in the project.

The relocation of residents was typical of subsequent government actions. After an area was designated, a construction zone the government assigned values to the properties it was expropriating. However, many were significantly lower than market value, and compensation for seemingly identical properties has been inconsistent.[1479]

Double standards and randomness in dealing with the issues at hand did not suggest the presence of a standard criteria.

"In March 2009, residents of the village Akhshtyr were told that they would receive the rouble equivalent of USD16,000 for each 1/100th of a hectare, but some residents inexplicably receive nearly double that amount. Those who felt they had been cheated staged a hunger strike. Rather than communicate with the residents, authorities refused to negotiate officially or to recognize that there was a dispute." The human factor and dealing with the affected people who had to leave their areas of residence to allow building the Olympic structures: "The situation finally stabilized, and residents were eventually moved to Nekrasovskoe. Seven new villages were constructed for people being relocated from other construction sites, and the process became less stressful for everyone. In what turned out to be a rare exception, the Russian government seemed finally to deal responsibly with its citizens."[1480]

In May 2010 was the relocation of the first batch of families affected by the Olympics construction: "On May 4, four families from the Imereti Lowland, whose houses and land plots had been alienated because of building Olympic objects, marked their housewarming parties in new cottages in Nekrasovskoe village, Krasnodar Territory. At the same time, other Imereti residents were surprised to learn that their resettlement to new houses in Nekrasovskoe is postponed, or cancelled whatsoever."[1481]

At the same time, "others were evicted from their homes and left with literally no place to go. They were residents of a cooperative building constructed in 2004, which had been built 'illegally', as they were informed, just before its demolition was scheduled. The construction firm is long gone, but since the residents were living in an 'illegal' structure the authorities told them they had no responsibility to find them new housing. As a result, they had to seek shelter in garages and other makeshift locations throughout the city."[1482]

Gulf Cooperation Council Countries

In another scope, various media outlets have published news about Saudi prince Bandar Bin Sultan, then head of Saudi Arabian intelligence, during a visit to the Russian Federation and his meeting with the Russian president Vladimir Putin. He presented attractive offers for the Russian leadership in the form of a deal that included generous offers worth tens of billions of dollars pouring like rain, which included for example but not limited to political, military, economical, and security matters that relate in a process of barter of positions and interests in order to obtain mutual concessions that include Syria, Iran, Egypt, and other interests.[1483]

According to the media, the talks that took place in one of Putin's houses on the outskirts of the Russian capital city addressed topics including terrorism, the situation in Egypt, deals of sale of Russian weapons between the two sides, joint investment, and economic cooperation. It included oil and gas "the areas of establishing refineries and petrochemical industries."[1484]

The Russian president's response, the presented proposals or other details on the margin of the meeting will not be repeated in this context, but what matters the circumstance of these articles is the part that concerns the Caucasus, where the same source reported that the Saudi prince said in overall what he told Putin: "As-Safir said Prince Bandar pledged to safeguard Russia's naval base in Syria if the Assad regime is toppled, but he also hinted at Chechen terrorist attacks on Russia's Winter Olympics in Sochi if there is no accord. 'I can give you a guarantee to protect the Winter Olympics next year. The Chechen groups that threaten the security of the games are controlled by us', he allegedly said."[1485]

How could a guarantee to protect the Olympic Games in Sochi be granted when it is the last capital of Free Circassia before its occupation by Tsarist Russia? What would Chechnya have to do with a Circassian subject and why shuffle cards as such? This seems like offering property of others that necessarily lead to entanglement and loss of rights by misplacing them! We will not complete here to the end of the pledge (protection) submitted to Putin because the Syrian affairs overall are not of a Circassian concern. Hence, neither Circassians nor logic would accept the bargains on Circassia while they are offered in the absence of the prerogative of indigenous people, where "withholding the truth will never be possible."

In a related subject and in the midst of the rush of oil-producing countries to invest in Russia, it can be noted that agreements in the field of investment, where investors from the United Arab Emirates, specifically Dubai, signed agreements in Sochi on the Black Sea to attract 800 million dollars of investments from the United Arab Emirates and were signed in September of

2010 and to focus on the importance of that, Putin personally attended the signing ceremony when he was a prime minister.[1486]

Another example was investing 300 million dollars by Damac of Dubai.[1487] It was also announced in the Kremlin that "Abu Dhabi expects to deposit five billion dollars in a joint investment fund with the Russian authorities in order to finance infrastructure projects in Russia, which falls in increasing the volume of the Arab investments in Russia."[1488]

The most fiscal convergence of the Gulf States toward Russia has continued beyond Sochi. The most important deals were signed in July 2015.

> The State Investment Fund of Saudi Arabia invest 10 billion USD in Russia, sending a strong signal of convergence of views between Moscow and Riyadh. The fund signed a contract with the Russian Direct Investment Fund for the largest amount of foreign direct investment in the history of Russia, Moscow announced late Monday."[1489]

The deal has proven a trend for the possibility of improving relations in the economic sectors.

> "The first seven projects received preliminary approval and we expect to achieve ten deals before year end", said Kirill Dmitriev, Chief Executive Officer of the Russian Direct Investment Fund. Dmitriev said that the Saudi defense minister Mohammed bin Salman Al Saud has played a "huge" role in the deal. The Prince visited St Petersburg with a large delegation during the economic forum and met with President Vladimir Putin and with the world leaders of investment funds.[1490]

The Sochi Aftermath

Paul Goble initiated his "Window," saying, "No nation more skillfully used an international event than did the Circassians during the Sochi Olympiad to call attention to the Russian-orchestrated genocide of their people 150 years earlier. Despite Moscow's best efforts, few independent reporters talked about Sochi without talking about the continuing crimes against the Circassians."[1491]

The expectations built on the Winter Olympics in Sochi by the Russian president did not match the predicted results.

> RUSSIAN PRESIDENT Vladimir Putin hoped to win the world's respect with his staging of the Winter Olympics. But a ruler who does not respect his own people will never be truly respected. One day after the Olympics ended, Mr. Putin showed, with the sentencing of eight protesters in Moscow, that he fears his people more than he respects them.[1492]

Human rights breaches in the Russian Federation were practiced before and after the games, against anyone who wanted to say or show nonviolent opinions in accordance with legal rules and regulations; they collided with the brutality of the regime's security forces.

> What's the difference between then and now? Today's Russian Federation professes to uphold constitutional guarantees of human rights and dignity. The words are in Article 29 of the Russian constitution: "Everyone shall be guaranteed the freedom of ideas and speech". It does not say that everyone shall agree with the president. It does not say that those who protest the president shall be imprisoned. But two decades after its adoption, that constitution is fraying under Mr. Putin's rule.[1493]

Promises made before the start of the project didn't materialize and were not met, where glittering pledges of uniqueness proved the lack of seriousness and applicability.

> Sochi-2014's website states that, "97% of construction waste was reused immediately at the Olympic construction sites," and that, "Sochi became a city without landfills; that 2 sites (with about 7 million cubic meters of waste) were closed and reclaimed". In reality, the scrap hard rock and construction waste became the biggest problem for Olympic construction, which was solved by creating large scale landfills and dumps.[1494]

Illegitimate and illegal applications and behaviors have affected everything, even polluting the environment and the water, besides the impact on conserving soil solidity and stability.

> In April of 2011, two large illegal dumps of soil, rock and construction debris were found near the village of Nizhnyaya

Shilovka, which is in the Valley of the Psou River. One of the dumps provoked a powerful landslide, which uprooted hundreds of trees and blocked the flow of springs into the river. Another illegal dump site was discovered in May 2012 in the Valley of the Mzumta River. The exact amount of illegally buried construction waste in Sochi is unknown. The contractors estimated that between 2013–2014 over 217 million tons of construction waste was generated. According to the Russian Ministry of Natural Resources' website, over 35 illegal dump sites were reported in and around Sochi.[1495]

It is worth highlighting a report mentioning the ecological impacts of the Winter Olympic Games, which stated the beginning stages until it was accepted by the International Olympic Committee, plus a "Statement from Environmental Watch on North Caucasus," which included a 13 point call:

> Damage from the Olympic construction is unfortunately irreversible; it is not possible to restore the lost ecosystems in Sochi National Park and the Imereti Lowlands. But we can carry out valuable lessons for the future. Environmental Watch on North Caucasus urges the President and the Russian government to take measures to prevent the destruction of unique ecosystems during future construction in the North Caucasus and in Russia in general. This can be achieved by making appropriate changes in environmental laws, expanding natural protected areas, and preventing future environmentally destructive projects in protected areas.[1496]

Ecologist Suren Gazaryan, a prominent expert in the field of environment and natural reserves, shared with other experts and NGOs, who were interested in this endeavor. Their intention was to preserve the nature of the earth that includes the forests, plains, mountains, valleys, rivers, parks, and caves, also, to maintain the variety of plants and species, in addition to pure water, trees, flowers, wild animals, birds, fish, and rare creatures.

Gazaryan was not in an enviable position.

> In a country increasingly known for its authoritarian-style crackdown on activists and dissidents, a bat scientist has won a number of impressive victories to protect the dwindling forests of the Western Caucasus. Beginning in the 1990s, Russian chiropterologist Suren Gazaryan led a number of

campaigns to fight illegal development, including mansions for then-president Dmitry Medvedev; regional Governor of Krasnodar, Alexander Tkachev; and even a project allegedly intended for president Vladimir Putin.[1497]

Authorities continued to crack down on activists by changing the laws to fit the authorities' policies, which are harmful to nature and the environment: "Meanwhile, recently passed legislation has placed enormous pressure on Russian environmental activists. The law targets NGOs that receive overseas funds and deemed to be politically active, requiring them to register as foreign agents or face heavy fines, suspension, closure, and criminal charges."[1498]

The Quality of Structures

Just after the end of the Sochi Olympic Games, the situation deteriorated as "Apartment buildings from Sochi's $50 billion Olympics are abandoned and falling apart. Apartment blocks that housed volunteers and media during the 2014 Sochi Olympics have been abandoned a year and a half later, Reuters reports."[1499]

The Environmental Effects of the Sochi Olympics

Arbitrary steps were taken during the planning and preparation of getting the Olympic facilities in the Sochi and Krasnaya Polyana region ready. They were in line with the nonobservance of protecting the natural reserves and forests, water resources, and settlement due to construction and paving of roads, railway construction, developing ski areas, building resorts and hotels, entertainment facilities, and service centers.

The environmental and ecological damage produced by the industrial toxics and chemical waste originating from the construction works of the Olympic facilities, roads and associated services is beyond repair in such a unique and fascinating natural beauty of Sochi and its surroundings. Environmental activists[1500] and Greenpeace Russia[1501] indicated worries that there is a dangerous increase of concentration of high-risk of toxic elements such as arsenic, phenol and a number of oil derivatives. The environmentalists say, "Pollution levels have risen dramatically around Sochi since the city was selected to host the 2014 Winter Olympic Games."[1502]

An article titled "The Sochi 2014 Madness Must End Now!" criticized the whole Sochi process: "Russia is recklessly destroying the regional ecology to build the Olympics venues. The United Nations had issued a scathing report condemning Russian atrocities against the natural environment, and the IOC was forced to investigate," but the findings were not announced. The article continued, "Allowing Russia to build the Olympic venues in Sochi will do irreversible environmental harm to Sochi. The invaluable Paul Goble documents that harm in today's issue, and Russian environmentalists on the front lines confirm that the Kremlin is butchering the natural world on the Black Sea coast in order to build venues of absolutely no value to ordinary Russians, at horrifying expense."[1503]

A blog called Sochi Watch posted a summary of the current ecological situation in Sochi, from an AFP article:

> Caught on vancouversun.com. Essentially, it covers the basics: that Russia is saying the gargantuan building project to prepare Sochi is "70%" finished and that this will be the "greenest" Olympics ever vs the Ecological Watch on North Caucasus saying that that ain't exactly the case. "In general, environmental damage in Sochi is much worse than what we expected in the early stages of construction planning," said Suren Gazaryan of the Environmental Watch on North Caucasus. The regional NGO continues to monitor Olympic construction sites after both Greenpeace and the World Wildlife Fund announced they were withdrawing from the process last year. "Right now construction crews have no oversight, they simply do what suits them, and this landslide is a good example," Gazaryan said as he walked along a river in Sochi National Park whose shores have become encrusted with asphalt-like mud. A mudslide from an illegal dump up the hill tore through the park and filled the river's banks with debris from tunnel construction and other waste in January. "Clearly leaving thousands of tons of waste on a steep hillside is not a good idea, but it's convenient, and it can't be stopped," Gazaryan said as he picked off a chunk of the black substance for testing.[1504]

The article mentioned difficulties and hard times faced by the environmentalists, as they carried out their duty of watching and monitoring all the irregularities and infringements on nature reserves, wild life, forests, and Sochi National Park. A conclusion said, "Russia remains an unsafe place to do business for those who attempt to speak out and who have a platform."[1505]

Russian authorities violated world heritage and UNESCO protected sites and forests: "The Russian government is preparing to allow construction of a cluster of ski resorts and roads in the Caucasus region that will alter one of Europe's few untouched mountain wilderness areas. The development is expected to impact two biosphere nature reserves, two national parks, wildlife sanctuaries and a World Heritage Site."[1506]

UNESCO followed and addressed the irregularities and breaches committed where the Sochi area and its surroundings had been exposed to changes resulting from changing the nature of the landscape and environment of the Olympic complex in the 'Western Caucasus' world reserve, which had been on the UNESCO World Heritage List, but ignored and disregarded by building the Olympiad facilities.

The World Heritage Committee "notes with concern the reports on proposed changes to Russian Federal protected area's legislation, which could significantly weaken the level of protection of State Nature Reserves and affect the protection regimes of more than half of the Russian natural World Heritage properties, including the Western Caucasus, and also requests the State Party to provide more information on the proposed law and take all appropriate legal measures to maintain a high level of protection of natural World Heritage properties on its territory, in accordance with Paragraph 15(f) of the Operational Guidelines."[1507]

The competent authorities moved and jumped to another site for changing its natural features:

> The World Heritage Committee stated that it: "Notes with serious concern the continued reports of infrastructure developments within the property as well as the announcement of a possible new ski resort on Lagonaki plateau. Also urges the State Party to submit copies of Environmental Impact Assessments to the World Heritage Centre conducted for all proposed developments which could affect the property, in line with Paragraph 172 of the Operational Guidelines, including an assessment of their potential impacts on the property's Outstanding Universal Value."[1508]

Article 3 of Resolution 2, of the World Natural Heritage Properties in the Russian Federation of the International Conference of the UNESCO World Heritage and the Role of Civil Society states,

> 3. To request the UNESCO World Heritage Center to request from the State Party of the Russian Federation in

shortest terms to submit to the Center the information about plans of the construction of tourist and sport objects inside the area of "Western Caucasus" World Heritage property as well as about planned changes of the protected area boundaries inside the composition of the property for further examination by the World Heritage Committee on its 40th Session in 2016, reserving in the case of confirmation of an existing or potential threat to its Outstanding Universal Value, its inscription in the "List of World Heritage in Danger.[1509]

After questioning: "How Sochi sought the Olympics the art of diplomacy and a little criminal pressure," the report on the ecological shock of Sochi 2014 Winter Olympic Games, it mentioned that

> in February 2003, the Chairman of the Russian Government, Mikhail Kasyanov, signed Decree No. 238:r:
> The description of the boundaries of Sochi National Park that can be leased for construction of sport and tourism resort Krasnaya Polyana. This document actually became the starting point for all subsequent Olympic lawlessness. Kasyanov ordered valuable natural areas, such" as the mountain ridges of Aibga, Psekhako, Gryshevui, and the area of Hmelevskih Lakes, to be earmarked for construction.[1510]

The importance of ignoring the environmental situation by the authorities was mentioned in the following by Tunne Kelam, member of the European Parliament: "Blatantly ignoring environmental standards has damaged the ecological balance and caused severe deterioration of the environmental situation with probably irreversible consequences for the local people."[1511]

[1423] http://ngm.nationalgeographic.com/2014/01/sochi-russia/forrest-text
[1424] The Fire Below: How the Caucus Shaped Russia (Edited by Robert Bruce Ware)
[1425] The Sochi Predicament: Contexts, Characteristics and Challenges of the Olympic Winter Games in 2014 (Edited by Bo Petersson and Karina Vamlig)
[1426] The Fire Below: How the Caucus Shaped Russia (Edited by Robert Bruce Ware)

1427 The Fire Below: How the Caucus Shaped Russia (Edited by Robert Bruce Ware)
1428 The Fire Below: How the Caucus Shaped Russia (Edited by Robert Bruce Ware)
1429 The Fire Below: How the Caucus Shaped Russia (Edited by Robert Bruce Ware)
1430 https://www.swp-berlin.org/fileadmin/contents/products/comments/2014C37_hlb.pdf
1431 https://www.swp-berlin.org/fileadmin/contents/products/comments/2014C37_hlb.pdf
1432 The New Tsar, The Rise and Reign of Vladimir Putin (Steven Lee Myers)
1433 http://www.independent.co.uk/news/world/europe/kremlin-cranks-up-the-propaganda-for-putins-60th-birthday-8201344.html
1434 http://olympics.time.com/2012/08/14/qa-sochis-olympics-chief-on-the-2014-winter-games/
1435 The New Tsar, The Rise and Reign of Vladimir Putin (Steven Lee Myers)
1436 The New Tsar, The Rise and Reign of Vladimir Putin (Steven Lee Myers)
1437 The New Tsar, The Rise and Reign of Vladimir Putin (Steven Lee Myers)
1438 The New Tsar, The Rise and Reign of Vladimir Putin (Steven Lee Myers)
1439 The New Tsar, The Rise and Reign of Vladimir Putin (Steven Lee Myers)
1440 http://sputniknews.com/russia/20121205/177931767.html
1441 The New Tsar, The Rise and Reign of Vladimir Putin (Steven Lee Myers)
1442 The New Tsar, The Rise and Reign of Vladimir Putin (Steven Lee Myers)
1443 The New Tsar, The Rise and Reign of Vladimir Putin (Steven Lee Myers)
1444 The New Tsar, The Rise and Reign of Vladimir Putin (Steven Lee Myers)
1445 http://www.zoominfo.com/p/Suren-Gazaryan/1665260147
1446 http://www.goldmanprize.org/recipient/suren-gazaryan/
1447 http://justicefornorthcaucasus.info/?p=1230735300
1448 http://justicefornorthcaucasus.info/?p=1230735300
1449 http://ngm.nationalgeographic.com/2014/01/sochi-russia/forrest-text
1450 http://www.businessinsider.com/apartment-buildings-from-sochis-olympics-are-abandoned-2015-10
1451 https://www.greengrants.org/wp-content/uploads/2014/02/Environmental-Watch-Sochi-2014-Report-Summaries-English.pdf
1452 https://www.greengrants.org/wp-content/uploads/2014/02/Environmental-Watch-Sochi-2014-Report-Summaries-English.pdf
1453 https://www.greengrants.org/wp-content/uploads/2014/02/Environmental-Watch-Sochi-2014-Report-Summaries-English.pdf
1454 http://eng.kavkaz-uzel.ru/articles/5978/
1455 https://www.greengrants.org/wp-content/uploads/2014/02/Environmental-Watch-Sochi-2014-Report-Summaries-English.pdf

Circassia 585

1456 https://www.greengrants.org/wp-content/uploads/2014/02/Environmental-Watch-Sochi-2014-Report-Summaries-English.pdf
1457 https://www.greengrants.org/wp-content/uploads/2014/02/Environmental-Watch-Sochi-2014-Report-Summaries-English.pdf
1458 https://www.greengrants.org/wp-content/uploads/2014/02/Environmental-Watch-Sochi-2014-Report-Summaries-English.pdf
1459 http://ngm.nationalgeographic.com/2014/01/sochi-russia/forrest-text and http://ngm.nationalgeographic.com/2014/01/sochi-russia/circassia-map
1460 http://windowoneurasia2.blogspot.com/2013/02/window-on-eurasia-sochi-countdown-51.html
1461 http://eng.kavkaz-uzel.ru/articles/5978/
1462 http://www.businessinsider.com/photos-of-sochi-russias-forgotten-circassian-people-2014-1
1463 https://www.youtube.com/watch?v=2wcKCkjy6hk
1464 http://justicefornorthcaucasus.info/?p=1251677051
1465 http://eng.kavkaz-uzel.ru/articles/5950/
1466 http://www.preventgenocide.org/law/convention/text.htm
1467 http://www.slate.com/blogs/the_world_/2014/02/05/the_circassians_and_the_olympics_did_the_age_of_genocide_begin_in_sochi.html
1468 The Circassian Genocide (Walter Richmond)
1469 The Circassian Genocide (Walter Richmond)
1470 The Circassian Genocide (Walter Richmond)
1471 The Circassian Genocide (Walter Richmond)
1472 The Circassian Genocide (Walter Richmond)
1473 https://www.greengrants.org/wp-content/uploads/2014/02/Environmental-Watch-Sochi-2014-Report-Summaries-English.pdf
1474 https://www.greengrants.org/wp-content/uploads/2014/02/Environmental-Watch-Sochi-2014-Report-Summaries-English.pdf
1475 https://www.greengrants.org/wp-content/uploads/2014/02/Environmental-Watch-Sochi-2014-Report-Summaries-English.pdf
1476 https://www.greengrants.org/wp-content/uploads/2014/02/Environmental-Watch-Sochi-2014-Report-Summaries-English.pdf
1477 http://www.americanrhetoric.com/speeches/vladimirputiniocsochipitch.htm
1478 http://ngm.nationalgeographic.com/2014/01/sochi-russia/forrest-text
1479 The Fire Below: How the Caucus Shaped Russia (Edited by Robert Bruce Ware)
1480 The Fire Below: How the Caucus Shaped Russia (Edited by Robert Bruce Ware)
1481 http://eng.kavkaz-uzel.ru/articles/13211/

1482 The Fire Below: How the Caucus Shaped Russia (Edited by Robert Bruce Ware)
1483 http://frontpagemag.com/2013/dgreenfield/saudis-offer-russia-opec-membership-terror-immunity-for-olympics/
1484 http://www.al-monitor.com/pulse/politics/2013/08/saudi-russia-putin-bandar-meeting-syria-egypt.html#ixzz2d5UVLSNv
1485 http://www.telegraph.co.uk/finance/newsbysector/energy/oilandgas/10266957/Saudis-offer-Russia-secret-oil-deal-if-it-drops-Syria.html and http://www.al-monitor.com/pulse/politics/2013/08/saudi-russia-putin-bandar-meeting-syria-egypt.html#ixzz2d5UVLSNv
1486 http://www.themoscowtimes.com/business/article/putin-welcomes-arab-cash-in-sochi/416584.html
1487 http://www.tradearabia.com/news/real_185899.html
1488 http://www.itar-tass.com/en/c142/875415.html
1489 http://financefeeds.com/saudi-arabia-invest-10-billion-usd-in-russia/ http://tass.ru/en/economy/806425
1490 http://financefeeds.com/saudi-arabia-invest-10-billion-usd-in-russia/
1491 http://windowoneurasia2.blogspot.com/2015/05/151-years-after-genocide-and-one-year.html
1492 https://www.washingtonpost.com/opinions/putins-repression-resumes-now-that-the-olympics-have-ended/2014/02/25/071f010a-9e5a-11e3-b8d8-94577ff66b28_story.html
1493 https://www.washingtonpost.com/opinions/putins-repression-resumes-now-that-the-olympics-have-ended/2014/02/25/071f010a-9e5a-11e3-b8d8-94577ff66b28_story.html
1494 https://www.greengrants.org/wp-content/uploads/2014/02/Environmental-Watch-Sochi-2014-Report-Summaries-English.pdf
1495 https://www.greengrants.org/wp-content/uploads/2014/02/Environmental-Watch-Sochi-2014-Report-Summaries-English.pdf
1496 https://www.greengrants.org/wp-content/uploads/2014/02/Environmental-Watch-Sochi-2014-Report-Summaries-English.pdf
1497 http://www.zoominfo.com/p/Suren-Gazaryan/1665260147
1498 http://www.goldmanprize.org/recipient/suren-gazaryan/
1499 http://www.businessinsider.com/apartment-buildings-from-sochis-olympics-are-abandoned-2015-10
1500 https://themoscowtimes.com/articles/sochi-landfill-waste-threatens-drinking-water-29103 and http://www.smh.com.au/world/sochi-winter-olympics-arrest-of-protesters-puts-focus-on-russian-suppression-of-dissent-20140217-hvcs8.html
1501 http://www.greenpeace.org/russia/en/press/releases/olympians-who-avoid-struggle/

[1502] http://www.rferl.org/content/black-sea-ecologists-alarmed-by-dolphin-deaths/24591773.html
[1503] https://larussophobe.wordpress.com/2010/03/18/editorial-the-sochi-2014-madness-must-end-now/
[1504] http://sochiwatch.blogspot.com/2011/05/ecological-destruction-continues-in.html
[1505] http://sochiwatch.blogspot.com/2011/05/ecological-destruction-continues-in.html
[1506] http://ens-newswire.com/2012/02/03/russia-allows-ski-resort-in-caucasus-world-heritage-site/
[1507] http://whc.unesco.org/en/decisions/4432/
[1508] http://whc.unesco.org/en/decisions/4432/
[1509] http://www.world-heritage-watch.org/images/sampledata/PDF-Dateien/14-5-Resolution-2-On-Natural-Properties-Russia.pdf
[1510] http://www.greengrants.org/wp-content/uploads/2014/02/Environmental-Watch-Sochi-2014-Report-Summaries-English.pdf
[1511] http://www.kelam.ee/in-english/news/circassians-standing-up-for-their-rights-and-cultural-identity-deserve-eu-support

16

Appendices

a. The Declaration of Circassian Independence

b. Circassia: Adygs Ask European Parliament to Recognize Genocide

c. Circassian Genocide: The History of Problem, Chronicles of Events, the Scientific Conclusion

d. 10 Stages of Genocide

e. A Letter to the Estonian Leadership

f. Circassians Handed a Letter to the Estonian Parliament

g. Members of the Riigikogu Met with the Representatives of the Circassian Community

h. The Circassians Refuse the Hostile Attitude Statement

i. Address to the Queen of England by Circassians

==

a. The Declaration of Circassian Independence

ADDRESSED TO THE COURTS OF EUROPE

The inhabitants of the Caucasus, instead of being subject to Russia, are not even at peace with her, but have for many years been engaged in continual war. This war they have maintained single-handed. They have received at no period encouragement or assistance from any power. While the Porte held the supremacy of these Provinces they were left for their means of defense to themselves, but lately the Porte has in every way betrayed and abandoned them. One Pasha opened the gates of the Anapa to Muscovite gold, telling the Circassians that the Russians marched as friends to support the Sultan against the Rebel Chiefs of Arminestan. Another Pasha again betrayed them, and left their country by night. Since then the Circassians have sent repeated deputations to the Sultan, to offer their devotion, to request assistance: they have, however, been treated with coldness. They have also applied to Persia with no better success, and finally to Mehemet Ali, who, although appreciating their devotion, was too far off then to support them.

In all these cases the deputies of Circassia had been instructed to tell to those who, being at a distance, did not know, how intolerable was the oppression of Russia, how hostile she was to the customs, the faith and happiness of all men (or why should the Circassians have fought so long against her), how treacherous were her generals, and how savage her soldiers, _ that therefor it was the interest of no one that the Circassians should be destroyed. On the contrary, that it was the interest of all the Circassians should be supported. A hundred thousand Muscovite troops occupied now in fighting with us, or in watching and blockading us, will then be fighting with you. A hundred thousand men now scattered over our barren and steep rocks, and struggling with our hardy mountaineers, will then be overrunning your rich plains, and enslaving your Rayas and yourselves. Our mountains have been the ramparts of Persia and Turkey, they will become, unless supported, the gate to both they are now the only shelter for both. They are the doors of the house, by closing which alone the hearth can be defended. But, moreover, our blood, Circassian blood, fills the veins of the Sultan.

His mother, his harem, is Circassian. His slaves are Circassians. His ministers and his generals are Circassian. He is the chief of our faith, and also of our race' he possesses our hearts, and we offer him our allegiance; by all these ties we claim from him countenance and support, and if he will not, or cannot defend his children and his subjects, let him think of the Khans of the Crimea, whose descendants is among us.

Such were the words our deputies were instructed to pronounce, but they were unheeded. They would not have been so, if the Sultan knew how many hearts and swords he can command, when he ceases to be the friend of the Muscovite.

We know that Russia is not the only power in the world. We know that there are other powers greater than Russia, who, though powerful are benevolent, who instruct the ignorant, who protect the weak, who are not friends to the Russians, but rather their enemies, and who are not enemies of the Sultan, but his friends. We know that England and France are the first among the nations of the globe, and were great and powerful when the Russians came in little boats, and got from us permission to catch fish in the sea of Azof.

We thought that England and France would take no interest in a simple and poor people like us, but we did not doubt that such wise nations knew that we were not Russians, and though we know little, and have no artillery, generals, discipline, ships, or riches that we are an honest people, and peaceable when let alone, but that we hate the Russians with good cause, and almost always beat them. It is, therefore, with the profoundest humiliation that we have learnt that our country is marked, on all the maps printed in Europe, as a portion of Russia; that Treaties, of which we know nothing, should have been signed between Russia and Turkey, pretending to hand over to the Russians these warriors that make Russia tremble, and these mountains where her footsteps have never come; that Russia tells in the West that the Circassians are her slaves, or wild bandits and savages whom no kindness can soften, and no laws can restrain.

We most solemnly protest in the face of heaven against such womanish arts and falsehood. We answer words with words, but it is truth against falsehood: for forty years, we have protested triumphantly against accusations with our arms' this ink, as the blood we have spilled, declares our independence; and these are the seals of men who have known no superior save the decision of their country-men who understand no subtle arguments_ but who know how to use their weapons when the Russians come within reach.

Who has power to give us away? One allegiance is offered to the Sultan, but if he is at peace with Russia he cannot accept it, for Circassia is at war. Our allegiance is a free offering, he cannot sell it, because he has not bought it.

Let not a great nation, like England, to whom our eyes are turned, and our hands are raised, think of us at all if it be to do us injustice. Let her not open her ear to the wiles of the Russian, while she closes it to the prayer of the Circassian.

Let her judge by facts between the people that is called savage and barbarous, and its calumniator.

We are four million, but we have unfortunately been divided into many tribes, languages, and creeds; we have various customs, traditions, interests, alliances, and feuds. We have hitherto never had one purpose, but we have modes of government, and habits of submission and command.

The chief chosen by each body during war is implicitly obeyed, and our princes and our elders govern according to the customs of each place with greater authority than in the great states around us' but from our wanting a common chief amongst ourselves, we who have ruled throughout the east have chosen always a foreign leader. We have thus voluntarily submitted to the dominion of the Khans of the Crimea, and afterwards to the Sultans of Constantinople.

Russia has attempted, whenever she had overpowered any portion of our territory, and in some she has succeeded, to reduce us to the condition of serfs, to enroll us in her armies, to make us spend our sweat and our blood to enrich her' to fight her battles, and to enslave to her others, even our own countrymen and co-religionaries. Hatred has, therefor, grown up between us, and bloodshed is unceasing, otherwise we might long ago have submitted to a Muscovite chief.

It would be a long and sad story to relate the acts of her cruelty, her faith violated, her promises broken; how she has encircled our country on every side; cut us off from the necessaries of life' how she has intercepted our commerce; how she has caused to fall under the knife of the hired assassin the last remnants of our ancient houses, and left us without chiefs to obey; how she has exterminated whole tribes and villages' how she has bought the treacherous agents o ft he Porte; how she has reduced us to poverty, and driven us unto hatred and exasperation against all the world, by the horrors she committed, while by her falsehoods she degraded us in the eyes of the Christian nations of Europe.

We have lost the stocks that formerly could have collected hundreds of thousands of men under their banners but we are now at last united all as one man in hatred to Russia 200,000 alone of our people have been subjected by her during this long contest, of the remainder not one has voluntarily served Russia. Many children have been stolen, and sons of nobles taken as hostages; but such as could recollect a country, have made their escape.

We have amongst us men who have favored and flattered and honored by the Emperor, and who have preferred to that favor the dangers of their country. We have amongst us thousands of Russians, who prefer our barbarism to the civilization of their country. Russia has built forts on points of our territory, but they dare not venture beyond the reach of their guns_ 50,000 Russians have lately made an inroad, and they have been beaten.

It is by arms, not by words, that a country can be conquered. If Russia conquers us, it will not be by arms, but by cutting off our communications, and making use of Turkey and Persia as if they were already hers; by rendering the sea impassable, as if it were her own; by blockading our coast; by destroying not only our vessels, but those of other states which approach us; by depriving us from obtaining slat, gunpowder, and necessaries of war, which to us are necessaries of life by depriving us of hope.

But we are independent we are at war_ we are victors. The representative of the Emperor, who numbers us in Europe as his slaves, who marks this country as his on the map, has lately opened communications with the Circassians not to offer pardon for rebellion, but to bargain for the retreat of 20,000 men enveloped by our people, and to make arrangements for exchange of prisoners.[1512]

=======================================

b. Circassia: Adygs Ask European Parliament to Recognize Genocide

October 16, 2006

Circassian public organizations have sent the President of the European Parliament the reference with request for recognition of the genocide against Circassian people.
Below is an article published on the adygeanatpress website presenting the appeal of Adygeyan Organization to the European Parliament.

Adygeyan (Circassian) public organizations of Russia, Turkey, Israel, Jordan, Syria, the USA, Belgium, Canada and Germany have sent the president of the European parliament Mr. Joseph Borrell Fontelles the reference with request for recognition of the genocide against Adygeyan (Circassian) people within and after the Russian-Caucasian war of the XVIII–XIX centuries. The reference was sent yesterday, but already today, as the vice-president of the public movement of Adygeya «Circassian congress» Zaur Dzeukozhev informed, the organization

– initiator of the action received the confirmation in reception of the reference signed by Annika Lopez Lotson, the secretary of the president.

In total in the signers' list there are 20 organizations, said Dzeukozhev. A compact disc with the archival documents written in due time by the Russian imperial war commanders was enclosed to the reference. Natpress publishes the full text.

«To the President of the European parliament Mr. Joseph Borrell Fontelles

The reference of the Adygeyan (Circassian) organizations to the European parliament

We, Adygs (Circassians) are the aboriginals of the Northwest Caucasus. Our customs, ceremonies, traditions, language, the way of life were developed during the millennia in this territory. Vitality of our traditions is one of the brightest features of our people, and its material and spiritual achievements—the Maykop and the dolmen cultures, the heroic epos «Narts» - are universal heritage of the mankind.

During its formation, the Adygeyan (Circassian) ethnos, often becoming an object of aggression, stood for protection of its freedom and independence. The military expansion of the Russian empire initiated in the second half of the XVIII century became for our people a real national tragedy, which consequences affect so far.

During the military actions of that time they carried out: occupation of territories, purposeful deprivation the peaceful population of the basic means of life-support—destruction of gardens and crops, stealing of cattle, burning completely of the peace settlements. Massacre of the peace population—women, children, and old men—was committed, too.

For the middle of the XIX century any organized resistance of Adygs (Circassians) was broken down. Since 1862 mass violent deportation of the indigenous population was started. Hundreds thousand people, pushed down to the coast of the Black Sea, perished because of colds, famine, epidemics. According to underestimated information of Adolph Berge (1828–1886)—who was considered at that time as the official historian of the Russian-Caucasian war—from among over one million Adygs (Circassians) they lost in the war over 400 thousand people; 497 thousand people were deported; in their historical native land only about 80 thousand people remained. However, the troubles of our people had not ended with that.

Huge masses of Adygs-emigrants appeared to be scattered on the extensive territory of the Ottoman Empire. Great inflow of the immigrants and impreparation of the Turkish administration to their reception and accommodation caused mass extermination of the people.

In the numerous archival documents there are data of the participants of those tragical events that allow to make the key conclusion: the war the Russian state unleashed in the XVIII–XIX centuries against Adygs (Circassians) in their historical territory is impossible to consider as usual military actions. Russia had as the main purpose not only capture of the territories, but also utter extermination or eviction of the indigenous people from the historical lands. It is impossible to explain in any other way the reasons for such inhuman cruelty the Russian armies demonstrated in the Northwest Caucasus.

The process of Adygs' violent deportation—both of separate families, and entire settlements—proceeded till the World War I. Small groups of Adygs (Circassians) that staid in their historical territories suffered from the policy of the violent cultural assimilation the imperial administration implemented.

The present Russian Federation, having proclaimed the democratic way of its political development for the country actually continues the policy pursued earlier by the Russian state. By the silent approval of the federal center during the last years in Adygeya Republic, as well as across all the Russian Federation, public organizations preaching the ideas of the national-chauvinism actively work. The final goal of such organizations is carrying out of a referendum on the status of the republic by the principle of the mechanical majority, that is to take advantage of the quantitative superiority appeared as a result of the Russian-Caucasian war (the indigenous Adygeyan population in Adygeya Republic now makes 24 percent).

Today on their ancestors' lands Adygs (Kabardians, Circassians, Adygs, Shapsugs)—about 700 thousand people—live in 4 subjects of Russian Federation (Kabardino-Balkarian Republic, Karachaevo-Circassian Republic, Adygeya Republic, Krasnodar territory) and now have no more than 20 percent of the territories from the historical lands they had occupied.

Over 3 million representatives of our people live outside the Northwest Caucasus in 50 states. Owing to that artificially created dissociation of the ethnic Adygs (Circassians) they gradually lose their culture and language.

During 142 years after the end of the Russian-Caucasian war Russia repeatedly changed its political system, but the attitude to Adygs (Circassians) remained constant—the violent cultural assimilation of the remained indigenous population in the historical territory and banning on returning for the Adygs (Circassians) expelled from the Northwest Caucasus.

On July 1st, 2005, the Reference to the State Duma of Russian Federation concerning recognition of the genocide against Adygeyan (Circassian) people was submitted. However, deputies of the Russian legislature could not have overcome religious and ethnic prejudices, having refused to recognize the moral and the legal responsibility for the brutal acts the Russian state had committed in the past.

According to the Convention on prevention and punishment of genocide adopted by the United Nations Organization (New York, December 9th, 1948) and the Convention on inapplicability of limitation period for war crimes and crimes against humanity of November 26th, 1968

- following the standard principles of equality of all the peoples irrespective of religious and ethnic elements and origin,

- basing on the incontestable historic facts testifying to the extermination and the violent deportation of Adygs (Circassians) from the territory of the Northwest Caucasus,

- proceeding from that Russian Federation is the assignee and the successor of the Russian state,

We ask the European Parliament to consider in comprehensive and objective way our Reference and to recognize the genocide against Adygeyan (Circassian) people, being committed by the Russian state since the end of the XVIII till the beginning of the XX centuries.[1513]

===================================

c. **Circassian Genocide: The History of Problem, Chronicles of Events, the Scientific Conclusion**

West-Caucasus tragic events of the 19th century as a result of which a million and half of Circassian nation appeared in front of existential threat, is actual even today due to its historic-scientific as well as political standpoint. In order to demonstrate whether the genocide took place against the Circassians during the wide scale aggressive military operations by the Russian colonizers I will present only those materials which are based on documentary facts and findings of authoritative expert—historians.

It is obvious that I cannot ignore my colleague's Professor Bezhan Khorava's multilateral noteworthy work—the Circassians, which was specially created for the purpose of studying in complex this problem of interest for us. The final section of the work is written:

"During the Russian-Circassian War the Russian Empire purposefully carried out the forced expel of the population residing in Western and Central parts of the North Caucasus—Abaza-Circassian population from the region, with the means of military attacks on civil population. During the war, the Russian authorities were executing the ethnic cleansing of the population. They were deliberately creating such conditions, which aimed at full or partial physical annihilation of the population from this region. As a result, the big part of Abaza-Circassian population perished, the other part was coerced to flee abroad and the very small part remained on the territory of the Russian Empire. As a consequence, multi ethnic groups vanished from the historic arena. In so far as, the Russian Empire actions may be evaluated as genocide and ethnic cleansing."

Heretofore, in 1929 while traveling in the Caucasus Acad. Simon Janashia met a direct participant of the famous events, and recorded the following testimony from Napsau Iabarakhqu Hansakhqu: (1862 year) after the exile "for seven years human bones were spread over the seashore. Ravens were making nests from men's beard and women's hair, for seven years the Sea was drifting to the shore the human skulls as a watermelon. I do not wish the enemy to see what I have seen." (Simon Janashia, Works, vol. IV. Tbilisi; 1968, Page 124).

At that time, the witness of Adige's tragedy I. Drozdov attested:

"Horrifying sight appeared in front of us, on the way all the way through scattered corpses of children, women, old people, devastated and torn to pieces by the dogs, exhausted with hunger and diseases the migrants, barely lifting their feet from weakness, falling from exhaustion but still alive, felt a prey of hungry dogs. . . . Alive and healthy had no time to think about the moribund: as they confronted unfavorable perspective:

Due to greed, Turkish skippers piled Circassians as freight, who were hiring their boats to the shores of Asia Minor and were throwing the Circassians overboard as excess freight at the slightest sign of their illness.

The waves cast ashore the corpses of those unfortunates along the coast of Anatolia. . . . almost half of them, who left for Turkey, reached the place. Such a disaster and to such an extent rarely stroke the mankind. (I. Drozdov; The final fight with the Highlanders in the West Caucasus//Caucasian Collection, Tiflis, 1877. Vol. 2; page 457)."

Adolf Berzhe, the Russian Empire military historian, terrified with the same reality wrote:

"I will never forget what an overwhelming impression the Highlanders in Novorossiysk Bay made on me, where about 17,000 people were gathered on the shore. Later on, during the rainy and cold seasons of the year, with almost complete lack of means of subsistence, raging epidemic of typhus and smallpox among the Highlanders made their conditions desperate. Indeed, whose heart would not be shaken at the sight, for example, of a young Circassian woman in rags lying on the damp soil, under the open sky, with two babies, one of whom fought in the death throes with the death, while the other looking to satisfy hunger from the breast of stiff corpse of mother." (Ad. P. Berje; Eviction of mountaineers from the Caucasus.// Russian antiquity. 1882. Vol. 33, Book second, page 362–363).

It is noteworthy that in the 50s of the 20-th Century, the British Security services displayed great interest in the Circassian history. It was partially due to activation of West in the direction of Caucasus within the framework of a new doctrine of "cold war". Circassian problematic is extensively depicted in the following politico-diplomatic publications:

Peter Brock, The Fall of Circassia: A Study in Private Diplomacy. The English Historical Review, Vol. 71, No. 280 (Jul., 1956), pp. 401–427; Charles Webster, Urquhart, Ponsonby, and Palmerston, The English Historical Review, Vol. 62, No. 244 (Jul., 1947), pp. 327–351 (Confirmed by Abraham Shmulevich's letter: Abraham Shmulevich, How the Russian bear overslept the Circassian question 2011-05-17 HTTP://WWW.APN.RU/AUTHORS/AUTHORS37.HTM)

In the following period, a number of foreign historians and experts used to discuss the issue of Circassian genocide. Among them, first and foremost, I would like to name an American Researcher-Analyst Stephen D. Shenfield, according to whose researches the total number of modern Circassians in the World is determined as 6 248 000. The majority of them—690,000, live in Circassian Republic: in Kabardo-Balkaria—500 640, in Karacha-Circassia- 83 525, in Adyge Republic- 109 137. Thus, only 10% of Circassians live in their historic homeland, the rest 90 % of the people are distributed in the rest of the world in the following manner: Turkey—5 000 000, Germany – 100 000, Jordan – 100 000, Syria – 100 000, France – 15 000, the USA—5 000, Israel -5 000 and the Netherlands – 3000.

Professor Shenfield's data reflects the reality, that is why during the genocide, or in the period of May 21, 1864 the situation was the same: in occupied Circassia 10% of the local population survived from death, but the rest 90% were forced to flee from their homeland (note: more then 200 Circassian civic organizations spread throughout the foreign countries are actively fighting for the protection of the rights of Adyge people to obtain the right of their return to their motherland). Asto Shenfield's answer to the question whether genocide was committed in Circassia, the answer was the following: While familiarizing oneself with the facts presented by different authors, it is very difficult to ignore the positive answer:

"Was it genocide? Reading some authors, it is hard to avoid answering yes" (The Circassians—A Forgotten Genocide? By Stephen D. Shenfield 1999; article from «Studies on War and Genocide», Vol. 1, in the series "War and Genocide", Oxford and New York: Berghahn Books).

The other also well-known American diplomat and expert Paul B. Henze in his monograph dedicated to the Circassians' fight against the Russian Empire, concluded: the things that happened were at least equal to and compared to genocide (it can be compared only with genocide): 'What happened was at least comparable to genocide' (Paul B. HENZE, THE NORTH CAUCASUS BARRIER. CIRCASSIAN RESISTANCE TO RUSSIA. "The North Caucasus Barrier", edited by Marie Bennigsen Broxup, published by HURST & CO. 2007, page 111).

Although, Michael Mann, (an expert from Belfast University) calls the Circassian bloody tragedy, the deadly ethnic cleansing and not the genocide, but the factual materials provided by him equal the genocide indeed. It cannot be called differently, when 1,500,000 people were banished from their homeland, among them only 500 000 reached Turkey, and the vast majority died from the remaining 1 million, according to the author: "This leaves almost a million unaccounted for. Most of them probably amounting to the half from total Circassian population. Most deaths resulted from malnutrition and disease. Murderous cleansing was certainly intended, but not genocide." (The Dark Side of Democracy: Explaining Ethnic Cleansing, by Michael Mann. CUP, 2005, pages 98–100).

The American professor Walter Richmond has also dedicated to the Circassian Genocide and deportation special monograph, which was published in 2008 (see: Walter Richmond "The Northwest Caucasus: Past, Present, Future." Routledge Press, 2008).

In conclusion, it was Professor Antero Leitzinger, who classified the national tragedy of Circassians as most unambiguous genocide among all foreign scholars. He, without hesitation concludes that the genocide of Circassian people committed by the Czarist Russia, in the 19th Century was the biggest genocide by that time. Finally, the conclusion of the researcher shapes into following:

The genocide committed against the Circassian nation by the Czarist Russia in the 1800s was the biggest genocide of the nineteenth century. Yet it has been almost entirely forgotten by later history, while everyone knows the later Jewish Holocaust and many have heard about the Armenian genocide. Rather than of separate, selectively researched genocides, we should speak of a general genocidal tendency that affected many—both Muslim and Christian—people on a wide scene between 1856 and 1956, continuing in post-Soviet Russia until today. (Antero Leitzinger, The Circassian Genocide "Turkistan News". (The Eurasian Politician—Issue 2, October 2000).

And now I will elaborate namely on documentary materials based on Russian and Circassian sources.

The first thing that one can notice without any efforts is that the punishment activities that took place in Circassia were absolutely scheduled, pre-planned military actions led by the Russian autocrat emperors. At the beginning, this kind of approach officially was expressed by Nikolay I, who wrote to General I. P. Paskevich (the Russia's special representative in the Caucasus, the Special Caucasian Corps Commander):

"Thus, having accomplished the nice work, the new assignment is ahead of you, in my opinion glorious as well, and in terms of its direct benefits much more important—to suppress forever the mountain people and to obliterate disobedient" (See.: General A. P. Sherbatov—Field Marshal-Paskevich – Erivanski. – St. Petersburg, 1891, Vol. II. Page 229).

As we can observe, in this official letter, the Head of the country was ordering to his subordinate military units and army commanders to subdue or physically annihilate the Highlanders (Circassians).

In addition, the subsequent Russian Emperor Alexander II in his special rescript underlined the fact that Russia's the military expansion launched 150 years ago completed successfully in 1864: 'The enviable fate fell to the share of your Imperial Highness to accomplish the case of conquest of the Western Caucasus began the half-century ago and for the first time proclaim to the Russian people that henceforth in the Caucasus there no longer remains a single rebellious tribe' (Order of the Caucasian Army of July 27, 1864 with the announcement rescript of Alexander II about the end of the Caucasian War//Problems of the Caucasian War and expulsion of the Circassians to the Ottoman Empire (in 20s and 70s of XIX cent.): Collection of archive documents/ comp. Professor Kumykov T.H.- Nalchik, 2001- page 311).

In March of 1864 the Grand Duke Mikhail Nikolaevich reported to the Defense Minister: "the entire space of the Northern slope to the West from the river Laba and the Southern slope from the mount of Kuban to Tuapse is free from the hostile population". On this document there is a manual script made by the Emperor Alexander II: "Thank God" (Problems of the Caucasian War and expulsion of the Circassians to the Ottoman Empire; Collection of archival materials, Nalchik, 2001, page 260).

In November 1863, Alexander II gave special instruction to General Evdokimov, who then commanded the Russian forces in the North-West Caucasus): "it is absolutely necessary to bring the border of the Russian settlements on the bank of the river Bzyb, because otherwise even a small part of Highlanders, remaining on the shore, on any conditions, will be the bait for our enemies in case of the war with foreign countries." (The attitude of Chief of Staff of the Caucasian Army Kartsov to Yevdokimov, the Commander of the Kuban region.// Problems of the Caucasian War and expulsion of the Circassians to the Ottoman Empire; Collection of archival materials, Nalchik, 2001, page 233).

The remarkable fact is that the Russian military leadership had an alternative plan to solve the Circassian problem. In particular, in October 1860—that is, the next year after the imprisonment of Shamil—when General A.I.

Circassia

Bariatinsky, (Commander-in-chief) the Caucasus Army's Military Chief in Vladikavkaz together with four other generals assigned in the Caucasus (D.A. Miliutin, G.I. Philipson, N.I. Evdokimov, D.I. Mirski) discussed the ways of solving of Circassian issue, there existed the more human action plan as well lobbied by the General Philipson. According to Philipson's presented necessary to implement plan of short term activities, with the help of Shamil's former combatant Mohamed-Emin, the Russian authority would be of easier arrangement, which envisaged the placement of military garrisons in several important populated centers, wood cut, road construction and establishment of governance combined with local populations' everyday elements, within which the Circassian were allowed to trade with the Turkish state (at one time A. Miliutin recalled about this: D.A. Milutin "My trip to the Kuban region and the Black Sea coast"// The tragic consequences of the Caucasian war for Adygei (second half of XIX century–early XX centuries): Collection of documents and materials; Nalchik, 2000. page 29).

But Philipson's proposal was resisted by General N. I. Evdokimov, who supported driving out of Circassian population from their native lands, their oust to Turkey, and settlement of Cossacks on their vacant territories; especially in regard of Shapsughs, the population residing in the north of Sochi, along the Black Sea coast.

Evdokimov supposed to complete the eviction of the Circassians from the Caucasus in duration of two-three years (also see pages 29–30). The position of General Evdokimov was shared by Bariatinsky and Maliutin. Finally, the plan of majority was accepted, envisaging physical destruction of Circassians and their exile from their homeland and (i.e., today's terminology, the genocide): "The only reliable way for a firm assertion of our dominion in the Western Caucasus is the occupation of mountainous and foothill spaces by our Cossack population on the both sides of the ridge. . . ." (Acts collected by the Caucasian Archeological Commission. –Tiflis, 1904.-Vol. XII. Page 665).

And what is most important, this plan of Evdokimov was approved as an action plan by the country's leader, the Emperor Alexander II, who in all cases demanded from his subordinates driving out of Circassians from their mother land and their exile to Turkey on the marshlands near Kuban area. General N. I. Miliutin recalled about this: "Inscribed in 1860, the idea of the action plan for Kuban was to finally clean up the mountain zone from the native population by forcing them to choose one of two things: either to move to indicated places on the plane and completely submit to Russian rule, or just to abandon the homeland and go to Turkey; the mountain line was supposed to be taken by advanced Cossack's villages and fortifications all the way from upper Laba to Black Sea coast"(D.A. Milutin. Memories // The Siege of the Caucasus. Memories of the participants of the Caucasian War of the XIX century- Saint-Petersburg, 2000. pages 593–594)

Realization of the genocide was held according to the preliminarily strictly defined rules; reduction of total amount of the local population was planned by the following means:

— Murder of people;
— Burn of the villages of survived to ashes;
— Destruction of food reserves and crops;
— Expulsion of the population.

"The war was implacable, ruthless and austere. We moved forward slowly step by step, but firmly, cleaning every land, where the soldiers passed, from the mountain-dwellers, to the last human being. Hundreds of "Auls' (mountain villages) were burnt to ashes just after the snow melted, however before the trees bloomed in green (in February and March); crops were exterminated and even trampled down by the horses. The residents of Auls, if they were caught aback, were immediately taken under escort to the nearest stanitsas and afterwards departed to the Black Sea shores and then to Turkey" (Venyukov M.I. To the history of colonization of the West Caucasus. 1861–1863//Russian history. 1878, June. Page 249).

General Velyanimov A.A. considered provoking the wide-scale artificial starvation as the effective and necessary measure to override Circassian people in the shortest period: "Velyanimov A.A. considered . . . starvation is the only method to conquer the mountain-dwellers in the shortest time" (Caucasus and Russian Empire: project – you, ideas, illusions and reality. Beginning of the XIX cent. – beginning of the XX cent. St. Petersburg, 2005. page 74).

Exercising the same method, the General Geiman V. hoped that the local Circassian population either would die of starvation or move to the seaside to settle in Turkey. The General wrote in his report in 1864: "Auls and reserves of bread and fruit are burnt down; it can be authentically presume that the population will have to either die of hunger during winter or move to our seaside points for expulsion to Turkey" (Problems of Caucasian war and expulsion of Circassians within the scope of the Ottoman Empire, Nalchik. 2001. page 336).

At the same time, during the same period, other General held exactly the same actions. Namely, in 1864, Orekhov I. supposed that in order to timely accomplish the planned operation: "It was necessary to onset the expedition in late autumn, when they (Circassians – M. Ch.) have the resources for winter ready and then, destructing these resources, to put the tribe under necessity either to be expelled or die of hunger. Exactly this method was fulfilled this autumn" (Orekhov I.I. To the South slope of the West Caucasus.//Military collection. 1869, № 9. page 97).

Despite the ruthlessness, committed by the Czarist Russia, the leaders of the Circassian confrontation never lost the sparkle of hope and expressed their commitment to access the Russian Empire under the condition that they would be allowed reside on their own land. In order of peaceful solution of the issue, the Circassian-Ubikhs delegation was composed with Abadzekh Hasan Bitkhev, Ubikh Keren-Tuk-Berzeg and Shapsugh Islam Tkhashev. They, on behalf of the Mejlis of Circassian people, arrived in Tbilisi, and later on, with the same proposal, demanded the audience with the Emperor Alexander II, who was in Kuban. However, unfortunately, this peaceful initiative of Circassians and Ubikhs had the same fate as the project by General Phillipson; Russia was not interested in solution of this issue by political means. Position of Russia is consequently reflected in the appeal of the Military Minister Miliutin D.A. to the Emperor Alexander II, where General insisted not to deviate from the policy of already planned genocide. On August 29, 1861 the Minister wrote:

"Your Emperor Highness, allow me perceive that the recently formed union of three nations of the West Caucasus, remained intractable: Shapsuls, Ubikhs and Abadzekhs, has sent the delegation to Tbilisi for negotiations and that the mentioned deputation is willing to have the audience with Your Highness during Your trip to Kuban region . . .

Arrival of Circassian deputation and their pacific assurances shall not affect fulfillment of our action plan in the West Caucasus. We shall emphatically continue colonization of that land with Cossacks, since I cannot deviate from my usual credo, that only displacing natives from the mountains, thus occupying their place with Cossacks, we can be substantially established in that region . . ." (Acts, collected by the Caucasian orthographic commission. Vol. XII. Page 932–933. Overall note of Administrator of the Military Ministry, General-adjutant Milyutina, of August 29, 1861).

The Commander of Kuban Military Troops, General N.I. Evdokimov also underlined inevitability of Circassian genocide and the greatest state significance of it:

"Resettlement of intractable mountain-dwellers to Turkey, without doubt is the important state measure, allowing accomplish the war in the shortest period, without efforts from our side . . ." (Berzhe Ad.P. Eviction of mountain-dwellers from Caucasus//Russian history. St. Petersburg, 1882. Vol. 33. page 342).

This General, in 1864, himself confessed the committed crime and openly wrote of the scales:

"In 1864 the fact has been committed, the example of which does not exist in history. The largest mountain settlement, once possessing the greatest value, armed and able to military arts, occupying the vast Zakubanski area from upper Kuban to Anapa and south slope of Caucasus gorge from Sudjuksi bay to the river Bzyb, having the most unassailable places, has suddenly disappeared from this land . . ." (Report of Evdokimov. page 88).

The aim of the Commander of Caucasus Army, the count Mikhail Nikolaevich was extermination of the major part of the local population. On November 10, 1863, he was once again trying to convince the Military Minister, A. Milyutin in necessity of such actions:

"Meanwhile, the nature of the coastal zone and habits of the population, occupying it at such extent, are not similar to what we can offer to the mountain-dwellers, that is, life on the steppe near Kuban, as a result of which the most of the population will have to be exterminated, as they will not agree to fulfill our demands" (Problems of Caucasian war and eviction of Circassians within Ottoman Empire. Collection of archive material. Nalchik, 2001. page 228).

The military historian of the XIX cent. R.A. Fadeev consumed that Russian Empire needed only the Circassian land, and no need they had of Circassians themselves:

"The land of Zakuban people was necessary for the state; the state did not need the circassian population" (Tragic consequences of Caucasian war for Adygians (the second half of the XIX cent. – the beginning of the XX cent.) Nalchik, 2000, page 162).

The direct participant of the Caucasian war of the XIX cent., M.I. Venyukov confirmed that the author of the "Settlement project of West Caucasus,' the count Evdokimov did his best to make the living conditions for Circassians maximally unbearable. He also considered drastic reduction of the local population as inevitable event by means of their decease and tried his best to achieve it:

'... the count Evdokimov, who was the direct executive of the official "project of settlement of West Caucasus", did not care about the fate of mountain-dwellers, who ere evicted to the plain near Kuban. He strongly believed that the best consequences of longstanding, expensive war for Russia, was expulsion of all dwellers overseas. Thus, he considered the people, remained in Kuban in capacity of peaceful nationals, just as inevitable evil and did his best to reduce their number and constrain their living conditions' (Venyukov M., Caucasian recollections (1861–1863)// Russian Archive – Moscow, 1880. Book I, pages 435–436).

The military historian of the XIX cent. R.A. Fadeev wrote about this fact: it was necessary to exterminate one half of the total number of the mountain-dwellers (Circassians), in order to make the remained half end all resistance and obey to the colonialists:

"It was necessary to exterminate the half of the mountain-dwellers, to make another half lay down arms' (Tragic consequences of Caucasian war for Adygians (the second half of the XIX cent. – beginning of the XX cent.). Nalchik, 2000. page 160).

And deeds of the General P.D. Babich, committed against the Bzhedug tribe, give us a clear picture about ruthlessness of conquer of Circassian sub-ethnic groups, fighting for independence. He exterminates 44 Bzedughian villages from January 18 till February 7, 1859 (For comparison: 50 thousand people, the whole population of Abazians reside in 29 villages of the modern Karacha-Circassian Republic instead of 44(!)) :

"General Babich made cutting through the forest, covering the dwelling of Bzhedukhs and this invading into the lands of this tribe, conquered and exterminated all 44 auls. The local population remained in the snow, in the middle of own burnt villages, without roof and food, in the country, open with cutting for constant invasion from our side. They understood impossibility to uphold own places from us" (Report of the General-Field-Marshal, the count A.I. Baryatinskiy for 1857–1859. page 1285).

As an example, I consider it necessary to describe one more genocide, committed by the military criminal, General G.Kh. Zass. As the participant of Caucasian war, Fedorov M.F. describes, in 1834-36, General Zass demolished the peaceful auls: Sout, Khoist, Khochelk, Lezerok, Tailis, Tlabghai, Tamov, Fesfir etc.

(Fedorov M.F. Battle notes in Caucasus from 1835 to 1842//Caucasian collection. 1879. Vol. III. Pages 50-52. See also Sherbina F.A. History of Kuban Cossack troops. Vol. II. Reprint reproduction. Krasnodar, 1992. page 406).

General Zass aimed to psychologically terrorize Circassians; he kept the peaceful population under constant fear, so on the places of gathering in the conquered villages, there always were exhibited the cut heads of Circassians, put on the lances. Historically we also know that Zass bargained Circassian skulls as in Russia, so in Germany. Such deeds of General Zass are described in notes of Decembrist N.I. Lorer:

"Zass, in order to maintain propagated idea of fear, kept the Circassian heads put on lances on the purposely made barrow near "Prochny Okop" (the name of the place), and their beard were uncurled in the wind. It was a sad and disgusting sight' (See "Notes of Decembrist N.I. Lorer" – Moscow, 1931. page 248).

These and other facts, reflecting Circassian genocide, were earlier qualified by the experts as attempt of physical extermination—genocide of this people. Such ruthlessness caused the feeling of protest event in the commanders of Russian occupation standing army. For instance, General N.N. Raevski, indignant at the scales of Circassian tragedy, retired and stated in his report:

"I am the first and the only one currently, rebelled against fatal military actions in Caucasus and so I am forced to leave this land. Our actions in Caucasus remind all disasters of the initial conquer of America by Spanish, but I can neither see here deeds and heroism, nor success of conquer of Pitsar and Cortess. Let's hope that conquest of Caucasus did not leave the bloody trace in Russian history, similar to which these conquerors did in history of Spain" (Acts, collected by the Caucasian Archaeographic Commission. Tiflis. Vol. IX, document 434, page 504).

In this regard, the fact is of utmost importance, that Circassian ethnos cannot forget the events of XIX cent. and Circassian conscious of these tragic events, perceiving it adequately, unconsciously gives it the classification of genocide. Though, Russian historian I.I. Kutsenko explained these facts in more expedient manner and more skillfully: "It is impossible to conceal the truth about genocide. Recollections of it are still alive in Adygian Republics, and they acquire new details, thus entail increased interest. Recollections on tragic, bloody past become the most painful on May 21, on every anniversary of accomplishment of Caucasian war. This day became the mourning date for many people. Thus, genocide has been long ago recognized by the main instance—mass conscious of the indigenous population, and the considerable number of Russians as well. It remains unrecognized officially solely by the political authority of Russia and the local administration, obedient thereto" (Kutsenko I.Ya. Truth and fraud. Nalchik, 2007. page 82).

It may seem surprising but the event under the Soviet censorship, Russian historian Pisarev V.I. also objectively wrote about Circassian genocide in 1940:

"During almost 100 years (from the end of 70s of the XVIII cent. till 1864), the mountain auls, bread and hay were systematically devastated and burnt by Tsar Troops and Cossacks, kettle was stolen, women, children and aged were enslaved. Peaceful population was mercilessly exterminated, the blood flew like water" (Pisarev V.I. Methods of conquest of Adygian people by Tsarism in the first half of the XIX cent.//Historical notes. Moscow, 1940. Vol. 9. page 155).

Russian scientists, Mints S.S., Gromov V.P., Shcherbina F.A. and others do not avoid the topic of genocide and dare to speak about it. Tradition of objective research undoubtedly existed in Russian Soviet historiography, the classical example of which were the events, described by Jacob Abramov in 20s of the XX cent, which totally, as in case of Academician Simon Janashia, were based on recollections of witnesses.

This historian describes the scenes of displacement to Circassian Black Sea coast in details:

"All this time, Circassians remained at the sea side, under the open sky without any living means. Sufferings, through which the mountain-dwellers had to pass, cannot be described. Thousands of them, word for word, were dying of hunger. In winter, hunger was added with cold. The whole North-East coast of the Black Sea was full of corpses and dying people, amongst which the other alive half was lying, but they too were extremely weakened, waiting when they would be sent to Turkey. The witnesses tell the terrible stories of that time. One tells about the corpse of mother, holding the frozen infant, another tells about the heap of human bodies, nestling up to another, hoping to keep the warmth of their bodies, and frozen in this position etc." (Abramov Ya. Caucasian mountain-dwellers. Krasnodar, 1927. Page 7).

Similar evaluations are characteristic of the article of the Russian researcher, which was recently published, and is distinguished with plentitude of factual material and emotions of the author (See Tamara Polovinkina: Circassia—my pain and hope. 2011).

I would also like to touch upon one important issue, which is significant for research of Circassian genocide. For some reason it was established that only 1763–1864 are considered as the most active period of Circassian genocide, which we categorically cannot agree with. True, this period of time was very active in regards of military operations, but Circassian genocide continued up to the beginning of the XX century, until 1907, when the most important document in the history of mankind was adopted—the Hague Convention of October 18, 1907 "On Rules and Habits of Land Battles".

The following historical facts speak about necessity of such conclusions:

In 1871–1881 428 households of Adygians were resettled from Kuban region, and 1381 households in 1882–1883.

In 1887, the Russian Government decided to conscript the Adygian-Circassians, residing in Kuban region, which entailed the protest from the local population. In the end, the parties agreed that Adygian auls would be resettled to Ottoman area; in October of 1888, 3 333 residents of Khajimukov aul were resettled to Ottoman land.

On November 7, 1889, the population of 6 Adygian auls was resettled to Ottoman land on the basis of the "permit" by the Emperor.

In 1890, 7 auls were resettled from Labi and Ekaterinodar units, as the Government needed their lands.

In 80-90s of the XIX cent. Approximately 20 000 people were resettled from Kuban region to Ottoman Empire.

In the end of 1890, 260 Kabardians, resettled from Tergi region, arrived to Damascus.

In 1900–1907, approximately 8 000 Kabardians were resettled to Ottoman Empire. This was one of the last acts of Circassian genocide by the Russian Empire.

Activation of Adygian scientific opinion is particularly noticeable in regards of recognition of Circassian genocide since the end of 80s of the XX cent. uptoday, when almost every year (on the regular basis), the scientific and social forums and meetings are held in all three Circassian autonomies. It is also noteworthy that on April 24–25, 1990, the participants of Koshehable Forum ("History – common property") adopted the joint recommendation, providing the competent conclusion on the fact that colonial acts of Tsarist Russia of the XIX cent. in West Caucasus shall be estimated as the policy of genocide, and struggle of Adygians was anti-colonial and was of progressive character, their effort was directed to maintain freedom and independence:

"To consider that Tsarism held the policy of genocide in regards with Adygian people in the XIX cent., to recognize struggle of Adygians for freedom and independence as mass, national, anti-colonial and progressive" (Circassia in the XIX cent. (material of the I Kashelbakh Forum "History—common property"). Maikop, 1991, page 263)//note: Koshehabl is the Circassian settlement, which in 1918 was practically demolished by the Red Army, 214 Circassian patriot died in this struggle against the aggressors//.

On October 24–26, 1990, the All-Union Scientific- Practical Conference "National-Liberating Struggle of North Caucasus people and Mohadjir problems" was held in Nalchik, where the recommendation of Nalchik Conference was adopted, providing the objective conclusion that policy of Russian Tsarism in Caucasus region was aggressive, with colonial character, which was related to enslavement, genocide and Adygian (and other nations) forceful expulsion and eviction from their homelands:

"As it is clear from material of this Conference, policy of Russian Tsarism in this region was aggressive, colonial, connected with conquest, genocide and expulsion of the major part of Adygian people and the part of other nations from their homeland" (National-Liberating Struggle of North Caucasus people and Mohadjir problems: Material of the All-Union Scientific-Practical Conference of October 24-26, 1990. Nalchik, 1994. Page 260).

The topic of Circassian-Adygian genocide was openly and exhaustively considered various times in the following scientific conference working programs:

Caucasian war: lessons of history and the present days (Krasnodar, May, 1994); "Adygian ethnos: history and prospects" (Maikop, October 24-25, 1996);

"Caucasian war in the history of North Caucasus people" Maikop, May 5–8, 1999);

"Besleney in historical and ethno-cultural context of Adygian ethnos" (Maikop, June 1, 2001); "Caucasian war: lessons and the present days" (Maikop, May 20–21, 2004);

International Round Table "Adygians (Circassians) in the XIX cent.: Problems of war and peace" (Maikop, May 21, 2009).

Upon considering the Circassian genocide, the scientists and experts of Circassian ethnicity, in their conclusions, are unanimous. Almost all historians as in Adyghe, Karacha-Circassia, so in Kabardo-Balkaria, consider that the Russian Empire held the genocide of Circassian people in the XIX cent., which implied extermination of 90% of this nation, or their expulsion from their homelands and forceful settlement to the Near East countries (See Asker Sokht, Circassian history and the present days. Parts 1 and 2. Political News Agency, 2010.04.22).

Even the scientists, who consider Adygian future only under Russian Empire, think so. For instance, the experienced historian from Maikop, Askhad Chirg, considering Circassian genocide (on the basis of the rich empiric material), wrote: "We need only truth about Circassian genocide, we cannot build friendship between the nations with lies. Adygian Republic remains the integral part of Russia, Circassians have the future only along with Russian people, in the Russian Empire". (Empire officials try to justify the genocide of Circassian people – kavkasia.net/Russia/article/1272517654).

At the same time, the active member of the Circassian national-liberating movement and one of the authors of the Circassian national project, Ruslan Kesh (Keshev), expresses similar attitude towards the genocide in his article "Genocide of Circassian People" (Tbilisi, 2010).

The results of the scientific research by Circassian Diaspora echo the conclusions of the local people. In this regards, the monograph, issued in 2010 by the older writer and historian, Kadir I. Natho, living in the USA, is noteworthy: CIRCASSIAN HISTORY, USA, Library of Congress. Xlibris Corporation. The chapter 6 of the book is totally dedicated to the issues of Circassian genocide. With the fail observation of the author, Russian Empire settled the Russians and Cossacks on the lands, "cleared" from Circassians as a result of the genocide, thus conducting colonization of these territories:

Evidently, to accomplish the genocide against the Circassian nation, Russia had to follow the policy of total physical destruction of the indigenous Circassian population and the colonization of the "cleared" Circassian territory by the Russo-Cossack, People,' Kadir I. Natho. Page 366.

The historical fact shall be considered as the victory of public opinion and Circassian movement, that on February 7, 1992, the Parliament of Kabardo-Balkaria Autonomous Republic, adopted the special resolution (N 977-XII-B), which recognized the fact of Circassian genocide by Russian aggressors during Russian-Caucasian war:

THE SUPREME COUNCIL OF KABARDO-BALKARIAN SSR RESOLUTION of February 7, 1992, N 977-XII-B ON CONDEMNATION OF GENOCIDE OF ADYGIANS (CIRCASSIANS) DURING THE YEARS OF RUSSIAN-CAUCASIAN WAR

The centennial colonial Russian-Caucasian war (1763–1864), bringing to Adygians (Circassians) innumerable disasters and sufferings, does not have the similarities in the history of new era. The major part of the Adygian ethnos, including over 90% of population of Kabarda, was exterminated, more than 500 thousand Adygian population was expelled by Tsar autocracy to the Ottoman Empire.

Giving the historical and politico-legal evaluation of Russian-Caucasian war, the Supreme Council of Kabardino-Balkarian Soviet Socialist Republic resolved:

1) To consider the mass extermination of Adygians (Circassians) during the Russian-Caucasian war and forceful expulsion thereof from their historical homeland to the Ottoman Empire as the act of genocide, the grave crime against the mankind.

2) To submit the proposal to the Supreme Council of Russian Federation to consider the issue on recognition of the genocide of Adygians (Circassians) during Russian-Caucasian war and granting the foreign compatriots thereof the dual citizenship.

3) To assign the Presidium of the Supreme Council of Kabardino-Balkarian SSR and the Council of Ministers of Kabardino-Balkarian SSR to elaborate the program of measures on rehabilitation and repatriation of foreign Adygians (Circassians).

4) To obtain the status of the exile nation for the foreign Adygians (Circassians) through the Supreme Council of Russian Federation and the relevant international organizations.

5) To declare May 31 as the Day of Memory of Adygians (Circassians) – the victims of the Russian-Caucasian war, as the day-off.

The Chairman of the Supreme Council of Kabardino-Balkarian ASSR KHACHIM KARMOKOV

Later on, on April 29, 1996, the 'State Council 'Khase' of the Republic of Adyge adopted the special resolution (№ 64-1), appealing to the State Duma of Russian Federation for official recognition of Circassian genocide, committed by the Tsarist Russia in the XIX cent:

The State Council – Khase of the Republic of Adyge RESOLUTION of April 29, 1996, N 64-1 ON APPEAL TO THE STATE DUMA OF RUSSIAN FEDERATION

The State Council – Khase of the Republic of Adyge resolves:

1. To adopt the Appeal of the President of the Republic of Adyge and the State Council – Khase of the Republic of Adyge to the State Federal Duma of Russian Federation on official recognition of the fact of genocide of the Adygian (Circassian) people during the Caucasian war.
2. To submit the said Appeal to the State Duma of Russian Federation.

The Chairman of the State Council – Khase of the Republic of Adyge E. SALOV

The dynamics of events during the subsequent period of recognition of the genocide of Circassian people by Russian conquerors during the Russian-Caucasian war by the Parliament of Kabardo-Balkarian Autonomous Republic developed with the following consequence around the problem of Circassian genocide:

On May 18, 1994, the President of Russian Federation, Boris Yeltsin published the address to the North Caucasian people ('Address to the Caucasian people'), where he recognized justice of struggle of Circassian people for freedom and independence in the XIX cent. The document condemned the policy of genocide, held by Russian Empire, but this recognition did not entail the efficient steps from the Russian authorities to suppress the results of this crime; the question of repatriation of the displaced persons (Muhadjirs) to the homeland has not been raised on the state level.

On July 15–17 of 1997 the Netherlands based high ranking organization THE GENERAL ASSEMBLY OF THE UNREPRESENTED NATIONSAND PEOPLES ORGANIZATION adopted special resolution 'On Situation of Circassian Nation'. The organization, based on this document, appealed to the Russian Federation and to the International Community to recognize the genocide of Circassian nation that took place in the 19th century and was asking to entitle Circassian people with a status of an exile nation:

RESOLUTION OF THE GENERAL ASSEMBLY OF THE UNREPRESENTED NATIONS AND PEOPLES ORGANIZATION FIFTH GENERAL ASSEMBLY

Fifth Session

Otepää, 15-19 July 1997

General Assembly Resolution 1

RESOLUTION ON THE SITUATION OF THE CIRCASSIAN NATION

The General Assembly,

HAVING HEARD the report of the International Circassian Association representative on the state of the Circassian nation that The Circassians have been partly exterminated during the Russian-Caucasian war and 90 percent of those remaining have been forcefully deported abroad to Turkey, Jordan and Syria;

The nation faced genocide for a long period;

The Circassian people living abroad have difficulty preserving their language, culture and identity;

THEREFORE,

CALLS UPON the Russian Federation and the international community to acknowledge the genocide of the Circassian nation that took place in the 19th century and to grant the Circassian people status of an exile nation.

CALLS UPON the Russian Federation to grant the Circassian people dual citizenship, both that of Russia and of their respective countries.

CALLS UPON the Russian Federation to ensure the Circassian people of the possibility to return to their historical land.

On May 28 of 1998, Teuvezh Kazanoko, Chairman of the International Circassian Association, at the Session IV of the commission of the UN raised the issue of recognition of genocide of Circassian People and the problem of repatriation of Circassian Diaspora:

TEUVEZH KAZANOKO, of Society for Threatened People, said that the history of the Adygh (Circassian) diaspora outside the Russian Caucuses originated from the nineteenth century. According to unsubstantiated sources, there were between 3 to 4 million Circassians living today in Turkey; they were subjected to prosecution and repression simply for being Circassian. To date, this problem had not been considered by the international community. Interested organizations should begin to consider this issue. The tend to return to the Caucasus was predominant among the Diaspora, but there was the difficult economic situation, and problems with the Russian legislative procedure did not facilitate obtaining Russian citizenship. Russian officials did not apply articles of the "Admission to the Citizenship of Russian Federation" to the Circassians – thus dooming them to existence without the right to a historical homeland. It was hoped that the UN would involve itself in the sufferings of the Circassian people.

On June 1st, of 2005 public movement 'Circassian Congress of Adyge Republic' applied to the State Duma of the Russian Federation to recognize the genocide of Circassians by the Russian state in 1763-1864. The appeal of Circassians was supplemented by more than 500 documentary files, collected by Murat Berzeg, chairman of 'Circassian Congress', evidences of cruelties, committed by the political and military leaders of the Russian empire, the facts of mass demolition of Circassian settlements and extermination of peaceful people were described in detail. The reply from the Russian Duma was cynical, stating that 'Circassians (Adyge people), were not victims of genocide during the II World War.'

On July 15, 2005, the known western expert on Circassian problems (genocide), Paul Goble, prepared the special coverage on radio 'Liberty,' dedicated to Circassian problems that were later also published as an article: "Circassians Demand Russian Apology For 19th Century Genocide."

Embracing Circassia, Building Our Future.

On October 11, 2006, 20 Circassian organizations of the 9 countries of the world appealed to the European Parliament with a request to recognize the genocide of Circassians.

On November 17, 2006, Circassian organizations of the Russian Federation applied with a request to Vladimir Putin, then President of Russia to facilitate the positive solution of the Circassian issue. These organizations received in response the following answer: "In the legislation of Russia there are no respective legislative provisions that determine the procedure for solution of the problem".

On May 21st of 2007 in Washington, in Jamestown Foundation (President Glen E. Howard) and Circassian Cultural Foundation (President Iyad Youghar) was organized a conference, named "Circassians: Past, Present and Future";

On October 4, 2007, the representatives of Circassian Diaspora in the USA applied with a demand to the President of Russia Vladimir Putin to recognize the Circassian genocide on the official level and in compliance with International Law, to study with attention and to revise the Circassian issue from overall perspective.

On April 13, 2008, in USA, New Jersey. William Paterson University was held the international conference

On March 20, 2010, in Tbilisi was held the international conference where the main attention was drawn to the issue of recognition Circassian genocide. The representatives of Circassian people applied to the President and the Parliament of Georgia with a request to recognize Circassian genocide.

On May 25, 2010, The Institute of Ethnology and Anthropology of the Russian Academy of Sciences published official conclusion that modern Adyges, Kabardinians, Circassians and Shapsuls are one Circassian nation.

In June of 2010, in Washington under the initiative of "Jamestown Foundation," was held one more conference on Circassian issue.

In November of 2010, the second Tbilisi conference discussed the new aspects of Circassian problem, including the organization of Olympic games in Sochi in 2014 in order to commemorate 150 year anniversary of victory over the Circassians "On Krasnaya Polyana" on May 21st of 1864.

In November of 2010, representatives of "the Circassian Congress" applied to the President and the Parliament of Georgia to speed up the procedures on recognition of the issue of Circassian genocide. Subsequently, there was established information cooperation with Diaspora and Caucasus issues committee of the Parliament of Georgia.

On May 2, 2011, organization "The Circassian Patriots" applied to the Parliament of Georgia to recognize the Circassian genocide.

On May 3, 2011, the Parliament received the address with similar content from the Circassian Diaspora of Israel as well: "The Circassian Diaspora of Israel applies to you with the request to recognize the genocide of Circassians, committed by the Russian state in the 19th century,"—it was written in the letter of Adnan Orkizh, chairman of the Circassian Congress of Israel.

On May 3, 2011, the Circassian Congress of Germany (chairman Zaur Ghedwaje) also applied to the Parliament. The authors of the letter were assuring of: 'The recognition of Circassian genocide by the Caucasian state, Georgia, will advance the relations between Georgian and Circassian nations to the new level and will further reaffirm historic ties between the two nations.'

On May 5, 2011, the Circassian Congress of Belgium applied with a request of recognition of the Circassian genocide to the Parliament of Georgia. The letter was signed by the Chairman of the organization Kuban Khatukai.

On May 6, 2011, Kabardo-Balkarian public movement "Adigha Khekuzj—Circassia" applied to the Parliament of Georgia with a request of recognition of the Circassian genocide. The letter was signed by the member of the coordinating council Abubekir Murzakanov.

On May 8, 2011, the Chechen Human Rights International Organization 'The World and Human Rights' ('МИР И ПРАВА ЧЕЛОВЕКА') applied with a request of recognition of the Circassian genocide to the Parliament of Georgia. The letter was signed by the President of the organization, well-known defender of Human Rights Said-Emin Ibragimov.

On May 9, 2011, the Georgian nongovernmental organization 'Independent Caucasus' applied with a request of recognition of the Circassian genocide to the Parliament of Georgia. The letter, on behalf of the members of the organization, was signed by the chairman Giorgi Sabedashvili.

On May 10, 2011, 'The Young Chechens International Organization' applied with a request of recognition of the Circassian genocide to the Parliament of Georgia. The members of the organization also expressed hope that the Parliament of Georgia would pay attention to the previous incoming letters of the Chechen and the Ingush organizations, with a request of recognition of genocide of these peoples.

On May 11, 2011, the Jordanian Circassian Organization 'Minute of Loyalty and Duty' ('МИНУТА ВЕРНОСТИ И ДОЛГА') (city of Amman) applied with a request of recognition of the Circassian genocide to the Parliament of Georgia.

On May 12, 2011, the famous Ingush dissident, writer and humanist Issa Kadzoev applied with a request of recognition of the Circassian genocide to the Parliament of Georgia. The author in his letter was emphasizing the fact that recognition of the Circassian genocide by Georgia would be continuation of famous Georgian-Caucasian love of fellow-men tradition and restoration of justice.

On May 12, 2011, Abraham Shmulevich published a vary interesting article about the Circassian genocide: How the Russian bear overslept the Circassian question HTTP://WWW.APN.RU/AUTHORS/AUTHORS37.HTM

On May 13, 2011, in the Parliament of Georgia, at the joint sitting of various committees, we submitted the following scientific conclusion about the genocide of Circassians. In the introductory part to it I said: The things, committed by the Russian Empire against Adyges, were the obvious genocide. The Parliament of Georgia has a chance to restore justice and to pay tribute to the memory of millions of suffered and hundreds of thousands of depressed Circassians."

THE Scientific conclusion

In 19th century, during the Russian-Caucasus War, Russian military-political leadership deported thousands of Circassian tribal groups from their lands to the Ottoman Empire, as Russia could not imagine coexisting with Circassians within the space of the Russian Empire. The Empire wanted Circassian territories without Adyghe people. Constrained deportation to Middle East countries was preceded with long, obstinate armed resistance of Circassian tribal groups. Their stubborn resistance turned to be Russia's justification for their bloody mass killing of Circassian tribes. Tsarist Russian strategists used their brutal tactic methods right against peaceful Circassian tribal groups. During "the demographic attacks" Russia used different brutal methods: mass killing, armed attacks on peaceful population, ethnic cleansing and deportation, burning forests and crops, starvation and deliberate spread of disease.

World history knows various genocide cases: Bosnia, Chechnya, Ruanda, but Circassians' genocide is unique, as Circassians lost ¾ of their population, sovereignty and the main – their homeland. So, Circassians are scattered in more than 50 countries in the world. They deserve refugees status, but unfortunately cannot benefit from it.

Based on the above-mentioned and relying on factual materials, historic documents and also sharing assessments of famous and independent expert-researchers, I conclude that in the 19th century, during the Russian-Caucasian war (1763-1864) the Russian political and military leadership has initially planned and then conducted the ethnic cleansing of Circassian territories. In the deserted settlements of Circassians were especially settled Kazaks and Russians, meanwhile as a result of numerous punitive military expeditions were killed or expelled from their homeland more than 90% of approximately million and half of Circassian population. It has been determined that during the conquering wars, conducted by Russia, the entire loss of genetic fund of Circassian people, amounted to more than 20% murdered out of the total population of this nation. Consequently, these actions are clearly qualified as genocide, as the purposeful extermination of representatives of any nation, when the casualty equals to more than 20%, automatically mean act of genocide, by any definition of this term.

The Genocide is proved out alternatively according to the data from Adolf Berzhe (1828-1886), who represented an official source of the Russian Empire. Berzhe claimed that amongst over million Circassians, above 400 thousand died in the war, 497 thousand people were banished, about 80 thousand people stayed in their historical homeland; that is, according to the official data of the Empire by itself, the number of victims of the civilian population amounted more than 40 percent.

The genocide of Circassians in Russia continued till the beginning of the twentieth century and stopped only in 1907. At that time the revolution drew the focus of attention of the Russian political elite in the other direction.

Circassia

At that point, I attached to my report the draft resolution on the abovementioned genocide. that was proposed as a working version in case, if the Parliament of Georgia would express commitment to recognize the issue of vital importance to Adyge peoples – **the Act of Genocide of Circassians.**

Draft

Resolution of the Parliament of Georgia

Recalling the colonial policy of the Russian Empire towards Circassians during the Russo-Caucasuswar (1763–1864), when the Russian political and military leadership planned and executed ethnic cleansing of Circassian territories, subsequently especially settling the territories with Kazaks and Russians, when as a result of multiple punitive military expeditions, more than 90% of the million and a half Circassian population was annihilated;

Recalling the 7 February 1992 Decree of the Supreme Council of Kabardino Balkaria Republic(№977–XII-B) on the Condemnation of the Act of Genocide of Adyge (Circassians) During the Russian-Caucasian War;

Taking into consideration numerous official documents of the Russian Empire confirming its aggressive actions, such as artificially engineered famines and epidemics amongst the civilian population, aimed at the physical annihilation of representatives of the Circassian people and giving historic and legal-political assessment to the results of the Russian-Caucasian (1763-1864) war that was fatal for the Circassian people;

The Parliament of Georgia resolves:

1. **Recognizes** the mass murder of Circassians (Adyge) during the Russo-Caucasus War and their forceful eviction from their homeland to Ottoman Empire (as well as to other countries of the Middle East), as an act of genocide, in accordance with the IV Hague Convention of October 18, 1907 and the UN Convention of 9 December 1948;

2. **Recognizes** the Circassians, forcefully deported during and after the period of the Russo-Caucasus War, as refugees//Internally Displaced persons, in line with the UN Convention on the Status of Refugees of 28 July 1951 and to entitle Circassian people with a status of an exile nation;

3. **Applies** to the international organizations (the UN, The European Parliament, The Councilof Europe, the OSCE), with a request to elaborate the respective mechanisms for political, material and humanitarian support of the descendants of the forcefully deported Circassians in the 19th century, in order to achieve their free repatriation on the homeland in the Northern-Western Caucasus, including Circassian republics.

4. **Addresses** the Government of Georgia with a request to elaborate the working plan, within the frame of which will be commemoration of victims of genocide that means creation of special educational, museum, memorial and other types of programs.

P.S. On May 20, 2011 the Parliament of Georgia at the plenary session voted for the adoption of Resolution On the Recognition of Genocide of Circassians by the Russian Empire. The legislative body was unanimous in its decision. 95 votes were in favor and none against. The resolution was submitted to the Parliament by Chairman of Diaspora and Caucasus Issues Committee Nugzar Tsiklauri.

The draft resolution, which we submitted, as a result of the committee hearings was formed as the following text:

Resolution of the Parliament of Georgia On the Recognition of Genocide of Circassians by the Russian Empire

Recalling the colonial policy of the Russian Empire towards Circassians during the Russo-Caucasus war (1763 -1864), when the Russian political and military leadership planned and executed ethnic cleansing of Circassian territories, subsequently settling the territories with other ethnic groups;

Recalling the fact that as a result of multiple punitive military expeditions, more than 90% of the Circassian population was annihilated;

Recalling numerous official documents of the Russian Empire confirming its aggressive actions, such as artificially engineered famines and epidemics amongst the civilian population, aimed at the physical annihilation of representatives of the Circassian people;

Recalling the 7 February 1992 Decree of the Supreme Council of Kabardino Balkaria Republic(№977–XII-B) on the Condemnation of the Act of Genocide of Adyge (Circassians) During the Russian-Caucasian War, and legally and politically assessing the results of the Russo-Caucasus War (1763-1864);

Recalling extensive legal and historic research which established presence of both fact and intent of genocide in the case concerned;

The Parliament of Georgia:

1. **Recognizes** the mass murder of Circassians (Adyge) during the Russo-Caucasus War and their forceful eviction from their homeland, as an act of genocide, in accordance with the IV Hague Convention on Laws and Customs of War on Land of October 18, 1907 and the UN Convention on the Prevention and Punishment of the Crime of Genocide of 9 December 1948;

2. **Recognizes** the Circassians, forcefully deported during and after the period of the Russo-Caucasus War, as refugees, in line with the Convention on the Status of Refugees of 28 July 1951.

Tbilisi, May 20, 2011

On July 12, 2011, The Georgian Parliament's recognition of Circassians genocide was **followed by the logical extension of corresponding Decree of Georgian Government (N1446) on the Memorial for Respecting Immortal Memory of Victims of the Circassians' Genocide. The memorial, which will be dedicated to the Caucasian political victims, annihilated by the Russian Empire, will be mounted in Anaklia resort. It is the place where refugee Circassian tribes, forced to flee from their homeland, passed through the territory in the 19 century during their deportation to the Ottoman Empire.**

Author: Prof. Merab Chukhua"[1514]

======================================

d. **10 Stages of Genocide**

"By Gregory H. Stanton, President, Genocide Watch

The Ten Stages of Genocide
By Dr. Gregory H. Stanton
President, Genocide Watch
Classification → Symbolization → Discrimination → Dehumanization → Organization → Polarization → Preparation → Persecution → Extermination → Denial

Genocide is a process that develops in ten stages that are predictable but not inexorable. At each stage, preventive measures can stop it. The process is not linear. Stages may occur simultaneously. Logically, later stages must be preceded by earlier stages. But all stages continue to operate throughout the process.

1. CLASSIFICATION: All cultures have categories to distinguish people into "us and them" by ethnicity, race, religion, or nationality: German and Jew, Hutu and Tutsi. Bipolar societies that lack mixed categories, such as Rwanda and Burundi, are the most likely to have genocide. The main preventive measure at this early stage is to develop universalistic institutions that transcend ethnic or racial divisions, that actively promote tolerance and understanding, and that promote classifications that transcend the divisions. The Catholic church could have played this role in Rwanda, had it not been driven by the same ethnic cleavages as Rwandan society. Promotion of a common language in countries like Tanzania has also promoted transcendent national identity. This search for common ground is vital to early prevention of genocide.

2. SYMBOLIZATION: We give names or other symbols to the classifications. We name people "Jews" or "Gypsies", or distinguish them by colors or dress; and apply the symbols to members of groups. Classification and symbolization are universally human and do not necessarily result in genocide unless they lead to dehumanization. When combined with hatred, symbols may be forced upon unwilling members of pariah groups: the yellow star for Jews under Nazi rule, the blue scarf for people from the Eastern Zone in Khmer Rouge Cambodia. To combat symbolization, hate symbols can be legally forbidden (swastikas) as can hate speech. Group marking like gang clothing or tribal scarring can be outlawed, as well. The problem is that legal limitations will fail if unsupported by popular cultural enforcement. Though Hutu and Tutsi were forbidden words in Burundi until the 1980's, code words replaced them. If widely supported, however, denial of symbolization can be powerful, as it was in Bulgaria, where the government refused to supply enough yellow badges and at least eighty percent of Jews did not wear them, depriving the yellow star of its significance as a Nazi symbol for Jews.

3. DISCRIMINATION: A dominant group uses law, custom, and political power to deny the rights of other groups. The powerless group may not be accorded full civil rights, voting rights, or even citizenship. The dominant group is driven by an exclusionary ideology that would deprive less powerful

groups of their rights. The ideology advocates monopolization or expansion of power by the dominant group. It legitimizes the victimization of weaker groups. Advocates of exclusionary ideologies are often charismatic, expressing resentments of their followers, attracting support from the masses. Examples include the Nuremberg Laws of 1935 in Nazi Germany, which stripped Jews of their German citizenship, and prohibited their employment by the government and by universities. Denial of citizenship to the Rohingya Muslim minority in Burma is a current example. Prevention against discrimination means full political empowerment and citizenship rights for all groups in a society. Discrimination on the basis of nationality, ethnicity, race or religion should be outlawed. Individuals should have the right to sue the state, corporations, and other individuals if their rights are violated.

4. DEHUMANIZATION: One group denies the humanity of the other group. Members of it are equated with animals, vermin, insects or diseases. Dehumanization overcomes the normal human revulsion against murder. At this stage, hate propaganda in print and on hate radios is used to vilify the victim group. The majority group is taught to regard the other group as less than human, and even alien to their society. They are indoctrinated to believe that "We are better off without them." The powerless group can become so depersonalized that they are actually given numbers rather than names, as Jews were in the death camps. They are equated with filth, im purity, and immorality. Hate speech fills the propaganda of official radio, newspapers, and speeches.
To combat dehumanization, incitement to genocide should not be confused with protected speech. Genocidal societies lack constitutional protection for countervailing speech, and should be treated differently than democracies. Local and international leaders should condemn the use of hate speech and make it culturally unacceptable. Leaders who incite genocide should be banned from international travel and have their foreign finances frozen. Hate radio stations should be jammed or shut down, and hate propaganda banned. Hate crimes and atrocities should be promptly punished.

5. ORGANIZATION: Genocide is always organized, usually by the state, often using militias to provide deniability of state responsibility (the Janjaweed in Darfur.) Sometimes organization is informal (Hindu mobs led by local RSS militants) or decentralized (terrorist groups.) Special army units or militias are often trained and armed. Plans are made for genocidal killings. Acts of genocide are disguised as counter-insurgency if there is an

ongoing armed conflict or civil war. The era of "total war" began in World War II. Firebombing did not differentiate civilians from non-combatants. The civil wars that broke out after the end of the Cold War have also not differentiated civilians and combatants. They cause widespread war crimes. Mass rapes of women have become a characteristic of all modern genocides. Arms flows to states and militias (often in violation of UN Arms Embargoes) facilitate acts of genocide. States organize secret police to spy on, arrest, torture, and murder people suspected of opposition to political leaders. Motivations for targeting a group are indoctrinated through mass media and special training for murderous militias and special army killing units. To combat this stage, membership in these militias should be outlawed. Their leaders should be denied visas for foreign travel and their foreign assets frozen. The UN should impose arms embargoes on governments and citizens of countries involved in genocidal massacres, and create commissions to investigate violations, as was done in post-genocide Rwanda, and use national legal systems to prosecute those who violate such embargoes.

6. POLARIZATION: Extremists drive the groups apart. Hate groups broadcast polarizing propaganda. Laws may forbid intermarriage or social interaction. Extremist terrorism targets moderates, intimidating and silencing the center. Moderates from the perpetrators' own group are most able to stop genocide, so are the first to be arrested and killed. Leaders in targeted groups are the next to be arrested and murdered. The dominant group passes emergency laws or decrees that grants them total power over the targeted group. The laws erode fundamental civil rights and liberties. Targeted groups are disarmed to make them incapable of self-defense, and to ensure that the dominant group has total control. Prevention may mean security protection for moderate leaders or assistance to human rights groups. Assets of extremists may be seized, and visas for international travel denied to them. Coups d'état by extremists should be opposed by international sanctions. Vigorous objections should be raised to disarmament of opposition groups. If necessary they should be armed to defend themselves.

7. PREPARATION: National or perpetrator group leaders plan the "Final Solution" to the Jewish, Armenian, Tutsi or other targeted group "question." They often use euphemisms to cloak their intentions, such as referring to their goals as "ethnic cleansing," "purification," or "counter-terrorism." They build armies, buy weapons and train their troops and militias. They indoctrinate the populace with fear of the victim group. Leaders often

claim that "if we don't kill them, they will kill us," disguising genocide as self-defense. There is a sudden increase in inflammatory rhetoric and hate propaganda with the objective of creating fear of the other group. Political processes such as peace accords that threaten the total dominance of the genocidal group or upcoming elections that may cost them their grip on total power may actually trigger genocide. Prevention of preparation may include arms embargoes and commissions to enforce them. It should include prosecution of incitement and conspiracy to commit genocide, both crimes under Article 3 of the Genocide Convention.

8. PERSECUTION: Victims are identified and separated out because of their ethnic or religious identity. Death lists are drawn up. In state sponsored genocide, members of victim groups may be forced to wear identifying symbols. Their property is often expropriated. Sometimes they are even segregated into ghettoes, deported into concentration camps, or confined to a famine-struck region and starved. They are deliberately deprived of resources such as water or food in order to slowly destroy them. Programs are implemented to prevent procreation through forced sterilization or abortions. Children are forcibly taken from their parents.

The victim group's basic human rights become systematically abused through extrajudicial killings, torture and forced displacement. Genocidal massacres begin. They are acts of genocide because they intentionally destroy part of a group. The perpetrators watch for whether such massacres meet any international reaction. If not, they realize that the international community will again be bystanders and permit another genocide.

At this stage, a Genocide Emergency must be declared. If the political will of the great powers, regional alliances, or U.N. Security Council or the U.N. General Assembly can be mobilized, armed international intervention should be prepared, or heavy assistance provided to the victim group to prepare for its self-defense. Humanitarian assistance should be organized by the U.N. and private relief groups for the inevitable tide of refugees to come.

9. EXTERMINATION begins, and quickly becomes the mass killing legally called "genocide." It is "extermination" to the killers because they do not believe their victims to be fully human. When it is sponsored by the state, the armed forces often work with militias to do the killing. Sometimes the genocide results in revenge killings by groups against each other, creating the downward whirlpool-like cycle of bilateral genocide (as in Burundi). Acts of genocide demonstrate how dehumanized the victims have become. Already dead bodies are dismembered; rape is used as a tool of war to

genetically alter and eradicate the other group. Destruction of cultural and religious property is employed to annihilate the group's existence from history. All men of fighting age are murdered in some genocides. All women and girls are raped. In total genocides all the members of the targeted group are exterminated.

At this stage, only rapid and overwhelming armed intervention can stop genocide. Real safe areas or refugee escape corridors should be established with heavily armed international protection. (An unsafe "safe" area is worse than none at all.) The U.N. Standing High Readiness Brigade, EU Rapid Response Force, or regional forces should be authorized to act by the U.N. Security Council if the genocide is small. For larger interventions, a multilateral force authorized by the U.N. should intervene. If the U.N. Security Council is paralyzed, regional alliances must act under Chapter VIII of the U.N. Charter or the UN General Assembly should authorize action under the Uniting for Peace Resolution GARes. 330 (1950), which has been used 13 times for such armed intervention. Since 2005, the international responsibility to protect transcends the narrow interests of individual nation states. If strong nations will not provide troops to intervene directly, they should provide the airlift, equipment, and financial means necessary for regional states to intervene.

10. DENIAL is the final stage that lasts throughout and always follows genocide. It is among the surest indicators of further genocidal massacres. The perpetrators of genocide dig up the mass graves, burn the bodies, try to cover up the evidence and intimidate the witnesses. They deny that they committed any crimes, and often blame what happened on the victims. They block investigations of the crimes, and continue to govern until driven from power by force, when they flee into exile. There they remain with impunity, like Pol Pot or Idi Amin, unless they are captured and a tribunal is established to try them. The response to denial is punishment by an international tribunal or national courts. There the evidence can be heard, and the perpetrators punished. Tribunals like the Yugoslav, Rwanda or Sierra Leone Tribunals, the tribunal to try the Khmer Rouge in Cambodia, or the International Criminal Court may not deter the worst genocidal killers. But with the political will to arrest and prosecute them, some may be brought to justice.

This processual model demonstrates that there is a logic to the genocidal process, though it does not proceed in a linear order. By helping us understand the logic of genocide, people can see the early warning signs of genocide and know when it is coming. Leaders can design policies to counteract the forces that drive each of the stages.

I am grateful to many people for improvements in my original eight stage model, in particular to Prof. Alan Whitehorn of the Royal Military College of Canada, who suggested the terms Stigmatization for what I have called Discrimination, and Extreme Victimization for what I have called Persecution. I have chosen the more familiar terms Discrimination and Persecution because they fit better into the law of discrimination and the international law of persecution.

No model is ever perfect. All are merely ideal-typical representations of reality that are meant to help us think more clearly about social and cultural processes. It is important not to confuse any stage with a status. It is more like a fluctuating point on a thermometer that rises and falls as the social temperature in a potential area of conflict rises and falls. It is crucial not to confuse this model with a linear one. In all genocides, many stages occur simultaneously.

The purpose of this model is to place the risk factors in Barbara Harff's pioneering analysis of country risks of genocide and politicide into a processual structure. Risks of political instability are characteristic of what Kuper called "divided societies," with deep rifts in Classification. Targeted groups of state-led discrimination are victims of Discrimination. An exclusionary ideology is central to Dehumanization. Autocratic regimes foster the Organization of hate groups. An ethnically polarized elite is characteristic of Polarization. Lack of openness to trade and other influences from outside a state's borders is characteristic of Preparation for genocide or politicide. Massive violation of human rights is evidence of Persecution. Impunity after previous genocides or politicides is evidence of Denial.

Ultimately the best antidote to genocide is popular education and the development of social and cultural tolerance for diversity. That is why Genocide Watch and the Alliance Against Genocide hope to educate people around the world to resist genocidal forces whenever they see them. Finally the movement that will end genocide must come not from international armed interventions, but rather from popular resistance to every form of discrimination; dehumanization, hate speech, and formation of hate groups; rise of political parties that preach hatred, racism or xenophobia; rule by polarizing elites that advocate exclusionary ideologies; police states that massively violate human rights; closure of borders to international trade or communications; and denial of past genocides or crimes against humanity against groups within or without the state that is in denial.

The movement that will end genocide in this century must rise from each of us who have the courage to challenge discrimination, hatred, and tyranny. We must never let the wreckage of our barbaric past keep us from envisioning a peaceful future when law and democratic freedom will rule the earth.

For those who doubt there is any direction in history, our common humanity is enough to give meaning to our cause. To those of us who know that history is not some directionless accident, this is our calling and our destiny. John F. Kennedy said, 'On earth, God's work must truly be our own.'

© 2013 Gregory H. Stanton. Originally presented as a briefing paper, 'The Eight Stages of Genocide' at the US State Department in 1996. Discrimination and Persecution have been added to the 1996 model."[1515]

=====================================

e. A Letter to the Estonian Leadership

"08.05.2015

His Excellency, President of the Republic of Estonia, Toomas Hendrik ILVES

His Excellency, President of the Estonia Parliament 'Riigikogu,' Eiki NESTOR

His Excellency, Prime Minister, Taavi RÕIVAS

In Re: A Request for Recognizing the Circassian Genocide committed by the Tsarist Russian Empire

In 18th and 19th centuries, genocide against the Circassian (Adygean) people had taken place where significant majority of Circassians were exterminated by the Russian Empire to take over our country, the Circassian (Adygean) homeland. The ones who survived were forced to leave their homeland and were deported and exiled as a whole, and as the Russian Empire planned, hundreds of thousands of people died during the exile process. According to a motto belonged to Russian generals and Russian authorities, the Russian Empire needed "the land that belonged to the Circassians, not the Circassians themselves".

Exile continued also after 1864 with different excuses and different disguises, all kinds of pressure was implemented to make a handful of Circassians left behind by some means to leave their homeland as well. Relevant documents are in the archives in addition to published documents by eyewitnesses in propria persona.

Today, only one tenth of the Circassian (Adygean) population, around 700,000 people; is living in a piece of land that can be delineated as a small piece of historical Circassia, scattered and divided around. Circassian People, although they are one nation, have been condemned by the Soviet administration and by its successor, the administration of the Russian Federation, to live disconnected from each other, in different political and administrative enclaves, with different names as if they are different nationalities and isolated from each other.

At the present time, and due to the Circassian Genocide and Exile, 90% of the Circassian population has been forced to live outside of their homeland, scattered in more than fifty countries around the world. "Indigenous population's right to be in contact with its own country" as a basic human right for Circassians in exile is restricted almost as much as nonexistence. The Russian Federation refuses to allow Circassians in exile to return to their Circassian homeland even if it is for urgent humanitarian purposes. The Request of Circassians in Syria who are caught in the fire of the civil unrest between the two sides in ongoing intestine war and still going on through all the pains of the conflict to return to their own homeland due to risk of death is not even taken into consideration by the Russian Federation.

Besides, activists who expressed their thoughts about the 'Circassian Problem' through totally democratic, legal and peaceful ways and means have been detained, harassed and have been put under pressure by open and undercover threats. This situation of the issue is still continuing in different forms.

The decisions of The Russian Federation's units, Kabardino-Balkarian Republic Parliament dated 7, February, 1992 and numbered (№977–XII-B), and the Republic of Adygea Parliament dated 29, April, 1996 and numbered 64-1, have both recognized the Genocide committed against the Circassians, which took place during the Russian-Circassian War that lasted for 101 years and they have condemned it. They also requested from the Russian Federation to recognize the Circassian Genocide.

Georgia, on 20, May, 2011, with the decision reached in its parliament upon the request of the Circassian People, was the first country as a member of the United Nations to recognize the Circassian Genocide.

According to that decision reached by the Georgian Parliament, the Russian Empire, during the war that took place between 1763-1864 years, had also performed Ethnic Cleansing against the Circassians and were replaced by other ethnic group (Russian population) on the Circassian (Adygean) homeland by means of state policy. By embarking into military activities aiming to punish the civilians, it completely annihilated a huge part of the Circassian population according to independent observers. Artificial famine was created and infectious diseases were spread amongst the civilian population.

The Georgian Parliament, in accordance with the Hague Agreement number IV, dated 18, October, 1907, and Prevention and Punishment of Genocide Crime Agreement, dated 1948, announced that the acts committed against Circassians were genocide.

The Circassian (Adygean) civil rights defenders and activists from around the world have applied to the Government of Ukraine on 21/06/2014 to recognize the Circassian Genocide. The Ukrainian Government responded to this application whereupon His Excellency, the President of Ukrainian, Mr. Petro Poroshenko, has instructed the Ukrainian Ministry of Foreign Affairs to investigate the issue. In their brief reply dated 07/07/2014, the representatives of the Ministry expressed the Mr. Poroshenko's instructions and stated that Congressman Oleg Lyashko has submitted to the Supreme Rada of Ukraine the legislative Proposal No. 4203 for 'discussing and recognizing the Circassian Genocide.' The purpose of the proposal is stated to be 'initiating a political and legal process regarding recognition of the genocide of the Circassian (Adygean) nation caused by the colonial policy of the Russian Empire between 1763 and 1864, and supporting the process by scientific and historical data.' Said legislative proposal has been renewed with Proposal number 2140, dated 13.02.2015 by MP Mr. Dmytro Volodimirovich in the new legislation session of Verkhovna Rada of Ukraine. It is being proceeded before the Committees on Human Rights, National Minorities and International Relations.

The administrative units Wayne, Prospect Park and Haledon of New Jersey, USA have recognized the Circassian Genocide on May, 21, 2014, July, 19, 2014 and July, 17, 2014, respectively on concrete grounds.

Another application has been presented on 11.11.2014 to Poland to recognize the Circassian Genocide by Circassian (Adygean) civil rights defenders and activists throughout the world.

The latest submission was sent to Lithuania on 11.03.2015 so as to recognize the Circassian Genocide. Upon said application, a response dated 30.03.2015, was sent by the Office of President of the Republic of Lithuania, Mrs. Dalia Grybauskaitė, which indicated that the application was received and transferred to the Ministry of Foreign Affairs since said ministry is responsible for the mentioned issue. In this context, a reply was sent by the Office of Prime Minister Mr. Algirdas Butkevičius, it was highlighted that application was transferred to Prime Minister Algirdas Butkevičius in propria persona.

The Circassian Question is a problem that had occurred as a result of the Circassian Genocide and Exile, and the country that is obligated to solve this problem is the Russian Federation. It became obvious that the Russian Federation, acting with the same arguments as the Russian Empire about the Circassian Problem even in the 21st century, is acting in the same manner in all subjects with its occupation of the Crimea, which is a land located within the territorial integrity of Ukraine and by groundlessly pleading suppression towards Russian speakers living in Eastern Ukraine in reality, aiming to occupy the whole Ukraine and right after by open threatening towards Poland and Eastern Europe. An old world practice "land-conquest growing by occupation" thought to be an old world way of thinking has been moved to the modern world by the Russian Federation, with furthermore leaving the whole world in astonishment.

At this point, as Estonia was the first state to restore its "sovereignty" in 1988 from the Soviet Union, it is an important country for Circassians. The destinies of Circassians and Estonians are intersected at their freedom aspirations. From 1987 to 1991, Estonians defiantly sang national songs forbidden by the Soviet authorities which are called as "Singing Revolution".

Circassians (Adygeas), throughout the world, peacefully demonstrated against Sochi Winter Olympics of 2014 on the grounds that the genocide was committed against Circassians in their own land-Sochi, which is part of Circassia. One of the demonstrations was held in Nalchik, capital city of Kabardino-Balkaria Republic which is a divided and isolated Circassian Republic, but peaceful demonstration was broken up by the Russian security troops through the use of harsh vehemence, demonstrators were detained and they were excruciated. Detained Circassians (Adygeas) were singing an epic heroic song called 'Nart Badinoqua,' when dreadful tortures were perpetrated on their bodies.

The 'Circassian Question' is related to 'values' as much as its national and international characters, thus we regard 'Circassia' within the 'Baltic-Black Sea-Caspian' area. Circassians are in favor of European values pursuant to Borjomi Declaration.

We, the undersigned, respectfully submit our request to Your Excellency, for the recognition of the Circassian Genocide:

175 signatures"¹⁵¹⁶

======================================

f. **Circassians Handed a Letter to the Estonian Parliament**

The International Circassian Council

"Honorable Members of the Estonian Parliament,

As members of the Circassian nation speaking in behalf of many in homeland and Diaspora people of our nation. we convey our sincere respect and best wishes to the Estonian people. The Circassians appreciate the opportunity to submitting to you facts about the continuing tragedy of our nation.

The plight of our Circassian nation, as one of the most ancient nations of the world and the most indigenous to the Caucasus is certainly one of the saddest episodes of humanity. The ongoing Russian evil imperial greed for the past 151 years has nearly eliminated our nation from existence. Ninety percent of our people live in scattered Diaspora throughout the world not allowed to repatriate to our homeland. And less than ten percent are allowed to remain in our motherland. This imposes grave consequences in the present and the future of our victimized nation. The Genocide the Russian state inflicted upon us, has eliminated more than half of our population and subsequently drove the remaining survivors into fetal ethnic cleansing and forced exile. Our Diaspora population is deprived from any direct association with culture, history and relations with our brothers and sisters in Circassia.

The past and current Russian state policies are in direct and clear violation of all internationally recognized laws and norms. Including the Universal Declaration of Human Rights, the International Law and and the United Nations Declaration on the Rights of the Indigenous Peoples.

More than two hundred thousand ethnic Circassians suffer today in the bloody Syrian civil war. Not less than 22 Circassian villages and large residential communities have been completely destroyed. Tens of thousands of Circassians have been forced to live without shelter, food or medical care.

Only a small fraction of this small oppressed ethnic European minority have been able to escape the civil war and return to Circassia to live in the relative safety of our motherland. Yet, all returnees are subjected to fabricated and discriminatory measures by the authority intended to force them leave our motherland and discourage other suffering Circassians to repatriate.

Despite the tragic and dark history of our Circassian Genocide, Russia had invited the world to celebrate the 2014 Sochi Winter Olympic Games over the mass graves of our people. Russia is planning to hold more festivities in Sochi in the upcoming events of World Cup of 2018 and Formula One in October 2015.

Russia has destroyed all mass grave and historical sacred sites of the victims of our people in order to erase any evidence of its historical crime, denying us the memorial observance we must have as part of our culture and tradition to remember the men women and children whose lives were taken in the Circassian Genocide.

All this while Human Rights conditions for Circassians in the North Caucasus are harsh and deteriorating as a result of Russia's intended hostile policies towards homeland Circassians and any Human Rights activism.

Circassians today are in dire need to make the free world aware of our enduring tragedy and honest people of the world support our cause.

We call upon the people of Estonia represented by its Parliament to follow similar approach made by the Parliament of the people of Georgia in recognizing the Circassian Genocide and the ethnic cleansing of our people as a Genocide and a as crime against humanity.

Adel Bashqawi   Nusrat Bas

Iyad Youghar   Serdar Bas

Tallinn, Estonia.

June 4th, 2015."[1517]

==================================

g. **Members of the Riigikogu Met with the Representatives of the Circassian Community**

"04.06.2015/Press releases

The members of the Riigikogu (Parliament of Estonia) met with the representatives of the Jordanian, Turkish and US communities of the Circassian diaspora. The meeting focused on the fate of the Circassian people through history.

Chairman of the Foreign Affairs Committee of the Riigikogu Hannes Hanso said that the fate of the Circassians is a historical issue that by today has acquired a clearly international character. In Hanso's opinion, the Circassians support the European values.

Member of the Riigikogu Eerik-Niiles Kross said that Estonians have a certain debt of honour to the Circassians, because the Estonian settlers near the Black Sea, for example, in Krasnaya Polyana, were settled on the Circassian lands. Kross noted that during the 150 years of living in exile, this North-Caucasian nation has preserved both its language and its culture, and added that today the communication of the Circassians with their historic homeland is hindered, several hundreds of thousands of Circassians live as refugees as a result of the Syrian War.

In the opinion of the Member of the Riigikogu Artur Talvik, Estonia should consider the possibility of receiving Circassians with refugee status, which would help reduce our debt of honour.

Members of the Riigikogu Jüri Adams, Mart Nutt and Johannes Kert also took part in yesterday's meeting. The Circassians also visited the Riigikogu in 2010.

According to the Circassian community, most of the nearly three million Circassians live in exile in more than 50 countries all over the world, and about 700,000 Circassians live in only a small part of historical Circassia.

The present city of Sochi is also a part of Circassia, and the Circassians all over the world organised peaceful demonstrations against the Winter Olympics held there in 2014. Currently they are protesting against holding the World Cup football tournament of 2018 in Sochi, because the games would take place on their historical lands.

In their letter to the President of the Riigikogu, the Circassians ask the Estonian Parliament to recognise the genocide on Circassians committed by the Russian Empire during the Russo-Circassian War in 1763–1864. They have sent a similar appeal to the parliaments several countries. Of the member states of the UN, Georgia has so far recognised the genocide."[1518]

==

h. The Circassians Refuse the Hostile Attitude

The Russian authorities have routinely turned a blind eye on the problems and the implications of the tragedies that befell on the Circassian nation ever since the end of the devastating war waged by the Tsars of the Russian Empire, which led to occupation, genocide and displacement. The Russians went a long way to ignore all the disastrous results, and the necessity to solve all their wrong doings. In the sense of legal and legitimate rights, the consequences of calamities and tragedies that have befallen on the Circassian people will not be forgotten before Circassians get their denied rights, which are guaranteed by the International Law, the Universal Charter of Human Rights and the United Nations Declaration on the Rights of Indigenous Peoples.

Circassians have long been exposed, in a constant and planned manner, to the effects of a hostile propaganda machine that has implanted a skepticism-based process, along with falsehood and redirecting attention. This process was orchestrated by well-known circles and parties that employ under-cover agents and proxies. They monitor Circassians everywhere, even in scientific centers and universities, both at the homeland and in the Diaspora, to know the trend of Circassia-related topics in order to influence, steer or change the concept.

In a publicity stunt, an article was published in 2015, by Sochi State University, funded by the Ministry of Education and Science of the Russian Federation, with the title "Circassian Question: Transformation of Content and Perception."

(http://www.academia.edu/15285565/Circassian_Question_Transformation_of_Content_and_Perception).

The purpose of issuing such information is to produce a fabricated work, while depending on some reliable references, but at the same time imposing information related to official Russian policies that contradict reality. The following are some of the mentioned contradictions:

— It uses official Russian terminology, such as using the name "the Caucasian War," instead of the Russian-Circassian War, while using made-up dates, ignoring the fact that the war extended from 1763 to 1864.

— They claimed that "the so-called Circassian question became extremely hot in the mid-2000s and in connection with the significant event of the 2014 Winter Olympics in Sochi." This only mentions half of the truth, because the other half involves the Circassian outrage in 2007 due to opposition of the Russian celebrations of the anniversary of the so-called "450 years of Circassians' voluntary association with Russia," which has never happened at all.

— The Russian president made a mistake (in 2007) while delivering a speech to the International Olympic Committee, when he mentioned the Greeks arriving to the Circassian coast in the distant past, without mentioning the original homeland of the indigenous Circassians.

— The Circassian Question was hot since Circassia was occupied, and will stay extremely hot until Circassians restore their legitimate rights.

— The Sochi Games had some positive results because of the publicity the Circassians got, when more people in the world knew about Circassia and the tragedies inflicted on the Circassians. This information spread in all languages of the world.

— The Circassian Question has existed before the Sochi Olympics, and will prevail until it is solved. The "historical and cultural context" is only one element of the problem.

— The main actors for solving the different issues of the Circassian Question are the Circassians themselves, in all their locations. They are backed by documents, laws and legality, provided that a retrospective approach is followed.

— The Circassian national movements were always in the arena and will continue to be there until they get their rights. Circassians do, and will continue to, observe the 21st of May, as a day of respect to the Circassian forefathers.

— Circassians will continue their nonviolent struggle, regardless of what obstacles are placed on their path to Circassia. The prediction that, "foreign policy factors and the Circassian question perception in the international arena has historically had a predetermined outcome," is true in the sense that Circassians will not let go on their rights on the soil of their homeland.

— The Russian Empire has achieved its dream of occupying the Circassian homeland, but the Russian authorities always wanted to put the blame on others, while the Russian state is occupying the Circassian homeland still refuses to restore the rights to the indigenous Circassians.

— Russia has imposed itself as a fierce enemy of the Circassians, while the Circassians will not be looking for other enemies; logic imposes that they seek friends who will recognize the tragedies incurred on them, and assist them to obtain their rights in international forums.

— The unilateral analysis that describes "the web-space in Russian, Circassian, Turkish, Arabic and English languages", reveals something different than what is depicted, because the trend towards social media (especially Facebook and Twitter) resulted in hundreds of Circassian pages and websites.

— There is a hostile attitude against any person who is concerned with the Circassians' rights, seeks to think of, or attempts to address the crucial Circassian issues of identity, historical heritage and the very survival of the Circassian nation. The process is even extended to cast unsubstantiated accusations against scholars, historians, writers, human rights activists, political analysts and institutes of research and analysis. Frantic criticism is directed at whoever dares to address or tackle the Circassian Question subject in an academic and historical manner.

The impact of the recognition of the Circassian genocide has worried those who claimed to be held accountable by local and international laws. This worry is not for committing the atrocities and genocide themselves, but for accepting the legal and material responsibility incumbent upon the State. The failure to deal with the real issues of the Circassian people has led to a policy of ignoring the issues and insisting on the denial process, despite the tangible facts that are available, which cannot be circumvented.

That is in disregard to international laws and norms regarding the continued non-recognition of genocide and to hold the Winter Olympic Games (in February 2014) in Sochi on the land that contains the remains of Circassians killed by the invading forces.

Circassians around the world believe in "Free Circassia Now."

The International Circassian Council.

January 16, 2016

    Iyad Youghar   Adel Bashqawi[1519]

=========================

i. Address to the Queen of England by Circassians

The Address that was sent by twelve hundred and fifty four of the most influential chiefs and elders throughout the provinces of Circassia:

ADDRESS TO THE QUEEN OF ENGLAND

To the reigning Sovereign, the highly venerated Potentate, the Possessor of the provinces and the crown, and the magnificent Monarch of England (of the imperial brilliant threshold), this humble representation of her servants the Circassians.

We have long suffered from the outrages of the Russians; yet the falsehoods they promulgate against us are more injurious, inasmuch as they assert that, from the one sea to the other, all the territory of the provinces of Circassia has been bestowed on them by the Sublime Porte; that hostages have been given them, and that it is entirely in their power; that the tribes of Circassia are under their domination – slaves subjected to their supreme orders; that from one sea to the other they have long since conquered the country by surrounding it with fortresses. Thus they seek to exalt themselves in the eyes of the other powers, while it is as apparent as the mid-day sun that all their statements are false. Thus, they have long continued to harass us, in the hope of at length acquiring the absolute mastery.

The truth is, that formerly Persian merchants came and went, and made sales and purchases; but since the Russians intruded themselves this commerce is cut off.

In reply to the allegations of the Russians, your humble servants, the Circassians, solemnly protest, that never since its commencement did the Ottoman power conquer us with the sword; never did it bring us succour in our distress; and never at any time did we pay it tribute: on the contrary it took our children and sold them as slaves in its bazars. And such having been the case, how could the Sublime Porte bestow us upon the Russians? If it had friendship for them, it might have given them some of the countries under its sway, but it had not either the power or the right to give them ours.

As to the forts which the Russians have constructed, they do us neither good nor harm. We are disposed to be in amity with our neighbours, but never shall we in any way be subject to the Russians. We hope in God that we shall never be subjugated by them, and through the help of the Almighty this hope may be fulfilled, for the Lord is a just God, and He will grant us his aid, that to the last among our tribes we may sustain the war against the Russians, and through His almighty succour never submit to them.

Although the governor of Anapa failed in performing his duty, he was a servant of the sacred and illustrious Chief of the Mussulman faith, and with the help of God we trust, that our connexion with that sacred and illustrious religion may remain unimpaired. If therefore the Ottoman government will now accept of our adhesion, we will henceforth submit ourselves voluntarily to it and to its orders, on these conditions: 1mo. That it shall entirely desist from taking and selling us as slaves. 2d. That it shall furnish us with cannons, soldiers, ammunition, and the other appurtenances of war, sending us also treasure, and assisting and succoring us faithfully; then we will be obedient to it. Let it send us also officers that we may begin the war with the Russians in earnest; and then, with the aid of the Almighty, we pledge our lives and our souls, that we shall take vengeance on the enemy. We engage moreover on the part of our tribes, that when the war is finished we will repay the Ottoman government the whole of the expense it shall have incurred: it shall be reimbursed for everything. And these matters having been thus arranged with the aforementioned government, we will remain submissive to its orders, and under its entire direction.

But if the Ottoman government will not aid us and furnish us with cannons, ammunition, troops, appurtenances of war and treasure; and if it shall not cease as in time past to take us for slaves, then we shall not subject ourselves to it, nor recognise its sovereign as ours; but if it furnish us with cannons, ammunition, troops, appurtenances of war and treasure, and aid and protect us, then shall we be submissive to its imperial orders, and will begin in earnest to take vengeance on the Russians in war, and at the termination of the war, we bind and oblige ourselves to repay all the expense which the Ottoman government may have incurred, and never to submit to the Russians; for in fine, if the war should render us feeble, we will disperse ourselves upon the mountains sooner than surrender to them.

If, however, your Majesty should not deem these arrangements advisable, we trust that your Majesty, and the other Powers, will issue orders that we may continue free and independent like Persia, Affghanistan, and other mountain-countries; and when your Majesty has thus definitively ordered and arranged, we will consider how we shall next proceed. If, however, the above arrangements could be made with the Ottoman government, we should esteem it a special favour, and we should be perfectly satisfied.

Sefir Bey, our minister, has been ordered to present our humble petition to your Majesty, and to the Ottoman Emperor, and we well act in conformity with what may be done and spoken by him.

May your Majesty, whose person is endowed with every exalted quality – with intelligence and with compassion – deign to receive this the humble address of our tribes. On your Majesty's supreme will our destiny depends.

1254 (Year of 1838)

(N.B. – To this address were appended the signatures of about twelve hundred and fifty of the most influential chiefs and elders throughout all the provinces of Circassia) pages 445, 446, 447 and 448, Journal of a Residence of Circassia During the Years 1837, 1838 and 1839. By: James Stanislaus Bell VOL. II."[1520]

[1512] http://justicefornorthcaucasus.info/?p=1251669883
[1513] http://www.unpo.org/article.php?id=5634
[1514] http://www.parliament.ge/files/1544_32742_536746_genocidi-en.pdf
[1515] http://genocidewatch.net/genocide-2/8-stages-of-genocide/
[1516] http://www.cherkessia.net/news_detail.php?id=6664
[1517] http://justicefornorthcaucasus.info/?p=1251675400
[1518] https://m.riigikogu.ee/en/press-releases/others/members-of-the-riigikogu-met-with-the-representatives-of-the-circassian-community/
[1519] http://justicefornorthcaucasus.info/?p=1251676982
[1520] http://justicefornorthcaucasus.info/?p=1251678058

INDEX

A

Abadzekhs, 95, 98, 103, 118, 124, 126, 128–29, 603
Abkhazia, 1, 3–4, 19, 50, 52, 57–58, 126, 324, 336, 425, 466–67, 517, 519–20
Adigha language, 145, 301, 325, 431
Adyghe, 2–3, 6, 8, 10, 13, 113, 134–35, 150, 293, 312–13, 351, 425, 462, 610, 617
Adyghe language, 3, 272, 313, 316–17, 405, 488
Adygs, 241, 287, 320, 366, 434, 487
Alexander II, 42, 77, 101, 127–29, 600–601, 603
Amman, 158, 354, 377
Anaklia, 148, 457–58
apartheid, 89, 234, 334, 362–63
Armenia, 59–60, 66, 137, 199, 243, 255, 308, 338, 371, 417
Armenian Genocide, 246, 253, 338–39, 346, 417, 446, 456, 467, 599
Armenians, 254–56, 258–59, 339, 414, 418
Atazhukin, Izmail-Bey, 177–78, 183, 185–87, 192, 194

B

Battle of Krasnaya Polyana, 111, 111–13
Black Sea, 92, 106, 172, 216, 451
Bolsheviks, 61–62, 66–68, 163, 212, 371
Bosporus, 11, 28–29, 76, 91, 106, 271–72
Bosporus state, 11, 13, 28–29, 76
Bulgakov, Sergei, 183, 185–93, 200

C

Caucasia, 31, 33, 59–60, 62–66, 68, 121–22, 132, 235, 256, 409, 463
Caucasians, 27, 61–63, 137, 190, 237, 352
Caucasian War. *See* Russian-Circassian War
Caucasus, 24–27, 32–36, 40–43, 60–65, 67–69, 91–94, 103–9, 127–29, 138–39, 163–67, 169–73, 195–200, 261–62, 459–63, 527–31
Caucasus Mountains, 2, 7, 164, 198, 271, 319, 321, 359, 555
Chechens, 40, 49, 64, 68, 108, 203–4, 454, 462, 466, 511–12, 617
Christianity, 13, 18, 224, 237, 341
Cimmerian Empire, 26–28, 76

641

Circassia, 1–5, 23–29, 31–35, 45–47, 51–53, 89–97, 99–107, 115–19, 121–25, 133–37, 215–29, 271–79, 399–403, 587–93, 631–39

Circassian activism, 337, 348, 422, 477, 502

Circassian activists, 55, 72, 288, 342, 393, 424, 428, 432, 443, 451, 464, 467, 496, 503–4

Circassian Association, 397, 428, 446, 495–96

Circassian Congress, 289, 364, 401, 406, 433–34, 486, 532, 570, 592, 614, 616

Circassian Deputies, 44, 126–28

Circassian Elders, 121, 127, 129, 248

Circassian flag, xiii, 59, 270, 273–75, 277, 353, 403, 434, 442, 457

Circassian Genocide Memorial, 335, 340, 444, 457

Circassian homeland, xii, 1, 10, 30, 50–51, 53, 73, 106, 321, 336–37, 422–23, 431–32, 481–82, 488–89, 637

Circassian identity, xiii, 115, 270, 283–84, 324, 396, 407, 445, 455

Circassian language, ix, 294, 307, 312

Circassian Memorial Day, xiii, 59, 251, 333, 335, 344–45, 349, 353–54, 459, 467, 478

Circassian National Movement, 426, 490

Circassian question, xiii, 46, 58–59, 73–75, 138–39, 352–53, 372–73, 410–13, 420–22, 427, 431–32, 488–90, 501–2, 521–22, 635–37

Circassians, ix–8, 11–14, 33–34, 51–54, 56–58, 73–75, 99–101, 112–14, 149–52, 158–66, 168–69, 214–17, 247–50, 341–44, 379–81

Circassian tribes

Abzakhs, 3, 32, 147–48, 154, 175, 240, 249

Besleney, 3, 125, 239, 310, 610

Bjedugh, 3

Hatuqwai, 3

Jana, 3

Kabarday, 3

Mokhosh, 3

Natkhwaj, 3

Shapsughs, 3, 32, 39–40, 42, 126, 147, 154, 157, 175, 215, 220–22, 225, 240, 366, 434

Temirgoy, 3, 310

Ubykhs, 2–3, 6, 32, 39–40, 42, 97, 105, 112, 118, 126–27, 147, 175, 310–11, 351, 454

Yedjerikway, 3

Cossacks, xii, 64, 96–97, 102–4, 112, 125, 128–31, 135, 188–89, 206–7, 212–13, 221–25, 231, 532–35, 603

Crimea, 41, 43–44, 50, 69, 104, 138–39, 216, 235–36, 350, 364, 369, 414, 511–12, 515–16, 518–19

D

decolonization, 26, 370, 373–74

Denikin, Anton, 62, 64, 67–68

diaspora, 241, 279–80, 300–301, 307–8, 312–13, 316, 326–27, 335, 366–67, 390–95, 397–400, 422–24, 472–74, 488–89, 494–95

Circassian, 74, 325, 334, 337, 342, 395, 410, 413, 432, 453, 474, 486, 488, 493, 614–16

E

Ermolov, Aleksey, 36–37, 92, 108, 116, 120, 146, 150, 163, 165–66,

195–209, 211, 213–16, 228–29, 232, 515
ethnic cleansing, 41, 49, 52–53, 77, 238–39, 242, 333–35, 359–60, 380, 413, 415–16, 443, 454, 596, 618
European Union, 54, 304–5, 307, 385–86, 488–89, 516, 544
Evdokimov, Nikolai, 41, 102, 111, 114, 122, 125–27, 157, 172, 239, 248–50, 601, 603–5
exile, xii, xiv, 2, 284, 301–2, 326–27, 421–22, 445–46, 462, 486–88, 494–95, 522–23, 601, 628–29, 634

F

falsifications, 286–87, 363–64, 384, 435, 484–85, 492
fascism, 212, 362, 537
First Russian-Chechen War, 324, 512
First World War, 66, 255, 258, 372

G

Gazaryan, Suren, 562, 579, 581
genocide, ix–x, 232–34, 242–48, 250–54, 413–15, 441–43, 446–49, 451–55, 457–63, 569–71, 598–99, 605–7, 609–14, 617–23, 625–35
  Circassian, 253, 260–68, 339–41, 344–46, 411–12, 423–25, 442–43, 446, 449–50, 455–58, 585, 606–8, 610–12, 615–17, 628–31
genocide recognition, 344, 354, 381, 444–45, 448
Genocide Watch, 233, 621, 627

Georgia, ix, 59–60, 66, 91, 137–38, 148–49, 254, 335–36, 341, 441–44, 457, 465–67, 501–3, 615–17, 619–21
Georgian parliament, 378–80, 393, 414, 424, 442–44, 621, 629–30
Georgians, 149, 259
Greeks, 2–3, 10–13, 17, 20, 23, 28–29, 58, 87, 323–24, 574, 636

H

Holocaust, 243–44, 415
human rights, 58, 197, 343, 361, 374–75, 407, 420, 431, 447, 450, 487–88, 522–25, 544, 546–47, 578

I

ICA (International Circassian Association), 74, 287, 314–15, 367, 372, 385, 390, 392–99, 423, 425, 428–29, 434–35, 473–74, 494–95, 613–14
ICC (International Circassian Council), 406–8, 457, 475–76, 632, 638
imperialism, 53, 84, 132, 205, 252, 280, 338, 399, 409, 524, 526, 532
  Russian, 252, 338, 399
independence, 23–29, 33, 42, 45, 48–50, 53–57, 59–61, 63–64, 66–70, 75, 92, 104, 370–71, 517–19, 609
  national, 370–71, 411, 532
India, 45, 85, 91, 105, 529
indigenous peoples, 7, 52, 54, 70–72, 147, 169, 215, 259, 284, 294, 342–43, 351, 370, 373, 376–77
International Association of Circassian Peoples, 312

International Circassian Language Conference, 313
international laws, xiv, 47, 52, 54–55, 74, 145, 196, 208, 232–33, 251, 253, 278, 343, 373–74, 637
IOC (International Olympic Committee), 46, 291, 403, 559, 564, 566–68, 573, 579, 581, 636
Islam, 13, 18–19, 32–33, 100–101, 224, 311, 341, 511, 547
Istanbul, 38, 65, 99–101, 135, 139, 161, 236, 272–73, 354, 403, 410, 423, 425, 486, 494
Ivan the Terrible, 4, 84, 88, 164, 286

J

JACCF (Jordanian Association of Caucasus Circassians' Friends), 474
Jamestown Foundation, 421, 424, 441, 480, 615
Jews, 244, 259, 537, 622–23
Jordan, x–xi, 6, 89, 101, 158, 283, 313, 332, 342, 377–79, 385–86, 426, 474, 525–27, 530–31

K

Kabardia, 177–81, 183–87, 189, 191–92, 201–3, 205–7, 210–12, 214–15
Kabardians, 14, 37, 95–96, 108, 110, 176, 179–81, 184–86, 188, 190–93, 201–5, 208–12, 310, 312, 427
KAFFED, 346, 395, 397, 482, 493–95
Khuade, Adnan, 419–21, 448, 481, 504, 546
Krasnaya Polyana, 111–12, 345, 425, 449–50, 467, 482, 557, 563–64, 566, 572, 574, 583, 634

Kuban, 3, 9–10, 12, 14, 18, 27, 37, 102–3, 109–10, 128–29, 210, 222–25, 319, 600–601, 603–5

L

Lenin, Vladimir, 69, 195, 335, 476
Levant, 91, 105, 161, 466

M

Markov, Sergei, 364, 366, 484–87
Maykop, 9, 107, 138, 302, 354, 367, 401, 403, 493, 531–32, 535–36, 593, 609–10
medals, 75, 77, 214
Medvedev, Dmitry, 42, 404, 517, 561, 580
mejlis, 47–48, 126
Minority Rights Group Europe, 70, 294
Mongol invasion, 24, 88–89, 104
Moscow, 56, 287–88, 314–15, 337, 350–51, 367–69, 404–5, 407–8, 454, 463–65, 477–78, 500–505, 542–44, 577–78, 605–7
mountaineers, 46, 90, 94, 107, 117, 120–21, 123, 125, 128, 133, 151, 155, 188, 219–20, 228
Muscovites, 4–5, 48, 84, 136, 164, 169, 408, 418, 590

N

Nalchik, 37, 211, 353–54, 397, 428, 430, 451, 486–87, 493–94, 536, 547–48, 550–51, 600–602, 604–5, 609
Natukhais, 95, 98–103, 118
natural law theory, 361
navy, 113–14, 134, 198

Nazism, 362
Nemtsov, Boris, 407
North Caucasians, 10, 30, 65, 117, 147–48, 294, 327, 334, 337, 515, 558, 612
North Caucasus, 7–9, 19, 49–50, 195–96, 314–16, 337, 350–51, 423–25, 429–32, 450, 452–54, 459–61, 496–500, 514–15, 526–28
Northwest Caucasus, 1, 7–9, 12–13, 18, 31, 46, 48, 58, 83, 95, 101, 103, 140–43, 241–42, 593–95

O

Ottoman Empire, 7, 31–33, 35, 38, 55, 88–89, 91–92, 135–37, 218–20, 241–43, 271, 345–46, 452–55, 457–60, 600
Ottomans, 18, 32–34, 36, 38, 44, 55, 57, 60, 91, 99, 101, 161, 174–75, 271–72, 415

P

Pasha, Tala'at, 256, 258
Paskevich, Ivan, 155–56, 599
Peter the Great, 43, 85, 87, 90–91, 105, 111, 179–80, 223
Poland, 59, 223, 244, 371, 410, 412–13, 421, 448, 630
Poles, 244, 409–12
Polonezköy, 410, 412
Porte, 34, 93, 96, 100, 108, 149, 161–63, 217, 219, 589, 591
Putin, Vladimir, 20, 42–44, 69, 72, 252–53, 338, 417, 430, 463–65, 516–18, 524–25, 558–62, 576–78, 584, 615

R

Republic of Adygea, 138, 275, 396, 420, 426, 428, 445, 453, 482, 493, 496, 542
resistance, Circassian, 4, 221, 477, 598
rights
  legal, 72, 250, 349, 361, 368, 475
  legitimate, xiii–xiv, 23, 35, 50, 52–55, 57, 73, 124, 146–49, 200, 288–89, 384–85, 473–75, 488–91, 635–36
  natural, xiv, 54, 204, 304, 361–63
Russia, 38–39, 43–45, 58–59, 92, 105–7, 164, 216, 218–21, 368, 384–85, 454, 495, 513–14, 550, 580–81
Russian army, 68, 109, 238, 410, 460, 518
Russian-Caucasian War. *See* Russian-Circassian War
Russian-Circassian War, 4–5, 46, 83–85, 90, 93–94, 101–4, 111–12, 137–38, 146, 235, 447–53, 498, 600–602, 604–5, 609–13
Russian Duma, 428, 496, 498, 614
Russian Empire, xii, 90–92, 96–98, 130, 169–71, 198–200, 212–20, 371, 420–21, 448–50, 569–71, 596–98, 610, 617–21, 628–31
Russians, 33–36, 53–54, 88–89, 94–96, 99–100, 106, 111–13, 129–30, 179–81, 183–85, 201–2, 220–23, 238–39, 248–49, 417–18
Russian State Duma, 246–47, 344, 400, 497–99, 595, 612, 614
Russian Tsarist Empire, 59, 349, 380
russification, 50, 260, 284
Russo-Circassian commerce, 116, 151, 227, 229

Rwanda, 243, 622, 626

S

Scassi, Rafael, 116, 151, 227–28, 230
Scythes, 27–28, 76
Sea of Azov, 1, 10, 95–96, 103
Seferbi, Zan, 272–74
self-determination, xiv, 23, 52, 54, 71, 73, 138, 146, 151, 240, 253, 280, 368–72, 374–76, 519
self-government, 71–72, 154, 370
Shapseghs, 95, 98–101, 103, 118, 500
Sinds, 10–11, 26–29, 56, 76, 322
slavery, 368–69, 374
Sochi, 126, 129–30, 250–51, 386, 394–95, 416, 482–83, 485, 526–27, 532, 555–62, 564–69, 573–74, 576–81, 633–34
Sochi Olympics, 291–92, 345–46, 364, 388, 394–95, 403, 416–17, 428, 430–32, 454–55, 483–86, 555–59, 563–70, 572–73, 578–80
South Caucasus, 60, 71, 103, 108, 181, 254
South Ossetia, 50, 517, 519
Soviet Union, 5, 50, 69, 87, 91, 117, 284, 311–12, 324, 369, 390–91, 397, 423, 444, 493
St. Petersburg, 93, 96, 98, 100, 102, 108, 110, 172, 177, 190–92, 212, 219, 226–27, 303, 401
Syria, xi, 6, 89, 91, 101, 105, 159–62, 361, 366–67, 369, 425–26, 463, 492, 495–98, 576

T

Tatars, 14–15, 32, 169, 235–37, 315, 346–49, 415, 418, 460, 464–65, 515, 519

Tbilisi, x–xii, 344, 378, 380, 394, 423, 441–44, 596, 603, 610, 615, 621
Terek, 109, 111, 131, 204, 207
Trabzon, 45, 123–24, 132, 527
Transnistria, 517–19
Transparency International, 561
Treaty of Adrianople, 33, 39, 91, 93, 99–100, 106, 116, 119, 151–52, 168, 217–18, 220, 254, 270, 272
Treaty of Belgrade, 54–55, 179
Treaty of Bucharest, 36
Treaty of Edirne. *See* Treaty of Adrianople
Tsitsianov, Pavel, 181–83, 336
Turkey, 112, 122–23, 125–26, 236, 255–56, 271–72, 295–96, 337–39, 416–18, 446–48, 452–55, 462–63, 500–503, 527–30, 601–2
Turks, 31, 33, 60

U

Ukraine, 49, 59, 139, 224, 253, 260, 347, 371–72, 408, 450, 484, 511–12, 515–17, 546, 630–31
Ukrainians, 459, 461
UNESCO (United Nations Educational, Scientific, and Cultural Organization), 291, 295, 307–8, 317–18, 567–68, 582
United Nations, 54, 58, 232, 234, 246, 280, 307, 341, 370, 374, 376, 380, 488–89, 525, 569
UNPO (Unrepresented Nations and Peoples Organization), 400
Urquhart, David, 115, 170, 272–77, 597

W

war crimes, 199, 233–34, 428, 549, 595, 624
White Russians, 62, 64, 67
Winter Olympics. *See* Sochi Olympics

Y

Yeltsin, Boris, 68, 498, 612

Z

Zass, Gregory, 92, 120, 157, 605–6

Printed in the USA
CPSIA information can be obtained
at www.ICGtesting.com
LVHW092015210124
769550LV00008B/23/J